Discarded
University of Cincinnati
Blue Ash College Library

LATINO AMERICA

LATINO AMERICA

A State-by-State Encyclopedia

VOLUME 1

Alabama–Missouri

**Edited by
Mark Overmyer-Velázquez**

Foreword by Stephen Pitti

GREENWOOD PRESS
Westport, Connecticut • London

Library of Congress Cataloging-in-Publication Data

Latino America : a state-by-state encyclopedia / edited by Mark Overmyer-Velázquez ; foreword by Stephen Pitti.
 v. cm.
 Includes bibliographical references and index.
 ISBN 978–0–313–34116–8 (set : alk. paper) — ISBN 978–0–313–34117–5 (vol. 1 : alk. paper) — ISBN 978–0–313–34118–2 (vol. 2 : alk. paper)
 1. Hispanic Americans—Encyclopedias. 2. Hispanic Americans—History—Encyclopedias. 3. Hispanic Americans—Social conditions—Encyclopedias. 4. U.S. states—Encyclopedias. 5. United States—History, Local—Encyclopedias. I. Overmyer-Velázquez, Mark.
 E184.S75L35555 2008
 973'.0468—dc22   2008026044

British Library Cataloguing in Publication Data is available.

Copyright © 2008 by Mark Overmyer-Velázquez

All rights reserved. No portion of this book may be reproduced, by any process or technique, without the express written consent of the publisher.

Library of Congress Catalog Card Number: 2008026044
ISBN: 978–0–313–34116–8 (set)
    978–0–313–34117–5 (Vol. 1)
    978–0–313–34118–2 (Vol. 2)

First published in 2008

Greenwood Press, 88 Post Road West, Westport, CT 06881
An imprint of Greenwood Publishing Group, Inc.
www.greenwood.com

Printed in the United States of America

The paper used in this book complies with the
Permanent Paper Standard issued by the National
Information Standards Organization (Z39.48–1984).

10 9 8 7 6 5 4 3 2 1

To *mis hijos y sobrinos,* living in several of the states of Latino America, all recipients and integral parts of this history in one way or another.

Contents

VOLUME 1

Foreword *by Stephen Pitti*	ix
Acknowledgments	xiii
Introduction	xv
1. Alabama	1
2. Alaska	13
3. Arizona	25
4. Arkansas	63
5. California	77
6. Colorado	105
7. Connecticut	125
8. Delaware	145
9. District of Columbia	157
10. Florida	167
11. Georgia	197
12. Hawaii	215
13. Idaho	225
14. Illinois	239
15. Indiana	269
16. Iowa	289

17.	Kansas	311
18.	Kentucky	335
19.	Louisiana	347
20.	Maine	363
21.	Maryland	373
22.	Massachusetts	385
23.	Michigan	405
24.	Minnesota	427
25.	Mississippi	445
26.	Missouri	463

VOLUME 2

27.	Montana	475
28.	Nebraska	489
29.	Nevada	501
30.	New Hampshire	519
31.	New Jersey	531
32.	New Mexico	549
33.	New York	577
34.	North Carolina	611
35.	North Dakota	627
36.	Ohio	639
37.	Oklahoma	657
38.	Oregon	667
39.	Pennsylvania	687
40.	Rhode Island	703
41.	South Carolina	715
42.	South Dakota	731
43.	Tennessee	745
44.	Texas	759
45.	Utah	791
46.	Vermont	811
47.	Virginia	821
48.	Washington	839
49.	West Virginia	855
50.	Wisconsin	867
51.	Wyoming	883

Appendix: Census Data of Latinos, 1870–2000	897
Index	901
About the Editor and Contributors	953

Foreword

This important encyclopedia proves that Latinos have a history in all 50 U.S. states, and it anticipates how and why residents of Latin American descent will continue to play critical roles throughout the hemisphere. Its publication follows up on announcements that Latinos have recently become the nation's largest minority population and on predictions about what this fact will mean for rural America, for race relations in U.S. cities, for future Democratic and Republican political campaigns, and for the cultural industries of New York, Miami, and Los Angeles. It also follows up on new attention paid by Latin American countries to emigrants: those family members, wage earners, and fellow citizens who have for decades been in the United States as students, labor migrants, or refugees from violence. It therefore contributes to critical national and hemispheric debates about our shared past and future, about the causes and consequences of migration, about the ways in which governments respond to demands by citizens and noncitizens, and similar issues of central importance.

The remarkable essays solicited by editor Mark Overmyer-Velázquez portray the dynamics, past and present, of changing migrant and native-born populations, and they explain the varied nature of Latino neighborhoods, workplaces, theaters, places of worship, and political organizations. Providing the first sustained accounts of Latinos in many regions of the United States and bringing essays of this sort together for the first time, *Latino America: A State-by-State Encyclopedia* should serve as a standard reference work for years to come. Because the contributors emphasize diverse Latino experiences, it seems clear that students, educators, and members of the general public will find much to admire in this collection. Some readers will turn to these regional studies for information about particular locales or prominent individuals. Others will depend on the demographic and statistical data that they offer. Teachers will also make good use of this encyclopedia. Instructors in middle schools and high schools will use it to integrate Latino materials into established curricula, or to develop new teaching units that respond to the changing demography of classrooms in the United States. Students in various academic settings, in high schools, colleges, and graduate programs, will turn to these volumes as starting points for new local, national, or international studies of Latinos. Like other readers, new generations of readers will find the bibliographies included in these essays indispensable for future research.

These are volumes of considerable intellectual range. As *Latino America: A State-by-State Encyclopedia* presents new, richly informative essays about all 50 U.S. states, it manages also to push our interpretation of those places and their residents. These contributions to local history, in fact, demand a rethinking of broad issues of national and international importance. As essayists explore how Latinos came to play such central roles in states as different as Arizona, Florida, and Mississippi, they tell us a great deal about patterns of national incorporation, about the ways in which, for example, the United States expanded its territorial borders and its influence into Latin America, and how the Mexican War of 1846–1848 and subsequent U.S. interventions in the Caribbean shaped the Latino past and present. They also address how new migration patterns connecting the United States and Latin America emerged from the mid-nineteenth century into the present, and how governmental, religious, and other officials nationwide responded in different ways to recent arrivals and their children. Students and scholars can hardly think about these topics at local levels without engaging other fundamental questions about regional and national identity, about the causes and consequences of migration, and about the intersecting histories of race, gender, and class. Attention to Latino communities from Maine to Hawaii focuses new attention on the ways in which Latin Americans have been seen as threats to U.S. national culture, and how Mexicans and others came to embody racial stigmas, which in turn defined their own individual and collective opportunities, their health and survival, and their identities.

Attentive to histories and changing contemporary circumstances, these essays also highlight the many different ways in which Latinos have responded to residency in the United States. The pages that follow, therefore, document the fascinating public and private lives of women, men, and children who struggled to make the best of difficult local circumstances, including some who contributed in remarkable ways to cities and towns across the country. Contributors show us Latinos who have long been deeply rooted in various locales and many who have articulated strong feelings of national identity for generations. From the Revolutionary War forward, these essays suggest that Latinos have fought and died in military campaigns in and for the United States, contributed labor to home front industries, and supported U.S. patriotic causes. But many others, as these essays also make clear, have concurrently remained Latin Americans within U.S. borders, committed to the homeland politics of Cuba or Colombia, and eager to influence nations elsewhere in the hemisphere. Some of the scholars in this encyclopedia call such political tendencies transnational, emphasizing the ways in which many Latinos have affirmed their connections with nations abroad. Thanks to *Latino America: A State-by-State Encyclopedia,* we know a great deal more both about the U.S. residents who have emphasized U.S. citizenship and national belonging, and about those who have drawn different cognitive maps of Latin America across the United States over the last century and more.

Published at a time when students, academics, policy makers, and others engage in heated new discussions about immigration and citizenship, race and labor, and the future of the United States and the broader hemisphere, this important encyclopedia deserves broad attention. *Latino America: A State-by-State Encyclopedia* contributes in fundamental ways to policy debates in the United States and Latin America, and it should guide new academic efforts to understand our shared past and future. Its wide-ranging portraits of Latino communities will no doubt inspire new and better ways of thinking about populations that have long been misunderstood or simply ignored in the United States.

Stephen Pitti
Professor of History and American Studies
Director of the Program in Ethnicity, Race, and Migration
Master of Ezra Stiles College
Yale University

Acknowledgments

The further I progress into my academic career, the more I learn that the scholarly enterprise of research and writing is an exciting and challenging one of building intellectual communities and enduring collaborative partnerships. I was not only very fortunate that Wendi Schnaufer of Greenwood Press contacted me to embark on this audacious project, but also that she skillfully and with a generous sense of humor guided me through what has been at times a labyrinthine process. I greatly appreciate the diligent work of all the contributors to these volumes and their patience with me as I pestered them with e-mails requesting the latest draft of their chapters. Their pioneering work will be a resource and inspiration for others in the years to come. My academic community throughout this adventure has included many of the administrative and custodial workers, students and faculty at the University of Connecticut. I am very grateful to the diligent custodial staff members—all of them Latinas—that continue to maintain my office in a semblance of order. I have been inspired and challenged by my undergraduate and graduate students over the past four years, and I thank them for their participation as critical readers of various ideas and writings present in this encyclopedia. In particular, Damian Nemirovsky and Michael Neagle merit special credit for their work on the census data chart and respective chapters. My colleagues in the history department and elsewhere have been very welcoming and giving of their time and encouragement. In particular, I have been blessed to receive large doses of critical insight and advice from my *compañeros* and mentors Blanca Silvestrini, Guillermo Irizarry, and Enrique Sepúlveda.

The Institute of Puerto Rican and Latino Studies at the University of Connecticut has served as a virtual home for this project over the past two years, for which I thank Anne Theriault and her student assistants. I owe a long overdue debt to Stephen Pitti. In addition to crafting the Foreword to the encyclopedia and working as an invaluable interlocutor with other contributors, Steve has been my long-term advisor, beginning with my graduate student days, when he first introduced me to the possibilities and responsibilities of studying and teaching Latino history. My greatest support in this project has been, as always, Jordanna Hertz. Jordi patiently and enthusiastically tolerated the fact that I completed most of the editing of these volumes at night, after our precious children, Sarai Dov and Maceo Ilan, were not-so-fast asleep.

Introduction

Puerto Rican *reggaetón* and Mexican *corridos* (ballads) have never had such popular attention. Supporters of party candidates in the 2008 U.S. presidential election have harnessed these popular music forms to mobilize an increasingly politically powerful Latino constituency. Reminiscent of the Viva Kennedy Clubs of the 1960s, Latinos have organized across national origins to work and sing in support of their preferred candidate. At the same time, politicians such as Governor Mike Huckabee of Arkansas have resurrected racist and erroneous narratives of the Alamo to champion the supposed patriotism and moral victory of white Americans over an invisible Latino enemy. In the context of intensified and unresolved debates around migration from Latin America and the Caribbean to the United States, these campaign fragments highlight the central importance of Latinos today and raise fundamental questions about who exactly this dynamic and heterogeneous population is and what their histories can teach us about the United States and their countries of origin.

Experiencing a demographic explosion since the 1960s, Latino/as are now the "majority minority" in the United States, for the first time outnumbering African Americans. One of every seven people in the nation identifies herself or himself as Latina/o, a group that has accounted for about half the growth in the United States population since 1990. The presence of over 47 million people of Latin American and Caribbean origins in the United States has profound implications for the future of this country and for the countries from which they originally came.

People of Latin American and Caribbean heritage have shaped the social, political, economic, and cultural landscape of the United States for centuries. Rather than merely returning another misplaced episode to the story of the United States, the chapters in *Latino America: A State-by-State Encyclopedia* confirm that the story of Latinos is central to U.S. history, and as such it challenges us to reimagine the fundamental constitution, development, and future of the country. Although more exploratory and suggestive than encyclopedically encompassing in its approach to knowledge, *Latino America: A State-by-State Encyclopedia* provides new routes to encounter Latino/as' longstanding contributions to and struggles with people and life in the United States. In *Latino America: A State-by-State Encyclopedia*, scholar-specialists provide individual chapters on each of the 50 states and the District of Columbia. This introduction briefly examines the multiple meanings and implications of the term *Latino*, and it discusses the major forces that have shaped the historical experiences of Latino/as in the United States. It concludes by introducing the encyclopedia's scope, coverage, and importance and by providing the reader with a key with which to navigate each chapter's constituent parts.

WHAT'S IN A NAME?

The demographic statistics outlined above elide the fact that Latino/as can be simultaneously an extremely diverse and fluid assortment of self-conscious individuals and a unified ethnic community. The strategic definition as Latino/a—at once external and self-identifying—is inherently political, and it is complicated by several factors, including historical context, generation, language, gender, race, class, location, and country of origin.

Emerging in the 1980s, the term *Latino* refers to people, either male or female, living in the United States with at least one parent of Latin American or Caribbean descent, and it is often used in contrast to groups such as Asian, African, and Anglo Americans. According to the official classificatory schemes of the U.S. census, *Latino* is applied to migrants and their descendents in the United States originating from the Spanish-speaking countries of North, Central, and South America, as well as from countries in the Caribbean and from Spain.[1] This definition often excludes countries such as Haiti, Brazil, and Belize, but it includes U.S. territories such as Puerto Rico. As a Spanish-language term, it takes masculine and feminine endings. Although the masculine versions of the term, *Latino/Latinos*, are commonly used to refer to both men *and* women, it is important to consider the meaning and power of using *Latina/Latinas* in place of, or in addition to, *Latino/Latinos*. In an effort to avoid masculine-only descriptions, some authors in the encyclopedia use hybrid terms such as *Latino/a*. The other popular term used to describe this population, *Hispanic*, was adopted in 1977 by the U.S. Office of

Budget and Management for purposes of data collection as a simplified way to categorize people of Latin American and Caribbean descent. However, many individuals of Latin American and Caribbean heritage or origin reject the term *Hispanic* to identify themselves, considering the label a denial of gains made by U.S. ethnic rights struggles and something that improperly identifies them more with Spain than with Latin America and the Caribbean.

As with all identities, Latinos/as choose their identifiers among a shifting and mutable repertoire that varies depending on the individual's political, historical and spatial contexts. Most Latinos first identify with their own national or subnational origins. For example, a woman with roots in Puerto Rico might first identify herself as *una puertorriqueña* and then as a Latina.[2] The term *Latino* is made further problematic by the thousands of non-Spanish-speaking indigenous migrants in the United States who may identify primarily with their small village or perhaps state of origin, and not with a Spanish-language heritage, as is the case with Mixtec migrants from the state of Oaxaca, Mexico, who have developed Oaxacan hometown associations in places such as Los Angeles.

The term *Latino America* in this publication's title additionally complicates the conundrum of identity and identifying by insisting on a transnational dynamic between Latin Americans and U.S. Latino/as. Although perhaps seeming at first glance a malapropism, *Latino America* suggests a shared hemispheric historical experience among North, Central, and South American as well as Caribbean populations that challenges us to reconsider fixed regions of study that divide the United States and Latin America into discrete units of inquiry.[3] Furthermore, by closely resembling its Spanish-language cognate, *Latinoamérica* (Latin America), Latino America makes a direct connection with Latino/as' region of origin.

LATINA/O HISTORY AS U.S. HISTORY

Latina/o history is central to the history of the United States. Just as we might learn about indigenous populations, Anglo-European settlement on (that is, migration to) the East Coast, or African slavery as part of the history of the United States, Latino/as have also played a critical role in shaping this country's history. From the sixteenth-century Spanish settlements in states such as Alabama, California, and Florida, to the role of state residents in nineteenth- and twentieth-century U.S. military campaigns in Latin America, to the contemporary surge of Latino/a populations in the Carolinas, Oklahoma, Oregon, and Connecticut, *Latino America: A State-by-State Encyclopedia* clearly demonstrates that Latina/os have been intimately connected to every historical stage and to every region in the United States.

U.S. economic and military imperialism, liberalized immigration laws, population expansion in Latin America, and comparatively higher wages in the

United States have determined the historical presence of Latino/as in the United States since the mid-nineteenth century. The years 1848, 1898, and 1965 exemplify these factors in history.

Mexicans refer to the 1846–1848 war with the United States as the North American Invasion. As a young country, the United States' first significant effort at economic and military imperialism cost Mexico over half of its territory—including the present-day U.S. states of California, Nevada, Utah, and parts of Colorado, Arizona, New Mexico, and Wyoming—which led some Mexican citizens left on the new U.S. side of the border to proclaim, "We didn't cross the border, the border crossed us." Mexico, weak from years of independence and civil wars, and the United States, eager to expand its borders to the west past Texas, built the right environment for war between the two countries. The annexed Mexican territory brought not only new citizens of Mexican heritage to the United States but also enormous mineral and land wealth. The mining prospectors made wealthy in the famous 1848 gold rush dug their mines on former Mexican territory in California. U.S. government officials and others viewed that event and the vast expanse of agricultural and pasture lands as fundamental to the country's westward expansion. In theory, the culminating Treaty of Guadalupe Hidalgo (1848) promised that Mexicans on the north side of the new Rio Bravo/Rio Grande border could become U.S. citizens; it was a promise rarely fulfilled as Anglo-European settlers frequently manipulated the law to remove Mexican access to land and citizenship rights. Ironically, as the West industrialized and demand for labor grew, it was often Mexican American and migrant Mexican workers who labored in the fields and factories of the growing economy.

The arrival of migrants from Latin America and the Caribbean to the United States was a direct result of U.S. imperialistic activities, starting with the invasion of Mexico in 1848. The United States' "harvest of empire" peaked with the 1898 Spanish-American War. With all of the continent's land colonized by the end of nineteenth century, the United States government looked to the remnants of Spain's overseas possessions to expand its economic empire. At the conflict's end and the signing of the Treaty of Paris on December 10, 1898, the United States had conquered not only Puerto Rico but also the Philippines and Guam, and irrevocably linked Cuba and Cubans to its trans-Caribbean future. When the United States' military was in the process of "freeing" the island of Puerto Rico from Spanish colonial rule in 1898, General Nelson Miles declared, "Our purpose is not to interfere with the existing laws and customs which are beneficial for your people." The island's inhabitants would have never imagined that two years later; with the passing of the Foraker Act in 1900 Puerto Rico would become a colony yet again, this time of the United States. The Act made the island a U.S. territory and gave the president power to appoint the governor and other high-level administrators. In 1917 Congress passed the Jones Act, imposing

U.S. citizenship on all Puerto Ricans. For the next 35 years the island would exist as a colony of the United States and provide cheap labor for the mother country's industries. In the 1950s, after the island's status had changed to a neo-colonial commonwealth model permitting some limited political autonomy, migration to the United States rapidly accelerated; in fact, this was the largest migration of Latin Americans to the United States the hemisphere had ever witnessed. But that was only the beginning of the migrant flood to the north. New legislation in the 1960s would not only increase the numbers of Latin American migrants to the United States, but it would also radically reshape the contours of North American society.

On October 3, 1965, President Lyndon B. Johnson signed the Hart-Celler Immigration Bill, inaugurating a new era of mass migration. The legislation, which phased out the national origins quota system first instituted in 1921, created the foundation of today's immigration laws. Prior to 1965, 70 percent of all migrant slots were allotted to natives of just three countries—United Kingdom, Ireland, and Germany—and most slots went unused. But there were long waiting lists for the small number of visas available to those born in Italy, Greece, Poland, Portugal, and elsewhere in eastern and southern Europe. The Hart-Celler Act eliminated the various nationality-based criteria, supposedly putting people of all nations on an equal footing for migration to the United States. The new legislation put in place a system based primarily on family reunification and needed skills. The long-term result of the Act was to reverse the composition of migrants coming to the United States in the last four decades of the twentieth century. In 1960, 75 percent of all the foreign-born population came from Europe, and only 14 percent came from Latin America, the Caribbean, and Asia. These numbers had been essentially inverted by 2000, when only 15 percent of migrants arrived from Europe, and over 77 percent arrived from Latin America and Asia. This trend only promises to continue in the future.

Latin America and the Caribbean also contributed to the massive flow of migrants to the United States during this period. Between 1960 and 2000 the region's population skyrocketed from 218 million to over 520 million. Political instability in Latin America and the Caribbean, combined with this growing population, meant increased needs for out-migration and work; thus many turned to the economic opportunities of the United States. On the other hand, for most of the twentieth century, agricultural, industrial, and domestic employers in the United States depended upon cheap migrant labor from Latin America, the Caribbean, and elsewhere to make enough profits to sustain their successes.

Though the events surrounding the years 1848, 1898, and 1965 help us to understand how and why Latin American and Caribbean populations migrated to the United States, they do not tell us much about what happened once they arrived. Despite their many shared experiences of U.S. military and economic imperialism, migration, and racial and ethnic discrimination once in the United States, Latina/os are anything but a uniform population. In fact, their broad diversity in terms of national origin, generation, gender, sexuality, class, and political affiliation—to name a few variables—has as much divided as it has united this growing demographic. Although popular cultural representations of Latina/os on TV and in film have tended to portray them as a unified and homogenous group with similar cultural sensibilities and linguistic, religious, and political affiliations, Latinos, as we have seen from this brief historical introduction, differ both in origins and destinations. Before even entering the United States, Latin Americans and Caribbeans themselves represent a large range of class, national, ethnic, and racial backgrounds—including black, brown, white, Asian, Indian, and any combination of these as well. Mexicans started migrating to the United States in the nineteenth century and Puerto Ricans in the early twentieth century, whereas South and Central Americans from countries such as Chile, Argentina, El Salvador, and Guatemala made their way north, seeking asylum from brutal military dictatorships—most supported by the U.S. government—in increasing numbers starting in the 1960s. Once in the United States, Latino/as of all backgrounds have continued to mix with local populations, forging a whole new set of identities and ethnic, national, and political allegiances. Far from being uprooted from their original cultures and assimilating into the American melting pot, diverse Latino/a communities maintain and develop their distinct cultures in new and innovative ways in the United States, adding to the rich diversity and complexity of the country. Indeed, Latina/os have contributed to U.S. society in ways that reach beyond their investments in the country's economy and labor. In the realms of politics, education, sports, and the arts, Latina/os are a growing presence helping to frame the future of the United States and their countries of origin.

In an ill-conceived attempt to stop or stem the flow of Latin American and Caribbean migrants to the United States, many U.S. politicians have sought to redraw the map of the country by effectively extending the border beyond the Rio Bravo/Rio Grande line deeper into the United States. In the wake of the terrorist attacks of September 11, 2001, U.S. officials and pundits have positioned Latino migration and migrants as central causes of national anxiety and insecurity. Increased surveillance and raids by Homeland Security officers have only further increased apprehension among the country's migrant communities. Despite renewed unilateral, anti-immigrant legislative intensification, the consistent and constant need of and demand for labor—fueled by an enduring imperial connection between the two regions—have proven the historical inefficacy of each new regulation and law. At the same time, our Latin American and Caribbean counterparts have continued to recast their countries' relationship with their neighbor to the north through the lives of their transborder citizens. If history has taught us anything about this protracted transnational relationship, it is that what is urgently required are multilateral negotiations that address and remedy long-standing economic and structural inequalities between the two regions. As the maps of the United States and Latin America increasingly overlap one another, we need to turn to histories such as those found in *Latino America: A State-by-State Encyclopedia* to redraw our conceptual and geopolitical maps of the country, hemisphere, and world, and to expand rather than restrict our access to new routes and possibilities for freer movement and lives.

ABOUT THE ENCYCLOPEDIA

Authored by an interdisciplinary group of scholars, *Latino America: A State-by-State Encyclopedia* is uniquely conceptualized to address the historical significance of the growing Latino/a American population throughout the United States. The set contains geographically distinct entries according to individual states and the District of Columbia.[4] Clearly presented for a general audience, this comparative method of organizing material importantly and appropriately moves the focus of the Latino/a experience from studies of gateway states in the Southwest to a national level. Besides paying careful attention to the transnational dimensions of Latin American migration to the U.S, individual entries critically examine the wide range of different Latino/a identities, ethnicities, and social and political positions at the state level. In doing so, the authors engage a broader understanding of the central role of people of Latin American and Caribbean origin and heritage in the United States.

As with all large edited works, there is a creative tension between uniformity and consistency on the one hand, and the uniqueness of the subject and its authors' scholarship on the other. The varying historical experiences of Latinos/as in each state challenged authors to examine different chronological and thematic emphases. Additionally, authors came to this project with their own disciplinary lenses and approaches. With all of this in mind, authors sought to incorporate themes that surpass national and intercultural boundaries, while simultaneously revealing some of the more salient sources of internal division among Latinas/os. Themes analyzed include the trans- and international dimension of Latin America's relationship with U.S. Latinas/os, cultural nationalisms, identity formations, political membership, gender relations, race and racism, labor and immigration law, and religion and expressive cultures.

Certain elements have been omitted while privileging others. For example, a decision was made not to have Puerto Rico as one of the chapters in this encyclopedia, because, despite the fact that inhabitants of the island of Puerto Rico were made U.S. citizens in 1917, they continue to be perceived as "foreign to the United States in a domestic sense" by the U.S. government, which makes them occupy a liminal status between state and colony. Although not the subject of a separate chapter, readers will discover the complexities of nationality and citizenship among Puerto Ricans in many of the individual state chapters.

Rather than include additional essays that examine political, economic, social, and cultural themes that transcend national and state boundaries, *Latino America: A State-by-State Encyclopedia* allows readers to conduct their own comparisons of themes and national groups among the states. As such, the publication's subtitle *State-by-State* could also read *State-to-State*, underscoring the movement between and within the states of the United States that so aptly characterizes the historical experience of Latino/as.

Every chapter is divided into distinct sections that approach the history of Latinas/os from multiple perspectives. The historical **Chronology** section that opens each essay offers an annotated timeline of the role and impact Latino Americans have had in the particular state. The **Historical Overview** examines in narrative form the extended presence of Latinas/os in the United States, emphasizing political, social, and economic histories unique to the region, from the earliest days of settlement of Latin American and Caribbean explorers to the present day. In the section **Notable Latinos**, authors document in chronological birth order select and representative individuals from the state's Latino population. These notable people are resourceful pioneers—past and present—who have created new possibilities and avenues of discovery and achievement for both Latinos and non-Latinos alike. Conceptualizing cultural production as a mutually constitutive aspect of political power, the section entitled **Cultural Contributions** explores cultural expressions, rituals, and traditions among each state's Latino/a populations. The **Notes** and **Bibliography** sections provide a critical resource for students and researchers seeking to expand their study of Latino American history. And finally, the **Appendix** provides a table with census data on Latinos from 1870 to 2000.

NOTES

1. Here and throughout the encyclopedia the terms *migrant* and *migration* are often used in place of *immigrant* and *immigration*. The latter terms imply a unidirectional path to the United States, and as such, they are linked to a historical privileging of assimilationist and melting-pot theories that ignore both the transnational movement of people back and forth across borders and their varied national and regional claims to identity and citizenship. Unless noted otherwise, *immigration* is only used when referring to official government policies or legislative or organizational titles, as in *immigrant rights laws*.

Similarly, when possible, the term *America* is avoided as a substitute for the term *United States*. Because Latinos are also of (Latin) American heritage and descent, it is inaccurate to believe that the term *America* refers uniquely to the United States. At times authors use *North American* to mean a citizen or inhabitant of the United States, although that term can also include Mexicans and Canadians.

2. National and subnational Latino groups often use separate categories to identify themselves. For example, Mexican Americans might use the term *Chicano/a* and Puerto Ricans the term *Boricua*. Each term has its own particular historical, political, and regional meaning.

3. The term *Latin(o) America* was first coined by Diane Taylor, and it has been used in similar ways by other authors to theorize issues of *mestizaje* (mixed race) and hybridity among Latin American and U.S. Latina/o subjects. See also works by Spitta and Poblete.

4. Entry lengths (roughly four, seven, or thirteen thousand words) vary depending on the number of Latinos as a percentage of the state's total population, as determined by the 2000 U.S. census.

SELECTED BIBLIOGRAPHY

Gonzalez, Gilbert, and Raul Fernandez. *A Century of Chicano History: Empire, Nations, and Migration*. New York: Routledge, 2003.

Gonzalez, Juan. *Harvest of Empire: A History of Latinos in America*. New York: Viking Penguin, 2000.

Gutiérrez, David. *The Columbia History of Latinos in the United States since 1960*. New York: Columbia University Press, 2004.

Oboler, Suzanne. *Ethnic Labels, Latino Lives: Identity and the Politics of (Re)Presentation in the United States*. Minneapolis: University of Minnesota Press, 1995.

Oboler, Suzanne, and Deena J. González, eds. *The Oxford History of Latinos and Latinas in the United States*. New York: Oxford University Press, 2005.

Overmyer-Velázquez, Mark, ed. *History of Latinos in the United States*, 6 vols. New York: Chelsea House Publishers, 2007.

Poblete, Juan. *Critical Latin American and Latino Studies*. Minneapolis: University of Minnesota Press, 2003.

Ruiz, Vicki. "Nuestra América: Latino History as United States History." *Journal of American History* 93, no. 3 (December 2006): 655–672.

Sánchez, George J. *Becoming Mexican American: Ethnicity, Culture and Identity in Chicano Los Angeles, 1900–1945*. New York: Oxford University Press, 1993.

Spitta, Silvia. *Between Two Waters: Narratives of Transculturation in Latin America*. Houston, TX: Rice University Press, 1995.

Taylor, Diana, and Juan Villegas, eds. *Negotiating Performance: Gender, Sexuality, and Theatricality in Latin/o America*. Durham, NC: Duke University Press, 1994.

1
Alabama

Helen Delpar

CHRONOLOGY

1540	Hernando de Soto leads a Spanish expedition that spends part of the year traversing Alabama. They are the first Europeans to visit the future state.
1559–1561	A Spanish expedition headed by Tristán de Luna explores part of Alabama during an unsuccessful effort to found a colony in territory still considered part of Florida.
1780–1813	Spanish forces commanded by Bernardo de Gálvez capture Mobile on March 14, 1780. This and other later victories allow Spain to regain control of Florida, which was lost to the British in 1783. Mobile and other portions of the future Alabama become part of West Florida, which extends from the Apalachicola and Chattahoochee rivers on the east to the Mississippi on the west, and north to 32°28′N. latitude. All of West Florida falls under U.S. control in 1811–1813.
1921	A sensational trial takes place after a Methodist minister, Edwin R. Stephenson, kills a Roman Catholic priest who had married his daughter to a Puerto Rican, Pedro Gussman. In his successful defense of Stephenson, attorney Hugo L. Black makes much of Gussman's supposed African ancestry.
1990s	A Latino influx to Alabama begins. Latinos, mainly from Mexico and Central America, many of them undocumented, come to the state to work in the poultry industry and in other low-wage, nonunion jobs.
1996	A lawsuit is initiated to force Alabama to offer driver's license examinations in Spanish and other languages besides English.

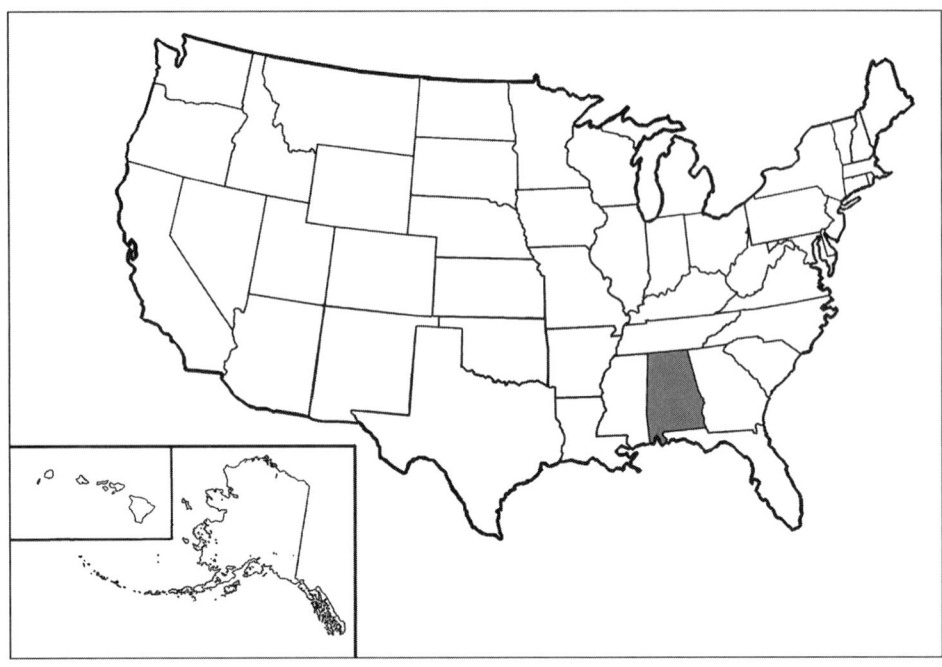

2001	The U.S. Supreme Court rules that Alabama is not required to offer driver's license examinations in languages other than English. By then, however, the state had already been offering the exam in Spanish and other languages, a policy upheld by the Alabama Supreme Court in 2007.
2007	A new Spanish-language radio station goes on the air in Birmingham. It is one of several new businesses and services targeted at the state's growing Latino population.
2008	Data from the Census Bureau demonstrate that more than half of Alabama's Latino population is of Mexican origin, and that 71.5 percent of Alabama's Latino population is under 35 years of age.
	Alabama's Joint Interim Patriotic Immigration Commission—created by the state legislature in 2007—issues a report listing 25 recommendations for enforcing immigration laws and cracking down on undocumented immigrants. These include finding out whether public medical facilities are being abused, denying bond to undocumented migrants, and impounding vehicles of drivers without licenses or proof of insurance. The report is issued after the commission holds public hearings in four cities.

HISTORICAL OVERVIEW

Alabama began to receive relatively large numbers of Latinos only after 1990, and they tended to congregate in certain areas of the state. Some residents welcomed the new arrivals, but others regarded them warily, fearful of the economic and social consequences of their presence. Moreover, the Latinos represented a novel cultural and racial element in a state that had traditionally defined itself in terms of black and white.

Hispanic Beginnings

Alabamians who were uncomfortable about the presence of Latinos in their midst often overlooked the fact that Spanish was the first European language heard in what is now Alabama. In the mid-sixteenth century two large expeditions traversed most of the territory of the future state. Little remains of the brief Spanish presence, though scholars debate the routes followed and pore over contemporary accounts of the expeditions to glean information about the American societies encountered by the Spaniards.

In 1537 the Spanish Crown authorized Hernando de Soto to launch an expedition to Florida, whose contours were still unclear. Landing with nine ships, 237 horses, and some 650 persons on Florida's western coast, probably at Tampa Bay or Charlotte Harbor, the expedition traveled to the panhandle and into present-day Georgia, the Carolinas, and Tennessee before entering Alabama. In 1935–1939 the U.S. DeSoto Commission retraced the expedition's route, but modern scholars have questioned its findings. For example, de Soto spent a month in Coosa, the central town of an important native chiefdom. The commission placed Coosa in modern Talladega County, but others argue that it was located in northwestern Georgia. Later the expedition moved through the territory of another important chief, Tascaluza. On October 18, 1540, de Soto engaged Tascaluza's forces in a bloody battle in Mabila, during which perhaps as many as 3,000 Indians were killed. The site of Mabila is still uncertain, but it may have been located near the Alabama River or on the lower Cahaba River. The expedition then moved north and made camp for the winter in northeastern Mississippi, among the Chickasaw.

Although the expedition is credited with the European discovery of the Mississippi River, overall it is considered a failure, as it not only cost the life of de Soto himself and those of many of his companions, but it also failed to yield the gold and silver sought by the Spaniards. Relations with the Indians were uniformly bad, no converts to Christianity were made, and no colonies were established. The expedition introduced pigs to the region as well as Old World diseases, such as smallpox and typhoid fever.

A second Spanish expedition that traversed much of what is now Alabama was equally unsuccessful. Led by Tristán de Luna, the expedition left Veracruz, Mexico, on June 11, 1559, with 11 ships, 240 horses, and 1,500 men, women, and children (including Indians and blacks) for the purpose of exploring and colonizing what was still called Florida. The expedition settled along Pensacola Bay, where, on September 19, a hurricane destroyed most of the ships; but the expedition also spent time on Mobile Bay (then called Bahía Filipina), which had been visited by Guido de Lavazares in 1558. Parties from the expedition traveled to an Indian community called Nanipacana, on the Alabama River, and reached Coosa as well. The expedition proved a failure for several reasons, including food shortages and Luna's deficiencies as a leader, and no permanent Spanish colony was established in Alabama.

Two centuries later, another Hispanic episode in what is now Alabama occurred when Spain acquired West Florida from the British in 1783. This region, stretching from the Apalachicola and Chattahoochee rivers to the Mississippi, extended from Mobile as far north as 32°28'N. latitude. During the 20-year Spanish occupation, top officials were Spanish, and consequently the official language became Spanish, but many of the residents were French, British, or American. For the Spanish authorities, the main preoccupation was twofold: the expansionist tendencies of the United States and the need to maintain friendly relations with the Indians, who also feared North American encroachment on their lands. These concerns prompted the Spaniards to establish Fort San Estevan (St. Stephens) in 1789, about 60 miles north of Mobile, on the Tombigbee River, but in 1795 Spain ceded the territory north of 31°N. latitude to the United States. Between 1811 and 1813 the United States occupied Mobile and the rest of West Florida. With these additions, ratified by the Adams-Onís Treaty of 1819, all of present-day Alabama was included within the territory of the United States.

The Nineteenth and Early Twentieth Centuries

Alabama entered the Union as a slaveholding state in 1819. It was part of the "Cotton Kingdom" of the pre–Civil War South, with a labor force made up largely of black slaves, who represented more than 45 percent of the total population of 964,201 in 1860. The free black population numbered only 2,690 in that year. Few foreign-born migrants settled in Alabama, except in Mobile, which was the principal outlet for the state's cotton exports. In 1850 the foreign born made up 31 percent of the city's free population of 13,712. Among them were 22 Mexicans and 144 Spaniards (including three described as "free colored"). A few Cubans and Mexicans, especially from the Yucatan Peninsula, also enrolled in Spring Hill College, a Jesuit institution in Mobile.[1] During the nineteenth and early twentieth centuries Mobile was also an important port of entry for sugar and cigars from Cuba and for bananas from Central America.

If few Latinos settled in the state, Alabamians had occasional contacts with Latin America, often in a wartime context unlikely to foster friendly feelings. Alabamians volunteered to fight for Texas independence, and some 140 were executed at Goliad in March 1836. Alabamians took part in the war against Mexico in 1846–1848 and in the war against Spain in 1898. During the latter conflict Richard Pearson Hobson, a naval officer from Greensboro, distinguished himself for a daring effort to bottle up the Spanish fleet in the harbor of Santiago, Cuba. Another Alabamian, William Crawford Gorgas, of the U.S. Army Medical Corps, was named chief sanitation officer for Havana in 1898. In this capacity he made use of the theory of the Cuban physician Carlos Finlay, according to which yellow fever was spread by mosquitoes. Gorgas was thus able to eradicate that deadly tropical disease in Cuba. Later Gorgas conducted a similar campaign against yellow fever during the construction of the Panama Canal.

Journalists and other writers displayed sentiments toward Mexicans and Latin Americans in general that were at best ambivalent. When a crisis arose over Pancho Villa's 1916 raid on Columbus, New Mexico, during the Mexican Revolution, Alabama newspapers conveyed a negative image of Mexicans. However, an editorial writer in the *Birmingham Post* predicted, during the centenary of Mexican independence, that in 2021 Mexico would be a greater power than any of the European nations because of its "vast territory and tremendously rich resources." Hudson Strode, a well-known teacher of fiction writing at the University of Alabama, published four books on travel and popular history related to Latin America in the 1930s and 1940s. Although he described Mexican peasants stereotypically as submissive fatalists easily transformed into "savage fanatics," he also declared the notion of Mexico's "inexhaustible riches" to be a "fallacy" and stressed the importance for the United States of a peaceful and prosperous neighbor. According to Strode, Cubans were fatalists too, but there was much in the Cuban character that North Americans might emulate, particularly "a basic joyousness that will not be suppressed."[2]

In the late nineteenth century and early decades of the twentieth century Alabama remained a largely rural state where agriculture was predominant. Because farm prices, especially for cotton, were often low during this period, most rural Alabamians, both black and white, lived in poverty. By 1930 nearly 65 percent of the state's farmers were either sharecroppers or cash tenants who usually found themselves at the mercy of landlords. White tenants frequently left their farms for jobs in textile mills, which grew rapidly after the Civil War. Alabama had also become an important coal-producing state, with 26,200 miners, by 1920; many black miners were convicts leased by the state to mine operators, a system that persisted until the late 1920s. Demand for Alabama's coal was stimulated in part by the rise of iron and steel production, which used coke as fuel. The iron and steel industry developed around the new city of Birmingham, founded in 1871, and it became a major source of nonfarm employment.

During this era the African American population remained large, even after the start of the Great Migration of blacks to the North, reaching nearly 36 percent of the total population in 1930. Racial segregation was the norm in schools, public accommodations, and most other areas of life, and blacks were effectively disenfranchised by the constitution of 1901. In this environment and given the poverty of the state, few foreign-born migrants moved to Alabama. In 1910, when the foreign born accounted for nearly 15 percent of the total U.S. population, they represented less than 1 percent of the Alabama population. Alabama's foreign born, mainly from central and southern Europe, usually found employment in the iron and steel and related industries in the Birmingham area.

There had long been a Roman Catholic presence in Mobile, and many of the recent foreign migrants in Birmingham were Catholics as well. By the 1920s, however, anti-Catholic, anti-immigrant sentiment had emerged with unprecedented virulence, articulated by U.S. Senator J. Thomas Heflin (1920–1931) and by groups such as Birmingham's Society of True Americans and the revived Ku Klux Klan. In 1921 a Puerto Rican migrant played a leading role in a notorious case that epitomized the racism and anti-Catholicism characteristic of the state and the era.

In August 1921 Pedro Gussman—who had migrated to the U.S. mainland from Puerto Rico at the age of 20—was a 42-year-old wallpaper hanger living in Birmingham. Several years earlier he had become acquainted with the much younger Ruth Stephenson, daughter of Edwin R. Stephenson, an ordained Methodist minister extremely hostile to Catholicism. The previous April, Ruth, then eighteen, had defied her father by joining the Catholic Church, and on August 11 she was married to Gussman by Father James E. Coyle, pastor of St. Paul's Cathedral in Birmingham. Upon hearing of the marriage, the outraged Stephenson went to the cathedral rectory and gunned Father Coyle down. When Stephenson was tried for murder, his defense attorney, Hugo L. Black, the future U.S. senator and Supreme Court justice, claimed that Stephenson had killed Coyle in a fit of temporary insanity. Although Gussman asserted that his parents had been born in Spain and that he was white, Black was at pains to suggest that the Puerto Rican was of African ancestry, thereby exploiting fears of interracial marriage. On one occasion Black had the courtroom dimmed to highlight Gussman's supposedly dark complexion, and on another he asked whether the Puerto Rican had had his hair straightened recently. In his closing argument Black declared that if Gussman was of Castilian descent, he had descended a long way. The jury quickly acquitted Stephenson.

Latino Influx in the Late Twentieth Century

Prior to 1990 few Latinos lived in Alabama, and they were mainly professional people, such as physicians and college instructors. Among the latter were many of the several hundred Cuban refugees who settled in Alabama during the 1960s. In addition, temporary workers were recruited to pick fruits and vegetables and to plant pine trees, but they usually returned to their place of origin after completing their assignments. In fact, the U.S. Census Bureau offered only sample-based estimates of the Latino population until 1980. In that year the Census Bureau counted only 33,299 Latinos in the state, or less than 1 percent of a total population of 3,893,888.

The years after 1990 witnessed a substantial influx of Latinos, who became permanent residents of Alabama. According to the Census Bureau's American Community Survey for 2006, there were 111,432 Latinos in Alabama, or approximately 2.4 percent of the total population of 4,599,030. The actual number of Latinos living in Alabama was undoubtedly much higher. In 2005 the Pew Hispanic Center estimated the number of "unauthorized migrants" living in Alabama at between 30,000 and 50,000.

By the time Latinos began arriving in the late twentieth century, the economy of Alabama had undergone substantial changes. The state was still relatively poor, but its economy was much more diversified than it had been earlier in the century. Although cotton remained a major crop, poultry raising and processing had become the most important activity in the agricultural sector, and Alabama ranked third in U.S. broiler production, behind Arkansas and Georgia. Other new products included farmed catfish and soybeans. Though experiencing declines in Alabama as elsewhere, textile and iron and steel production was still a major part of the industrial sector. These traditional industries were, however, supplemented by new manufacturing activities. Most notable perhaps was the establishment, beginning in the 1990s, of automobile plants by several foreign makers—including Mercedes, Honda, and Hyundai—and of factories for the production of auto parts.

Latinos initially settled in the northern section of the state—mainly in rural, sparsely populated, overwhelmingly white counties.[3] One such county was Marshall County, where the Latino population in 2006 was estimated at 8,100, or 9.3 percent of a total population of 87,185. In neighboring DeKalb County, there were 6,460 Latinos in 2006, or 9.5 percent of a population of 68,014. Other northern counties where Latinos were numerically significant included Franklin and Cullman counties.

Farther south, the more populous Jefferson County, where Birmingham is located, and Shelby County had sizable Latino populations too. In Jefferson County, Latinos numbered 17,337, or 2.6 percent of the total population in 2006. In Shelby County 5,934 Latinos, or 3.3 percent of the total population, were counted. There was also a Latino presence in parts of the 12-county Black Belt (so called because of its rich soil), the most impoverished and heavily African American section of the state, even as the region was losing population.

Approximately 64 percent of the Latinos counted in the 2006 survey were Mexicans; the others came mainly from Central America and the Caribbean. Most of these Latinos originally went to northern Alabama to work in poultry-processing plants. By the late 1990s, for example, in the tiny town of Collinsville, in DeKalb County, approximately half of the workers in the local poultry plant were Latinos. They also found employment in a local sock factory, a nursing home, and in retail establishments. By 2000, 23.5 percent of Collinsville's 1,644 residents were Latinos. Poultry-processing plants drew Latinos to other areas of the state, such as the town of Union Springs in the Black Belt's Bullock County. In 2006 Latinos accounted for about 2.7 percent of the county's approximately 11,714 people. Throughout the state Latinos also found work in construction, landscaping, restaurants, and other service industries.

In addition, many Latinos opened restaurants, groceries, clothing stores, and other businesses to serve their communities, and by 2002 there were more than 2,500 Latino-owned businesses in the state. A Hispanic Business Council was established in 2001 as part of the Birmingham Area Chamber of Commerce to assist Latino entrepreneurs and companies doing business with Latinos. In 2003 an Alabama Hispanic Chamber of Commerce was formed in Birmingham. Affiliated with the U.S. Hispanic Chamber of Commerce and made up solely of Latino entrepreneurs, its members included retailers, mortgage brokers, insurance agents, and others.

Mixed Reception

The growing number and visibility of Latinos in a state where the foreign-born population had traditionally been minuscule produced mixed feelings. On the one hand, Latinos were praised for their work ethic and for revitalizing depressed business areas. According to a *Birmingham News* article from January 10, 2004, Collinsville's Main Street was the site of several Latino-owned businesses—such as grocery store–restaurants, a shipping and travel agency, and a food products distribution center. The mayor was quoted as saying that the Latino businesses had "brought the downtown area back to life" and boosted the town's sales tax receipts. The Latino influx occurred when economic conditions in the state were generally good and unemployment was below the national average. As a result, relatively few complained that Latinos were depriving native Alabamians of desirable jobs.

On the other hand, many native Alabamians expressed unhappiness over the growing Latino population, particularly the undocumented among them. The principal grievance was that they represented a burden on taxpayers because of their utilization of public services. Because undocumented workers usually lacked health insurance, they turned to public hospitals and public health departments for prenatal and other forms of medical care. In 1994 there were only 44 visits by Latinos to Jefferson County Department of Health centers, but by 2000 the figure had risen to more than 13,000. The number of interpreters employed by the department increased from one to six in the same period.[4] Between 1993–1994 and 2002–2003, according to a Pew Hispanic Center estimate, the number of Latinos enrolled in Alabama public schools increased by nearly 380 percent. In counties of high immigration, public school teachers and administrators, especially at the elementary level, were confronted with the arrival of children with limited English-language skills; yet federal and state funding for ESL (English as a Second Language) and other services was deemed inadequate.

Some Alabamians complained that Latino residents lowered neighborhood property values through overcrowding or by producing excessive noise or other disturbances. As a result, Pelham (Shelby County) and other communities adopted ordinances limiting the number of adults who could legally occupy a single-family dwelling. In Hoover, an affluent suburb of Birmingham, the congregation of day laborers in front of a city-owned building became an issue in municipal elections in 2005.

The sound of Spanish or the sight of bilingual signs offended other Alabamians. As early as 1990 nearly 90 percent of voters approved an amendment to the state constitution declaring English to be Alabama's official language and requiring officials to preserve and enhance its role. As a result, the state ended its practice of offering the driver's license test in Spanish and other foreign languages. In 1996, backed by the Southern Poverty Law Center and other groups, Martha Sandoval, a permanent U.S. resident originally from Mexico, initiated a class-action suit against the state for the right to take the driver's license test in Spanish. Federal district and appeals courts agreed with the plaintiff's contention that the English-only policy violated Title VI of the Civil Rights Act of 1964. But in 2001 the U.S. Supreme Court ruled by a 5-4 vote that Sandoval could not sue the state for discrimination (*Alexander v. Sandoval*). By that time, however, the state had resumed testing in languages other than English, leading to new litigation in 2005 by the Southeastern Legal Foundation. In October 2007 the Alabama Supreme Court upheld the state policy by a 5-4 vote. The majority accepted the state's contention that the policy encouraged the assimilation of foreign-language speakers by facilitating access to education, employment, and other activities.

Alabamians unhappy about the increased number of Latinos among them sometimes resorted to vandalism. In July 2006 gunshots were fired into the windows and glass doors of Latino businesses in the Marshall County town of Albertville. The following October trailers occupied by Latinos in Tuscaloosa County's Northport were vandalized and a Mexican flag set on fire. At another trailer park, obscenities were spray-painted on a mobile home, and the occupants were told to leave.

In response to large pro-immigrant demonstrations throughout the United States in the spring of 2006, including one in Birmingham and another in Albertville, some Alabamians took part in counterdemonstrations. In Cullman a crowd of 300–400 held signs with such sentiments as "Illegals cost taxpayers thousands of dollars a year." A Ku Klux Klan anti-immigration rally in Russellville (Franklin County) attracted some 300 supporters. In 2003 the desire to reduce illegal immigration led Alabama to become the second state (after Florida) to sign an agreement with the U.S. Immigration and Customs Enforcement to use state troopers to enforce federal laws; 70 troopers were expected to be authorized to arrest undocumented aliens by the end of 2006.

As of 2006 few Latinos were registered voters in Alabama, and the Latino community as a whole had little political influence. However, churches and other nonprofit groups provided legal, medical, and educational services to recent migrants. Among the latter were the Hispanic Interest Coalition of Alabama, which was established in 1999 to assist Latinos in the Birmingham metropolitan area, and the Huntsville-based Alabama Hispanic Association, founded in 2002, which focused on northern Alabama.

As Alabama's Latino population rose, the city of Mobile maintained a close relationship with Cuba. In 1993 Mobile and Havana became sister cities, the first such U.S. "twinning" since the Cuban Revolution. Through the work of the Society Mobile–La Habana, numerous conferences and people-to-people exchanges took place. After Congress passed legislation in 2000 permitting limited U.S. exports to Cuba, Mobile again became an important port for the shipment of agricultural goods to the island, many of them produced in Alabama and ranging from poultry to wooden utility poles.[5]

NOTABLE LATINOS

Soto, Hernando de (c. 1500–1542). Spaniard who led the first European expedition in the future Alabama. Born in Jerez de Badajoz, de Soto came to the New World around 1514, settling in Panama, and took part in the conquest of Nicaragua (1524). He played a major role in Francisco Pizarro's campaign against the Inca Empire (1531–1533); but eager for an independent command, he secured appointment as governor of Florida (1537). During his trek through the future U.S. Southeast, he fell ill and died on May 21, 1542. His body, weighted with sand, was sunk in the Mississippi River.

Luna y Arellano, Tristán de (c. 1510–1573). Spaniard who tried unsuccessfully to found a colony on the Gulf Coast of Alabama and Florida. From a distinguished Aragonese family, Luna had been a long time resident of Mexico when the viceroy appointed him governor of Florida in 1558. Because of the problems that plagued Luna's efforts, he was relieved of his command in March 1561 and returned to Mexico. His successor, Angel de Villafañe, was also unsuccessful in establishing a permanent Spanish presence on the Gulf Coast.

Gálvez, Bernardo de (1746–1786). Army officer who gained control of West Florida for Spain in 1780. Born near Málaga to a prominent family, Gálvez had extensive experience when he was appointed governor of Louisiana in 1777. After Spain declared war on England during the American Revolution (1779), he defeated the British at Baton Rouge, Mobile, and Pensacola, thereby enabling Spain to retain control of Florida in 1783. Gálvez later served briefly as governor of Cuba and viceroy of Mexico.

Gussman, Pedro (ca. 1879–?). Puerto Rican who became enmeshed in a sensational murder trial in Birmingham in 1921, after his marriage to Ruth Stephenson led her father, Edwin R. Stephenson, to shoot to death the priest who had married them. During the trial, Stephenson's attorney, Hugo L. Black, made much of Gussman's supposedly negroid physical appearance. He and Ruth soon separated, and both disappeared from view after the trial.

Sandoval, Martha (1946–). Mexican-born resident of Mobile who was lead plaintiff in a class-action suit seeking the right to take the state driver's license examination in Spanish. When the suit was filed on December 31, 1996, the test was administered only in English. Sandoval, a permanent legal resident, was insufficiently proficient in English to pass the test and suffered hardship because she lacked a license. After tests became available in Spanish and other foreign languages in 1998, she passed the examination on her first try.

CULTURAL CONTRIBUTIONS

The increase in the Latino population exposed Alabamians to Latin American food, music, and culture in general. Mexican restaurants soon dotted the landscape throughout the state, and supermarkets began to stock Latino products on their shelves. Spanish-language radio stations went on the air in Birmingham and other cities, and Spanish-language and bilingual newspapers also circulated in the state—among them *El Latino*, a free weekly established in 1996. Roman Catholic churches began to schedule Sunday masses in Spanish and to hold special celebrations in honor of the feast day of the Virgin of Guadalupe. Baptists and other Protestant denominations also reached out to Latinos by launching ministries and offering English-language classes and other services. Since 2003 Birmingham's Hispanic Business Council has sponsored an annual Fiesta that attracts thousands. It aims at acquainting Alabamians with the culture of Latin America while offering various services to Latino attendees. Soccer acquired a Spanish accent as teams for Latino adults were formed and organized into leagues. In Jefferson County in 2005 there were three such leagues with more than 70 teams, as well as a Latino baseball league with ten teams.

NOTES

1. Thompson, 168–169; Kenny, 153–154, 277–278, 302.
2. *Birgmingham Ledger*, March 30 and April 11, 1916, cited in Sterkx, 168–169; Strode, *Timeless Mexico*, xiv–xv, 416–417; Strode, *Pageant of Cuba*, xx–xxi.

3. Mohl, 243–245; Moseley, 45–46.
4. Patino, 31–32.
5. Society Mobile–La Havana. http://www.havana-mobile.com.

BIBLIOGRAPHY

Badger, R. Reid, and Lawrence A. Clayton, eds. *Alabama and the Borderlands: From Prehistory to Statehood.* Tuscaloosa: University of Alabama Press, 1979.

Birmingham News, 2000–2007, passim.

Kenny, Michael. *Catholic Culture in Alabama: Centenary Story of Spring Hill College, 1830–1930.* New York: America Press, 1931.

Mohl, Raymond A. "Latinization of the Heart of Dixie: Hispanics in Late-Twentieth-Century Alabama." *Alabama Review* 55 (October 2002): 243–274.

Moseley, Edward H. "Growing Hispanic Influence in the United States: The Case of Alabama." In *El triángulo económico España-USA-América Latina.* Eds. Saturnino Aguado-Sebastián and Rosa María García Barroso. Alcalá de Henares, Spain: Instituto de Estudios Norteamericanos, 2002, 43–50.

Patino, Fausto. "Maternal and Child Health Services Utilization by Hispanics in Alabama." PhD diss., University of Alabama at Birmingham, 2002.

Pew Hispanic Center. http://pewhispanic.org.

Pruitt Jr., Paul M. "Private Tragedy, Public Shame." *Alabama Heritage* 30 (Fall 1993): 6–20.

Society Mobile–La Habana. http://www.havana-mobile.com.

Sterkx, H.E. "Unlikely Conquistadores: Alabamians and the Border Crisis of 1916." *Alabama Review* 24 (July 1971): 163–181.

Strode, Hudson. *The Pageant of Cuba.* New York: Harrison Smith and Robert Haas, 1934.

———. *Timeless Mexico.* New York: Harcourt Brace, 1944.

Thompson, Alan Smith. "Mobile, Alabama, 1850–1861: Economic, Political, Physical, and Population Characteristics." PhD diss., University of Alabama, 1979.

U.S. Census Bureau. 2006 American Community Survey. http://factfinder.census.gov/home/saff/main.html?_lang=en.

Weddle, Robert E. *Spanish Sea: The Gulf of Mexico in North American Discovery, 1500–1685.* College Station: Texas A&M University Press, 1985.

2

Alaska

Edna Jiménez-Lugo

CHRONOLOGY

1774 The viceroy of New Spain (Mexico), Don Antonio Maria Bucareli y Ursua, orders Juan José Pérez Hernández, a Spanish captain, to lead the first Spanish expedition to Alaska departing from San Blas, Mexico.

1775 During the second Spanish expedition to Alaska, the Peruvian Juan Francisco Bodega y Quadra, as commander of the vessel the *Sonora*, anchors in a harbor known today as Bucareli Bay, named in honor of Viceroy Bucareli.

1779 The third Spanish expedition to Alaska, commanded by the Spanish explorer Ignacio Arteaga and Juan Francisco Bodega y Quadra, sails to Bucareli Bay and then stops in Prince William Sound, Gulf of Alaska.

1788 The Nootka Controversy develops. The dispute is between the Spanish and British governments over lands explored in 1774 by Spanish explorers and later claimed in 1778 by the British. It takes from 1790 to 1794 to solve the Nootka Controversy, as various agreements are signed by the Spanish and British to define possession of the lands.

The Spanish explorers on the fourth Spanish expedition to Alaska encounter the first Russians at what is now called Unalaska Island, off the southwest coast of Alaska.

1790 The Spanish explorer Salvador Fidalgo commands the fifth Spanish expedition from San Blas, Mexico, to Nootka. After several stops along Prince William Sound, Fidalgo and the crew members of the *San Carlos* take possession of several regions and assign them Spanish names.

1791–1792	The Italian explorer Alejandro Malaspina and the Spanish explorer José Bustamante sail from Cádiz, Spain, to visit Spanish colonies, and to the Northwest Coast in search of the Northwest Passage.
1792	The Spanish explorers Jacinto Caamaño and Juan Pantoja survey the area of Bucareli Bay in search of the Northwest Passage. This is the end of the Spanish explorations to Alaska.
1795	Due to problems encountered by Spanish explorers in Europe and New Spain, the Spanish decide to withdraw from Alaska at the port of Nootka.
1899–1916	The Alaska Mexican Gold Mining Company operates in Douglas Island, Alaska, during the early mining history of the state.
1975–1977	Latinos are a part of the workforce that builds the 800-mile Trans-Alaska Pipeline from the North Slope to the south central port of Valdez.
1981	Latinos Unidos del Norte is founded as a community organization that promotes Latino culture and language in interior Alaska.
1990–2000	Latinos account for 10.5 percent of the population growth in Alaska—one of the highest rates recorded for Latinos in Alaska.
2001	The Council of Latin Americans in Alaska for Special Services (CLASE), a community organization, starts providing assistance in the areas of adult education, health, and migrant rights to Latinos in Anchorage.
2004	Many Latinos from other states assist firefighters during a wildfire season that burns 6.7 million acres in interior Alaska.

2005   Latinos are recorded as the second-largest minority group in Alaska. Population estimates record that Latinos account for 5.1 percent of the state population.

HISTORICAL OVERVIEW

An increase of the Latino population in Alaska since 2001 makes them the second-largest minority group in the state. By 2005 there was an estimated 31,000 Latinos living in Alaska.[1] Approximately 19,000 live in the Anchorage borough, one of the most populated urban cities in Alaska. Nearly 5,000 enjoy living in other urban areas, such as Fairbanks and Juneau, the state capital. Hundreds of Latinos face the challenges of living in rural Alaska in remote areas inaccessible by road, such as Angoon, Barrow, Nome, and Bethel. Some Latinos who work in the fish-processing industry prefer smaller areas, such as Kodiak Island and the Aleutians.

The early migration of Latinos to Alaska resulted from a rapid growth in the state's economy. For instance, the 1902 gold rush boom in Fairbanks, the strong military presence in Alaska since the 1950s, the oil boom in the 1960s, and the construction of the Trans-Alaska Pipeline in the 1970s all contributed to the growth of Alaska's Latino population.

The social context of Latino life in Alaska is different from that of states where Latinos are the largest minority population. In Alaska, the majority of political and social minority issues are associated with Alaska Natives' cultural preservation, education, health, and improvement of basic services in rural areas. Little attention is given to Latino culture and society. However, Latinos and Natives share a concern with policies that affect language issues in the state.

LEGACY OF SPANISH EXPLORATIONS

The Spanish influence in Alaska is less evident than in many other states in the Southwest. From 1774 to 1792, Spanish explorers conducted expeditions to Alaska with the hopes of finding the Northwest Passage—a supposed link between the Pacific and Atlantic oceans believed to be navigable through North America. Before the era of aviation, the hypothetical discovery and dominion over the Northwest Passage was considered of great economic and strategic importance. Expansion of the Russian fur trade to the Spanish-colonized west coast of California was another reason for the early Spanish incursion into Alaska.

The majority of the Spanish expeditions to Alaska departed from San Blas, Mexico. The viceroy of New Spain (today's Mexico), Don Antonio María Bucareli y Ursua, was one of the most influential in the Spanish expeditions to explore the northern coast in search of the Northwest Passage and Russian settlements. In 1774, the Spanish captain Juan José Pérez Hernández, following

Bucareli's instructions, sailed north in search of latitude 60°, which is approximately where Prince William Sound is located in the Gulf of Alaska. This 1774 expedition failed to reach Alaska, as the sailors did not pass beyond Queen Charlotte Islands, Canada.

In 1775 a second expedition departed with two vessels: the *Santiago*, led by the Spanish Captain Bruno de Hezeta, and the *Sonora*, commanded by the Peruvian Juan Francisco Bodega y Quadra. Although their mission was to reach latitude 65° north, the crew members of the *Santiago* and the *Sonora* were ambushed by the Chinook Indians along the northern coast of United States, close to what is now known as the state of Washington. After that skirmish, the vessels went in opposite directions. Hezeta returned to San Blas with the *Santiago*'s crew, while Bodega y Quadra headed north up the southeast coast of Alaska with the *Sonora*'s crew, toward the contemporary town of Sitka. In search of a better place to anchor than Sitka, Bodega y Quadra continued to the Southeast and anchored in quiet waters later named by Bodega and known today as Bucareli Bay. Neither Bodega y Quadra nor the crew members of the *Sonora* ever returned to San Blas, landing instead in a Spanish settlement in the Monterey Bay of California.

From 1776 to 1778, Spanish explorers repaired and built ships to continue these expeditions to the north. In 1779 the vessels *Princesa*, commanded by the Spanish explorer Ignacio Arteaga, and the *Favorita*, led by Bodega y Quadra, departed from San Blas. The vessels stopped in the recently discovered Bucareli Bay, where they interacted with Native Americans. Encounters with Tlingit Natives in the Southeast led to violence, including the first and only recorded Native Alaskan death caused by Spanish explorers. That same year, the *Princesa* and the *Favorita* sailed in search of a safer anchorage. They arrived in Prince William Sound, where the crew members met with another group of Natives in Alaska, the Aluttiq. The expedition then headed south and west to the Kenai Peninsula.

During the expeditions from 1774 to 1779, Spanish voyagers traded food and artifacts with natives. Some believe potatoes and other crops arrived in Alaska during exchanges between explorers and natives, but little evidence is available to substantiate these theories. Expeditions to the north were expensive, risky, and dangerous, causing many deaths among the Spanish crews. The Northwest Passage was never found, and Spanish exploration to the north was put on hold until 1787. In 1788 another vessel departed from San Blas, heading north to Prince William Sound. Crew members of the 1788 expedition documented one of their first encounters with Russian explorers during a stop at what is now called Unalaska Island. The Spanish-Russian encounter ended when the Spanish explorers returned to San Blas.

The year of 1788 was of great controversy between the Spanish and British crowns. A dispute on sovereignty over an area discovered and named by the

Spanish during the 1774 expedition led to what is known as the Nootka Controversy. Nootka was the name given by the British to a place that the Spanish had explored and named Surgidero de San Lorenzo (Anchorage of Saint Lawrence). Although the Nootka Agreement was signed in 1790, preventing a war between the two nations, confusion remained over what land area pertained to the British and what to the Spanish. After further disputes, both the British and the Spanish had free access to the area in 1794, but by 1795 the Spanish had withdrawn from the port of Nootka.

The search for the Northwest Passage still was intriguing for some Spanish explorers. A 1790 expedition commanded by the Spanish explorer Salvador Fidalgo sailed to Prince William Sound, where he named various sites on his way north. In 1791 the Italian Alejandro Malaspina and the Spanish explorer José Bustamante y Guerra sailed from Cádiz, Spain, to visit Spanish colonies and search for the Northwest Passage. They later learned the passage was a myth. Nevertheless, in 1792, the Spanish explorers Jacinto Caamaño and Juan Pantoja started a voyage to Bucareli Bay from San Blas with the goal of finding the so-called Northwest Passage. Caamaño and Pantoja surveyed the area of Prince of Wales Island, then headed west, arriving in the Queen Charlotte Islands. The voyage of 1792 was the last expedition to the Northwest and the end of 18 years of Spanish exploration in Alaska.

Spanish Names in Alaska

Similar to the case in other areas colonized by Spaniards, the Spanish legacy in Alaska is recorded in the names of towns, rivers, and glaciers sighted by early explorers. The best-known examples are the towns of Valdez and Cordova, two small cities located in the southern area of Alaska.

Salvador Fidalgo named the town of Valdez, located in the northeast of Prince William Sound, in honor of a minister of the Spanish Navy, Antonio Valdés y Basán. Modern-day Valdez is a tourist destination known for its natural beauty, waterfalls, glaciers, fishing industry, and marine life. Historical events such as the Viernes Santo (Good Friday) Earthquake in 1964 (which forced the relocation of the city) and later the Exxon Valdez oil spill in 1989 significantly and negatively affected the economy and progress of Valdez.

Cordova, another small city in southeast Alaska, was named by Salvador Fidalgo during his 1790 expedition in search of Russian settlements in the Pacific Northwest. Fidalgo proclaimed the land east of Prince William Sound to be Puerto Cordova, in honor of Luis de Córdova y Córdova, a famous captain general of the Spanish Royal Navy. This small town, accessible only by plane or boat, is home to hundreds of Latinos.

Other places named by Spanish explorers along the east coast of Alaska include Gravina Island, the name of which honors another illustrious Spaniard, Federico Carlos Gravina. Over time, Spanish names were changed by other explorers or translated by Russians or North Americans. Under North American influence, U.S. sailors and the U.S. Geological Survey renamed parts of Alaska honoring the original Spanish names, while some were translated into English.

Latinos in the Alaskan Context

Alaska is a very popular tourist destination, visited for its astonishing and pristine landscapes, glaciers, mountains, wildlife, and tundra. Tourism in Alaska makes a major contribution to the economy during the summertime and stands only second to oil revenues in overall economic importance. Tourists, including Latinos, are visible in Fairbanks, Anchorage, Juneau, Barrow, and southeast Alaska. Although tourists are less evident during the harsh winters, Latinos visit relatives in Alaska during all times of the year.

Alaska's geographic isolation and harsh climate contribute to the relatively low migration of Latinos to the state. Access by road is limited within the state's largest cities (Anchorage and Fairbanks) and communities. Because Alaska, along with Hawaii, does not connect physically with the 48 other states, migrants accessing the state by land have to cross through Canadian territory by a rough road with limited services. In addition, permafrost and extreme temperatures during winter contribute to the lack of public utilities (water, energy, and phones); the limited availability of education; and the lack of medical facilities and paved roads in many areas of Alaska, especially in rural sites. This situation makes the wilderness unattractive to some looking for an urban lifestyle or job opportunities.

Despite the limitations and conditions of living in Alaska, some Latinos enjoy living in remote towns and are able to find job opportunities in rural areas. This is the case for about 200 Latinos living in the famous town of Barrow, in the North Slope borough. Barrow is the northernmost town in the United States, located on the shores of the Arctic Ocean. The majority of Barrow's approximately 5,000 residents are Alaskan Natives of Iñupiat Eskimos descent. For Latinos living in Barrow, the lifestyle differs dramatically from that of other urban areas in Alaska. U.S. Latinos in Barrow live according to the context of rural life in Alaska, which includes engaging in traditional subsistence practices of seal hunting and bowhead whale hunting. Although Barrow is a tourist destination, visitors and locals can only access it by air. One of the limitations Latinos face in Barrow is the transportation of goods and high costs of living. For instance, just one barge arrives in town every August, loaded with equipment, diesel, vehicles, and goods that cannot be transported by aircraft. The movement of the barge is limited by ice in the Arctic Ocean. Because vehicles can only be shipped in this way once a year, their cost is prohibitive for personal use, forcing noncommercial users to rely on all-terrain vehicles during summer and snow machines during winter as a method of transportation within the small town.

Another remote site is in the Yukon-Kuskokwim region, where 85 percent of the population is Yupik Eskimos and Athabaskan; approximately 100 Latinos live there. As an additional challenge for Latinos living in this region of rural Alaska, the Yukon-Kuskokwim region has the highest rate of infectious diseases in the state due to a lack of running water and proper sewer facilities.

Although some Latinos decide to migrate to rural Alaska, most choose urban areas, such as Anchorage, Fairbanks, and Juneau. More than half of the Latino population in Alaska lives in the Anchorage Borough, where many are connected to the military community. By 2005, Latinos active at the Elmendorf Air Force Base and Fort Richardson in Anchorage accounted for 5.7 percent of the Anchorage military population.

There are about 5,000 Latinos residing in the Fairbanks Borough. The second-largest city in Alaska, Fairbanks attracts Latinos with its dynamic economic and educational opportunities. Although temperatures in Fairbanks can drop to −45°F for about two weeks in January and darkness reigns during winter, the city has many attractions.

Fairbanks has a highly regarded school district, where Spanish is offered as an elective to local students. The Fairbanks North Star Borough School District assists non-English speakers, including Latinos, who require a tutor or interpreter at school until they become proficient in English. The presence of the University of Alaska at Fairbanks (UAF) is another asset that attracts Latinos because of education and employment opportunities.

Fairbanks is a city where traffic jams are almost nonexistent and where people can enjoy the privacy of living in the wilderness and having the pleasures of city life nearby. As compared to other states, the crime rate in Alaska is very low, making the state a very attractive and peaceful place for Latinos to live and raise children in a relatively safe environment.

NOTABLE LATINOS

Reyes, María Elena (1947–). In 2003, María Elena Reyes, a Mexican American from Texas, was the first Latina to earn tenure at the University of Alaska at Fairbanks. The Latino community at UAF knows Dr. Reyes for her contribution as faculty advisor to the Latina/o Culture Club, the first Latino college student organization in Alaska. She was Alaska's chairperson and national board member for the National Association of Hispanic and Latino Studies from 1999 to 2006.

Pantoja, Alberto (1956–). Puerto Rican–born Alberto Pantoja is an entomologist well known for his scientific research in South America, Central America, and the Caribbean.

In 2003 he was appointed as research leader for the Subarctic Agricultural Research Unit of the United States Department of Agriculture (USDA), the Agricultural Research Service (ARS) in Alaska. Pantoja is the first Latino research leader in the history of ARS in Alaska, and currently is the highest-ranked Latino working for USDA-ARS in Alaska.

Fernandez, Ivette (1975–). In 2001, Ivette Fernandez became the first Latina to receive the title of Miss Alaska and was honored with the Miss Congeniality award. In 2001 she was a legislative aide for a state senator; in 2007 she worked as the associate director for Latin American Affairs at the U.S. Department of Homeland Security. Fernandez is of Mexican descent and active in the Latino community. She was the feature speaker for the 2006 scholarship fund-raiser event hosted by the Latinos Unidos del Norte (United Latinos of the North) during the Hispanic Heritage Month, celebrated at the University of Alaska Fairbanks. In October 2006, she was also the guest speaker at the Eielson Air Force Base for a luncheon celebrating the importance of Latinos in the Air Force. Recently, Fernandez participated in the 2006 Young Hispanic Leaders Program in Spain with fourteen other Latino Americans.

Gomez, Scott (1979–). Scott Gomez, of Mexican and Colombian heritage, was born in Anchorage, Alaska. In 1998 he became the first Latino player to be drafted by a National Hockey League (NHL) team. As a professional ice hockey player with the New Jersey Devils during the 1999–2000 NHL season, Gomez was awarded the Calder Memorial Trophy as the league's rookie of the year. Other awards received by Gomez included team First All-Star, Top Scorer, and Most Valuable Player. He and his teammates won the Stanley Cup in 2000 and 2003. During the 2004–2005 lockout year, he returned to Alaska and joined the Alaska Aces Team. For the 2006–2007 NHL season, Gomez became the first Latino to have a million-dollar contract for his superb performance as a hockey player.

CULTURAL CONTRIBUTIONS

For many Alaskans, "Latino" is synonymous with "Mexican." Occasionally, some Alaskans assume that all Latinos are of Mexican descent, perhaps because the majority of Latinos in Alaska are Mexicans. However, the population of Alaska includes Latinos from Central America, South America, and the Caribbean. Such confusion is also part of the history of Fairbanks. An Italian who discovered gold in 1902 in the Tanana Valley, near Fairbanks, is known as Felix Pedro, but his real name was Felice Pedroni. The use of the name "Felix Pedro" leads many to believe that he was Latino, not European.

Alaskans' confusion with Latinos' ethnic origins probably arises from the strong presence of Mexican cuisine in the interior of the state (Fairbanks), south central Alaska (Anchorage Borough, Soldotna, Kenai, Homer, and Valdez), southeastern Alaska (Juneau, Petersburg, Sitka, and Ketchikan), the North Slope (Barrow), and Kodiak Island. Approximately 7 percent of the restaurants in Anchorage offer primarily Mexican cuisine. Certainly, Mexicans have lived in Anchorage for decades, as is evidenced by a factory named Taco Loco that assumed operations in the 1960s. Currently, Taco Loco products include tortillas, chips, and salsa that are distributed across Alaska. Anchorage is the only city with Latino markets (Bodega Hispana and La Flor de Tijuana) offering products that are difficult to come by for Latinos in other Alaskan cities. However, large chains of supermarkets in Fairbanks and Anchorage contain modest sections of ethnic foods for Latinos.

Latino cuisine in Alaska attracts people from the Latino community, as these restaurants are one of the few places where Spanish is spoken and the cultural diversity of Latinos is evident. Latino culture and identity are represented in the names of Latino restaurants. Names such as Jalapeños and Cilantros are representative of Latino condiments in food, while other names, such as El Chicano, Azteca, El Sombrero, and Acapulco, are representative of Mexican culture. In North Pole, a small town in the interior near Fairbanks, the Mambo Grill offers Latino cuisine from South and Central America, including the Caribbean (Cuba, the Dominican Republic, and Puerto Rico), making it a must-visit restaurant for the Latino community.

In the Mexican restaurants of Fairbanks and Anchorage, it is common to hear guests and employees speaking Spanish. However, the situation in Pepe's North of the Border, a Mexican restaurant in Barrow, is slightly different, because the owner is of European descent—although employees at the restaurant do speak Spanish. Pepe's North of the Border is influenced by the Mexican friends of Fran Tate, who established the restaurant in 1978. The restaurant is very famous among locals and tourists visiting Barrow from all over the world, because it is the only Mexican restaurant in town and the northernmost Mexican restaurant in the United States. In the 1980s an article about Tate and her Mexican restaurant was published in the *Wall Street Journal,* and Tate was a guest on Johnny Carson's *Tonight Show.*

Besides the evident influence of Latinos throughout Mexican and Latin American cuisine in Alaska, various Latino organizations sponsor events, such as Cinco de Mayo celebrations, that enrich cultural identity during Hispanic Heritage Month. Because Anchorage is the state's most populous city, most Latino organizations are located there. These include the Anchorage Latino Lions, Anchorage Hispanic Cultural Committee, Alaskans Concerned About Latin America, Association of Latin American Students, and Consejo de Latinamericanos en Alaska para Servicios Especiales (Council of Latin Americans in Alaska for Special Services, or CLASE). CLASE focuses on meeting the needs of the Latin American community with social services and programs related to education, migration, and citizenship, among other issues related to public policy.

Eielson Air Force Base, near Fairbanks, also holds several events during Hispanic Heritage Month to celebrate the culture, traditions, and contributions of the Air Force's Latinos. In 2006, Ivette Fernandez, a Mexican American who is active in Latino community events in Fairbanks, was the guest speaker for one of the Air Force events.

Eielson Air Force Base Latinos and Latinas: Princess Rivera, Gloria Wilson, Gloria Harrison, Johanna Gonzalez, Alex Paz Rivera, Ray Hernandez, Robert Palos, Victor Valencia, and Enrique Carrillo. Courtesy of Office of Multicultural Affairs and Diversity (OMAD) from the University of Alaska Fairbanks.

In Fairbanks, Latinos Unidos del Norte, a community organization, and the Hispanic or Latino Awareness Organization (HOLA) a student organization, together with the UAF Office of Multicultural Affairs and Diversity, sponsor fundraising events for two scholarships awarded to two Latinos at the University of Alaska at Fairbanks. One scholarship goes to a college freshman, and the other to a continuing student; both include a tuition waiver for a year and $1,000 from Latinos Unidos del Norte.

During the spring of 2007, the group Tezkatlipoka Danza Azteca, from Southern Mexico, performed traditional and ceremonial dances as part of the Festival of the Native Arts in Fairbanks. Most of the music on the radio stations of Fairbanks is in English, but Latino music can be requested on Friday afternoons at the UAF campus station, KSUA, which features a Latino disc jockey, José Cruz-Gómez. In Anchorage, KSKA hosts radio shows in Spanish from Sunday to Tuesday.

Religious services in Spanish are available in Fairbanks at the Sacred Heart Cathedral, at UAF for students who are Catholics, and at the Kingdom Hall of Jehovah's Witnesses. In Anchorage, Our Lady of Guadalupe is one of the churches visited by some of the Latinos. The Virgin of Guadalupe is the patron saint for Mexicans—and, increasingly, for many Latinos.

NOTE

1. Population percentages and other demographic statistics reported in this chapter are based on data compiled from the U.S. Census Bureau—specifically, the 2000 and 2005 population estimates. The "State and County QuickFacts of Alaska" are available online at http://quickfacts.census.gov/qfd/states/02000.html (accessed January 17, 2007), and the 2005 American Community Survey is available online at http://factfinder.census.gov (accessed February 3, 2007).

BIBLIOGRAPHY

Alaska Conservation Foundation. *Guide to Alaska's Cultures.* Anchorage, AK: Alaska Conservation Foundation, 2004.

Alaska United Gold Mining Company. "Seventeenth Annual Statement. Superintendent's Report, Balance Sheet, and Profit and Loss Account." Douglas Island, AK, 1912.

Baker, Rachel, John Boucher, Neal Fried, and Brigitta Windisch-Cole. "Long-Term Retrospective: Alaska's Economy since Statehood." *Alaska Economic Trends* 19 (December 1999): 3–21. http://almis.labor.state.ak.us.

Ben-Yosef, Tamar. "Rural Villages Living with Effects of No Running Water." *Fairbanks Daily News-Miner,* January 3, 2007, A1, A8.

"Chronological History of Alaska." Statewide Library Electronic Doorway. http://sled.alaska.edu/akfaq/akchron.html (accessed January 15, 2007).

Curteich, John H. *History of Alaska: Land, People, and Events.* Westlake Village, CA: John Hinde Curteich, 2002.

Ferrell, Nancy Warren. *Destination Valdez.* Minneapolis, MN: Lerner Publications Company, 1998.

Fried, Neal, and Brigitta Windisch-Cole. "The Military Is Big Business in Anchorage." *Alaska Economic Trends* 26 (June 2006): 4–14. http://almis.labor.state.ak.us.

Kidder, Lyn. *Tacos on the Tundra: The Story of Pepe's North of the Border.* Anchorage, AK: Bonaparte Books, 1996.

Legislative Bulletin #19-6. "Mayor Rocky Gutierrez, A Pioneer in Municipal Government." Juneau, AK. April 14, 1995.

Olson, Wallace M. *The Spanish Exploration of Alaska, 1774–1792.* Auke Bay, AK: Heritage Research, 2004.

———. *Through Spanish Eyes: Spanish Voyages to Alaska, 1774–1792.* Auke Bay, AK: Heritage Research, 2002.

Rey-Tejerina, Arsenio. "Spanish influence in Alaska and Spanish Place Names." http://www.explorenorth.com/articles/rey/reyindex.html (accessed January 3, 2007).

Richardson, Kirsten. "Eating Out." *Anchorage,* November 16–22, 2006. http://www.anchoragepress.com/archives-2006/eatingoutvol15ed46.html (accessed December 7, 2006).

Williams, Greg. "Migration." *Alaska Economic Trends* 24 (July 2004): 3–12. http://almis.labor.state.ak.us.

———. "Population Projections." *Alaska Economic Trends* 25 (February 2005): 4–15. http://almis.labor.state.ak.us.

———. "Race and Ethnicity in Alaska." *Alaska Economic Trends* 21 (October 2001): 11–21. http://almis.labor.state.ak.us.

3

Arizona

Geraldo L. Cadava

CHRONOLOGY

1539	Franciscan Friar Marcos de Niza crosses through southeastern Arizona on his way to Zuni pueblos in New Mexico.
1540	The Coronado expedition, led by Spanish explorer and conquistador Francisco Vázquez de Coronado, is the first by Europeans to systematically explore Arizona.
1687	Francisco Eusebio Kino establishes Mission San Xavier del Bac at a Tohono O'odham settlement near Tucson.
1775	On August 20, Hugo O'Connor, a colonel in the Spanish army, founds the Tucson Presidio.
1821	Mexico wins independence from Spain.
1826	On December 31, Anglo-Americans visit the Tucson Presidio for the first time.
1838	A 6-year civil war in Sonora begins between federalists (represented by José Cosme de Urrea) and centralists (represented by Manuel María Gándara).
1846–1847	Between October 1846 and January 1847, the Mormon Battalion of Stephen Watts Kearney and Philip St. George passes through Tucson and southern Arizona in the midst of the Mexican-American War.
1848	The Treaty of Guadalupe Hidalgo makes central and northern Arizona part of the United States.
1853	On December 30, the Tratado de la Mesilla makes the portion of Arizona south of the Gila River part of the United States. Known in the United States as the Gadsden Purchase, the treaty is ratified on June 24, 1854.

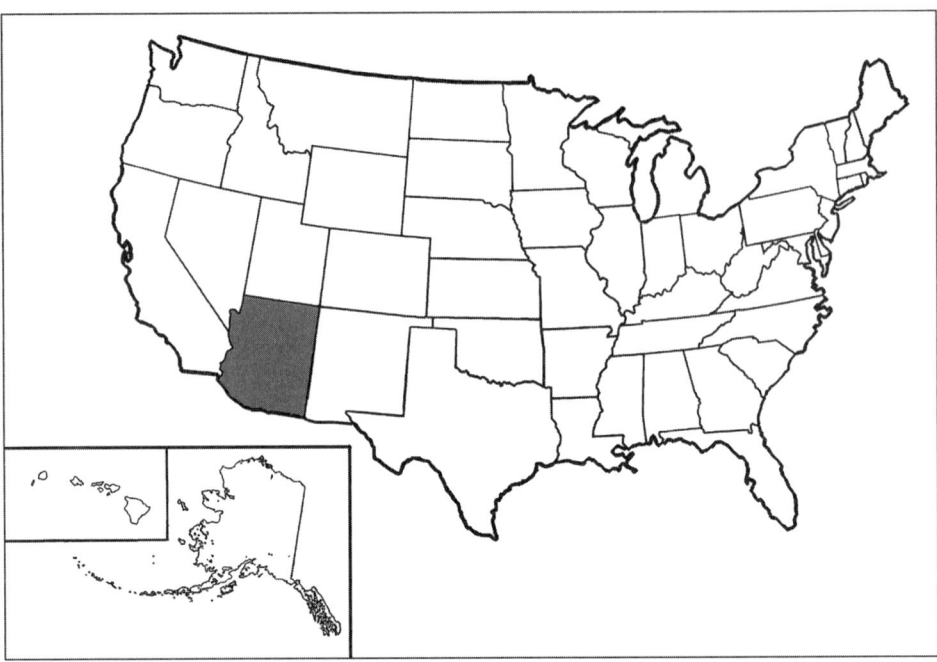

1856	The last Mexican troops leave the Presidio of Tucson on March 10.
1857–1858	A gold strike along the Gila and Colorado rivers, near Yuma, gives rise to Arizona's first mining boom.
1862	A gold strike even bigger than the one in 1857 prompts another boom in Yuma.
1863	Arizona becomes a territory of the United States.
1871	A total of 144 Apaches, all but eight of whom were women and children, are murdered by a group of Anglos, Mexicans, and Tohono O'odham Indians in the Camp Grant Massacre.
1877–1881	Mexican and Mexican American workers lay tracks for the Southern Pacific Railroad across Arizona. The railroad arrived in Yuma in 1877 and in Tucson in 1880, connecting with Lordsburg, New Mexico, in 1881.
1894	On January 14, La Alianza Hispano-Americana, an ethnic Mexican mutual aid society, fraternal insurance organization, and civil rights organization, is founded in Tucson.
1903	A copper-mining strike in Bisbee is the first major labor strike in Arizona.
1911	The Roosevelt Dam is completed, leading to Arizona's World War I–era agricultural boom.
1912	Arizona becomes a state on February 14.
1915–1916	Anglo and Mexican employees of Phelps Dodge go on strike in Clifton and Morenci.

1917	Citing the supposed communist influence of the Industrial Workers of the World (IWW), Phelps Dodge Corporation deports copper workers from Bisbee to New Mexico.
1927	Future farm labor leader Cesar Chávez is born on March 31 in Yuma.
1946	In Morenci, Mexican American veterans of World War II lead a strike against Phelps Dodge to lobby for fair treatment and equal wages for ethnic Mexican workers.
1952	*Sheeley v. González* desegregates public schools in the farming community of Tolleson, setting a precedent for the state as a whole.
1972	In May, Cesar Chávez holds a Fast of Love, refusing to eat for 24 days in protest against Arizona House Bill 2134. The bill outlaws boycotts and strikes by farmworkers during harvest season.
1980s	The church-based Sanctuary movement in Tucson provides safe haven to refugees from war-torn Central American countries in the early 1980s.
1983	Strikes occur against Phelps Dodge in Clifton and Morenci.
2004	Arizona voters, including almost half of all Latino voters, pass Proposition 200. The initiative requires proof of citizenship before registering to vote or applying for public benefits and denies social services and education to undocumented migrants.
2005	Democratic Governor Janet Napolitano declares a "state of emergency" in Arizona, owing to migration and other border issues.
2006–2007	Thousands of demonstrators march on May Day for comprehensive immigration reform.

HISTORICAL OVERVIEW

Arizona's Latina and Latino population is predominantly Mexican—mainly from the states of Chihuahua and Sonora—which has had a significant impact on the culture, social life, and political economy of ethnic Mexican communities in the state. Only during the late twentieth century did migrants from Central and South America arrive in Arizona in large numbers, seeking sanctuary from wars in their home countries and providing labor to support Arizona's economic and demographic boom.

Arizona north of the Gila River became part of the United States following the 1848 Treaty of Guadalupe Hidalgo, which also formally ended the Mexican-American War. The area south of the Gila, which at the time included the only towns in Arizona with settled Mexican populations—such as Tucson, Tubac, and Tumacácori—remained part of Mexico until 1854. In that year, the United States purchased for $10 million an additional 29,000 square miles of Mexican land in a treaty known in the United States as the Gadsden Purchase and in Mexico as El Tratado de la Mesilla. In 1856, Mexican soldiers finally vacated the Tucson Presidio, the last city in the United States with a Mexican military presence. Arizona became a territory of the United States in 1863, and then a state in 1912.

The Spanish Colonial and Mexican Periods

Arizona's Latino history dates back at least to the sixteenth century, when Franciscan friar Marcos de Niza entered southeastern Arizona in 1539 to explore what was then an uncharted corner of northwestern New Spain. From a distance, de Niza saw the Zuni pueblo of Cíbola—mythically described as a city of gold—and later he wrote that it was larger than Mexico City. These descriptions led Francisco Vázquez de Coronado to retrace de Niza's footsteps in 1540, searching in vain for the sight that had impressed his predecessor. Coronado and his followers, including hundreds of Native Americans, became the first to systematically explore the Arizona territory. As part of the Coronado expedition, García López de Cárdenas became the first European to see the Grand Canyon, and Hernando de Alarcón the first to navigate the lower Colorado River. Though other Spaniards entered Arizona over the next two centuries, none settled permanently there until the 1700s.

By the time of the Mexican independence in 1821, Spaniards and native groups (including Tohono O'odham, Apaches, and Pimas) had already established many of the religious, military, farming, and ranching communities that shaped Arizona's history into the twentieth century. Jesuit missionary Eusebio Francisco Kino had traveled throughout northern Sonora and southern Arizona to set up the first missions; these became one method used by the Spanish empire not only to convert Native American souls but also to acclimate Native Americans to village life and teach them European stock-raising and farming techniques. Kino established San Xavier del Bac near Tucson in 1687 and Guevavi near Tumacácori in 1701, though both missions were abandoned and then reestablished in 1732, after Kino had already died. The establishment of these missions, along with the 1736 silver strike at Arizonac, a few miles south of Nogales, spurred the first wave of non–Native American settlement in Arizona. Kino introduced various grains, vegetables, fruit trees, and herds of livestock to the state; yet, many perceived him and later Spanish missionaries as unwelcome colonizers. The Pima Revolt of 1751—during which Pima Indians, led by Luis Oacpicagigua, killed more than a dozen men, women, and children—was an early example of Native American resistance against Spanish settlement in Arizona. Pima Indians briefly regained control of Tubac as the surviving non–Native Americans fled, but the Spanish Crown reasserted its authority the following year by establishing Arizona's first presidio, or military garrison, at Tubac in 1752. In 1775 a second presidio was established in Tucson.

The pattern of colonial settlement—cooperation and conflict with the Native Americans—and military response recurred throughout the Spanish, Mexican, and early United States periods. Spanish colonists developed several methods of negotiating contact with Apaches, such as forming alliances with Tohono O'odham and Pima Indians; developing a rationing system that rendered Apaches militarily and economically dependent; and setting up *establecimientos de paz,* or peace camps, near military garrisons in order to incorporate Native Americans within village boundaries.

Life for Arizona's first non–Native American inhabitants was highly unstable—resulting, out of necessity, in highly flexible migration patterns and the frequent abandonment and resettlement of villages. During periods of relative peace, Spanish colonists worked as subsistence farmers and small ranchers along the Santa Cruz and San Pedro rivers, but when Apache raids and other conflicts arose, many sought refuge near the presidios at Tubac and Tucson. Tucson was an example of a typical community, as many *vecinos* (civilians who lived near military garrisons) grew crops of wheat, corn, beans, and vegetables, and raised cows and sheep to feed their families and presidio soldiers. The early nineteenth century was relatively peaceful, and many of southern Arizona's ranching, farming, and mining communities prospered, even though the total non–Native American population of the area was only 1,000, with 300 to 500 living in Tucson, 300 to 400 living in Tubac, and less than 100 living in Tumacácori.[1]

The situation changed during Arizona's Mexican period, when Mexico's political instability again exposed the area's vulnerability. The Mexican War of Independence, from 1810 to 1821, had several consequences for Mexicans in Arizona and Sonora. First, the war depleted Mexico's treasury and destroyed its silver-mining industry, which meant the government had little money with which to provision the presidios. Second, in 1824 the Mexican government dismembered the Spanish empire's *provincias internas* and turned control over to independent Mexican states, setting the stage for multiple civil wars between centralists and federalists. War broke out in Sonora in 1838, as centralists (under Manuel María Gándara) and federalists (under José Cosme de Urrea) struggled for power. Third, in 1831 Mexico ended the rationing system that Spain had established to maintain peaceful relations with Apaches. In 1825, approximately 2,500 Apaches received weekly supplies of beef, corn, sugar, and other goods from commanders in Chihuahua, Sonora, and New Mexico. When the Native Americans stopped receiving such rations, they left the peace camps and resumed raiding as a means of livelihood.[2] During the 1830s and 1840s, Mexicans therefore abandoned many of southern Arizona's missions, farms, ranches, and land grants made by the Spanish and Mexican governments (including San Rafael de la Zanja, Babocómari, and San Bernardino), leaving their cattle to roam freely throughout the region. By the late 1840s, even Tubac was deserted temporarily, leaving Tucson as Arizona's only military settlement.

The increased presence of outsiders in southern Arizona by the late 1840s was another source of regional instability. French and Anglo fur trappers—such as Bill Williams, Ceran St. Vrain, Antoine Leroux, and Christopher "Kit" Carson—first entered Arizona territory during the 1820s and 1830s, which led many Mexicans in Sonora to worry about U.S. designs on their land. The outbreak of the Mexican-American War in 1846 confirmed their suspicions, as U.S. troops under Stephen Watts Kearney and Philip St. George Cooke—called the Mormon Battalion—passed through Tucson in 1846 and 1847. Even though Cooke assured the Sonoran governor, Manuel María Gándara, that his troops meant Sonora no harm, the United States annexed half of Mexico's land, including most of Arizona, only a year later. For the first time, this split Arizona and Sonora in two.

Following Mexico's cession of land under the Treaty of Guadalupe Hidalgo, Mexico tried to secure what remained of its northern frontier by granting plots of land to soldiers in exchange for 6 years of military service. In 1854, however, the United States acquired the rest of Arizona (south of the Gila River) through the Gadsden Purchase. In 1856, as Mexican troops left Tucson, many Mexicans stayed in Arizona, as it had been their lifelong home. Others returned to Mexico, in part because they recognized the racism Mexicans had experienced in Texas and California after the United States annexed those territories, and they were aware that the same fate might befall them if they stayed.[3]

The Post-Gadsden and Early Territorial Periods

Before Arizona became its own territory in 1863, it formed part of the territory of New Mexico, and the Mexicans who stayed there after the Treaty of Guadalupe Hidalgo and the Gadsden Purchase became Arizona's first ethnic Mexican citizens. Nevertheless, during the immediate post-Gadsden era, such categories were relatively fluid, as families continued to move freely between Arizona and Sonora. The two states worked as one social, cultural, and economic region, despite the international border that had recently separated them.

Sonoran politics was a key factor driving migration between Sonora and Arizona during the 1850s and 1860s. After Mexican president Antonio López de Santa Anna resigned, following the Mexican-American War, a succession of temporary governments divided Mexico into various liberal and conservative factions. In Sonora the struggle was between liberal Ignacio Pesqueira and conservative Manuel María Gándara, who had been a central figure in Sonora's political infighting years earlier. They traded governance of the state several times during the 1850s and 1860s, until Porfirio Díaz became Mexico's president in 1876 and installed his own governors. The battles between Pesqueira and Gándara, combined with the French occupation of Sonora during the 1860s, led Sonorans to emigrate en masse, particularly between 1848 and 1849, 1852 and 1853, and 1865 and 1868.

Continued conflict with Native American groups in Sonora and Arizona also caused ethnic Mexicans in both states to migrate. As in earlier periods, Native American raids during the post-Gadsden era led farmers to abandon their land and move within and between Sonora and Arizona. Tensions caused by Anglo and Mexican conflicts with Native Americans increased during the 1850s and 1860s as Apaches and other Native Americans began to use the new international boundary to play each side against the other, participating in an illicit trade in arms, cattle, and other goods that had been stolen from the United States and Mexico. Anglos, Mexicans, and Pima and Tohono O'Odham Indians often formed alliances against Apaches; the most notorious example of such interethnic alliance was the Camp Grant Massacre of 1871, during which prominent Anglos, Mexicans, and Tohono O'odham from the Tucson area killed more than 100 Apaches, all but eight of whom were women and children.

Despite such tensions, Arizona's mining, ranching, and agriculture industries developed significantly during the early territorial period, though they did not boom until the late nineteenth century (following technological developments such as the arrival of the railroad). Ever since Spanish explorers searched for Cíbola during the sixteenth century and then struck silver at Arizonac in 1736, Arizona had been thought of in terms of its potential mineral wealth.

Shortly after the Gadsden Purchase, Anglo entrepreneurs reopened mines that had been dormant for decades. The Sonora Exploring and Mining Company, near Tubac, founded in 1856 by Charles D. Poston and Samuel P. Heintzelman, purchased property from Mexican landholders with backing from investors in New York, Ohio, and other states to the east. It was Arizona's first mining corporation, though many others would follow. Mexican workers—primarily from Sonora, but also from Chihuahua, Durango, and Sinaloa—filled most of the company's labor needs, which included clearing out old abandoned shafts and digging new veins.

For 12-hour workdays, Mexican miners earned 16 ounces of flour and $15 to $30 per month, depending on the type of labor they performed. At the low end of the wage scale, pick and crowbar men (*barrateros*) and ore carriers (*tanateros*) earned $15 a month, whereas those who tended the furnace and smelters made $25 to $30. These wages were still higher than the $6 to $8 per month Mexican workers earned on haciendas in Sonora, though they earned only half the $30 to $70 per month that Anglo miners made.[4] Most Anglo mine owners saw ethnic Mexicans as a cheap, efficient, docile, and permanent source of labor. One way they tried to make Mexican labor permanent was to charge a 300 percent markup on goods sold at the company store, which forced many to live month to month on lines of credit that bound them to the company. Nevertheless, many Mexicans simply left the mines when they desired, or when they were mistreated, even if they owed money to the company store. Though many Mexican miners worked for Anglo-owned companies, some operated mines for themselves. One leased the Picacho Mine from Poston, and when he closed it during the 1860s (because heavy rains had flooded the mine shafts), Mexican *gambusinos,* or ore thieves, stayed behind and mined an additional 240,000 ounces of silver over several years.

Far more common during the early territorial period than a relatively large operation such as the Sonora Exploring and Mining Company were the individual placer miners, or *placeros,* who traveled from camp to camp as various sites boomed and busted. They struck veins of ore, exhausted them, and moved on to the next strike. In general, mining progressed clockwise around the state, from Tubac to Yuma, to Wickenburg and Prescott, to Clifton and Morenci, and back down to Bisbee. Because of anti-Mexican racism in central and northern Arizona mining towns—as well as long-standing cultural connections between Mexican miners and southern Arizona—the proportion of Mexican miners in Arizona decreased considerably as the mining frontier moved from south to north. Mexican and Mexican American men and women established camps that were generally separate from the camps of Anglo miners. According to the 1870 territorial census, the women were predominantly single and young; they were from Sonora, Arizona, and New Mexico, and they worked as cooks, housekeepers, boarding-room operators, and seamstresses.[5]

Gila City became Arizona's first boomtown in 1858, but by the mid-1860s, it was already a ghost town. Jacob Snively discovered gold there in 1857, and in less than a year, more than 1,000 independent Anglo and ethnic Mexican prospectors were earning $50 a day from veins in the area. Just a few years later, in 1862, an even bigger placer strike gave rise to the town of Yuma. Many of the Sonoran miners who first settled Yuma during the 1860s were returnees from California's gold fields. After hearing of the California gold rush, more than 10,000 Sonorans passed through Arizona on their way to northern California. Some returned seasonally to Sonora throughout the 1850s to plant and harvest their crops, but many stayed in California until the 1860s, when news of the Yuma placer strike and the experience of anti-Mexican racism in California led them to return south.[6]

Towns throughout Arizona established several businesses to support the development of Arizona's early mining industries. Freighting companies were established in Tucson to haul materials to and from the mines. Ferry businesses started in Yuma to carry miners across the Colorado River. Lumber outfits in the Chiricahua Mountains opened to supply wood for furnaces, and farm produce from the region fed miners. Men such as Estevan Ochoa, Mariano G. Samaniego, and Leopoldo Carrillo migrated from Sonora during this period and started merchant and freighting companies that profited greatly from the growth of Arizona's mines. Most of their trade—conducted mainly in Mexican pesos, called "dobey dollars"—was between Arizona and Sonora. Though most Mexicans worked as unskilled or semiskilled laborers, these men formed the core of Arizona's Mexican middle and upper class during the early territorial period.

Cattle ranching also developed following the Mesilla Treaty. A group of investors from Providence, Rhode Island, organized the Sopori Land and Mining Company near Tubac in 1859, later renaming it the Sopori Land and Cattle Company. Prior to the arrival of Anglos, Mexicans controlled Arizona's ranch land. Many ranches were established on Spanish and Mexican land grants that had been passed down from generation to generation, then sold or abandoned during the nineteenth and twentieth centuries. For example, the ranch operated during the late nineteenth century by Sabino Otero, the so-called Cattle King of Tubac, sat on land originally granted by Spain to his grandfather Toribio in 1789. The Pacheco family ranch was on land granted by Spain to their ancestor Ignacio Antonio Pacheco in 1813.

Other Mexicans bought ranches when they migrated from Sonora during the 1870s and 1880s. Although some of the best ranch land was in southern Arizona, Mexican ranchers worked land in other areas as well. José María Redondo, for example, owned La Hacienda de San Isidore, located north of Yuma, near the Arizona-California border; Teodoro Ocampo, and his wife, Mariana owned a ranch near Wickenburg.

In many ways, the Oteros, Pachecos, and other ethnic Mexican ranchers taught Anglo ranchers the trade, which they had practiced for centuries before Anglos arrived. This included the Spanish terms Anglos adapted and made their own. Words used by Anglo cowboys such as buckaroo (vaquero), lariat (*la reata*), chaps (*chaparreras*), and dally (*dar la vuelta*), all had their origin in the vernacular of Mexican ranch work.[7] Each spring, ranchers from Arizona and Sonora gathered for a roundup at the Elías Ranch, near San Pedro, where they returned to their rightful owners the cattle that had wandered onto the land of neighboring ranches across the border. More than business meetings, the roundups were festive occasions; ranchers raced their horses, held cockfights, and performed the *saco de gallo*, during which a rider on horseback swiped from the ground a rooster buried up to its neck in dirt. *Charrería*, a Mexican cowboy competition, evolved separately from rodeo from the early twentieth century forward, but they intersected during the nineteenth century at roundups and other gatherings.

By the 1870s and 1880s, Anglo businessmen had begun to buy and consolidate wide swaths of Mexican ranch land in Arizona, which sold for $200–$300 an acre.[8] In 1870, there were approximately 5,000 head of cattle in all of Arizona, and by the mid-1880s, there were more than 650,000.[9] In less than two decades, Arizona's ranch lands had been transformed—with grave consequences for most

Mexican ranchers. By the early twentieth century, Emilio Carrillo had lost La Cebadilla Ranch; Anglo businessmen had bought the San Bernardino and San Rafael de la Zanja land grants; and, following a severe drought, Bernabé Robles was forced to sell his Rancho Viejo, which stretched from Florence to the U.S.-Mexican border. After selling their ranches, many ranchers moved to Tucson and Phoenix, and their migrations constituted an important part of Arizona's urbanization during the early twentieth century. Some continued to operate small ranches well into the twentieth century, and a few maintained larger ranches that competed with Anglo-owned corporations. However, by the mid-twentieth century, much of the ranch land once owned by Mexicans in the Santa Cruz, San Pedro, and Sonoita valleys had been sold to various Anglo interests that converted it into large-scale ranching and farming corporations, mines, guest ranches for tourists, and modern housing developments.

Along with mining and cattle ranching, agricultural industries also developed significantly after the Gadsden Purchase. Commercial farming increased during the late nineteenth century, but it was the federal dam projects of the early twentieth century that transformed Arizona's landscape and led to impressive booms in cotton and other crops. Phoenix, drawing on the surrounding Salt River Valley, became Arizona's first primarily agricultural settlement in the 1860s, and it quickly became Arizona's most productive agricultural region. Like other towns north of the Gila River, Phoenix was settled by Anglos—in this case, farmers who hired Mexicans to improve and build upon the canals, or *acequias,* first dug by Hohokam Indians centuries earlier. Mexicans and Mexican Americans came to Phoenix from the 1860s forward to perform most other farm labor as well, first setting up tents near fields and later moving into Phoenix's barrios. They planted, cultivated, and harvested crops; cleared land and plowed fields; and cared for livestock and draft animals. As Phoenix's farms grew, other businesses that relied on Mexican labor moved to the area as well, creating additional job opportunities for blacksmiths, carpenters, leather workers, construction workers, and merchants. According to the 1870 census, Phoenix had 240 residents, 124 of whom were listed as Mexican.[10]

Many Mexicans worked for Anglo farmers, but others bought or leased farmland to work for themselves. José María Redondo, for example, in addition to grazing 2,500 head of cattle, grew crops of barley, oats, wheat, alfalfa, and corn on his farm north of Yuma. And after Francisco Valenzuela moved to Phoenix in 1877, he acquired 160 acres in the city's western suburbs through the Homestead Act. By the early twentieth century, Valenzuela was growing alfalfa and maize, and raising dairy cows, horses, chickens, and turkeys.

If they were unable to buy their own land, some Mexicans leased small parcels on larger farms, where they grew food both to feed their families and to sell at the market. Women shared this labor as well, raising chickens, selling eggs, milking cows, and churning butter. Like Mexican cattle ranchers, however, the number of Mexican farmers decreased by the twentieth century as Anglo-owned corporations gained control of many of Arizona's agriculture industries. In Phoenix, for example, the 1870 territorial census listed 30 Mexican farmers and ranchers in Phoenix, but by 1900, there were only nine.[11] By the early twentieth century, farming communities such as Tolleson and Glendale sprouted up around Phoenix. These were home to canal companies; creameries and dairies; flour mills; hay and grain companies; ice companies; nurseries; and produce distributors.

THE COPPER BOOM AND THE ARRIVAL OF THE RAILROAD DURING THE LATE NINETEENTH CENTURY

If core industries such as mining, cattle ranching, and agriculture grew during the early territorial period, they exploded from the 1880s forward, following the arrival of the Southern Pacific and other railroad lines. Copper, cotton, cattle, and railroads became mutually dependent industries that transformed Arizona's economy during the late nineteenth century. Copper companies, such as Phelps Dodge, depended on railroads to deliver the heavy equipment and new technology that allowed them to produce more copper and bring it to market, whereas railroads depended on copper mines for their contracts to deliver equipment, food, timber, laborers, and other goods.

The simultaneous development of the railroad and other industries led to unprecedented economic growth, which transformed towns such as Clifton, Bisbee, Tombstone, and Douglas within the span of a few decades. Clifton, for example, produced 5 million pounds of copper in 1881, 15 million pounds in 1882, and 24.5 million in 1883. Production there peaked in the early twentieth century when, in 1904, the town produced 29 million pounds of copper—more than the total copper production in Arizona in 1883.[12] Part of the demand for copper during the 1880s and 1890s was driven by the electrification of the United States, which depended on that metal as a conductor.

As the mines seemed to have unlimited potential for profit, capital poured into southern Arizona and northern Sonora as never before, primarily from investors in Europe and eastern states such as New York. In addition to mines in Arizona, they invested in Sonoran cities such as Cananea, Nacozari, and Agua Prieta. International railroad tracks connected Sonora and Arizona; various labor migrations supplied workers to mines in both Mexico and the United States; and the capital flows that invested in mines in Cananea and Bisbee converted a once isolated region into an industrial crossroads of capital, labor, and international political cooperation.[13]

Mexicans provided much of the labor for corporations such as Phelps Dodge, the Arizona Copper Company, and the Greene Consolidated Copper Company in

Cananea. During the 1870s, copper companies relied on Mexican familiarity with the region's resources and basic extraction and smelting techniques, but as new equipment arrived during the 1880s, Mexican miners struggled to compete for jobs. New technologies first decreased the need for Mexican labor in mines, but many workers found new jobs with the railroads when work in mines was unavailable. When copper production increased throughout the 1880s and 1890s, the labor needs of the mines increased as well, which again created a demand for cheap Mexican labor—often recruited in gangs.

Some mining towns—such as Clifton and Morenci—were known as Mexican towns, whereas others—such as Bisbee, Tombstone, Globe, and Miami—were thought of as Anglo towns, populated mainly by migrants from western and northern Europe. The different pay scales of each town reflected the wage disparity between Anglo and Mexican copper miners. In Globe and Miami, the lowest wage was $3 per 10-hour day, whereas the lowest wages in Clifton and Morenci were $1.75 to $2.00 for the same amount of time.[14] Anglos and Mexicans also generally performed different types of labor. Mexicans and Mexican Americans did most of the smelting and dangerous underground work, whereas Anglos received the majority of management and other high-paying positions. Finally, mining camps were segregated; most Mexican miners lived in neighborhoods such as Ragtown (in Douglas) or Bajo (across the border, in Agua Prieta). Segregated mining camps and differential wages, in addition to late pay, lead poisoning, and abusive overseers, frequently led Mexican miners to strike or walk off the job. Major strikes, often ending in ethnic and racial violence, occurred throughout the twentieth century: at Clifton and Morenci in 1903; at Cananea in 1906; at Bisbee in 1915 and 1916; and again at Clifton and Morenci in 1946 and 1983.

The Southern Pacific railroad, which arrived during the late 1870s, made Arizona's late-nineteenth-century copper boom possible. Freighting had become an important industry in Arizona; companies such as Tucson's Tully and Ochoa transported machinery, lumber, and copper ore back and forth from the mines and supplied food, clothes, and other goods to agricultural and military settlements. Because freight wagons pulled by horses were slow, expensive, vulnerable to robbery, and unable to support the heavy machinery that drove Arizona's mines from the 1880s forward, many freighting companies went out of business after the railroad arrived.

Railroads also increased trade with areas east and west of Arizona, which decreased trade with Sonora, once Arizona's foremost trading partner. Tracks first crossed into Yuma in 1877, then progressed eastward, using the work of Mexican and Chinese laborers. These tracks reached Tucson in 1880 and Lordsburg, New Mexico, in 1881. Anglo, Irish, and Scandinavian workers laid most of northern Arizona's railroad tracks, but Mexicans and the Chinese (until the latter were excluded during the early 1880s) laid practically all the tracks in southern Arizona. By the twentieth century, the Southern Pacific connected the state's mines, ranches, farms, and timberlands. Railroads penetrated deeper into Arizona when Mexican labor built feeder lines such as the Maricopa, Phoenix, and Nacozari railroads to connect the main Southern Pacific line with cities throughout Arizona and northern Sonora. Copper mines and railroad companies remained two of Arizona's largest employers of Mexicans well into the twentieth century. In 1911, 60 percent of Arizona's smelter workers were Mexican, and in 1920 the Southern Pacific employed over 25 percent of Tucson's Mexican male workforce.[15]

Barrios, Urbanization, and Early Mutual Aid Societies

The development of cattle ranches, copper mines, and railroads also affected cities such as Tucson and Phoenix. The Southern Pacific brought thousands of new Anglo migrants into Arizona, where they reconfigured the social, political, economic, ethnic, and racial character of the state. One important marker of this shift was the transfer of the capital from Tucson, most of which remained ethnically Mexican through the early twentieth century. The capital moved to Prescott in the late 1870s and then to Phoenix in the late 1880s; both of those cities were primarily Anglo towns by the late nineteenth century. Railroads boosted Tucson and Phoenix as centers of trade, leading to new business opportunities for Mexican and Mexican American butchers, bricklayers, grocers, launderers, and other workers looking for employment even as they signaled the beginning of Arizona's urbanization from the late nineteenth century forward.

Ethnic Mexicans became increasingly segregated in barrios as Anglos gained social, political, and economic control of Tucson and Phoenix. On the one hand, their segregation was a sign of subordination. As marginalization depended in part on racism for justification, barrios became stereotyped as havens of gambling, prostitution, and disease. Eventually, such racial thinking led to the destruction of some of Tucson and Phoenix barrios during the twentieth century. On the other hand, barrios were economically diverse centers of Mexican culture and family life; racially diverse neighborhoods with Chinese and Indian—and later, African American—inhabitants; and vibrant artistic, intellectual, and political centers. For example, dozens of Spanish-language newspapers emerged in Phoenix and Tucson during the 1880s and 1890s, and they attest to the intellectual energy of Arizona's Mexican and Mexican American communities. In Phoenix, *La Guardia* was established by José García in 1881, *El Democrata* by Pedro G. de la Lama in 1898, and *El Mensajero* by Jesus Meléndez, among many others. In Tucson, Carlos Velasco started *Las Dos Repúblicas* and *El Fronterizo* in the late 1870s, whereas others started *La Sonora*, *La Colonia Mexicana*, and *La Alianza*. Even more Spanish-language newspapers were established during the twentieth century, such as *El Tucsonense*, published by Francisco Moreno. The best Mexican writers in Arizona and Sonora wrote for these papers, which kept Mexicans and Mexican Americans well informed of local and regional news, as well as developments throughout Latin America.

Tucson's Barrio Libre in particular was home to an economically and politically diverse community at the turn of the century. In the 1860s and 1870s, during the first wave of migration following the Gadsden Purchase, many members of Sonora's middle and upper classes—journalists, lawyers, doctors, and politicians—took up residence in Tucson. Even though they started new lives in Arizona, they maintained connections with politicians, businessmen, and relatives in Sonora. Members of Sonora's working class migrated to Arizona during the 1860s and 1870s as well, but they looked for work primarily at farms, ranches, and mines in more rural areas, rather than in Tucson. Joining these *sonorenses* were the ranchers who moved to Tucson after selling their land, and together they formed Tucson's Mexican middle and upper class. They established some of Arizona's first literary societies, philharmonic clubs, and leisure resorts, helping make Tucson the largest and most sophisticated center of ethnic Mexican society between Los Angeles and El Paso.

Many middle-class *tucsonenses* also held conservative political ideologies, carried over from their lives in Sonora or cultivated by their privileged class positions in Arizona. Carlos Velasco, for example, arrived in Tucson during the 1870s after having lived under the influence of Sonora's relatively rigidly stratified society, and his experience there informed the ideas his newspapers printed about organized labor, fiscal conservatism, and other issues. In general, these newspapers opposed organized labor as a threat to their own class interests, which more often than not were aligned with those of Arizona's Anglo elite.

Still, Tucson's Mexican middle class worked in several contexts to address the prevalence of racism in Arizona. Criminal records demonstrated that Mexicans were arrested and convicted for murder, larceny, and robbery more often than Anglos; Mexican, Chinese, and Native American laborers continued to occupy positions at the bottom of the wage scale; and nativist organizations, such as the American Protective Association and the Society of American Workers, formed in Arizona during the 1890s. One important way that ethnic Mexicans dealt with anti-Mexican racism in Arizona was to form political groups and mutual aid societies, which spread across the U.S. Southwest during the late nineteenth and early twentieth centuries. Some examples were the Mutual Benevolent Society of the Latin American Races in Phoenix, Club Mexicano Republicano in Tucson, and the Sociedad Mexicana de Protección Mutua in St. Johns. Such groups charged their members dues in exchange for low-cost sickness, accident, and death benefits; they were also active in many community affairs, including political and social events, such as dances and charity benefits.

Perhaps the most significant of Arizona's mutual aid societies was La Alianza Hispano-Americana, formed in Tucson in 1894. The organization's founding members—including Estevan Ochoa, Mariano Samaniego, and Carlos Jácome—were representatives of Tucson's Mexican middle class. As the organization grew, however, it gained working-class members as well—particularly in rural mining and agricultural communities, such as Douglas, Bisbee, Tolleson, and Glendale. From the few chapters that spread across Arizona by the early twentieth century, La Alianza became a regional organization with lodges (or *logias*) in California, New Mexico, Colorado, and Texas, and then an international organization with lodges in Sonoran cities such as Nogales, Hermosillo, and Guaymas. At its peak during the 1920s and 1930s, La Alianza claimed well over 10,000 members as it evolved from a fraternal insurance organization into a political advocacy and civil rights organization by the mid-twentieth century. It promoted both Americanism (through celebrations of George Washington's birthday and the Fourth of July) and pride in its members' Mexican heritage (through celebrations of Benito Juárez's birthday and Mexican independence).

Migration, the Mexican Revolution, and the World War I Era

In addition to segregation in barrios and the development of *mutualistas,* the early twentieth century also marked a period of mass migration from Mexico to Arizona, and to many other areas of the United States. Between 1900 and 1920, more than 47,000 Mexicans settled in Arizona—which, in addition to migrants from Mexico, included Mexican American citizens of the United States from California and other areas—primarily to work as railroad and migrant farm laborers.[16] The greatest number migrated between 1910 and 1920, both because the Mexican Revolution caused many Mexicans to seek refuge in the United States, and because the economic boom of the World War I era created new job opportunities for Mexican workers. During the nineteenth century, the vast majority of Mexican migrants to Arizona were men from Sonora and Chihuahua. During the early twentieth century, however, whole families came from other areas as well, such as Guanajuato, Aguas Calientes, and Michoacán.

Different groups of migrants settled in different parts of Arizona, depending on the kinds of employment and cultural opportunities available to them. For example, because Tucson's economic base during the early twentieth century was primarily commercial, rather than agricultural or industrial, and therefore it could not absorb as many laborers as other parts of the state, it never attracted the same number of laborers that cities such as Phoenix did. Tucson became a haven for members of Mexico's revolutionary elite, such as Pancho Villa, Plutarco Elías Calles, Adolfo de la Huerta, and Alvaro Obregón, each of whom visited Tucson between 1913 and 1917.[17] Most Mexican migrants to Arizona during this period, however, were workers looking for jobs in Arizona's agricultural, railroad, and other industries.

The opening of the Roosevelt Dam in 1911 gave Phoenix's Salt River valley its first steady water supply to cultivate crops. With the new source of water, as well as increased wartime demands for food and cotton—a key ingredient of rubber tires and other war matériel—agricultural production in Arizona skyrocketed during World War I. Arizona growers harvested 400 acres of Yuma Long Staple cotton in 1912, 33,000 acres in 1917, and 180,000 acres in 1920.[18] The dramatic rise in production, combined with the service of many Arizona farmers in World War I, prompted growers to plead with government officials and the Arizona Cotton Growers Association (ACGA) to permit the importation of Mexican labor, lest their crops wither unpicked. The Alien Contract Labor Law of 1885 and the Immigration Act of 1917 had made it difficult for employers to hire foreign contract labor. The critical labor shortage cited by growers across the United States, however, led Secretary of Labor William Bauchop Wilson to allow Mexican laborers to work in the United States on a temporary basis, exempting them from literacy tests, head taxes, and other restrictions. During this first Bracero program—a concerted effort by the United States and Mexico to supply temporary Mexican labor—growers throughout the southwestern United States imported thousands of Mexican farmworkers to plant and harvest crops during the 1910s. For its part, the ACGA recruited more than 35,000 Mexicans to labor in Phoenix's fields between 1918 and 1921 alone, marking the largest migration to date of Mexican workers to the Salt River valley.[19]

After particularly successful harvests from 1918 to 1921, the cotton market crashed during the early 1920s, and many Arizona farmers abandoned their fields and dismissed their workers, even though they had hired those workers under contract. The Mexican consulate in Phoenix estimated that the cotton crash left between 15,000 and 20,000 migrant workers stranded in the valley without pay or way of getting home. La Liga Protectora Latina (LPL)—formed in 1915 by Phoenix businessmen Pedro G. de la Lama, Ignacio Espinoza, and Jesus Meléndrez—and several Mexican and Mexican American civic organizations opened soup kitchens to help the stranded farmworkers, but such measures did not solve the problem. Mexican officials negotiated for the ACGA to pay workers' unpaid wages and send them back by train to Mexico, free of charge, but growers never made good on the agreement. Eventually, Mexican president Alvaro Obregón arranged for the Mexican government to repatriate workers. Mexican newspapers criticized the ACGA for treating Mexico's farmworkers shamefully, and the incident had a lasting effect on Arizona-Mexico relations—especially when Arizona growers again sought to negotiate temporary labor contracts during the World War II era.

Racial and class conflict also characterized the experience of Arizona's Mexican and Mexican American communities during the early twentieth century—perhaps nowhere so violently as in mining communities. In 1903 thousands of ethnic Mexican workers in Clifton and Morenci walked away from their jobs with Phelps Dodge to participate in the first major strike in Arizona history. The labor movement in Arizona had successfully lobbied the territorial legislature to reduce miners' workdays from 10 to 8 hours per day with no cut in pay. Phelps Dodge scaled back the workday, but in violation of the new law, they scaled back wages as well, which led workers to strike. The Western Federation of Miners (WFM) did not organize workers in Clifton and Morenci, because they were so-called Mexican towns, so some of the *mutualistas* formed during the late nineteenth century helped organize workers. The strike ended in a standoff between workers and National Guardsmen, federal troops, and the Arizona Rangers, who were used throughout the early twentieth century to suppress labor unrest.

Racial prejudice in Clifton and Morenci was manifest in other aspects of life as well, as members of a 1904 Anglo-led posse confiscated Irish Catholic orphans from the ethnic Mexican families who had adopted them, claiming that Mexicans were unfit to raise white children. In 1906, arguing that it was not in the best interest of white orphans to have Mexican parents raise them, the United States Supreme Court upheld the actions of the white vigilantes and decided that the orphans would remain with white parents. The same year, a strike rocked the Sonoran mining town of Cananea, where 2,000 Mexican employees left their jobs when the Greene Consolidated Copper Company failed to meet their demands for an increased minimum wage, eight-hour workday, and pay rates and promotions commensurate with those of Anglo miners. Arizona Rangers helped suppress this strike as well, and more than 20 strikers were killed in the action. Another strike erupted in Clifton and Morenci in 1915, amid labor activism that also swept across other areas of the United States. This time, with the backing of unions such as the WFM and International Workers of the World (IWW), as well as the support of thousands of Euro-American miners, more than 3,000 ethnic Mexicans struck for improved working conditions and wage parity with Anglos.

Although the 1915–1916 strike resulted in a wage increase, another incident in 1917 ended in tragedy. Citing the communist influence of the IWW, Cochise County sheriff William Wheeler formed the Bisbee Citizens' Protective League, which imprisoned 1,186 striking mine workers—268 of which were ethnic Mexican.

Mexicans and Mexican Americans negotiated such instances of ethnic and racial conflict during the early twentieth century through increased social and political activism. *Mutualistas* similar in function to La Alianza formed during the World War I era—including the Liga Protectora Latina (LLP), a fraternal insurance organization that also offered broad educational, moral, social, and material support to Phoenix and Arizona's ethnic Mexican communities. The immediate impulse for its establishment was discriminatory legislation, such as the 1913 law requiring an English literacy test in order to vote. In response, the LPL and other organizations taught ethnic Mexicans how to read the preamble to the Constitution. Later, it rallied community opposition against the Claypool-Kinney Bill, which sought to prohibit employers from hiring "anyone deaf or dumb, or who could not speak or read the English language."[20] Though the bill did not name Mexicans in particular, it was widely understood to target them. In part because of the efforts of the LPL, the Arizona Supreme Court overturned Claypool-Kinney. Placing great emphasis on education in addition to political organization, the LPL also lobbied the Arizona State Legislature to approve bilingual education in elementary schools.

Americanization and the Great Depression

The Friendly House, established in Phoenix during the early 1920s by teacher and social worker Carrie Green, was another important organization that focused on Mexican communities. Offering courses in English, citizenship, hygiene, and homemaking, it worked for the Americanization of Mexicans without denying participants' Mexican heritage. Along with the Phoenix Americanization Committee and similar groups in Tucson, the Friendly House was a local manifestation of a national Americanization movement that began during the World War I era. Arizona's public schools also launched Americanization programs, such as the 1C program—which until the mid-1960s made English-only language instruction and courses in American culture mandatory for many ethnic Mexican schoolchildren. Estevan Ochoa and other ethnic Mexicans had played a key role in establishing Arizona's public schools during the 1870s, but by the end of the nineteenth century, the state's school boards were dominated by Anglo administrators, many of whom argued that Mexican schoolchildren were developmentally behind their Anglo peers. Originally intended to address issues of educational development, the 1C program in effect segregated Mexican schoolchildren.

Economic hardship caused by the Great Depression had a significant impact on Mexicans and Mexican Americans in Arizona. By the early 1930s, 59 percent of Phoenix's Mexicans and Mexican Americans, compared with 11 percent of Anglos, received some form of public welfare.[21] Anti-Mexican sentiment throughout the state increased as Mexicans and Mexican Americans, citizens or not, became viewed as burdens. The Friendly House assisted ethnic Mexicans by providing day care and helping thousands of men and women find jobs as seamstresses, domestic workers, or bricklayers. The federal government—through the Unemployment Relief Bureau, the Federal Emergency Relief Administration, and the Civil Works Administration—also provided work for Mexican Americans on construction and maintenance projects, if they could prove U.S. citizenship.

Not all Mexicans and Mexican Americans experienced equal hardship during the 1930s, as many still found work as ranch hands and in factories, laundries, and other service industries. Some small-business owners, such as Pete Romo, owner of a butcher shop in Phoenix, and Rafael Granados Sr., a veteran of the Mexican Revolution who owned Phoenix's first Mexican-operated drugstore, remained afloat during the Depression. So did many owners of larger businesses, such as Tucson's Alex G. Jácome, whose department store continued to serve its Anglo and Mexican clientele. Nevertheless, thousands of Mexicans in Arizona repatriated to Mexico during the Depression, either forcibly or voluntarily. Even though repatriation, economic depression, and racial discrimination characterized the experience of many in Arizona during the 1920s and 1930s, the persistent efforts of organizations such as La Alianza, the LPL, and the Friendly House also shaped Arizona's Mexican and Mexican American communities as they entered the pivotal World War II era.

The World War II and Postwar Eras

One of the key turning points in Arizona's history, the World War II era, initiated a period of economic and demographic boom that had important consequences for ethnic Mexicans. Cities such as Phoenix and Tucson became Sun Belt metropolises through the arrival of military bases, the presence of other defense-related industries, and increased efforts by chambers of commerce and other booster organizations to attract visitors and new residents.

The population of Arizona's two major cities increased by 400 percent between 1940 and 1960, largely because of these developments. Several trends characterized Arizona's Mexican and Mexican American communities during the World War II and postwar eras. First, because of the rapid influx of primarily white migrants from eastern and midwestern states and the West Coast, by mid-century ethnic Mexicans represented only 15 and 22 percent of Phoenix and Tucson's populations, respectively—their lowest proportion of any period, before or since. Second, and partly because of Arizona's sustained economic and demographic booms, many Mexicans and Mexican Americans during the postwar era enjoyed new social, political, educational, and economic opportunities. Third, despite these new opportunities, persistent challenges and racism led a growing constellation of Mexican and Mexican American civic organizations to continue to struggle for first-class citizenship and civil rights.

During the 1940s and 1950s, mining, agriculture, railroad freighting, and ranching remained important sectors of Arizona's economy. However, Arizona's sunny climate, available labor pool, right-to-work legislation, and tax laws favorable to corporations attracted high-tech and defense industries as well. Davis-Monthan Air Force Base, in Tucson, and Luke Air Force Base, in Phoenix, were built during the early years of the war to serve as training facilities for allied pilots from around the world. They were also buffers in the U.S.-Mexican border region, protecting against a feared invasion by Germany and Japan through Mexico. Mexicans and Mexican Americans from all over the United States and Mexico worked and trained at these bases. During the war years—and even more so during the postwar era—military defense industries built up around Davis-Monthan and Luke, including Consolidated Vultee and Hughes Aircraft in Tucson, and AiResearch and Goodyear in Phoenix. These and other companies quickly became the largest employers in their respective cities, but they primarily hired Anglos to work in management and skilled positions, whereas ethnic Mexican men and women worked as machinists, metalworkers, and other lower-paid jobs.

Work in defense industries was just one way that Arizona's Mexican and Mexican American communities contributed to the allied war effort. They also volunteered for the Red Cross, held fund-raisers, and joined organizations such as La Asociación Hispano-Americana de Madres y Esposas (a women's organization in Tucson that bought and sold war bonds), sent letters to soldiers, and published a community newsletter, among other activities. Also, at Phoenix's Immaculate Heart Church, Mexican American women hung American and Mexican flags to honor those who served; they also placed a silk banner on an altar to the Virgin of Guadalupe bearing the names of all the soldiers who had died.[22] Finally, social and political groups such as La Alianza, the League of United Latin American Citizens (LULAC, a national organization founded in Corpus Christi, Texas, in 1929), and others sold and bought war bonds; collected rubber, paper, metal, and other rationed goods; and hosted dinners and dances for Latin American troops training at Arizona's military bases.

Thousands of braceros contributed to the war cause as well, working primarily in Maricopa, Pinal, and Pima counties to harvest Arizona's cotton, citrus, and vegetable crops. In Arizona's fields, braceros joined year-round farmworkers as well as Mexican American volunteers, such as the Victory War Volunteers, who during a three-week period in 1942 harvested more than 35,000 pounds of cotton.[23] Under the provisions of the 1942 Emergency Farm Labor Program, the Arizona Farm Bureau Federation contracted 5,975 Mexican men between 1943 and 1947 to work in Arizona's fields.[24] Though the program was originally intended to fill the void of American farmworkers who left to serve in the war, a coalition of growers and politicians in the United States and Mexico extended the program until 1964—well beyond the war years, despite the program's shortcomings. These problems included worker exploitation and a spike in the number of undocumented migrants, who had come looking for work as well.

Although precise numbers are unavailable for the period after 1947, thousands of Mexican workers harvested Arizona's crops during the postwar era. These workers provided labor that was vital to the maintenance of Arizona's agriculture industry, but their presence was nevertheless a polarizing issue that often divided Arizona's Mexican American communities. In 1946, hundreds of Mexican Americans identifying themselves as "citizens, taxpayers, and agricultural workers" petitioned Arizona governor Sidney P. Osborn to stop importing bracero labor, offering the common argument that braceros drove down wages, took jobs, and inspired racism toward all ethnic Mexicans—including those who were U.S. citizens. Many workers in farming communities—such as Phoenix, Tolleson, Guadalupe, and Tempe—continued to oppose bracero labor throughout the postwar era, receiving support from such groups as the Fresh Fruit and Vegetables Workers Union Local 78, an affiliate of the Congress of Industrial Organizations, and the Community Service Organization (CSO).

Many Mexicans and Mexican Americans from Arizona also served in World War II. Because of their patriotism toward the United States and participation in a war against racism abroad, they expected to receive treatment as equals when they returned home. Benefits from the Servicemen's Readjustment Act of 1944—popularly known as the GI Bill—helped many ethnic Mexican men and women buy new homes and enroll at the Arizona State Teachers College (later renamed Arizona State University), the University of Arizona (U of A), and trade schools. However, employers, city planners, and civic organizations continued to discriminate against them.

During the postwar era, Mexican American veterans became particularly active in fighting for civil rights through organizations such as the GI Forum, the American Legion, and Veterans of Foreign Wars.[25] In 1946, for example, the American Legion's Thunderbird Post 41 in Phoenix took a lead role in efforts to desegregate the Tempe Beach community swimming pool, which had exercised an unofficial ban on Mexicans from its opening in 1923 to 1946. The local LULAC chapter, Council 110, took up the issue in 1942 after two young Mexican American women and their dates—pilots from Mexico—were denied entry and told to leave. Despite pressure from LULAC, Tempe Beach did not desegregate until 1946, when American Legion members convinced Tempe Beach to drop its discriminatory policy.

The same year, American Legion members organized to fight for integrated housing after they learned that city planners had drawn blueprints for three separate housing projects: one for whites, one for African Americans, and another for Mexican Americans. The members filed suit against the Garfield Property Owners Protective Association, and on December 11, 1946, the Arizona Supreme Court decided that housing had to be integrated. Also in 1946, veterans in Clifton and Morenci struck against Phelps Dodge for wage parity with white miners. Throughout the post–World War II and Korean War eras, ethnic Mexican veterans were highly respected in their communities, and former soldiers often boasted about having joined the military voluntarily, rather than waiting to get drafted.

New job opportunities and increased demands for equality during the postwar era also led to a significant expansion of Arizona's Mexican American middle class. For the first time, significant numbers of ethnic Mexicans, including many World War II veterans, moved from Tucson and Phoenix's barrios into parts of town that had been inhabited almost exclusively by whites. Some experienced discrimination upon arriving. They persisted nevertheless, even in some of Tucson and Phoenix's most exclusive, upper-class neighborhoods. However, most Mexicans and Mexican Americans—because of enduring discrimination, economic inequalities, and distinct cultural opportunities—continued to live in Tucson and Phoenix's barrios.

Other evidence of the growth of Arizona's Mexican American middle class included the increased efforts of Mexican (and later, "Hispanic") chambers of commerce to promote Mexican American business interests, social organizations, enrollment in Arizona's universities, and political participation and representation. In part because of the GI Bill, more Mexican Americans pursued degrees at the University of Arizona and Arizona State University, even though their proportional enrollment remained extremely low. Mexican and Mexican American students joined groups such as the Spanish Honorary Club, the Newman Club for Catholic Students, and Los Universitarios, a club for students interested in Latin American affairs.[26] Phoenix's Vesta Club, established in 1954, also helped increase educational opportunities for Mexican Americans by raising college scholarship funds for local youth.

Other groups focused on increasing political participation among Arizona's ethnic Mexican communities. In addition to older groups, such as La Alianza, Friendly House, and others that predated World War II, newer ones, such as local chapters of LULAC and the CSO, became important parts of Arizona's ethnic Mexican communities. LULAC's Council 110 was established in 1940, and Plácida García Smith, who directed the Friendly House during the 1930s, served as one of its earliest presidents. The California-based CSO operated in Phoenix from 1952 to 1958. LULAC and the CSO focused primarily on increasing political participation through voter registration drives, but they also held citizenship classes, formed neighborhood improvement committees, and engaged in multiple civil rights struggles. The Spanish American Democratic Club and the Latin American Club of Arizona also focused on political participation. These groups achieved some success, and Anglo politicians in Arizona came to regard Mexican Americans as important voters and candidates. The vast majority of Mexican Americans during the postwar era voted for Democratic candidates, though a few prominent Mexican Americans—such as department store owner Alex G. Jácome and bank president Louis Felix—were active members of the Republican Party.

The postwar era also saw the proliferation of ethnic Mexican social clubs, such as Tucson's Monte Carlo Men's Club; Club Cienna, a group for single women; and Club Mavis, a women's auxiliary of La Alianza. Even though these clubs were primarily social groups, many of their members went into politics. By 1960, two Monte Carlo members were state legislators, and another was the vice chairman of the Pima County Democratic Central Committee. In addition, ethnic Mexican youth formed car clubs—such as Club Belmont, the Playboys Club, and Los Dukes—and attended dances at Tucson and Phoenix's many ballrooms. Another organization, the Cuauhtémoc Club, celebrated Arizona's cultural connection with Sonora by planning celebrations of Mexican Independence Day and yearly trips to Hermosillo. They joined many ethnic Mexican families in Tucson that made regular trips to Sonora to visit family members, shop in Nogales or Agua Prieta, or visit dentists and doctors who charged less than their counterparts in Arizona. Finally, a few middle-class Mexican Americans were members of the Rotary Club, the Kiwanis Club, and the Lions Club. In many ways, Tucson in 1960 still retained its Sonoran character, as more than 70 percent of ethnic Mexicans there were of Sonoran descent.[27]

Despite these trends toward social and economic equality, challenges remained. The majority of ethnic Mexican workers in Arizona were still near the bottom of the wage scale, and Arizona's 1946 right-to-work law made it difficult for them to organize; very few Mexicans or Mexican Americans served on Arizona's school boards or as teachers; they were arrested at higher rates than members of other ethnic and racial groups; and the loan provisions of the GI Bill often discriminated against them. Also, de facto segregation policies separated Mexicans from Anglos in theaters, swimming pools, and public schools. To address such issues, La Alianza's Richard Estrada and Greg García, among others, filed important antisegregation lawsuits such as *Baca v. Winslow* (1944), which desegregated Winslow's public swimming pool, and *González v. Sheeley* (1952), which legally ended segregation in Arizona's elementary schools. In *González v. Sheeley*, Mexican and Mexican American plaintiffs sued the superintendent of schools in the rural farming community of Tolleson, a western suburb of Phoenix, for segregating their children. The school system acknowledged segregation and unequal facilities, but claimed the situation resulted from segregated housing patterns, rather than any conscious efforts of discrimination on the part of school board administrators, adding that language deficiencies necessitated instructing Mexican children in separate classes. Plaintiffs, however, borrowed the logic of *Méndez v. Westminster,* a 1947 desegregation case in California, to argue that segregation violated their children's constitutional rights. Arizona Supreme Court judge David Ling sided with them, ruling that segregation violated Mexican children's rights under the Equal Protection Clause of the Fourteenth

Amendment. *Sheeley v. González* became an important precedent for other desegregation cases in the state—such as *Ortiz v. Jack*, which ended segregation in Glendale, another farming suburb of Phoenix—and the desegregation of public facilities in the mining community of Miami, Arizona.

THE CHICANO MOVEMENT ERA

Building on the activism of the 1940s and 1950s, ethnic Mexicans in Arizona during the 1960s and 1970s—who often identified themselves as Chicanas and Chicanos—continued to struggle for social, economic, cultural, and political justice. Chicanas and Chicanos supported regional and national Chicano movements, but Arizona's Chicano movement remained primarily defined by local issues.

During the 1960s, many older organizations, such as La Alianza and the Friendly House, struggled to remain relevant as new groups—including the Mexican American Student Organization (MASO), the Movimiento Estudiantil Chicano de Aztlán (MEChA), and Chicanos Por La Causa (CPLC)—organized Mexican and Mexican American youth. Even though the membership of organizations such as La Alianza declined during the Chicano movement era, prominent Mexican Americans of an older generation remained committed to their relatively conservative ideas about political change, economics, and ethnicity. La Alianza finally folded in 1965, in part because of corruption charges and political infighting. LULAC and the Friendly House, however, were more successful in rejuvenating their message by taking up President Lyndon B. Johnson's War on Poverty and other issues.

During the Chicano movement, national political organizations formed local chapters in Arizona, such as the Mexican American Political Association (MAPA, founded in 1960 by Mexican Americans in California) and the Political Association of Spanish Speaking Organizations (PASSO, founded in Texas in 1961 by Hector García, who also founded the GI Forum). But many local and statewide organizations particular to Arizona formed as well, such as the Phoenix-based American Coordinating Council of Political Education (ACCPE) and Chicanos Por La Causa (CPLC). The Southwest Council of La Raza (SCLR), another civil rights organization, started in Phoenix with a small grant from the Ford Foundation. It later became a national organization based in Washington, DC, called the National Council of La Raza (NCLR). Each of these organizations had local objectives, such as improved housing, as well as statewide and national goals, such as the election of Chicana and Chicano political candidates and increased voter registration.

In part because of the efforts of such groups, several Latino Democratic candidates were elected during the 1960s and 1970s to the Arizona state legislature, including Leonardo Calderón Jr. (1964–1966), David Valenzuela (1964–1966), and Tony Abril (1967–1970, 1973–1982). As a response to such political activism, organizations and individuals—including future U.S. Supreme Court justice William Rehnquist—began to monitor ethnic Mexican participation at the polls during the 1960s.[28] These monitors claimed they were only interested in protecting against voter fraud, many Mexican Americans nevertheless viewed such actions as discriminatory efforts to bar them from the political process.

Perhaps the most important political organization to form during Arizona's Chicano movement was Chicanos Por La Causa (CPLC), established in 1969, which by the early twenty-first century had 30 offices in 23 cities and served 45,000 individuals. CPLC's annual operating budget skyrocketed from $676,000 during the early 1970s to $6.3 million by the end of the decade, sparking the ire of many who disapproved of government support for what they called special-interest groups. Founded by Arizona State University student movement leaders Alfredo Gutierrez and Joe "Eddie" López, CPLC drew together diverse elements of Phoenix's Chicano movement to build community service programs focusing on housing, education, counseling services, small-business development, job training, migration, and public health.

Student activism was also a key component of Arizona's Chicano movement. At the University of Arizona and Arizona State University, students established the MASO during the late 1960s, which they incorporated into the national MEChA during the early 1970s. At both universities, Chicano students called for the development of courses on Chicano history and culture; more Chicano faculty members; and increased cultural opportunities. Students at the U of A, including Salomón Baldenegro, Raúl Grijalva, and Guadalupe Castillo, formed the Mexican American Liberation Committee (MALC), which led the effort to organize walkouts at Tucson and Pueblo high schools, similar to the walkouts that rocked Los Angeles high schools in 1968. Even though participation in the Tucson walkouts was less than in Los Angeles, students in Tucson nevertheless brought attention to issues of overcrowding and bilingual education. They also formed the El Río Coalition Front, which during the summer and fall of 1970 successfully pressured the Tucson city government to convert El Río Golf Course into a public park and community center. Students at Arizona State University engaged in similar community-based struggles, such as the successful protest against the Phoenix Linen Towel Supply Company, which paid discriminatory wages to its Mexican workers and failed to promote them. Because of these students' efforts, Arizona State University promptly ended its contract with Phoenix Linen.

Operating alongside and often in concert with political and student activism, farmworker organizations formed another key element of Arizona's Chicano movement. Arizona's farmworker organizations were most active in Phoenix's Salt

River valley. During the 1960s and 1970s, the Maricopa County Organizing Project (MCOP), Migrant Opportunities Program (MOP), and United Farm Workers (UFW) of Arizona provided job training for migrant workers and focused on sanitation, access to safe drinking water, migrant health, protection from pesticides, child labor, and wage discrimination. Like farmworkers throughout the United States, farmworkers in Arizona did not get state unemployment insurance, workers' compensation, or overtime pay; moreover, under the National Labor Relations Act, they could not organize. The UFW in Arizona, led by Gustavo Gutiérrez, often organized in solidarity on these and other issues with UFW members in other areas. For example, following César Chávez's famous strike against Delano grapes and his subsequent march to Sacramento, the UFW in Arizona led a boycott of Arizona's grape growers and organized a 20-mile march from Tolleson to the capitol building in Phoenix.

One of the most important events of Arizona's Chicano movement, which brought national media attention to the state, was Chávez's 1972 Fast of Love, during which Chávez fasted for 24 consecutive days as a protest against Arizona House Bill 2134, which proposed to outlaw strikes during harvest. The bill, Chávez and the UFW argued, would negatively affect farmworkers' ability to fight for fair labor conditions. By the time Chávez was admitted to Phoenix's Memorial Hospital because his organs were failing, his fast had already gained media attention from the *New York Times,* the *Los Angeles Times,* and the *Washington Post;* support from national celebrities, including Joan Baez and Coretta Scott King; and a daylong sympathy strike organized by 1,500 farmworkers in Yuma. Despite Chávez's fast, HB 2134 passed the state legislature, at which point the UFW led an unsuccessful movement to recall Governor Jack Williams. The Fast of Love nevertheless mobilized Phoenix and Arizona's Mexican and Mexican American communities, which had a significant impact on the outcome of state elections in 1974. In part because of the widespread support of Mexican American voters, Raúl Castro became the first Mexican American governor of Arizona; Democrats captured control of the state senate; and Alfredo Gutiérrez of MASO and CPLC became the senate majority leader.

Several urban-renewal projects also inspired community activism during Arizona's Chicano movement era, such as freeway construction through Tucson and Phoenix barrios, along with supposed neighborhood improvement projects that destroyed Mexican and Mexican American neighborhoods. Interstate 10 displaced many homes in Tucson's El Hoyo barrio, and the Maricopa Freeway split Phoenix's Cuatro Milpas in half. Then, during the late 1960s, city developers razed Tucson's Barrio Libre, building the Tucson Convention Center where houses once stood. Urban-renewal projects ripped through Phoenix barrios when the expansion of Phoenix's Sky Harbor International Airport led to the destruction of the Golden Gate barrio, where many ethnic Mexican families had lived from the

1920s forward. Multiple organizations, such as Tucson's Save La Placita Committee (led by longtime resident and community organizer Alva Torres), collected signatures, raised funds, and solicited legal advice in order to prevent the destruction of these neighborhoods, but to little avail.

POST–CHICANO MOVEMENT

From the 1970s forward, the primary concerns of Arizona's Latino communities have revolved around political representation, access to services, and migration. Latinas and Latinos made several gains as a result of the Chicano movement, including the establishment of the Mexican American Studies and Research Center at the University of Arizona in 1983. In 1991, Manuel T. Pacheco became the University of Arizona's first Mexican American president. Then, in 1992, Arizona State University established a Chicano Studies program, which was renamed Transborder Chicana/o and Latina/o Studies in 2006. Additionally, more Latinas and Latinos were elected to political office following the Chicano movement than during any other period of Arizona's history. Despite the gains of the post–World War II and Chicano eras, Latinas and Latinos in Arizona continued to face many challenges. Phoenix Union High School was forced to close temporarily in 1982, because it continued to segregate ethnic Mexican students. Also, of ASU's 40,000 students, only 2 to 3 percent during the early 1980s were of Latin American birth or heritage.

Migration from Latin America has perhaps been Arizona's most divisive social and political issue since the Chicano movement. Migration was a matter of local and national concern during earlier eras as well, but debates in Arizona reached peak intensity during the late twentieth and early twenty-first centuries as Arizona became the busiest point of migration along the U.S.-Mexican border. Setting the tone for much of the late twentieth century was the 1976 Hanigan Case, in which George, Patrick, and Thomas Hanigan went on trial for torturing, beating, and robbing three Mexican nationals—Manuel García Loya, Eleazar Ruelas Zavala, and Bernabe Herrera Mata—whom they caught crossing over their ranch land in 1976 in Elfrida, just north of Douglas. George Hanigan, the father of Patrick and Thomas, died before the trial began, but an all-white jury acquitted Patrick and Thomas in 1977. Phoenix's Mexican consul said the verdict "declared open season on illegal immigrants." In response the National Coalition on the Hanigan Case formed as a human rights advocacy group to protect Mexicans and Mexican Americans from suffering similar attacks.[29]

During the early 1980s, Latin American migration to Arizona was again at the forefront of local and national attention as a coalition of community leaders—including Jim Corbett, Guadalupe Castillo, Presbyterian minister John Fife, and Roman Catholic priest Ricardo Elford—offered sanctuary to Central American refugees who fled their war-torn homes in Guatemala, El Salvador, and other countries. Though it began as a church-based initiative in Tucson, the Sanctuary movement expanded to more than 500 congregations across the United States. During the mid-1980s, the U.S. Department of Justice indicted 16 participants in the Sanctuary movement; 11 went on trial, and 8 were eventually convicted of smuggling charges, even though the activists argued that humanitarian considerations justified their actions. At the same time, by the mid-1980s, undocumented Mexican migration had become a divisive issue in Arizona, as the 1986 Immigration Reform and Control Act (IRCA) granted amnesty to thousands of Mexicans in Arizona. Many civil rights activists in Arizona generally favored IRCA's amnesty provisions but argued that they were not being properly implemented, whereas both Anglo and Mexican anti-immigration activists argued that amnesty only encouraged Mexicans to continue migrating illegally.

In part as a backlash against IRCA, several anti-immigration organizations formed in Arizona during the late twentieth and early twenty-first centuries, such as Save Our State (SOS), an Arizona spin-off of a California-based organization; the Minuteman Project; Border Guardians; and Protect Arizona Now. Several immigrant rights and humanitarian groups formed as well, including No More Deaths, Border Action Network, and the Coalición de Derechos Humanos (cochaired by immigration lawyer Isabel García). The work of both sides intensified during the early twenty-first century as Arizona, in part because of the funneling effect of immigration crackdowns in California and Texas, became the most traversed point of crossing for undocumented migrants into the United States. The Tucson and Yuma sectors of the U.S. Border Patrol apprehended more than 500,000 undocumented migrants every year during the late twentieth and early twenty-first centuries, and hundreds more died of heat in the Arizona-Sonora desert. The intensification of immigration debates led 56 percent of Arizona voters, including 47 percent of the state's Latina and Latino voters, to pass Proposition 200 in 2004. Many observers compared the initiative with California's Proposition 187. This led Democratic governor Janet Napolitano to declare a state of emergency in Arizona in 2005, and it also led thousands of immigrant rights activists to march in Tucson and Phoenix on May Day in 2006 and 2007 in support of comprehensive immigration reform. By the early twenty-first century, Arizona had become the focal point of the national debate over migration.

Since 1990, Arizona has been one of the fastest-growing states in the nation. During the 1990s alone, its population increased by 40.1 percent. Even more impressive was the 88.2 percent growth of Arizona's "Hispanic" and "Latino" populations, as U.S. census takers classified members of those groups. Mexicans and Mexican Americans continued to be the dominant Latino group in Arizona, constituting approximately 90 percent of the total Latino population, whereas Puerto Ricans represented 1 percent, Cuban Americans 0.4 percent, and all others (primarily from Central America) approximately 8 percent. According to the 1990 U.S. census, Arizona's population was 18.8 percent "Hispanic" (688,338 of a total population of 3,665,228); according to the 2000 U.S. census, the number had increased to 25.3 percent (1,295,617 of a total population of 5,130,632). Most of that growth took place in the counties and cities that experienced the greatest overall growth, including Maricopa County (Phoenix) and Pima County (Tucson). However, traditionally Latino-dominated areas, such as Santa Cruz, Cochise, and Yuma counties (which, in addition to Pima County, form southern Arizona's border with Mexico), experienced impressive growth as well. This was especially true in border towns such as Douglas, Nogales, and Yuma, which capitalized on the North American Free Trade Agreement's increase in cross-border commerce, the growth of agriculture industries, and tourism.[30] By 2005, Arizona's Latina and Latino population had grown to represent 28.6 percent of the state's total population, and reports during the fall of 2006 proclaimed Phoenix and Tucson majority-minority cities for the first time since the late nineteenth (in Phoenix's case) and early twentieth (in Tucson's case) centuries.

In addition to occupying familiar positions in Arizona's agriculture and mining industries, Latinos have filled Arizona's construction, domestic service, janitorial, and landscaping jobs. New Latino migrants to Arizona have joined those whose families have lived there for several decades, if not centuries, and their cohabitation has led to both conflict and cooperation over issues such as migration, labor, bilingualism, and social services for migrants.

NOTABLE LATINOS

Vázquez de Coronado, Francisco (1510–1554). An explorer of New Spain (Mexico), Coronado was born near Salamanca, Spain, and first traveled to Mexico at the age of 25. Between 1540 and 1542, and in search of the mythical golden cities of Cíbola and Quivira, he led an exploration of the present states of Arizona, New Mexico, Texas, Oklahoma, and Kansas. His expedition greatly enhanced knowledge of the geography and peoples of Arizona.

Kino, Eusebio Francisco (1644–1711). Born in Italy, Kino became one of the New World's foremost missionaries, establishing dozens of missions in the territory that became northern Mexico and southern Arizona. Often called the Father of Arizona, Kino arrived in Sonora in 1687. In what would become Arizona, he established missions at San Xavier del Bac, Guevavi, and elsewhere. In addition to his missionary work, Kino was a mapmaker, an astronomer, a mathematician, and an agro-pastoralist who introduced cattle into the region.

Elías, Eulalia (1788–1865). With her brother Ignacio Elías, Eulalia Elías managed the horses and cattle on the San Juan de Babocómari land grant in Cochise County from 1833 to 1849.

Redondo, José María (1830–1878). A pioneer of Yuma, Redondo was a prominent miner, rancher, and landowner during Arizona's territorial period. He served three terms in the territorial legislature and was mayor of Yuma. Redondo's 1,000-acre ranch north of Yuma was one of Arizona's largest.

Ochoa, Estevan (1831–1888). Born in Chihuahua, Mexico, Ochoa became one of Tucson's most prominent ethnic Mexicans during the late nineteenth century. Making his fortune as co-owner of the Tully and Ochoa freighting company, he is also generally credited as the founder of public education in Tucson. In 1875 he became Tucson's only Mexican elected mayor from the Gadsden Purchase forward. Ochoa also raised sheep and owned mines. He was one of the first to experiment with Pima cotton, planting acres of cotton crops and sending samples to New York.

Carrillo, Leopoldo (1836–1890). Born in Moctezuma, Sonora, Mexico, Carrillo moved to Tucson in 1859, where he became the owner of several businesses and ranches throughout southern Arizona. During the 1880s, he developed Carrillo Gardens, which became Tucson's most popular resort park during the late nineteenth century.

Velasco, Carlos (1837–1914). Born in Hermosillo, Sonora, Mexico, Velasco contributed to Tucson's intellectual and cultural life during the late nineteenth century, founding newspapers such as *Las Dos Repúblicas* and *El Fronterizo*. In 1894 he cofounded La Alianza Hispano-Americana.

Samaniego, Mariano (1844–1907). A native of Sonora, Samaniego attended St. Louis University and moved to Tucson in the 1860s. During the late nineteenth century, he was one of Tucson's foremost businessmen, ranchers, and politicians. In 1891 he became a member of the University of Arizona's Board of Regents, and in 1894 he cofounded La Alianza Hispano-Americana. Samaniego served four terms in Arizona's territorial legislature from the 1870s to the 1890s. He also cofounded the Arizona Pioneers Historical Society.

Gárfias, Enrique (1851–1896). Born in Mexico and raised in California, Gárfias moved to Phoenix in 1874, where he became the city's only ethnic Mexican elected official during the nineteenth century.

Bonillas, Ignacio (1858–1944). Originally a schoolteacher from Tucson, Bonillas became mayor of Nogales, Sonora, and then a Mexican diplomat to the United States. He was the favorite candidate of Venustiano Carranza in Mexico's 1920 election.

Vásquez, Carmen Soto de (1863–1934). In 1915, Carmen Soto de Vásquez founded Tucson's famous Teatro Carmen. Until it closed in 1924, Teatro Carmen was Tucson's foremost theater for Spanish-language productions and a central gathering place of Tucson's ethnic Mexican community.

Ronstadt, Federico (1868–1954). Born in Las Delicias, Sonora, Ronstadt moved to Tucson at the age of 14, where he became one of the city's most prominent businessmen, musicians, and citizens during the late nineteenth century. He opened a carriage-manufacturing shop in 1888, which eventually became one of Tucson's biggest businesses. The Ronstadt family, from the time of Ronstadt's arrival forward, has been considered one of Tucson's foremost pioneer families.

Rebeil, Julia (1891–1973). A graduate of Tucson's St. Joseph's Academy, Rebeil earned her master's degree at Chicago Musical College, then attended the Fountainbleau Conservatory near Paris before returning to Tucson in 1920 to teach piano at the University of Arizona. When she retired in 1953, she was the head of the university's piano department.

Espinel Ronstadt, Luisa (1892–1963). Daughter of *tucsonense* Federico Ronstadt, Luisa Espinel became an internationally renowned singer who gave concerts in Los

Angeles, New York, and Europe. She was most famous for her interpretations of Spanish folk songs; late in her career, she also became an actress.

Garcia Smith, Placida (1896–1981). A longtime resident of Phoenix and the director of the Friendly House during the 1930s, García Smith led efforts to provide job opportunities and social services to the city's ethnic Mexican communities. Also during the 1930s, she helped form the Phoenix's Southside Improvement organization. In 1941 she served as president of Phoenix's newly formed LULAC chapter, and in 1962 she was honored as the Phoenix Woman of the Year.

Jácome Sr., Alex G. (1904–1980). A native of Tucson, Alex Jácome Sr. became president of Jácome's Department Store in 1932, after his father, Carlos Jácome, died. In addition to running his commercial business, Jácome became Tucson's foremost diplomat to Mexico during the mid-twentieth century, serving as the city's honorary vice-consul to Mexico. He was also a U.S. delegate to the 1954 Inter-American Indian Conference in La Paz, Bolivia, and to a 1959 trade mission to Spain. Also active in Arizona affairs, Jácome was a member of the University of Arizona's Board of Regents from 1952 to 1960, serving as its president in 1959.

Urquides, María (1908–1994). A teacher and administrator in Tucson's public school system during the twentieth century, Urquides became a nationally renowned advocate for bilingual education. She was the first Latina to serve on the YWCA's board of directors, and in 1974 the Tucson Unified School District recognized her lifelong service by naming Urquides Elementary School in her honor.

Díaz, Adam (1909–). Originally from Flagstaff, Díaz moved to Phoenix as a child, and in 1948 he became the first Mexican American elected to the Phoenix City Council. He served 4 years on the council and one as vice-mayor of Phoenix. He began his community service during the 1930s and 1940s as an active member of the Latin American Club, the Spanish American Club, and as a co-worker of Plácida Garcia Smith at the Friendly House. During the postwar era, he was a member of American Legion Post 41 and was the president of Friendly House in 1948. He later served as chairman of the board of Chicanos Por La Causa. In 1964 he won the Phoenix Sertoma Club's Service to Mankind Award, and in 1977 he received the first Plácida Smith Award for his service to the Friendly House. In 2007 the Phoenix Westside Senior Center was renamed the Adam Díaz Senior Center.

Castro, Raúl (1916–). Born in the midst of the Mexican Revolution, in Cananea, Sonora, Castro moved to Arizona in 1926, where he became a prominent Mexican American politician. After receiving his law degree from the University of Arizona and becoming a member of the Arizona Bar Association in 1949, Castro was elected Pima County attorney general in 1954, and he served as judge of the Pima County Superior Court from 1959 to 1964. Before serving as Arizona's first ethnic Mexican governor from 1974 to 1976, he was a U.S. ambassador to El Salvador and Bolivia. Castro's term as governor was cut short in 1977, when Jimmy Carter appointed him U.S. ambassador to Argentina.

Guerrero, Eduardo "Lalo" (1916–2005). Guerrero was born and raised in Tucson's Barrio Viejo district, and as a youth, he was a pachuco and car gang member. He started his musical career in Tucson as a member of Los Carlistas. Although he moved his family to California during the 1940s, Tucson remained an important source of inspiration for his music.

Cordova, Valdemar A. (1922–1988). Born in Phoenix, Cordova became a decorated U.S. Army Air Corps veteran of World War II before receiving his law degree from the University of Arizona in 1950. After serving on the Phoenix City Council from 1956 to 1958, in 1965 he became the first Mexican American Maricopa County Superior Court judge. In 1979, President Jimmy Carter appointed Cordova as a federal district court judge, and in 2002, Phoenix renamed its municipal court the Valdemar A. Cordova Building.

Chávez, César (1927–1993). Perhaps the most famous Mexican American in the United States from the Chicano movement forward, Chávez was born in Yuma and spent a considerable portion of his career supporting Arizona's farmworkers—most famously during his 1972 Fast of Love, organized as a protest against Arizona House Bill 2134. The bill outlawed boycotts and strikes by farmworkers during harvest season. Apparently the chant "¡Si Se Puede!" originated at Phoenix's Santa Rita Hall during the fast. For his lifetime of work, Arizona State University awarded Chávez the honorary degree of doctor of humane letters on May 8, 1992. Chávez died where he was born, in Yuma, on April 22, 1993.

Olivárez, Graciela Gil (1928–1987). Born in Phoenix and raised in Barcelona, Arizona, Olivárez was Phoenix's first female disc jockey. She brought attention to local issues of poverty and working conditions for migrant farmworkers. In 1965 she became state director of the Office of Economic Opportunity for Arizona. She then received a law degree from the University of Notre Dame in 1970, becoming the first woman to graduate from that school. In 1977, President Jimmy Carter appointed her as director of the Community Service Administration; she was the highest-ranking Mexican American woman in the Carter administration.

Torres, Alva (1932–). A native of Tucson, Torres has been a member of several ethnic Mexican civic organizations, such as the Mexican American Unity Council and the League of Mexican American Women. During the 1960s, she helped form the Save La Placita Committee, which tried to prevent the so-called urban renewal of Tucson's Barrio Libre.

Rubio-Goldsmith, Raquel (1936–). Born in Douglas, Rubio-Goldsmith received an undergraduate degree in law and philosophy from the National Autonomous University of Mexico (UNAM) before becoming a history professor at Pima County Community College in 1969, and at the University of Arizona in 1983. In addition to her academic work, Rubio-Goldsmith has worked as an activist promoting migrant and women's rights.

López, Joe Eddie (1939–). Born in Duran, New Mexico, López traveled with his family of migrant farm laborers around the U.S. Southwest before settling in Maricopa County in 1939, where he attended Peoria High School and Arizona State University. During the Chicano movement era, López organized construction workers and farmworkers, cofounding Chicanos Por La Causa. Before he was elected in 1996 to the Arizona state Senate, he served on the Maricopa County Board of Supervisors from 1972 to 1976, the

Arizona House of Representatives from 1991 to 1992, and the Phoenix Union High School District Governing Board from 1990 to 1996.

Martin, Patricia Preciado (1939–). Born and raised in Tucson, writer Patricia Preciado Martin received her degree in elementary education in 1960 from the University of Arizona. The author of books such as *Images and Conversations, Songs My Mother Sang to Me,* and *Beloved Land,* Martin has spent a lifetime documenting the lives of Arizona's ethnically Mexican women and men. During the 1980s, she developed the Mexican Heritage Project at the Arizona Historical Society with Thomas E. Sheridan, an anthropologist and historian at the University of Arizona.

Castillo, Guadalupe (1942–). Castillo received her BA and MA at the University of Arizona before becoming a history professor at Pima County Community College. During the 1960s and 1970s, she was an active member of Tucson's Chicano movement, helping organize efforts to introduce a Mexican American Studies curriculum at the University of Arizona and to convert El Río Golf Course into a public park and community center. From the 1970s forward, she became involved with several immigrant rights organizations, such as Derechos Humanos and No More Deaths.

Marín, Christine (1943–). A native of Globe, Marín is the archivist and curator of the Chicano Research Collection at Arizona State University's Hayden Library. Marín earned a BA in English in 1974, an MA in U.S. history in 1982, and a PhD in U.S. history in 1997, all from Arizona State University. Her scholarship has focused primarily on the mining community of Miami and on Mexican Americans in Arizona during the World War II era.

Pastor, Ed (1943–). Born in the mining town of Claypool, Pastor received his BA in chemistry from Arizona State University in 1966, as well as his law degree in 1974. Before he became Arizona's first Latino representative in the U.S. Congress, Pastor served as a member of Governor Raúl Castro's staff and the Maricopa County Board of Supervisors. His Fourth District includes most of downtown Phoenix and Glendale.

Gutierrez, Alfredo (1944–). Born in Miami, Gutierrez became one of Phoenix's foremost civil rights activists during the Chicano movement and beyond. During the 1960s, he was a leader of Arizona State University's MASO, founder of a Brown Beret chapter in Phoenix, and founder of Chicanos Por La Causa. In 1974 he became the youngest person ever elected to the Arizona state legislature, and in 2002 he ran an unsuccessful campaign for governor.

Baldenegro, Salomón (1945–). Originally from Douglas, Baldenegro cofounded MEChA at the University of Arizona in 1969. He organized many other efforts as well, including walkouts at Tucson and Pueblo high schools and protests for the conversion of Tucson's El Río Golf Course into a public park and community center. During the 1970s, Baldenegro was a candidate for mayor of Tucson, supported by La Raza Unida Party, and after the Chicano movement, he continued to advise the University of Arizona chapter of MEChA.

Ronstadt, Linda (1946–). A native of Tucson and granddaughter of Federico Ronstadt, Linda Ronstadt became an influential American folk rock singer. In 1964, at the age of 17, Ronstadt moved to California, where she has spent much of her life. But she has maintained a home in Tucson, and her music remains influenced by her roots there. A winner of several Grammy awards, Ronstadt's *Canciones de mi Padre* won the 1988 award for Best Mexican American Performance.

Grijalva, Raúl (1948–). Born in Tucson, Grijalva attended Sunnyside High School before receiving his BA in sociology from the University of Arizona. While at the University of Arizona, he was a founding member of MEChA. In 1974, Grijalva became a board member of the Tucson Unified School District, and from 1975 to 1986, he directed the El Pueblo Neighborhood Center. Grijalva served on the Pima County Board of Supervisors from 1988 to 2002, and in 2000 he was elected as a Democratic member of Congress from Arizona's Second District.

García, Isabel (1953–). Born in Tucson, García became one of southern Arizona's foremost immigrant rights activists, serving as Pima County public defender and cochair of the Coalición de Derechos Humanos. She has served on the board of directors of the National Network for Immigrant and Refugee Rights, testified before the United States Congressional Sub-Committee on Immigration, and organized the Border Summit held in Tucson in 2000.

CULTURAL CONTRIBUTIONS

Latina and Latino cultural contributions have extended well beyond Tucson and Phoenix barrios, shaping much of Arizona history through a year-round calendar of national and religious celebrations, along with other community activities, ranch culture, and art and music. Mexicans and Mexican Americans have celebrated Mexican national holidays—such as Cinco de Mayo, Mexican Independence, and Fiestas Patrias—even as they have celebrated U.S. national holidays, such as Independence Day and President's Day. Many of these are festive occasions that involve fireworks, bonfires, dancing, singing, drinking, eating, and other activities. Mexicans and Mexican Americans have demonstrated the binational character of their celebrations by wearing the national colors of both the United States and Mexico, reading aloud passages from the American Declaration of Independence, or marching to the music of Mexican bands. Many Anglo-led organizations, such as the Tucson Festival Society and the Tucson Rodeo and Parade Committees (which organize the annual Fiesta de los Vaqueros), have drawn inspiration from the cultural contributions of Arizona's ethnic Mexicans, reinterpreting celebrations such as *charrería* and incorporating them into broader social and cultural life.

A variety of religious celebrations also punctuate the year, such as Las Posadas, Easter, Día de los Muertos, and the appearance of the Virgin of Guadalupe to Juan Diego. There celebrations include annual pilgrimages in October from Tucson to Magdalena, Sonora, to pay homage to Saint Francis Xavier. Active participation in these and other religious occasions reflects the predominance of Catholicism among Arizona's ethnic Mexicans. In Tucson around 1960,

90 percent of ethnic Mexicans were Roman Catholic, amounting to 50 percent of the city's Catholic community in general—even though Mexicans and Mexican Americans represented only about 25 percent of the city's population. Although the majority of Arizona's ethnic Mexicans are Catholic, some are Protestant.

Because ethnic Mexicans in southern Arizona incorporate religious folk practices and prayers to *curanderos* and *curanderas* (or faith healers) into their worship, many have referred to their particular brand of Catholicism as Sonoran Catholicism, again linking the cultures of Arizona and Sonora.[31] The primary churches that have served ethnic Mexicans in Arizona are San Agustín Cathedral, Santa Cruz, and San Xavier del Bac in Tucson, and St. Mary's, St. Anthony's, and Immaculate Heart Church in Phoenix. Some of these, such as San Xavier and San Agustín, were built during the eighteenth and nineteenth centuries. However, many were built during the 1910s and 1920s through local fund-raising efforts, volunteer labor, and donations. In addition to religious services, churches have also provided many social services and helped with political organization. Other important sites of worship are southern Arizona's folk religious shrines—such as Tucson's El Tiradito, or Wishing Shrine, where Mexicans and Mexican Americans light votive candles in prayer for loved ones.

Mexicans and Mexican Americans also have made many contributions to Arizona's artistic and intellectual life. Philharmonic clubs, newspaper publishers, and literary societies of the late nineteenth century have made an impact, along with singers such as Lalo Guerrero and Linda Ronstadt, art organizations such as Phoenix's Movimiento Artístico del Río Salado, and Arizona's Mexican and Mexican American artists and intellectuals. For example, the annual Tucson International Mariachi Conference, established in 1982, has become a world-renowned celebration of mariachi music and *baile folklórico*. In addition, ethnic Mexicans such as Ernesto Portillo Sr., in Tucson, and Pete Bugarín, in Phoenix, helped pioneer broadcast radio in Arizona. Many popular deejays were from Sonora, Zacatecas, and other Mexican states, and some had experience working in Arizona's mines and fields before they worked in radio. Delivering news from Mexico, playing *orquesta* and *corridos*, and hosting local personalities, they broadcast early morning shows such as *La Hora Mexicana*, which appealed to a broad range of listeners as they got ready for work. Another popular disc jockey was Graciela Gil Olivárez, Phoenix's first female disc jockey, who brought attention to issues such as poverty and living conditions among migrant laborers.

Mexicans and Mexican Americans have also engaged in other community activities, which have contributed to Arizona's culture. Many of these have been held at community parks, ballrooms, theaters, and barrios. Parks such as Grant Park in Phoenix and Kennedy Park in Tucson have been important gathering spots for sporting events, barbecues, concerts, holidays, and various educational opportunities. Similarly, dances at ballrooms such as Maravilla in Phoenix and Del Río in

Tucson have provided opportunities for ethnic Mexican youth to socialize, and for Latina and Latino musicians—many of whom traveled on the so-called Taco Circuit throughout the U.S. Southwest—to make a name for themselves. It was from this milieu that individuals such as Eduardo "Lalo" Guerrero emerged as one of the most popular ethnic Mexican singers of the post–World War II era.

NOTES

1. Sheridan, *Arizona: A History*, 38.
2. Sheridan, *Arizona: A History*, 45–46.
3. Sheridan, *Los Tucsonenses*, 31.
4. Poston, quoted in Park, 62.
5. Susan L. Johnson, "Women in Central Arizona Mining Towns, 1863–1873," unpublished essay dated May 1981, in the Arizona Collection (Tempe, AZ: Hayden Library, Arizona State University), 3.
6. Park, 99, 101, 103.
7. Sheridan, *Los Tucsonenses*, 32.
8. Sheridan, *Los Tucsonenses*, 73.
9. Sheridan, *Los Tucsonenses*, 90.
10. Luckingham, 17.
11. Dean and Reynolds, *Hispanic Historic Property Survey*, 16.
12. Park, 205, 208.
13. See Truett.
14. Sheridan, *Los Tucsonenses*, 176.
15. Park, 265; and Sheridan, *Los Tucsonenses*, 181.
16. Dean and Reynolds, 2006, 28.
17. Sheridan, *Los Tucsonenses*, 250, 166.
18. Dean and Reynolds, *Hispanic Historic Property Survey*, 38.
19. Dean and Reynolds, *Hispanic Historic Property Survey*, 38.
20. Dean and Reynolds, *Hispanic Historic Property Survey*, 50.
21. Luckingham, 39.
22. Dean and Reynolds, *Hispanic Historic Property Survey*, 97.
23. Dean and Reynolds, *Hispanic Historic Property Survey*, 77.
24. Wayne D. Rasmussen, *A History of the Emergency Farm Labor Supply Program, 1943–1947*, Agricultural Monograph No. 13 (Washington, DC: U.S. Department of Agriculture, Bureau of Agricultural Economics, September 1951), 226.
25. In 1960, for example, the Tucson American Legion's Morgan-McDermott No. 7 claimed 110 ethnic Mexican members of a total membership of 1,500 (7.3 percent), while Post No. 549 of the city's Veterans of Foreign Wars had 200 ethnic Mexican members of a total membership of 895 (22.3 percent). In 1946, because of such low representation in the Morgan-McDermott chapter, Mexican Americans from that group formed their own organization especially for Mexican American veterans, naming it Cocío and Estrada for two ethnic Mexicans from Tucson who died during service. Tucson's Post No. 4903 of the Veterans

of Foreign Wars also had Mexican American members, but the numbers were far fewer, because this post was based on Tucson's east side, and very few ethnic Mexicans lived on the east side in 1960. See Officer, "Sodalities and Systemic Linkage: The Joining Habits of Urban Mexican-Americans," 262, 264.

26. Officer, "Sodalities and Systemic Linkage," 207.
27. Officer, "Sodalities and Systemic Linkage," 73–74.
28. Dean and Reynolds, *Hispanic Historic Property Survey*, 110.
29. Christine Marín, "They Sought Work and Found Hell: The Hanigan Case of Arizona," *Perspectives in Mexican American Studies* 6 (1997): 96–122
30. 1990 census figures were calculated based on information provided at the state of Arizona's Web site: "Hispanic Origin and Race for Arizona, Counties and Places," at http://www.workforce.az.gov/?PAGEID=67&SUBID=129 (accessed May 14, 2007). It cites 1990 Census of Population and Housing, PL 94-171 Data File. Census figures from 2000 were calculated based on information provided at the state of Arizona's Web site: "Total Population by Hispanic or Latino and Race; Counties, Incorporated and Census Designated Places, Arizona's Indian Reservations," at http://www.workforce.az.gov/?PAGEID=67&SUBID=127 (accessed May 14, 2007). It cites the Census 2000 Redistricting Data (PL 94-171) Summary File.
31. Officer, "Sodalities and Systemic Linkage," 124, 151.

BIBLIOGRAPHY

Brady, Mary Pat. *Extinct Lands, Temporal Geographies: Chicana Literature and the Urgency of Space*. Durham, NC: Duke University Press, 2002.

Browne, J. Ross. *Adventures in the Apache Country: A Tour through Arizona and Sonora, with Notes on the Silver Regions of Nevada*. New York: Harper and Brothers, 1869.

Dean, David R., and Jean A. Reynolds. *Hispanic Historic Property Survey, Final Report*. Phoenix, AZ: City of Phoenix, Historic Preservation Office, and Athenaeum Public History Group, 2006, 28.

Luckingham, Bradford. *Minorities in Phoenix: A Profile of Mexican American, Chinese American, and African American Communities, 1860–1992*. Tucson: University of Arizona Press, 1994.

Martin, Patricia Preciado. *Images and Conversations: Mexican Americans Recall a Southwestern Past*. Tucson: University of Arizona Press, 1983.

———. *Songs My Mother Sang to Me: An Oral History of Mexican American Women*. Tucson: University of Arizona Press, 1992.

———. *Beloved Land: An Oral History of Mexican Americans in Southern Arizona*. Photography by José Galvez. Tucson: University of Arizona Press, 2004.

Meeks, Eric V. *Border Citizens: The Making of Indians, Mexicans, and Anglos in Arizona*. Austin: University of Texas Press, 2007.

Mowry, Sylvester. *Arizona and Sonora*. New York: Harper and Brothers, 1864.

Officer, James E. "Sodalities and Systemic Linkage: The Joining Habits of Urban Mexican-Americans." PhD diss., University of Arizona, 1964.

———. *Hispanic Arizona, 1536–1856*. Tucson: University of Arizona Press, 1987.

Park, Joseph F. "The History of Mexican Labor in Arizona during the Territorial Period." Master's thesis, University of Arizona, 1961.

Sheridan, Thomas E. *Arizona: A History*. Tucson: University of Arizona Press, 1995.

———. *Los Tucsonenses: The Mexican Community in Tucson, 1854–1941*. Tucson: University of Arizona Press, 1986.

Truett, Samuel. *Fugitive Landscapes: The Forgotten History of the U.S.-Mexico Borderlands*. New Haven, CT: Yale University Press, 2006.

Vélez-Ibáñez, Carlos. *Border Visions: Mexican Cultures of the Southwest United States*. Tucson: University of Arizona Press, 1996.

4

ARKANSAS

Steve Striffler and Julie M. Weise

CHRONOLOGY

1541	Spanish explorer Hernando de Soto arrives at Parkin, Arkansas, and erects a cross near present-day Helena. His party ultimately travels through much of the state.
1800	Spain cedes the Louisiana colony, including present-day Arkansas, to France.
1920	Pittsburgh Reduction Company (Alcoa) brings 655 Mexican workers from south Texas to Bauxite, Arkansas, to mine aluminum ore.
1930–1932	Mexicans in Bauxite and the Arkansas Delta find themselves out of work due to low cotton and aluminum prices; many repatriate to Mexico at their own expense.
1940s	Arkansas Delta farmers begin recruiting bracero workers to chop and pick cotton.
1952–1964	Some 251,298 Mexican nationals chop and pick cotton in Arkansas.
1950–1952	The Mexican consulate in Memphis fights discrimination against Mexicans in Osceola and Marked Tree.
1954	Memphis's African American leader, George W. Lee, alleges that Mexicans earn more than African Americans for picking cotton in Arkansas.
1960	A migrant labor camp opens in Hope, Arkansas, to serve migrant workers (including Mexicans and Mexican Americans) on their way between Texas and the upper Midwest or Florida.
1962	About 600 Arkansas Delta farmers pack a Department of Labor hearing in West Memphis to protest a proposed bracero wage increase from

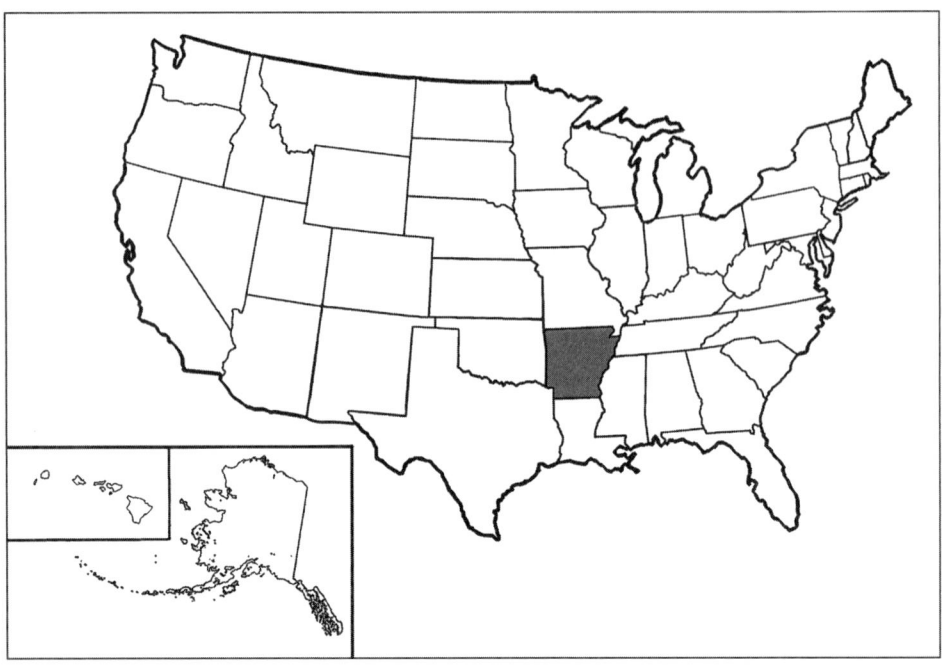

	50 cents to 70 cents per hour. A compromise of 60 cents is reached, but bracero contracting to Arkansas declines significantly.
1964	The Bracero program ends, and picking cotton becomes more mechanized; many Mexicans and Mexican Americans move on to pick fruit in Florida.
1971	The Migrant Farm Labor Center in Hope processes 48,000 migrants, most of whom are Mexican.
1980s	The most recent wave of Latin American migration into Arkansas begins.
1990–1991	The first League of United Latin American Citizens (LULAC) council is formed in Little Rock. A council in Rogers is formed shortly after.
1998	Americans for an Immigration Moratorium of Rogers and other organizations support federal legislation that calls for a five-year moratorium on immigration. Their goal is to halt the flow of undocumented migrants into northwest Arkansas. Organizations run anti-immigration radio, television, and newspaper ads in Arkansas.
1999	The INS announces it will open an enforcement office in northwest Arkansas because of an increase of Latino population. The first Cinco de Mayo celebration in Little Rock is held. The Hispanic Women's Organization of Arkansas is founded in the northwest section of the state.
2000	Governor Mike Huckabee announces the start of the statewide Hispanic Assimilation Program. A $50,000 study will focus on the needs of Arkansas's growing Latino population.

2001	A suit is filed against Rogers police for racial profiling against Latinos.
2003	A branch of LULAC forms at the University of Arkansas at Fayetteville in order to increase Latino enrollment.
2005	LULAC holds a national convention in Little Rock.
2006	An estimated 10,000 protesters hold pro-immigration rallies in Springdale, Arkansas. The mayor of Rogers, Arkansas, asks for federal money to train local officers so that they may question, detain, and process suspected undocumented migrants encountered in daily police work.
2007	The Guatemalan consulate comes to northwest Arkansas to provide passports and identification to Guatemalans living in the area. Newly elected Democratic Governor Mike Beebe appoints Maria Elena de Avila Peters as the Hispanic liaison to the governor's office.

HISTORICAL OVERVIEW

Though the Spanish crown nominally controlled present-day Arkansas for most of its colonial period, Spanish culture exerted little influence on this early frontier society. The beginnings of slavery-based plantation agriculture in the antebellum years more critically influenced the future course of Arkansas's Latino history. Though no significant Latino communities existed in the state until the twentieth century, Arkansas's early patterns of agriculture, labor, and African American history help explain the course of its Latino history.

As Reconstruction faced its final death knell in the South at the turn of the twentieth century, African Americans remained subject to violence and coercion that kept them available as a labor source. Thus, Latino migration to the South as a region was low through the mid-twentieth century. Yet, in periods of African American migration out of the state, farmers and other employers have looked to Latin American migrants and U.S.-born Latinos to meet their labor needs.

Mexican workers first came to Arkansas in the 1920s to pick cotton and mine aluminum ore. While their presence in the central Arkansas mining town of Bauxite lasted only a decade, their arrival to work the rich soil of the delta region of northeast Arkansas initiated a half century of migrations. Because the Arkansas Delta was late to mechanize production, Mexican and Mexican American workers stayed in the area through the 1960s, making Arkansas more dependent on Mexican labor than any southern state besides Texas. By the 1970s, most Latino workers in Arkansas were passing through on their way to harvest crops on the Atlantic Coast or in the upper Midwest.

Finally, Latinos have played a critical role in Arkansas's new service economy, moving to every part of the state and powering the state's massive chicken-processing industry. At the turn of the twenty-first century, a Latino middle class was also establishing itself in Arkansas.

Mexicans in Bauxite

The Great Migration of African Americans out of the South prompted some Arkansas farmers and employers to seek Mexican laborers immediately following World War I. The Pittsburgh Reduction Company (later known as Alcoa) recruited Mexican, Italian, and Chinese workers, in addition to African Americans, to mine aluminum ore during the interwar years. By the end of 1920, it had recruited 655 Mexicans to live and work in Bauxite. The company built segregated housing for its workers, naming the respective areas Mexico Camp, Africa Camp, and Italy.

While the company received some criticism for hiring Mexican rather than native-born workers, Mexico Camp housed Mexican and Mexican American families in Bauxite through the early 1930s. The local newspaper began publishing a Spanish-language page to cater to this relatively settled community of Mexican workers. Mexicans in Bauxite were separated from both whites and blacks, despite the Treaty of Guadalupe Hidalgo's promise to consider Mexicans as whites under the law. Mexicans in Bauxite's Mexico Camp attended Mexican-only schools, shopped at Mexico Camp's own branch of the company store, and used recreational facilities separate from blacks, whites, and Italians.

When ore production nearly stopped in the early years of the Depression, Mexicans were the first to be laid off. While the company transported many workers back to Laredo, others were stranded and had to return to Texas or Mexico at their own expense.

Mexicans in the Arkansas Delta

For most of the twentieth century, the fate of Arkansas's Latinos and its cotton were intertwined. Rapid Mexican migration to the United States during the 1920s—and the expansion of this migration beyond Texas, to locales such as California and the Midwest—reverberated in Arkansas, albeit on a drastically smaller scale. Indeed, it was Californian and Texan farmers' access to plentiful Mexican labor that Arkansas farmers hoped to emulate.

The Lee Wilson Plantation, which dominated Mississippi County, Arkansas, was the most active in pursuing Mexican laborers. The Depression notwithstanding, baptism records suggest that small numbers of ethnic Mexican families lived and worked in the Arkansas Delta throughout the 1930s. Largely ignored by white and black society, these migrants neither received the benefits of the New Deal nor suffered the forced deportations that affected Mexican communities elsewhere. World War II, however, would bring thousands of Mexican workers to the same parts of Arkansas, generating deliberate attempts to exclude them from white society.

WORLD WAR II AND THE BRACERO PROGRAM

In 1942 the U.S. and Mexican governments negotiated a guest worker program that would come to be known as the Bracero program. While the program is best known for its presence in the Southwest, Arkansas at times trailed only California and Texas in the number of braceros recruited. This was due primarily to the state's unusually slow pace of mechanization, as well as the migration of both white and African American rural workers to cities during World War II. Braceros began arriving in Arkansas in the late 1940s; by the early 1950s, they had become ubiquitous throughout the Arkansas Delta. Between 1952 and 1964, Arkansas farmers employed 251,298 braceros in picking cotton, in addition to an unknown number of Tejanos.[1] Statistics available from 1957–1959 suggest that braceros performed a quarter of the cotton-picking labor in Arkansas during that period.[2]

The arrival of thousands of Mexicans to the Arkansas Delta forced the question of whether these racially ambiguous newcomers would be treated as whites, blacks, or something else under the region's Jim Crow system. Initially, Mexicans' exclusion from white institutions was widespread, though not universal, varying from town to town and establishment to establishment. In both Osceola and Marked Tree, workers complained to the Mexican consulate in Memphis that they were being excluded from white restaurants and forced to sit with blacks in movie theaters. Said one proprietor in Osceola, "We have a very high class trade that would leave if my place was filled up with Mexicans. I would close up before I would serve them."[3] Police in Marked Tree would stake out bars where Mexicans were served to make arrests, regardless of whether individuals had caused any particular disruption.

Some Mexican Americans made their way to the delta as well, and their U.S. citizenship did not affect their treatment. In 1951, for example, Corpus Christi native Bonifacio Nieto, a cook, traveled to Marked Tree in search of work. When Nieto entered a restaurant called Prince to inquire about employment possibilities, the first person he encountered shouted at him that "Spanish people" were not welcome. Thus, Tejano families migrating to work the delta's cotton fields faced the same discrimination as their bracero counterparts.

Though bracero contracts included an array of guarantees and protections regarding wages, housing, and working conditions, stating that discrimination based on ancestry or nationality would not be tolerated, the Mexican government's power to enforce these guarantees declined significantly during the late 1940s and early 1950s. Although Mexican government attempts to stymie discrimination took the form of drawn-out battles, they did have limited success in securing Mexicans' access to white establishments. For example, in November 1949, bracero complaints prompted Mexico's consul in Memphis, Ruben Gaxiola, to investigate alleged discrimination against Mexicans in Marked Tree. He recorded his findings with a camera: "No Mexicans" signs prominently displayed in front of the town's 11 establishments. Additionally, one of the town's two movie theaters seated Mexican patrons only in the area reserved for blacks. Attaching the photos as evidence in his report to Mexico City, Gaxiola immediately recommended that Marked Tree's employers—most prominently, E. Ritter—have their bracero contracts cancelled. Gaxiola hoped that swift action would set an example for the rest of Arkansas, "as an energetic protest against these discriminatory acts against Mexicans."[4]

Though it took 2 years and the cancellation of Ritter's contracts, once local officials became convinced that their labor source was imperiled, they employed inventive means to stymie discrimination. The Marked Tree City Council published an ordinance in the Marked Tree *Tribune* stating that any person or business discriminating against Mexicans would be fined between $10 and $50. The police department changed its compensation structure to remove officers' incentive to make superfluous arrests of Mexican workers. The farmers' association even purchased two restaurants that refused to comply with the mandate.

During the mid-1950s, the consulate's constant interventions and its limited control over the supply of Mexican labor had placed Mexicans in a social and economic position that was de facto superior to that of local blacks. In 1952 the Mexican government secured a raise in the minimum bracero wage to 50 cents per hour or the local prevailing wage, whichever was higher. In an era when agriculture in the United States had no minimum wage, braceros became the only laborers in Arkansas's fields to have such a guarantee. In 1954, African American leaders lodged a formal protest against the wage disparity, claiming that African American laborers were paid 30 cents per hour for cotton chopping, while Mexicans were paid 50 cents. Unlike Mexican nationals who could rely on the power of the Mexican government, blacks in Arkansas had little power, and their grievance never was addressed.

Mexican government lost its power to withhold workers over the course of the 1950s, but in the early 1960s, the U.S. Department of Labor responded to liberal opposition to the Bracero program and began to enforce bracero housing codes more strictly while proposing an increase in bracero wages to 70 cents per hour. Some 600 Arkansas Delta farmers packed a hearing in West Memphis on March 2, 1962, to protest the proposed increase. In the end, a compromise of 60 cents was reached, but contracting of Mexican nationals to Arkansas dropped drastically in these waning years of the Bracero program. The program formally ended in 1964. While delta farmers recruited a few Mexican Americans from Texas to operate their gins over the course of the 1970s, all but a handful of the region's Latinos left the delta. Many moved on to pick fruit in northern Florida's increasingly productive orchards.

Migrants in the 1960s–1980s

Though no longer picking cotton in the delta, Mexican workers continued to enter Arkansas during the 1960s and 1970s. Southwestern Arkansas became a way station for Mexican and Mexican migrant workers moving between Texas and the Midwest or the Atlantic Coast. In 1960 the Migrant Farm Labor Center opened on Highway 67 just west of Hope, later expanding under federal direction in response to growing national attention to the plight of migrant farmworkers.

The Migrant Farm Labor Center processed tens of thousands of migrants every year (nearly 50,000 in 1971), but few went on to work or stay in Arkansas. For those who did remain and work in Arkansas, the options were limited to seasonal agriculture, including limited cotton work in the delta, fruit in north Arkansas, and tomatoes in various parts of the state. In fact, by the mid- to late 1970s, Arkansas tomato farmers were complaining of labor shortages and insisting that migrant labor from Mexico was the foundation of successful tomato farming. Federally certified migrant labor, which required luxuries such as housing and mediocre wages, was simply too expensive for Arkansas farmers. A young attorney general named Bill Clinton helped tomato farmers in their search for a cheap and available labor force. This image—Latinos as migrants—would endure even as more and more Latinos began to make the state their home beginning in the 1980s.

Arkansas as a New Receiving Site

The mid-1980s, and particularly the 1990s, marked the first time Arkansas received relatively large numbers of migrants from Latin America, as well as Latinos from other U.S. states. Between 1990 and 2000, while the U.S. Latino population increased by nearly 60 percent and hundreds of thousands of Latinos left traditional receiving sites (such as California), Arkansas's Latino population more than tripled and was surpassed in growth only by that of North Carolina. In 1990 less than 1 percent of Arkansas's population was Latino; by 2000 that figure was nearly 4 percent; and by 2005 almost 5 percent of Arkansas (or more than 125,000 people) was Latino. The vast majority of Arkansas's Latinos are migrants, typically coming either directly from Mexico and Central America or spending time in other U.S. states before making their way to Arkansas. Many of these have responded to the saturation of low-wage labor markets in California and an economic boom in the U.S. South. Among migrants, at least 70 percent are from Mexico; slightly less than 10 percent are from Central America (mainly El Salvador and Guatemala); and much smaller percentages came from South America and elsewhere.[5]

Latinos and Poultry

In the case of Arkansas, greater numbers of Latinos were initially drawn to the state in the mid-1980s largely because of employment opportunities in the poultry industry. The state produces more chicken than any other, and poultry is Arkansas's largest industry. Tyson Foods, the largest poultry producer in the world, is headquartered in the state, and most of the industry's major players have operations in Arkansas. As a result, the surge in Latino population during the 1990s was geographically concentrated in towns or regions with significant poultry-processing facilities. Although the speed and timing of Latino entry into poultry plants varied somewhat depending on region, the latinization of the state's industry was undeniable by the mid-1990s.

In most cases, and especially in the economically booming and poultry-producing region of northwest Arkansas, whites and blacks left poultry plants in the 1980s as more attractive jobs became available. Latinos, many of whom moved from California, quickly obtained poultry jobs that, although difficult and dangerous, provided benefits, the potential for overtime, and relative job security, especially when compared to seasonal agriculture. As one migrant recounted,

> I am the Christopher Columbus of Arkansas. I discovered Arkansas for my pueblo [in Mexico]. I came to Arkansas in 1987 or 1988. I had been working in California for more than twenty years. The first day [in Arkansas] Tyson hired me. There were ten Mexicans in the plant. . . . Right away I told my two other sons to come to Arkansas. I said quit your job [in California] tomorrow and come. Then the whole town [in Mexico] stopped going to California and started coming to Arkansas.[6]

Reception of Latinos in Arkansas

In the most rural and impoverished state in the country—a state that is characterized by one small town after another—the influx of Latinos has been transformative. Rogers, Arkansas, a midsize town of about 40,000 in the northwest corner of the state, saw its Latino population swell to nearly 10,000 by 2003. Likewise, in DeQueen, in southwest Arkansas, the Latino population went from 506 (or roughly 10 percent of the population) in 1990 to more than 2,000—close to 40 percent of the town's total population. Although small, such numbers represent profound cultural shifts, especially when multiplied across the state. One migrant put it this way:

> When I first came to Arkansas it was tough working in poultry because there were no *Hispanos*. I made some friends at work. We never socialized outside of work, though. Just going out was a struggle. It was like people had never met someone who

didn't speak English. I almost couldn't get my children registered in school. No one at the school spoke Spanish! And there was no ESL [English as a Second Language]. I'd been in California for ten years so I was accustomed to the United States. But here was like another country.[7]

Arkansas has experienced its share of nativist and racist impulses with respect to the Latino population, including fears about schools, the use (or lack thereof) of the English language, the taking of jobs by migrants, declining property values, and crime. Overall, however, Arkansans' reaction to unauthorized immigration has been more subdued than that of the federal government.

INS Raid of Poultry Plant

In July of 2005, immigration agents raided a poultry plant in Arkadelphia, a city in southwest Arkansas, arresting more than 100 workers—or about half the day shift. As officials told everyone to "freeze," some workers began to cry, while others called relatives on cell phones in order to ensure that their children were cared for when they got deported to Mexico. The impact of the raid, as well as the possibility of future raids, was undermined by two subsequent events.

First, about 60 percent of the deported workers returned to Arkansas and were working in the area within the year. These workers belong to churches, have kids in school (who are often U.S. citizens and have never seen Mexico), own homes, and are stable members of the community.

Second, the small-town environment of Arkadelphia prompted many local residents to be sympathetic with migrants and their employers—and angry with the government for removing members of their community. In some cases, they even thwarted government officials in their efforts to crack down on document fraud and illegal hiring. Some members of the community had not even been aware that their friends were undocumented until the raid. For years these community members had been sharing food, vacationing together, playing on sport teams, and attending church with their Mexican friends. As a result, after the raid, some residents helped immigrants fight deportation or return to southwest Arkansas from Mexico.

As prominent citizens of the town, Republican governor (and presidential hopeful) Mike Huckabee and Democratic Senator Blanche Lincoln both strenuously resisted federal officials on the issue of workplace raids. When asked by federal officials to charge workers with the forgery of Social Security cards, the local county prosecutor—who by now counted Mexicans among his friends—told the agents he would think about their request. His reluctance to prosecute (and essentially deport) people who paid taxes, raised families, and had kids in schools was supported by the town sheriff. These prominent townspeople did nothing and were subsequently left out of the loop when the raid finally happened. For his part, Governor Huckabee, instead of jumping on the anti-immigration bandwagon, called for a White House investigation into why this particular poultry plant was targeted: "Our first priority should be to secure our borders. I'm less threatened by people who cross the line to make beds, pick tomatoes or pluck chickens than by potential terrorists."[8] Huckabee also donated $1,000 to the workers' families.

LATINOS IN TODAY'S ARKANSAS

Although the Latino population remains concentrated in Little Rock, northwest Arkansas, and poultry-producing areas in Arkansas, by the early 2000s, the Latino presence was felt throughout much of the state. Latinos now work in the service economies, light industry, agriculture, landscaping, construction, government, and many other sectors of the economy. Although the Latino population remains relatively poor, there is a well-established middle-class in certain areas of the state, many of whom own independent businesses, are business executives, or occupy important positions within state and local governments. Many of these have begun sending their children to college. Indeed, if the 1990s saw Latinos preoccupied with the nuts and bolts of settlement in Arkansas, the current decade has been characterized by diversity, increased assertiveness, and better organization. The Latino population has moved well beyond poultry. Economically, they are vital to many sectors and present virtually everywhere. Culturally, they are visible not only in the form of Mexican restaurants and Cinco de Mayo celebrations, but also fundamental to cultural life within the state. Politically, they are not only a constituency that is pursued by political parties, but also one that has formed its own advocacy organizations—such as LULAC—in many parts of the state.

NOTABLE LATINOS

Garcia, Joe (c. 1925–). A native of south Texas, Joe Garcia spent the 1940s as a migrant worker in Arkansas and the upper Midwest. In 1945 he came to Parkin, Arkansas, where farmer E.D. McKnight contracted him to recruit and oversee Mexican bracero workers. For nearly 20 years, Garcia went to Texas to recruit crews of 20–25 workers to Parkin. Once these workers arrived, Garcia served as an interpreter and intermediary between McKnight and the workers. Choosing to settle in Arkansas with his wife, Garcia was unique among the tens of thousands of Mexicans and Mexican Americans who came through Arkansas on a seasonal basis between the 1940s and 1960s. In fact, in 2000, Garcia proclaimed himself "the only Mexican in Parkin, Arkansas." Garcia went on to serve on Parkin's City Council.

Lopez, Al "Papa Rap" (1955–). Since moving to Arkansas in 1994, Al "Papa Rap" López has used music to help people from different cultures find common ground in communication, education, health issues, and more. He has been northwest Arkansas's most prominent and effective cultural broker, helping North Americans and Latinos understand each other. In addition to his radio show, *What's Up, Que Pasa?* on Spanish radio's La Zeta station, he also writes a weekly column, "Papa Reporte," which appears in several Spanish-language newspapers in Arkansas.

Treviño, Robert P. (1958–). Treviño arrived in Arkansas in 1990 and served as the economic development, diplomatic, and Hispanic affairs advisor to former governor Mike Huckabee. He has also served as the commissioner of Arkansas rehabilitation services under governors Huckabee and Beebe. As former director of LULAC, Treviño led the successful effort to bring the 2005 LULAC national convention to Little Rock, helped establish the largest Hispanic student scholarship fund in state's history, and helped create the state's first and largest Cinco de Mayo festival.

Solorzano, Margarita (1959–). Born in Mexico, Solorzano moved to the United States in 1990 and began living in Arkansas in 1996. In 2002, Solorzano, a founding member of the Hispanic Women's Organization of Arkansas, received recognition from the National Campaign for Tolerance, "honoring those who are leading the way towards a more tolerant and just America." In 2006 she received the Civil Rights Leadership Award from the Arkansas Citizens First Congress.

Restrepo, Luis Fernando (1962–). A dual citizen of Colombia and the United States, Restrepo was born in Washington, DC, to Colombian parents and grew up in Medellin, Colombia. Restrepo arrived in Fayetteville in 1995 to join the University of Arkansas, where he is a professor of Latin American literature and directs the Comparative Literature and Cultural Studies program.

Avila-Peters, Maria Elena de (1965–). Born in Mexico, Maria Elena de Avila-Peters moved to Little Rock, Arkansas, in 1991. Trained as a certified public accountant, she is Governor Mike Beebe's liaison to the Hispanic community in the state of Arkansas.

Alemán, Lucía Hernández (1967–). Born in Mexico City, Hernández Alemán graduated as an attorney-at-law from the Autonomous University of the State of Mexico and moved to Arkansas in 1999. She was the first director of the Northwest Arkansas Workers' Justice Center, an organization dedicated to immigrant rights.

Muñoz, Christina (1980–). Muñoz is coanchor for Channel 7 *News at 6* and *Nightside* in Little Rock. Born in South Dakota, Muñoz, whose mother is Chilean, is active in community organizations such as the American Cancer Society and LULAC. She has also been president of the board of Ballet Arkansas and performs each year onstage in the annual production of *The Nutcracker*.

Aviles, Alejandro (1982–). Aviles was the first Latino elected as a delegate from Arkansas to the Democratic National Convention (2004). Chicago-born Aviles has spent most of his life in Arkansas, and was a founder of LULAC at the University of Arkansas (2003). He was also nominated by Congressman Boozman and appointed by

Governor Huckabee as one of fifteen inaugural members of Arkansas's first state board to improve the lives of the Hispanic community (Arkansas Task Force on Latino and Hispanic Affairs).

CULTURAL CONTRIBUTIONS

While Arkansas is commonly defined as a place of black and white, the influx of hundreds of thousands of Mexicans during the 1940s through the 1960s left a permanent mark on race relations in the state. "No Mexicans" signs represented the first discriminatory policies that white farmers, restaurant owners, and local authorities in Arkansas's black belt were forced to dismantle—several years before *Brown vs. Board of Education* set off the South's violent and contentious desegregation process. Mexicans arrived in an Arkansas already unsettled by blacks' increasing power and mobility as a result of World War II. Their presence and the antidiscriminatory interventions of the Mexican consulate contributed to the inevitability of Jim Crow's death. Farmers praised Mexicans for having a work ethic and moral values superior to that of the blacks, relying on them to avoid paying the higher wages that might have lured blacks back to rural areas. In effect, these farmers hoped the Bracero program would help prolong the reign of white supremacy and family farming. Yet the mandate to admit these dark-skinned foreigners to white establishments and pay them a minimum wage for their work undermined the very system they had been imported to protect.

As the Arkansas economy diversified beyond agriculture, the growing Latino presence in the closing decades of the twentieth century contributed substantively to the state's cultural landscape. Although this cultural influence shapes the daily lives of all Arkansans, the ubiquitous presence of Mexican food and Latino music and celebrations does not necessarily represent a sea change in relationships between Latinos and non-Latinos. More meaningful interaction and understanding remains relatively limited because of language and cultural barriers; the segregation of Latinos into certain jobs, neighborhoods, and churches; and a general lack of public spaces for cultural interface of any kind.

At the same time, interest has grown among both Latinos and non-Latinos in creating spaces for cultural interaction. Cultural events such as Cinco de Mayo are now often accompanied by public lectures and other efforts to educate Arkansans about the history and meaning of such activities. Hispanic Heritage Month at the University of Arkansas has become an important annual series of lectures, dances, and other cultural expressions that simultaneously celebrate, educate, and unite people. Recently, the Historic Arkansas Museum in Little Rock even showcased the work of accomplished Latino artists living in Arkansas in the exhibit *Arkansas Arte Latino*. Such nascent efforts promise to foment popular understanding of Latino culture that moves beyond chips and salsa, J-Lo, and Taco Bell. As Latinos become further integrated into Arkansas, their influence on education, food, work, and religion will inevitably grow. The question is how such influence will be received by the rest of the state.

NOTES

1. See Holley.
2. See Grove.
3. See Weise.
4. See Weise.
5. All statistics are from the U.S. census. When filling out a census, many Latinos simply check "Hispanic" and do not note their country of origin. As a result, the percentage of Latinos who are Mexicans or Central American in Arkansas is likely even higher than statistics suggest.
6. Steve Striffler's interview with Poultry Worker #9, December 28, 2000. Names withheld to protect informants.
7. Steve Striffler's interview with Poultry Worker #5, March 3, 2000.
8. Hennessy-Fiske.

BIBLIOGRAPHY

Grove, Wayne Allison. "The Economics of Cotton Harvest Mechanization in the United States, 1920–1970." PhD diss., University of Illinois, 2000.

Hennessy-Fiske, Molly. "The Town That Didn't Look Away." *Los Angeles Times*, July 23, 2006.

Holley, Donald. *The Second Great Emancipation: The Mechanical Cotton Picker, Black Migration, and How They Shaped the Modern South*. Fayetteville: University of Arkansas Press, 2000.

Keltner, Robert W. "Tar Paper Shacks in Arcadia: Housing for Ethnic Minority Groups in the Company Town of Bauxite, Arkansas." *Arkansas Historical Quarterly* 60, no. 4 (2001): 341–359.

Striffler, Steve. *Chicken: The Dangerous Transformation of America's Favorite Food*. New Haven, CT: Yale University Press, 2005.

Weise, Julie. "Al Sur: Mexicans and Mexican-Americans in the U.S. South, 1918–1935." Paper presented at the Pacific Coast Branch of the American Historical Association, Corvallis, OR, 2005.

———. "Against Discriminatory Acts against Mexicans: White Supremacy, Discriminación, and the Bracero Program in Arkansas." Paper presented at the UCLA Graduate Student Conference on Migration and Race, Los Angeles, April 27, 2007.

Whayne, Jeannie M. *A New Plantation South: Land, Labor, and Federal Favor in Twentieth-Century Arkansas*. Charlottesville: University Press of Virginia, 1996.

Whayne, Jeannie M., Thomas A. DeBlack, George Sabo III, and Morris S. Arnold. *Arkansas: A Narrative History*. Fayetteville: University of Arkansas Press, 2002.

Woodruff, Nan Elizabeth. "Pick or Fight: The Emergency Farm Labor Program in the Arkansas and Mississippi Deltas during World War II." *Agricultural History* 64, no. 2 (1990): 74–85.

5
CALIFORNIA

Lourdes Gutiérrez Nájera

CHRONOLOGY

1542	Sailor Juan Rodríguez de Cabrillo from Portugal is commissioned by Viceroy Antonio de Mendoza to sail north along the coast of Mexico. Cabrillo lands in the port of San Diego.
1602	Spanish explorer Sebastian Vizcaíano is sent by the Spanish viceroy to look for repair ports in California. Vicaíano finds the entrance to Monterey Bay.
1769	Junípero Serra, a Franciscan missionary, establishes the first mission in California, named Alta California. Along with Captain Gaspar de Portolá, he establishes 21 missions and converts approximately 6,800 people along the coast of California.
1774	Pedro de Garcés, a Spanish Franciscan missionary, founds the first overland route to California.
1776	Juan Bautista de Anza founds the presidio of San Francisco.
1781	La Placita Olvera, the heart of the Mexican community, is established.
1829	The Old Spanish Trail, facilitating trade between Los Angeles and Santa Fe, New Mexico, is established.
1846	The Mexican-American War begins. Although the United States is victorious in almost every battle fought in California, the Californios (people of Spanish, Indian, and Mexican ancestry who were incorporated into California after it became a state) win the Battle of San Pasqual in 1846.
1848	The Mexican-American War ends in 1848 with the Treaty of Guadalupe Hidalgo. The treaty grants the United States 55 percent of Mexican territory, including present-day California. When the U.S. Senate ratifies

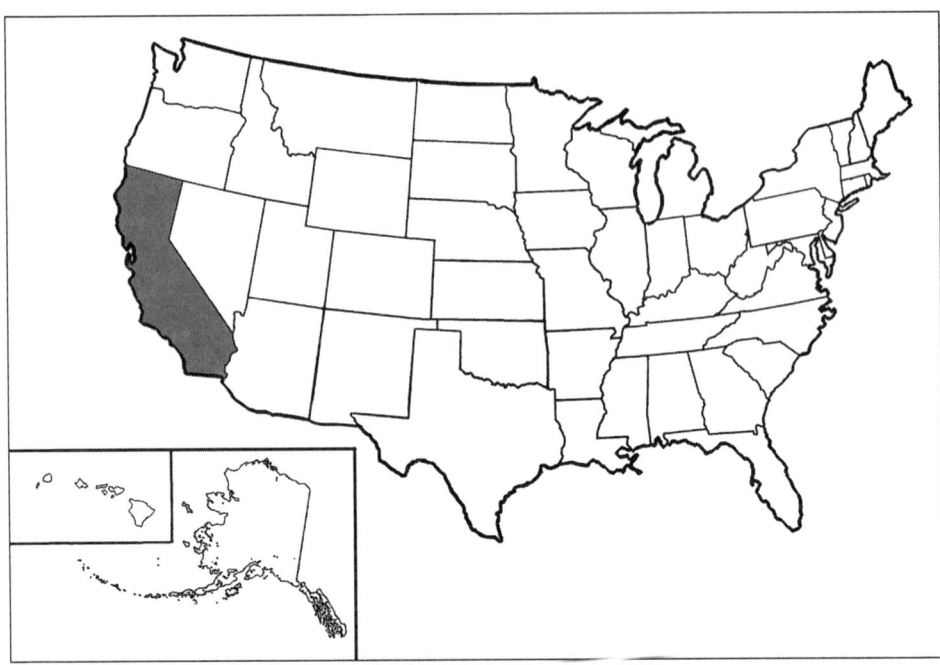

	the treaty, they remove Article 10, an article that guarantees protection of Mexican land grants. Of these grant claims by Mexicans, 27 percent are rejected. Under the treaty, Mexican nationals are given a year to decide if they want to have Mexican or U.S. citizenship. About 75,000 Latinos choose U.S. citizenship.
	The gold rush begins when Californian landowner John Sutter finds gold in the Sierra Nevada foothills in California. Many Mexicans are forced off their land by the gold seekers.
1849	Many Mexicans participate in the mining of gold in the hills, rivers, and countryside of northern California. Migrant communities begin to form and take root in California.
1850	The Foreign Miners Tax, which levies a fee on any miner who is not a U.S. citizen, is enacted. The tax affects over 15,000 Mexican miners in California.
1851	Congress passes the California Land Claims Act to help Mexican Americans prove their land claims. The act is unsuccessful because of the expensive legal costs involved; consequently, many Mexicans lose their land.
1855	The Greaser Act, an anti-Mexican law, is enacted. Vagrancy laws and so-called greaser laws (referring to a derogatory term for a Mexican) are passed. The laws prohibit cockfights, bullfights, and bear baiting—traditional customs of many Mexican Americans.
	Spanish-language newspaper *El Clamor Público* is founded in Los Angeles.

1862	The Homestead Act is passed in Congress. The act allows squatters in the West to settle and claim vacant lands—often those owned by Mexicans.
1866	Cristóbal Aguilar is elected mayor of Los Angeles.
1875	Romualdo Pacheco is elected as the first, and only, Latino governor of California. Pacheco later becomes the first Latino to chair a standing committee in Congress.
1910	The Mexican Revolution begins, and hundreds of thousands of Mexicans seek refuge in California.
1917	In response to labor shortages during World War I, many Mexicans move to California to labor in farms, mines, and railroads on a temporary basis. Congress passes the Immigration Act of 1917, requiring migrants to pass a literacy test. Mexicans are exempt, because they are needed as laborers. In May the Selective Service Act is enacted, requiring that Mexican noncitizens register for the draft.
1920s–1930s	Mexican farmworkers organize agricultural strikes throughout California—for example, in the Imperial Valley melon fields (1928, 1930), El Monte strawberry fields (1933), Hayward pea fields (1933), and the San Joaquin valley cotton fields and fruit orchards (1933).
1926	*La Opinión,* a daily Spanish-language newspaper, begins publication.
1928	Chicanos living California establish the Confederación de Uniones Omberas Mexicanas (Confederation of Mexican Labor Unions, or CUOM) to combat wage and racial discrimination in the workplace.
1929	The stock market crash and the inception of the Great Depression contribute to growing anti-immigrant sentiment, leading to the deportation of over one million Mexicans living in California—many of them United States citizens.
1930s	During the Great Depression, thousands of people from the Dust Bowl migrate to California in search of better living conditions, displacing Mexican workers, especially in the agricultural sector.
1931	Mexican American parents sue the school board in Lemon Grove for segregating their children from Anglo children. The court deems racial segregation among children illegal. This is the first successful desegregation court case in the United States.
1933	Chicanos establish the La Confederación de Uniones de Campesinos y Obreros Mexicanos (Confederation of Mexican Farm Worker and Labor Unions, or CUCOM), the largest agricultural union.
1942–1943	The Sleepy Lagoon case exposes judicial discrimination against Chicanos in Los Angeles. In the case, seventeen Chicano youth are found guilty of charges that range from assault to first-degree murder. The California District Court of Appeals reverses the convictions in 1944.
1942–1964	The Bracero program establishes a contract labor agreement between Mexico and the United States. The program brings over four million

	Mexican farmworkers to work in the agricultural sector of the United States. The majority of these Mexicans work in California.
1943	The Zoot Suit Riots occur in east Los Angeles, in the aftermath of the Sleeping Lagoon Case. Mexican youth are exposed to Anglo criticism, prejudice, and violence.
1946	In Santa Ana, Gonzalo Mendez, a Mexican American, files a lawsuit (*Mendez v. Westminister School District*) against segregation in the Westminster public school system. The federal district court rules segregation in schools unconstitutional, and this ruling sets the precedent for the *Brown v. Board of Education* case.
1950	Residents of the Chávez Ravine Mexican American community are forced to sell their homes to the city of Los Angeles to make way for a public-housing project. The housing project is cancelled, and a stadium for the Dodgers baseball team is built on the land.
1954–1958	Operation Wetback, a government program to deport undocumented workers, is established. The program leads to the deportation of 3.8 million people of Mexican descent, many of whom were living California.
1962	The National Farm Workers Association (NFWA) is founded by César Chávez and Dolores Huerta in Delano, California, to organize, serve, and protect farmworkers. The organization later becomes the United Farm Workers of America.
	Democrats Phil Soto from La Puente and John Moreno from Los Angeles become the first Latinos to be elected into the California state legislature. They are known for their commitment to serving their communities.
1964	The government terminates the Bracero program and the contracted importation of laborers from Mexico.
1965	Luis Valdez founds El Teatro Campesino (Farm Workers' Theater); drawing on a blend of Spanish and English, this theater portrays Anglo discrimination and Chicano resistance.
	César Chávez launches a nationwide strike and boycott of California table and wine grapes.
1966	Professor Rudy Acuña teaches the first Mexican-American history class in Los Angeles.
1967	The Brown Berets, a Chicano activist organization, is established in east Los Angeles. The group actively protests police brutality and the U.S. war in Vietnam. They also establish and run a free medical clinic and publish the newspaper *La Causa*.
1968	In what is referred to as the Los Angeles Blowouts, thousands of Chicano High School students walk out of their classrooms in protest of poor school conditions.
1970	A Chicano moratorium is held in Los Angeles to protest the disproportionate amount of Latino casualties in the Vietnam War. Approximately 25,000 demonstrators participate. Three Chicanos, including well-

	known Mexican American journalist Ruben Salazar, are killed when the police break up the demonstration.
1973	Five Latinos serving in the state legislature establish the Chicano Legislative Caucus to foster the political empowerment of Latinos in California by developing legislative priorities that protect their rights.
1982	A group of Chicana/Latina women establish the Mujeres Activas En Letras Y Cambio Social (MALCS) organization at the University of California Davis campus. The organization aims to support and promote education about the issues of Chicana/Latina and Native American women.
1986	Congress passes the Immigration Reform and Control Act (IRCA). The act establishes a process for undocumented migrants who have been in the United States since January 1, 1982, to become legal citizens. Latinos living in California are able to take advantage of this legislation by establishing legal residency.
	California voters pass Proposition 63, declaring English the official language of California.
1990	On June 15, 400 janitors, many of whom are Latino migrants, go on strike for improved wages and benefits in the Century City area of Los Angeles. They are attacked by the Los Angeles Police Department during a peaceful demonstration, and 24 janitors are injured. This event leads to the establishment of Justice for Janitors Day, organized by Justice for Janitors, a section of the Service Employees International Union.
	The census reveals that Latinos make up over 25 percent of the Californian population.
1993	Activist César Chávez dies. His funeral becomes the most widely attended Mexican American political demonstration.
1994	On November 8, Proposition 187 is passed. The proposition bans undocumented migrants from receiving public education and public benefits and makes it a felony to sell, distribute, or use false citizenship or residence documents. It also requires teachers, doctors, and state officials to report suspected undocumented migrants to the INS. The U.S. District Court rules the proposition unconstitutional in September 1999.
	In October, Operation Gatekeeper, a border enforcement strategy aimed at deterring illegal migration around the San Diego-Tijuana border, is enacted. As security is reinforced through an increase in border patrol agents, modern technology, and the building of reinforced fences, undocumented migrants are forced to cross through more desolate areas, increasing risk of death.
1995	The University of California Regents vote to end affirmative action, affecting the lives of thousands of Latinos in higher education.
1996	California voters pass Proposition 209, an initiative that bans preferential treatment based on race or gender in all state and local public programs.
1998	Proposition 227 is passed by California voters. This proposition bans bilingual education and English as a Second Language (ESL) programs

	in public schools, replacing them with a one-year intensive English immersion program.
1999	Minority groups make up the majority of the population of California. Latinos are the largest minority group.
2000	César Chávez Day becomes a state holiday in California.
	The U.S. census reveals that Latinos constitute 32.4 percent of California's population.
2001	Ron Gonzáles is elected mayor of San Jose, becoming the first Latino mayor of the city since California became a state in 1850.
2003	Lieutenant Governor Cruz Bustamante runs for governor. He receives one-third of the votes in the gubernatorial race.
2005	Antonio Villaraigosa is elected the first Latino mayor of Los Angeles since Cristóbal Aguilar in 1866.
	The state of California passes the Apology Act for the Mexican repatriation program that took place in the 1930s. This act recognizes the unlawful nature of the forcible removal of U.S. citizens of Mexican descent and offers a public apology for the violation of their civil rights as citizens.
2006	Approximately one million migrants and their supporters march in cities throughout California to protest anti-immigrant legislation.
2007	Antonio Villaraigosa, mayor of Los Angeles, forms a cross-border alliance with Antonio Saca, president of El Salvador, to combat gang violence. Mara Salvatrucha, also known as MS 13, is one of the most violent gangs in Los Angeles. MS 13 originated in El Salvador and, in addition to Los Angeles, has groups in Guatemala and Honduras.

HISTORICAL OVERVIEW

The most populous state in the country, with an estimated 35.5 million residents according to the 2000 census, California has long been a Latino stronghold. Its first Latino presence came under Spanish rule beginning in the sixteenth century, and before being integrated into the United States in 1850, California formed part of Mexico's northern frontier.

To date, the Latino population in California remains overwhelmingly Mexican.[1] There is, however, a growing presence of Central Americans, Puerto Ricans, and people from other Latin American and Caribbean nations. The Latino presence in California is the largest of all the states. Despite the large presence of Latinos in California and their contributions, the history of Latinos in this state has been one marked by struggle for economic, racial, and political equality. Nevertheless, Latino cultural, economic, linguistic, and political contributions are fundamental to California's fabric. Today the state's Latino legacy remains embedded in the Spanish place names and architecture, Latino migrant presence, cultural celebrations, and cuisine.

Early Latino Settlements

California's colonization began first with the arrival of Portuguese sailors exploring the coastline and continued with Spanish soldiers and Franciscan missionaries who accompanied them. Juan Rodríguez Cabrillo, a Portuguese sailor, was the first sailor to explore the coast of California in 1542, sailing into the San Diego bay and describing its port. Later expeditions by the Spaniard Sebastian Vizcaíno in 1602 uncovered Monterey Bay. Vizcaíno's explorations of the coastline were extensive; as he ventured inland, he charted his visit to the coastline meticulously. His expedition reports underscored the suitability of California colonization and proposed Monterey as a port of call. However, more than a century would pass before settlements were established.

It was not until the eighteenth century that Spain undertook full ownership of California. Settlement occurred largely in response to growing incursions of Russian and European-American traders and explorers into Spain's northern territories. In order to defend itself from foreign incursions, Spain relied on three primary institutions to settle the region: presidios, missions, and towns (pueblos). Presidios were self-contained forts, including armories, stables, resident dwellings, and chapels set up to defend Spain's claim to California. To facilitate their maintenance, presidios were often located near dependable water supplies, as well as pastoral and agricultural lands. The Spanish built four presidios in California: in San Diego, Santa Barbara, Monterey, and San Francisco.

In contrast, missions, often located close to presidios for protection, were established to convert (and supposedly civilize) Native Americans living in California. Staffed by Franciscans, these missions held conversion to the Catholic faith as the primary goal. But once Native Americans were converted and brought into the sphere of influence of the mission, progress could begin toward the secondary goal: creating proper Spanish citizens. Native Americans were thus expected to learn Spanish language and culture. Native Americans also became the main source of labor for maintaining the missions. Frontier town settlements were also encouraged by Spain. Many towns sprung up near missions and presidios, attracting a diverse group of people with varying skills and crafts to help sustain them. These towns eventually grew in size and have become recognized centers of Latino culture.

The first mission, established in San Diego, was the result of an expedition by Don Gaspar de Portolá, who was accompanied by Father Junípero Serra in 1769. The San Diego mission became the foundation for the colonization of California. The settlement in San Diego was followed by a later expedition in 1770 to Monterey, where Father Serra founded a second mission. Alongside the construction of the missions, a presidio was also built in each of these locations to help guard Spain's territorial claims. The San Francisco mission and presidio were founded in 1776. At the time of his death in 1784, Father Serra had founded nine missions. Other missions built by fellow Franciscans followed. In all, 21 missions were built between San Diego and San Francisco.

Native Americans living in the missions were circumscribed to the physical limits of the missions after they were baptized. While many resisted and escaped, they were often recaptured by soldiers. Native Americans endured life under Spanish rule in California until the Mexican War of Independence from Spain in 1821. With the end of the war, the new sovereign Mexican state was formed, gaining tenuous political control over California. Under a Mexican California, missions and presidios lost most of their power and land. The missions were secularized, and Native Americans were emancipated. Lands were sold off and redistributed to Mexicans; few Native Americans received any land. The presidio also lost its function under Spanish rule.

After Mexican independence, the privatization of mission lands helped to transform California's economy. Between 1834 and 1846, the Mexican governors of California awarded 700 private land grants to mostly elite Mexicans. These elite landowners established large ranching estates throughout California. Mexican Californians created a new economy and new identities for themselves as Californios. While Mexico tried to exert control over its population in California, it demonstrated little control. In fact, Californios increasingly demanded autonomy from the Mexican government in the mid-1840s. At the same time, the privatization of land also encouraged Anglo-American settlers attracted to California's rich agricultural lands and new economic opportunities. Consequently, by the 1830s, migrants from the United States outnumbered Mexicans in California.

By the 1840s, the United States government had become increasingly interested in acquiring California for access to the Pacific Ocean in order to facilitate trade and whaling, among other reasons. The United States offered to buy California from Mexico, but the Mexican government refused. At the same time, a sentiment was growing in the United States that California should be absorbed into the United States. Guided by principles of manifest destiny, the United States declared war on Mexico in 1846.

Shifting Allegiances: The Gold Rush and Latino Discrimination

The Mexican-American War ended in 1848 with the signing of the Treaty of Guadalupe Hidalgo. The treaty transferred California to the United States with the explicit provision that all Mexicans who wanted to remain would become United States citizens at the end of one year's residency. But within a year of the signing of the treaty, gold was discovered in northern California. As waves of U.S. citizens stormed into California, there resulted an escalation in conflicting land claims. Though they demonstrated valid proof of their land claims, many Mexicans were denied their claims and consequently lost their lands. Still other Mexicans lost their lands piece by piece to armed squatters who took land forcibly, through violence. While some fought to retain their land holdings through the court system, another group of Mexican land holders sold off their lands to avoid violence.

Thus the gold rush set the stage for an emerging pattern of discrimination against Latinos. As Mexicans were forced off their lands, local authorities were often unwilling to aid Mexican landowners, thereby perpetuating and condoning discriminatory practices. But Mexicans were not the only targets. The gold rush had also attracted experienced Mexican, Peruvian, and Chilean miners to the region; their success created tremendous animosity.

As a result of this overt discrimination, Latinos were often victims of violence in mining camps. Latinos involved in any disturbances were often expelled from mining camps, if not subjected to violence—including murder and lynching. When European foreigners or Anglo-Americans caused disturbances, they were not subjected to similar forms of punishment. This discrimination against Latinos was to some degree publicly sanctioned, if not reinforced, by the passage of discriminatory measures. These included the Foreign Miner's Tax, passed by the state legislature in 1850, shortly after California gained its statehood. This law deemed all foreigners working in the mines trespassers and required that foreigners pay $20 per person per month. This law spawned resistance, and the penalty was lowered to between $3 and $4 per month. Despite being based on racial prejudices, this tax was imposed on Latinos and Asians. The unequal and violent treatment of Latinos—not to mention the exorbitant tax—led thousands of Mexican miners to return to Mexico, while others fled to southern California.

The climate of violence against Latin Americans, particularly in northern California, spurred retaliation as Latinos formed armed (bandit) groups. Banditry, as it was often called, became commonplace throughout the 1850s. While many groups of armed Latinos surfaced, some have become legendary. Perhaps the most recognized Latino who rose to legendary status during the gold rush was Joaquín Murrieta (c. 1829–1853). Though Murrieta's background is often disputed, he came to symbolize Latino American resistance. It is rumored that his success as a miner produced much Anglo resentment toward him. One day, while mining for gold, he and his wife were attacked by a group of Anglo-American men who resented his success. They are purported to have raped his wife and beaten him. Although Murrieta sought justice through the legal system, he was not allowed to testify as a witness, because he was Mexican. Angered by the injustice, Murrieta set out to seek revenge, forming a gang with friends to find and punish his wrongdoers. They killed several men. Murrieta is said to have led various robberies and stolen thousands of dollars' worth of gold. In May 11, 1853, the governor of California, John Bigler, created the California State Rangers to set out and arrest Murrieta and the members of his posse. On July 25, 1853, a group of California Rangers is said to have encountered a group of men near Monterey. When all was said and done, two of the Mexicans had been killed. The Rangers believed one to be Murrieta and carried the head as proof. But legend has it that the head did not belong to Murrieta; his own sister denied it was the head of her beloved brother. In subsequent months and years, others claimed to see Murrieta, and so Murrieta became a legendary figure epitomized in songs and written lore.

Despite the turbulence that accompanied U.S. annexation and the harsh discrimination that accompanied Latinos during the gold rush in northern California, the Latino experience appears to have been very different in southern California. In Los Angeles, Latino landowners like Don Pío Pico, who served as California's governor after the Mexican-American War, were able to hold on to large ranch estates. Latinos were also able to exert power and respect. For example, prominent political figures, including Jose Miguel Covarrubias, Pablo de la Guerra, and Andres Pico, held office in the state legislature and in local governments. It was not until the end of the 1850s that their prominence in politics began to wane as more Anglo-Americans entered the legislature. Nevertheless stories like those that typified Latino experience in northern California are absent, and Los Angeles is described as being a place where Mexicans and Anglos interacted and intermarried freely. In the 1870s, Mexican Americans still constituted a majority of the population in the Los Angeles region.

From Economic Prosperity to Depression

At the turn of the twentieth century, California's economy was booming as a result of several factors. First, the transcontinental railroad was completed. The construction of this railroad facilitated the movement of people and goods across the country. As a consequence, Los Angeles was transformed into a bustling commercial hub. The railroad also contributed to the development of agriculture by facilitating transportation to processing and distribution locations. For ranchers, the railroad eased the burden of transporting cattle and sheep while opening up markets. Second, huge oil deposits were uncovered throughout the state, but mostly in southern California—in places like Huntington Beach, Santa Fe Springs, and Long Beach. California became a large oil producer, helping to stimulate its economy. Third, agriculture took on growing significance in California's expansive economy, to a large extent facilitated by the construction of the railroads, irrigation, and technological advances. In the central valleys, wheat became the most important farm product, while in southern California, citrus production came to predominate.

California's prosperous and growing economy required more labor. The railroads facilitated the movement of Mexican migrants to help fill those needs. Soon Mexican migrants became indispensable to California's agricultural economy. Also notable during this time period is the importation of Puerto Ricans to work in agricultural fields. Together, Latino and Asian labor provided the backbone of agricultural production.

The expansion of cities like Los Angeles, San Francisco, and San Jose was also facilitated by economic growth. Cities emerged around agricultural centers, railroad labor camps, and other economic industries throughout California. Latinos formed part of the integral fabric of these cities, settling near their places of work. In the cities, Latinos formed their own neighborhood enclaves, providing an environment where people shared a similar language, customs, and culture. While many Latinos chose freely to live in Latino enclaves—or barrios, as they have come to be known—many more were forced to live there through segregation. In Los Angeles, Latinos were excluded from white neighborhoods through racialized forms of exclusion that included violence and harassment.

Mexican migration to California increased significantly between 1910 and 1930. The largest contributor to rising Mexican migration was the Mexican Revolution; large numbers of Mexicans fled the violence and sought refuge in the United States. Even with this influx, California's growing industries required more laborers. By 1915, the United States was busy mobilizing for war, stimulating the growth of new businesses that contributed to these efforts. These business opportunities also relied on Latino labor in California. However, as U.S. entry into World War I approached, the Immigration Act of 1917 was passed, largely in an effort to restrict European migration into the country.

Specifically, the law included an entry fee (head tax) and introduced a literacy test for prospective migrants. This act had a tremendous impact on Mexican migration—and hence on California's economy. Because many Mexicans could neither afford the exorbitant head tax nor read, migration dropped severely. California's agricultural industries were particularly affected by the sudden shortage of labor. Given the importance of agriculture for feeding a population ready for war, a proviso was enacted that exempted Mexican agricultural and railroad workers from the requirements of the 1917 Immigration Act until 1921. It was later extended for one more year, until 1922. As a direct consequence of the proviso, the first labor program was initiated. Thousands of Mexicans registered to work; many more came undocumented. At the end of the program, many Mexicans did not return, but no overt pressures were placed upon them to return, because they filled an occupational niche not coveted by most U.S. citizens, including returning soldiers after the war.

In 1924 another immigration law was passed that set limits on Asian and southern European migrants; again Mexicans were excluded from such restrictions. By the mid 1920s, California's Latino population had skyrocketed. By 1930, more than 30 percent of the Mexican migrant population resided in California.

The Depression and the Mexican Repatriation Program

The Depression had a profound and immediate impact on Latinos in California. As North Americans lost their jobs, Mexicans and Mexican Americans in the state became targets of growing resentment and were increasingly accused of taking jobs from U.S. citizens. Subsequently, many employers were forced to discharge Mexican employees. As the Depression worsened, anti-immigrant sentiment flourished, culminating in a xenophobic campaign that resulted in the forced repatriation of Mexicans. Mexican workers were no longer welcomed.

Between 1929 and 1930, an estimated 500,000 Mexicans were repatriated without any deportation hearings—many of them U.S. citizens. Railroad transportation facilitated the repatriation process across the Mexican border. While the impact of repatriation was felt across the country, California had the highest number of repatriates, with Los Angeles County feeling the largest effects. As documented in *Decade of Betrayal*, a recent historical account, 50,000 Mexicans and their children departed from Los Angeles within a five-month period in 1931.

For Mexicans living in California, repatriation was internalized as a form of betrayal. Needless to say, for many Mexican Americans who remained in California, the repatriation program spawned both distrust and protest. For many of the repatriated, this act produced great shame. While some Mexican American citizens and legal residents eventually returned to the United States, others remained in Mexico, unable to overcome feelings of betrayal and loss.

The recent passage of California's Apology Act of 2005 may help repair the sting left behind in the wake of Mexican repatriation. Through the Apology Act, the state of California offered formal apology for the forceful and illegal removal of Mexicans who were legal residents and citizens at the time. More importantly, it recognized the denial of their civil liberties and constitutional rights.

World War II and the Importation of Mexican Labor

In the 1940s, World War II produced a shift in the tide of Mexican migration. As the United States entered the war, Mexican Americans responded to a call of duty. Mexican Americans served in the military overseas and upon their return; seventeen received Congressional Medals of Honor. In California, World War II brought tremendous labor shortages as men were called to war. Here also, Mexican Americans responded by filling these jobs. As a result, many were able to gain entry into jobs and industries previously closed off to them. However, at the same time they were achieving some upward mobility, they also were leaving behind less skilled jobs, like farmwork.

Labor shortages produced by World War II were particularly felt in agriculture, though other industries, like steel manufacturing, meatpacking, and processing, also suffered. Once again, the United States turned toward Mexico to fill these shortages. In 1942 the U.S. Department of State reached an agreement with the Mexican government to create a temporary labor program. The Mexican government built in provisions to protect its citizens from the types of discriminatory exploitation that

Mexican laborers had previously incurred in the United States. The U.S. Department of State conceded to Mexican demands for protective measures. Both the United States and Mexico, having signed the Mexican Labor Program (more typically referred to as the Bracero program), implemented this new system in August 1942.

Under the Bracero program, Mexicans were provided with temporary permits that allowed them to work legally in the United States for short periods of time. In the United States, growers were provided a cheap labor force. Despite provisions for the humane and fair treatment of Mexican laborers, braceros endured less-than-ideal working and living conditions. In the agricultural fields, they lacked toilets and running water; they were also exposed to dangerous pesticides, like DDT. The agricultural camps where braceros lived tended to provide substandard housing, and the tenants were frequently overcharged for their board.

While the program was intended to attract a documented Mexican labor pool, it also resulted in a large migration of undocumented workers. California, having attracted the highest percentage of braceros, experienced the significant growth of its Latino population. In 1952 the United States experienced a recession that brought attention to the rise in undocumented Mexican migrants in the country. Again, the United States carried out a mass deportation campaign, called Operation Wetback. In California, the Immigration and Naturalization Services, along with local officials, carried out raids in which Mexican migrants were rounded up and deported. In the course of 3 years, more than one million Mexicans and Mexican Americans were expelled from the United States. Ironically, even in the midst of deportations, the U.S. Congress approved the continuity of the Bracero program until 1964. Mexicans continued to migrate to California in search of jobs.

When the program ended, Mexicans had once again become an indispensable part of California culture. Also noteworthy: at the program's end, several well-established patterns of Mexican migration had emerged. Many braceros chose not to return to Mexico, settling in California, where they continued to work and live in ethnic enclaves. Later some braceros encouraged further migration of relatives and friends to California. A pattern of cyclical migration also emerged as Mexicans moved to California for short stints at a time in order to earn money. Finally, the Bracero program contributed to a growing trend of undocumented migration through California's southern border. These patterns of Mexican migration and settlement would take on new significance in the 1980s and 1990s, as Mexicans once again become targets of nativism.

Ethnic Tension in the Aftermath of World War II

For Latinos living in California, World War II brought both opportunities and challenges heightened by ethnic tensions between Mexican Americans and Anglo-Americans. In part these tensions were a response to entry into World War II and the forced removal and internment of Japanese and Japanese Americans in California. For some Anglo-Californians, fear and suspicion of the Japanese was also extended to include Mexicans and Mexican Americans.

In Los Angeles, much of the tension was focused on Mexican American males, known as pachucos, who were part of a youth counterculture centered on popular jazz culture. As part of this counterculture, pachucos wore the distinctive zoot suit, including a long topcoat with broad shoulders and a loose, high waist; pleated pants tapered at the bottom; and a brimmed hat—an iconic clothing style of the jazz era. These Mexican American youths tended to hang together in small groups, flaunting their suits and dance moves. Their style and ways, largely disapproved of by Anglo-Americans, drew public criticism in the press; they were accused of being hoodlums and criminals.

In 1942 public disdain for pachucos contributed to the unlawful conviction of 17 Mexican American youths in the Sleepy Lagoon Case; the group was accused of murdering a young Mexican American found dead near the site of a house party. While the details of the death were unknown, Los Angeles police arrested and accused a group of pachucos who had been involved in a fight at the party the dead youth had attended. The conviction of the youth was widely publicized and helped create a hostile environment for young Mexican Americans.

In the wake of the convictions, a conflict broke out in Los Angeles between white American sailors stationed in the city and Mexican American zoot-suiters, as they were called. Violent incidents between the sailors and the Chicanos were frequent from 1942 to 1943. On May 31, 1943, a group of U.S. sailors on leave fought with a group of Mexican American youth in the Los Angeles downtown area. Joe Dacy Coleman, one of the U.S. sailors, was seriously injured; in retaliation, a group of 50 sailors went to the primarily Mexican neighborhood of east Los Angeles and attacked zoot-suiters and other Mexicans in the vicinity. These acts of racialized violence came to be referred to as the Zoot Suit Riots. In the end, the riots were blamed primarily on the Mexican-American population, while the sailors were praised for cleaning up the streets of Los Angeles.

Despite the troubling events of 1942, Latinos demonstrated resilience and strength throughout the 1940s and 1950s. It was during this time period that Latinos challenged segregation through the legal system. In 1946 *Mendez v. Westminster District* banned school segregation. In the 1950s, residential desegregation also began to occur as Latinos moved out of ethnic enclaves and into more integrated communities. In part this process was facilitated by the 1944 GI Bill, which provided government loans to many Latino veterans. With the loans, Latino veterans were able to buy homes and start new businesses. Many Latinos also took advantage of the program to attend college. Finally, during this time period, many American-born Latinos transitioned into skilled and semiskilled occupations. In all, the strides made by Latinos for social equality throughout the

40s and 50s contributed to a growing ethnic consciousness that helped to foster the social movements of the 1960s and 1970s.

Chicano Social Movements

Throughout the 1960s and 1970s, Latino youth of Mexican descent reclaimed their ethnic identity and mobilized around it. Referring to themselves as Chicanos (a derivative of Mexicano and members of *la raza*, or "the people") Mexican Americans used the label as a symbol of ethnic pride. As a politicized concept, the Chicano movement drew attention to the economic, social, and political marginalization of Latinos. Chicanos banded together to demand their right to fair treatment and equal access to education, political participation, and employment opportunities, as well as the right to claim membership in an ethnic community without prejudice.

In California, as in other places throughout the country, Chicanos mobilized around various causes, adding to the complexity and vibrancy of the multiple struggles that constituted the Chicano movement, which took root in the 1960s.

In part, these struggles drew on earlier examples of Mexican American activism. In 1931, for example, Mexican American parents called for a boycott to fight school segregation in Lemon Grove. Since the 1920s, Mexican Americans had also organized agricultural strikes throughout California in order to gain better wages. These precedents no doubt contributed to the defining struggle of the Chicano movement in California, which began with the efforts of labor organizers and the United Farm Workers Union (UFW).

Bringing together the concerns of mostly Filipino and Mexican agricultural workers in rural California, César Chávez and Dolores Huerta shed public light on the plight of agricultural labor. Having experienced agricultural farmwork as a youth, Chávez knew of the inherent racial and economic inequalities. After serving in World War II, Chávez returned to California with a desire to change the quality of life of farmworkers. He gained valuable organizing experience in the 1950s working for the Community Service Organization (CSO) in San Jose. However, Chávez wanted to create an organization that would benefit farmworkers. Dolores Huerta, a native of Stockton, had also gained organizing experience through the CSO, and in 1955 she cofounded the Sacramento CSO chapter. Huerta shared a common drive to empower Chicano farmworkers.

In 1962, Chávez and Huerta cofounded the National Farm Workers Association (NFWA)—later renamed the United Farm Workers Union Organizing Committee—in Delano, California. The NFWA developed a strong membership of farmworkers who sought equality and justice and drew support from public figures and community members. In 1965 the NFWA initiated a grape pickers' strike and later called for a national boycott of California table and wine grapes.

Five years later, in 1970, the NFWA scored its greatest victory when their strikes, boycotts, and other efforts finally won a contract with the largest grape growers in California. Subsequently, Latino farmworkers with NFWA contracts received higher wages and benefits.

The struggle for social justice and equality was not confined to the fields. High schools, colleges, and university campuses throughout California also became political battlegrounds for Chicanos. In their respective educational settings, Chicano students called for administrators to open the doors of universities to people of color, hire minority faculty, and include minority perspectives in their curricula.

The largest high-school student protest in the history of the United States is exemplary of younger student involvement in the Chicano movement. In 1968 more than 1,000 students peacefully walked out of Abraham Lincoln High School in Los Angeles with Chicano teacher Sal Castro to protest of the deplorable conditions in their school. This walkout sparked similar walkouts across Los Angeles in what is now referred to as the blowouts of 1968. In all, more than 10,000 high-school students walked out in protest of a lack of suitable school conditions, lack of minority teachers, and high dropout rates for Latinos.

Universities became another focal point of protest. Across California campuses, including UCLA, Berkeley, and Cal State Northridge, students and faculty pushed for scholarships for minorities, an increase of minority faculty, and the creation of Chicano studies. In 1969 a coalition of student groups meeting at the University of California at Santa Barbara established the Movimiento Estudiantil Chicano de Aztlán (the Chicano Student Movement of Aztlán), best known as MEChA. Throughout California university campuses, MEChA became a strong advocate of Chicano studies. MEChA continues to uphold the original goals of the Chicano movement and has chapters in nearly every university across the country.

The movement also confronted popular media representations of Mexican Americans, promoting scholarly, literary, and artistic productions that validated the identity and experiences of Mexican Americans. Rodolfo Acuña, a professor of history at California State University at Northridge, for example, wrote *Occupied America*, refuting widely held assumptions of Chicanos. Artists like Luis Valdéz, who formed *El Teatro Campesino* (the Farm Worker Theater), also became active participants in the movement.

Diversification of Latino Population

Throughout the 1970s, Latinos continued to be integrated into California's growing economy. Many Latino migrants settled in California, especially in Los Angeles. By 1980, the Latino population of the state had grown to over 4,544,331 and accounted for 19.2 percent of the total population. It is estimated that more than half of the Latino population was living in Los Angeles county alone. While the predominant flow of migrants continued to be from Mexico, in the 1980s, the migrant flows showed new patterns of diversification.

Beginning with the Mexican migrant population, the 1980s saw flows of people from nontraditional sending regions of the country. Whereas Mexican migration had typically been associated with people from northern regions, like Michoacan, Zacatecas, Durango, and Chihuahua, an increasing number of Mexican migrants throughout the 1980s came from more southern regions of the country, including Mexico City and Guerrero. Most notably apparent, however, was a migrant stream of indigenous Mexicans from Oaxaca and Puebla. Among the latter were Mixtec migrants who were overwhelmingly absorbed by California's agricultural economy and Zapotec migrants who integrated themselves into Los Angeles's service economy. So many Oaxacan migrants were present in the state that by the 1990s, notable anthropologist Michael Kearney had coined the phrase Oaxacalifornia to describe the relationship established between indigenous Oaxacan sending communities and communities of settlement in California.

Beginning in the 1980s, new migrants also came from Central American countries, including El Salvador and Guatemala—countries escaping U.S.-supported civil wars. To date, Central Americans constitute the second-largest percentage of Latinos in the state. When Salvadorans fled their country, many eventually settled in Los Angeles. A well-established community of Salvadorans in the Los Angeles Pico-Union districts was thriving in the 1990s with *pupuserias*, local restaurants that served handmade corn flour cakes stuffed with cheese or meats and topped with pickled cabbage and vegetables, a traditional Salvadoran dish. Salvadorans also established several refugee resource centers in that area of Los Angeles that provided services to the Central American community. They were also engaged in activism in California that shed light on the atrocities of the civil war in El Salvador. Today there are more Salvadorans living in Los Angeles than in the capital of San Salvador.

Guatemalan migrants also fled the ravages of war. In contrast to Salvadoran refugees, however, Guatemalans settling in Los Angeles and San Francisco were largely indigenous. Like Salvadorans, they also established close-knit communities throughout Los Angeles and integrated themselves into the local culture and economy.

Other groups of Latino migrants are also present in the state. Puerto Ricans, for example, have been living in California since the late 1800s. However, their unique status as U.S. citizens has often differentiated them from other Latino groups. They are peppered throughout the state, but their presence has often been overlooked. However, their contributions to California's Latino culture are equally important. Today, California's Latino population also boasts growing numbers of migrants from South American countries, including Ecuador, Colombia, Peru, Argentina, and Bolivia.

While new patterns of migration include a growing number of migrants from countries beyond Mexico, Latino migration is also unique today for its increasingly transnational character. Today's Latino migrant population is not one that is typified solely by a permanent movement from their country of origin to settlement in California. Rather, Latino communities today may include people who have permanently relocated, temporary migrants or sojourners here for short periods of time, and also people who move back and forth between their places of origin and those of settlement in California. This movement back and forth has facilitated the increased flow of goods and services that span across geographic space. Thus, money transfers occur every day between Oaxaca and Los Angeles; Salvadoran delicacies are shipped daily to Los Angeles; and print media is available in California as well as countries of origin that cover events in both locations. Important holidays and celebrations from the country of origin may be celebrated in California. Terms such as *Oaxacalifornia* and *Mexifornia* capture the uniqueness of transnational Latino cultures.

Migration Backlash

In California, as in other states across the country, Latino migration has always been met by ambivalence. On the one hand, California's economic industries have welcomed Latino laborers throughout its history as a source of cheap labor. On the other hand, during times of economic recession or resource scarcity, a popular response to Latino presence has been to adopt restrictive anti-immigrant measures. For example, in the 1930s (during the Depression) and in the 1950s (at the height of the Cold War), Mexicans and Mexican Americans were repatriated across the border. During both repatriations, California deported the highest number of people of Mexican descent.

More current measures passed in California are much less extreme than those of the past. Yet ambivalence toward Latino migrants continues to surface in the form of restrictionist and anti-affirmative-action measures within the state of California. Throughout the 1990s, California constituents approved several measures that impacted the lives of both migrant and native-born Latinos alike. The legality of some of these measures continues to be debated.

Several of the most notable anti-immigrant pieces of legislation drafted throughout the 1990s were Proposition 187, Proposition 209, and Proposition 227. Proposition 187, passed in the California state legislature in November of 1994, denied undocumented migrants and their children access to publicly funded programs, including health care and K–12 education. The successful passage of this proposition was based on an inflammatory anti-immigrant campaign that blamed undocumented Mexican migrants for flooding the state and overtaking public resources. The campaign's successful use of images of undocumented migrants crossing into San Ysidro and dashing across the freeway to avoid being stopped by migration swayed California's residents to vote for the measure. Convinced by the rhetoric, people did not question either the racist undertones of the campaign or the figures presented.

A consequence of this legislation is that all Latinos became suspect under the law; distinctions between migrant and native-born Latinos were lost. Consequently, Proposition 187 resulted in mounting resentment among Latinos who felt they were unjustly depicted as parasites to the system, neglecting their many positive contributions, including the payment of taxes. Many more resented that Latino had become synonymous with "illegal" or "undocumented," when many Latinos living in California were citizens who had been in California for generations. The passing of Proposition 187 was followed by injunctions filed by the Mexican American Legal Defense and Educational Fund (MALDEF), the American Civil Liberties Union (ACLU), and other civil rights groups, citing the unconstitutional nature of its provisions. Proposition 187 would eventually be declared unconstitutional in 1998, 4 years after its passage.

The passage of Proposition 187 produced a conservative fervor that contributed to the creation and passage of a proposition passed in 1996, Proposition 209. Called the Civil Rights Initiative, this proposition eliminated affirmative action in state-run agencies and educational institutions. This measure won by a larger majority than Proposition 187. Finally, in 1998, California voters also passed Proposition 227, requiring that all public-school instruction be conducted in English. This act effectively eliminated bilingual education, with the exception of intensive yearlong English immersion programs developed for new migrant youth.

While not directed exclusively at Latinos in the state, these pieces of legislation had enormous consequences for both migrant and native-born Latinos living in California. Certainly a negative consequence was that Latinos continued to feel targeted by exclusionary measures regardless of their legal status in the United States. Latinos felt stigmatized by Proposition 187 and further marginalized by Proposition 209. But rather than rendering Latinos victims, the passage of Proposition 187 stirred a new wave of Latino consciousness. Latinos, who by 1995 represented more than 26 percent of the population, responded in two significant ways: registering to vote and attaining citizenship. As a result of these actions, Latinos became a major voting constituency that has helped to transform the face of state and local politics. At the state level, currently one in four assembly members is Latino, and Lieutenant Governor Cruz Bustamante became the first Latino to be elected speaker of the assembly. At local levels, California voters elected Latino mayors in several of the largest cities, including San Jose and Los Angeles, not to mention all the city councilmen and councilwomen who were also elected into their positions.

LATINOS AT THE MILLENNIUM

In a similar fashion to the anti-immigrant campaigns of the 1990s that triggered the passing of Proposition 187, the popular discourse presented in the media in the new millennium has again created sensationalist rhetoric that targets Latinos in similar ways. Moreover, in a post-9/11 environment, Latino migrants are increasingly characterized in the media as linked to terrorism, drug trafficking, and other crimes. Terrorism and drug trafficking have become the new staging grounds for political debates focusing on the growing presence of Latinos in this country—more specifically, on the U.S. border with Mexico. With the largest Latino population residing in California, the state has received increased attention in print, radio, and television campaigns targeting undocumented migrants. CNN's Lou Dobbs, for example, has run a series titled *Broken Borders*, which constantly depicts migrant paths through southern California as a "terrorist alley."

These recent representations of Latinos have sparked an immigration debate that has polarized the nation. One response has been a rise in anti-immigrant sentiment that targets migrants while hiding behind the veil of border protection. Such a view is represented by a group of volunteers who call themselves the Minuteman Project; they have organized civil patrols "to protect the nation's borders from illegal immigration," as frequently reiterated by the media. On the other side are migrants and U.S.-born citizens who resent the ways that they are being negatively depicted and criminalized.

At the national level, conservatives and liberals in Congress have continued to debate the future of migration across the nation's borders. In 2005 several pieces of legislation were proposed in Congress to stem the flow of undocumented migration through Mexico. Proposals in Congress ranged from amnesty programs for undocumented laborers living and working in the United States, to guest worker programs to allow a temporary flow of a legalized labor pool, to more restrictionist measures that would continue to reinforce the nation's southern border by sealing off the United States from Mexico through reinforced steel and concrete barriers.

Latinos have been caught in the crossfire. As in decades past, one of the ironies remaining is that there continues to be a demand for cheap Latino labor in this country. In particular, California's agricultural industry is still dependent on Latino manual labor. But since the 1990s, California's booming economy also contributed to the increasing integration of Latinos into its service economy as custodians, gardeners, housekeepers, and nannies, among other occupations. Latinos resented the public hostility directed toward them and in response began to organize. Documented and undocumented Latino migrants and U.S. citizens banded together around a campaign that stressed human rights over the question of legality, boldly asserting that "*all* immigrants have rights."

During the last week of March 2006, over one million Latinos across the country in various cities took to the streets in response to proposed anti-immigration legislation threatening to pass through Congress at the time. More than 500,000 Latinos marched in Los Angeles alone. The march represents one of the largest recent political demonstrations calling for an end to Latino racism and injustice. Moreover, it calls for a critical perspective on Latino migration—one that is historically informed and is inclusive of migrant voices. In a break from the past, however, recent movements signal the ushering of a new historical moment for Latinos in California. As demonstrated by recent trends, Latinos in the state currently account for 32.4 percent of the population; according to projections, they will account for 47.8 percent of the population by the year 2040, becoming the ethnic majority in California. While the social problems of the past have not disappeared, at the closing of the first decade of the new millennium, Latinos are making strides in all areas of life, including education, occupational advancement, professionalization, and politics. The future looks promising.

NOTABLE LATINOS

Rodríguez Cabrillo, Juan (1499–1543). Portuguese by birth, Juan Rodríguez de Cabrillo sailed for the Spanish crown and was the first to explore the California coast in 1542.

Vizcaíno, Sebastián (1548–1624). Sebastián Vizcaíno explored the California coastline in the early 1600s, making detailed charts. He is also noted for exploration of the Monterey Bay area.

Serra, Junípero de (1713–1784). Junípero de Serra was a Franciscan missionary who, along with soldier Gaspar de Portolá, founded 21 missions in California, including the first.

Portolá, Gaspar de (1716–1784). As a soldier in the Spanish Army, Gaspar de Portolá led an expedition that founded San Diego and Monterey. Portola also served as governor of Baja and Alta California from 1767 to 1770.

Requena, Manuel (1804–1876). Manuel Requena became the second Latino to become mayor of Los Angeles when he took his place as acting mayor for two weeks (September 22, 1856–October 4, 1856).

Aguilár, Cristóbal (1816–1886). The third Latino mayor of Los Angeles, Cristóbal Aguilár served two separate terms, from 1866 to 1868 and from 1871 to 1872.

Coronel, Antonio Francisco (1817–1894). In 1853, Antonio Francisco Coronel became mayor of Los Angeles. Born in Mexico City, Coronel came to California as a young man. During the Mexican occupation of California, Coronel was appointed assistant secretary of tribunals for the City of Los Angeles, and in 1843 he became a justice of the peace in the city. During the Mexican-American War, Coronel served as a captain and sergeant-at-arms in the Mexican Artillery. After the war, he continued to be involved in politics and served as county assessor and member of the Los Angeles Council for several years between 1854 and 1867.

Murrieta, Joaquín (1829–1853). Joaquín Murrieta was an infamous and legendary figure of the California gold rush during the 1850s who has come to symbolically represent early opposition to white, European-American domination.

Pacheco, Romualdo (1831–1899). Romualdo Pacheco is the only Latino who has served as governor of California; he held the office from 1877 to 1883. In 1876 Pacheco was elected to the House of Representatives, but he did not serve, because the House Committee on Elections refused to accept his certificate of elections. He was reelected to the House of Representatives and served until 1883. In 1879 he was appointed chair of the Committee on Private Land Claims. After leaving Congress, Pacheco was named the U.S. envoy extraordinary and minister plenipotentiary to the Central American states.

Ruiz de Burton, María Amparo (1832–1895). María Amparo Ruiz de Burton was the author of *The Squatter and the Don* (1885). Written in English, the book is regarded as the first Mexican American novel.

Lozáno, Ignacio (1886–1953). Ignacio Lozáno founded the Spanish-language newspaper *La Opinión* in 1926, and it has been published continuously since then. The newspaper focuses on news from Spanish-speaking parts of the world. Before founding *La Opinión*, Lozáno established the *La Prensa*, a Spanish-language periodical read by Mexican political refugees.

Galarza, Ernesto (1905–1984). A historian, labor organizer, and activist, Ernesto Galarza migrated to Sacramento, California, from Mexico at the age of eight. He grew up working in the fields with his parents and excelled in education. He is one of the first Mexican Americans to have received a college education, which culminated in a PhD in history from Columbia University. Galarza dedicated his adult life to organizing farm laborers and raising awareness of their exploitation through his teaching. He wrote several books, including *Barrio Boy*, about his own childhood. He was nominated for the Nobel Prize in literature in 1976.

Díaz, José (1919–1942). José Díaz was a 22-year-old farmworker murdered on the morning of August 2, 1942, on the way home from a neighbor's birthday party in what government officials called the growing Mexican American frenzy of the time. A fan of the contemporary jazz music era, he often wore a zoot suit, an outfit that had become increasingly symbolic of an unruly Mexican American youth gang culture. His murder in 1942 was used to rationalize government intervention, both violent and nonviolent, to quell a chaotic and supposedly threatening population.

Soto, Philip (1926–1997). Philip Soto was one of the first two Latinos to be elected to the California state legislature. From 1962 to 1966, Soto, a Democrat from La Puente, served as the state representative for the Fiftieth Assembly District. During his terms, he helped organize the United Farm Workers and was active in protesting the Vietnam War. After leaving office, Soto became the director of operations of a nonprofit vocational and job training program in east Los Angeles called SER: Jobs for Progress.

Chávez, César (1927–1993). Activist César Chávez, cofounder of the National Farm Workers Association (NFWA, later known as the United Farm Workers Association) spent most of his adult life in California. In 1965 Chávez and the NFWA organized a California grape picker's strike to demand higher wages and encouraged U.S. citizens to boycott table grapes to show support. Chávez also organized strikes and boycotts for the rights of migrant workers in several different agricultural sectors.

Moreno, John (1927–1999). A Democrat from Los Angeles, John Moreno was one of the first Latinos to be elected to the California state legislature. As the representative for the Fifty-First Assembly District from 1962 to 1964, he served as vice chair of the Constitutional Amendments Committee.

Gonzáles, Pancho (1928–1995). Professional tennis player Pancho Gonzáles was born in Los Angeles to Mexican parents. Gonzáles won, among other awards, the men's singles at the United States Championships of 1948 and 1949; the men's doubles at Wimbledon in 1949.

Salazar, Rubén (1928–1970). As a Mexican American journalist for the *Los Angeles Times,* Rubén Salazar focused on issues that affected Latinos. His reports included stories about the Bracero program, the U.S.-Mexican border, racial discrimination, and ethnic politics. He was killed by police during the National Chicano Moratorium March in protest of the Vietnam War.

Escalante, Jaime (1930–). Prized Bolivian-born Los Angeles math teacher Jaime Escalante was the subject of the 1988 book *Escalante: Best Teacher in America* and the 1988 film *Stand and Deliver.* He was inducted into the Teachers Hall of Fame in 1999 and is the recipient of numerous prestigious awards, including the Presidential Medal for Excellence in Education, the George Forster Peabody Award, and numerous honorary doctorate degrees.

Huerta, Dolores (1930–). A cofounder of the National Farm Workers Association, Dolores Huerta played vital role in organizing farmworkers. Raised in Stockton, Huerta became the coordinator for the East Coast table grape boycott, led the political sector of the farmworkers' union, and was involved with the feminist movement of the late 1960s. Huerta continues to fight for labor rights and spread awareness of farmworker injustices today.

Valens, Ritchie (1941–1959). Considered the first Chicano rock and roll star, Ritchie Valens is best known for his hit song "La Bamba," which was influenced by Mexican folk music. Born in San Fernando, he died when he was 17 years old in a plane crash. Valens received a star of the Hollywood Walk of Fame in 1990 and was inducted into the Hollywood Hall of Fame in 1991.

Rodríguez, Richard (1944–). Best known for his 1982 memoir *Hunger of Memory,* a book that describes how learning English distanced him from the native culture of his parents, Richard Rodríguez is an accomplished author. As a public intellectual, he appears frequently on the *MacNeil/Lehrer News Hour* and is a contributing editor for *Harper's* magazine.

Marin, Richard "Cheech" (1946–). Born in South Central Los Angeles, comedian and actor Richard "Cheech" Marin is perhaps best known for his role as half of the comedy duo Cheech and Chong. Marin wrote, directed, and starred in the comedy *Born in East LA* (1987). He has also appeared in numerous films and television shows. Additionally, Marin is active in Latino politics and volunteers for the Hispanic Scholarship Fund and the Inner City Arts Council.

Olmos, Edward James (1947–). Most known for his roles in the film *Stand and Deliver* and more recently the PBS miniseries *Mi Familia* (My Family), Mexican American Edward James Olmos is an Emmy-winning actor hailing from east Los Angeles. In 1998 he founded Latino Public Broadcasting Company with the goal of supporting diverse perspectives on public television and providing funding for programming about issues that affect Latinos.

Molina, Gloria (1949–). A native Angelina, Gloria Molina is a member of the Los Angeles County Board of Supervisors and the chairwoman of the Los Angeles County Metropolitan Transportation Authority. In April of 2006, she was voted Hispanic Businesswoman of the Year by the *Hispanic Business Magazine*. Other important positions she has held are deputy for presidential personnel; deputy director for the Department of Health and Services; and California state assemblywoman.

Gonzáles, Ronald R. (1951–). Ron Gonzáles was elected the first Latino mayor of San Jose since California gained statehood in 1850. Gonzáles has received several national honors, including the Point of Light Award, in recognition of his contributions to his community.

Moraga, Cherrie (1952–). Cherrie Moraga was born in Los Angeles in 1952, and her Chicana roots have informed her experiences as a lesbian poet, playwright, essayist, scholar, and activist. Her work in the theater has contributed to the growth of Chicano theater, and she is the recipient of numerous prestigious honors and awards, including the National Endowment for the Arts Theatre Playwriting Fellowship Award. In 1983 Moraga cofounded the group Kitchen Table: Women of Color Press. She is also coeditor of the pivotal Chicana feminist text *This Bridge Called My Back: Writings by Radical Women of Color*, coauthored separately with Gloria Anzaldua and Ana Castillo.

Soto, Gary (1952–). Born in Fresno, award-winning Gary Soto has written numerous books of poetry as well as young adult and children's books. Soto won the American Book Award for his 1985 memoir *Living Up the Street* (1985) and was a National Book Award finalist for his 1995 book *New and Selected Poems*.

Bustamante, Cruz Miguel (1953–). Until 2003, Cruz Miguel Bustamante held the highest-ranking elected position among Latinos living in the United States. Bustamante has served as a California assemblyman (1993–1996), speaker of the assembly (1996–1998), and lieutenant governor (1999–2007). In 2003 he ran for governor of California, but lost to Arnold Schwarzenegger. As a Democrat, Bustamante focused on education, the environment, racial tolerance, diversity, and the support of migrant and agricultural communities.

Villaraigosa, Antonio (1953–). An east Los Angeles native, Antonio R. Villaraigosa was elected the forty-first mayor of Los Angeles on July 1, 2005. Prior to becoming mayor, Villaraigosa served in the California state assembly and in 1994 was elected the first assembly speaker from Los Angeles in 25 years. In 2003 he was elected part of the Los Angeles City Council.

Cervantes, Lorna Dee (1954–). Lorna Dee Cervantes, an accomplished and award-winning poet, was born and raised in California. Her poems and novels offer deep insight into the lives and experiences of Mexican Americans living in the northern

California communities she was raised in. Her works include *From the Cables of Genocide: Poems on Love and Hunger* (1991), a collection of poems; and *Emplumada* (1981), her first book that received an American Book Award. In 1995 she received a Lila Wallace-Reader's Digest Writers' Award.

Solis, Hilda L. (1957–). As a congresswoman in the House of Representatives, Hilda L. Solis has been recognized for her leadership. Among her many accomplishments, Solis's dedication to environmental justice earned her a John F. Kennedy Profile in Courage Award (2000). She was the first woman to receive this honor. Solis has also served as the first Latina on the Committee on Energy and Commerce (2003).

Ochoa, Ellen (1958–). Southern California native Ellen Ochoa is the first female Latina astronaut for NASA. In 1993, Ochoa went on her first space shuttle mission aboard the *Discovery*. Ochoa has won many awards, including two Space Act Tech Brief Awards, three Space Flight Medals, an Outstanding Leadership Medal, an Exceptional Service Medal, the Women in Aerospace Outstanding Achievement Award, and the Hispanic Heritage Leadership Award.

Escobedo Cabral, Anna (1959–). Born in San Bernardino, Anna Escobedo Cabral is the forty-second treasurer of the United States. Cabral, a second-generation Mexican American, was confirmed and sworn in to the position on December 13, 2004. As president and CEO of the Hispanic Association on Corporate Responsibility, Cabral worked with Fortune 500 companies to increase Latino presence in leadership, employment, philanthropy, and governance. She has served as deputy staff director for the U.S. Senate Judiciary Committee (1993–1999) and as executive staff director of the U.S. Senate Republican Conference Task Force on Hispanic Affairs (1991–present).

López, George (1961–). George López, a Mexican American comedian and actor known for his satirical representations of Mexican American culture in the United States, is the fourth Latino male to headline a sitcom in the United States. As an active member of the Latino community, López also started the George and Ann López-Richie Alarcon CARE Foundation, an organization that provides educational community and arts resources.

Tobar, Hector (1963–). Born to Guatemalan parents in Los Angeles, Hector Tobar is a noted author, journalist, and foreign correspondent of the *Los Angeles Times*. He is author of *Translation Nation: On the Trail of a New American Identity* (2005) and *Tattooed Soldier* (1998). His work for the *Los Angeles Times* earned him a Pulitzer Prize in 1992. In 2006, *Hispanic Business Magazine* named Tobar one of the 100 Most Influential Hispanics in the United States.

Alcaraz, Lalo (1964–). Lalo Alcaraz is a Mexican American cartoonist best known for his daily syndicated comic strip *La Cucaracha*. Alcaraz's work focuses on Latino political issues, like migration, border politics, and race relations. Alcaraz is also host of *The Pocho Hour of Power*, a Pacifica Radio weekly political humor show.

De La Hoya, Oscar (1973–). One of the best contemporary boxers from the United States, Oscar De La Hoya was born to Mexican migrant parents in east Los Angeles. He captured a gold medal in the 1992 Olympics and since then has won five boxing titles in five different weight classes.

Gutiérrez, Oscar (Rey Mysterio Jr.) (1974–). Better known as Rey Mysterio Jr., Oscar Gutiérrez, a professional wrestler, is known for the mask he wears during his World Wrestling Entertainment appearances.

Furcal, Rafael Antoni (1977–). Dominican American baseball star Rafael Antoni Furcal currently plays shortstop for the Los Angeles Dodgers. Known for his strong throwing arm, he was awarded the National League Rookie of the Year Award in 2000.

Rodríguez Jr., Paul (1984–). Paul Rodríguez Jr. won a gold medal in skateboarding in the 2005 X Games. Rodríguez was born in Chatsworth, California, and is the only Latino to have a professional model show sponsored by Nike.

CULTURAL CONTRIBUTIONS

Latinos have contributed to the vibrancy of California culture. They have contributed to the socioeconomic, political, and cultural life of California in multiple ways through the arts, culinary traditions, architecture, music, politics, popular culture, and everyday activities that bring life, character, and continued vitality.

In California kitchens, Mexican and other types of Latin American food have become ubiquitous in California; it is not uncommon, especially in southern California, to find Latin American supermarkets, restaurants, *puestos* (food vendor stands), traditional foods, and Latin American candies. Tacos, tamales, empanadas, *pupusas, clayudas,* and various salsas are evidence of a much larger culinary tradition that is the result of the cultural and ethnic hybrid that defines California cuisine.

One notable form of contemporary Latino artistic expression has been muralism. Murals decorate the walls of buildings throughout cities like Los Angeles, San Francisco, San Diego, and San Jose, with portraits of Latinos and images chronicling Latino history and struggle. The artistic creations, like those found in Chicano Park in San Diego, provide living testament of Latino cultural and artistic expression. Located under the San Diego freeway, Chicano Park contains a conglomeration of outdoor murals, sculptures, earthworks, and architectural pieces. The importance of this site was officially recognized as a San Diego Historical Site in 1980. In Los Angeles, works like the Great Wall of Los Angeles, depicting the history of ethnic people of California, is another example of notable cultural contribution by Latinos.

California Latinos have also produced award-winning literary contributions. Poets like Cherrie Morraga and Lorna Dee Cervantes; essayists like Richard Rodriguez; and novelists like Maria Amparo Ruiz de Burton have produced works that capture the Latino experiences of discrimination, exploitation, and perseverance. The literary works by Latinos have contributed significantly to critical reexaminations of feminist theory, gay and lesbian studies, Latino studies, and American history.

Other contributions to popular culture include Latino theater, movie, and film productions. In 1979 Luis Valdez's *Zoot Suit,* commemorating the riots of 1943, became the first Chicano play to appear on Broadway. The performance troupe Culture Clash (Richard Montoya, Ric Salinas, and Herbert Sigüenza), founded in San Francisco in 1984, attained national recognition in 1993 through their sketch comedy television series, also called *Culture Clash*. More recently, *George Lopez*, the syndicated situation comedy that aired on ABC from 2002 to 2007, represents another significant cultural contribution by Latinos in the media. Latinos have also made inroads in the field of motion pictures, an important California cultural industry, producing documentaries and feature films.

Beyond these contributions, the Latino presence in California has made unmistakable linguistic contributions toward increasing the rise of bilingualism in California. According to the U.S. Census Bureau, 26 percent of people in California speak Spanish at home. The prominence of Spanish language throughout the state is evident on billboards, street signs, radio channels, and print media.

The cultural contributions made by Latinos have been so significant that in recent years, scholars and others have used terms such as *Mexifornia* and *Oaxacalifornia* to acknowledge the transformation of California by migrants into a dynamic, transnational cultural space.

NOTE

1. According to a recent survey by the Pew Hispanic Center, Mexicans account for 84 percent of the Latino population in the state. Source: "Survey Brief: Latinos in California, Texas, New York, Florida and New Jersey." Pew Hispanic Center, March 2004. Available online at: http://pewhispanic.org (accessed March 25, 2007).

BIBLIOGRAPHY

Acuña, Rodolfo. "Greasers, Go Home: Mexican Immigration, the 1920s." In *The Latino Condition: A Critical Reader.* Eds. Richard Delgado and Jean Stefancic. New York: New York University Press, 1998, 86–91.

———. "Early Chicano Activism: Zoot Suits, Sleepy Lagoon, and the Road to Delano." In *The Latino Condition: A Critical Reader.* Eds. Richard Delgado and Jean Stefancic. New York: New York University Press, 1998, 309–319.

Alvarez Jr., Robert. "The Lemon Grove Incident: The Nation's First Successful Desegregation Court Case." *Journal of San Diego History* 32 (1986). http://www.sandiegohistory.org/journal/86spring/lemongrove.htm.

Balderrama, Francisco E., and Raymond Rodriguez. *Decade of Betrayal: Mexican Repatriation in the 1930s.* Albuquerque: University of New Mexico Press, 1995.

Blackmer-Reyes, Kathy. "History of MALCS." MALCS Web site. 2004. http://malcs.net/history.htm.

California Latino Caucus. "Historical Overview of the Latino Caucus." 2007. http://democrats.assembly.ca.gov/latinocaucus/history_purpose.htm.

California Missions Tourist Information. http://www.californiamissions.com.

Carrasco, Gilbert Paul. "Latinos in the United States: Invitation and Exile." In *The Latino Condition: A Critical Reader.* Eds. Richard Delgado and Jean Stefancic. New York: New York University Press, 1998, 77–85.

César Chávez Foundation. http://www.Chavezfoundation.org/cesareChávez.html.

Civilrights.org. "Civil Rights: A Chronology." 2002. http://www.civilrights.org/library/permanent_collection/resources/crchron.html.

Democracy Now! "Between 500,000 to 2 Million Take to the Streets of L.A. to Demonstrate against Anti-Immigrant Bill." 2006. http://democracynow.org/article.pl?sid=06/03/27/1449257.

Driscoll, Barbara. *The Tracks North: The Railroad Bracero Program of World War II.* Austin: University of Texas, CMAS Books, 1999.

Ganster, Paul, and David E. Lorey. *The U.S.-Mexican Border into the Twenty-First Century.* Boulder, CO, and New York: Rowman and Littlefield Publishers, 2008.

Garrahan, Matthew. "LA and El Salvador Act over Gang Crime." MSNBC, 2007. http://www.msnbc.msn.com/id/18425327.

Hayes-Bautista, David. *La Nueva California: Latinos in the Golden State.* Berkeley: University of California Press, 2004.

Justice for Janitors. http://www.seiu1877.org/articles/article.cfm?ID=3660.

Marentes, Carlos, and Cynthia Marentes. "We Have Fed You All for a Thousand Years." Farmworkers Web site, 1999. http://www.farmworkers.org/strugcal.html.

Muñoz, Rosalio. "1970: Chicano Moratorium—2005: Latinos for Peace." *People's Weekly World Newspaper,* August 12, 2005. http://www.pww.org/article/view/7591/1/283.

National Park Service. "A History of Mexican Americans in California." In *Five Views: An Ethnic Historic Site Survey of California.* http://www.cr.nps.gov/history/online_books/5views/5views5.htm.

Nevins, Joseph. *Operation Gatekeeper: The Rise of the Illegal Alien and the Making of the U.S.-Mexico Boundary.* New York: Routledge, 2002.

Oboler, Suzanne, and Deena González. *The Oxford Encyclopedia of Latinos and Latinas in the United States, Volume 1.* New York: Oxford University Press, 2005.

Olvera Street. http://www.olvera-street.com.

PBS. "The Border: History (Text Timeline)." http://www.pbs.org/kpbs/theborder/history/index.html.

PBS. "The History of Chávez Ravine." http://www.pbs.org/independentlens/Chávezravine/cr.html.

PBS. "People & Events: The Zoot Suit Riots of 1943." http://www.pbs.org/wgbh/amex/zoot/eng_peopleevents/e_riots.html.

Pew Hispanic Trust. http://www.pewhispanic.org.

Pitti, Stephen. *Devil in Silicon Valley: Northern California, Race, and Mexican Americans.* Princeton, NJ: Princeton University Press, 2004.

Schevitz, Tanya. "California Minorities Become Majority: Census Reflects Surge among Latinos, Asians." *San Francisco Chronicle,* August 30, 2000. http://www.sfgate.com/cgi-bin/article.cgi?file=/chronicle/archive/2000/08/30/MN3103.DTL.

6

Colorado

Tom I. Romero II and Nicki M. Gonzales

CHRONOLOGY

1776	Spanish priests Francisco Atanasio Dominguez and Silvestre Velez de Escalante, along with eight other men—en route to California—lead an expedition through western Colorado, traversing through the San Juan Mountains of Colorado.
1779	New Mexican Governor Don Juan Bautista de Anza, along with 573 men, sets out to attack Comanche Indians, traveling over Poncha Pass, through South Park, and over the Front Range to Colorado's eastern foothills.
1786	Governor Anza negotiates peace treaty between the Comanches and the Utes.
1787	Governor Anza selects site—near present-day Pueblo—to begin first (and last) Spanish settlement in the area; it eventually fails.
1821	Mexico wins independence from Spain.
1822	Mexico opens trade with foreign nations. Santa Fe Trail links the Mexican southwest with St. Louis, cutting through southeastern Colorado.
1833	Bent's Fort is constructed on the northern bank of the Arkansas River, between present-day La Junta and Las Animas. It later becomes an important economic, social, and cultural meeting place—along the Santa Fe Trail—for Anglos, Mexicans, and Native Americans. Mexican government issues the Conejos Land Grant, which sits in the southwestern part of the San Luis Valley and includes today's town of Alamosa. This same year, 80 Mexican families attempt to settle an area

	of the Conejos Grant, but are chased back to Abiquiu, New Mexico, by raiding Navajo Indians.
1842	El Pueblo (or Fort Pueblo), a small village, is founded at the confluence of Fountain Creek and the Arkansas River. One of the founders is a Latina from Taos, Teresita Sandoval; married to an American man, she challenges many of the gender attitudes of the day. The small village of El Pueblo is later home to "mountaineers" and their Latina wives from New Mexico. This multi-racial trading post is a center of trade between whites, Latinos, and Indians. This later becomes Pueblo, Colorado, a city with a long history of Latino settlement and civil rights activism.
1843	Governor Manuel Armijo of New Mexico grants the one million-acre Sangre de Cristo Land Grant to two naturalized Mexican citizens. About three-fourths of the grant sits in what later becomes the state of Colorado, and would become the most contested piece of land in the state's history.
1846	War breaks out between the United States and Mexico
1848	The Treaty of Guadalupe Hidalgo ends the Mexican-American War. Mexico cedes 529,017 square miles to the United States for $15 million, including southern Colorado. Seventy-five thousand Spanish-speaking inhabitants—many in Colorado—become U.S. citizens. The treaty guarantees the civil, political, and land rights of these new citizens.
1849	Latino settlers make first attempt to settle Sangre de Cristo land grant, near present-day San Luis, without the permission of grant owner Car-

	los Beaubien. This settlement fails. Settlements may have existed as early as 1847, on areas of the grant lands. Two permanent settlements may pre-date San Luis: Old San Acacio in 1850 and Garcia in 1849.
1851	Carlos Beaubien brings Spanish-surnamed settlers to found the first permanent settlement at San Luis, Colorado—"Colorado's Oldest Town"—promising them 50–100 varas of private land, as well as access to thousands of acres of mountain land. These communal land rights would become the basis for a lengthy lawsuit in the late twentieth century.
1852	San Luis People's Ditch claims the earliest water rights in Colorado under the doctrine of prior appropriation. Today, the San Luis community still operates an intricate acequia irrigation system, which relies on snow melt from the mountains to irrigate their lowland farms.
1858	Latino settlers establish the Our Lady of Guadalupe Catholic Church in Conejos. It is the first church structure in what would become the state of Colorado.
1860s	Rise of profitable sheep industry in Spanish American villages on the old Mexican land grants.
1860	United States Congress validates the Sangre de Cristo Grant, essentially recognizing Carlos Beaubien's promises to the Latino residents on the grant's lands.
1861	U. S. Congress creates the Territory of Colorado.
1862	At the Battle of Glorieta Pass, the Colorado Regiment helps to defeat the Confederate Army. A number of Spanish Americans from the San Luis Valley fight in the battle on the Union side.
1868	Colorado Territorial Supreme Court objects to the use of the Spanish language in Territorial courts.
1871	El Comité de la Merced (the Land Grant Committee) forms in the town of San Luis, Colorado. It is one of the earliest grassroots political organizations in Colorado, and likely the earliest formal grassroots Latino organization in the state.
1876	Latino politicians, such as Casimiro Barela, Jesus Maria Garcia, and Agapito Vigil play crucial roles in the creation of Colorado's Constitution at the Constitutional Convention and lobby successfully to have the document published in Spanish and English, as well as German.
1880s	Conflicts arise between Spanish American sheep herders and Anglo-American cattlemen over grazing lands.
1900	Sugar beet companies establish successful farms in southeastern Colorado, near towns such as La Junta, Rocky Ford, and Lamar. Mexican migrant workers provide the majority of the labor for the industry by 1920.
1900–1920	Colorado Fuel and Iron Corporation brings the state's first Mexican migrants to work in its steel mills. Pueblo's Mexican-born population increases by 2,500 in 20 years.

1900–1930	About 45,000 Mexicans migrate to Colorado in search of jobs, mostly in the agricultural, steel, mining, and smelter industries.
1903–1904	United Mine Workers (UMW) leads a strike in the coalfields of southern Colorado. Striking workers are replaced by Mexican and Japanese workers.
1910s	Sugar beet companies begin to recruit Latino laborers from southern Colorado, New Mexico, and Texas to work in the fields in northern Colorado. Mexicans fleeing the upheaval of the Mexican Revolution also arrive in northern Colorado to work in the fields, especially during the World War I years. Latino laborers also find work in the railroad industry in Colorado.
1913–1914	United Mine Workers calls a strike in the coalfields in southern Colorado, demanding higher wages, shorter work days, and better conditions. Miners—many of Mexican descent—and their families abandon their company houses and move into UMW-supplied tent colonies.
1914	Ludlow Massacre results when state militiamen descend upon the UMW's miners' tent colony, leading to the deaths of two women, eleven children, five miners, and one militiaman.
1916	Small group of Latino community members leads a successful informal grassroots movement in San Luis against the Costilla Estates Development Company, which had tried to violate the community's legal land rights.
1920s and 1930s	Latinos continue to work in large numbers in the beet fields, living in *colonias* in beet-growing communities. To combat the prejudice and exploitation that they often face, Mexican migrant communities in northern Colorado and nonmigrant Spanish Americans in southern Colorado form mutual aid societies.
1927	Spanish-speaking workers make up 60 percent of the labor in the beet fields.
1930s	Nativist sentiment toward Mexican laborers intensifies. As the Great Depression rages on, whites from the southern plains migrate west and compete with Mexican laborers for farm jobs.
1935–1936	Nativist calls to deport illegal aliens from Colorado put American-born Spanish Americans and Mexican Americans on the defensive. As a result, many support Governor Johnson's call to deport the undocumented workers.
1936	Colorado Governor Edwin C. Johnson declares martial law, ordering the Colorado National Guard to the New Mexican border to prevent migrant workers from entering Colorado. His actions are later declared unconstitutional.
1940s	Latinos in Denver forge interracial efforts with other marginalized groups to advocate for equal civil rights.
1947	Denver's new mayor, Quigg Newton, forms the Mayor's Commission on Human Relations. The commission's work throughout the 1950s and

	early 1960s highlights the intense discrimination suffered by Denver's Mexican American community.
1949	Chama Citizens Committee formed. This grassroots committee organizes resistance in the town of Chama—a small town on the Sangre de Cristo land grant in the San Luis Valley—to protect its rights to use the communal lands of the land grant.
1959	La Asociacíon de los Cívicos Derechos (the Association for Civil Rights) is formed in San Luis to protect the community's unique set of legal land rights on the lands of the Sangre de Cristo Land Grant.
1960s and 1970s	Conflict erupts in San Luis over conflicting notions of land use and ownership, as Latino residents assert their historic communal land rights while large land owner Jack Taylor asserts his private property rights—all over a piece of property that will become known as the "Taylor Ranch."
1965	In *Taylor v. Jaquez*, the Colorado District Court issues a ruling that essentially extinguishes the unique land use rights—granted to the Latino residents of San Luis under the Sangre de Cristo Land Grant. This ruling would be the first of many regarding those legal rights.
1966	The Crusade for Justice is formed largely through the efforts of Rodolfo "Corky" Gonzales. The Crusade spearheads calls for Chicano nationalism throughout Denver and the Southwest.
1969	Chicano Youth Blowouts in West High School and First National Chicano Youth Liberation Conferences. Charges of racism and discrimination lead Denver's Chicano youth to walk-out of their classes and protest discrimination in the public school system. The walk-out culminates in a violent riot with the police. Weeks later, Chicano youth from around the nation meet in Denver and draft *El Plan Espiritual de Aztlán* (the Spiritual Plan of Aztlan).
1970s	Chicano activism spreads to towns on the Western Slope, as activists protest educational and employment inequalities. At the same time, in the state's metropolises, Chicano activists find their influence waning after a series of violent, and at times deadly, clashes with police.
1970	UFW calls for national lettuce boycott. Chicano activists in Colorado support the strike statewide. Dicho y Hecho lettuce strike begins in Center, Colorado, where over 80 percent of Latinos live in poverty.
1971	Escuela Tlatelolco (Tlatelolco School) is incorporated to provide an alternative education for young Latinos centered on developing and nourishing cultural pride, confidence, and developing leadership among Latino youth. El Centro Su Teatro is founded as a Chicano theater organization aimed at building Chicano community through art and culture.
1973	*Keyes v. [Denver] School Board Number One* is decided by the United States Supreme Court. Filed originally in 1969, the case involves a school district that is largely Mexican American. It is the first non-southern school desegregation case to reach the high court because of Denver's "tri-ethnic" racial demographics.

1978	Land Rights Council of San Luis is founded to defend the community's historic communal land rights. The LRC goes on to form coalitions with state, regional, and national civil rights activists and organizations to create a formidable, persistent, and ultimately successful social movement.
1981	The Land Rights Council of San Luis revives its legal battle to regain the land rights lost in the 1965 *Taylor v. Jaquez* ruling, by filing *Rael v. Taylor*.
1983	State Senator Federico Peña, a relatively recent newcomer to politics, becomes mayor of the City and County of Denver.
1987	After a bitter and at times racially-charged election, Peña wins a second term. Under his leadership the city and county become revitalized through the Denver International Airport, the redevelopment of lower downtown (LoDo), and the expansion of support for the arts and diversity.
1993	Colorado Governor Roy Romer forms the Sangre de Cristo Land Grant Commission, whose task is to come up with a compromise solution to the San Luis land grant problem.
1994	The Colorado Supreme Court issues its ruling in *Rael v. Taylor*, essentially sending the case back to the District Court, where Constitutional issues of due process of law would be considered. This ruling allowed the San Luis community to reopen the legal battle for the San Luis community's land rights.
2002	The Colorado Supreme Court issues its ruling in the San Luis land conflict. By this time, the case is known as *Lobato v. Taylor*.
2006	El Centro Su Teatro unveils its plans to build a new, $3.5 million regional Latino performing-arts center—El Corazón de la Ciudad (the Heart of the City)—in Denver's hip Westside Santa Fe arts district.

HISTORICAL OVERVIEW

Spanish and Mexican Eras

The earliest Spanish forays into the land that would become the state of Colorado began as early as 1776—the year North American revolutionaries issued their Declaration of Independence. That year, two Spanish priests, Francisco Atanasio Dominguez and Silvestre Velez de Escalante, along with eight other men, led an expedition through western Colorado, traversing through the San Juan Mountains of Colorado. They were followed in 1779 by New Mexican Governor Don Juan Bautista de Anza, along with 573 men, who set out to attack the Numunah (Comanche Indians) over the Front Range to Colorado's eastern foothills. Governor de Anza also attempted to establish the first Spanish settlement, near present-day Pueblo, in 1787. He did this by first negotiating peace with native communities in the area, which was an extraordinary feat at the time.

Although the settlement eventually failed, it was the first attempt at permanent settlement by a group of Europeans in what is today Colorado. These early racial encounters would begin a complex process of negotiation among racial, ethnic, and cultural groups, which would dominate the history of Colorado.

After Mexico won independence from Spain in 1821, its leaders opened up trade with foreign nations along the newly established Santa Fe Trail. This trade route brought U.S. and French Canadian traders into the soon-to-be U.S. Southwest, altering the power dynamics in a region that had been populated mainly by Mexicans and Native Americans. Places such as Bent's Fort and Fort Pueblo would become centers of cultural exchange between Mexicans, Indians, and Anglos.

By the 1830s, the Mexican Governor of New Mexico began to implement a policy of distributing large land grants to Mexican citizens along its northern frontier—what is today northern New Mexico and southern Colorado. Mexico intended the land grants to form a buffer against a rapidly expanding, Manifest Destiny–inspired American nation. This policy was in place until the beginning of the Mexican-American War in 1846. Present-day southern Colorado included portions of some of the largest land grants: the Vigil & St. Vrain Grant, the Conejos Grant, the Beaubien & Miranda Grant, and the Sangre de Cristo Grant. These land grants left a legacy of legal and political confusion that Colorado courts would continue to grapple with throughout the twentieth century and into the twenty-first.

On these grant lands, Spanish-surnamed settlers founded the first permanent (nonindigenous) towns in Colorado. These settlements would become the bedrock for Latino history and culture in Colorado, especially that which would dominate southern Colorado. The history of Colorado's oldest town offers a glimpse into the richness and complexity that characterized Colorado's early Latino settlements.

San Luis de la Culebra was founded in 1851 by a small group of settlers from New Mexico. The town was situated in the San Luis Valley, on the 1 million acre Sangre de Cristo land grant. Manuel Armijo, Mexican Governor of New Mexico, had issued the grant to two naturalized Mexican citizens in 1843, but immediate efforts to populate the grant were allowed by the outbreak of war between the United States and Mexico. After the two original grantees were killed in 1847, the grant fell into the hands of Carlos Beaubien, a naturalized Mexican citizen of French Canadian descent, who had risen to political and social prominence in New Mexican society. Beaubien would face many challenges as executor of the grant—one of them being the arrival of a new political system.

THE U.S. ERA

As the grant owner, Beaubien not only had to begin fulfilling his obligations to settle the grant, but he had to do so under a new political and legal regime. The

Treaty of Guadalupe Hidalgo ended the Mexican-American War in 1848 and ushered in the U.S. era for Latino Colorado. The treaty ceded 529,017 square miles to the United States for $15 million, which included the southern part of Colorado. Seventy-five thousand Spanish-speaking inhabitants in the region—many in Colorado—become U.S. citizens, and under the treaty they were guaranteed their civil, political, and land rights.

In 1850, Beaubien began efforts to populate the grant land. He offered single men 50 varas of land and married men 100 varas of land.[1] The land was divided in long, narrow strips to conform to the region's natural topography. All strips touched both a river and the resource-rich mountain land, providing settlers with the resources to survive the harsh climate conditions of the San Luis Valley.

In addition to individual vara strips, Beaubien also granted settlers communal use-rights to the mountain lands, which they would eventually name "La Sierra." Settlers could use La Sierra's resources—grazing lands, timber, and plants and animals on the mountain. Beaubien eventually recorded these land rights in a legal, Spanish-language document in 1863. This document would become the basis for the ongoing litigation legal conflict over land rights between Anglo land owners and the Latino residents of San Luis.

Once settled, San Luis residents began shaping a devoutly Catholic community based on communal principals regarding resource use. In 1852 community leaders claimed the earliest water rights in what would become the territory of Colorado. Prefiguring what would become known as the doctrine of prior appropriation in American law, Latinos built an intricate acequia irrigation system, relying on snow melt from the mountains to irrigate their lowland farms.

By the time that Colorado was established as a territory, many Latino communities in southern Colorado were already thriving. A regional sheep industry had emerged in these Latino villages. Colorado's Latinos were also distinguishing themselves in military campaigns in holding the fragile U.S. republic together. In 1862 at the Battle of Glorieta Pass, the Colorado Regiment—which included a number of Latinos from the San Luis Valley—helped to defeat the Confederate Army.

A LATINO POLITICAL VOICE EMERGES

Meanwhile, Latinos were also making waves in territorial politics, as politicians debated the use of the Spanish language in government proceedings. In 1868, Colorado's Territorial Supreme Court objected to the use of the Spanish language in Territorial courts. This was a blow to Latino communities, as they were attempting to find their way in the new Anglo-dominated world of Colorado politics and law.

As communities began encountering the challenges of U.S. hegemony, grassroots organizations surfaced to protect those rights. El Comité de la Merced (the Land Grant Committee), formed in 1871 in San Luis, Colorado, offers one example. It was likely the earliest formal grassroots Latino organization in the state. Community leaders formed this group to defend the community's legal communal land rights, granted to them under the original Sangre de Cristo land grant and protected by the 1848 Treaty of Guadalupe Hidalgo. The communal land at the center of this activity was the mountainous portion of the original grant—named "La Sierra" by the locals.

In addition to such grassroots activity, in the 1870s Latino politicians mobilized their influence in state government. In 1876, Casimiro Barela, Jesus Maria Garcia, and Agapito Vigil played crucial roles in the creation of Colorado's Constitution at the Constitutional Convention. They lobbied successfully to have the state's Constitution published in Spanish, English, and German. This apparent shift in the political winds—from the 1868 Territorial Court Ruling—underscores the ambivalence surrounding issues of race and citizenship in Colorado, as well as the political power wielded by Latino politicians. Interestingly, Latino politicians, such as Casimiro Barela and Agapito Vigil, also lobbied for women's suffrage in Colorado.

Latinos and Colorado's Segmented Labor Force

In addition to political challenges and accomplishments, the Gilded Age and Progressive Era in Colorado also brought industrialization. Latinos played crucial roles in the shaping of a modern industrialized Colorado. Many—especially those who had owned land in southern Colorado and who had depended on small-scale agriculture to make a living—soon found themselves without land. Crop failures, a poor cattle market, unscrupulous Anglo creditors, lawyers, and land speculators all contributed to this loss of land, forcing Latinos to seek work in other industries. Although some Latinos weathered the storms and remained on their own land—raising sheep and cattle—others migrated in search of wage work, to areas where mining, smelting, meat packing, and large-scale agriculture dominated.

During the 1870s and 1880s, when the railroad arrived in southern Colorado, so did the coal mining companies. Latinos flocked to both industries in search of steady work. Those who found jobs with the railroad companies were relegated to low-wage track maintenance or section work. Latinos in the mining industry found similarly unskilled, low-paid work. Yet their numbers in the mining industry, in particular, continued to rise. By 1905, Latinos represented 11.5 percent of all Colorado Fuel and Iron mine workers, and by 1914, that number increased to 17.4 percent.[2] By sheer numbers, they were a formidable presence. Mining companies also looked to Mexican labor to break strikes, especially during the 1903–1904 strikes in the coalfields of southern Colorado.

The first 30 years of the twentieth century witnessed the diversification of Colorado's Latino population, when about 45,000 Mexicans migrated to Colorado in search of jobs. These migrants were fleeing the economic and political chaos of the Mexican Revolution and were searching for opportunity in "El Norte," especially during World War I, when labor demands were at an all-time high. They represented historical experiences that were quite different from Colorado's native-born Latinos, and those differences would play out politically and socially. Nevertheless, both groups sought work in the agricultural, mining, steel, and smelter industries.

By 1900, sugar beet companies, such as the National Sugar Company, were recruiting Mexican and Mexican American labor to work the beet fields in southern and northern Colorado. These companies established successful farms near southern towns such as La Junta, Rocky Ford, and Lamar, as well as northern towns such as Greeley, Erie, and Brighton. By 1927, Spanish-speaking workers made up 60 percent of the labor in the beet fields, as newspapers touted the biological characteristics that made Mexicans well-suited for such labor.

As migrant laborers, Latinos encountered exploitive conditions and intense nativism. They found themselves living in segregated neighborhoods. And their children—considered unsanitary and intellectually inferior—were not welcome in "white" schools.

Meanwhile, Latinos continued to work in Colorado's mines, and they would do so well into the twentieth century. They worked the mines of southern Colorado, around the towns of Trinidad, Pueblo, and Walsenberg, as well as the northern coal fields in and around Boulder County—in towns such as Erie, Louisville, and Serene. Latinos partook in some of the most important labor strikes in the state's history, such as the strike that led to the Ludlow Massacre, in which two women, eleven children, five miners, and one militiaman were killed.

Latinos entered the steel industry in significant numbers. Like mining and agricultural companies, the Colorado Fuel and Iron Corporation recruited Mexican immigrants and native-born Latinos to work in its steel mills. Triggered by the railroad and the influx of investment monies, the city of Pueblo became the iron and steel center of the west—an accomplishment made possible by foreign and native-born Latino labor. In the early twentieth century, the city's Mexican migrant population increased by 2,500, in a period of 20 years.

The smelting industry also drew many Latino wage workers. Smelters sprung up in many places throughout the state, such as Leadville and Durango, attracting Latino laborers. Within a few years, many of these smelter companies began to relocate to Denver to minimize their production and labor costs. As a result of this and other factors, Latinos arrived in Denver in larger numbers around the turn of the twentieth century, contributing to the ethnic and racial diversity of the city. Again, Latinos found themselves relegated to the bottom rungs of society and to certain sections of the city. By the mid-1920s, Latinos dominated the Auraria neighborhood on the west side of Denver. They formed a close-knit community, with neighborhood events revolving around St. Cajetan's Catholic Church.

Repression and Regeneration: Depression and World War II

The Great Depression during the 1930s proved extremely challenging for Colorado's Latino community on a variety of levels. Most obvious was the economic impact of the Depression on Latino wage-laborers, who were often the first employees released as Colorado's industrial enterprises reacted to the economic crises. Moreover, persistent drought, combined with long-term unsustainable land use, exacerbated the dust bowls that afflicted the sugar-beet, cantaloupe, and other agricultural industries in the state's eastern plains. This drove thousands of Latino laborers to seek relief from the state's already over-taxed public welfare system.

Nativism made Latinos the scapegoat for the social and economic disruptions that Coloradoans faced during this time. Such anger intensified when Colorado Governor Edwin C. Johnson declared martial law, ordering the state's National Guard to the New Mexican border to prevent Latino migrant workers from entering Colorado. He also issued a call to deport undocumented workers. In other cases, local newspapers advocated for the internment of Latino "aliens" to "concentration camps." In every instance, United States citizenship afforded Colorado's Latinos little protection against public and private discrimination. Such actions reflected a series of national repatriation campaigns during the 1930s. In response, Latinos in both northern and southern Colorado formed mutual aid societies to combat the prejudice and exploitation that they faced.

World War II proved to be a transformative time as wartime activities in the early 1940s rejuvenated the economy. As a result, thousands of Latinos permanently found their way to Colorado to work in wartime factories, meat-packing plants, iron-foundries, construction projects, federal government jobs, agriculture, and railroads. Denver, in particular, saw its Latino community burgeon from approximately 15,000 persons in 1940 to nearly 45,000 by 1950. Indeed, by the end of the 1940s, Denver possessed one of the largest concentrations of Latinos in New Mexico and Colorado.

Denver's Latinos encountered ambivalence in regard to their status as full and equal citizens. For example, throughout World War II Denver's public bathhouses and swimming pools maintained an informal segregation policy that included separate days for Latinos. Similarly, Latinos encountered recalcitrant landlords who refused to lease or sell residential property to them. As a result, Latinos found themselves segregated (along with blacks and Japanese Americans) to some of the oldest and most poorly maintained neighborhoods in the west and east sides of the city. Yet Latinos also encountered a city that was ripe for change. In 1943, James Fresques became the first Latino to serve on Denver's City Council. Three years later, Fresques's council colleagues voted him as president of the council, where he served until 1958.

Latinos continued to migrate to Denver and Colorado to work in an emerging Cold War economy, in which nonagricultural wage and salary employment rose at twice the rate of the national average. Latinos, however, did not share in the Cold War economic largesse. Remarkably, seven out of every ten residents in Denver's poorest neighborhoods were Latino.[3] By the 1960s, Latinos represented the most impoverished, most segregated, and least employable group in Colorado's largest city.

LATINOS AND RACISM

In response to the racial prejudice that they encountered, Colorado's Latino communities maintained grassroots efforts to strengthen their communities. Though Colorado's Latino community did not have active local chapters of national Latino organizations (e.g., GI Forum, League of United Latin American Citizens) until the middle of the 1960s, Colorado's Latinos engaged in efforts to forge interracial coalitions, with other marginalized groups and organizations such as the Unity Council, Urban League, and the Anti-Defamation League of B'nai B'rith to advocate for equal civil rights. Mexican Americans such as Bert Gallegos, Bernard Valdez, and Lino Lopez were instrumental in the movement for fair employment and fair housing legislation in the state. Other Latinos joined with the state's small, but influential, black community in protesting police brutality and police profiling.

By the 1950s and early 1960s, Colorado's Latinos also recognized the importance of intra-community organization. Accordingly, organizations such as the Good Americans Organization, Latin American Educational Fund, and the United Latin American Organization served as the precursors to a more sustained Latino politics. The United Latin American Organization, for instance, provided insight into the politics that would emerge out of Denver's segregated and racialized barrios. Accordingly, the organization challenged publicly held perceptions about the "criminality" of the city's Latino community. Organizing its members around the concept of *la raza* (the people), the United Latin American Organization invoked a nascent concept of race in its rights agenda, which came to also include discrimination in employment, housing, and public education.

In rural areas, grassroots activities continued as well. Such activity reflected the complexity and confusion created by layers of legal and political conquest in the Southwest. In the 1940s and 1950s, the town of San Luis mobilized again to protect its land rights and to seek legal validation of them. The community formed organizations that would provide a foundation for later, more radical Latino political organizing in the 1960s and 1970s, which surfaced as a result of many factors.

This more radical Latino activism arose in both rural and urban centers in the 1960s and 1970s, with certain areas emerging as hotbeds of Chicano activism. Among rural areas, San Luis saw some of the most intense political organizing. The issue was again land rights—an issue stemming from the Mexican land grant system. In 1965, the Colorado District Court dealt a blow to the San Luis community when it ruled in favor of a process to extinguish the town's communal land rights to a portion of the original Mexican grant, which had become known as La Sierra. Following this moral and legal defeat, organized political activity gave way to vigilante-type violence between residents who refused to submit to the ruling and those who fought to uphold it.

Violence similarly marked the experiences of Latinos in Denver after a series of deadly altercations between police and Latinos in the city in the early 1960s. Such tensions compelled Latinos to consider radically different alternatives to securing the civil rights of the community. The most visible spokesman in this regard was Rodolfo "Corky" Gonzales. A former prize-fighter who had achieved prominence in the local Democratic Party, Gonzales organized Denver and southwestern Latinos around the concept and term *Chicano*.

In 1966, Gonzales and other Denver area activists established the Crusade for Justice (Crusade) to promote the interests and values of the city's Chicano community. Significantly, the organization was founded on the belief that Mexican Americans represented a distinct racial group. In his epic poem "Yo Soy Joaquin" (I Am Joaquin), Gonzales outlines the mosaic of different cultures and different racialized people that make up the Chicano community.

Young Latino activists march in Rudolfo "Corky" Gonzales' funeral procession, April 2005, Denver. Courtesy of Nicki Gonzales, Regis University.

Moreover, the Crusade embraced the concepts of self-determination and nationalism to mobilize the Latino community. In March of 1969, the Crusade organized Latino youth from throughout the United States for the First National Youth Liberation Conference in Denver. During this conference, participants drafted *El Plan Espiritual de Aztlán*–a Chicano declaration of independence. Accordingly, the preamble to the document focused directly on the importance of race to the Chicano political project:

> In the spirit of a new people that is conscious not only of its proud historical heritage, but also of the brutal "Gringo" invasion of our *territories*, We, the Chicano *inhabitants* and civilizers of the northern *land* of Aztlán, from whence came our forefathers, reclaiming the *land* of their birth. . . . We are free and sovereign to determine those tasks which are justly called for by our *house*, our *land*, the sweat of our brows, and by our hearts. Aztlán belongs to those that plant the seed, water the fields, and gather the crops, and not the foreign Europeans. We do not recognize capricious frontiers on the Bronze continent.[4]

The project of Chicano nationalism was further fleshed out in two subsequent National Youth Liberation Conferences, in Denver in 1970 and 1971, where Latino youth committed themselves to creating an independent La Raza Unida political party, to establishing land banks for economic development, and to petitioning the United Nations for partition of 54 percent of the lands held by the U.S. government in the forests of New Mexico. Constant violence between the police and cultural nationalists in Denver's Latino community throughout the 1970s, however, sapped much of the energy out of some of the most transformative elements of Colorado's urban Chicano Movement.

As a result, the battle for equity and access turned to nonpolitical, but equally contested, forums. Particularly acute was the segregation of Latinos in Denver's neighborhoods and public schools, which in 1973 compelled the U.S. Supreme Court to decide the first non-southern school desegregation case in *Keyes v. School District Number One*. One issue that particularly troubled the courts was whether Latinos were to be considered white or non-white for school desegregation purposes. As the court ultimately concluded, Latinos experienced the same consequences as black students of segregation. Though the origins of racial segregation were different, the case revealed that predominantly black and Latino schools received the oldest textbooks, the poorest equipment, and, often times, only vocational curriculums that made the academic level in such schools lag a year or two below that of the white schools.

Moreover, Latino students encountered hostile attitudes to Mexican culture and the Spanish language in the classroom. Tension had become so great that in 1969, hundreds of Latino students walked out of schools to protest such discrimination. The walk-out and subsequent violent suppression by the Denver Police Department highlighted the various ways that Latino students became educationally, as well as physically, segregated from their white peers.

In response, the court in *Keyes* fashioned a district-wide remedy for the entire Denver Public School System that recognized the distinct needs of Latino students in the city. Ordering not only bussing, the court also adopted a plan that provided for bilingual and multicultural programs in the entire district. Though this decision to provide a Chicano-centered desegregation plan was overturned on appeal, Denver's Latinos fundamentally repositioned the way that the nation's courts would understand the legal rights of the community.

Equity and Access at the End of the Twentieth Century

The same radical politics of Chicano nationalism spilled over into rural San Luis when, in 1978, three Chicano activists formed the Land Rights Council of San Luis to fight for the return of the town's communal land rights—rights that were taken away in a 1965 District Court decision. The LRC's founders—Ray Otero, Shirley Romero-Otero, and Apolinar Rael—seized upon the electric atmosphere of the day and formed an organization dedicated to using the legal system as a tool to achieve validation of their lost rights. Twenty-four years after its founding, the LRC emerged victorious. In 2002 the Colorado Supreme Court ruled in favor of the Latino residents of San Luis and validated their communal land rights—essentially overturning the 1965 District Court ruling. The precedent-setting decision changed the way the state's courts view Spanish-language documents, Mexican law and customs, and Mexican land grants. In 2004, the United States Supreme Court further legitimized the State Court's ruling when it refused to hear appeals by the other side, allowing the lower court's ruling to stand. Within hours of the decision, descendants of the original settlers on the Sangre de Cristo Land Grant entered La Sierra for the first time in decades. The San Luis victory stands as one of the most significant events in the history of Colorado's Latino population.

At the same time, Colorado's Latinos made other notable accomplishments. Of all of the achievements, the most prominent was the election of Democratic State Senator Federico Peña as Mayor of Denver in 1983. Peña was born in Laredo, Texas and moved to Denver in 1973 to work with the Mexican American Legal Defense and Education Fund on desegregating Denver's public schools. In 1979 Peña was elected to the state legislature, where, in his second term, he became the leader of the State Senate's minority Democrats. Although a fast riser in the Democratic Party's ranks, Peña was still relatively new to the city and did not have the long-standing political ties of his opponents. In spite of the odds against him, Peña ran his mayoral campaign on a broad-based platform that focused on civil rights, city planning, and economic development. As the centerpiece of his vision, Peña asked Denver voters to "imagine a great city" centered on an ambitious center-city concept that mixed new construction, historic preservation, and racial as well as social equality of the City and County of Denver's diverse groups.

Peña's vision resonated with Denver's electorate. On Election Day in 1983, more than 63 percent of registered voters in the City and County of Denver came out to vote—a record that has yet to be matched in Denver's mayoral history. Peña, with the near unanimous support of Latinos and other groups of color, became the City and County of Denver's first Latino mayor. The Peña administration proved to be a watershed in Denver's history, preparing the city for the challenges of the new millennium. In his 8 years as mayor of Denver, Peña tirelessly promoted nationally renowned large-scale public works projects—including the Denver International Airport, the Denver Convention Center, the upscale Cherry Creek shopping district, development of a new main library, and the completion of the Denver Center for the Performing Arts as the largest theater complex in the nation outside of New York's Lincoln Center—while also driving a realignment in the racial politics of the city. Most importantly, Peña and his administration quietly pushed racial and social equality in all levels of city government. Although Peña's administration was not without controversy, his detractors conceded that he opened "the door so wide that when two black men ran to succeed him, the color of their skin never became a campaign issue."[5]

In spite of the many accomplishments of Latinos at the end of the twentieth century, many long-standing residents and recent Spanish-speaking newcomers to the state continued to encounter political, social, and institutional barriers in the state. As was true throughout most of the twentieth century, Latinos are Colorado's largest and fastest-growing non-White community. Yet poverty, nativism, racial profiling, and educational inequity too often define the contemporary experiences of Latinos in the state. As they have done historically, Latinos undoubtedly will continue to resist their marginalization and stake their claim in shaping the history of Colorado and of the nation.

NOTABLE LATINOS

Sandoval, Teresita (1811–1894). Sandoval was one of the founders of El Pueblo trading center in 1842. This multiracial trading and agricultural community would later be known as Pueblo, Colorado.

Chacon, Raphael (1833–1925). A farmer, rancher, merchant, sheriff, politician, soldier, and author, Chacon's memoirs in the early 1900s provide a unique and rare glimpse of this tumultuous period from a Latino perspective. Chacon served several terms in the Colorado Territorial Legislature. He resided in Trinidad, where he operated a ranch until his death.

Barela, Casimiro (1847–1920). Barela was a politician, newspaperman, community leader, Las Animas County Justice of the Peace, assessor, and territorial representative. In 1875 he served as a delegate to Colorado's Constitutional Convention. In 1876 he was elected to his first term as state senator. He printed two Spanish-language newspapers—one in Trinidad and one in Denver. He served 37 years in the Colorado Senate.

Rael, Apolinar (1899–1993). Rael, a native of San Luis, served as a community organizer, a Chicano movement-era activist, a rancher, and cofounder of the Land Rights Council of San Luis in 1978. He would be the heart and soul of the San Luis land rights movement, even after his death.

Valdez, Bernard (1912–1997). The Manager for the Denver Department of Social Services from 1963 through 1979, Valdez served on the National Council of Community Relations (Department of Justice), National Advisory Committee on Mexican-American Education, and select committees on Educational Opportunity and Bilingual-Bicultural Education.

Sanchez, Francisco "Paco" (1915–1973). Born in Guadalajara, Mexico, Sanchez was the radio voice of Denver's Mexican and Mexican American communities until his death. Along with Levi Beall, Sanchez founded Denver's first Spanish-language radio station, KFSC, in 1954, where he was known for his biting commentary.

Tafoya, Charles (unknown–1999). The executive director of the Latin American Research and Service Agency from 1967–1973, Tafoya was a leader in Denver's American Federation of State, County and Municipal Employees, the AFL-CIO, Latin American Education Foundation, American G.I. Forum, Metropolitan Fair Housing Center, Westminster Elks, East Side Health Board, American Legion, Colorado Business Advisory Council, Adams County Improvement Association, and the Disabled American Veterans.

Gonzales, Rodolfo "Corky" (1928–2005). Gonzales, an author, activist, and prizefighter, organized Denver's and the Southwest's Mexican American community around Chicano nationalism. Born and raised in Denver's east side, where he had a dramatic rise and eventual break with the local Democratic Party, Gonzales and the organization he founded—the Crusade for Justice—symbolized widespread discontent with the tenants of modern liberalism.

Otero, Ray (1945–). Born in Fruita, Colorado, Otero served as an army paratrooper during the early years of the Vietnam War. After military service, he became active in the Chicano Movement. He first became a vocal advocate for educational equity on Colorado's Western Slope. He later joined ranks with Reyes Tijerina in the New Mexican Land Grant Movement. Recruited by local activists in San Luis, Colorado, he relocated to that community and became integral to its land grant movement. As cofounder of the Land Rights Council of San Luis in 1978, Otero would help bring about the legal victory in 2002 that ended the struggle over land rights.

Peña, Federico (1947–). Peña served as the City and County of Denver's first and only Mexican American mayor. A former state-senator and lawyer for the Mexican American Legal Defense and Education Fund (MALDEF), Peña served as secretary of transportation under President Bill Clinton.

Falcón, Ricardo (1950–1972). Falcón today stands as one of the most well-known martyrs of the Chicano Movement. A Chicano activist, focused mainly on Chicano issues in rural northeastern Colorado, he was murdered at age 22 en route to the La Raza Unida Party convention in El Paso, Texas, in 1972. Today, his name is synonymous with the Chicano struggle for justice.

Romero-Otero, Shirley (1950–). A native of San Luis, Romero-Otero first learned of the Chicano Movement through a college Chicano history class. She took what she learned and became an inspiring advocate for the San Luis land rights movement. In 1978 she cofounded the Land Rights Council of San Luis and became a lifelong Chicana civil rights activist and community organizer. She is also a dedicated educator and advocate for educational equity on Colorado's Western Slope.

Falcón, Pricilla (1951–). The widow of slain activist Ricardo Falcón, Pricilla Falcón is a Chicano studies professor at the University of Northern Colorado and a well-known community activist.

Garcia, Tony (1953–). Since 1974, Garcia has served as the artistic director of El Centro Su Teatro—Denver's Chicano theater troupe. In 1991 he became Executive Director, and assumed both titles in 1996. El Centro Su Teatro is the third-oldest Latino theater troupe in the country. Garcia is also a well-respected playwright, author, professor, and recipient of numerous national theater awards.

CULTURAL CONTRIBUTIONS

Whether one is driving along Denver's Federal Boulevard in September, enjoying the smell of roasting *chiles verdes,* or watching the Aztec dancers perform at Denver's annual Cinco de Mayo celebration, one cannot help but relish the rich cultural contributions of Latinos in the religious, leisure, and architectural realms, as well as on the nomenclature of the state.

Latinos have left an indelible mark on Colorado religious practice. Urban Catholic parishes—among them St. Cajetan's and Our Lady of Guadalupe—have served Denver's Latino neighborhoods and provide a forum in which residents celebrate their cultural uniqueness and, at times, organize themselves around political issues, such as civil rights or immigrant advocacy. Traditional religious institutions—such as Los Hermanos Penitentes, a lay brotherhood with roots in rural Southern Colorado in the mid-nineteenth century—still exist. Meanwhile, religious rituals such as "Las Posadas"—the Christmas Eve reenactment of Joseph and Mary's search for shelter—continue to thrive in both rural Latino communities and urban Latino parishes.

The Latino influence on Colorado's cultural celebrations is vast. Denver's annual Cinco de Mayo celebration is one of the largest in the nation, as the city sponsors a three-day fiesta in its Civic Center Park—complete with Mexican music, dances, food, and an outdoor Catholic mass. Although not as large, events surrounding 16 de Septiembre commemorate, in particular, the lives of Latino activists who have struggled for justice and equality.

In the arts, Latinos have certainly made their mark on Colorado. In 1971, Su Teatro was founded. Today it is known as El Centro Su Teatro—the third-oldest

Chicano Theater troupe in the United States. The group is currently raising money to build a $3.5 million arts complex along Denver's Santa Fe Drive, which in recent years has become a haven for art galleries and theater, including the renowned Museo de las Américas.

Colorado is well known for its active lifestyle, and Latinos have contributed to this lifestyle through their contributions to various sports. A long tradition of boxing—both in rural and urban Latino communities—exists, and Latino boxers trained in local programs have achieved national prominence. An equally rich tradition of wrestling at the high school level exists, and Latino wrestlers have consistently been at the top of the sport.

More recently, the meteoric rise in the popularity of soccer in Colorado has mirrored the growth of its Latino population. Some of the best-attended sporting events are those in which Mexican soccer teams play against the Major League Soccer franchise, the Colorado Rapids. Perhaps most telling of all, the world-famous National Western Stock Show in Denver is highlighted by the Mexican Rodeo Extravaganzas that celebrate the significant reliance on Latino vaqueros to Colorado's cattle culture and industry.

To be sure, the name of the state of Colorado, and vivid place names such as La Junta, Las Animas, Buena Vista, Del Norte, Alamosa, and Sangre de Cristo, speaks to the ubiquitous influence of Latino life in the mile high state.

NOTES

1. A vara is an archaic unit of Spanish land measurement. One vara strip was about 33.3 inches wide and up to several miles long.
2. Deutsch, 1987, 26–33.
3. U.S. Department of Commerce, Bureau of the Census, *Current Population Reports*, "Characteristics of Families Residing in 'Poverty Areas,'" March 1966.
4. http://studentorgs.utexas.edu/mecha/archive/plan.html.
5. Borderick and Ann Carnahan, "Mayor Built on Dreams of Great City: Even Detractors Agree He'll Be Remembered for Big Projects, Topped by 2.4 Billion Airport," *Rocky Mountain News*, June 23, 1991.

BIBLIOGRAPHY

De Baca, Vincent C. *La Gente: Hispano History and Life in Colorado.* Denver: Colorado Historical Society, 1998.
Deutsch, Sarah. *No Separate Refuge: Culture, Class, and Gender on an Anglo-Hispanic Frontier in the American Southwest, 1880–1940.* New York: Oxford University Press, 1987.
Gonzales, Nicki M. "'Sin Tierra, No Hay Libertad': The Land Rights Council and the Battle for La Sierra, San Luis, Colorado, 1863–2002." PhD diss., University of Colorado at Boulder, 2007.

Johnston, Dick. *The Taylor Ranch War: Property Rights Die*. Bloomington, IN: Authorhouse, 2006.

Latin American Research and Service Agency (LARASA). http://www.larasa.org/about/History/LARASA-History/history.htm.

Lee, Chungmei. "Denver Public Schools: Resegregation, Latino Style." Harvard University, Civil Rights Project, 2006. http://www.civilrightsproject.harvard.edu/research/deseg/denver_reseg.php.

Lopez-Tushar, Olibama. *The People of El Valle: A History of the Spanish Colonials in the San Luis Valley*. Pueblo, CO: El Escritorio, 1997.

Romero II, Tom I. "Colorado's Centennial Constitution and the Ambivalent Promise of Human Rights and Social Equality." *Albany Law Review* 69, no. 101 (2006): 569–579.

———. "Of Race and Rights: Legal Culture, Social Change, and the Making of a Multiracial Metropolis, Denver, 1940–1975." PhD diss., University of Michigan, 2004.

———. "'Our Selma is Here': The Political and Legal Struggle for Educational Equality in Denver, Colorado, and Multiracial Dilemmas in American Jurisprudence." *Seattle Journal of Social Justice* 3 (Fall–Winter 2004): 73–142.

Vigil, Ernesto B. *The Crusade for Justice: Chicano Militancy and the Government's War on Dissent*. Madison: University of Wisconsin Press, 1999.

7

Connecticut

Tricia Gabany-Guerrero

CHRONOLOGY

1524	Estevam Gomes de Santo (Portuguese Mariner) is sent by the Spanish Crown to explore the northeast coast of the New World.
1654	The General Court of Connecticut becomes so alarmed by the number of barrels of rum flooding into its ports that it bans the import of "whatsoever Barbados liquors" to protect the small distillers of New England and begins confiscating the cargos of "rum runners."
1733	England's parliament passes the Molasses Act, which imposes a duty on molasses in an attempt to control manufacture of rum. New England colonists ignore it, smuggling supplies for their distilleries from the French and Spanish West Indies.
1752–1758	The Spanish Ship Case is heard in the court of New London. A local, unnamed "Spanish Jew" is a key translator in a case involving Spanish ships with valuable cargo from Honduras destined for Cadiz, Spain.
1795	Caesar Shaw, "a free Negro Mariner," receives a Seaman's Protection Certificate in New London. Shaw then sails aboard the Sloop Betsy, John Webb, master, for a voyage from New London to the West Indies.
1796	The cargo of brig *Caroline* (master Elihu Cotton)–on her return to Middletown, Connecticut, from a voyage to Jamaica—consisted of rum and sugar.
1812	Rum and Molasses imported from Puerto Rico to New London, Middletown, and Glastonbury.
1830	The first Latin American student enrolls at Yale University.

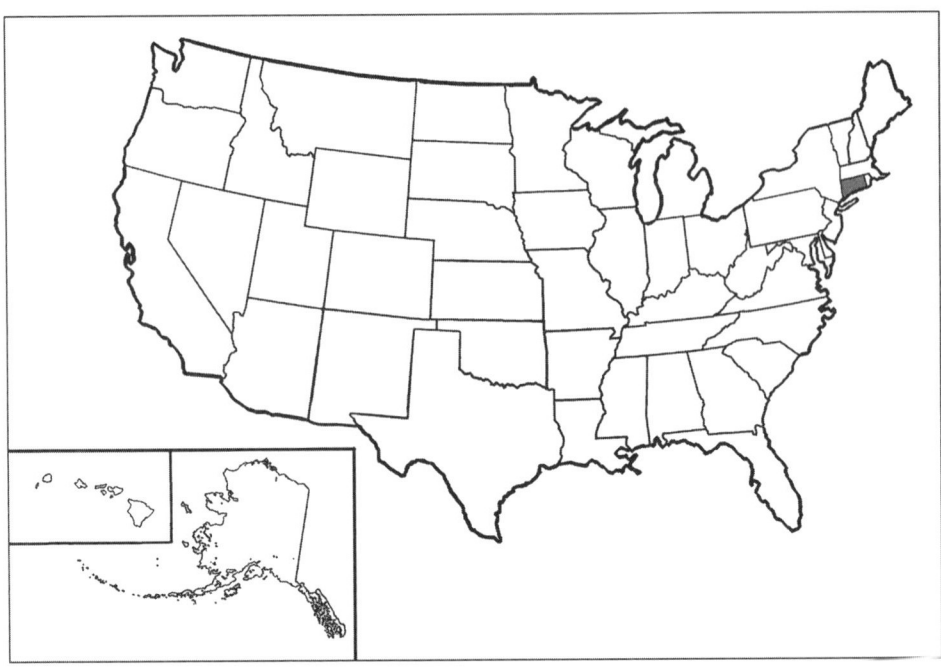

1839	The *Amistad*, a Spanish slave ship that sailed from Cuba, arrives in New Haven.
1847	A logbook kept by Abanson Fournier on board the ship *Stonington* of New London, George W. Hamley, master, for a voyage from Tasmania to the Pacific Ocean whaling grounds, documents that during the voyage the ship was commandeered at San Diego, California, for Mexican war service. Captain Hamley was captured at San Blas, Mexico, and Alanson Fournier took command for the passage home.
1870	U.S. census reveals that New Haven and Hartford rank among the top 50 cities for population in the nation. Both cities register foreign-born populations from Latin America and the Caribbean. New London County records more people (167) from the Atlantic Islands than any other place in Connecticut.
1914–1915	Hiram Bingham directs expedition from Yale University to Peru and excavates Machu Pichu.
1916	A soldier in Bridgeport, who identifies himself as Portuguese (originally from St. Vincent in the Caribbean), serves as a Buffalo Soldier in the U.S. invasion of Mexico at the Battle of Carrizal, Chihuahua, Mexico.
1917	Jones Act: Recognition of Puerto Ricans as having U.S. citizenship rights increases migration from the island to the mainland, including Connecticut.

1952	First Puerto Rican farmworkers are flown in to Hartford.
1967	The Hispanic Center of Greater Danbury is founded by a group of Latino community leaders as a civic center to preserve their languages and culture. The Spanish Action Coalition is founded in Hartford.
1969	Urban protests and rioting occur in Hartford. Junta for Progressive Action, Inc. is founded as New Haven's oldest Latino, community-based organization.
1972	La Escuelita, the first bilingual/bicultural school, is founded in Hartford as a result of the efforts of María Sánchez, Professor Perry Alan Zirkel (University of Hartford), and community members such as Esther Jiménez, Antonio Soto, and Edna Negrón.
1974	Casa Boriqua is created at Yale University to provide cultural center and living space for Puerto Rican students.
1974–1975	The San Juan Center, under the direction of Yasha Escalera, is founded to provide community services to Puerto Ricans. Connecticut Association for United Spanish Action (CAUSA) is founded. CAUSA is a membership organization for Latino social service agencies. Governor Ella Grasso establishes the first Special Assistant for Puerto Rican Affairs under the Governor's Office.
1977	La Casa de Puerto Rico files suit against the Hartford Fire Department for discrimination against Puerto Ricans. Three Kings Day, January 6, is made an official school holiday in Hartford.
1978	The Hispanic Health Council is founded in Hartford to integrate public advocacy; high-level, community-based research; and research-based service to provide outstanding care to the poor and underserved.
1979	The Connecticut Association of Latinos in Higher Education (CALAHE) is established as a nonprofit organization dedicated to promoting the participation of Latinos in different areas of post-secondary education in Connecticut. Membership is composed of Latino and non-Latino personnel and students from institutions of higher and secondary education, as well as other professional organizations that share in the spirit of the organization.
1980	Humanidad Inc. is founded in Rocky Hill to provide bilingual/bicultural educational and residential services, as well as advocacy and health care for persons with disabilities.
1984	American Thread Company closes in Willimantic and many Puerto Rican workers become unemployed.
1996	Connecticut has 13 elected and appointed Latino officials.
1997	The Bridge Academy, an important educational institution for Latinos, is established in Bridgeport.
2001	Eddie Alberto Pérez is elected the first Latino Mayor of Hartford and is reelected in 2007.

2006	Day laborers from Ecuador are detained by immigration raids in Danbury and become known as the Danbury 11.
2007	Connecticut has 27 elected and appointed Latino officials.
	From June 6 to 11, Immigration and Customs Enforcement (ICE) conducts immigration raids that detain 32 people in New Haven after passage of the Elm City Resident Card (New Haven ID card open to all residents). The card provides the opportunity for people without a driver's license or other form of identification to access municipal and banking services.
	Connecticut legislature passes the Dream Act to allow undocumented students, with special criteria, the option to apply for and enroll in state higher education institutions by paying in-state tuition. The measure is vetoed by Governor Jodi Rell.
2008	The State of Connecticut Latino and Puerto Rican Affairs Commission releases a socioeconomic report based on a statewide study.

HISTORICAL OVERVIEW

Connecticut's relationships with Latin American and Caribbean populations are riddled with U.S. historical engagement in the political and economic affairs of the peoples of this geographic region. From the early trade relationships established during the Connecticut Colony to recent demands for low-wage laborers in the twentieth and twenty-first centuries, Connecticut has played an important role in the migration histories of contemporary Latino populations.

Connecticut's largest ethnic minority is Latinos, surpassing African Americans for the first time in the 2000 census. Within this population, the majority of Latinos in 2000 were Puerto Ricans (194,443), followed by Mexicans (23,484), and Colombians (12,009). The Puerto Rican population has historically been and currently is the largest Latino population in the state. The composition and heterogeneity of the Latino population, however, is changing rapidly.

Connecticut individuals of Latin American or Caribbean origin whose populations were estimated to have grown at greater than 50 percent rates during the period from 2000 to 2006 were: Uruguayans, Guatemalans, Brazilians, Ecuadorans, Bolivians, Salvadorans, Argentineans, Peruvians, and Mexicans. The highest population increases, as opposed to growth rates, were from Brazil, Mexico, Ecuador, and Guatemala, in that order. Negative growth rates were registered for people from Barbados, Cuba, Venezuela, Guyana, Chile, Nicaragua, Costa Rica, and Panama.

In Hartford, 40 percent of the population is Latino; the majority of residents is Puerto Rican and second is Peruvian. Peru was the first Latin American country to establish a permanent consulate in Hartford.

Although growing in number, South Americans, especially from Peru, Ecuador, and Brazil, still remain minority populations and are concentrated in the western part of the state. As examples, the largest population of Guatemalans is found in Stamford (3,971), and Brazilians are concentrated in Danbury (4,158). Although research on urban populations predominates in the literature, rural communities in Connecticut have also seen increases in more economically marginalized populations from Latin America, particularly from Amerindian communities. Working on dairy, chicken, vegetable, and flower (green) farms and hidden from public view, it is likely that many rural workers were not counted in the 2000 census.[1] The high cost and scarcity of housing in Connecticut also facilitates cross-border housing arrangements in New York, Massachusetts, and Rhode Island for Latin American and Caribbean day-workers in Connecticut.

Background

The earliest known explorer to the Connecticut coastline was a Portuguese captain, Estevam (Estevão) Gomes de Santo (name changed in Spain to Esteban Gomez). Gomes sailed with Ferdinand Magellan and returned on a mutiny ship. Although he was imprisoned in Spain until Magellan's remaining crew testified to the horrors of the trip, he was given command of an exploratory Spanish voyage to the northeast coast of the New World in 1524.[2] Commanding the ship *La Anunciada*, Gomes produced the most accurate known maps of what became the New England coastlines. Gomes's descriptions and maps were documented by Diego Ribero,[3] and his records were used by Humfray Gylbert (Gilbert). After the initial European territorial disputes[4] over the colonization of Native American lands in New England, and specifically Connecticut, British domination prevailed by the 1700s. The circuits of trade between Europe, the Caribbean, and New England, especially at port centers such as New London, New Haven, and Bridgeport, served as important places for interaction for British commerce. The sea trade of rum, molasses, tobacco, sugar, and slaves was an important part of Connecticut's early history.

Once England declared sovereignty over the Connecticut colony, foreign ships were forbidden to land except in distress. Such was the case in an instance in 1752, when damaged Spanish ships loaded with gold, silver, indigo, and other precious cargo were basically shipwrecked at New London. Although the case surrounding the ship itself is the focus of the pamphlet (Mather Hooker, 1934), the fate of the crew—probably the first Spanish-speaking migrants into the New London region—and an intriguing unnamed personality referred to as a "Spanish Jew" who serves as a local translator, represent the first known instances of Spanish-speaking migrants into the Connecticut region.[5]

The Connecticut colony was deeply engaged with the West Indies trade (over 43 percent of cargo in 1769). Connecticut shipped livestock, packed meat, poultry, flour, wood, and cheese, principally to the ports of Barbados,

Antigua, Turks Island, Saint Kitts, Saint Martin, and Saltanilla. Molasses, tobacco, sugar, and rum were the principal imports. With only a brief decline during the disruptions in trade during the Revolutionary War and the War of 1812, Connecticut continued to strengthen its trade ties with the West Indies during the nineteenth century.[6]

Because tobacco became an important product in trade and labor involving Connecticut, it receives special treatment here. Tobacco is one of the defining commodities for the history of Connecticut Latino populations. Tobacco was cultivated along the Connecticut River Basin by Native Americans long before European colonization, but the demand for tobacco both within the colony and in England grew quickly during the seventeenth century. It appears that as the tobacco industry grew and consolidated, particularly during the nineteenth century, federal taxes on tobacco became an important source of revenue for the U.S. government. Whereas the southern tobacco industry was directly connected to slave labor, in Connecticut the industry appears to have depended on new migrants and, within this group, on children and women laborers for processing.

A hallmark event in the history of relations between the Caribbean and Connecticut occurred when the Spanish ship *Amistad*, which, bound for Cuba with illegally procured slaves from Mendeland (Africa), was escorted into the New London harbor by a U.S. ship in 1839. The ensuing trial of the slaves who had rebelled against their Spanish captors engaged and mobilized the abolitionist movement in Connecticut and centered Connecticut within a national debate about slavery.[7] Although the slave trade was abolished in England and the British Colonies in 1807 and in Mexico in 1829, the Spanish Caribbean colonies, as well as the United States, continued to depend upon this institution until late in the nineteenth century.[8]

Despite the relationship between slavery and commodities, trade between Connecticut and the Caribbean continued to flourish. The trade connections between Puerto Rican and Connecticut ports may have involved direct migration from both Mayaguez and Ponce to New Haven, Connecticut. An example of migration is evidenced by the wealthy Puerto Rican family of José de Rivera Sanjurjo, who established an elegant residence in Bridgeport, Connecticut in 1844.[9]

Connecticut soldiers were directly engaged in the war with Mexico (declared in May, 1846) with recruits in the First and Second Artillery regiments as well as the infantry. The Ninth Regiment (the Irish Brigade) specifically served in the war with Mexico. An important figure in the political history of Connecticut, Major Seymour, was directly involved in the invasion of Mexico City and led one of the charges on the Castillo de Chapultepec. He later returned to Connecticut to become governor in 1850. Later in the nineteenth century (1898), Connecticut soldiers serving in the First Connecticut National Guard were deployed to fight in the Spanish-American War, which resulted in the acquisition of Puerto Rico as a territory of the United States.

Although a few elite Latin American and Caribbean students attended Yale University during the 1800s, it is believed that most migrants to Connecticut were a result of trade relations. It is unclear exactly how many people of Latin American and Caribbean origin lived in Connecticut during its early history, but the 1870 census illustrates that migration had already begun.[10] Ship records from Connecticut ports provide a rich record of passengers and trade relations. Several records show transport of Puerto Ricans to New Haven, specifically.[11] Perhaps surprisingly, New London County recorded the largest number of people (169) from the "Atlantic Islands," presumably the West Indies, in Connecticut.[12] The relationship between the "Atlantic Islands" and Connecticut is perhaps best reflected in the documentation of the importance of trade in rum and sugar. The Connecticut economy in general, and the ports and rivers in particular, focused on the trade in rum, dry goods, tobacco, and sugar.[13]

The early twentieth century is pocketed with Connecticut interaction with the peoples and places of Latin America and the Caribbean. Yale University professor Hiram Bingham directed an expedition to Peru in 1914 and 1915. His partial excavation of the site of Machu Pichu, high in the Andes, resulted in the importation of thousands of artifacts from Peru. The intellectual exchanges as a result of Hiram Bingham's expeditions resulted in long-term connections between Peru and Connecticut. In 2006, Peruvian officials began discussions with Yale University for the return of artifacts about 90 years after Bingham's expedition.

One of the earliest cases of Latin American and Caribbean migration to Connecticut involves a soldier by the name of Apolinario Pinkeiro. Pinkeiro was born on the Caribbean island of St. Vincent in 1893 and registered his ethnicity as Portuguese. He migrated to Bridgeport, enlisted in the Army, and was honorably discharged in 1919. His service is recorded as a Buffalo Soldier in the U.S. invasion of Mexico at the Battle of Carrizal, Chihuahua, Mexico. Pinkeiro's experience illustrates how his multicultural background was translated into one racial category; according to his skin color and the social construction of race in Connecticut, Pinkeiro was considered "colored" and inscribed into the Buffalo Soldier unit, despite his registration as a Portuguese native of St. Vincent.

In 1917, the passage of the Jones Act provided U.S. citizenship rights for Puerto Ricans who migrated from the island to the mainland, including Connecticut. This increased the benefits for laborers who decided to make the transition to the mainland and discouraged the maintenance of residence in Puerto Rico, where neither an elected governor nor the right to vote in federal elections existed.

A military service record for Alescander Cornelius from Bridgeport is an example of the service of Caribbean migrants in World War I. He was born in St. Croise, Virgin Islands, and listed himself as colored and Episcopal. Cornelius was married to Nanie Scott from Danville at A.M.E. Zion Church in Bridgeport and worked as a laborer at American Tube and Stamping Co.[14] Another military service record lists Horton Dockendorff as born in the United States, but his father Abel was from Lima, Peru. Dockendorff characterizes himself as white, Congregationalist, and single. He served as a sergeant in World War I in France and worked as a clerk at Winchester Repeating Arms Co. in New Haven both before and after the war.[15]

When child labor laws forbade the use of children in the tobacco industry, recruitment of African Americans from the South by tobacco agricultural firms supplied the growth of the industry during World War I. During the depression, newly migrated European laborers (youth and adults) also labored in the tobacco fields. Connecticut's child labor laws had no statutory age limits and therefore, up through 1944, Connecticut's farmers brought children, up to 1,000 African American boys each summer from the South, to "work camps" on farms.[16] The University of Connecticut's agricultural experiment stations played key research roles in providing the tobacco industry with enhanced techniques for cultivating shade tobacco and in managing the tobacco agricultural operation.

Relationships between Latin America, the Caribbean, and tobacco growers were evident in the growth of the industry. Although the shade tobacco industry's best profits were during the 1920s, several large companies operated profitable operations in Connecticut within the Shade Tobacco Growers Association. The growers housed workers in migrant camps along the Connecticut River Valley in northern Connecticut.[17] Some of the tobacco was grown and processed in Connecticut, but after World War I tobacco was also shipped to the Dominican Republic, where workers processed the tobacco into smokable commodities that were reimported into the United States for sale. Connections with South America also existed as newly developed Ecuadorian seed cultivars were annually imported to Connecticut.

During World War II, Jamaicans were recruited to work in the tobacco industry in Connecticut and they settled just outside the tobacco farms in Bloomfield. As part of the War Food Administration, Connecticut was one of the largest importers (2,053 workers in 1945) of Jamaican labor to support the tobacco industry. An additional 1,001 Jamaicans were recruited to work in over 24 industrial businesses in Connecticut in 1945.[18] Jamaicans risked their lives to come to work in Connecticut during World War II. After many Jamaicans served building and maintaining the Panama Canal under the direction of the United States, they were shipped on war boats through the Gulf of Mexico, while evading German U-boat attacks, and up the Mississippi River.[19] In 1957 Kenneth Jones, a member of the House of Representatives in the Jamaican Parliament, made a visit to the mayor of Hartford to lobby for more Jamaican workers in Connecticut. He commented on potential tensions between Jamaicans and Puerto Ricans over work opportunities in the tobacco industry and emphasized that Jamaicans would work harder to retain the privilege of annually returning to the United States.[20]

Puerto Ricans were recruited as part of Operation Bootstrap. This industrial stimulation plan decreased Puerto Rican sugar and agricultural production and attempted to stimulate industrial production by granting tax breaks to companies that relocated to Puerto Rico. The number of Puerto Ricans displaced from farming, however, did not match the low numbers and low wages of jobs created through the industrialization program. In order to mediate the growing labor force and income deficit, Puerto Ricans were flown into Connecticut in 1952 to support tobacco, textile, metalwork, and agricultural industries in Windsor, Hartford, and Waterbury. There appears to have been virtually no state-wide planning for the educational, health, and cultural needs of the new Puerto Rican population in the state.[21] The influx of the large number of Puerto Ricans in Connecticut grew exponentially from 1950 to 2007, with Connecticut now ranking with the largest percentage of Puerto Ricans in the United States and Hartford with the largest per capita population outside of Puerto Rico.

Puerto Ricans were employed in four major areas of Connecticut's economy: a declining manufacturing sector, that included the textile industry (such as American Thread in Willimantic); small manufacturing in Waterbury; the poultry industry (dominated by Hartford Poultry[22] and later Kof-Koff Egg Farms); and tobacco farms. Hartford became the closest urban center for Puerto Ricans who decided to settle in Connecticut after participating in the tobacco industry, whereas Waterbury and Bridgeport became destinations for the Puerto Rican out-migration from New York City that largely began in the 1960s. The service industry, tobacco seasonal work, and blue-collar jobs provided the basis for the community's economic survival in Hartford.

The religious community, including both Roman Catholic and Protestant denominations, participated in serving the growing Spanish-speaking community in Hartford. In 1959, the director of the San Juan Puerto Rican Catholic Center in Hartford, Attorney Joseph Kenny, in collaboration with the Connecticut Council of Churches, called for the Connecticut legislature to investigate the living and working conditions of migrant farmworkers. Raoul Mercado, a social worker at the center, also testified that thousands of Puerto Rican migrant farmworkers were forced to live in conditions without running water, sanitation, or cooking facilities.[23] In 1960, The Greater Hartford Council of Churches provided leadership in creating positions to serve the community, at both staff and pastoral levels.[24]

Willimantic's Latino population became predominately Puerto Rican in the 1960s, as they were recruited to work in the thread mill and then in the surrounding poultry and landscape agribusinesses. With the decline and eventual closure of the thread mill, Willimantic became an increasingly economically depressed community. With very few options for advancement in the workforce, many Puerto Ricans remained in the changing poultry industry and found new employment venues in agriculture—such as the mushroom industry (closed in 2007)—education, and the landscape (green) industry.

During the 1940s Cubans were reported to have participated in foundry work in Waterbury.[25] Perhaps this is why Connecticut was chosen as one of the many destinations for political refugees in the 1960s. The largest influx into Connecticut occurred as part of the U.S. airlift of Cubans exiting after the success of the Cuban Revolution. From 1965 to 1966, 1,627 Cubans were formally resettled in Connecticut.[26]

Migration from the Dominican Republic, frequently through New York City, also became part of the growing heterogeneity of the Latino population in Waterbury, Connecticut during the 1960s. In this case, urban women appear to have formed the backbone of this new immigrant group into the Waterbury economy, in contrast with the largely rural farming experience of the first Puerto Rican migrants into the community.[27] Expatriate participation in D.R. elections has substantially increased since the granting of dual citizenship status in 1996.

The Hartford riots, which broke out in 1969, provide a venue for discussing the difficulties that the Puerto Rican community faced in terms of police brutality, political neglect, and community representation. In 1970 the *Hartford Courant* began a Spanish-language column that addressed the specific concerns of the growing Latino community. The first issue noted the continued low levels of Puerto Rican and black employees on the police force. The monumental changes that occurred as a result of Puerto Rican community organization and leadership development in managing community ethnic relations, as a result of the explosive situation in 1969, made possible the leadership that came to fruition in the twenty-first century.[28]

The economic conditions of Latinos in the northeast worsened from 1970 to 1990, particularly in urban areas. This was a result of the general decline in industrialization in the northeast as well as poor economic growth in the United States. Also, during this period it became evident that prison sentences and conviction rates for Latinos in general, and specifically Black Latinos, were higher than the either African American or European American populations in the United States. Perhaps significantly, within the Latino population, Cubans received lower sentences, when compared with similar crimes, than either Puerto Ricans or Mexicans.[29]

The tobacco industry became fertile ground for community organizations, such as the Puerto Rican Migrant Support Committee (CAMP), which struggled to protect migrant worker rights under increasingly difficult field conditions. With the support of the United Farmworkers Union in 1974, the Agricultural Workers Association (ATA) had hoped to unionize the workers. The ATA pulled out of the Northeast, however, before that dream could be accomplished, leaving in its wake the exposure of the Puerto Rican Secretary of Labor's deals with the Tobacco Growers' Association. Gradually Puerto Rico reduced its worker exports to the tobacco industry, down to 1,954 participants in 1984, and the industry in turn sought workers who were not part of the union effort.[30]

The founding of the Hispanic Health Council in Hartford in 1978 marked a concerted effort to address the health problems of the Latino community. The long history of community health research, education, and treatment promoted by the Hispanic Health Council has provided a wealth of resources to mitigate the specific problems of the Hartford community. There is also a tendency, however, within the social work literature about Latinos and health, to fetishize the specific practices of Latinos with respect to alcohol, drugs, and health. This has resulted in an enormous volume of studies that attempt to explain the "drinking behavior" of Latinos without placing this behavior in the larger context of U.S. society, conducting similar studies among other populations, or examining the structural and systemic economic and political factors that impinge upon Latino communities.[31] The Connecticut Center for Eliminating Health Disparities among Latinos, founded by Rafael Pérez-Escamilla (University of Connecticut, Nutritional Sciences) in 2006, seeks to change the research and clinical agendas with respect to Latino populations in Connecticut.

During the 1980s Guatemalan and Salvadoran populations, in particular, found refuge within Connecticut, as their countries were engaged in civil wars. During this period a new trend in immigrant education developed with several academic projects, such as Victor Montejo's (Guatemalan Maya leader) doctoral dissertation about the impact of Guatemalan and U.S. governmental intervention in Maya communities.

Since the major devaluations of the Mexican peso in 1982 and again in 1994,[32] Mexican migrants to Connecticut have increased exponentially. Two towns, Willimantic and Wallingford, are examples of the diversity of this population and the changes in industry that have occurred in the past 20 years. Despite the local high unemployment rate, agribusiness industries recruited laborers from Mexico, specifically the state of Puebla, and largely indigenous peoples from Guatemala. Wallingford's history reflects an interesting twist in migration patterns. Whereas NAFTA provided the fodder for major steel industries, such as U.S. Steel and Bethlehem Steel,[33] to close in major industrial centers, such as Pittsburgh, Pennsylvania, Wallingford's steel industry thrived by importing Mexican workers and specializing in high-technology sheet metals.[34]

In 1972, La Casa Borinqueña (now the Puerto Rican/Latin American Cultural Center) was established at the University of Connecticut to provide support for the growing Puerto Rican student movement. By 1974, the Center for Latin American and Caribbean Studies was formed at the University of Connecticut, offering a major and minor as well as a graduate program concentration in Latin American Studies under International Affairs. In 1974, Yale University students and faculty organized La Casa Boriqua (changed to La Casa Cultural in 1977). Yale University currently offers a BA in Latin American Studies and a graduate certificate in Latin American and Iberian Studies through the Council on Latin American & Iberian Studies of the Whitney and Betty MacMillan Center for International and Area Studies. By 1994 Scott Cook, an anthropologist and former director of the Center for Latin American & Caribbean Studies at UConn, organized the Institute of

Puerto Rican and Latino Studies. Other universities, such as Southern Connecticut State University, now offer specialized programs in Latin American Studies. In 1995 Connecticut was one of the first states in the country to establish a State Commission on Puerto Rican and Latino Affairs. This commission reviews and monitors the impact of state legislation on the Latino community. One of the critical leaders in this institution is Commissioner Fernando Betancourt, who has held his position since the commission's inception.

In 2001, Eddie Perez became the first Puerto Rican and Latino mayor of a capital city in the United States. His victory in Hartford was monumental for the Puerto Rican community, which had gained many leadership seats on the City Council but had not been able to obtain this critical position for Latino leadership in the city. In 2007 Mayor Perez was elected to a second term in office.

During the past 18 years, from 1990 to 2008, the differences between the immigration statuses of Latin American and Caribbean populations working in Connecticut have divided populations and prevented labor organization. Recent crackdowns on "trafficking in persons" by the U.S. Department of Labor (April 2007) on nursery operators (such as Imperial Nurseries in Granby) illustrate one example of a vertically integrated U.S. agro-industry that employs large numbers of Latino and Latin American workers.[35]

New Haven has recently made national news for the decision to provide a city identification card (CID) to all residents, without respect to their immigration status.[36] This controversial measure at the national level has received positive endorsement from immigrant rights groups nationwide. Although the CID provides identification necessary for banking and other services, the CID could also be used to identify those who are undocumented migrants if the data is available under the Freedom of Information Act. Also in 2007, the Connecticut Legislature passed "The Dream Act" to allow undocumented students with special criteria the option to apply for and enroll in state higher education institutions by paying in-state tuition. The measure was vetoed by Governor Rell.

Contrastingly, Danbury is the site of a new policy, approved in February 2008, which consolidates the authority for immigration enforcement in both state and local police to supplement ICE (Immigration and Customs Enforcement). This is the first such policy adopted in the United States. The policy was created in response to the labor recruitment of migrants from Brazil, Ecuador, Colombia, Mexico, and the Dominican Republic to fill growing blue-collar jobs in the Danbury regional economy (population approximately 80,000). Latinos now represent approximately 15.8 percent of the population in Danbury, and this population grew at a rate of 133.7 percent from 1990 to 2000.[37] The visibility of Latin American and Caribbean workers organizing soccer games and waiting on street corners for day-labor jobs at Kennedy Park drew the attention of ICE (Immigration and Customs Enforcement) to Danbury. On September 19, 2006, eleven migrants from Ecuador were detained and promptly shipped to Harlingen, Texas. The National Lawyers Guild, the ACLU, and the Yale Law School Clinic provided legal assistance to the families and workers of the nicknamed Danbury 11.

These two measures have serious implications for the state's growing undocumented Latin American and Caribbean populations, who will form the future Latino communities of Connecticut.[38]

NOTABLE LATINOS

Negrón, Edna (1944–). An educator and a politician, Negrón was born in Puerto Rico and came to the United States in 1955. Her family settled in Hartford, where she attended Weaver High School. Negrón went on to graduate from Hartford College for Women and then the University of Hartford, where she was awarded a BS degree in 1973 (summa cum laude) and an MS in 1974. She holds an honorary doctorate degree from Trinity College. She served for many years as the Coordinator of the Bilingual/Bicultural Education Program for the Hartford Public Schools. As principal of the Ramón E. Betances School in Hartford, she founded the Family Resource Center, which became a national model for family-based, multi-generational social services housed in public schools. In 1989, after a long term on its Board, Negrón was elected President of the Board of Directors of La Casa de Puerto Rico. A year later, Negrón became the representative for the State's 6th House District, after winning a special election for the seat vacated by the death of María Sánchez.

Pérez, Eddie (1957–). Mayor of Hartford, Pérez is originally from Puerto Rico. He graduated from Hartford Public High School and later earned an Associate's Degree from Capital Community Technical College. After spending many successful years as a community organizer, Pérez earned his degree in economics at Trinity College (while working there full-time). He then spearheaded the completion of the Learning Corridor—recognized as a national model for comprehensive community revitalization. Pérez has made history by being not only Hartford's first Latino mayor, but also the first Latino mayor of a state capital.

Betancourt, Fernando (1959–). Executive director of the State of Connecticut Latino and Puerto Rican Affairs Commission, Betancourt develops and recommends public policy as it affects the Latino and Puerto Rican communities throughout Connecticut to the Executive and Legislative branches of State government. Some issues on which his expertise is particularly valued include: welfare and welfare reform; racism; housing rights; Puerto Rico's political history and status; the AIDS epidemic and services; civil rights; language rights; voting rights; discrimination by gender, sexual orientation and national origin; bilingual education; and campaign finance reform.

Pérez-Escamilla, Rafael (1960–). Originally from Mexico, Pérez-Escamilla obtained his BS in chemical engineering from the Universidad Iberoamericana in Mexico City and his masters in food science and PhD in nutrition from the University of California at Davis. He is the principal investigator and director of the Connecticut Center of Excellence for Eliminating Health Disparities among Latinos, and a professor of nutritional sciences at the University of Connecticut. He also holds the title of Nutrition Extension Scientist for the State of Connecticut and a joint appointment with the Department of Community Medicine and Health Care (MPH program) at the University of Connecticut Health Center in Farmington. Pérez-Escamilla is an internationally recognized scholar in the areas of domestic and international community nutrition.

Matos, Kica (1966–). The community services administrator of the City of New Haven. Matos was executive director of Junta for Progressive Action, New Haven's oldest Latino, community-based organization. She is also a clinical visiting lecturer in law at Yale Law School. For most of her adult life, she has devoted herself to advocacy in the area of human rights and civil rights, working in nonprofit organizations including Amnesty International and the NAACP Legal Defense Fund. In 2005 she was the recipient of the New Haven Register Person of the Year award. Prior to joining JUNTA, she was an assistant federal defender in Philadelphia, Pennsylvania, where she represented death-sentenced inmates in state courts and federal habeas corpus proceedings. She has a BA from Victoria University of Wellington, New Zealand, an MA from The New School, and a JD from Cornell Law School.

Cotto, Luis (1967–). Cotto is an artist and Hartford city councilmember (2008–2011) with a long history of community activism in the Puerto Rican community. He is the former co-owner of La Paloma Sabanera, a coffee shop and political center for community activists in Hartford.

González, Jose B. (1967–). Born in San Salvador, El Salvador, migrated to New London, Connecticut at the age of eight, and has been the recipient of such honors as Connecticut's Higher Education Multicultural Faculty of the Year Award. González has published poetry in such journals as *Callaloo, Teacher's Voice, Palabra, Calabash,* and *Colere,* and anthologies including *Coloring Book, Nantucket: A Collection,* and *Latino Boom: An Anthology of U.S. Latino Literature,* which he also coedited. He is the recipient of the 2006 Poet of the Year Award, presented by the New England Association of Teachers of English. In addition, he has contributed critical and nonfiction essays to such journals as New England Quarterly and to National Public Radio. He holds a master's in English from Brown University and a PhD in English from the University of Rhode Island.

Soto, Balam (1970–). An artist, Soto was born in Mixco, Guatemala, into his native tribe Pocomam Maya. In his mixed media images, he has combined shamanic training with his experience as a Native Central American to develop a unique style of contemporary native art. He is the owner of Nahual Balam Studio, where he exhibits and sells his paintings and masks. He currently resides in an artists' community with his family in Hartford.

CULTURAL CONTRIBUTIONS

Vast changes have occurred in the opportunities and cultural venues for Latinos in Connecticut. From cultural clubs, which predominated in the 1950s and 1960s, to the twenty-first century's rich cultural milieu of artists, restaurants, performers, and festivals, Latino culture is thriving in Connecticut.

Specific cultural education programs were initiated in the 1950s. The most notable is the work of the New Haven State Teachers' College, which offered a summer school exchange for teachers at the Inter-American University in San German, Puerto Rico. Citing the need for teachers to better understand the 20,000 Puerto Ricans living in Connecticut, the program provided cross-cultural education for teachers in 1959.[39] Later, federal education grants to the University of Connecticut and, currently, Yale University, provide educational opportunities for teachers to continue learning about Latin American and Caribbean cultural roots.

In the 1960s, articles in the *Hartford Courant* described the growth in cultural opportunities for the Puerto Rican community, noting a Spanish-language movie theatre and pastors (Protestant and Roman Catholic) in Bridgeport, a new "Spanish" restaurant in Meriden, the distribution of *La Prensa* on Hartford streets, and social clubs in Wallingford and New Britain.[40] Over 40 Puerto Rican–owned businesses, including grocery stores, blossomed in Hartford by 1970. *La Prensa Gráfica*, the first bilingual newspaper in New England, began in Hartford in 1973, and local television featured two Spanish-language broadcasts, *Adelante* and *Barrio*.[41]

The current diversity of artists, performers, and restaurants is evident at annual festivals such as the Areyto Latino Festival, established in 1996, which coincides with the Puerto Rican Day Parade every June in New Haven. Many other festivals exist, such as the Puerto Rican Parade (since 1993) in Bridgeport and Three King's Day Parade (January 6) in Hartford.[42] Although WCUM, 1450 AM, is the only known Latino-owned radio station in Connecticut, Univisión and Telemundo have both expanded their markets and coverage of Connecticut. Important writers of Spanish- and English-language fiction and historical and cultural works are part of the growing intellectual cadre of Connecticut higher education, in both private and public institutions. Current Latino performers based in Connecticut include: the Alturas Duo, Ray González, Los Trovadores de America, and Mariano Cotto.

NOTES

1. Gabany-Guerrero, Guerrero-Murillo, and Legrand, 2004.
2. "The Gilbert Map of c.1582-3."
3. The full title of this world map is *Carta Universal En que se contiene todo lo que del mondo Se ha descubierto fasta agora: Hizola Diego Ribero Cosmographo de Su Magestad: Año de 1529. La qual Se devide en dos partes conforme a la capitulcio que hizieron los catholicos Reyes de españa, y El Rey don Juan de portugal e la Villa de tordessilas: Año de 1494* [General chart containing the whole of the world that has hitherto been discovered; complied by Diego Ribero, cosmographer to His Majesty, which is divided into two parts according to the agreement made by the Catholic Majesties of Spain and King John of Portugal at Tordessilas, A.D. 1494].

4. England, the Netherlands, Spain, and France.

5. More research needs to be conducted on ship logs, specifically from Caribbean and Latin American locations to Connecticut ports, for the picture of trade in persons and commodities to be complete.

6. Daniels, 1980, 429–450.

7. Horton and Horton, 1997.

8. Brazil was the last country in the Americas to abolish slavery (1888).

9. Glasser, 2005, 176.

10. Detailed research on surnames for ship passenger lists and census data in Connecticut is needed to provide a more detailed view of this important history.

11. Glasser, 2005. "Lists of ships' passengers from the 1800s show that other visitors and settlers went back and forth between Connecticut and Puerto Rican ports. Ships ferried wealthy tourists, merchants, planters, and skilled workers of both nationalities between Bridgeport or New Haven, Connecticut, and Mayagüez, Ponce, or Guayanilla, Puerto Rico . . . New Haven census records for 1860 show that ten Puerto Ricans lived in the city at that time. One of them was Augustus (probably Augusto) Rodríguez, who joined the Fifteenth Connecticut Regiment in 1862. Fighting in the Civil War, Rodríguez reached the rank of lieutenant before he was mustered out in June of 1865. When he returned from battle, Rodríguez became a New Haven firefighter."

12. Migration from the Atlantic Islands was also recorded for the cities of Hartford and New Haven.

13. A century ago, the Connecticut River was an important artery in the transportation system of all this section of New England, and the stories of the time when the boatman's song echoed through the valley, instead of the locomotive whistle or the honk of the automobile driver, are increasingly interesting as those days recede further into the past, and the present generation knows less of the problems of those days. In about 1970, Sumner L. Howard, recorded the following:

> The boats carried down loads of freestone, shingles and other produce, bringing back heavy freight such as iron, sugar, molasses, grindstones, salt, etc., while a specialty was made of new rum during the last of June . . . At practically all points along the river, where boats were supposed to stop, the country stores carried a stock of rum in addition to their other merchandise. There was a store building about where Granger Block on Westminster Street now stands, the front door opening on Westminster Street and a flight of stairs leading down the back side to the canal. They sold rum, in addition to dry goods, and often disposed of a barrelful in one morning to the boatmen and rafts men. This rum was made from distilled molasses and seldom caused drunkenness or fighting. It was sold at twenty-five cents a gallon, or three cents a tumbler (1/2 pint). Brandy, gin, and West India rum sold at five cents a glass, while whiskey was unknown. In spite of the large amounts of liquor consumed, there was not as much drunkenness as at *the present time.*

14. Archive of the State Library of Connecticut, RG 12: War Records Department, World War I Veterans, Box 46.

15. Archive of the State Library of Connecticut, RG 12: War Records Department, World War I Veterans, Box 31.

16. Tucker, 1994.

17. Glasser, 2005.

18. Ransom, 1946.

19. For detailed oral histories see Fay Clarke Johnson's book *Soldiers of the Soil*.

20. *Hartford Courant*, "Jamaica Political Figure is Welcomed by Mayor," February 15, 1957.

21. In an article by Craig Pearson, "'Too Little, for Too Many' Brings Puerto Rican Migrants to State" (*Hartford Courant*, May 2, 1954), a stereotypical view of Puerto Ricans was presented to the public that included the U.S. political perspective that Puerto Rico is devoid of natural resources.

22. Hartford Poultry was the largest supplier of kosher chickens in the state of Connecticut.

23. Kravsow, 1959.

24. *Hartford Courant*, "Worker Named by Council for Puerto Ricans," August 6, 1960.

25. Glasser, n.d.

26. Thomas, 1967.

27. Glasser, n.d. "Puerto Ricans had struggled in the 1950s to form cultural beachheads such as St. Cecilia's Church, for many years the only Hispanic parish in Waterbury. Dominicans and other Latinos slowly began to enter these institutions and make them more multicultural. After a long time of participating side by side with Puerto Ricans in church and watching the development of Dominican communities in other parts of the state or region, a group of Dominican women decided to celebrate their culture's uniqueness within the larger context of *hispanidad*. In the late 1980s, they started the celebration of the festival of the Virgen de la Altagracia, the patron virgin of the Dominican Republic, inside St. Cecilia's Church."

28. Cruz, 1997.

29. Steffensmeier and Demuth, 2000.

30. Glasser, 2008.

31. See, for example, Christina S. Lee.

32. Vidal, 1994.

33. Bethlehem Steel moved to the port city of Lazaro Cárdenas, Michoacán, Mexico.

34. Allegheny Ludlum Stainless Steel operates in Wallingford and Waterbury.

35. Bernstein, 2007.

36. Carpenter, 2007. "Besides serving as identification for bank services and if police ask for ID, the card can be used at municipal locations such as libraries, beaches, and parks—and as a debit card for city parking meters and at 15 downtown shops."

37. Vásquez, 2003.

38. Spencer, 2008.

39. *Hartford Courant*, "College offers Summer Study in Puerto Rico," March 5, 1959.

40. Pearson, 1954.

41. See Cruz, 1997, 63.

42. For details on the history of specifically Puerto Rican cultural celebrations, see Glasser's *Aquí me quedo*.

BIBLIOGRAPHY

Archive of the State Library of Connecticut. RG 12: War Records Department. World War I Veterans. Box 31.

Archive of the State Library of Connecticut. RG 12: War Records Department. World War I Veterans. Box 46.

Atwood, Frank. "Connecticut Farm News." *Hartford Courant*, March 25, 1953.

Bernstein, Nina. "Suit Charges That Nursery Mistreated Laborers." *New York Times*, February 7, 2007.

Bishop, R.P. "Lessons of the Gilbert Map." *Geographical Journal* 72 (1928): 237–243.

Carpenter, Caitlin. "New Haven Opts to Validate its Illegal Residents." *Christian Science Monitor*, July 17, 2007.

Collection of Louis F. Middlebrook. Mystic Seaport Museum. Collection 50, Box 1, Folder 1.

Cruz, José. "María Sánchez: Godmother of the Puerto Rican Community." *Hog River Journal*, Summer 2003. http://www.ctheritage.org/encyclopedia/HRJ/MariaSanchez.htm (accessed March 19, 2008).

———."A Decade of Change: Puerto Rican Politics in Hartford, Connecticut, 1969–1979." *Journal of American Ethnic History* 16, no. 3 (1997): 45–81.

Daniels, Bruce C. "Economic Development in Colonial and Revolutionary Connecticut: An Overview." *William and Mary Quarterly* 37 (1980): 429–450.

Gabany-Guerrero, Tricia, Narcizo Guerrero-Murillo, and Ana Legrand. "Educational Needs Assessment of Non-English Speaking Agricultural Workers in Connecticut: A Pilot Study." Paper presented to the Cooperative Extension Service at the University of Connecticut, Storrs, October 22, 2004.

Glasser, Ruth. "From 'Rich Port' to Bridgeport: Puerto Ricans in Connecticut." In *The Puerto Rican Diaspora: Historical Perspectives*. Eds. Carmen Teresa Whalen and Victor Vázquez-Hernández. Philadelphia, PA: Temple University Press, 2005, 174–199.

———. "Waterbury, Connecticut: An Evolving, Multi-Latino City." Working paper. University of Connecticut, Urban Studies Program. N.d.

———. "Tobacco Valley: Puerto Rican Farm Workers in Connecticut." *Hog River Journal*, March 2008. http://www.hogriver.org/issues/v01n01/tobacco_valley.htm.

———. *Aquí me quedo: Puerto Ricans in Connecticut*. Hartford, CT: Connecticut Humanities Council, 1997.

Hartford Courant. "College Offers Summer Study in Puerto Rico." March 5, 1959.

———. "Jamaica Political Figure Is Welcomed by Mayor." February 15, 1957.

———. "'Too Little, for Too Many' Brings Puerto Rican Migrants to State." May 2, 1954.

———. "Worker Named by Council for Puerto Ricans." August 6, 1960.

Hooker, Roland Mather. *The Spanish Ship Case*. Hartford, CT: Tercentenary Commission of the State of Connecticut, Committee on Historical Publications, 1934.

Horton, James Oliver, and Lois E. Horton. *In Hope of Liberty: Culture, Community, and Protest among Northern Free Black*. New York: Oxford University Press, 1997.

Johnson, Fay Clarke. *Soldiers of the Soil*. New York: Vantage Press. 1995.

Judd, Sylvester. *History of Hadley*. Springfield, MA: H.R. Huntting & Co., 1905.

Kravsow, Irving. "Probe into Farm Conditions: Asked by Puerto Rican Center." *Hartford Courant*, March 7, 1959, 1A.

Lee, Christina S., "Social Processes Underlying Acculturation: A Study of Drinking Behavior among Immigrant Latinos in the Northeast United States." *Contemporary Drug Problems* 33 (2006): 585–609.

Logbook of *Stonington* (Ship), 1846, February 28–1847, September 29. Mystic Seaport Museum.

Manifests and entry papers. *Caroline* (Brig). Mystic Seaport Museum Records. 1796.

Manuel-Scott, Wendi. "Soldiers of the Field: Jamaican Farm Workers in the United States during World War II." PhD diss., Howard University, Washington, DC, 2003.

Pearson, Craig M. "'Last Migration' Brings 12,000 Puerto Ricans to Connecticut, Revives Old Problem." *Hartford Courant*, April 25, 1954, A1.

Ransom III, Reverdy C. "Jamaican Workers in the State of Connecticut." *Journal of Negro Education* 15 (1946): 717–721.

Shaw, Ceasar. "Seaman's Protection Certificate." Mystic Seaport Museum Records. December 30, 1795.

Spencer, Mark. "Cordial Talk on a Hot-Button Issue." *Hartford Courant*, March 13, 2008.

Steffensmeier, Darrell, and Stephen Demuth. "Ethnicity and Sentencing Outcomes in U.S. Federal Courts: Who Is Punished More Harshly?" *American Sociological Review* 65, no. 5 (2000): 705–729.

Thomas, John F. "Cuban Refugees in the United States." *International Migration Review* 1 (1967): 46–57.

Tucker, Barbara M. "Agricultural Workers in World War II: The Reserve Army of Children, Black Americans, and Jamaicans." *Agricultural History* 68 (1994): 54–73.

U.S. Census Bureau. U.S. Census 1870. Selected Nativities by Counties. Table VII.

Vásquez, Daniel W. "Latinos in Danbury, Connecticut." Latinos in New England. Boston, MA: University of Massachusetts, Mauricio Gastón Institute for Latino Community Development and Public Policy, 2003. http://www.gaston.umb.edu/

Vidal, Gore. "The Economy at a Time of Crisis: Mexico, 1995." *Mondes en Developpement* 22 (1996): 77–84.

8

DELAWARE

Milton R. Machuca

CHRONOLOGY

1525	Spanish explorer Estevan Gomes passes by and notes the mouth of Delaware Bay.
	Slave trader Pedro de Quejo's expedition reaches the entrance of Delaware Bay and lands on the Delmarva Peninsula.
1639	The first African on the Delaware, Anthony Swart, is brought from the Caribbean to Fort Christina.
1763–1767	Charles Mason and Jeremiah Dixon survey the line later named after them to resolve a border dispute between William Penn and Lord Baltimore that had lasted for almost 100 years.
1950s	Puerto Rican contract laborers arrive in Delaware to follow employment opportunities in agriculture and industry.
1961	The Puerto Rican Association meets in the basement of Saint Paul's Roman Catholic Church, in Wilmington.
1969	The Latin American Community Center (LACC) is founded by a group of Puerto Ricans.
1970	The state population is 548,104 people, of whom 4,820 are Latinos.
	LACC's La Fiesta child care center opens in Wilmington.
1977	The Delaware and Pennsylvania Advisory Committees to the U.S. Commission on Civil Rights publish *The Working and Living Conditions of Mushroom Workers*, a report on the mushroom industry in Chester County, Pennsylvania, and New Castle County, Delaware.
1980	The state population is 594,338 people, of whom 9,540 are Latinos.

1985	Governor's Advisory Council on Hispanic Affairs (GACHA) is formed by an executive order signed by Governor Michael Castle.
1990	The state population is 666,168 people, of whom 15,510 are Latinos.
1995	An executive order is reissued by Governor Thomas R. Carper to continue the Governor's Advisory Council on Hispanic Affairs (GACHA).
2000	The state population is 783,600 people, of whom 37,321 are Latinos.
2002	LACC receives a 3-year JUMP mentoring grant totaling $220,000. LACC receives a 5-year, $1.3 million federal education grant (administered by the State Department of Education) under the auspices of the Leave No Child Behind program.
2003	LACC operates with a $2.2 million budget and offers over 40 programs to the community.
2006	The state population is 865,051 people, of whom 56,131 are Latinos. On May 1 (May Day), after a season of protest and as part of the national immigrant general strike, or "A Day without Immigrants," four of the five poultry-processing plants in Sussex County shut down.

HISTORICAL OVERVIEW

Efforts by Spain in the sixteenth century to establish, and later maintain, a foothold along the Atlantic coast between Florida and Chesapeake Bay—a region considered vital to the protection of Spain's successful Caribbean establishments—

brought the earliest Spanish-speaking peoples to present-day Delaware. In 1525 Pedro de Quejo, a Spanish slave trader, piloted a preliminary expedition composed of two caravels and some 60 crewmen for Lucas Vásquez de Ayllón, one of the Auditors of Hispaniola. The purpose was to explore the coastal area of land granted to Ayllón by the King of Spain in search of the mythical land of Chicora. It appears that Quejo entered present day Delaware Bay and sailed along much of its western side, then passed down the east coast of the Delmarva Peninsula to the lower portion of Chesapeake Bay.[2]

After this brief incursion, Spanish-speaking peoples would not return to Delaware until the mid-twentieth century. Meanwhile, during the 400 years in between, Dutch, Swedes, Finns, and Britons settled and colonized the region, in the process decimating, dispossessing, and displacing the Algonquin-speaking group known as Leni-Lenape, Delaware's aboriginal population.[3] Thus from its very beginnings, Delaware, one of the original thirteen British colonies, had a remarkably varied and complex ethnic composition and settlement.

Next to Rhode Island, Delaware[4] is the second-smallest state in the Union. Delaware is made up of three counties: Kent in the center (800 square miles, established in 1664), New Castle in the north (494 square miles, established in 1680), and Sussex in the south (1,196 square miles, established in 1664). This small state, in the middle of the United States Atlantic Seaboard, not quite part of the South nor the North because of the way the Mason-Dixon Line bisects it, has until recently often been isolated and in many ways even deemed an unimportant place. The Mason-Dixon Line proved to be an effective cultural boundary in the state; key issues in U.S. history have consistently divided the state's population. The Civil War, for example, divided sympathies in the state between Union and Confederation to the point that it resembled a miniature version of the country.[5]

For Latinos, Delaware was not a traditional point of destination; however, as explained below, this situation changed rapidly during the last quarter of the twentieth century.

Puerto Ricans were the first Latino group to arrive in the area. They came in the late 1940s (after War World II) and early 1950s as contract laborers hired to work in the agricultural and industrial sectors. These workers provided the base from which sprang the Puerto Rican community in Delaware. Some of them settled in Wilmington and Newark (New Castle County), where they shared the historic misfortunes and hopes of the Irish, Germans, Poles, Italians, Jews, Ukrainians, rural African Americans, and other newcomers who had arrived over the past century and a half. Puerto Ricans were the dominant Latino presence until the mid to late 1970s (122,000 persons migrated between the 1940s and 1970s).

During this period, mushroom growing in New Castle County (although not as big as in neighboring Chester County, Pennsylvania) attracted Puerto Rican workers.

But in the mid-1970s and 1980s, the pull for jobs in the local mushroom industry coupled with the push of a declining rural economy in Mexico contributed to the rapid arrival of Mexican workers to Chester County, Pennsylvania, and New Castle County, Delaware.

In 1977, the Delaware and Pennsylvania Advisory Committee to the United States Commission on Civil Rights published its report on the mushroom industry in Chester County, Pennsylvania, and New Castle County, Delaware (hereafter referred to as 1977 DPAC Report). This report indicated that in the 1970s, there were 25 to 50 mushroom growers in New Castle County whose labor force was composed of Puerto Rican and Mexican workers. The Mexican worker profile was quite similar to those of earlier migratory waves to the state: they were mostly young, male, single, and Spanish speaking. A few were married, and there were even fewer women. Assessing accurately how many Mexicans were working in the industry is simply impossible. The 1977 DPAC Report recognized that there were no accurate statistics for mushroom workers in general, let alone for Mexican workers. The American Mushroom Institute calculated a figure of between 2,000 and 3,000 workers. For the next two decades, however, the regional mushroom industry experienced repeated shocks, and it had to adapt and reconfigure over and over again to changing economic and social conditions. It succeeded in Pennsylvania, but it almost disappeared in Delaware.[6]

In the south of the state a different story started to unfold in the late 1980s and early 1990s. Although during this period each county in the state exhibited faster population growth than the rest of the nation, it was Sussex County that grew the fastest, at a rate double the growth of Delaware as a whole. New residential housing near the inner bay attracted retirees to homes near the beaches, and low-paying jobs on farms and in chicken-processing plants brought a wave of Latin American migrants.[7] Initially, migrant workers—including Mexicans and Mexican Americans, Central Americans (mostly Indigenous Mayans from Guatemala), and some Haitians—came from Florida and Texas to work in the seasonal fruit-and-vegetable farms in the county.[8] Some of them were hired at the border in the late 1980s under H2B visas, some were beneficiaries of the 1986 Immigration Reform and Control Act or IRCA, and others were undocumented individuals fleeing civil unrest in their countries.[9] Some of these workers, mostly Guatemalans, broke away from the stream each summer, preferring year-round employment in the county's poultry-processing plants.

Although the Latino population is still higher in the northern part of the state (New Castle County), a new Latino community has been forming for the past 20 years in the south. Their impact in the area is unquestionable, and they have affected housing, language, business, and culture. Non-Latino residents were caught by surprise in this seemingly overnight process and found themselves a numerical minority. Tensions have been inevitable. In the post-9/11 world, immigration status has become an issue; for example, Delaware's governor, Ruth Ann Minner, shortly after 9/11, blocked the issuance of vehicle tags to individuals who could not prove their citizenship with a Social Security card.[10]

Despite these difficulties the Latino community in the state has flourished during the past decade as never before. In Delaware the reported migrant population has nearly doubled to 67,000 since 2000. Although this figure includes other groups (for example, the Chinese and eastern Europeans), a significant percent of this population is Latino. Compared to other areas of the country these figures may not look so significant, but they have been enough to bring about an unprecedented change to many towns in the state.

Census figures reveal interesting changes and trends in the Latino population in Delaware in the past four decades. In 1970, Delaware had 548,104 residents; 4,820 of these were Latinos (0.87 percent of the total population), concentrated in New Castle County only, mostly in Newark and Wilmington. In 1980, the total state population was 594,339 residents (an increase of 8.4 percent), of which 9,540 were Latinos (1.61 percent of the total population and almost double that of the previous decade). New Castle County still had the lead (6,825), followed by Kent County (1,800, mostly in Dover) and Sussex County (915, mostly in Georgetown). In 1990, the state population was 666,168 (an increment of 12 percent), and the Latino population had reached 15,510 (2.33 percent of the total population and an increment of 65 percent compared to the previous decade). Distribution by county maintained the previous trend: New Castle County (11,075), followed by Kent County (2,854), and Sussex County (1,221).

A big change occurred between 1990 and 2000. Whereas the total population of the state was 783,600 residents (an increment of 17 percent), Delaware's Latino population grew 140 percent, to 37,321 residents. This population was also distributed differently when compared to the previous trend: New Castle County (26,307), followed by Sussex County (6,736) and Kent County (4,278).[11]

NOTABLE LATINOS

Villamarin, Juan A. (1939–). Villamarin is an emeritus professor of anthropology and former chairperson of the Department of Anthropology at the University of Delaware. He continues to mentor students and teach some courses at the university. Villamarin guides undergraduate and graduate students, ushering in class after class of Latino professionals to the Delaware arena.

Miró, Joseph (1946–). Miró, a Republican state representative in Delaware of Cuban ancestry, spent 31 years as a teacher for the Christina School District/Wilmington School District and served as chair of the World Language Department. After retiring, he became president and consultant of Miró Diversified Services. He serves in many leadership roles, including state representative (R), 22nd District; vice chair of the

Health and Human Development Committee; chair of the Business/Corporations/Commerce Committee; chair of the Homeland Security Committee; and member of the Education Committee, Bond Bill Committee (alternate), Joint Finance Committee (alternate), and Appropriations Committee (alternate). He previously served as councilman in the New Castle County Council, 3rd District.

Rivera, Jaime "Gus" (1950–). Rivera, a physician, was born in Puerto Rico and migrated to the United States in 1957. He graduated from Aviation High School in Queens, New York. He attended the City College of New York, graduating with honors in 1972. He received his MD degree from Harvard Medical School in 1976 and completed residency training in pediatrics in 1979. In 1972, Rivera cofounded the Latino Boricua Health Organization at Harvard Medical School. This organization currently has 13 chapters in medical schools across the country and is dedicated to increasing Latino enrollment in medical school and serving their needs while in medical school. Rivera serves as an appointed member of Delaware governor Ruth Ann Minner's administration in the capacity of chairman of the Governor's Advisory Council on Hispanic Affairs. He serves on the board of directors of the United Way of Delaware, and he is a director of the Grand Opera of Delaware. Rivera is cofounder of the Delaware Hispanic Political Action Committee and the Delaware Friends of ASPIRA Committee.

Pilonieta Blanco, Gabriel (1955–). Gabriel Pilonieta Blanco, originally from Venezuela, is a historian. He worked as a reporter after coming to the United States and then decided to start his own publication, *El Tiempo Hispano*, a weekly bilingual newspaper. Pilonieta renders an invaluable service to the Delaware region in that he provides the community with a forum to highlight accomplishments, express concerns, and debate important issues.

Rodríguez, Havidán (1959–). Rodríguez, born in Puerto Rico, is a sociologist with academic training in demography and statistics. He has expertise in both quantitative and qualitative research methodology. Rodríguez is the University of Delaware's vice provost of Academic Affairs and International Programs and the former director of the Disaster Research Center (DRC). He joined the University of Delaware in 2003 as director of the DRC and professor in the Department of Sociology and Criminal Justice. Rodríguez has published in the areas of disasters, diversity in higher education, and Latinos in the United States.

Delgado, Milton (1962–). Born in New York City, Delgado is a U.S. Navy veteran, a former instructor at the U.S. Naval Academy. He works for Nemours Health and Prevention Services as a community relations associate. He helps community leaders build an infrastructure that will sustain community-based, long-term educational programs focused on healthy eating and physical activity. Delgado sits on the board of directors of the Latin American Community Center and of Westside Health, and he chairs the Health Committee for the Governor's Advisory Council on Hispanic Affairs.

Matos, Maria (1962–). Matos, a native of Puerto Rico, has been the executive director of the Latin American Community Center (LACC) in Wilmington since 1995. Major accomplishments include the selection of LACC by the National Council of La Raza as the regional affiliate of the year for 2005 and 2006; the development of a high school reentry program at LACC to reduce the number of high school dropouts among Latino youth; and the designation as a supplementary education provider for the state of Delaware.

CULTURAL CONTRIBUTIONS

Latinos have indisputably had a strong influence on the cultural landscape in Delaware. Earliest efforts to organize the Latino presence in the state resulted in the creation of the Latin American Community Center (LACC), which was founded in 1969 by a small group of Puerto Rican migrants seeking to address the immediate needs of members of their community as they adapted to life in a new country and, in most cases, to a new language. Its main offices are located in Wilmington. LACC offers different programs aimed at different age groups and needs, including La Fiesta I, Early Childhood Assistance Program (ECAP/La Fiesta II), Adult Education Center, DeLead Delaware, and La Oficina de los Niños. LACC organizes three annual events: the Outstanding Hispanic Student Recognition Awards (April/May), the Hispanic Heritage Month Open House (September), and the Grand Ball (September/October).

In 1977 a group of Puerto Ricans started the Semana Hispana, a weeklong celebration that consisted of a Food Festival on Market Street, the Miss Hispanic Delaware Pageant at Saint Paul's Catholic Church, a Grand Ball, a three-mile run, and the Puerto Rican Parade. Thirty years later, the Semana Hispana has evolved into the Hispanic Festival of Wilmington, an annual three-day event that reaches the Latino and greater Delaware community. It has become a much-anticipated community tradition and a highlight of the Hispanic Heritage Month. It is organized by Nuestras Raíces Delaware.[12]

In 1985, the Governor's Advisory Council on Hispanic Affairs (GACHA) was formed by an executive order signed by Governor Michael Castle; the order was reissued by Governor Thomas R. Carper in 1995. The council has the critical roles of advising the governor of Delaware and serving as a bridge between Latino Delawareans and their state government.[13] Its members include Delaware Latinos from all walks of life. The council organizes its work through the Hispanic Student Recognition Program (a joint effort with LACC) and the Economic Development, Health, Education and Social Justice Committees.[14]

After the passage of IRCA in 1986, the rapid growth of the Latino community in Delaware has become apparent, and so has its impact on the state's cultural landscape; local and regional journalists periodically report on this topic.[15] The local school districts, for example, found themselves dealing with a rising enrollment of migrant children. The Roman Catholic Church has also experienced this growth in Spanish mass attendance and its catechism classes. Local agencies have experienced an increasing Latino clientele seeking social services. The local supermarkets are regularly stocked with ethnic food such as tortillas, chilies, corn, and so forth. Latino restaurants and grocery stores (which offer money wiring services, Spanish music CDs, and calling cards) have mushroomed almost overnight.

In the southern part of the state, the Latino presence has also contributed to the local culture. Since 1995, the all-volunteer-run Hispanic Festival in Georgetown (Festival Hispano de Georgetown), organized by El Centro Cultural in Georgetown, has been held annually in September at St. Michael's Catholic Church. The festival includes instrumental, vocal, and dance performances, an art exhibit, a costume parade, children's activities, and traditional Hispanic foods. In 2004, the Library of Congress designated the Festival a Delaware Local Legacy.[16]

Also in Georgetown, La Esperanza Community Center was founded in 1996, primarily to provide support to the increasing number of migrant workers arriving in Sussex County from Mexico and Guatemala. Since then, it has evolved into a multi-service support organization that assists with the assimilation of Latinos into the broader Sussex County population.[17]

Voices Without Borders/Voces Sin Fronteras is a faith-based, grassroots advocacy nonprofit organization based in Wilmington, committed to improving the quality of life of Latinos and Latin American migrants living in Delaware. Founded in 2000, Voces seeks to promote social and institutional change by establishing a space for dialogue and exchange among its members, members of other organizations, and the government.

In the academic arena, the La Raza Alumni Association (LRAA) at the University of Delaware was created in 2006. LRAA is an organization that serves many purposes; most notably, it offers oversight and expertise to La Raza undergraduate executive boards, fosters social and intellectual development of La Raza members, works to maintain unity among under-represented communities, and raises money to support future generations of minority students in higher education. LRAA also serves as a forum for La Raza alumni to engage each other in the public, private, and nonprofit sectors to increase the wealth, power, and influence of the La Raza Familia. The ultimate goal of LRAA at the University of Delaware is to raise money to establish an endowment to support the La Raza Center for Latino and Minority Affairs (La Raza Center).

The pervasive presence of the Spanish language has become apparent in media. There are at least five Spanish newspapers: *El Tiempo Hispano* (bilingual weekly); *El Mundo Hispano* (bilingual monthly); *El Sol Delaware* (Philadelphia's El Sol created a Delaware edition); *Hoy en Delaware* (bilingual monthly); and *Unidad Latina* (bilingual semi-monthly in Oxford, Pennsylvania, covering southern Chester County, Pennsylvania, and Delaware). *El Tiempo Hispano* is particularly important. It began in January 2006 with a run of 3,000 for each edition. In just over a year, that number grew to 10,000. Written in both Spanish and English, *El*

Tiempo Hispano looks at issues of importance to Delaware's Latino community, covering most of the Delmarva Peninsula. The newspaper features community events as well as information about local communities and leaders. Because one of the goals of the newspaper is to build bridges for new migrants coming to the area, it is intentionally published in both English and Spanish. Additionally, an online version is available.[18]

There is one radio station, La Exitosa/930 AM, which offers round-the-clock Spanish-language programming in Milford.[19] Other stations have individual Spanish programs: *En Español,* 10:30 A.M.–noon on Sundays, WGMD/92.7 FM in Rehoboth Beach; *La Invasora,* 9 A.M.–midnight on Saturdays, WJWL/900 AM in Georgetown and WJWK/1280 AM in Seaford; *The Latin Beat,* noon–1 P.M. on Sundays, WDEL/1150 AM in Wilmington; and Radio Uno, 4–6 P.M. on Saturdays, WVUD/91.3 FM in Newark. There are also three television programs: *Con Sabor Hispano, Dando la Vuelta,* and *¡Viva la Vida!*

Finally, Delawarehispanic.com was created in 2002 as the first Hispanic Internet magazine in Delaware; it serves as a resource for Latinos to progress and improve their lives. It aims at teaching the state's Latinos about voting, getting driver's licenses, and gaining access to political leaders. It also includes information on Spanish-language church services, leaders in the state's Latino community, and jobs for bilingual workers.

NOTES

1. http://www.geolytics.com/projection.
2. Hoffman, 1990.
3. Weslager, 1972.
4. In 1610 English sea captain Samuel Argall sailed into the bay and named present-day Cape Henlopen Cape La Warre, giving rise to the name *Delaware* for the bay, the river, the Native American group, and later, the state.
5. Munroe, 2006, 130–143.
6. Garcia, 1997, 12.
7. Munroe, 2006.
8. Griffith and Kissam, 1995.
9. Borland, 2001.
10. Caldwell, 2006.
11. Unofficial estimates indicate that these figures might be even higher. See, for example, Horowitz and Miller, 1999.
12. http://nuestrasraicesde.org.
13. http://www.dhss.delaware.gov/dhss/dssc/gacha/index.html.
14. GACHA's Annual Report 2006.
15. See, for example, Caldwell 2006 and Nefosky 2006. Annie Nefosky, a Wilmington-based radio journalist, won 1450 WILM NEWSRADIO 2006 awards in the categories

for National Federation of Press Women (Special Programming) and the National Edward R. Murrow Award (News Series) for her radio program "Chasing Dreams in the First State: An In-Depth Look at the Latino Population in Delaware."
16. http://lcweb2.loc.gov/diglib/legacies/DE/200002825.html.
17. http://www.laesperanza.org.
18. http://www.eltiempohispano.com.
19. http://www.wyusam.com.

BIBLIOGRAPHY

Borland, Katherine. *Creating Community: Hispanic Migration to Rural Delaware*. Wilmington, DE: Delaware Heritage Press, 2001.

Caldwell, Christopher. "Hola, Delaware! How Guatemalan Immigrants Changed a Small American Town." *Weekly Standard*, August 14, 2006.

Delaware Federal Writers' Project. *Delaware: A Guide to the First State*. Compiled and written by the Federal Writers' Project of the Works Progress Administration for the State of Delaware. New York: Hastings House, 1955.

Delaware Governor's Advisory Council on Hispanic Affairs (GACHA). Annual Report. Wilmington, DE. 2006.

Ferris, Benjamin. *A History of the Original Settlements on the Delaware: From Its Discovery by Hudson to the Colonization under William Penn, to Which is Added an Account of the Ecclesiastical Affairs of the Swedish Settlers, and a History of Wilmington, from Its First Settlement to the Present Time*. Wilmington, DE: Wilson & Heald, 1846.

Garcia, Victor Q. "Mexican Enclaves in the U.S. Northeast: Immigrant and Migrant Mushroom Workers in Southern Chester County, Pennsylvania." JSRI research report #27. East Lansing, Michigan State University, Julian Samora Research Institute, 1997.

Griffith, David Craig, and Edward Kissam. *Working Poor: Farmworkers in the United States*. Philadelphia, PA: Temple University Press, 1995.

Higgins, Anthony, ed. *New Castle on the Delaware*. Delaware Federal Writers' Project, New Castle Historical Society, 1973.

Hoffecker, Carol E. *Delaware: A Bicentennial History*. New York: Norton, 1977.

Hoffman, Paul E. *A New Andalucia and a Way to the Orient: The American Southeast during the Sixteenth Century*. Baton Rouge: Louisiana State University Press, 1990.

Horowitz, Roger, and Mark J. Miller. "Immigrants in the Delmarva Poultry Processing Industry: The Changing Face of Georgetown, Delaware, and Environs." JSRI occasional paper #37. East Lansing, Michigan State University, Julian Samora Research Institute, 1999.

Louhi, Evert Alexander. *The Delaware Finns; or the First Permanent Settlements in Pennsylvania, Delaware, West New Jersey, and Eastern Part of Maryland*. New York: Humanity Press, 1925.

Munroe, John A. *History of Delaware*. Newark: University of Delaware Press; London: Associated University Presses. Fifth edition, 2006 (originally published in 1979).

———. *The Philadelawareans, and Other Essays Relating to Delaware*. Newark: University of Delaware Press, 2004.

United States Commission on Civil Rights, Delaware Advisory Committee and United States Commission on Civil Rights, Pennsylvania Advisory Committee. "The Working and Living Conditions of Mushroom Workers: A Report." Washington, DC: Commission on Civil Rights, 1977.

Weslager, Clinton Alfred. *The Delaware Indians: A History.* New Brunswick, NJ: Rutgers University Press, 1972.

Wuorinen, John H. *The Finns on the Delaware, 1638–1655: An Essay in American Colonial History.* New York: Columbia University Press, 1938.

9

DISTRICT OF COLUMBIA

Enrique S. Pumar

CHRONOLOGY

1800	The federal capital is transferred from Philadelphia to the District of Columbia. Two years later, Congress provides the city with its first municipal charter.
1822–1823	Joseph Marion Fernández (1783–1857) becomes the first Hispanic to serve in Congress as a delegate from the territory of Florida.
1960s	Many Latin American political exiles settle in Washington, DC, escaping a new wave of dictatorships throughout Latin American.
1960	With the outbreak of the Cuban Revolution, many Cuban exiles begin to settle in the Washington, DC, metro area.
1967	The Washington Metropolitan Area Transit Authority is created.
1970s	Economic crises and political instability in Central America increase the number of Central American migrants in the Washington, DC, metro area.
1973	Congress approves the District Self-Government and Governmental Reorganization Act, which establishes the current governance structure with an elected mayor and a 13-member council.
1976	The Mayor's Office of Latino Affairs (OLA) is organized to act as liaison between the District government and the Latino community. To date, this office—along with the Commission on Latino Community Development—is the only political voice for Latinos in the District government agencies.
1978	The nonpartisan Congressional Hispanic Caucus Institute is established.

1979	The Salvadoran civil war and the Nicaraguan Revolution contribute to the increase of these two Latino groups in Washington, DC. The decade of the 1980s witnesses the largest wave of Latino migrants to the District.
1986	The Hispanic Chamber of Commerce is founded, reflecting the increasing presence of Hispanics in the business sector of the state and the purchasing power of this group.
2000	The Latino population reaches 39 percent of the foreign-born population of the District of Columbia; by 2002, Latinos constitute 9.4 percent of all the District's residents.
2003	The Latino population in the District reaches 53,289.

HISTORICAL OVERVIEW

The early Latino presence in the nation's capital was shaped by the very unique historical identity of the District. Washington, DC, was founded to house the federal government, and as such its demographic growth has been driven by the peculiar nature of politics. This means, among other things, that a portion of the residents in the city is transient as it circulates in and out of the city according to electoral cycles. In addition, the population of the District has grown proportionally to the size of the federal government. After the Great Depression in the late 1920s and early 1930s, when the federal bureaucracy expanded with the insertion of New Deal programs, the population and character of the District of Columbia changed, gradually becoming the metropolitan city that is today. However, Latinos did not settle in large numbers in the city until much later. Although events in the District had an immeasurable impact in the historical destiny of Latin American nations, the Latino population in the city was not sizeable until the latter part of the twentieth century. With the exception of foreign diplomats, a few professionals and politicos[1] who lived in the city during political transitions, and the occasional public intellectual (for example, Fernando Ortiz, who came to reside briefly in Washington, DC, during his exile in the United States in the 1930s), Latinos tended to congregate in nearby cities such as Philadelphia and New York, where the economic and cultural ties with their home countries had been solidified since the early days of the nineteenth century.

Historically, first-generation Latinos tend to congregate in areas with large manufacturing districts where there are ample opportunities to work and the cost of entering the labor force is considerably less. In addition, Latinos have traditionally been underrepresented in professional careers, such as law and engineering, associated with public service. Additionally, civic activists began to flow in numbers into the District after the 1960s. For example, the National Council of La Raza, the largest of the Latino civil rights and advocacy organizations in the country, with some 300 affiliated community-based organizations throughout the nation, did not open its Washington, DC, offices until 1968.

One of the major area's engines of growth—in addition to the federal government, international, and nonprofit advocacy organizations—did not become well established until after World War II, when institutions such as the Organization of American States and the Inter-American Development Bank were created.

THE LATINO POPULATION BOOM

Like most other cities in the nation, the bourgeoning number of Latinos settling in Washington, DC, has been in large part the result of transnational ties and political and economic events in Latin America. Before the 1980s, the Latino community of the District was primarily composed of a few professionals from throughout Latin America who came to work in the growing number of international and regional organizations. As such, the civil servants and other professionals who came to live in the District composed one of the most ethnically diverse Latino populations in the nation. Although no single Latin American nation predominated, this population shared high levels of education and professional status.

Along with this professional group, a growing number of service workers gradually settled in the city, taking advantage of the growing service-sector employment opportunities. As in other neighborhoods of the DC metro area, the biggest jump in the Latino population occurred after 1980. Between 1990 and 2002, the population of Latinos residing in the District increased by 56 percent, becoming the area's fastest-growing ethnic minority. Demographers estimate that by 2010, Latinos will total about 70,000. Several political and economic factors contributed to this transformation. Civil wars, economic devastation, and a succession of natural disasters provoked a mass migration from Central America, primarily from El Salvador. In the rest of Latin America, the downward mobility caused by the financial crises of the 1980s also brought many new economic migrants to the city at a time when the metro regional economy was booming. Many Latinos who had ties with relatives and acquaintances in the city learned about the historically low unemployment rate in the District and surrounding jurisdictions. Finally, the growth of the service-sector economy during the 1980s also attracted many newcomers, and by 2000, Central Americans already accounted for 22.4 percent of the foreign-born population in the District, South Americans for 10.1 percent, and migrants from the Caribbean for 6.2 percent. Of these three regions, almost 13 percent came from El Salvador alone.

CURRENT ISSUES

In a number of ways the dispension of the new social class and professional status of the recent wave of Latino migrants is reflected in the residential clustering of the newcomers. The great majority of Latinos reside in working-class neighborhoods east of 16th Street, one of the major thoroughfares along the north-south corridor in the city, in such districts as Columbia Heights, Adam Morgan, and Mount Pleasant. Neighborhoods populated by poor Latinos are among the most violent and the most dilapidated. In 1991, the lack of sufficient affordable housing and mounting political frustrations in the Latino community fueled the riots in Mount Pleasant, one of the predominantly Latino neighborhoods in the city. The proliferation of Latino street gang activity in the District between 1999 and 2003 prompted the mayor and the DC Police Department to form the Gang Intervention Partnership Program, which has drastically reduced the reported gang violence among Latino youth.

Latino enrollment in public schools around the city has doubled since the 1980s. However, Latino students continue to score lower than other ethnic groups in most criteria of educational achievement. The levels of schooling and language proficiency among parents and immediate family members are highly correlated with at least some of the dismal scores among Latino students. The basic reading and math skills among Latino children did not improve between 1990 and 2000, and their scores were among the lowest in the nation. Clearly, the performance of Latino students in school is closely related to the question of family wellness and human capital. The first report on the state of Latino children in Washington, DC (2003), issued by the Council of Latino Agencies found a close correlation between poverty, economic deprivation, and educational attainment in the Latino population. In 2000, 23 percent of Latino children of school age (6–17 years old) and 26 percent of the preschool age (6 years old or younger) were living in poverty in the District. Although this figure is lower than the poverty rate among African American children and, as one might expect, substantially higher than the rate among whites, the report concludes that the condition of poverty affects educational attainment most visibly when it contributes to the high degree of student absenteeism, the low levels of parental involvement in school and school work such as homework, and the alarming dropout levels among Latino students. Between 1991 and 1999, the dropout rate among Latino students was cut in half; however, in 1999, this group still had the highest dropout rate of any ethnic group in the District public school system.

Poverty, together with the hardships associated with selective assimilation, has also contributed to the near crisis in public health among Latino youth in Washington, DC. This group of Latinos has the highest percentage of drinking and cocaine consumption among the District youth population. But Latinos have the lowest percentage of marijuana use, which declined more drastically in this group than in any other during the 1990s. In addition to language and communication impediments, the single most alarming obstacle to receiving adequate health care for Latino families is the low level of insurance coverage.

Interracial tensions have also been more evident in the District recently. The sources of tensions between Latinos and African Americans derive primarily from the underrepresentation of the former in the governing institutions of the District government. In recent decades, no Latino representative has been elected to the city hall or the city council. In addition, the Office of Latino Affairs falls under the mayor's purview and lacks political independence. On the other hand, politics in the city are controlled by African American groups and politicos. The voice of the Latino population has been impaired by the migratory status of the majority of this population. There has been little attempt to overcome the miscommunication and cultural stereotypes that permeate the perceptions these two groups have of each other. The relationship between the two groups is further complicated by their competition for affordable housing and service jobs in the city.

Unlike other areas of the United States where one of the major divisions among Latinos is their political affiliation, in the District, with its overwhelming Democratic force and its nonvoting status in presidential elections, the major source of intra-ethnic tensions among Latinos relates to their immigration status and the biased treatment various groups of Latin migrants receive from federal agencies. Political asylum continues to be granted to refugees from leftist revolutionary regimes (for instance, Cubans and Nicaraguans) at a much higher rate than to refugees from other nations (primarily El Salvador and Guatemala), regardless of their level of suffering or the validity of their residency claims. For example, in 1997 Congress passed the Nicaraguan Adjustment and Central American Relief Act, which permitted Nicaraguans and Cubans residing in the United States since 1995 to become permanent legal residents through a relatively effortless status adjustment procedure. However, Salvadorans and Guatemalans had to prove they had been living continuously in the United States since 1990 in addition to meeting other stringent requirements.

NOTABLE LATINOS

Fernández, Joseph Marion (1783–1857). Fernández was the first Hispanic to serve in Congress and the first delegate from the territory of Florida. From 1835 to 1838 he served in the U.S. Army, and in 1845, after being defeated when he ran for the U.S. Senate, he moved to Cuba and managed his family sugar estate near Matanzas.

Farragut, David Glasgow (1801–1870). Son of Jorge Farragut, a merchant captain from Minorca, Spain, who migrated to America in 1776, Farragut entered the Navy, where he distinguished himself as a midshipman defending the District of Columbia during the war of 1812. He later rose to the rank of admiral.

Garesche, Julius (1821–1862). Garesche attended Georgetown College and West Point and later rose to a distinguished military career. While residing in Washington, DC, he helped found the Society of St. Vincent de Paul.

Garcia-Menocal, Aniceto (1836–1908). A U.S. Navy admiral and Cuban-born civil engineer who, after graduating from the Rensselaer Polytechnic Institute in Troy, New

York, in 1862, became subchief engineer on the Havana water works. In 1870, he was appointed engineer of public works in New York City, and between 1873 and 1885 Menocal worked as chief engineer responsible for drawing surveys in search of the best route for a canal in Panama and Nicaragua. The Garcia-Menocal family produced several generals and admirals and one president of Cuba. In 1900 he oversaw the plans for the naval station in the Philippines.

Yzaguiree, Raul (1939–). Born in San Juan, Texas, Yzaguiree is a civil rights activist who served as president and CEO of the National Council of La Raza from 1974 to 2004.

Melendez, Sara (1940–). An educator and community activist, Doctor Melendez, a native of Puerto Rico, has served on the boards of the Ethics Resource Center, the Points of Light Foundation, the National Puerto Rican Forum, the MS Foundation for Women, and the Aspira Association. Doctor Melendez has published numerous articles on education, leadership, and diversity, and he has coauthored a book on bilingual education.

Medrano, Hugo (1943–). Medrano is the founder and artistic director of the GALA Theater Company. Already an accomplished actor and director in his native Argentina, Medrano created GALA in 1976 shortly after arriving in the nation's capital. He has been involved in one way or another in promoting and developing Latino actors in Washington ever since.

Velazco, Anna (1952–). A nonprofit executive and social entrepreneur, Velazco is currently the executive director of the DC Public Library Foundation. She recently served 5 years in the District of Columbia government, primarily as director of planning and analysis in the Office of the Deputy Mayor for Children, Youth, Families, and Elders. She began her career as an adult educator in the fields of literacy, English as a second language, and adult basic education, culminating in managing a network of 18 alternative learning centers in New York City. She holds degrees in literature and the classics from Oberlin College and Harvard University.

Leiva, Rodrigo (1956–). Leiva is president of the Board of Trustees of Latino Fiesta DC 2007 and director of membership services of the Latino Federation of Greater Washington.

Arene, Eugenio (1960–). Arene is the president and executive officer of the Latino Federation of Greater Washington. A native of El Salvador, in 2002 Arene became the executive director of the Council of Latino Agencies (CLA), a nonprofit membership organization comprising 40 multicultural, community-based agencies in the Washington Metropolitan Area that provides direct services to the Latino community and low-income residents. In addition, he serves on the boards of the Center for Nonprofit Advancement, the Greater Washington Ibero-American Chamber of Commerce, and the Youth Build Charter School in Washington, DC.

Vivero, Mauricio (1966–). Vivero is the executive director of Ayuda Inc. and president of 501 (c) Strategies. A native of Cuba, Vivero has built a distinguished community service and nonprofit career, having served as director of government relations for Independent Sector, a national coalition representing more than 600 foundations, charities, and corporate giving programs. From 1998 until 2003, he was vice president of government relations and public affairs at the Legal Services Corporation. He also served as director of grassroots lobbying for the American Bar Association (ABA) and as director of leadership development for the National Council of La Raza.

Reinoso, Victor (1969–). Reinoso serves as the deputy mayor for education in the District of Columbia and is the principal policy advisor to the mayor on issues related to education. He was elected to represent the Second District on the Board of Education in November 2004 and elected as chief operating officer of the Federal City Council, a nonprofit, nonpartisan membership community development organization in the District. Reinoso was a founding staff member of the Fair Employment Council, now the Equal Rights Center, a civil rights advocacy group. He earned his undergraduate degree from Georgetown University and his MBA from the MIT Sloan School of Management.

CULTURAL CONTRIBUTIONS

Multiple community-based Latino associations hold community festivals celebrating the Latino culture heritage and national identity. One of the oldest community festivals is the Latino Festival Fiesta DC in Mt. Pleasant. Held in one of the neighborhoods with the strongest historic Latino ties, the festival celebrates the rich multicultural tradition of Latin America and showcases the growing Latino businesses in the city. In addition, several institutions throughout the city sponsor cultural festivals such as the Latin American Film Festival. The many public affairs programs and cultural centers from Latin American embassies and international organizations also enrich the city's cultural life. One such center is the Inter-American Cultural Center at the Inter-American Development Bank. The Cultural Center was created in 1992 with the mission of advancing the cultural heritage of Latin American and Caribbean nations in Washington, DC. The center also contributes to social development by administering a grants program that sponsors and cofinances small-scale cultural projects. Another such institution is the Smithsonian Latino Center. The center is part of the Smithsonian Institution and receives about $1 million per year in funding from Congress to promote Latino cultural heritage through museum exhibits and cultural programs. In the past 10 years alone, the Center has distributed approximately $10 million in congressional funds to more than 250 successful cultural art projects. Six Spanish-language dailies and magazines are published in the city. Some 50 restaurants and lounges catering to Latinos have opened in the city in the last decade. One of the oldest Latino theater companies, GALA (Grupo de Artistas Latinoamericanos), also operates in Washington, DC. GALA was founded in 1976 and was the outgrowth of Teatro Double, a bilingual children's

Latino commercial center in the Adams Morgan neighborhood. Courtesy of Enrique S. Pumar.

theater in Washington. GALA Hispanic Theatre has long been a groundbreaking and energetic performing center presenting classical and contemporary plays in Spanish and English, as well as an accompanying program of dance, music, poetry, spoken word, art, and, more recently, film. In January 2005, after 29 years of moving between venues, GALA moved into its permanent home in the historic Tivoli Theater. The move to a permanent home fulfilled the dream of its founder, Hugo Medrano, who had envisioned GALA as one of the more vibrant cultural outlets in the city.

NOTE

1. According to the Biographical Directory of the U.S. Congress, only 61 Hispanic delegates have served in the legislative branch since 1774. See http://www.loc.gov/rr/hispanic/congress/contents.html.

BIBLIOGRAPHY

Bean, Frank D., and Marta Tienda. *The Hispanic Population of the United States*. New York: Russell Sage Foundation, 1988.
Office of Latino Affairs, District of Columbia. http://ola.dc.gov/ola/site/default.asp?olaNav.
Portes, Alejandro, and Robert L. Bach. *Latin Journey: Cuban and Mexican Immigrants in the United States*. Berkeley: University of California Press, 1985.

Renteria, Rose Ann. "A Vibrant Latino Presence in Washington, DC." *Footnotes,* May–June 2000.

Repak, Terry. *Waiting on Washington: Central American Workers in the Nation's Capital.* Philadelphia, PA: Temple University Press, 1995.

Roy, Kishna, and Heather McClure. *The State of Latino Kids in the District of Columbia.* Washington, DC: Council of Latino Agencies, 2003.

Sanchez-Korrol, Virginia. *From Colonia to Community.* Westport, CT: Greenwood Press, 1983.

Singer, Audrey. *At Home in the Nation's Capital.* Washington, DC: Brookings Institution, Center on Urban and Metropolitan Policy, 2003.

———. *The Rise of New Immigrant Gateways,* Washington, DC: Brookings Institution, Center on Urban and Metropolitan Policy, 2004.

Valenzuela, Abel, Ana Luz Gonzalez, Nik Theodore, and Edwin Melendez. *In Pursuit of the American Dream: Day Labor in the Greater Washington D.C. Region.* Los Angeles: University of California at Los Angeles, Center for the Study of Urban Poverty, 2005.

10

Florida

Martin Nesvig

CHRONOLOGY

1513	Juan Ponce de León leads first Spanish exploration of Florida, but no permanent settlement is established.
1528	Explorer Pánfilo de Narváez leads a large expedition to Florida, making landfall near Tampa Bay. The exploratory mission results in disaster: of 300 men, only four survive. One of them is Alvar Núñez Cabeza de Vaca, who wanders from Texas to the Pacific and writes a narrative of the expedition and the shipwrecked survivors' travels.
1539	Explorer Hernando de Soto leads a larger exploration to Florida, making landfall at Tampa Bay; over 4 years he leads his expedition through Florida and southeast North America.
1565	Pedro Menéndez de Avilés establishes the first permanent Spanish settlement in Florida as the province's governor; St. Augustine is established.
1567–1705	Spanish Franciscan and Jesuit missions established throughout Florida.
1586	English corsair Sir Francis Drake raids St. Augustine.
1596–1597	Spain annexes Ais (above Cape Canaveral) and Guale (in present-day Georgia) as provinces; Guale Indian Rebellion lasts for 6 years, beginning in 1597.
1613–1617	Epidemic diseases kill most mission Indians.
1628	Dutch naval officer and privateer Piet Heyn captures the entire Spanish silver fleet off the coast of Cuba, along with all financing for Florida.
1668	English corsairs led by Robert Searles sack St. Augustine.

1670	Treaty of Madrid recognizes a boundary line between Spanish Florida and English Carolina.
1672–1695	Castillo de San Marcos, a massive stone fort, is built in St. Augustine.
1686	Spanish explorers Juan Enríquez Barroto and Antonio Romero explore Pensacola Bay.
1700–1713	The War of Spanish Succession, called Queen Anne's War in North America, pits Spain against England; the Spanish population of Florida is reduced to its lowest point, less than 1,000.
1763	During the French and Indian War, the English take Havana; Spain trades Florida to the English in exchange for Havana, and Florida becomes an English possession.
1783	Florida is returned to Spanish possession in imperial horse trading.
1821	After repeated invasions by President Andrew Jackson, Florida is ceded to the United States.
1868	Cuban and Spanish cigar workers and manufacturers leave Cuba and settle in Key West.
1885–1924	Thousands of Cubans come to Tampa and establish Ybor City as Florida's first migrant Latino community.
1959	Fidel Castro overthrows Fulgencio Batista in Cuba, spawning decades of migration from Cuba.
1961	Belen Jesuit Preparatory School, founded in Havana in 1854, opens in Miami after being expelled from Cuba by its alumnus Fidel Castro.

1966	Cuban Adjustment Act provides automatic permanent resident alien status to Cubans arriving in the United States.
1980s–1990s	Thousands of Colombians fleeing political violence in Colombia migrate to Florida.
1980s	Thousands of Nicaraguans flee civil war and the Sandinista regime for Florida.
	Billions of dollars worth of Colombian cocaine passes through southern Florida.
1980	In the Mariel boatlift, some 125,000 people leave Cuba in boats and arrive in Miami.
	Race riot in Liberty City (Miami-Dade County) erupts and 18 people are killed.
1989	Panamanian general Manuel Noriega is tried, convicted, and imprisoned for drug trafficking and money laundering in a Miami federal court.
	Ileana Ros-Lehtinen becomes first Latina and first Cuban American elected to the U.S. Congress.
2000s	Upper- and middle-class Venezuelans arrive in Florida after leaving Venezuela, following presidential victories by self-proclaimed socialist Hugo Chávez.

HISTORICAL OVERVIEW

Hurricanes and the fountain of youth were at the heart of the Spanish colonial enterprise of Florida, and in many ways, nearly 500 years later, those two physical phenomena continue to define Florida. In 2004 and 2005 several hurricanes hit Florida, leaving devastation in their wake. And although the fountain of youth was never found, anyone who takes a walk down the boardwalk in Palm Beach or Miami Beach would swear that the cosmetic surgeons have gotten close enough. But it was really hurricanes that in many ways defined Florida's earliest existence and also defined Florida's earliest Spanish presence. Too swampy for serious building in the colonial period, too subject to hurricanes for permanent structures, and lacking a densely settled imperial Indian population for taxation, Florida was for hundreds of years a kind of backwater and buffer zone against the imperial pretensions of the French and English to the north. Unlike Havana, with which Florida has had a long relationship, Florida was off the main trans-Atlantic commerce routes. Of course, Florida's status as a backwater and extension of the Old South changed dramatically in the second half of the twentieth century.

The twentieth century in Florida witnessed a radical re-Hispanization of the state. As of 2005 the state itself was home to more than 1 million Cubans, close to 650,000 Puerto Ricans, half a million Mexicans, almost a quarter million Colombians, 120,000 Dominicans, over 100,000 Nicaraguans, and thousands of

Hernando De Soto, soldiers, sailors, and priests landing in Florida, from 1855 engraving. Courtesy of the Library of Congress, Prints & Photographs Division.

Latinos from all over Latin America. Latinos now make up just under 20 percent (approximately 19.6 percent as of 2005) of the total population of Florida.[1] Miami-Dade County, home famously to the largest concentration of Cubans in the United States, is just over 60 percent Latino.[2] How Florida went from being a colonial outpost of the Spanish New World endeavor to being a U.S. territory and slave state, a state with the highest lynching rates of any southern state in the early twentieth century, to a state with a vast amalgamation of Latinos from all parts of Latin America, is the story of this chapter.

Like some parts of the U.S. Southwest—notably New Mexico and, to a lesser extent, California—Florida has a long political history as part of the Spanish Empire. But Florida did not have a historically consistent Latino presence. Prior to the nineteenth century, Florida had been sparsely populated, and the Spanish presence from the sixteenth through the eighteenth centuries, although consistent from an administrative and territorial perspective, was never deep or wide-ranging. Instead, even though Florida was a Spanish possession for nearly 300 years, it would take a revolution in Cuba in 1959, an exodus and migration to Miami, a booming cocaine trade from Colombia in the 1980s, counterrevolutionary migrations from Nicaragua and Venezuela, waves of migrations from Central and South America, and agricultural migrations from Mexico to transform Florida into one of the United States' most diverse Latino populations. One joke is that if one wants to lie on the beach and speak English, one should go to Cancún, and if one wants to lie on the beach and speak Spanish, one should go to Miami. In a highly globalized economy and world system in which Miami lies at the heart of the Caribbean basin, international borders and linguistic debates about English-only legislation seem to fall largely on deaf ears in Florida.

But despite this pluralism and diversity, Florida is also a deeply divided place—a place where accents determine business transactions, where national identities are held so dear that, rather than cosmopolitanism, Florida is better characterized by ethnic factionalism, provincialism, and racism. The Cuban Republican U.S. senator from Florida Melquiades (Mel) Martínez had this to say about the use of the Mexican flag on April 8, 2006, after hundreds of thousands of predominantly Mexican migrants staged rallies across the country for immigration reform: "I think it's terrible . . . But if what this is about is the opportunity to be an American, to be a resident of America, to work in America and, ultimately, to be a citizen of America, they need to be carrying American flags."[3] But Martínez is not to be found to protest when Cubans wave the Cuban flag on news of the potential demise of Castro, at the restaurant Versailles, or at the ubiquitous presence of Cuban flags from rearview mirrors of cars in Miami. The Cuban flag waves proudly at the entrance to downtown Miami from the Freedom Tower in front of the American Airlines Arena, and neither Senator Martínez nor any other Cuban political leader has ever protested this as "un-American" or somehow disparaging the preferential treatment that Cubans received from the United States as pawns in the Cold War.

What it really comes down to is a politicized division between Latinos and between Cubans, who are predominantly white, and African Americans, between individual Latino groups, and between Latinos and Anglos, in Florida. In the fall of 2006, Cuban Hialeah-based state legislator Ralph Arza repeatedly referred to Miami schools superintendent Rudy Crew (who is African American) as a "nigger," all the while enjoying the support and loyalty of his constituency and political cronies. Only after Arza and his cousin Gus Barreiro were caught on tape repeating the same language, threatening other legislators, and eventually charged with witness tampering felonies did Arza step down from the legislature.

Tellingly, part of his mea culpa was tempered with self-pity in which he said he "felt sad" that people considered him a racist.[4]

These are mere vignettes but they go a long way toward highlighting the deep ethnic, racial, and ideological divisions that drive Floridian Latino identity. Whatever one thinks of the political identity of Latinos in Florida, the issue of national identity and flags is a clear symbol for the division, not unity, of Latino identity in Florida.

Spanish Colonial Florida (1513–1763)

Unlike other parts of the Spanish imperial project in the Americas (such as Mexico, Peru, and the Caribbean), which were important for large Indian populations as tax and labor bases, silver deposits, or as sugar plantation sites, Florida never offered the Spanish Empire much of anything. Its principal purpose was as a territorial buffer between the lucrative trans-Atlantic silver fleet system, which disembarked from Havana before heading to Seville, and the imperial pretensions of the French and English in the Carolinas and Louisiana. Nor were the climate, land, or Indian populations much help in this regard. Hurricanes, swamps, mosquitoes, floods, and vicious semitropical sun all combined to make Florida less than salubrious. The Indian populations were largely composed of hunter-gatherer groups and as such, unlike the Mexicans and Andeans, offered little financial incentive for ambitious conquistadores or hacienda owners. Despite these drawbacks, Florida exerted a powerful tug on the collective imagination of early Spanish explorers. Juan Ponce de León, the former leader of the conquest of Puerto Rico in 1506 (and Puerto Rico's erstwhile Spanish governor) led the first Spanish expedition into Florida, in the now-famous search for the fountain of youth. He never found gold (or, it seems, the fountain of youth) but was named *adelantado* (governor) of Florida by the Crown in 1514. Delayed by administrative and family events in Spain (his wife had died) Ponce de León returned to Puerto Rico. In 1521, amid reports of Hernán Cortés's spectacular victory over the Mexican Empire, Ponce de León led a new expedition to Florida with some 200 settlers, missionaries, horses, and domestic animals, but on landing in Florida (probably in San Carlos Bay) he was wounded by an arrow shot by hostile Indians, fled to Cuba, and died of infections from the wound.

Ponce de León's experience in Florida would prove ominously predictive. For over 200 years the Spaniards struggled to make Florida a Spanish possession in the style of Cuba, Puerto Rico, Mexico, or Peru, and as a whole the effort was largely fruitless. Even by 1700 the Spanish population in Florida had not yet risen above 2,000. By contrast many of the larger Spanish cities alone in the Americas had Spanish populations well above that—Mexico City may have had as many as 50,000 Spaniards by the end of the eighteenth century.[5]

The Americas, for Spain, were important for both global and economic reasons. Although Spain had little difficulty keeping most of its possessions in the core areas of its American holdings (in Mexico and the Andes, for example), the peripheral and transitional regions were more susceptible to foreign intrusions and trade. The Spanish Crown established a mercantile trade system—or closed sea—in which only certain trade ports were licensed and in which free trade between nations was prohibited. This meant that Seville was the home port for all of the Spanish American trade—a highly lucrative international trade in American silver, European cloth, Chinese silk, and Asian spices, among other items. In the Americas, Lima, Panama, Veracruz, and Havana were the principal ports of entry or embarkation. Given the currents and winds of the Caribbean, and the need to transport the vast amount of silver coming from Zacatecas in Mexico and Potosí in upper Peru, Havana became the final port in the eastward flow of bullion. Ships laden with silver from the Caribbean ports of Panama and from Veracruz in Mexico would meet in Havana for provisioning and ship repairs; Havana also quickly became an important shipbuilding city. Having provisioned in Havana, the silver fleets traveled under military escort to Seville.

After Ponce de León, Pánfilo de Narváez and then Hernando de Soto made unsuccessful explorations in Florida, leading to no real permanent settlement. It was not until 1565 that Pedro Menéndez de Avilés was awarded a contract as *adelantado* of Florida. Virtually all conquest in the Americas by the Spanish was privately funded. Like Cortés and Ponce de León, Menéndez de Avilés put up the lion's share of the funding for conquest endeavors in the hopes that conquest and victory would bring untold wealth, fame, fortune, and power. This system was based on the old medieval system of patronage, in which vassals risked their fortunes and lives in exchange for titles of nobility and lands from the Crown. Menéndez de Avilés's Florida venture fit this pattern.

Menéndez de Avilés had convinced the Spanish Crown to grant him the title of *adelantado* (governor). It helped his cause that the French (many of whom were Protestants and therefore anathema to the Catholic king Phillip II of Spain) had set up forts on the Florida coast. Menéndez de Avilés went to Florida with 10 ships and 1,000 men and made landfall in St. Augustine on September 8, 1565. Thus began the first permanent Spanish settlement in Florida.

The Spanish presence was haphazard and spotty. Unlike conquest efforts in the Caribbean, which turned up gold, or in Mexico, which turned up large imperial societies with vast tax and labor base populations, Florida offered little. Nevertheless, over the next few years Menéndez de Avilés, along with his wife doña María de Solís, set up a string of semifortified Spanish towns. As with Peru and Mexico, a good portion of the Spanish settlers came from the relatively poor province of Extremadura and from upper Andalucía.[6] Like Pizarro, who was famously illiterate and viewed by his Old World rivals with scorn, the settlers of

Florida were social climbers, looking to move up the socioeconomic food chain from their relatively meager Spanish origins. Those at the top, like the *adelantado* and his household, would enjoy expensive Ming dynasty porcelain (imported from China via Manila and Acapulco), gold embroidery, marzipan from Toledo, dates, almonds, and, most assuredly, to remind themselves of their Spanish pedigree, vinegary wine from Spain.[7]

But these were isolated households. The experience of Spaniards in colonial Florida was one of isolation, raids by rival European corsairs and freebooters, tense relations with nomadic Indian groups, and poor funding from the Crown. Although the Crown saw Florida as important strategically, it did not invest heavily in fortifications or in the budgets of the presidios. Instead, these presidios were often marginal places where criminals served their sentences.[8] By 1600 St. Augustine was the only Spanish fortification in 600 miles of coastline. In the 1610s, epidemic disease dramatically reduced Indian populations, and labor shortages were common because the Spanish had demanded a kind of levy draft labor system from their Indian subjects. In 1622 a massive hurricane devastated trade. The year of 1628 was a low point for Florida. For the first and only time in its history, an entire Spanish silver fleet was captured, by Dutch naval officer and privateer Piet Heyn, off the coast of Cuba. Subsidies for the Florida presidio and mission systems were devastated.

In the wake of these events, a new push to expand Spanish presence came from governors Luis de Rojas y Borja and Luis de Horruytiner. What became known as Middle Florida (the area in the panhandle around Tallahassee) was settled, and Franciscan missionaries began to set up small missions. Tallahassee and the Apalachee area would provide food and harbor for Spanish ships fleeing corsairs in the Gulf of Mexico. In theory the expansion was a good idea, but like much of the history of early Florida, the Spanish were harassed by raids and unpredictable weather. The Apalachee rebelled against Spanish rule in 1647, and an internal war between Christianized and non-Christianized tribes broke out. In 1668 St. Augustine was sacked by English corsair Robert Searles. In 1670 English settlers from Barbados founded Charleston. The Spanish Crown responded to these events with increased investment in Florida. In the 1670s the building of the massive stone Castillo de San Marcos was begun in St. Augustine.

Despite the efforts of the Crown, Spanish Florida remained a place renowned for seemingly constant war and raiding. In fact the Spanish population of Florida may have fallen below 1,000 by the end of the War of Spanish Succession in 1713.[9] Even the missionaries, who were famed for their intrepid nature and willingness to live in the most extreme circumstances, fared poorly in Florida. By 1759, it is reported, there were less than 10 Franciscan priests in all of Florida. South of St. Augustine there was virtually no Spanish presence at all on the Atlantic coast.

In 1683, amid the various explorations and expansions into Middle Florida, Pensacola Bay was scouted by the Spanish. It was settled, and some argued that it should replace St. Augustine as the capital of Spanish Florida—a suggestion rejected by Charles II. As in the rest of Florida's early history (or modern history, for that matter), criminals settled Pensacola. Many of the settlers sent to work in the presidio had come from jails in Mexico or were press-ganged into service from the poorer sections of Mexico City and Veracruz. The Spanish priests who went to Pensacola often complained bitterly of the low moral standing of the presidio defenders, who had little incentive to defend imperial ambitions. Likewise, despite the efforts of the Crown to the contrary, Pensacola proved an excellent place for contraband international trade with the French of Louisiana and Mobile. By 1763 Pensacola had only barely survived after decades of raids, smuggling, disease, and neglect—this despite the fact that the Crown had sunk more than 4.5 million pesos into the endeavor. When Pensacola, along with the rest of Florida, went to the English, there were only a few hundred Spaniards there, compared with perhaps over 2,000 in St. Augustine.[10]

In 1763 Florida was ceded by the Spanish Crown to England in exchange for Havana, which the English had taken during the various imperial wars known as the French and Indian (or Seven Years') War. Spain saw Florida as increasingly less important, but more significantly it viewed Havana as much more important. Cuba was home to a burgeoning sugar plantation economy, and by 1763 Cuba had supplanted Brazil as one of the world's major sugar producers. Cuban plantation owners had adopted new technologies in production developed in Barbados and the island was fast emerging as an important piece in Spain's international economy—to say nothing of the Caribbean. Florida, on the other hand, produced virtually nothing. In the end this worked well for Spain, because Cuba emerged over the next three decades to become the world's major sugar producer, rising in importance after the Haitian Revolution, which ousted French slave owners.

In all, it appeared that Florida was a kind of lost land, a marshy bog forgotten by history and left out of the important shipping lanes between Panama, Veracruz, Havana, and Seville. How ironic this state of affairs seems now, when Miami is perched as one of the Caribbean basin's most important Latin cities, and when the relationship between Florida and Cuba has never been stronger.

Interim Years (1763–1821)

From Florida's incorporation into British America, and its temporary return to Spain from 1783 to 1821, the area was torn between competing imperial interests and the growing expansionist pretensions of the world's next great empire—the

United States. Although the economy of the Spanish period was marked by its dependence on Indian and slave labor, this tendency grew during the interim years (to be expanded more during the antebellum years). At the same time, this period, especially the second Spanish period, saw a highly diverse population, mixed between white Protestants, white Spanish Catholics, Indians, blacks, and mestizos and mulattos (persons of mixed descent).

St. Augustine, now under Catholic rule again, witnessed a kind of cultural revival. Spanish residents in 1789 staged a three-day celebration for the coronation of King Charles IV of Spain; a new cathedral church was built between 1793 and 1797; and the Spanish Crown began offering grants of land up to 150 acres for settlers from the United States to come to Florida. Nevertheless, this period never saw any substantial growth. When the War of 1812 broke out, Florida was increasingly caught in the crossfire of imperial interests. Likewise, in 1810 various groups in Mexico, and later in other parts of Latin America, rebelled against the Spanish Crown and established independent nations. In 1821 Florida was ceded to the United States and the era of the Spanish flag flying over Florida came to an end—even if, more than a century later, the Cuban flag would again fly over Miami and countless Latin American flags would dangle from rearview mirrors.

THE EARLY U.S. FLORIDA (1821–1959)

As a territory and later state of the United States, Florida would develop into one of the most conservative and economically and technologically underdeveloped states of the Old South. Developed on slave labor and harboring a deep-seated white supremacy, antebellum Florida remained relatively undeveloped. Nevertheless, it expanded considerably in population. In 1825 there were about 13,000 residents in all of Florida (excluding Indians), and within 5 years the non-Indian population grew to nearly 35,000. Centered on the upper-east coast and middle Florida, the territory developed a cotton industry.[11]

Some Spaniards remained in Florida, and St. Augustine, unlike the largely white Tallahassee, remained a fairly diverse town, retaining a mix of Anglo and Spanish residents. Joseph Hernández, a sugar planter, was made the territorial delegate to Congress in 1823. Although Spaniards retained their slaves after the transition in 1821, very few Spaniards migrated to Florida after this date. The result is that by the Civil War, most Spaniards had died, were subsumed into the population through intermarriage, or had migrated to other parts of the Spanish world. Overall, Florida took a turn toward being a territory (and a state in 1845) defined by slave plantation labor, stark black-white race relations, and poor infrastructure.

By the turn of the nineteenth century the Latino presence in Florida was negligible as the state went through the Civil War and Reconstruction. Literacy rates were among the lowest of all Southern states. Segregationists ruled with a politics of white supremacy, terror, and political favor. Lynching rates were higher in Florida than any other part of the South in the first decades of the twentieth century.[12] Education was formally segregated both by Jim Crow laws and by legislative decree.

There were some sporadic Latino migrations in this period. Cuban cigar workers and manufacturers had come to Key West in the 1860s, and in the 1880s they went in large numbers to Tampa, founding Ybor City as modern Florida's first Latino migrant enclave. Named after the Spanish industrialist Vicente Martínez Ybor, cigar workers and the cigar industry formed a close-knit Latino community. Spanish-language (and other languages—principally Italian) newspapers were founded, and cooperative fraternal and social organizations began to spring up. Later, by the 1910s and 1920s, political exiles from Latin America began to consider Florida, and Miami in particular, to be a potential place of refuge. Developed by canny railroad magnates such as Henry Flagler, southern Florida at long last was connected to the rest of Florida and the United States and developed—once the crocodiles and mangrove swamps were cleared out—as a kind of winter paradise. Former dictator-president of Mexico Porfirio Díaz, in exile in Paris, was rumored to have considered a comeback in Miami. By the end of the 1920s, more than 1,000 Cubans opposed to the rule of Gerardo Machado had come to Miami. When, after Machado was overthrown in a revolution in 1933, the exiles returned to Cuba, the *Miami Herald* prophetically said that "Miami's gates will always be open to Cubans, should the time ever come again when they need a refuge."[13] Of course, that time would come in 26 years, when another revolution spawned the single largest Latino migration in Florida's history.

MODERN FLORIDA (1959–2007)

On January 2, 1959, Fidel Castro and his supporters began a victorious march toward Havana, having successfully ousted Fulgencio Batista, who fled Cuba in the early morning of New Year's Day. With this shift began one of the Cold War's most notorious stories, and also the single greatest migration of Latinos into Florida in its history. The migrations across the now-famous "ninety miles" of the Florida straits would be massive. Hundreds of thousands of Cubans would eventually leave Cuba for Miami. And this migration also paved the way, in uneven ways, for future Latino migrations, because this ultimately transformed Miami from a relatively sleepy retirement town and enclave of Russian Jewish émigrés into a city where one could conceivably live and die without speaking a word of English.

The Cuban migrations to Miami were structured along class, socioeconomic, professional, and racial lines. The first wave of migrations came immediately in the wake of Castro's triumph. Fearing (correctly) that Fidel would turn Cuba communist, the Batista oligarchy, wealthy conservatives, business owners, and the right-wing professional class constituted, generally, the initial migration to Florida. Predominantly white and well-to-do, this group tended to integrate successfully into the Miami economic and political world. Unlike other migrant groups in U.S. history, Cubans have benefited from the circumstances of global politics. Eager to embarrass or eventually defeat Castro (and, one might add, to add Cubans to their voting rolls), formal U.S. policy has been exceptionally favorable to Cubans. The first wave of émigrés, who viewed themselves as political exiles, possessed an unusual profile for migrants: educated, propertied, and professional. In many cases they were from the highest ranks of the old Batista elite. The result is that this relatively upper-middle- and upper-class group set up shop quickly in Miami as a kind of oligarchy in wait for the hoped-for demise of Castro. Castro did not fall; in fact, he outlived assassination attempts, coups, an incompetent invasion at the Bay of Pigs, and even the Cuban Missile Crisis. The next wave of Cuban migrants consisted of children who were airlifted out of Cuba by the U.S. military, a program known as Operation Pedro Pan.

Until 1965 Cuba saw the first phase of the revolution and it became increasingly clear that things were taking an authoritarian turn. Castro surprised the United States and the exile community in September 1965, when he announced that anyone in Cuba who had relatives in the United States and who wished to leave was free to do so. The result was the so-called freedom flights over the next 9 years, in which close to 300,000 Cubans left for Florida.[14] Throughout this process Miami became the "front line in the Cold War."[15] In 1966 the United States implemented the Cuban Adjustment Act, which provided for immediate and automatic permanent resident status for all Cubans who arrived legally in the United States. The U.S. government also sponsored wide-ranging welfare programs to assist new arrivals. By the mid-1970s the United States government had spent more than $1 billion assisting Cuban migrants.

The result of the U.S. government's eagerness to discredit Castro and welcome enemies of world communism was to provide unprecedented opportunities for Cubans in Florida, who thrived as a result of strong familial and community solidarity, economic patronage, and their generally high socioeconomic profile prior to migration to Florida. By the late 1970s Cubans had come to form an economically and politically powerful group in Miami. By 1977 Cubans owned 8,000 businesses in Miami.[16]

Although Cubans would increasingly dominate Miami business and politics, 1980 marked a watershed in Florida history, in the collective dynamic of Latino identity in Florida, in Cuban identity, and in the ethnic balance in Florida. In April 1980 Castro announced that *gusanos* (worms—Castro's pejorative word for enemies of his regime) would be free to leave Cuba. Debarking from Mariel Harbor, some 125,000 Cubans left for Miami. It was nothing short of a debacle. Cubans in Florida organized fleets of "freedom boats" to ferry the émigrés. Among the Marielitos were a substantial amount of criminals and the mentally insane whom Castro had released from asylums and prisons. He remarked that he had "flushed the toilets of Cuba" on the shores of Miami and openly mocked the exile community in Florida. U.S. President Carter was caught off-guard and the entire incident made for salacious headlines—murderers and psychotics dumped on Miami's shores. From a demographic perspective, however, important shifts could be detected—Marielitos were generally poorer, younger, and less white than previous Cuban migrants. Significantly, unlike previous migrations, which tended to be for both economic and ideological reasons, by 1980 the promises of the revolution were souring on substantial portions of the population, and middle-class and working-class Cubans left Cuba out of discontent over the stagnant economy and the increasingly dictatorial rule of Castro.

In the midst of the Mariel boatlift, Haitian migrants were simultaneously attempting to cross the Florida straits and reach the United States. But Haiti did not have a communist government and Haitians, unlike Cuban émigrés of the 1960s, were overwhelmingly black and very poor. U.S. policy called for turning away Haitians. Bloated corpses of Haitian migrants began to wash up on Miami beaches. The African American community in Miami seethed; predominantly black Liberty City and Overtown were among the poorest cities in the United States. In the same year four white policemen were accused of beating a black man, Arthur McDuffie, to death. In May 1980 the officers were acquitted and Miami erupted in racial violence over four days, killing eighteen people and causing more than $100 million in property damages.[17]

The year 1980 was a turning point for Latino identity in Florida. It was the year when the clear inequities in U.S. immigration policy were laid bare, but it was also the beginning of a much more diverse Latino migration into Florida. Tens of thousands of Nicaraguans began to flee the Sandinista regime, which like Castro's, was unabashedly communist. But Nicaraguans did not receive the same open-armed welcome that Cubans had in the 1960s and 1970s. They had seen themselves as occupying similar circumstances as Cubans, but official policy did not reflect that perspective. Instead, Nicaraguans were left in a kind of legal and immigration limbo. In many instances unable to obtain visas or documentation, Nicaraguans were never able to achieve the kind of socioeconomic success that Cubans had.

The 1980s were also the years of Colombian cocaine in Miami. Billions of dollars worth of cocaine came through Miami, which was a porous harbor. Mayors and police welcomed the trade with virtually public smiles. Mayors were indicted. The city's homicide rate soared. Miami became Murder, U.S.A., as so-called cocaine cowboys—hit men for the Medellín Cartel, the principal operative in the cocaine trade in the 1980s—shot down people in the streets. Real estate values plummeted and tourists were warned to stay inside at dark. But at the same time violence in Colombia was worse. A lingering, decades-long, low-level civil war continued to claim thousands of lives and in the process thousands of Colombians fled the country for Florida. Today close to a quarter million Colombians reside in Florida, making them the fourth-largest Latino group in the state.

While the lurid stories of corruption, murder, and discos awash in cocaine made headlines, and while racial tensions boiled over to murderous mayhem in Florida in the 1980s, something else was happening. South Florida was increasingly looking southward to the Caribbean and South America politically, culturally, and economically. Banks sprang up like mushrooms in Miami in the 1980s as the need to launder drug money skyrocketed. General Manuel Noriega, the Panamanian dictator, was one of the principal operatives, staging a lucrative money-laundering scheme between Miami and Panama. In the end, of course, Noriega was captured by U.S. forces in an invasion of Panama in 1989 and extradited to Miami, where he was prosecuted and imprisoned in a U.S. prison. Also, after Mariel, the makeup of Cuban migrants, and Latino migration to Florida in general, changed. The 1990s saw the *balseros*, or rafters, from Cuba and, increasingly, widespread migration from South America pick up speed in the 1980s and 1990s. But apart from this, south Florida was also developing into a place where Latino migrants could arrive and not skip a beat, as it were. One could literally live and die in Miami without learning English. This meant opportunities for Latin American enterprises and for service industries.

By the end of the 1980s, crime levels in south Florida had dropped. Thousands of Latinos from all over Latin America came to Florida for education, work, family, political exile, economic exile, and to chase the enigmatic lure of Florida. Puerto Ricans, who are U.S. citizens, came to Florida for the same reasons people move from state to state within the United States—jobs, career, education, family—but given south Florida's increasing reputation as a place open to Latinos, Puerto Ricans saw Florida as a viable and desirable option. The same could be said of Peruvians, Argentines, Colombians, and Dominicans—they lacked U.S. passports but they came for the Latino presence and perceived opportunities. Much of this migration came from the middle classes, who saw in Florida economic or educational opportunities, familial ties, or career moves.

Other groups fared differently. Central Americans, especially from Honduras and El Salvador, as well as large numbers of Mexicans, have come to Florida since Mariel, largely in pursuit of a better life and job opportunities. Whereas Cubans came with the support of the U.S. government, migrants from Central America and Mexico have tended to arrive in Florida without documentation, with shaky migration status, or as members of extended families. They have often found work in the service sector, semi-skilled labor, domestic work, construction, and agriculture. Mexicans, for example, are the third-largest Latino group in Florida (over half a million) but are concentrated heavily in rural areas of south Florida. Many Salvadorans and Hondurans work in service sectors. Nicaraguans see the political and migration situation in Florida as especially bitter. Many were educated members of the middle and upper classes who left Nicaragua after the Sandinista takeover and assumed (wrongly) that they would receive the same welcome Cubans did. But the dynamics of the Cold War had changed, and many Nicaraguans who came to Miami in the 1980s remained in a kind of limbo, seeking out jobs well below their educational and career levels.

One final group that has made for an interesting phenomenon is Venezuelans. Like many South Americans who have come to south Florida for career opportunities, many Venezuelans have left their home country for both economic and political reasons. Hugo Chávez, a firebrand socialist, has increasingly imposed his own version of economic reform on Venezuela since his election in 1998 and his subsequent reelections in 2000 and 2006. Thousands of wealthy and professional middle- and upper-middle-class Venezuelans, seeing correctly that their vast fortunes are in peril, have left Venezuela for the more favorable tax and political climes of Florida. The 2006 election in Venezuela is instructive. Chávez won the election in a landslide, with over 60 percent of the vote. Miami set up the Orange Bowl stadium as a polling station for the election early in December 2006. When the results were tallied, Manuel Rosales—who opposed Chávez—received 10,679 votes, and Chávez, 242. Thus Rosales received nearly 98 percent of the U.S.-based Venezuelan vote—a fairly stark contrast from his paltry 30-some percent in Venezuela.[18] The election shows how closely Florida's Venezuelans have followed the rightward tilt of Cubans in south Florida.

After the multilayered migrations from every nation in Latin America to Florida over the last four decades, the state is home to one of the nation's most diverse Latino populations. Nearly 3.5 million Latinos now reside in Florida, surpassing New York as the state with the third-largest Latino population in the United States (California, with 12.5 million Latinos, is first; Texas, with 7.9 million, is second).[19] Unlike the U.S. Southwest, where Mexicans are by far the single largest Latino group, Florida's Latino population is more wide-ranging. Cubans still compose the lion's share of the state's Latino population, composing 29 percent of the total Latino population of Florida and nearly 6 percent of the total state population. But as noted, sizable Mexican, Puerto Rican, and Colombian populations form part of this mosaic, which literally includes every single country in the Hispanic Americas—Paraguayans represent the smallest single national group, with just over 1,400.

The diversity of Latino populations in Florida is geographically determined—that is, there are clear patterns to the migrations. There is no county north of Seminole (near Orlando) where Latinos compose more than 10 percent of the population, and the counties with the highest concentration of Latinos (Miami-Dade at 60 percent; Orange and Broward each near 20 percent) are in south Florida or around Orlando, Tampa, and inland south Florida. This is the result of the multiple migration patterns—Cubans and South Americans into Miami; Puerto Ricans into Tampa, Orlando, and Miami; and Mexicans into rural areas.

Cubans, as can be expected, are most heavily concentrated in Miami-Dade and Broward counties. They are the single largest ethnic group in Miami-Dade County, representing about 32 percent of the county's population, with about 740,000. Whites who would likely identify as non-Hispanics probably represent about 450,000–600,000 people, making it, along with African Americans/non-Hispanic blacks, the dual second-largest ethnic group in Miami-Dade.[20] As of 2005 in Miami-Dade, Cubans represent over half (about 52 percent) of all Latinos, whereas no other single Latino group represents more than 7 percent of the total Latino population of Miami-Dade—about 96,000 Nicaraguans live in Miami-Dade, making them the second-largest single Latino group in the county, far behind the some 740,000 Cubans. The highest concentration of Cubans is in Hialeah, where Cubans represent at least 71 percent of the total population (145,444 out of 203,575).

Other Latino populations in Florida, such as Puerto Ricans, the next largest Latino group in Florida (at over 600,000 total in all Florida), are more spread out. Puerto Ricans are the single largest Latino group in Orange County—of the 236,000 Latinos (out of a total population of 1 million) in Orange County, 115,000, are Puerto Rican. Likewise, Puerto Ricans make up the majority of Latinos in Osceola County—50,000 out of 87,000 Latinos. They compose a sizable portion of the Latino population in Broward County, which is home to the most diverse, in terms of percentages, of Latino populations in Florida. A sizeable Puerto Rican population also resides in Hillsborough County (65,000 out of 238,000 Latinos and a total population of 1.1 million). Approximately 81,000 Puerto Ricans also live in Miami-Dade.

Close to 390,000 Latinos live in Broward out of a total population of about 1.8 million. Of this Latino population, no single group composes more than 20 percent of the Latino population. Approximately 78,000 Puerto Ricans (about 20 percent), 69,000 Cubans (about 18 percent), 57,000 Colombians (about 15 percent), 34,000 Mexican (about 9 percent), 19,000 each of Dominicans, Peruvians, and Venezuelans (each about 5 percent), and 9,000 Ecuadorians (about 2 percent) and an undetermined number of Brazilians (mostly in Pompano Beach) live in Broward County, making it a very evenly divided county in terms of Latinos.

Mexicans, who compose the third-largest national Latino group in Florida, tend to be spread out, largely in rural areas. This is due to the migration patterns in general of Mexicans into Florida, who have largely been from poorer groups than Cubans, Venezuelans, Puerto Ricans, and Colombians. This does not mean that no wealthy Mexicans have migrated to Florida (there is a small and extremely wealthy Mexican enclave in Aventura, in north Miami-Dade), but in general it appears that Mexican migration in Florida has followed family routes or agricultural or semiskilled labor markets. And unlike migrations from Central America, which have largely settled in urban areas such as Miami, Mexicans have tended to settle in areas such as Hillsborough County (53,000 in the county of 1.1 million), a large county that includes Tampa and rural areas to the east. Mexicans have also migrated for agricultural and service jobs across central-south Florida, and the highest concentrations can be found in rural areas such as Homestead in southern Miami-Dade County (some 43,000 in the county) and rural parts of Palm Beach County (30,000, but perhaps more given the nature of agricultural work). In some rural counties Mexicans represent a large majority or a sizeable plurality of the Latino population: Polk County (more than 25,000 in a county of half a million in 2000, and half of the overall Latino population); Lee County (16,000 out of 42,000 Latinos and 440,000 overall); Hendry County (10,000 out of 14,000 Latinos and a total county population of 36,000); De Soto County (inland from Sarasota on the Gulf Coast, where 7,000 of 8,000 Latinos are Mexican out of a total population of 32,000); Hardee County (south of De Soto, with 7,500 out of close to 10,000 Latinos were Mexican in 2000, out of a total population of 27,000); and Highlands County (6,000 out of 11,000 Latinos in a county of 87,000).

But population figures on Mexicans can be difficult to track in Florida. Unlike Cubans, who are given visas on arrival in the United States, Puerto Ricans, who are U.S. citizens, and professional South Americans, who arrive with visas, many Mexicans in Florida remain undocumented. It is likely that the overall population of Mexicans in Florida is higher than the 2005 reported number of 532,000.

Other groups (South and Central Americans primarily, as opposed to Puerto Ricans and Mexicans) tend to be concentrated very heavily in Miami and Broward. For example, over 70 percent of all Colombians (the fourth-largest Latino group statewide) in Florida live in these two counties (57,000 in Broward and 90,000 in Miami-Dade, out of some 235,000 in the state). Sixty-three percent of the statewide Dominican population of about 122,000 lives in Miami-Dade and Broward. This trend holds true for several other groups from South America: Venezuelans (76 percent of the 82,000 statewide population), Peruvians (72 percent of the statewide population of about 78,000), and Argentines (77 percent of the statewide population of 52,000). Central Americans also follow this concentration in southeast Florida (statewide, 88 percent of 117,000 Nicaraguans, 68 percent of 88,000 Hondurans, and 60 percent of 47,000 Salvadorans live in Miami-Dade and Broward Counties).

But for all this diversity, Florida in many ways is the very opposite of cosmopolitanism. Rather than celebrating diversity and ethnic mixture, Latino identity in Florida is defined principally by national association and by divisive and tense relationships between Cubans and other Latino groups. Given Cubans' highly privileged immigration status, and their socioeconomically higher status than other groups, especially among those who arrived before Mariel, many Latinos in Florida see Cubans not as their natural allies but as their economic and political enemies. Politics is about perception, and the very perception that Cubans have turned Miami into a third-world city, as Colorado Republican congressman Tom Tancredo recently claimed, or that racial division and ethnic distrust had turned it into the "Beirut of the West," as Puerto Rican mayor of Miami Maurice Ferré once remarked, are telling indicators of Latino identity in Florida.[21] The question—heavily determined by the accented response—"where are you from?" is one of the most common first questions asked between Spanish speakers in Florida, and its underlying cultural implication writ large on the public stage can lead, as it did in Liberty City, to devastating consequences of racial violence.

NOTABLE LATINOS

Menéndez de Avilés, Pedro (1519–1574). Born in Avilés, in Asturias, Spain, Menéndez de Avilés came from the Spanish nobility and made a name for himself as a formidable naval officer. In 1554 he commanded the fleet that brought Phillip II to England to wed Queen Mary. By the 1560s he was operating as a commander in the Spanish trans-Atlantic military fleet system between the Americas and Spain. True to medieval and colonial methods of conquest, Menéndez de Avilés (not without some opposition and political troubles) was granted the title of *adelantado* of Florida. This meant that he would front the capital for the venture of conquest and colonization of Florida in the name of the Crown in exchange for a share of the spoils and potential title of nobility.

On August 28, 1565, he founded St. Augustine as the first successful permanent Spanish settlement in Florida. He also encouraged Catholic missionaries to come to Florida as part of the Hispanization project. Although the long-term success of St. Augustine was mixed, Menéndez de Avilés was important as the first successful colonizer of Spanish Florida. Also, his project fell in line with traditional approaches to colonization by the Spanish. Rather than being funded by a royal army or Crown-sponsored force, Spanish colonization efforts in the Americas were privately funded affairs, and Menéndez de Avilés's approach to conquest as a means of social advancement and financial gain fell within this cultural pattern.

Martínez Ybor, Vicente (1820–1896). Born in Valencia, Spain, Martínez Ybor moved to Cuba and became involved in the cigar-making business. He became quite successful, but in 1869 a revolution against Spain led him to leave Cuba for Key West.[22] He had a cigar factory there, but a fire destroyed it in 1880. He left Key West for Tampa shortly thereafter. In 1885 he purchased several city blocks of land on the outskirts of Tampa. He bought a cigar factory and developed a large cigar industry in Tampa. With the promise of steady work, many Spanish, Cuban, and Italian migrants came to Tampa to work in the cigar business or in the various satellite service industries spawned by the engine of the cigar industry.

Eventually the area where Martínez Ybor operated was named after him. It is a testimony both to his entrepreneurial spirit and to his role as the first leader of a Latino migration in modern Florida. Although the Latino community of Tampa–Ybor City would never rival that of Miami in later times, it is significant as a kind of foreshadowing of future migrations. Moreover, even during the nadir of Latino presence in Florida in the nineteenth century, the connections between Cuba and Florida were always very strong.

Ferré, Maurice (1935–). Born in Ponce, Puerto Rico, Ferré was the first Latino elected mayor of a major U.S. city in the modern era. Described by one historian as a "revolutionary in pinstripes," he was mayor during some of Miami's most tumultuous times between 1973 and 1985, having been reelected four times after his initial election in 1973.[23] Ferré oversaw Miami's transformation from Cuban exile enclave to Cocaine, USA, and was eventually consumed by the shifting ethnic lines of south Florida politics.

Ferré was from a wealthy family of politicians and construction company owners. He earned a bachelor degree in architecture from the University of Miami in 1957 and worked for his family's concrete business. He ventured into politics (a Democrat) and was elected to the Florida legislature and Miami-Dade county commissioner in the later 1960s and early 1970s. He ran for and was elected mayor of Miami in 1973. Although eventually the rightward shift in Miami politics and the increasing political clout of Cubans would force him from office, Ferré is significant as the nation's first Latino mayor of a major city.[24]

Ros-Lehtinen, Ileana (1952–). Born in Havana, Congresswoman Ros-Lehtinen came to Miami after Castro's rise to power and was educated at Florida International University in Miami, receiving a BA in 1975 and an MS in 1987, and received an EdD from the University of Miami in 2004. The daughter of a prominent anti-Castro activist, Enrique Ros, Ros-Lehtinen has been at the forefront of the anti-Castro lobby in both the Florida legislature and U.S. Congress for over two decades as a Republican. She served in the Florida state legislature (1982–1986) and senate (1986–1988) before running for Florida's 18th Congressional District in 1988, with future governor Jeb Bush as her campaign manager. She won the seat and has held it since then. When she was elected, she was the first Latina woman and first Cuban American elected to the U.S. Congress. Her candidacy was endorsed by the powerful anti-Castro activist Jorge Mas Canosa, who had once been head of the Cuban American National Foundation.

Ros-Lehtinen has been a consistent advocate of anti-Castro policies and has embroiled herself in several controversies concerning Castro over the years as a lawmaker. In the 1980s she lobbied for the pardon and release of Orlando Bosch, who had been implicated in the bombing of Cubana Flight 455 in 1976, which killed 73 people. She organized a "Free Orlando Bosch" day in her efforts. Recently, in 2006, the documentary *638 Ways to Kill Castro* was released by BBC, and in it Ros-Lehtinen twice openly called for the assassination of Castro. When pressed in various interviews, she denied having said this; the director released the full interview transcripts that clearly showed the congresswoman calling for the assassination of Castro. Ros-Lehtinen beat a hasty retreat but insists that her fundamental position is just.

Ros-Lehtinen has been consistently one of the most militant supporters of anti-Castro policies and one of the tireless advocates for regime change in Cuba. She operates from a powerful base of both political and popular support in Miami; in 2006 she was reelected to her seat with 62 percent of the district's vote. It is not clear what her future goals are, but she is an important voice for anti-Castro politics and is symbolically important as a Latina political leader of the right.

Estefan, Gloria (1957–). Born Gloria Fajardo in Havana, the now famous singer was a daughter of the Batista Cuba elite. Soon after her second birthday and shortly after Castro took over in Cuba, her family fled Cuba and came to Miami. When she was 18, she met her husband—Emilio Estefan, whose family name she took—at a wedding party. She joined Emilio's band, which would change its name to the Miami Sound Machine. They were married in 1978 and soon became one of Miami's cultural power couples. Miami Sound Machine produced some of the most memorable disco music of the late 1970s and early 1980s, and in 1984 the band produced its first English-language album. Shortly thereafter the band released "Primitive Love," which sold over 3 million copies in the United States and established Gloria and the Miami Sound Machine as bona fide stars.

Through the 1980s Estefan's star rose along with spectacular record sales, but in 1990 her tour bus crashed and she suffered severe injuries, which required a year of recovery and physical therapy. She made a comeback and through the 1990s established herself as one of the United States' premier Latina vocalists. She has won five Grammy Awards, among others, and has produced both Spanish- and English-language albums to critical and popular acclaim. In addition to her musical activities, she has become active as a restaurateur in Miami and a member of the Board of Directors of the University of Miami. Significantly, Estefan in many ways paved the way for the so-called Latin explosion in North American pop music made notable by the work of Ricky Martin, Shakira, and Jennifer Lopez. She is also noted for having helped create what is now known as the Miami sound, or the Miami Latin sound, a particular fusion of disco, Latin, and dancehall styles.

Cantero III, Raoul (1960–). The grandson of former Cuban dictator Fulgencio Batista, Cantero was appointed the first Latino on the Florida State Supreme Court by then governor Jeb Bush in 2002. Appointed as a strong conservative by Bush, his tenure on the court was intended to blunt what Bush and Cantero saw as judicial activism on the bench. Although prior to his appointment he had not served as a judge, he was known to have strong views on topics such as abortion. In 1993 he wrote a letter to the editor of the *Miami Herald* in which he said that "abortion kills children." He also weighed in on the Orlando Bosch case. In 1989 Cantero said on a Miami radio talk show that Bosch was a "Cuban patriot."[25]

Cantero was born in Madrid in 1960 after his parents (his mother is Batista's daughter) left Cuba in the wake of Batista's fall and Castro's rise to power. His family came to

Miami soon thereafter, in 1961.[26] He proved to be a brilliant student, graduating summa cum laude from Florida State University in 1982 and cum laude from Harvard Law in 1985. He served as a law clerk for Justice Edward B. Davis of the United States District Court for the Southern District of Florida. He worked in the appellate division of the Miami law firm Adorno and Yoss and was active in several bar association panels and committees, as well as community organizations such as the Coral Gables Planning and Zoning Board, serving as its president at one point. Being named to the State Supreme Court at the age of 41, he is poised to become an influential jurist and has been mentioned as a possible U.S. Supreme Court nominee, though he was recently passed over for this distinction in favor of Samuel Alito. In any case, Cantero's Florida court appointment is significant on numerous levels. He is the first Latino Supreme Court justice of Florida and, like Ileana Ros-Lehtinen, he symbolizes the rise of prominent Cubans to high-profile positions of political power.

Ayala, Jorge "Rivi" (1964–). Born in Colombia and raised in Chicago after age 11, Ayala went on to become one of the Medellín cocaine cartel's principal assassins in Miami in the 1980s, acting as the personal bodyguard and favored hit-man of Griselda Blanco, a major cocaine operator for the Medellín cartel in 1980s Miami.

The TV show *Miami Vice* and the movie *Scarface* made cocaine and Miami synonymous on the national stage, but beyond the lascivious stereotyping of Miami Latinos as drug-dealing murderers and money launderers, there was, in the end, quite a lot of cocaine trafficking, murder, and money laundering in Miami in the 1980s. Entire Miami City Police Academy classes did get arrested, and Miami mayors were indicted on corruption charges. At the center of this was a multibillion-dollar cocaine industry centered in Antioquia, Colombia, overseen largely by the Medellín cartel. Ayala came to Miami as a noted car thief from Chicago, and he had a reputation for fearlessness. His reputation quickly gained him entry into the world of organized crime and the cocaine trafficking industry of Miami. He was the enforcer of Griselda Blanco and is, by his own admission, responsible for several murder-assassinations on Blanco's orders.

Long known in Miami in the world of organized crime and investigative journalism, his story resonates as a real-life *Scarface*. Some may view him as a kind of worst-case stereotype of drug-trafficking Colombians, but there can be no underestimating his role in the transformation of Miami in the 1980s as the United States' most dangerous city and as a city built with billions of dollars of cocaine and laundered money. Eventually, the drug trafficking through Miami was compromised by law enforcement efforts; now travels principally across the U.S.-Mexican border, but in Miami in the 1980s, Rivi was the man to be reckoned with in what was, at the time, Miami's single largest source of income: Colombian cocaine.

CULTURAL CONTRIBUTIONS

RELIGION

Religion in Florida has been heavily influenced by Latinos. During the lengthy Spanish colonial presence, Franciscan and Jesuit missionaries established a far-flung missionary system throughout the coast and interior of Florida. However, in general, these missions were rarely successful in the ways that Spanish missionaries were in places such as Mexico and Peru. Instead, they suffered, as did the colonial enterprise in general in Florida, from underfunding. Moreover, the Indian groups often proved impervious to missionary efforts. The overall result was not the kind of widespread conversion of Indians that took place in densely settled areas of Latin America. Instead, the experience of Spanish missionaries in Florida was more akin to the perilous and shaky experiences in other peripheral regions, such as southern Chile, northern Mexico, and the Amazon, where highly mobile and nonurbanized Indians proved difficult to concentrate into mission settlements.

But if the colonial missionary efforts of the Spanish met with mixed success, the massive migrations of Latinos into Florida over the last four decades has made for a transformation of the religious landscape of Florida. Long a bastion of Anglo Protestantism, Florida now has been influenced by Latin American popular Catholicism and by Caribbean Catholicism in particular. Perhaps the most notable influence has been popular Cuban folk Catholicism. A mix of African *orixá* (spirit) worship and folk veneration of saints, Afro-Cuban religious influence is quite visible, especially in Miami. One can walk into virtually any grocery store and find candles for San Lázaro (a saint popular among Cubans) or Eleguá (the Yoruba *orixá*).

The mixture of African and Spanish elements in Cuban religion has become a flashpoint both culturally and politically. Anthropologists and historians debate whether *orixá* and spirit propitiation should be called syncretic or parallel. In any case, African slaves introduced the worship of *orixás* to Spaniards in Cuba. The mixing or parallel use of *orixás* and Spanish Catholic saints is called Santería in the Spanish Caribbean, Voodoo in Haiti, and *Candomblé* in Brazil. But whereas Mesoamerican gods were subsumed into Spanish saints (Tlaloc, the god of rain, became John the Baptist, for example), *orixás* remain highly visible in Latino folk religion in Florida.

The presence of Santería in Florida became an issue of political debate in Hialeah. The Church of Lukumi Babalu Aye, an organization that practiced and promoted Santería, intended to set up its base in Hialeah in the 1980s, but the city enacted an ordinance directed at the Church. Santería rituals involve animal sacrifice, and the city of Hialeah passed a law prohibiting this sacrifice. Although the unspoken motive may have been racial—Santería is derived from African rituals and white Cubans, many of whom, like Ralph Arza, are powerful political leaders in Hialeah—the implications went well beyond that. The Church of Lukumi Babalu Aye challenged the law and the law was upheld in U.S. Circuit Court. The Church then appealed to the U.S. Supreme Court, which heard the case and ruled, in 1993, in a 7-2 decision written by Justice Anthony Kennedy, that the Hialeah ordinance violated the Santeros' right to practice religion as protected under the First Amendment of the U.S. Constitution.[27]

Santería is not the only form of folk religion of Latin American origin that has come to become important in Florida, but the Hialeah case highlighted just how politically charged questions of religious practice could be in a highly diverse Latino population in Florida. The Virgin of Guadalupe, revered by Mexicans, is another visible sign of the changing landscape of religion in Florida. Located in central Florida, Mexicans have brought their own form of Catholicism with them. The recent trend of saint bracelets has become a highly visible marker of popular Catholicism in Florida. And so-called *botánicas* (religious paraphernalia stores) dot the Latin sections of Florida cities.

Food and Drink

Some of the most visible and tangible cultural changes in Florida stemming from Latinos come in the form of food and drink. Mojito—a delicious concoction of rum, sugar, lime juice, and mint leaves—has become nationally and internationally famous as a quintessentially Miami drink. Latin Caribbean food—in restaurants, take-out counters, and in stores—has dramatically changed the culinary landscape of Florida. And more recently, the influence of Latin fusion has become the next big thing in food and culinary trends.

One need only walk into a corner grocer in Miami to get a sense of just how dramatic the influence of Latinos on food culture has become. Badía, the spice and herb company, markets a vast selection of traditional non-Latin spices, such as tarragon, thyme, and black pepper, but has also become one of the largest spice companies in the United States, with widespread distribution in Florida. Badía offers everything from Mexican chiles, Puerto Rican *mojo* (a garlic-based marinade), and virtually any spice or seasoning from the Caribbean imaginable. Likewise, products by Goya Foods can be found in major supermarkets in Florida as well as in corner markets. The Meridian Market, on 6th Street by Meridian in Miami Beach, is a case in point in the incredible culinary diversity and cultural mixing of Florida. The deli hot food counter offers a wide range of traditional Caribbean foods such as *ropa vieja* (a meat stew with peppers and onions), fried yuca, black beans, Cuban-Chinese fried rice, and others. The girls who work the counter are predominantly Honduran migrants and do not speak English. The butcher counter is run by a Cuban and an Argentine who provide many typically Argentine and Latino meats such as beef sweetbreads, tripe (for Mexican *menudo*), *vacío* (an Argentine steak cut), and many others. The produce section offers a wide range of Latin, especially Caribbean, vegetables such as yuca, chayote squash, avocado, habanero chiles, jalapeño chiles, and papaya.

It would be easy to belabor the point, but perhaps yuca is most symbolic of the Latin and Caribbean influence on Florida's culinary landscape. A nutritionally poor but calorie-rich tuber, yuca is a starchy food, similar to a sweeter version of a Russet potato. Long used by the indigenous Tainos of the Caribbean for its caloric richness, yuca was quickly adopted into Spanish Caribbean food. A staple of Puerto Rican, Cuban, and Dominican diets, yuca can be found in most supermarkets and grocers in south Florida and is often found on menus in upscale restaurants, as well as being a standard at mid-range Caribbean restaurants.

In addition to the influence of Caribbean styles, Argentine food has also made impressive inroads in Florida. Long known for its high-quality beef, Argentine *parrillas* (grills) have proven wildly popular in Florida for their simple offerings of steak, red wine, and pasta. Mexican food, which is of course incredibly popular throughout the United States, has been more confined to regions of Florida such as Homestead, where there are large enclaves of Mexican migrants. Because the market audience is primarily Mexican, the nature of Mexican food in Florida has tended to be less internationalized and "Taco Bell-ized" as it has been in other parts of the United States, where the tendency of Mexican food to be very hot and spicy has been tamped down for American palates.

South American wine has also proven to be extremely popular in Florida. Whereas in other parts of the United States with large Latino populations, such as California, where Californian, Australian, and French wines tend to be more popular, the close demographic and financial links between Florida and Latin America have made for a booming industry in the export of Argentine and Chilean wine into Florida. Indeed, one is as likely to find an Argentine malbec or a Chilean cabernet in a wine store or restaurant list as a Californian pinot noir or French Bordeaux, both of which tend to be more expensive than their South American counterparts.

And then there is the rum. Caribbean rum has in many ways transformed the image of Miami and Florida into a place where the party never ends and the cocktails always remain full and the girls scantily clad, and the men pack pistols in nightclubs. This is in many ways testimony to the success of marketing campaigns that have associated rum, mojitos, and Cuba libres as symbolic of the Florida Latin experience. But it is also testimony to the financial and political influence of the Bacardí family and conglomerate, which came to Miami shortly after the fall of Castro.

Music

The Miami sound offers a refrain of the old saw: one may not know how to define it, but one knows it when one hears it. Exuberant, playful, and robust, Florida's Latin music has developed out of classical Cuban styles, dancehall, reggae, soul, and disco. Celia Cruz, the singer whose voice was truly larger than life, in many ways symbolized this new sound, even if it is Gloria Estefan who came to be its most visible representative for non-Spanish speakers. Celia Cruz was trained in mambo, salsa, and other forms and left Cuba after Castro's rise, but she was based primarily in Mexico City, though later in life she had homes in Miami and New York. The "new" Latin sound of Florida combined brash band music along with the big vocals of singers such as Cruz to produce a unique kind of Caribbean music.

Apart from this now signature music, numerous other styles of music have come to influence both Florida and even international musical styles. The most recent phenomenon is *reggaetón*, which is principally Puerto Rican in origin. *Reggaetón* combines rap, hip-hop, salsa, reggae, and heavy bass into a seductive mix that can now be heard in cafés, bars, clubs, and on the radio from Miami to Santiago, Chile. Among the noted artists of the genre are Calle 13, Wisín y Yandel, and Daddy Yankee. *Reggaetón* has its critics—it has been called misogynist and overly violent—but nevertheless it appears to be in for the long haul.

In addition to Caribbean musical forms, more staid musical styles also have made some inroads in Florida's culture, though with considerably less success. Mariachi, from Mexico, has not caught on much outside of Mexican communities. The same could be said of *criolla*, the Peruvian style of music from the coastal areas, which combines vocals and Afro-Peruvian elements. Nonetheless, these styles can be heard and found principally in south Florida. Perhaps most symbolic, and indeed financially significant, of the growing influence of Latinos in music culture in the United States and Florida is the presence in Miami of many of the high-end music awards ceremonies. The Latino Billboard and Grammy ceremonies are now frequently held in Miami, and it is fitting that Gloria Estefan has often led the way.

NOTES

1. http://factfinder.census.gov/servlet/DTTable?_bm=y&-geo_id=05000US12086&-ds_name=ACS_2005_EST_G00_&-redoLog=false&-mt_name=ACS_2005_EST_G2000_B03001.

2. http://factfinder.census.gov/servlet/DTTable?_bm=y&-geo_id=05000US12086&-ds_name=ACS_2005_EST_G00_&-redoLog=false&-mt_name=ACS_2005_EST_G2000_B03001.

3. *Miami Herald,* April 8, 2006.

4. *Miami Herald,* November 11 and 12, 2006.

5. Although it is not without controversy, a classic study of the population of the Valley of Mexico remains Charles Gibson's *The Aztecs under Spanish Rule: A History of the Indians of the Valley of Mexico, 1519–1810* (Stanford: Stanford University Press, 1964).

6. See, among others, Peter Boyd-Bowman's *Indice geobiográfico de cuarenta mil pobladores españoles de América en el siglo XVI,* 2 vols. (Bogotá: Instituto Caro y Cuervo, 1964; Mexico: Ed. Jus, 1968) and Ida Altman's *Emigrants and Society: Extremadura and America in the Sixteenth Century* (Berkeley: University of California Press, 1989).

7. See Eugene Lyon, "Settlement and Survival," in *The New History of Florida*, ed. Michael Gannon (Gainesville: University Press of Florida, 1996).

8. Amy Turner Bushnell, "Republic of Spaniards, Republic of Indians," in *New History*, 66.

9. Charles W. Arnade, "Raids, Sieges, and International Wars," in *New History*, 108.

10. Arnade, "Raids, Sieges and International Wars," 102, and William S. Coker, "Pensacola," in *New History*, 128.

11. For discussion of the early U.S. period in general and for statistics given here on the subject, see Daniel L. Schafer, "U.S. Territory and State," in *New History*, 207–230.

12. Mormino, 2005, 315.

13. Quoted by Raymond A. Mohl and George E. Pozzetta, "From Migration to Multiculturalism: A History of Florida Immigration," in *New History*, 401.

14. Mormino, 2005, 286.

15. Quoted in Mohl and Pozzetta, "From Migration to Mulitculturalism," 405.

16. Mormino, 2005, 288.

17. Mormino, 2005, 289.

18. *Miami Herald*, December 4, 2006.

19. For census data on Florida, I have relied on the U.S. Census Bureau Web site, which is interactive for state, county, and city statistics on population ethnic and racial identification. The principal location for the information on Florida, which can be searched for city and county statistics, is http://factfinder.census.gov/servlet/ACSSAFFPeople?_event=&geo_id=04000US12&_geoContext=01000US%7C04000US12&_street=&_county=&_cityTown=&_state=04000US12&_zip=&_lang=en&_sse=on&ActiveGeoDiv=&_useEV=&pctxt=fph&pgsl=040&_submenuId=people_10&ds_name=ACS_2005_SAFF&_ci_nbr=null&qr_name=null&reg=null%3Anull&_keyword=&_industry=.

20. The U.S. census has two forms containing ethnic/racial questions. The first asks for race and does not ask whether one is Hispanic. The second form does not ask for phenotypic or geographically linked racial categorization but rather about whether one is Hispanic or not, with options for nationally related categories. In the 2005 figures drawn by the community surveys in Miami-Dade, about 900,000 people are non-Hispanic of any race. In the race category, in which many Hispanics identify as white, about 460,000 people are identified as black or African American. One might reasonably guess that some portion of this came from Afro-Latinos, but not much, given the general composition of Miami Latinos, most of whom claim white status racially. Accounting for some shaving off of these numbers, we can remove 300,000–450,000 people from the non-Hispanic number of 900,000, given the preponderance of non-Hispanics in the Miami black community. This gives us approximately 450,000–600,000 non-Hispanic whites in Miami-Dade, a number still lower than that of Cubans as a distinct group.

21. Quoted in Mormino, 2005, 290.

22. For a standard biography, see L. Glenn Westfall's "Don Vicente Martínez Ybor, the Man and His Empire: Development of the Clear Havana Industry in Cuba and Florida in the Nineteenth Century" (PhD diss., University of Florida, 1977). Further studies include Gary Mormino and George E. Pozzetta, *The Immigrant World of Ybor City: Italians and Their Latin Neighbors in Tampa, 1885–1985* (Gainesville: University Press of Florida, 1998).

23. Mormino, 2005, 290.

24. See, for example, Raymond Mohl's "Maurice Ferré, Xavier Suarez [sic], and the Ethnic Factor in Miami Politics," in *Spanish Pathways in Florida, 1492–1992*, eds. Ann L. Henderson and Gary R. Mormino (Sarasota, FL: Pineapple Press, 1991).

25. http://www.sptimes.com/2002/07/11/State/Selection_a_swipe_at_.shtml.

26. http://sun6.dms.state.fl.us/eog_new/eog/library/releases/2002/july/appt_cantero-07-10-02.html.

27. The full transcript of the case *Church of Lukumu Babalu Aye v. City of Hialeah* can be found at http://caselaw.lp.findlaw.com/scripts/getcase.pl?navby=CASE&court=US&vol=508&page=520.

BIBLIOGRAPHY

Arnade, Charles W. *Florida on Trial, 1593–1602*. Coral Gables, FL: University of Miami Press, 1959.

Boswell, Thomas D., and James R. Curtis. *The Cuban-American Experience: Culture, Images, and Perspectives*. Totowa, NJ: Rowman and Allanheld, 1983.

Bretos, Miguel. *Cuba and Florida: Exploration of a Hispanic Connection, 1539–1991*. Miami: Historical Association of Southern Florida, 1991.

Burns, Allan F. *Maya in Exile: Guatemalans in Florida*. Philadelphia, PA: Temple University Press, 1993.

Bushnell, Amy Turner. *The King's Coffer: Proprietors of the Spanish Florida Treasury, 1565–1702*. Gainesville: University Press of Florida, 1981.

———. *Situado and Sabana: Spain's Support System for the Presidio and Mission Provinces of Florida*. New York: American Museum of Natural History, 1994.

Carr, Patrick. *Sunshine States: Wild Times and Extraordinary Lives in the Land of Gators, Guns, and Grapefruits*. New York: Doubleday, 1990.

Chatelain, Verne E. *The Defenses of Spanish Florida, 1565 to 1763*. Washington, DC: Carnegie Institute of Washington, 1941.

Coker, William S., and Douglas G. Inglis. *The Spanish Censuses of Pensacola, 1784–1820: A Genealogical Guide to Spanish Pensacola*. Pensacola, FL: Perdido Bay Press, 1980.

———. *John Forbes' Description of the Spanish Floridas, 1804*. Pensacola, FL: Perdido Bay Press, 1979.

Cruz, Arturo K., and Jaime Suchlicki. *The Impact of Nicaraguans in Miami*. Coral Gables, FL: University of Miami, Graduate School of International Studies, 1990.

Deagan, Kathleen. *Spanish St. Augustine: The Archeology of a Colonial Creole Community*. New York: Academic Press, 1983.

Galgano, Robert C. *Feast of Souls: Indians and Spaniards in the Seventeenth-Century Missions of Florida and New Mexico*. Albuquerque: University of New Mexico Press, 2005.

Gannon, Michael V. *The Cross in the Sand: The Early Catholic Church in Florida, 1513–1870*. Gainesville: University Press of Florida, 1965.

García, Genaro, ed. *Dos antiguas relaciones de la Florida*. Mexico City, Mexico: Tip. de J. Aguilar Vera y Comp., 1902.

García, María Cristina. *Havana, USA: Cuban Exiles and Cuban Americans in South Florida, 1959–1994*. Berkeley: University of California Press, 1996.

Geiger, Maynard. *The Franciscan Conquest of Florida (1573–1618)*. Washington, DC: Catholic University of America, 1937.

Grenier, Guillermo J., and Alex Stepick. *Miami Now: Immigration, Ethnicity, and Social Change*. Gainesville: University Press of Florida, 1992.

Greenbaum, Susan. *More than Black: Afro-Cubans in Tampa*. Gainesville: University Press of Florida, 2002.

Griffen, William B. "Spanish Pensacola, 1700–1763." *Florida Historical Quarterly* 27 (1959): 242–262.

Hann, John H. *Missions to the Calusa*. Gainesville: University Press of Florida; Florida Museum of Natural History, 1991.

Henderson, Ann L., and Gary R. Mormino, eds. *Spanish Pathways, 1492–1992. Los caminos españoles en la Florida, 1492–1992*. Translated by Carlos J. Cano, José A. Feliciano-Butler, and Warren Hampton. Sarasota, FL: Pineapple Press, 1991.

Hoffman, Paul E. *A New Andalucia and a Way to the Orient: The American Southeast during the Sixteenth Century*. Baton Rouge: Louisiana State University Press, 1990.

Landers, Jane G., ed. *Colonial Plantations and Economy in Florida*. Gainesville: University Press of Florida, 2000.

Lyon, Eugene. *The Enterprise of Spanish Florida: Pedro Menéndez de Avilés and the Spanish Conquest of 1565–1568*. Gainesville: University Press of Florida, 1976.

McEwan, Bonnie. *The Spanish Missions of La Florida*. Gainesville: University Press of Florida, 1993.

Milanich, Jerald T. *Florida Indians and the Invasion from Europe*. Gainesville: University Press of Florida, 1995.

Milanich, Jerald T., and Susan Milbrath, eds. *First Encounters: Spanish Explorations in the Caribbean and the United State, 1492–1570*. Gainesville: University Press of Florida, 1989.

Mohl, Raymond A. "Miami: The Ethnic Cauldron." In *Sunbelt Cities*. Eds. Richard Bernard and Bradley R. Rice. Austin: University of Texas Press, 1983, 71–89.

———. "Miami: New Immigrant City." In *Searching for the Sunbelt: Historical Perspectives on a Region*. Ed. Raymond A. Mohl. Knoxville: University of Tennessee Press, 1990, 81–98.

Mormino, Gary R. *Land of Sunshine, State of Dreams: A Social History of Modern Florida*. Foreword by Raymond Arsenault. Gainesville: University Press of Florida, 2005.

Mormino, Gary R., and George E. Pozzetta. *The Immigrant World of Ybor City: Italians and Their Latin Neighbors in Tampa, 1885–1985*. Champaign-Urbana: University of Illinois Press, 1987.

Oré, Luis Jerónimo de. *The Martyrs of Florida (1513–1616)*. Translated by Maynard Geiger. New York: Joseph F. Wagner, 1936.

Pérez Firmat, Gustavo. *Life on the Hyphen: The Cuban-American Way*. Austin: University of Texas Press, 1994.

Portes, Alejandro. *The Economic Sociology of Immigration: Essays on Networks, Ethnicity, and Entrepreneurship*. New York: Russell Sage Foundation, 1995.

Portes, Alejandro, and Rubén G. Rumbaut, eds. *Ethnicities: Children of Immigrants in America*. Berkeley: University of California Press, 2001.

Portes, Alejandro, and Rubén G. Rumbaut. *Immigrant America: A Portrait*. 3rd ed. Berkeley: University of California Press, 2006.

Portes, Alejandro, and Alex Steppick. *City on the Edge: The Transformation of Miami.* Berkeley: University of California Press, 1993.

Schafer, Daniel L. "'A Class of People Neither Free Men Nor Slaves': From Spanish to American Race Relations in Florida, 1821–1861." *Journal of Social History* 26 (1993): 587–609.

Stamps, S. David, Miriam Stamps, and Susan Greenbaum. *Comparative Study of Blacks, Whites, and Hispanics in the Tampa Metropolitan Area.* Tampa: University of South Florida, Institute on Black Life, 1990.

TePaske, John Jay. *The Governorship of Spanish Florida, 1700–1763.* Durham, NC: Duke University Press, 1964.

Weber, David J. *The Spanish Frontier in North America.* New Haven, CT: Yale University Press, 1992.

Weddle, Robert S. *Spanish Sea: The Gulf of Mexico in North American Discovery, 1500–1685.* College Station: Texas A&M University Press, 1985.

Zubillaga, Félix. *La Florida: La misión jesuítica (1566–1572) y la colonización española.* Rome, Italy: Institutum Historicum Societatis Iesu, 1941.

11

Georgia

Stephanie A. Bohon

CHRONOLOGY

1521	Explorers Francisco Gordillo and Pedro de Quexos explore the Atlantic Coast from Florida to Cape Hateras, North Carolina.
1526	Explorer Lucás Vazquéz de Ayllon founds the first named European settlement in the New World at San Miguel de Gualdape on the Savannah River. It lasts two months.
1527	Surviving members of the Gualdape colony return to Santo Domingo, Dominican Republic.
1539–1543	Explorer Hernando de Soto begins his exploration of the Southeast, including inland Georgia.
1566	The Spanish government establishes a fort on St. Catherines Island. Jesuit priests construct Mission Santa Catalina, Georgia's first church, within the fort.
1587	Puturiba, the first Franciscan mission in Georgia, is established on or near Cumberland Island.
1595–1597	The Franciscan Missions Talapo, Santo Domingo de Asao-Talaje, Santa Catalina de Guale, and Santa Clara de Tupiqui-Espogache, and the mission-presidio Nuestra Señora de Guadalupe de Tolomato, are established on the Sea Islands.
1597	The Guale Rebellion, a Native American uprising, results in the destruction of several Spanish missions and the burning of St. Catherines Island Presidio. All remaining Spanish missions are abandoned.
1605	Franciscans reestablish Georgia's mission system. The St. Catherines Island Presidio is rebuilt for their protection.

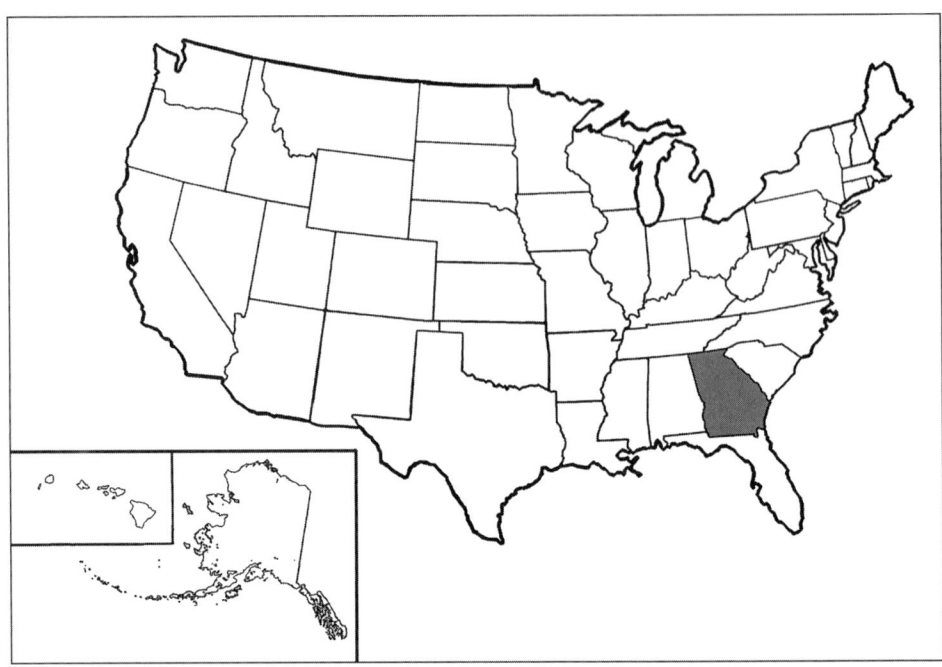

1670	St. Catherines Island Presidio is abandoned after attacks by English-controlled South Carolina forces.
1675–1680	Attacks by the Westo tribe and pirate raids destroy most of the Spanish missions in Guale and Mocama.
1702	An invasion of Spanish Florida by South Carolina troops destroys the remaining Guale and Mocama missionary systems.
1721	Fort King George is established by the British on the former site of Mission Santo Domingo de Asao as the southernmost British outpost in North America.
1733	The first English colony in Georgia is established by General James Oglethorpe, exacerbating hostilities between the Spanish and the English.
1739	The War of Jenkin's Ear begins between English and Spanish colonizing forces.
1742	The Battle of Bloody Marsh is fought on St. Simons Island, ending Spanish occupation of Georgia.
1898	Spanish-American War begins with the bombing of the USS *Maine*. Georgia supplies 3,000 troops for fighting in Cuba, Puerto Rico, and the Philippines.
1900	Georgia Senator Augustus Octavius Bacon introduces legislation to block U.S. annexation of the Philippines and Cuba.
1948	Cuban students at Georgia Tech organize the Latin Americans Club.
1960	Fidel Castro's rise to power results in a mass migration of Cubans to Miami and Atlanta.
1970s	Latino workers begin to find work in Georgia's chicken-processing industry.

1980s	Latino workers begin supplying labor in Georgia's textile industries.
1981	Cuban-born Roberto Goizueta becomes chairman and chief executive officer of the Atlanta-based Coca-Cola Company.
1996	The Olympic Games launches Atlanta's reputation as an international city; many Latin American-based companies move to Georgia.
1998	The Board of Regents of the University System convenes the Hispanic Task Force to determine how to best meet the needs of Georgia's Latino students.
2000	The U.S. census reports Latino numbers in Georgia are much higher than projected.
2002	The Georgia Supreme Court upholds a lower court decision that makes Latinos a cognizable (within court's jurisdiction) group for jury selection.
2003	Governor Perdue creates the Latino Commission for a New Georgia. In August two Mexican American college students, Desiree Smith and Beatriz Velez, create the Students for Latino Empowerment. It is the first student organization dedicated to encouraging upward mobility among Georgia's Latinos.
2004	Former employees file federal racketeering charges against carpet-maker Mohawk Industries, claiming that the hiring of Latino workers represents a conspiracy to depress wages.
2005	On September 30 robberies of four mobile home parks in Tift and Colquitt Counties result in the murder of six Mexican immigrants in an incident known as The Night of Blood.
2006	On April 17 Governor Perdue signs the Georgia Security and Immigration Compliance Act; many view the bill as anti-Latino. On November 5, Cherokee County officials unanimously enact the state's first ordinance, making English the official language of the county.

HISTORICAL OVERVIEW

Between 1990 and 2005, the Latino population in Georgia increased 474 percent; by 2000, there were Latinos living in every one of Georgia's 159 counties. African Americans, who compose almost 30 percent of Georgia's population, are now outnumbered by Latinos in some counties, despite the fact that Latinos only compose about 7 percent of Georgia's current population.[3] Latinos are now visible across the state; thus, many Georgians mistakenly believe that their presence in the state is a new phenomenon. In fact, Georgia has enjoyed 500 years of Latino presence, beginning with the very first Spanish pilgrims who arrived from what is now the Dominican Republic in the sixteenth century.

COLONIAL GEORGIA

In 1520, Francisco Gordillo and Pedro de Quexos began an expedition from Hispaniola (the island that today is home to Haiti and the Dominican Republic) up the coast of North America to explore the area north of Florida. After claiming for Spain land just south of what is today the Georgia-Florida border, Quexos went on to explore a considerable portion of the Atlantic coast. He is believed to be the first European in Georgia.

Back in Hispaniola, Lucás Vazquéz de Ayllon, who was responsible for organizing Gordillo's 1520 expedition, obtained a charter from Spain to create the first European settlement north of Mexico. With 600 colonists and an indigenous guide, they sailed north to land in Winyah Bay, South Carolina. Finding the area unsuitable for settlement, they traveled south, finally settling in an area around the Savannah River, probably on or near what is today Sapelo Island. They named the settlement San Miguel de Gualdape (the exact name of the settlement and its precise location are in dispute). The settlement did not last long. It was attacked by the indigenous people and plagued by disease and slave revolts. After only two months, the failed expedition returned to Santo Domingo with only 150 settlers remaining. De Ayllon died on the voyage home.[4]

Although the Gualdape colony was short-lived, it is important in that it set the stage for the creation of Spanish missions and garrisons along the coastal regions of Georgia in what are today called the Sea Islands. Beginning in 1574, Spanish priests and friars began settling in what they called Mocama (the area between Altamaha and Nassau Sound) and Guale (north of Altamaha Sound to St. Catherines Sound). Between 1587 and 1680 there were at least 18 Franciscan missions located throughout the Sea Islands and as far inland as the Okefenokee Swamp.

Although the primary purpose of the missionaries was to convert the Native Americans to Catholicism, friars often interfered with the political and social affairs of the indigenous people. Their presence allowed for the protection of illegal Spanish slaving expeditions, and many Native Americans were forced into servitude. Although slavery was prohibited under Spanish law, unmarried indigenous men were forced into servitude, working in the Spanish-controlled fields or fortifying the battlements around St. Augustine in Florida. Due to poor working conditions, many became ill and died. This situation led to numerous revolts, the most notorious of which was the Guale Rebellion that resulted in the death of all but one friar and the discontinuation of the Georgia mission system until 1605.

Between 1605 and 1680 the Jesuits, and later the Franciscans, rebuilt many of the missions, and the Spanish government created some garrisons for their protection. The primary mission-presidio was Santa Catalina on St. Catherines Island. Built in 1566, nearly two centuries before Spanish missions were built in California, it is assumed to be the oldest church in Georgia.

Despite the fortifications, the Spanish settlements were often attacked in English slave and pirate raids and were constantly under threat by the indigenous people. The Iroquoian Westo tribe, called the Chichimeco by the Spanish, was the most troublesome. Beginning in 1675, the tribe began attacking Spanish missions and presidios with the support of the English colonies in South Carolina and Virginia. By 1680, most of the Spanish settlements had been destroyed by the Westo. In 1702, South Carolina forces successfully invaded the weakened Guale strongholds to destroy the remaining outposts.

Although the Spanish outposts were primarily established in the coastal regions, some exploration occurred inland. Renowned Spanish explorer Hernando de Soto traveled through Georgia in search of gold and other valuables along a path now known as the De Soto Trail. The expedition, which resulted in an exploration of most of the Southeast and Midwest, was notorious for its mistreatment of the indigenous people, but it also served to provide Europeans with their first glimpse of native habits and cultures. One of de Soto's most valued guides on his expedition to the Mississippi River was Perico, a 17-year-old boy from one of the native tribes in Georgia.

De Soto's exploration of Georgia, however brief, was cause for conflict between the Spanish and the English, who had established a British colony in Savannah in 1733.[5] Georgia served as a buffer between Spanish forces around St. Augustine and well-established British colonies in South Carolina. Spain used de Soto's travels to make a claim on Georgia territory, and James Oglethorpe, the governor of the English Georgia colony, organized settlers and indigenous people to fight these claims. By 1739, hostilities between British and Spanish colonizing forces ultimately resulted in the War of Jenkins' Ear, with fighting mostly occurring in Florida.

It is thought that only one significant battle in this war occurred in Georgia, but it was pivotal. Although outnumbered five to one, General Oglethorpe's forces defeated Don Manuel de Montiano's troops in 1742 at the Battle of Bloody Marsh on St. Simons Island. The fight was short lived and resulted in few casualties, but it marked a turning point in the war because it demoralized Spanish troops. The Battle of Bloody Marsh represents the last Spanish offensive on Georgia and the beginning of the end of Spanish occupation of Georgia territory.

Georgia and Latin America

With the ousting of the Spanish in the eighteenth century, the history of Latinos living in Georgia remains largely unrecorded from 1742 until modern times. The history of relations between Georgia and Latin America is better documented. Certainly, the presence of the plantation system and the heavy reliance on slave labor created strong trading ties between Georgia port cities and many Caribbean islands, including Cuba and Hispaniola. It is estimated that between 1755 and 1767 more than 60 percent of the slaves brought into Savannah harbor were from the Caribbean.

There is also a strong Georgian thread throughout the history of the Spanish-American War. When the United States declared war on Spain on April 20, 1898, many Americans saw the war as an opportunity to claim the territories of Cuba, Puerto Rico, and the Philippines from the Spanish. Many Georgians, however, were opposed to annexation. Most outspoken among them was the U.S. Senator from Georgia, Augustus Octavius Bacon. Bacon called the U.S. occupation of Cuba unnecessary, extravagant, wasteful, and illegal, and he introduced legislation to block its annexation. When Cubans were allowed to decide for themselves whether or not to be annexed, the annexation effort was resoundingly defeated.

Half a century later, when Fidel Castro took control of Cuba in 1959, many Cubans fled to Atlanta. Like Miami, Atlanta was a prime relocation site because there were many strong historical and social ties between Georgia's capital and Havana. Since the turn of the twentieth century, the Atlanta business elite had frequented Cuba as a vacation destination, and many of the Cuban upper class educated their children in Atlanta schools, particularly the Georgia Military Academy, Georgia Tech, and Emory University. In fact, one of the first institutions in Georgia organized around Latino culture was the Latin Americans Club established by Cuban Georgia Tech students in 1948. It was the forerunner of a variety of Latino cultural organizations that would eventually spring up in Atlanta, such as the Latin American Association and the Mexican Center of Atlanta.

Cubans have regularly migrated between Atlanta and Havana since 1920. When former students were displaced as a result of the Cuban Revolution, Atlanta, like Miami, became a logical refuge. Migration from Cuba to Atlanta accelerated in the sixties, with as many as 2,500 Cubans (mostly upper-class whites) eventually settling in the Atlanta area by 1980. For many Atlanta was a secondary destination, after living for some time in Miami.

Among the new settlers fleeing first to Miami and then to Atlanta was Robert Goizueta. Born in Havana, Goizueta was educated at elite institutions in the United States, including Yale University. After returning to Cuba, he answered a newspaper advertisement for a chemical engineer at the Coca-Cola Company. Goizueta moved up the ranks in the company, first in Havana, then in Miami and the Caribbean, and eventually in Atlanta, where he was elected chairman and chief executive officer in 1981. He is largely credited for the marked success of the company in the eighties, its positioning as the worldwide soft drink giant, and for his philanthropic contributions to education. In 1994 Emory University renamed its business school in his honor.

Other former Cuban residents now living in Georgia have also prospered, and many have used their wealth to support anti-Castro movements and activities. Elena Diaz-Verson Amos, a former Cuban resident who moved to Columbus, Georgia in 1955, is prominent among them. Married to AFLAC insurance mogul John Amos, she used her considerable financial resources to advocate for humanitarian causes in Cuba. She also financed the smuggling of Cuban dissidents out of the country, including Alina Fernández Revuelta, the illegitimate daughter and outspoken critic of Castro. Fernández and her daughters lived with Amos in Georgia for several years before moving to Miami.

In the early 1980s, Amos lobbied the Department of Defense to move the School of the Americas (SOA) from Panama to Fort Benning (near Columbus). The SOA is a U.S. Army–operated training center for Latin American military and law enforcement personnel. Training is conducted in Spanish. In 1984 the SOA was moved to Fort Benning, and Amos is credited with being instrumental in this move.

Amos's involvement with SOA has lent an air of notoriety to her biography. Almost from its inception, the SOA has been controversial. Many detractors argue that the school is a training ground for state terrorism and that students are trained in torture and other human rights abuses. Certainly, long lists of Latin American dictators, including Manuel Noriega, were trained at the SOA. In response to these charges, Congress voted to withdraw its authority for the SOA in 2000. In 2001, the school reopened as the Western Hemisphere Institute for Security Cooperation (WHINSEC), and WHINSEC now requires students to take courses in human rights along with their other curriculum. Despite these changes, the governments of Argentina, Venezuela, and Uruguay have recently established official policies to cut ties with WHINSEC.

GEORGIA AS AN EMERGING GATEWAY

Although Latinos have had a presence in Georgia throughout most of the state's history, it was not until the 1990s that the state became a prime receiving location for both immigrants from Latin America and Latino migrants from other U.S. states.[6] Between 1990 and 2000, when the U.S. Latino population increased 58 percent, Georgia's Latino population tripled. Georgia is now the eleventh-largest state in total Latino population size, with more than 600,000 Latino residents. The majority of Georgia's Latinos, about 60 percent, are immigrants, whereas the remaining are U.S. born. Of the immigrants, about half are of Mexican origin. Cubans, Colombians, Guatemalans, and Peruvians make up most of the remaining half.

Georgia does not stand alone in the phenomenon of mass Latino migration to the Southeast that is often referred to as "the Dixie Diaspora." Most states in the South experienced a marked increased in their Latino population in the nineties, but Georgia stands out as the largest receiver, in total numbers, of all of the southeastern states except Florida. Georgia also differs from its neighbors in that the Latino newcomers are not geographically concentrated in one location but are scattered throughout the state.[7]

Most of the influx is attributed to the economy. Since 1972 the South has outperformed other regions in economic growth; Georgia, particularly Atlanta, has been at the forefront of this growth. Along with an increase in jobs in the service sectors, low-wage, low-skilled jobs continue to be created in agriculture and industry, and professional jobs are increasing as well. This growth has attracted many residents to Georgia. At the same time, recessions in cities such as Houston drove many Latinos to new destinations, including Atlanta.

In Georgia, two million new residents settled in the state between 1990 and 2004, and many of them were Latino. For the new residents who were Latino, the primary attraction was available jobs in construction, poultry, and textiles. Ambitious construction projects such as preparations for the 1996 Atlanta Olympics created additional new jobs, increasing an already large labor demand for builders. Much of this demand was filled by Latino labor.

In places such as Dalton, Georgia, communities were transformed seemingly overnight. This city had fewer than 1,500 Latinos living in it in 1990. By 2000, Latinos made up more than 40 percent of the total population and more than 60 percent of public school students. In Hall County, the population changed from nearly all white to 20 percent Latino in a 5-year period. In the Atlanta metropolitan area, the Latino population grew 370 percent between 1990 and 2000.

Although the Latino population is most heavily concentrated in the Atlanta metropolitan area and a few scattered cities such as Athens, Moultrie, Dalton, and Gainesville, the Latino presence was felt throughout the state by 2000. In most counties, immigrants compose the majority of the Latino population, and localities have had to adjust in order to provide services to people with limited English fluency. However, in some areas—particularly those with military bases such as Columbus and Hinesville—U.S.-born Latinos far outnumber the immigrants.

Included among the Latinos now living in Georgia are a relatively large number of unauthorized migrants. According to the Office of Homeland Security, between 2000 and 2005 Georgia had the largest percent increase in unauthorized immigrants (114 percent) of all of the states.[8] Certainly, only a fraction of Latinos are unauthorized immigrants, and not all unauthorized migrants are Latinos, but reliable reports suggest that more than 70 percent of unauthorized migrants are Latinos, mostly from Mexico. More importantly, the presence of unauthorized migrants in Georgia and the national attention the phenomenon has received has legitimized anti-Latino sentiment proffered under the guise of immigration policy reform. Georgia-based groups such as the Dustin Inman Society and the American Resistance Foundation warn about the possibility of the state becoming "Georgiafornia," making reference to the large Latino presence in California.

On December 5, 2006, officials in Cherokee County reacted to the growing Latino presence there by unanimously approving an ordinance that would allow the county to revoke the business licenses of landlords who rent properties to unauthorized immigrants. Although touted as an immigration (rather than a Latino) issue, commissioners at the same time approved a measure making English the official language of the county. More than 7 percent of the residents of Cherokee County are Latino, and most of them are recent immigrants who are still learning English.

LATINOS IN THE LABOR MARKET

Although there are undoubtedly many unauthorized Latino immigrants in Georgia, the majority of Georgia's Latinos are either U.S.-born or legal immigrants. What all of them have in common is that most are relative newcomers to the state. More than 80 percent of Georgia's Latino immigrants have been living in the state for less than 15 years. Many of them are new to the United States as well. For those who moved from other U.S. states, many came to escape the crime, crowding, unemployment, gangs, and high cost of living in places such as Los Angeles and New York. Others came to join family members who arrived before them. Most came to fill the demands for labor, particularly in the construction, poultry, and textile industries.

Preparations for the 1996 Olympics, paired with the influx of new (mostly non-Latino) residents from other states, created a mass demand for new housing, roads, hospitals, shops, and other infrastructure. Some of the jobs filled by Latino construction workers are new jobs created by this construction boom. Other jobs have been created by vacancies. Many of the previous non-Latino black and white construction workers saw opportunities in the expanding construction industry to leave their jobs as roofers, carpenters, and masons to become contractors, often hiring Latino labor. The high wages in the industry make it a particularly desirable sector in which to work.

New construction also created demands for construction auxiliary jobs. For Latinos, the most common auxiliary work is in landscaping. Latino men are commonly employed in landscaping in traditional gateway places such as Los Angeles, Houston, and Miami, so many of the new migrants to Georgia brought these skills with them. Some of these former landscape workers have begun their own small lawn service enterprises.

Another major employer of Latinos is the poultry industry. In Gainesville, Georgia (which bills itself as the Poultry Capital of the World), Latinos began replacing mostly white and a few black workers in the 1970s, but this replacement became widespread in the mid-1990s. It is important to note that jobs in the poultry industry were not going to Latinos at the expense of non-Latino workers; rather, as the economy grew in the 1990s, whites and blacks left jobs in the poultry industry, which often required back-breaking work in sub-zero refrigerators, for jobs with better working conditions in the service sector.

The transition of the poultry industry from non-Latino to Latino workers dramatically changed the landscape of Gainesville and other cities with large poultry-processing plants. Within 10 years, Gainesville and surrounding Hall County transformed from an almost all-white place to one that was one-fifth

Latino. Latino-owned businesses now line the main thoroughfares through Gainesville, and some of the local elementary schools are almost entirely composed of Latino students.

The overwhelming majority of Latinos in Gainesville are immigrants. This is particularly noticeable in the schools, where many students are second-language learners. Because the transformation of Gainesville happened so quickly, teachers have had little time to transition to teaching students with limited English proficiency. Despite this, change has been rapid and largely successful. Gainesville Elementary School and Fair Street Elementary School have received national attention for their high test scores, including accolades from President George W. Bush.

Another school district that made a rapid transition was the Dalton City Schools in northwest Georgia. Dalton, a textile city that produces half of this country's carpets, had operated under conditions of labor shortages since the sixties. As Latinos began migrating north from the poultry plants in Gainesville to work in a large chicken-processing plant in Whitfield County (of which Dalton is the county seat), some of them saw better opportunities in the carpet industry, which paid higher wages. The children of these Latino workers are now the majority of Dalton's school students.

The transition from poultry to textiles was gradual at first. Although Latinos began working in carpets in the eighties, only 3.1 percent of the Whitfield County's total workforce was Latino in 1990. By 2000, however, the county had the largest percentage concentration of Latinos in the state (over 22 percent), and Dalton City was almost half Latino. Although there are no official estimates, many speculate that Latinos are now the majority of carpet workers in Georgia.

The transition of the carpet industry from non-Latino to Latino workers has not happened without incident. In Calhoun, just miles from Dalton, Mohawk Carpet Mills was sued by a group of former workers alleging that the carpet manufacturer conspired with labor recruiters to artificially lower wages in textile jobs by recruiting and hiring unauthorized immigrant workers from Mexico. Mohawk denied this allegation. Executives at Mohawk and Dalton-based Shaw Industries maintained that they took pains to ensure that their workers held proper work permits. Furthermore, industry insiders assert that without the influx of Latino workers—most of whom are immigrants from Mexico—the textile industry would have been forced to close their doors in Georgia due to the inadequate labor supply. This claim was substantiated by economic analysts. In 2006, the U.S. Supreme Court declined to rule on the Mohawk case.

Latino Life in Georgia

Despite the concentration of Latinos in relatively high-paying, blue-collar jobs, Latinos remain at the bottom rung of the socioeconomic ladder in Georgia. On average nationally, Latinos fare better than African Americans in terms of personal and family income and occupational attainment. In Georgia, this is not the case. There are three reasons for this. First, Georgia is home to some of the most affluent African Americans in the country, and the state has a sizeable African American middle class; African Americans tend to be less well off in other states. Second, many of the Latinos in Georgia are recent immigrants who have not yet developed the English language skills or job credentials to gain higher-paying jobs. Third, there are barriers in the social structure to upward mobility for Latinos.

Because of the high rates of poverty among Latinos in Georgia, many find it difficult to obtain adequate transportation, housing, and health care. Georgia has a poor public transportation infrastructure, and Latinos who do not own a vehicle find it difficult to get around. Carpooling is the means by which 40 percent of employed Latinos get to and from work, and although this system is efficient, it limits the other places that Latinos can visit beyond their workplace. It also keeps many from obtaining better-paying jobs elsewhere. For those who own their own vehicles, getting a license to drive it is also a problem. Most places offer driving tests only in English, and identification requirements are strict. For those Latinos who are immigrants, these barriers make it more difficult to obtain drivers licenses in Georgia than in many other U.S. states.

Many Latinos also live in unsafe, dilapidated housing. Those without transportation may choose poorer quality housing because it is within walking distance of work. For recent Latino immigrants with undeveloped English skills, dilapidated housing may be the only housing that they know about because they lack access to good information. For Latinos who are poor—more than a quarter of Georgia's Latinos—bad housing may be all that they can afford.

One of the ironies of the fact that so many Latinos live in such poor quality housing stock is that many of them are employed in construction. They build homes that they cannot afford to buy. Additionally, some Latinos who can afford to buy homes have become victims of unscrupulous realtors. Housing fraud is a growing problem in Georgia, and Latinos are increasingly the victims.

For the poorest Latinos having several people living in a household is one means by which housing becomes affordable. This practice leads to problems of overcrowding, which is so widespread that Latinos in Georgia have a name for it, *camas calientes* (hot beds). The phrase refers to the situation whereby so many are sharing living quarters and sleeping in shifts that the mattresses never get cold. Some communities have reacted to *camas calientes* by enforcing housing codes that limit the number of people sharing living quarters. Such laws ignore the cultural tendency among Latinos to live in larger, multigenerational households. Additionally, these ordinances can lead to more overcrowding in other areas as residents are pushed from one locale to another.

Often Latinos live segregated from other Georgians in mobile home parks. Because of the heavy concentration of Latinos—especially immigrants—in these places, trailers parks are increasingly becoming the targets of criminals. Particularly problematic are home invasions. Because many recent immigrants are uninformed about U.S. banking practices, they keep their money at home. Knowing that there are likely to be large sums of money in the trailers, criminals will target these Latino communities.

In southern Georgia, a group of armed robbers invaded four mobile home parks one night in October 2005. Using guns and clubs, robbers assaulted the Mexican immigrant residents who had the misfortune to be home, resulting in the death of six immigrants and serious injuries to five more. The incident, known as the Night of Blood, heightened Georgians' awareness of the precarious position of new Latino immigrants, and many banks, in response, began accepting the Mexican *matrícula consular* card as sufficient identification to open a bank account. The mayor of Tifton County also flew the Mexican and U.S. flags at half mast to demonstrate the county's sorrow at the loss of these immigrants' lives.

Of course, although many Latinos remain in poverty in Georgia and tragedies do occur, many have also done quite well. *Hispanic Business* magazine lists several Georgians in their list of the 75 Wealthiest Hispanics in America. Topping the list is the Goizueta family, but also among them is Lou Sobh, an immigrant from Torreon, Mexico, whose automobile dealership is the largest minority-owned business in Georgia and one of the largest Latino-owned businesses in the country. Elena Diaz-Verson Amos was listed in 1997 as America's wealthiest Latina. Georgia's Latinos can also be found heading multinational advertising agencies, financial institutions, and research centers. Many prominent Latino physicians and scientists work at the Center for Disease Control and Prevention in Atlanta, and several are on faculty at the University of Georgia, Georgia Tech, and Georgia State University. Additionally, there are thousands of Latino-owned small businesses, as well as several Spanish-language radio stations and newspapers.

Starting a business in Georgia can sometimes be a challenge for Latinos, because most non-Latino Georgians are less familiar with Latino culture and the Spanish language than they might be in states such as California and Texas. For example, renowned artist Dan Vargas founded Vargas, Flores and Amigos in 1990 as the first Latino advertising agency in the Southeast. Vargas notes that in the early years of his operation, people would call his agency and ask to speak to Amigos.

However, as the Latino population grows, Georgians are becoming more used to seeing new Latino businesses next door to longer-established, black- or white-owned enterprises. Furthermore, Latino residents are increasingly viewed as a viable business market. In 2000 Roy Communications, an internationally renowned black-owned advertising agency, merged with Vargas's enterprise because Roy's president thought that her agency was ill-equipped to reach the Latino market. This move is indicative of a trend seen on a smaller scale among other businesses. Increasingly, businesses are working to position products and services to reach Latino buyers. According to projections by the Selig Center for Economic Growth, Georgia now has the tenth-largest Latino market in the nation.

Georgia's Response to Latino Migration

Although the business community has embraced the Latino market, other sectors of Georgian society have been slower to welcome the new residents. Overall, the rapid growth of the Latino population has forced many Georgians to reconceptualize the social dynamics of race in the state. In places such as Gainesville, the shift from being one of the whitest cities in the state to one that is sizably Latino has required meeting the challenges of diversity. In the counties where African Americans outnumber whites and dominate the power structure, room has had to be made for minorities of another color.

At first, several African American leaders were reluctant to share power with another minority group. In 2002 there was considerable debate over whether or not to officially recognize Latinos as a minority group. By 2006, however, when the General Assembly debated over the passage of the Georgia Security and Immigration Compliance Act (SB529), all of the African American legislators sided with the Latino legislators in opposing the bill. The bill, which was signed into law in April 2006, is intended to reduce the flow of unauthorized immigrants into Georgia. Minority leaders, however, saw it as a back-door attack on Latinos. One newspaper called it a "Latino witch hunt."

SB529 follows on the heels of a number of local ordinances designed to reduce or eliminate the changes that local communities are seeing in response to the increasing Latino population. Some municipalities have enacted ordinances that ban or restrict the use of foreign languages on signs. Others have used anti-loitering laws to restrict day labor, a practice that is common among Latino immigrants without regular jobs. In November 2006, Cherokee County passed the first local ordinance in Georgia making English the official language.

At the same time, many organizations have worked to expand their outreach to the Latino community. In 1998, the Board of Regents of Georgia's university system, which had long focused on increasing the representation of African American students in higher education, established a task force to study the unmet needs of Georgia's Latino population. By 2003, a consortium of six state colleges and universities was formed to create the Hispanic Pilot Project. This project is charged with meetings two goals: to increase the number of instructors certified in English as a Second Language, and to encourage Latinos to pursue higher education. This is one of several new initiatives to increase Latino educational attainment in Georgia.

In 2003 Desiree Smith and Beatriz Velez, two Mexican American freshman students at the University of Georgia, founded Students for Latino Empowerment

(SLE). This organization is the first Georgia-based student group organized around improving the socioeconomic position of Latinos. SLE sponsors a number of activities to help Latino adolescents find pathways to college. The inception of this organization followed closely on the heels of the founding of the Georgia Association of Latino Elected Officials (GALEO), a political advocacy group that aims to give a voice to Georgia's growing Latino population. GALEOs formation was largely in response to the 2002 elections, where Sam Zamarripa, Pedro Marin, and David Casas were the first three Latinos elected to the Georgia General Assembly. In 2005 GALEO was instrumental in organizing the Coalition for a New Georgia, an association of at least 25 groups fighting for Latino rights in Georgia.

These organizations have been influential in helping Latino voices be heard and in halting many anti-Latino bills that have been introduced in the state legislature. In 2002 the Georgia State Supreme Court heard arguments in *Smith v. the State*. As part of their ruling, the Court upheld a lower court's determination that Latino ethnicity must be considered in the make-up of jury pools. Prior to that ruling, courts only had to consider whether blacks and women were properly represented.

Because the Dixie Diaspora is a relatively new phenomenon, the Latino presence in Georgia is still viewed by many Georgians as a novelty. Among these Georgians, there is a sense that the Latino stay in the state is temporary. The history of states such as Texas, California, and New York suggest that this is not the case. It is more likely that the Latino population in Georgia will continue to grow, and Latinos will continue to make vital contributions to the history and culture of the state. It will take some time, however, before all Georgians accept Latinos as full and legitimate citizens of the state.

NOTABLE LATINOS

Vazquéz de Ayllon, Lucás (c. 1475–1526). Vazquéz de Ayllon was a Spanish conquistador who, with 600 settlers, founded the first European settlement in the New World at San Miguel de Gualdape on the Savannah River near Sapelo Island. He is best known for the discovery of Chesapeake Bay and the exploration of South Carolina.

Soto, Hernando de (c. 1500–1542). From 1539 to 1543, Hernando de Soto led 3,700 troops on an expedition of southeastern North America. In 1540 de Soto's party traveled through Georgia, making him the first European to explore Georgia's interior.

Diaz-Verson Amos, Elena (1926–2000). Diaz-Verson Amos was a Cuban-born philanthropist who moved to Columbus, Georgia in 1955. Named in 1997 as the wealthiest Latina in the United States, she was influential in lobbying the U.S. Army to relocate the School of the Americas (now the Western Hemisphere Institute for Security Cooperation) to Fort Benning. She also served on the board and as the director for a number of arts, advocacy, and humanitarian groups, including the Valladares

Foundation, a human rights organization. Amos was also instrumental in financing dissident Alina Fernández Revuelta's covert flight from Cuba. Fernández is the daughter of Fidel Castro.

Goizueta, Roberto C. (1931–1997). Cuban-born Roberto Goizueta was elected president and chief operating officer of the Coca-Cola Company in 1980. In 1981, he became Coca-Cola Company's chairman and CEO. Under his tutelage, the company's stock increased 7,200 percent, creating more shareholder wealth than any CEO in history and making Goizueta the first billionaire corporate manager in the United States. In 1992 Goizueta and his wife, Olga, established the Goizueta Foundation to provide assistance to Georgia-based charitable and educational institutions. The foundation has donated millions of dollars to assist in strengthening educational programs for Latino students.

Vargas, Daniel O. (1942–). Vargas, a noted community activist, is a former art director for Avon Products. In 1990 he founded Vargas and Amigos, Inc., the first Latino advertising agency in the Southeast. His art and advertising concepts are award-winning, including being listed among Advertising Age's "100 Best Ads Ever Created." In 1982 he designed the Georgia peach logo that is the centerpiece of Georgia's license plate design. His artistic rendering of famous Latino soldiers is on permanent display at the Pentagon.

Sobh, Lou (1944–). Lou Sobh, founder and president of Lou Sobh Automotive, is listed among the wealthiest Latinos in America. His company is the largest minority-owned business in Georgia and one of the twenty largest Latino-owned businesses in the United States. Sobh, who was born in Torreon, Mexico, is founder and chair of the National Association of Hispanic Automobile Dealers and is on the board of directors of the National Council of La Raza.

Zamarripa, Sam (1952–). In 2002 Zamarripa, an investment banker, became the first Latino elected to the Georgia State Senate. A Democrat from Atlanta, Zamarripa is known for his strong advocacy of immigration rights and as a proponent of issues of interest to Latinos. He resigned from the Senate in 2006.

Ginés, Venus (1961–). Puerto Rican–born Ginés is the founder and chief executive officer of Día de la Mujer Latina, a Georgia-based organization aimed at addressing health disparities among the Latino population. Along with providing a range of health services, the organization sponsors annual one-day health fiestas in 22 states, Puerto Rico, and the Dominican Republic in order to screen Latina women for breast cancer, help the uninsured gain access to health care, and address health risk behaviors among Latino adolescents.

Smith, Desiree (1985–) and **Velez, Beatriz (1985–).** Phoenix-born Smith and Houston-born Velez, student activists, spent most of their childhood in Georgia. In 2003 they entered the University of Georgia as freshman, where they organized the Students for Latino Empowerment (SLE), the first student group organized to improve the socioeconomic position of Georgia's Latinos. With the help of government and private funds, SLE sponsors two annual signature events to promote college enrollment among Latino students. SLE chapters are now forming in other universities in Georgia and in other states.

Sports broadcaster Fernando Palacios and two campers at Campo Nuestro, a baseball clinic for Latino youth sponsored by the Atlanta Braves. Courtesy of Atlanta National League Baseball Club.

CULTURAL CONTRIBUTIONS

In many states, Latinos have transformed the culture by introducing Latino products and services into everyday use and Spanish words into the common vernacular. Certainly this has happened in Georgia. More and more Georgians are eating salsa, speaking Spanish, and celebrating festivals such as Cinco de

Mayo. However, the biggest cultural contributions may be those that are less visibly Latino. Icons that people tend to think of as uniquely Georgian have been greatly influenced by Latinos. Peaches, peanuts, cotton, and Vidalia onions, all crops traditionally associated with Georgia, are harvested and packed by Latino migrant workers. Carpets, one of the state's leading exports, and poultry, one of its major agricultural commodities, would not have remained an integral part of the Georgia economy without Latino labor. Coca-Cola, the state's most ubiquitous soft drink, gained its market position, in part, due to Latino CEO Roberto Goizueta. Even the Georgia peach logo, seen both in the state's capitol and also on Georgia residents' license plates, is a design of Latino artist Dan Vargas.

NOTES

1. Historical documents give evidence that many Spanish missions were established in Georgia. Although some have been recovered through archeological investigations, the names, dates, and locations of many of these remain speculative.

2. Coca-Cola is a registered trademark of The Coca-Cola Company.

3. Demographic information reported in this chapter is calculated based on data from the U.S. Census Bureau, Census 2000 and Census 1990, Summary File 1 (SF1) and Summary File 3 (SF3), and U.S. Census Bureau, American Community Survey 2004, generated by Stephanie Bohon using American FactFinder, available online at http://factfinder.census.gov (accessed November 1, 2006).

4. The name of de Ayllon's settlement has been recorded as Gualdape, Guandape, and Guadelupe. The exact site is also unknown. Some historians place the settlement in South Carolina or Virginia. Based on archeological evidence, most scholars maintain that the original site was in the Georgia Sea Islands and was likely named Gualdape.

5. Georgia territory was also claimed by France.

6. The distinction between the terms *immigrant* and *migrant* are important. In this chapter, immigrants refer to people who move to Georgia directly from other countries. Migrants are those who move to Georgia from other U.S. states or territories who may or may not have been born in the United States.

7. The largest concentration of Latinos is in metropolitan Atlanta, but there are large Latino settlements throughout the state.

8. Hoefer, Rytina, and Campbell, 2006.

BIBLIOGRAPHY

Anrig Jr., Greg, and Tova Andrea Wang, eds. *Immigration's New Frontiers: Experiences from the Emerging Gateway States.* New York: Century Foundation, 2006.

Atiles, Jorge H., and Stephanie A. Bohon. "*Camas Calientes:* Housing Adjustments and Barriers to Social and Economic Adaptation among Georgia's Rural Latinos." *Southern Rural Sociology* 19 (2003): 97–122.

———. *The Needs of Georgia's New Latinos: A Policy Agenda for the Decade Ahead.* Athens, GA: Carl Vinson Institute, 2002. http://www.cviog.uga.edu/latinos.

Bayala, Charolette A. "Cuban Refugees in Atlanta: 1950–1980." Master's thesis, Georgia State University, 2006.

Bohon, Stephanie A., Heather Macpherson, and Jorge H. Atiles. "Educational Barriers for New Latinos in Georgia." *Journal of Latinos and Education* 4 (2005): 41–56.

Gill, Leslie. *School of the Americas: Military Training and Political Violence in the Americas.* Durham, NC: Duke University Press, 2004.

Greising, David. *I'd Like the World to Buy a Coke: The Life and Leadership of Roberto Goizueta.* New York: Wiley, 1998.

Hayes, Cassandra. "Media Meltdown." *Black Enterprise,* June 2000.

Hispanic Business. "75 of the Wealthiest Hispanics in America." September 2002.

Hoefer, Michael, Nancy Rytina, and Christopher Campbell. "Estimates of the Unauthorized Immigrant Population Residing in the United States: January 2005." Washington, DC: Office of Immigration Statistics, Department of Homeland Security, 2006.

Lanning, John Tate. *The Spanish Missions of Georgia.* Chapel Hill: University of North Carolina Press, 1935.

McMillan, Richard. "Savannah's Coastal Slave Trade: A Quantitative Analysis of Ship Manifests, 1840–1850." *Georgia Historical Quarterly* 78 (1994): 339–359.

Murphey, Arthur D., Colleen Blanchard, and Jennifer A. Hill, eds. *Latino Workers in the Contemporary South.* Athens: University of Georgia Press, 2001.

Passell, Jeffrey S. "The Size and Characteristics of the Unauthorized Migrant Population in the U.S." Washington, DC: Pew Hispanic Center, 2006.

Smith v. the State, 571 S.E.2d 740 (Ga., 2002).

Thomas, David H. *St. Catherines: An Island in Time.* Atlanta: Georgia Endowment for the Humanities, 1988.

Worth, John E. *The Struggle for the Georgia Coast: An Eighteenth-Century Spanish Retrospective on Guale and Mocama.* Washington, DC: American Museum of Natural History, 1995.

12

Hawaii

Lucía V. Aranda

CHRONOLOGY

1555	The Spanish sailor Juan Gaetano visits the Hawaiian Islands but charts them incorrectly.
1794	Francisco de Paula Marín (1774–1837) brings the first pineapple and coffee plants to the Islands. Manini, as he is known, stays on as an advisor to King Kamehameha I.
1832	Mexican cowboys are invited to teach Hawaiians about cattle ranching, giving way to the *paniolo*, the Hawaiian cowboy, a word derived from español.
1893	Queen Lili'uokalani (1838–1917) surrenders under protest, and the Hawaiian monarchy is overthrown.
1898	On July 7 President William McKinley signs the annexation of Hawaii by the United States.
1900	The first Puerto Ricans arrive in Hawaii sugar plantations.
1901	Approximately 5,000 Puerto Ricans are established on the Islands.
1921	A second wave of Puerto Rican migration arrives in Hawaii.
1931	The Puerto Rican Civic Club is founded.
1932	The Puerto Rican Independent Association is founded.
1959	Hawaii becomes the 50th state of the United States.
1973	The United Puerto Rican Association of Hawaii merges with the Puerto Rican Civic Club and the Puerto Rican Independent Association.
1980s	A new wave of Latino migrants come to Hawaii, especially to the islands of Maui and Hawaii.
1980	The Puerto Rican Heritage Society is established.
1994	The first Hawaii Hispanic Heritage Festival is celebrated.

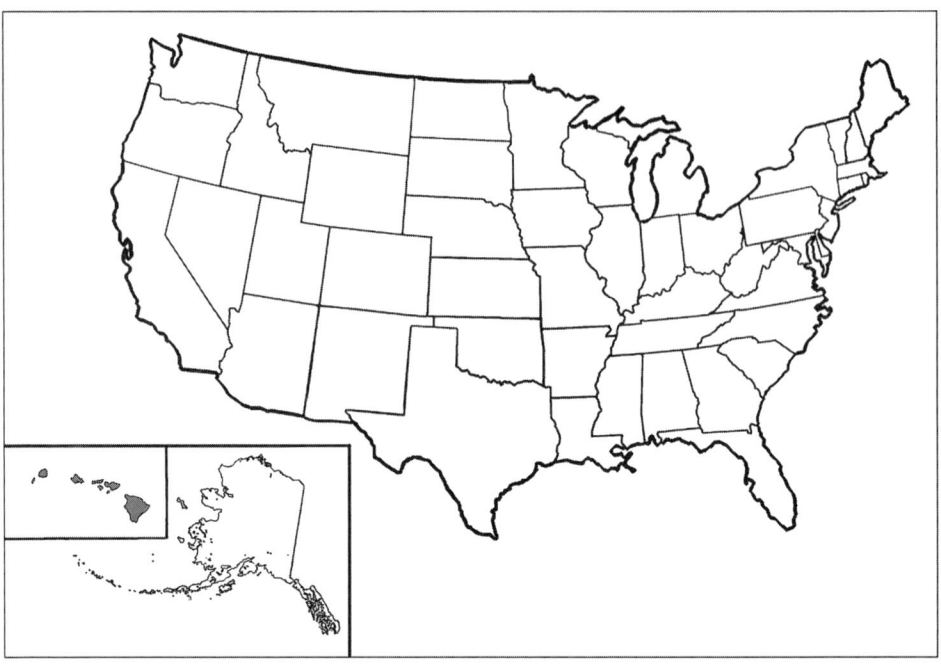

2000 According to the U.S. census 7.2 percent of the population in Hawaii is Latino. Centennial celebrations of the first arrival of Puerto Ricans in Hawaii take place.

2005 According to the U.S. Census Bureau the Latino population grows more rapidly than any other ethnic group, composing 8 percent of the population in Hawaii; however, community activists estimate the Latino population at 10 percent, including undocumented migrants.

HISTORICAL OVERVIEW

The state of Hawaii, composed of eight islands—Hawaii, Maui, Oahu, Kauai, Molokai, Lanai, Niihau, and Kahoolawe—is one of the most isolated territories in the world. However, by 1555, according to Spanish archives, the Spanish sailor Juan Gaetano had already been to the islands and charted them. A few longitudinal degrees off, Gaetano called the archipelago *Islas de Mesa* (Table Islands); Maui he named *La Desgraciada* (The Unfortunate One), the island of Hawaii (or the Big Island, as it is also known) *La Mesa* (The Table), and the islands of Molokai, Lanai and Kahoolawe *Los Monjes* (The Monks).

A less obscure but still fairly unfamiliar character in Hawaiian history is Francisco de Paula Marín, a Spanish sailor who came to Hawaii in 1794 and stayed on to work with King Kamehameha I as his physician, interpreter, and business manager. In fact, the 2006 proclamation of Hispanic Heritage Day by the governor of Hawaii celebrates Marín as the earliest Latino influence on the Islands.

A better-known Latino influence in Hawaii is that of a group of cowboys who came from Mexico at the turn of the nineteenth century. In 1793 the British explorer Captain George Vancouver had presented King Kamehameha I with half a dozen longhorn cattle, which were allowed to roam the island of Hawaii freely. By 1830 the *kapu*, or taboo, on the cattle was lifted, and 2 years later, when the cattle had multiplied and become a danger, King Kamehameha III and John Palmer Parker (who would establish Parker Ranch, one of the oldest and largest ranches in the country) arranged to have a handful of cowboys brought to the Islands from Veracruz to train Hawaiians in cattle- and horse-handling skills. These and the other Spanish-speaking men that followed brought with them their language, culture, and music, and as they embraced Hawaiian culture, a hybrid culture arose. Born of this contact an important cattle industry developed, and the quintessential *paniolo* culture of cattle ranching, vaquero clothes, and music was born.

Puerto Ricans would be the next Latino group to make its presence felt in Hawaii. The four factors that would lead to this were the Chinese Exclusion Act of 1882, which put a stop to cheap labor from China in the United States; the annexation of Puerto Rico by the United States in 1898; the precarious situation created by the devastating San Ciriaco Hurricane, which hit Puerto Rico in 1899; and the fact that Puerto Ricans were experienced sugar cane workers. On December 23, 1900, 66 Puerto Ricans got off the *Río Janeiro* in Honolulu Harbor. However, 50 more had escaped en route—forced by the poor living conditions endured on the voyage from Puerto Rico to New Orleans by steamship, from New Orleans to San Francisco by rail, and then from San Francisco to Hawaii again by boat. Between 1900 and 1901, 11 expeditions would bring 5,203 Puerto Ricans to Hawaii. The last group of Puerto Ricans would arrive at the Islands in 1921; the high cost of transporting the 683 men, women, and children offset any further attempts to bring Puerto Ricans as laborers to Hawaii.

The plantation culture that developed on the Islands and evolved into the multiethnic local culture of Hawaii would not have been the same without the presence of the significant Puerto Rican contingent that arrived at the turn of the twentieth century. Between 1852 and 1946 approximately 395,000 people were recruited to work in Hawaii on the sugar plantations. Although less numerous, the Puerto Ricans joined migrants from China, Japan, Korea, the Philippines, Samoa, and Portugal who had also come to work on the sugar plantations. The migration patterns were not alike for all the migrant groups either: some, such as the Spanish or Italians, used Hawaii as a stepping-stone to the continental United States; like the Puerto Ricans, the Portuguese—recruited as entire families—tended to stay on the Islands; the Japanese, Chinese, and Filipinos, who made up the majority of the migrants on the sugar plantations, arrived as single men and either intermarried, sent for picture brides, or returned to their homeland.

With the annexation of Hawaii in 1898, the mainland Unites States became Hawaii's main market, and sugar plantations would dominate the economy of the Islands well into the twentieth century. In the sugar (and later pineapple) plantations, which resembled small cities, life was stratified according to national origin—ethnic groups were pitted against each other, and animosity frequently stemmed from the fact that salaries depended on nationalities. The *lunas* (or overseers) belonged more often than not to the white and smaller European American migrant groups, who received, on average, higher salaries. The Puerto Ricans, who were used as labor scabs for the Japanese and Chinese (who were already attempting to form worker organizations and to go on strikes), fared somewhat better than their Asian counterparts. In fact, it was not too long before Puerto Ricans were not bound to one plantation like the Asians but were able to move from one plantation to another in search of better working conditions. In spite of the exacerbation of cultural differences on the ethnically segregated plantations, a local, multiethnic culture developed from the interaction of Hawaiians, Japanese, Chinese, Filipinos, Portuguese, Samoans, Puerto Ricans, and the other migrant groups—one that ultimately formed the basis of Hawaii's present-day multiethnicity. However, in the process the Hawaiian indigenous population dwindled from 97 percent, in 1853, to just 16 percent in 1923, by which time the Japanese had become the largest ethnic group in Hawaii.

IDENTITY: FACTS AND FIGURES

Identity in the state of Hawaii can be said to be more sui generis than in other states due to its past and present history. Hawaii is the most multiracial state in the nation and is slated to have the highest percentage of minorities (77.3 percent) by 2025.[1] The data from the 2000 Census Report indicates that a staggering 24.1 percent of its population defined itself as belonging to two or more races, followed by far by Alaska (with 5.4 percent) and California (with 4.7 percent). It is not surprising that Honolulu has now become the city with the largest mixed-race population in the United States, at 14.9 percent.

The largest ethnic group on the Islands identifies itself as Asian, at 41 percent (510,354), followed by Whites or Caucasians, at 23 percent (284,455); a third group, which considers itself multiracial, makes up 18 percent of the population (217,171); and in fourth place are Latinos, who make up 7.2 percent of the population (87,699).[2] The American Community Survey of 2005 figures indicate a growth of the Latino population in Hawaii to 98,699 people, or 8 percent of the total population. In fact, this figure jumps to 10 percent according to Latino activists, once legal and illegal migrants are taken into consideration.

Latinos are growing at a much faster rate than any other single ethnic group in Hawaii: of the 5–25 age population, 10 percent is Latino, whereas 40 percent is Asian, 16 percent white, and 2 percent African American. Those who consider themselves multiracial, a consequence of the high degree of intermarriages that are so common in Hawaii, and indicate "Other" on the census form, make up 31 percent of the 5–25 age population.

The proportion of Latinos and Native Hawaiians (as well as Pacific Islanders who are included in the same category) is presently balanced; however, economic factors such as the elevated price of housing have forced Native Hawaiians to move elsewhere. Data from the U.S. Census Bureau indicate that in 2004, 30.3 percent Native Hawaiians and other Pacific Islanders lived in California, whereas only 26.2 percent lived in Hawaii (5.7 percent lived in Washington; 4.9 percent in Texas; 3.4 percent in Utah.; and 3.2 percent in Nevada).

If the most numerous ethnic group among Asians is the Japanese, Puerto Ricans make up the largest Latino group on the Hawaiian Islands (34.2 percent), followed closely by Mexicans (22.6 percent). The fact that Latinos in Hawaii reported more than one race would explain how the third-largest group is a composite of "Others" (38.4 percent). Other Spanish-speaking groups are Spaniards (1.1 percent), Cubans (0.8 percent), Panamanians (0.5 percent), Colombians (0.5 percent), Peruvians (0.4 percent), Dominicans (0.3 percent), Salvadorans (0.3 percent), Guatemalans (0.3 percent), Argentineans (0.2 percent), Chileans (0.2 percent), and Ecuadorians (0.2 percent).

Oahu, the seat of the capital, holds the largest number of Latinos on the Hawaiian Islands, 7.1 percent of the population, whereas the island of Hawaii has the highest percentage of Latinos, 11.6 percent.[3] A significant number of Latinos on the Islands are stationed at the military bases; for example, on the island of Oahu 16.2 percent of the personnel on Schofield Barracks and 8.37 percent on Hickam Air Force Base are Latino.[4]

Economy

The economic development in postcontact Hawaii was dominated by the sugar and pineapple plantation industry. However, plantations disappeared in the 1990s, and the economy, which has since attempted to diversify, is sustained by tourism, defense, and highly technological innovation industries. The low unemployment rates (2.3 percent in 2006) have attracted Latino migrants to the construction and service industries, especially to Maui and the Big Island. According to the 2000 U.S. census, the foreign-born population of Hawaii arrived primarily from Asia (83.3 percent), Oceania (6.3 percent), Europe (4.9 percent), Latin America (3.2 percent), Northern America (1.8 percent), and Africa (0.5 percent). Interestingly, it is on the more sparsely populated islands of Maui, Lanai, and Molokai that there is a greater percentage of businesses owned by Latinos (5.1 percent vs. a 3.1 percent on the rest of the islands). On Maui, more than 100 Latino-owned companies have opened in the last 6 years, especially in the construction, landscaping, cleaning, and restaurant industries.

Government

Although Latinos make up the fourth-largest group in Hawaii, this 10 percent of the population has very little visible government representation and largely remains a politically invisible group. Although it is true that the number of Asian American appointments has declined, Latinos, in spite of the requisite population, have not been appointed to top policy positions. Two of the few local Puerto Ricans who have served the Hawaiian government are Faith Evans, a former state legislator, and Alex Santiago, a former Hawaii state representative.

NOTABLE LATINOS

Camacho Souza, Blase (1918–). Camacho Souza founded the Puerto Rican Heritage Society in 1980, and he is also the project director of the Puerto Rican House at Hawaii's Plantation Village. Born in North Kohala, Hawaii, to Puerto Rican parents and the first Puerto Rican graduate of the University of Hawaii, Camacho Souza is an authority on the Puerto Rican experience in Hawaii.

Carr, Norma (Gómez) (1927–). Carr's 1989 doctoral dissertation "Puerto Ricans in Hawaii: 1900–1958," from the University of Hawaii, is an obligatory reference for any study dealing with the Puerto Rican migration to the Islands. Carr, who was born to Puerto Rican parents in New York, moved to Honolulu with her husband in 1958.

Evans, Faith (1937–). A locally born Puerto Rican, Evans is a former state legislator and the first woman to serve as a U.S. marshal. A cofounder of the Puerto Rican Heritage Society, Evans was appointed by Governor Ben Cayetano as chair to the Puerto Rican Centennial Commission.

Ortiz, Nancy N. (Perry) (1942–). Ortiz is a radio host to *Alma Latina* (Latin Soul), "the longest running Latin music program in the Pacific." Born in Aiea, Oahu, Ortiz, whose grandparents arrived from Puerto Rico at the turn of the twentieth century, describes herself as a "Boricua Hawaiana." Ortiz created Alma Latina Productions to promote salsa and latin music in Hawaii. One of the cofounders and executive director of the Centro Hispano de Hawaii/Hawaii Latino Center, she remains active in the United Puerto Rican Association.

Dias, Austin (1946–). Born in Honolulu and raised on Kauai's Kilauea Sugar Plantation, Dias, professor of Spanish at the University of Hawaii, was chair of the Department of Languages and Literatures of Europe and the Americas for over 10 years. Dias, who is an honorary member of the Puerto Rican Heritage Society and was appointed to the state's Puerto Rican Centennial Commission, has been instrumental in bringing to the forefront the forgotten literature of the early migrants of Puerto Rico to Hawaii.

Valdez, Pedro (1946–). Valdez, a native of Texas, arrived to Hawaii in the 1970s after retiring from the U.S. Navy and became host of the only local Spanish-speaking television program ever broadcast in Hawaii, *¿Qué pasa Hawai?* which ran from 1991 to 1998.

Villa, José (1948–). From 1994 to 1999, Villa published the bilingual Spanish-English newspaper *Hawai'i Hispanic News*, also available in an online format from 1996 to

2000. He cofounded, and serves as secretary of, the Latin Business Association. Villa, who is involved in "providing a forum from which to educate Latinos with dignity and respect," presents "This Week in the Hispanic Nation" on Ray Cruz's *Sabor Tropical* show on Hawaii Public Radio.

Cruz, Ray (1951–). Cruz is undoubtedly the most important Latino DJ in Hawaii. Born in New York and raised in Puerto Rico, Cruz has promoted Latino music on the Islands for over 18 years, hosting the weekly *Sabor Tropical* on Hawaii Public Radio. Cruz has been extremely influential in maintaining the high profile of Latin music on the Islands.

Sánchez, Rolando (1951–). Sánchez, a native of Nicaragua, moved to Hawaii in 1984 and in 1987 formed the band Salsa Hawaii. With events such as the Hawaii International Latin Music Festival, Miss Latin-Hawaii Scholarship Pageant, and many other cultural events, this Honolulu-based percussionist, songwriter, singer, and producer has been instrumental in infusing the salsa scene in Honolulu with the vitality it has today.

Sánchez, Martha (1953–). Sánchez, from Cuernavaca, Mexico, opened the Mercado de la Raza in 1994, one of the first Latino markets on Oahu. Sánchez is a cofounder of Centro Hispano de Hawaii/Hawaii Hispanic Center and is so active in Latino affairs on that island that her business doubles as a Hispanic food market and Hispanic referral center for the community.

Ortiz, Eddie (1964–). Ortiz, a retired U.S. marine bandsman of Puerto Rican descent and a transplant from New York who has been on the Islands since 1997, formed the salsa band Son Caribe in 2002. Garnering the admiration of fans locally, nationally, and internationally, Son Caribe has opened for Celia Cruz and Tito Puente, and received a 2004 Grammy Award consideration for Best Salsa/Merengue Album of the Year.

CULTURAL CONTRIBUTIONS

As a result of the pervasive and ubiquitous ethnic diversity in the state of Hawaii, it would be difficult to affirm that there exists a distinct Latino identity on the Islands. The situation is such that many in the Latino community believe they garner too little respect from the other ethnic groups, largely because they are misunderstood. The fact that their purchasing power remains largely untapped attests to this invisible stature.

Latinos did start organizing themselves around cultural organizations early on in their arrival to the Hawaiian Islands. By 1931, Puerto Ricans had established the United Puerto Rico Association of Hawaii, and a year later came the Puerto Rican Independent Association. These would merge in 1973 to become the United Puerto Rican Association of Hawaii. Still active today, the United Puerto Rican Association of Hawaii, located at 1249 N. School Street in Honolulu, remains a social hall that hosts Latino activities. Like the Puerto Rican Heritage Society founded by Blase Camacho Souza and Faith Evans in 1980, it promotes a scholarship program for the grandchildren of Puerto Rican migrants. More recent is the Latin Business Association of Hawaii, which Ray Cruz, José Villa, his wife Marie Villa, and Jesús Puerto founded with the intention of becoming a link between Hawaii's Latino businesses and the global business community.

On Maui the service program for Latinos, called Enlace Hispano, founded in 1999, provides translation services, referrals, cultural events, and education and development opportunities for Maui's growing Latino community. As part of Maui Economic Opportunity (MEO), Enlace Hispano awards the César Chávez prize to recognize the effort of Hispanics on the island; recipients so far have been César Gaxiola (2005) and Silvia Naiberg (2006), present director of Enlace Hispano.

Although Latino cultures have blended into one larger "local" culture, Latinos are more visible in the food and names. Local dishes such as *pateles* (as *pasteles* are locally known) from Puerto Rico are found alongside *horchata, churros, malasadas,* Portuguese bean soup, and sausages. Across the islands there are numerous Latino restaurants; although the majority are Mexican, there are some Argentinean, Cuban, and Puerto Rican ones as well. In fact, the ethnic food aisles in many Hawaiian supermarkets stock a Mexican section alongside the Japanese, Thai, or Vietnamese sections. The fusion in food is such that *ka'lua* tacos or *taro* tortillas are staples on menus across the islands. Many of these can be found at the Hawaii Hispanic Heritage Festival, which usually takes place in October in Honolulu, and at the Somos Amigos Festival on Maui. These two festivals, the first launched by the once very active Centro Hispano de Hawaii/Hawaii Hispanic Center and the second by Enlace Hispano, showcase Latino music, dance, and food, although Somos Amigos incorporates Portuguese culture as well.

Insofar as a literary contribution to the Hawaiian Islands is concerned, the visibility of Latinos was strongest at the time of migration at the turn of the twentieth century. Puerto Rican migrants such as Carlo Mario Fraticelli, Salvador Hernández, Nicolás Caravallo Vegas, Justo Pérez Peña, Andalecio Troche, and Tanilau Dias wrote *décimas* in the *jíbaro* oral tradition and recited or sung them at social gatherings. Fraticelli, who migrated to Hawaii in 1901, seemed to be "conscious that he [was] the spokesperson for his Puerto Rican people."[5] As Fraticelli chronicled life in Hawaii in Spanish, and called Puerto Ricans to action against an unjust oligarchic plantation system, he could not help but pervade his poetry with deep nostalgia and regret for leaving his beloved Puerto Rico.

Rodney Morales, of Puerto Rican descent and professor at the University of Hawaii, recalls another perspective of the migrant experience: a Puerto Rican culture that, intertwined with that of the Japanese, Filipino, Portuguese, and Hawaiian communities, helped form the local culture that the plantation system gave way to. In "Ship of Dreams," Morales draws on the distinct ethnic differences that distinguished the diversity of the local culture of Hawaii, without the nostalgia of his parents' or grandparents' generations.

Latinos have achieved substantial visibility in the music that is heard on the Hawaiian Islands. Guitars, generally believed to have entered the Islands with the *paniolos* in 1832, and the 'ukelele—which has its precursor in the Portuguese *braguinha*, brought from Madeira by migrants at the turn of the century—have both had a profound influence on Hawaiian music. The Spanish influence on the slack-key guitar is likened to that of the falsetto singing, which also arrived with the *paniolos* from Veracruz and blended with ancient Hawaiian chants to become an essential element of Hawaiian music. An indication of how music blended life on the culturally diverse plantations is *kachi-kachi* (or *katchi-katchi*) music, the onomatopoeic name the Japanese used for the folkloric music of the migrants from Puerto Rico as they scraped the guiro. The *cuatro* is the focus of *jíbaro* music in Hawaii, and although *kachi-kachi* music is more infrequent every day, it can be said to link the traditional and contemporary music of the Boricua community in Hawaii.

For Ángel Santiago, president of the United Puerto Rican Association of Hawaii, "it was through sports and music that the Puerto Ricans on the Islands were able to hold on to their roots." There were a great number of groups playing the *cuatro*, guiro, box bass, maracas, *palitos*, or the bongos at the association's social hall until very recently, such as the Trio Borinque or Silva and His Rumba Kings in the 1930s, The Jolly Ricans in the 1950s, the Rumbacheros in the 1960s, or Boy and His Family of Troubadors from 1941 to 1986. Puerto Ricans excelled

Trio Borinque (circa 1930). Courtesy of United Puerto Rican Association of Hawaii.

in baseball: they were Territory Champions and had their own baseball leagues. However, due to a lack of players, the Puerto Rican baseball league has ceased to exist as such. Joseph Martin took Puerto Rican excellence in boxing one step further and became a Hawaii sumo wrestler champion in the 1950s.

There are a handful of Latino radio shows airing in Hawaii today, most notably *Sabor Tropical,* on Hawaii Public Radio, but without a doubt Latino music is more visible on the dance floor, where salsa dancing in clubs and classes can now be found almost nightly, sometimes in more than one venue. These local Hawaiian salsa bands are usually a composite of residents of Latino ancestry and, more often than not, Latino members of the military.

NOTES

1. Cheng and Ho, 2002, 12.
2. U.S. Census Bureau, 2000 Census.
3. U.S. Census Bureau, 2007 American Community Survey Reports.
4. U.S. Census Bureau, 2000 Census.
5. Dias, 2001, 100.

BIBLIOGRAPHY

U.S. Census Bureau, 2007. American Community Survey Reports. Race/Ethnicity Reports. The Hispanic Community–2004. http://www.census.gov/prod/2007pubs/acs-03.pdf.

Aranda, Lucía. "Latinos in Hawaii." In *Encyclopedia of Latinos and Latinas in the United States.* Eds. Suzanne Oboler and Deena J. González. New York: Oxford University Press, 2005.

Camacho Souza, Blase, and Alfred P. Souza. *De Borinquen a Hawaii, nuestra historia. From Puerto Rico to Hawaii.* Honolulu, HI: Puerto Rican Heritage Society, 1985.

Carr, Norma. "Puerto Ricans in Hawaii: 1900–1958." PhD diss., University of Hawaii, 1989.

Cheng, Susan M., and T. Linh Ho. "A Portrait of Race and Ethnicity in Hawaii: An Analysis of Social and Economic Outcomes of Hawaii's People." Hawaii: Pacific American Research Center, 2002.

Dias, Austin. "Carlo Mario Fraticelli: A Puerto Rican Poet on the Sugar Plantations of Hawaii." *Journal of the Center for Puerto Rican Studies* XIII, no. 1, (Spring 2001): 94–107.

López, Iris. "Borinkis and Chop Suey: Puerto Rican Identity in Hawaii, 1900 to 2000." In *The Puerto Rican Diaspora. Historical Perspectives.* Eds. Carmen Teresa Whalen and Víctor Vázquez-Hernández. Philadelphia, PA: Temple University Press, 2005.

Morales, Rodney. "Ship of Dreams." In *The Speed of Darkness.* Ed. Rodney Morales. Honolulu, HI: Bamboo Ridge Press, 1988.

Pukui, Mary Kawena, and Samuel H. Elbert. *Hawaiian Dictionary. Hawaiian-English, English-Hawaiian.* Honolulu: University of Hawaii Press, 1986.

U.S. Census Bureau. 2000 Census. 2000.

13

Idaho

Errol D. Jones

CHRONOLOGY

1820s–1850s	Mexican and other Spanish-speaking fur trappers work future southeastern Idaho.
1860	Discovery of gold attracts Mexican miners, muleteers, ranchers, and cowboys to the area.
1870	The census counts 60 Latin Americans (mostly Mexican) in what is Idaho today.
1890	Idaho statehood is established.
1910s	Railroads and the Mexican Revolution bring more Mexicans to Idaho. Idaho National Guard sent to Mexican border.
1917	Mexican government complains about treatment of Mexicans in beet fields.
1920s	Labor recruiters turn to Mexican migrants to meet needs of Idaho's expanding economy.
1930	Mexican Consulate in Salt Lake City investigates abuses of Mexican workers in eastern Idaho.
1935	In Teton pea fields 1,500 workers—mostly Mexican—strike. Governor declares martial law.
1942–1947	The Bracero program brings 15,600 Mexican workers to Idaho. Contract violations lead to strikes, and discrimination leads to termination of jobs.
1955	Governor creates Migratory Labor Committee to report on conditions in migrant camps. Increasing number of migrants settle permanently.

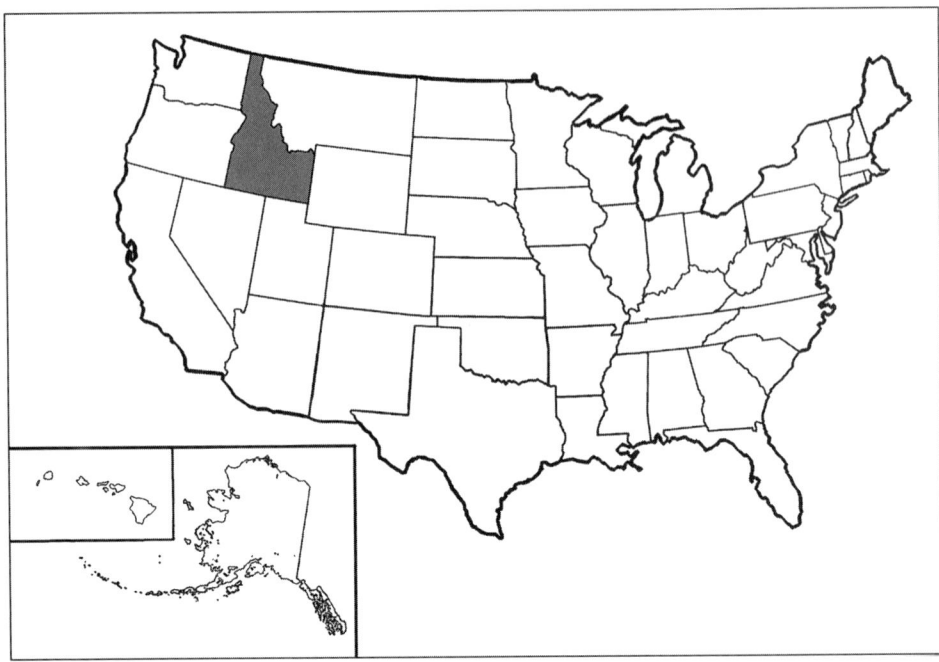

1961	Idaho Citizens Committee for Civil Rights successfully wins passage of antidiscrimination law.
1965	Idaho Farm Workers' Services incorporates, bringing Head Start programs to migrant camps.
1967	John Pino (Pocatello) elected Idaho's first Latino legislator.
1969	Idaho Human Rights Commission formed with Mexican representation.
1971	Idaho Migrant Council formed to promote rights of Idaho's Mexican Americans in health, education, and housing.
1987	Idaho Legislature creates Commission on Hispanic Affairs.
1990s	Jesse Berain becomes Idaho's second Latino legislator. Farm workers included in state's workers' compensation program. Hispanic Business Association formed. Workers Compensation extended to Idaho's farm workers.
2000–2007	New Hispanic Cultural Center built in Nampa. New minimum wage law extends federal minimum wage to farm workers. Farm Labor Contractor Registration and Bonding Act forces contractors to register and post bonds with state.

HISTORICAL OVERVIEW

Over the last quarter century the Latino population in Idaho has dramatically increased, as it has nationally. The 2000 Idaho census showed 101,690 people of

Workers at the Casa Valdez Tortilla Factory, 1979. *Idaho Statesman* photo, Boise State University Library, Special Collections.

Latino background living in the state, revealing a striking population growth of ethnic groups from Latin America. Most of that growth is attributed to migration. Accurate numbers, however, are difficult to determine. About 80 percent of Idaho's Hispanics (the official government term) are Mexicans or of Mexican heritage. In 1980, Idaho's total population of 943,985 contained about 36,560 (or 3.9 percent) Latinos. Over the next decade the Latino population jumped to almost 53,000 (or 5.3 percent) of a total of 1,004,000. Though significant, Latinos still represented a small percentage of the total population. Over the next 10 years their numbers almost doubled again, increasing from about 53,000 to 101,690, a growth of 92 percent. In 2000 Idaho's population had swelled to 1,293,953, of which 100,000 were Latinos, equaling 7.9 percent of the total population. Estimates for 2003 put the state's overall population at 1,367,034, with Latinos jumping to 119,066, or about 8.7 percent. Idaho's recent demographic increase is impressive, but growth of the Latino community is even more so, and it continues to soar. The most recent census estimates (2006) of Idaho's Latino population show 139,000 of a total 1,466,465, or an increase of 20,000 in only three years. If these estimates prove accurate, Latinos currently represent about 9.5 percent of the state's population, the largest minority group by far. These numbers may contain undocumented individuals, but it is difficult to say how many. The most reliable estimates range from 25,000 to 50,000, according to the U.S. Census Bureau and the Department of Labor's Current Population Survey.[1] These growth rates cast Idaho as a state whose ethnic complexion is undergoing a radical change, forcing the government, economy, and society to adapt.

Early Origins

Spain had claimed as part of its colonial empire the region that eventually became the state of Idaho. There is, however, little evidence that the Iberian power did anything to control or even explore the region. The first Euro-Americans (the Lewis and Clark Expedition) to set foot in Idaho encountered Spanish-speaking Native Americans who no doubt had picked up the language through trade. Mountain men, including some Spaniards and Mexicans, following in the footsteps of Lewis and Clark, lived off the land as trappers and hunters. Spain ceded its claims to the Idaho territory and the rest of the Pacific Northwest in 1819 in the Adams-Onis Treaty. The few Spanish settlers remaining did not relocate south of the 42nd parallel, the northern limit to Spanish territory. Instead, they formed part of the population that grew with the discovery of gold in the Northwest. Historical accounts after 1819 contain names such as Manuel, one of five merchants in Kootenai, Idaho, and Casildo Robles, owner of a dance hall. With the end of the Mexican-American War in 1848 the United States gained political control of all Mexican territory between the Rio Grande and the 42nd parallel, and with it over 75,000 Mexicans who had made their homes there. For Mexicans on both sides of the border the new boundary line was only a political fabrication and meant little to their ability to come and go. Although the Mexican population of those new U.S. states bordering Mexico grew after the war, Mexicans were slow to move north beyond the 42nd parallel until lured there by economic opportunity.

Opportunity came with the discovery of gold on Orofino Creek in 1860. Other discoveries followed and in 1863 Idaho became a territory independent of the Washington Territory. Almost 15,000 people lived in Idaho when the 1870 census was taken, 60 of them Latinos (including 10 women and 4 children), mostly of Mexican descent. Though not a large group, they played an important role in the region's economy, bringing with them Mexican traditions of handling horses and livestock. Many of these early Latinos were mule packers, ranchers, and cowboys. A smaller number were miners and laborers, and a few were soldiers in the U.S. Army. They and their children became solid members of Idaho's pioneer community. Spanish words and Mexican techniques and equipment permeated the cowboy and ranching cultures of southwestern Idaho, eastern Oregon, and northern Nevada. That influence continues to this day.[2] Here and there in these early years one catches glimpses of a richer, more diverse culture than it is usually portrayed in the standard accounts of that era. Mexican vaqueros, expert horsemen trained with the lasso, worked the isolated ranches. Skilled Mexican mule train packers hauled food and supplies into Idaho's mines high in the mountains. While on campaigns against resisting Native Americans, the U.S. Army occasionally relied on them to supply its troops with necessities.

Mexicans dominated the mule packing trade, making themselves an indispensable economic asset. Their traditions and Spanish vocabulary suffused the business. According to the 1880 census several Mexican mule packers lived in Lewiston, while others called Boise home, including "Idaho's premier muleteer" Jesús Urquides. Known as the "fast little packer," Urquides was born in Sonora, Mexico, in 1833 and, like so many other Sonorenses, migrated to the California gold fields during the 1849 gold rush. Having little interest in prospecting for gold and silver, Urquides turned to packing. In 1860 he transferred his operations from California to Walla Walla, Washington, and from there to Lewiston, Idaho. When gold was discovered in the Boise basin in 1862, Urquides snatched the opportunity to move to Boise to pack supplies into the surrounding mines. Near the Boise River Urquides built his own "Spanish village," with corrals and outbuildings for his mules, cabins for his packers and wranglers, and a home for his family. At the time of his death in 1928 Urquides was a prominent and prosperous Boise resident, lauded for contributions to the state's economy, photographed (with his mules) in Boise parades, and mourned by all who knew him. He was buried in Boise's Pioneer cemetery, a stone's throw from Spanish Village. Long after his death Spanish Village remained a landmark in the growing state capital until the city razed the buildings in 1972.

Railroad and Farm Laborers

In the late nineteenth and early twentieth centuries Mexican American pioneer families such as the Urquides, Fontes, Ortiz, Amera, Valdez, Galindo, Ocampo, Ursino, Escaso, Ruiz, and Carusia enjoyed relative prosperity, respect, and acceptance in their Idaho communities. But Idaho's economy underwent change during that time. The gold rush was short lived, and in its place emerged an expanding agricultural and livestock industry. Railroads penetrated the territory and the federal government made lands available to thousands of settlers attracted to Idaho by large-scale, government-financed irrigation projects. Southern Idaho's Snake River desert plateau now burst with sugar beets, potatoes, and other market crops.

When the Utah-Idaho Sugar Company built a rendering plant in eastern Idaho in 1904, it recruited Mexican workers. An economic boom in the southwest, west, and northwest regions of the U.S. took advantage of those who fled the chaos and turmoil of the Mexican Revolution (1910–1920). The outbreak of war in Europe in 1914 and U.S. entry into that war in 1917 created a labor shortage, leading the government to agree to a contract labor program with Mexico. Railroads and

Idaho sugar companies drafted some of these early workers to toil in the fields and lay rails in southern Idaho.

Rules of this first Bracero program compelled U.S. employers to hire Mexican workers at recruitment centers. The agreement stipulated the wages, length of contract, tasks to be performed, and worker accommodations. Moreover, growers and railroad companies were obligated to inform immigration officials when workers broke contracts. Because there were numerous violations of agreements and workers' complaints, among other problems, the program was ended on December 31, 1919.[3]

While investigating complaints of worker abuse in 1917, Idaho Labor Commissioner William J.A. McVety found more than 2,000 undocumented Mexicans, including 500 women and children, working in southern and eastern Idaho beet fields. In the Idaho Falls, Shelley, and Blackfoot regions "complaints were numerous regarding their accounts [wage agreements], living quarters and about winter clothing." The commissioner concluded that "too much [was] left to the supervision of the Sugar Company." He warned the governor that such labor abuses put the survival of the company and the industry in jeopardy.[4]

Mexican migration to Idaho continued after termination of the Bracero program. Suffering company abuse, low wages, unsanitary and inadequate living accommodations, corrupt labor contractors, and difficult and dirty work, Mexican workers came to the United States out of desperation. Their own country's economy could not sustain them. Throughout the 1920s railroad companies continued to hire Mexican migrants, until they made up the majority of maintenance crews in many western states. By 1930 Mexicans constituted nearly 60 percent of the section crews employed in Idaho.[5] Migrants coveted railroad jobs because no matter how menial, those jobs usually meant steady employment with wages higher than those in fieldwork. Farm labor was just the opposite: it paid less, and it was seasonal, with workers following the crops and living in tents, lean-tos, or deplorable camps. It exacted a heavy penalty from school age children who were both pulled from their studies in the early spring and prevented from returning to them until late fall.

Mexican consular officials from Salt Lake City, Utah, did what they could to help Mexican citizens working in Idaho. This protection did not extend to Mexican American migrants, who could only turn to the local justice system when problems arose. Consular officials intervened in wage disputes, complained about substandard working and living conditions, and tried to investigate personal tragedies such as injuries and deaths. A case in point occurred in Burley on July 4, 1920. Local police burst into a shack near the sugar beet factory and shot two (one fatally) Mexican beet workers playing poker with other men. Many irregularities and injustices swirled around this incident; yet, there was little the Mexican consul could do to see that his country's citizens were treated fairly and that justice was served. The Idaho National Guard's participation in U.S. retaliation against Pancho Villa's raid into New Mexico a few years earlier fueled a growing backlash against Mexicans.

In order to maintain a constant flow of inexpensive labor from Mexico, U.S. immigration policies in the 1920s treated Mexicans differently from the Chinese, the Japanese, and southern and eastern Europeans, all of whom were virtually excluded from entry into the United States. The farm lobby even succeeded in having Mexicans exempted from the immigration head tax. As a result, Mexican nationals and Mexican Americans continued to stream into Idaho in far larger numbers than the 1920 census figures show (only 1,215 Idaho residents born in Mexico, nine times greater than the count of 133 in 1910). Census numbers fail to show the North Americans of Mexican descent living or working in Idaho during the 1920s, but government sources and local newspapers reported large numbers of Mexicans and other Latinos working the state's mines, rails, forests, and farms.[6]

Throughout the 1920s, more and more Mexican Americans and Mexican nationals migrated into the state, and as they did, a pattern of discrimination and human rights abuses emerged. Xenophobia was one of the defining characteristics of American society in the 1920s, and Idaho was no exception. A Payette minister drew a crowd of some 500 to a Ku Klux Klan rally in Boise in June 1924. He praised the virtues of the Klan and its mission to end Jewish economic monopoly, prevent mixed marriages, bar Catholics from political office, and dry up the "flood of undesirables" pouring into the country.[7] During the decade newspapers reflected negative attitudes toward Mexicans in general.

Several large produce companies flocked to Idaho in the 1920s and 1930s to grow green peas. After being harvested, the peas were packed in ice and shipped by rail to markets as far away as Chicago and the East Coast. Companies contracted with Idaho farmers such as those in the Teton Valley to plant the peas and recruited large gangs of migrant pea pickers to harvest the crop. Because most of the harvesters—even during the Great Depression era—were Mexicans or Mexican Americans, complaints flooded the Mexican consulate of workers being abused, cheated on their wages, forced to live in subhuman conditions, and subjected to all sorts of indignities.

By August 1935 worker anger exploded during a strike in the Teton Valley's pea fields. The conflict had escalated from a dispute over wages between laborers and the produce companies to one in which the farmers became directly involved, because they feared losing their pea crops. In their anger they lashed out at the strikers. Violence erupted on both sides, forcing county officials to beseech the governor to declare martial law and send the National Guard. On August 15 and 16, Idaho Guardsmen entered labor camps and arrested about 125 "Mexicans who were causing the trouble." Another 30 or more were picked up on valley streets. Together with "a few American agitators and some parasites and camp followers," these Mexicans were held under guard until they were paid the wages still owed them. Troopers then loaded them into trucks furnished by the packing companies, or forced them into their own cars and trucks, and escorted them to the county line, warning them not to return. The next day the remaining workers returned to the fields. The strike was over. It was clear at the time, and it still is, that the authorities violated workers' civil rights regardless of their citizenship or ethnicity.[8]

The Great Depression was a nightmare for most North Americans and for countless Mexicans. Many U.S. citizens of Mexican heritage suffered profoundly when arrested and, together with their Mexican cousins, deported to Mexico. No official forced migrations of Mexicans or Mexican Americans from Idaho during the Depression occurred, but it became the policy of some communities to "hire whites only." Nevertheless, the Idaho Sugar Beet Growers Association brought so many Mexicans for spring thinning in 1935 that "local residents felt discriminated against." Growers responded that "white workers were amateurs who did the job poorly and were slower and less efficient than the Mexicans."[9] Signs posted at roads entering the state warned nonresidents that state social services would be denied them. Because they were Mexicans, one resident remembered, there was no relief for them. In spite of that, with demand for Mexican migrant labor in sugar beet production high, migrant workers may have flocked to Idaho in greater numbers during the 1930s.

WORLD WAR II BRACEROS AND THE MIGRANT STREAM

War mobilization effectively ended the Depression. Local Idahoans and domestic migrants left the fields to take well-paying jobs in factories and elsewhere. In 1941 national farm federations urged the United States Employment Service to import thousands of Mexican contract workers. As the country's wartime economy expanded, demand for farm labor grew. Recently completed New Deal reclamation projects added an additional 2,895,000 irrigated acres to Idaho's and Oregon's agricultural sectors by 1940. Two years later farm labor shortages were greatest in the Pacific Northwest. Unable to find workers, growers became desperate. The Idaho State Farm Bureau Federation petitioned for more than 1,000 Mexican farm laborers, and the Utah-Idaho Sugar Company requested braceros. Mexican workers began arriving the following year. From 1942 to 1947, 15,600 Mexican men entered Idaho.

U.S. farm federations wanted Mexican contract labor, but they resented the restrictions and rules imposed. Braceros vigorously protested contract violations and abuses, but some farmers ignored their complaints and forced them to do the most difficult and perilous tasks. Suffering serious accidents, exposed to chemical and lead poisoning in the fields, finding only contaminated water to drink on the job, braceros' health was constantly in jeopardy. Although some farmers' inattention to proper safety procedures at times led to worker death, they often reprimanded camp managers who took additional precautions to prevent accidents.[10]

The Bracero agreement did not give workers the right to strike for better conditions or pay. But in Idaho and elsewhere ill treatment and contract violations caused workers to protest and, at times, walk off the job. Farmers often brought strikes to an end by assaulting braceros and threatening them with jail, forced labor, or deportation. Wage disputes often strained farmer-bracero relations. Facing the lowest wages and the most "recalcitrant farmers" of any Northwest state, "braceros' strikes in Idaho were more serious and prolonged." Idaho earned a reputation for discrimination against braceros, especially in Canyon County, where Mexicans were routinely barred from stores and saloons. To its credit, the Notus Farm Labor Committee joined others in denouncing racist practices and warned they could lose their labor supply. Prejudice against the braceros became so pronounced in Idaho that the Mexican government threatened to cancel contracts in the state, finally doing so in 1948. On the other hand, some communities welcomed Mexican workers and treated them with kindness and respect.[11]

After the war, Idaho's need for agricultural labor persisted. Contributing to the labor demand were new techniques in deep well pumping, more acreage brought under cultivation, and new food processing plants. Low pay, harsh conditions, and seasonal employment, failed to attract many locals. Employers turned to Mexican American families, mostly from Texas's Rio Grande Valley, who journeyed north on a migrant circuit in search of work. Undocumented Mexicans joined the Mexican Americans in the migrant stream to Idaho. Their numbers increased after the war. A 1955 U.S. Public Health Service study of migrant life found over 8,000 workers and about 13,500 family members in the state. The number of migrant workers almost doubled to 15,000 ten years later. Idaho growers and the state's political leaders deemed them essential to the prosperity of the state's agricultural sector. Furthermore, these migrants proved to be ideal farm workers: they arrived on their own, were skilled and experienced, accepted lower wages than locals, took advantage of few social services, and moved on when the work was done. In brief, they were almost invisible.[12]

Finding Their Own Way

Although small communities of Mexicans and Mexican Americans had existed in Idaho cities for some time, the number of permanent residents grew as nonseasonal jobs for them became available. Anglo communities and public institutions, accustomed to migrants coming for a few months of the year and then leaving, adapted slowly to this new reality. Moreover, migrants continued to arrive during the agricultural season, and the Anglo community could not, or would not, distinguish between permanent Mexican American citizens and those recent arrivals who worked the fields. To the typical Anglo Idahoan they were all the same: poor, unable to speak English, and transient dwellers of labor camps. Mexican Americans eager to join mainstream Idaho society sent their children to school, rented or bought a house in a safe and decent neighborhood, went to church, and participated in community activities. Despite these efforts, they confronted language and education obstacles that had initially tied them to the migrant circuit.

Encouraged by the civil rights movement of the 1960s, Idaho's Latino activists struggled to create their own organizations to address their unique concerns. From these efforts emerged the Idaho Migrant Council in 1971. Run by a board of Mexican American farm workers, for over 35 years the Idaho Migrant Council championed the rights of migrant laborers and other low-income folk to decent housing, improved health care, and greater educational opportunities. Together with other ethnic and racial minorities, Latinos formed the Idaho Citizens Committee for Civil Rights and successfully won passage of an antidiscrimination law in 1961. By 1969 they persuaded the state legislature to create the Idaho Human Rights Commission with Mexican representation. After a four-year struggle, Latino activists convinced the legislature to establish the Commission for Hispanic Affairs in 1987.

Civil rights legislation and affirmative action programs opened the doors to state and federal employment, providing opportunities for Latinos to leave the migrant stream and achieve better-paying and higher-status jobs. Most who took these jobs, however, were two or three generations removed or from nonmigrant families. Nevertheless, Latinos could now be seen in positions that were previously the exclusive domain of Anglos. To promote improvements in the Latino community, activists working in government formed Image de Idaho, a statewide advocacy group linked with Latino organizations in other states. Image sponsors annual conferences to focus attention on social and economic issues confronting the Latino community.

Alarmed by the high proportion of Mexican American youth who dropped out of junior and senior high schools, the Idaho Migrant Council (IMC) conducted a study of six school districts in southern Idaho in 1978 and discovered that between 80 and 90 percent of Mexican American students dropped out before graduating. The following year IMC filed a class action lawsuit on the students' behalf against the State Board of Education and local school districts. The suit claimed that education officials were out of compliance with state and federal laws protecting the rights of limited English proficient (LEP) students. Under Title VI of the 1964 Civil Rights Act states received federal funds to ensure that schools provided educational services to all its students regardless of race, color, or national origin. Almost four years later, the courts worked out a settlement agreement between the IMC and the State Board of Education. Effective in 1983–1984, the settlement required each school district to identify students with limited English proficiency and submit a plan designed to enable them to participate in the school's standard curriculum within a reasonable period of time.

In June 1990 the State Board of Education created the Task Force on Hispanic Education to study the state's public education system and to recommend solutions to problems facing students in the state's growing Latino community. One of the Task Force's most notable findings was that 40–60 percent of Latinos still dropped out of school. The 1993 legislature allocated $1 million to improve services to LEP students and increased it to $2.25 million for the 1997–1998 school year, when the number of those students stood at 13,188. Unfortunately, the impact of increased funding and additional efforts did not produce the expected results. The U.S. Department of Education Office for Civil Rights reported in 1995 that language minority students in several of the state's districts were not able to participate effectively in the regular instructional program. The estimated dropout rate that year was over 43 percent. One writer concluded that it would take another lawsuit to force the state to remedy the situation.[13]

During the 1990s and the first few years of the twentieth century Latino activists have won many victories for Idaho's farmworkers, of whom 95 percent are Mexican nationals or Mexican Americans. A law passed in 1996 overturned a 1917 law that excluded agricultural workers from workers' compensation coverage. Lawmakers extended the federal minimum wage to farm workers effective in 2002. That same year the legislature passed the Farm Labor Contractor Registration and Bonding Act, which forces contractors to register and post bonds with the state.

Idaho's economic growth opened up opportunities for Latinos and others in every conceivable field. Mexican Americans and other Latinos are found in all professions, in business, in government, in skilled trades, and more. But they also endure unacceptable poverty, have persistently high dropout rates from junior and senior high school, and continue to face discrimination. Idahoans have made great strides in dealing with some of these problems, but much more needs to be done to overcome the lingering prejudices of the past. Mainstream Idahoans need to acknowledge the historic and important role played by Mexicans, Mexican Americans, and other Latinos in the creation of Idaho society. Their presence and their contributions go back as far as any other nonnative Idaho group.

NOTABLE LATINOS

Urquides, Jesus (1833–1928). Early pioneer and premier muleteer, Urquides built Spanish Village, from which he helped provision mining towns in the Boise Basin.

Hernandez Rodriguez, Antonio (Tony) (1920–2004). Ardent civil rights activist, Hernandez Rodriguez fought to end discrimination in the state through passage of an antidiscrimination law. He was instrumental in organizing cultural events and working with youth.

Berain, Jesse (1928–). Latino community leader since the mid-1950s and a key organizer of cultural events, Jesse has also served on the Human Rights Commission and in the State Legislature. He and his wife Maria work with at-risk youth and advocate for the elderly.

Fuentes, Humberto (1942–). A political activist and spokesman for Idaho's farm workers, Fuentes was a key participant in the establishment of the Idaho Migrant Council, also serving as its executive director from 1971 to 2001.

Schachtell, Ana Maria (1947–). Schachtell has served as cultural specialist for the Idaho Commission on Hispanic Affairs. She played a key role in establishing the Hispanic Cultural Center (opened 2003), and she has chaired its board: She is an ardent promoter of Latino culture and education in Idaho.

Gonzalez Mabbutt, Maria (1955–). A notable political activist and farm worker advocate, Gonzalez Mabbutt's work focuses on registering Latinos to vote and protecting their civil rights.

CULTURAL CONTRIBUTIONS

Starting in 2000, as more and more migrants of Mexican heritage found permanent work in Idaho, community activities such as parades, fiestas, and dances that expressed their unique cultural identity became more frequent. The celebrations continued on an annual basis. Complete with elaborate costumes, music, dances, piñatas, food booths, parade floats, queen contests, and baseball games between labor camps, these fiestas marked a new sense of stability in Idaho's Mexican American communities. Though newspapers drew a distinction between "migrant workers" and "residents," in truth many of the fiesta organizers already were residents.

Presently, fiestas such as Cinco de Mayo, Mexican Independence Day, and other cultural activities draw large crowds of non-Latinos, which seems to herald a level of acceptance by the dominant society of the growing Latino presence. The practice of showing appreciation to those who labor in the fields was revived recently by numerous groups working with migrant workers. Farm Worker Appreciation Day is one example of an annual event celebrating southwestern Idaho farming communities. As a capstone to the vitality of Latino cultural influences, Latinos joined forces with a broad spectrum of other interested citizens to raise money for a new Hispanic Cultural Center in Nampa, Idaho. Funded by grants from the Idaho state government, the Mexican state of Jalisco, individuals, and businesses, the new center opened its doors in 2003 and has become the venue for a vibrant display of Latino art, dance, lectures, fiestas, and a variety of other cultural events.

NOTES

1. Jones, "Invisible People"; Passel, 6; Wu.
2. Jones and Hodges, "Writing the History of Latinos in Idaho," 18.

3. García, 21.
4. Jones and Hodges, "A Long Struggle," 54.
5. Gamboa, "Mexican American Railroaders," 35.
6. Margo J. Anderson, *The American Census: A Social History*. New Haven: Yale University Press, 1988; *Idaho Farmer*, 13 October, 1921.
7. Ourada, 17, 20; Jones, "Shooting of Pedro Rodriguez," 40–55.
8. McConnel to Ross, Governor's Papers, August 14, 1935.
9. Gamboa, *Mexican Labor and World War II*, 14–15.
10. Gamboa, *Mexican Labor and World War II*, 68–73.
11. Gamboa, *Mexican Labor and World War II*, 83, 84, 112.
12. Salazar, 15; Jones "Invisible People."
13. Byrd, 131.

BIBLIOGRAPHY

Anderson, Margo J. *The American Census: A Social History*. New Haven, CT: Yale University Press, 1988.

Byrd, Sam. "The Plight of Mexican-American Students in Idaho's Public Schools." In *The Hispanic Experience in Idaho*. Eds. Errol D. Jones and Kathleen Rubinow Hodges. Boise, ID: Boise State University, 1998, 131.

Delgado, Max. *Jesús Urquides, Idaho's Premier Muleteer*. Boise: Idaho State Historical Society and Hispanic Cultural Center of Idaho, 2006.

Gamboa, Erasmo. *Mexican Labor and World War II: Braceros in the Pacific Northwest, 1942–1947*. Austin: University of Texas Press, 1990.

———. "Mexican American Railroaders in an American City: Pocatello, Idaho." In *Latinos in Idaho: Celebrando Cultura*. Ed. Robert McCarl. Boise: Idaho Humanities Council, 2003, 35–42.

García, Juan Ramon. *Operation Wetback: The Mass Deportation of Mexican Undocumented Workers in 1954*. Westport, CT: Greenwood Press, 1980.

Idaho Statesman. "Census: Hispanic Population Rises Across Idaho." August 11, 2007, Business 1.

Jones, Errol D. "Invisible People: Mexicans in Idaho History." *Idaho Issues Online*, Fall 2005. http://www.boisestate.edu/history/issuesonline/fall2005_issues/1f_mexicans.html.

———. "The Shooting of Pedro Rodriguez." *Idaho Yesterdays* 46, no. 2 (Spring–Summer 2005): 40–55.

Jones, Errol D., and Kathleen Rubinow Hodges. "Writing the History of Latinos in Idaho." In *Latinos in Idaho: Celebrando Cultura*. Ed. Robert McCarl. Boise: Idaho Humanities Council, 2003, 17–30.

———. "A Long Struggle: Mexican Farm Workers in Idaho, 1918–1935." In *Memory, Community, and Activism: Mexican Migration and Labor in the Pacific Northwest*. Eds. Jerry Garcia and Gilberto Garcia. East Lansing: Michigan State University, Julian Samora Research Institute, 2005, 41–84.

Ourada, Patricia. *Migrant Workers in Idaho*. Boise, ID: Boise State University, 1980.

Passel, Jeffery S. "Estimates of the Size and Characteristics of the Undocumented Population." Pew Hispanic Center Report, March 21, 2005, 6, Table 1. http://pewhispanic.org/files/reports/44.pdf. Accessed August 28, 2005.

Ross, C. Ben. Governor's Papers. Idaho State Historical Society, Library and Archives, AR2/15, Box 1. Boise.

Salazar, Maria. "Yo, También, He Estado Aquí." Unpublished article. 1991.

Wu, Huei Hsia. "By the Numbers: Mexican Workers and Idaho." *Idaho Issues Online*, Fall 2005. http://www.boisestate.edu/history/issuesonline/fall2005_issues/index.html.

14

Illinois

Sylvia Fuentes

CHRONOLOGY

1541	Spanish explorer Hernando de Soto first enters Illinois by crossing the Wabash River at Mount Carmel. This expedition was Spain's longest into Native America.
1850	The 1850 U.S. census reports that Illinois has 50 Mexican residents.
1884	The Mexican Consulate is established in Chicago.
1900	The 1900 census reports 156 people of Mexican descent in Illinois.
1906–1910	Mexicans and Chicanos are recruited to work on the Chicago railroad.
1910	The number of people of Mexican descent documented in Illinois is 672.
1916	Railroad companies bring hundreds of Mexicans to Chicago's Near West Side because this is where the hub of railroad companies are located and one of the few places where Mexicans find affordable housing.
1916–1919	The restriction on European immigration in concert with wartime economic boom and labor shortage results in a demand for railroad and industrial labor. This fuels a demand for Mexican labor.
1920	The number of people of Mexican descent in Illinois jumps to 4,592.
1920–1921	Postwar industrial depression. Chicago Packinghouse workers begin to strike and employers seeking relief hire Mexicans.
1924	Mexicans established the first local Mexican church, Our Lady of Guadalupe, in South Chicago.
1928	Dedication Ceremony of Our Lady of Guadalupe Church in Chicago on September 30.

1930	Approximately 21,000 Mexicans reside in Illinois.
1930–1940	Chicago Societies is the first Mexican American Political Club designed to promote informed voting in East Chicago.
1935	El Frente Popular Mexicano, a group with leftist ties to organized labor in Mexico, is established in Illinois.
1937	Mexican workers are among strikers and supporters beaten, arrested, and murdered by Chicago police during the infamous Republic Steel Mill Strike.
1940	The number of Mexicans in Illinois is 23,545.
1943	The Mexican Civic Committee is formed.
1950s	Mexicans establish branches of civil rights organizations already active in the Southwest. This includes the GI Forum and the League of United Latin American Citizens (LULAC).
1950	There are 34,538 Mexicans in Illinois.
1960	There are over 63,000 Mexicans documented in Illinois. Casa Aztlán is established in Chicago.
1966	On June 12, the Puerto Rican community—feeling a sense of neglect, marginalization, and despair and further fueled by police brutality—rebels in what became known as the Division Street Riots.
1970	There are 117,268 Mexicans living in Illinois.
1977	The Chicago-Colombia Lions Club is founded.
1978	The Puerto Rican People's Parade is first held in response to the murder of two youth by Chicago police.

1982	Wellington Avenue United Church of Christ located in Chicago, only the second Church in the United States to participate in the Sanctuary Movement, illegally houses Central American families attempting to escape political violence in their homelands. Casa Guatemala is founded in Chicago to provide support for Guatemalans and Latin Americans. Centro Romero is founded in Chicago in honor of Archbishop Oscar Romero by Salvadoran refugees to continue the archbishop's work of aiding Central American refugees escaping political and violent turmoil.
1987	The Mexican Fine Art Center Museum opens.
1992	The Puerto Rican Organization for Political Action files a suit to require the Chicago Board of Election Commission to provide Spanish-speaking voters with instructions and assistance in Spanish.
2002	The Illinois Legislative Latino Caucus Foundation is formed.
2006	Latino activists and Illinois residents join the Immigrant Rights Marches held in several cities and towns in Illinois.

HISTORICAL OVERVIEW

The history and experiences of Latinos in Illinois is a result of the economic, social, and political needs of Illinois citizens. Illinois has the fifth-largest Latino population in the United States and the fifth-largest increase in the same population between 1990 and 2000.[1] In 2000 the Census Bureau identified Mexicans as the majority of the state's Latino population, followed by Puerto Ricans, and lastly by those categorized as "Other Hispanic/Latino."

Tejanos, Cubans, Central Americans, and other Latinos have settled and played an important role in the development of Illinois. Groups of people representing less populated and well-known Latino countries have also contributed greatly to Illinois history; however, there is a dearth of information and even less recognition of such contributions.

In 2004, Latinos accounted for 14 percent of all Illinois residents. Between 1990 and 2004, the Latino population increased almost 96 percent. Latinos accounted for 63 percent of the total population growth during these 14 years.[2] The largest Latino groups in Illinois are Mexicans, Puerto Ricans, and Cubans, respectively, although the Census Bureau includes Cubans as the third-largest group with those categorized as "Other Hispanic/Latino."

Sixty-two percent of the state's Latino population is Mexican and lives in Chicago. While Puerto Ricans also have a history of settling in Chicago, most (48.7 percent) call New York City their home. The growth in the Latino community is occurring primarily in the suburbs and this trend is expected to continue.

In terms of county population, Cook County has the fourth-largest Latino population in the United States, with 1.1 million. This represents 70 percent of the entire Latino population in Illinois. With 753,644 Latinos, Chicago has the third-largest U.S. city population, outdistanced only by New York and Los Angeles. Currently, almost one-third of all children in the Chicago area are of Latino origin. Nearly 40 percent of the Chicago area school students are of Latino origin.[3]

Many of Illinois's Latinos live in the six-county metropolitan Chicago area, where 92 percent of the state's Latinos are concentrated. The six counties are Kane, Cook, DuPage, Lake, McHenry, and Will. In 2000, Kane County had the largest concentration of Latinos (23.7 percent). Between 1990 and 2000 McHenry County registered the fastest Latino growth rate: 223 percent.[4] At one time, Chicago was considered the most frequent port of entry into the United States. Traditional destinations from Chicago had been Cicero, Elgin, and Aurora. A trend toward outward migration from Chicago has been noted, and Naperville, Schaumburg, and Palatine are now ranking among the top 10 Illinois destinations for new migrants.[5]

In Cicero, there has been a rapid growth of the Latino population, which continues to grow. In the past ten years there has been a 40 percent increase in the town's Latino population, resulting in approximately 77 percent of the community residents being identified as Latinos. This remarkable growth is due primarily to migration and higher-than-average birth rates. Such growth is expected to continue in the future. In fact, in the 30 years between 1995 and 2025 the U.S. Census Bureau estimates that the Latino population in Illinois will double, reaching an estimated 2,275,000 people. The example of the large impact of Latino growth on the suburb of Cicero serves to underscore this point.

Latino growth in Illinois and around the country has been met with feelings ranging from apathy to abhorrence. Discussions of economic matters usually evolve into a debate about U.S. hardship at the hands of undocumented Latinos. An uninformed segment of the general population has difficulty separating undocumented workers from those who are lawful residents and citizens. Between 1990 and 2003 Illinois was well on its way to suffering a net loss of jobs. Increases in employment attributable to Latinos in Illinois provided relief. In 2002 there were 40,000 Latino-owned businesses generating over $7.5 billion in revenues.[6] The average age of the state's Latinos plays an important part in growth of the workforce. The Latino population in Illinois is overwhelmingly young, with a little over half aged 25 years or less. By comparison, the average age for non-Latino Illinoisans is approximately 36 years.[7]

Illinois became the 21st U.S. state in 1818. Prior to that, Illinois was part of a territory known as French Louisiana. The Illinois territory was later lost to England after the French and Indian war, and it was subsequently reclaimed from the British. In 1803, the North American explorers William Clark and Meriwether Lewis began their expedition from Illinois with help from the Spanish Louisiana governor.[8]

The State of Illinois soon found itself participating in a war with Mexico. In January 1846, U.S. President James K. Polk sent troops to the Rio Grande, declaring that Mexico started the war with the Spot Resolution (naming a particular location where U.S. blood had been shed). President Abraham Lincoln opposed the war indicating it was uncalled for, unconstitutional, and deliberately begun by the United States.[9]

Illinois contributed a total of 6,123 men between June 1846 and January 1848 to the Mexican-American war. The United States defeated Mexico, and it rewarded itself with over 500,000 square miles of new territory, which forms a great deal of the current U.S. Southwest.[10] Illinois troops participated in the battles of Buena Vista, Vera Cruz, and Cerro Gordo; they even participated in the march into Mexico City.[11]

During the 1890s, Illinois became a conglomerate in the agricultural and industrial fields. It was at the forefront in the production of wheat and corn, and second in livestock. Manufacturing, union stockyards, and meatpacking businesses also grew in cities like Joliet, Peoria, and Rockford, making Illinois the hub in the north central United States.[12] Illinois had great appeal for those seeking employment.

In 1898, Illinois would again find itself embroiled in conflict with those whose mother tongue was Spanish. The Spanish-American War had begun. After years of U.S. tension with Spain because of the Spaniards' rule over Cuba, the sinking of the U.S. battleship *Maine* in Cuban waters became the cause for the U.S. declaration of war.[13]

Governor John Tanner of Illinois offered "whatever moral and material support may be necessary in this emergency to maintain the honor of the U.S. flag and prevent or punish any attempt at hostile invasion of our common country."[14] Illinois became the first state in the Union to offer material support and troops for the coming war. In April of 1898, eight Illinois National Guard regiments, as part of U.S. forces, joined approximately 5,000 Cuban revolutionaries to free Cuba from Spanish rule.[15]

In the early part of the twentieth century the influx of Mexican and Latino migration to Illinois was driven by the demand for inexpensive, high-quality labor in the agricultural and railroad industries. By the early 1900s, employment opportunities emerged in other industrial sectors.[16]

Although many Latin Americans migrated to Illinois of free will, capitalists were luring them with the promise of better working conditions, better pay, and an abundance of employment opportunities. The most popular destination for persons of Mexican origin who were coming from the Southwest and Mexico was Chicago.[18] In fact, the city outside of the Southwest with the most Latin Americans was Chicago.

Forced deportation of Mexicans, some of whom were U.S. citizens, and federal repatriation programs to Mexico began in the early 1920s and reached into the

1940s. Recruitment by capitalists for inexpensive labor and the social ills of the time placed Latinos, as a whole, in a tenuous situation. The capitalist need for labor, the Latinos' need to earn a living, and the fear of being deported made for an atmosphere of fear and conflict.

On the one hand, Mexicans were viewed as cheap labor used to fill voids in the labor market; on the other, Mexicans and other Latinos became the scapegoats for social troubles. Aggravated by historical tension with countries where Spanish was the official language, the tone was set for discrimination and unspoken policies against Mexicans and other Latinos.[19]

New migrants to Illinois from Mexico, the Southwest, Puerto Rico, and Cuba arrived in the city in the 1950s. The Latino population did not become significant until the 1960s. Nevertheless, Latinos have embraced this country and given their lives for the freedoms that all U.S. residents enjoy. There was only one all-Latino infantry division serving during the Korean War. Its members were Puerto Rican and belonged to the 65th Infantry Division. Combined with those serving in World War II and Korea, the city of Silvis, Illinois, contributed the most men to these conflicts than any other community of its size. During these conflicts, Silvis lost eight Latino men and erected a tribute to them in the form of a monument dedicated to their sacrifices.[20]

The 1990 data for Illinois revealed that 14.2 percent of residents over age five spoke a language other than English at home. That number rose to 19.2 percent by 2000, translating to 2.2 million residents. Illinois is fifth among states with non-English speakers, preceded only by California, Texas, New York, and Florida.

According to 2005 data, 21.5 percent of Illinoisans speak a language other than English at home, and a total of 12.6 percent of Illinoisans speak Spanish at home. This ranks Illinois the state with the ninth-largest Spanish-speaking population behind Arizona, California, Florida, Nevada, New Jersey, New Mexico, New York, and Texas. Illinois is the only one of all nine states located in the Midwest.[21]

A number of socioeconomic issues have led to disparities in a number of areas where Latinos are concerned. For example, adult literacy skills—which affect a person's ability to obtain employment, function in health care systems, or function in general—are disproportionately lower among Latinos than among Whites and Blacks, respectively, in the United States.[22] According to data collected in 1992 and reported in 2004, Illinois Latino adults fell in the lowest two literacy category levels, being outperformed by their White and Black counterparts.[23]

The 2000 census data demonstrated that U.S. educational attainment levels were high and continuing to rise. In 2000, most people aged 25 years and over in the United States had earned a high school diploma or higher degree, and more than half the U.S. population aged 25 and over (52 percent) had completed at least some college education. Nine percent had an advanced degree.

By 2000, Illinois educational attainment numbers had risen and surpassed those reported for the U.S. in general: 81.4 percent had a high school diploma, 53.7 percent had some college, 26.1 percent had a bachelor's degree, and 9.5 percent had an advanced degree. By comparison, the disparity for Latinos in Illinois in educational attainment is significant. Data reveal only 52.4 percent having obtained a high school diploma, 30.3 percent having had some or more college, 10.4 percent having attained a bachelor's degree or more, and only 3.8 percent having obtained an advanced degree.[24]

Despite the gradual increase in numbers of Latinos in higher education, in Illinois there is a disparity in representation of Latino faculty and staff. In 2002 the Illinois Board of Higher Education indicated that hiring biases were likely one source of failure in increasing numbers of minorities. Beginning with narrow advertising of the position, racially homogenous search committees, biases in judging candidates, and flawed interview processes, the eventual hiring of Latinos is an irregularity.[25]

Data from 2001 reveals that the number of Latino faculty members in Illinois educational institutions was minimal. Community colleges claimed 1.4 percent of Latino faculty representation; private institutions revealed 1.9 percent, and public universities boasted 2.5 percent Latino faculty representation.[26]

The 2004 poverty data for the State of Illinois reveal that although Latinos comprised 12.1 percent of the population, 16.4 percent lived in poverty as defined by the state. People with disabilities fared worse. Of persons with disabilities, 16.3 percent living in poverty were non-Latino Whites, whereas the rate for Latinos was 28 percent. Unfortunately, senior citizens are not immune from being affected by poverty. Of seniors, 6.4 percent living in poverty were non-Latino Whites, but 17.1 percent were Latinos.[27]

A trend in Illinois and many other areas of the United States is the English-only movement. There has been significant growth in the Latino Spanish-speaking population in Carpentersville, Illinois. It has bred tension among residents with village officials proposing English-only ordinances to effectively erase Spanish documents in the village.[28] It has been widely reported that the real target of this ordinance are those perceived to be illegal migrants who at best refuse to acculturate.[29] In 1923 Illinois passed legislation making "American," not "English," the official state language. In 1969 the law was amended because of the obvious inability to punish Illinoisans who continued to use English.[30]

Although Latinos in Illinois are high in numbers and in a position to affect legislation and elections, voter registration for Latino citizens has been exceeding low. It lags behind registration rates for Blacks and Whites. Nevertheless, although data is not complete, turnout of Latinos registered to vote in Illinois elections during presidential election years is impressive. Voter turnout for Latinos ranged from 76.5 to 92.2 percent between 1984 and 2004, and for some of the elections that took place in those years it surpassed that of White voters.[31] Illinois politicians have been paying close attention to those numbers. With a little over half of Latino residents who are eligible to vote having registered, a surge in voter registration in combination with the traditionally high voter turnout will affect the outcome of any political race.

Mexicans and Mexican Americans

The census of 1850 reported that the state of Illinois had 50 Mexican residents. In 1900, the census showed that there were 156 people of Mexican descent in Illinois. This number increased to 672 in 1910, and then it increased drastically to 4,592 in 1920. By 1920, Illinois ranked eighth in the country in terms of the size of its Mexican population.[32]

The migration into Illinois occurred in three distinct phases. The first phase occurred in 1906–1910, and it was associated with the recruitment of Mexicans by the railroad companies already employing Mexicans in the Southwest. The second phase occurred in 1916–1919, and it was based on employer demands during World War I and labor shortage (as a result of immigration restrictions from Europe); several railroad companies brought hundreds of Mexicans to the Near West Side of Chicago in 1916. The third phase came about during the postwar industrial depression era: stockyard districts began to appear in Chicago, and employers looking to break the packinghouse workers strike of 1921–1922, sought out Mexicans.[33] Prior to the 1900s, a small number of Mexicans and other Latinos had come to Chicago looking for work wherever they could find it. Many did migrant work, whereas others went into the art and entertainment fields.[34] Mexican migrant workers were employed by the railroads in Chicago at least as early as 1907.[35] A small number of those initial laborers settled in the area, but soon they would be joined by a larger wave of Latino migrants.

In 1914 the U.S. Army comprised 98,000 men, and President Woodrow Wilson increased the number of the Army troops to 140,000, likely in anticipation of the mounting tensions overseas. The United States entered the war in 1917, and all males between the ages of 21 and 30 were required to register for military service. By 1918 almost 24 million men had registered, and 4 million of those registrants were drafted into service.[36]

An unprecedented opportunity arose for migrants as they were hired to replace workers serving as soldiers in World War I. Mexicans were the first group to arrive in the Midwest, more specifically in Chicago. The earliest new migrants were single young men who rapidly settled near their places of employment in close-knit groups. Industries that recruited the young men included the South Chicago steel mills, the meatpacking companies close to the Back of the Yards and the Near West Side, and the budding railroad system close to the Hull House area.[37]

Between 1912 and 1928, the ethnic composition of the workforce in various industries in Chicago changed drastically. Mexicans had gone from 0 percent of the steel industry's workforce in 1912 to 9.4 percent of workers in 1928. The packinghouses experienced the same growth.[38] Out of this labor shift came the *colonias* (communities), which were already commonplace in California, Texas, New Mexico, and Arizona.[39] One of the first Mexican-based *colonias* in Illinois was in South Chicago. Thereafter, many Mexicans and other Latinos began to form communities in proximity to their employment.

Historically, new settlement experiences have occurred due to personal economic need on the part of Mexican American and Mexican nationals as well as to fiscal security interests on the part of the United States. The 1900s employment opportunities had become bountiful, and Latinos were surreptitiously welcomed as they provided cheap labor. Thus, a pattern began to emerge: Mexicans, Chicanos, and other Latinos would primarily be used to fill the demand for cheap labor in agricultural and railroad industries.[40] The railroad expansion served as a catalyst for Mexican American employment in Chicago, and that city would later be identified as the Midwest Mexican Capital.[41] During the industrial and agricultural boom, many Mexican migrants lived in railroad camps, in and around Chicago. During the winter of 1927–1928, 950 Mexican people were found living in 20 camps. Men accounted for 423 of camp residents, 155 were women, and 372 were children. Among the railroads with camps were Atchison, Topeka and Santa Fe Ry. Co.; Chicago, Milwaukee and St. Paul Ry. Co.; Chicago and Northwestern Ry.; and Burlington Railroad.[42]

Midwestern Mexican *colonias* appeared in the early twentieth century—a period during which there was massive Mexican migration to the area—because there were no established Mexican communities. South Chicago had one such *colonia*.[43] The year of 1929 saw a sizable influx of Mexican and Mexican Americans into Illinois, most notably into Chicago. Chicago housed one of the largest and strongest Mexican populations outside the Southwest. Although the population was relatively small compared to the city's total population, it was a Midwest destination that drew Latinos by the largest numbers.[44]

By 1930, the number of Mexicans in Chicago had increased dramatically. Single men were no longer the only ones making the trip. Initially, groups of Mexican male workers came directly to Chicago, having been recruited by industries to fill voids caused by wartime labor shortages; others came as a result of the known demand for more laborers. Ultimately, Mexican men and women journeyed toward Chicago from the agricultural fields, looking for other opportunities. The lure of gainful employment in the United States and the desire to escape the revolution in Mexico were the primary reasons for the massive migrations north.

The movement of Mexicans to urban areas had thus begun. It is estimated that there were 1,265 Mexicans in Chicago in 1920, and that the number had jumped to 19,362 by 1930. The urban *colonias,* or barrios, were dreadful. Inundated by rodents, chronic disease, high infant mortality rates, lack of essential utilities, and lack of protection from the elements, the families huddled together to find comfort in supporting one another. Eventually, the rise of culturally familiar shops, restaurants, and churches added to the comfort level of the local residents.[45] By this time, one-third of the Mexican population was composed of women, children, and extended family members. These new families formed cultural and social networks that provided relief from discrimination and economic hardship. Their connection to their mother country remained strong, leading to local celebrations of holidays such as Mexican Independence Day.[46]

Thousands upon thousands of Mexican laborers had entered the industrial labor force in the Midwest. By 1930, the Mexican population of Illinois numbered 28,906.[47] However, the stock market crash of 1929 left the country in economic despair that lasted until World War II. The war also caused the loss of over half of the population of Mexican origin in Indiana, Illinois, and Michigan.

In the 1930s the U.S. secretary of labor, William N. Doak, initiated a nationwide campaign of terror against Mexicans.[48] Although this initiative was referred to as repatriation, many U.S. citizens of Latin American origin were deported. Local immigration officers and law enforcement agencies willingly supported implicit anti-Mexican sentiment as well as deportation raids that resulted in more losses of Mexican-origin residents and citizens.

During the 1930s and 1940s, as a result of this anti-Mexican campaign, the Mexican population dropped 40 percent in the United States. In Illinois it caused the Mexican population to decline to 21,449 in the 1930s and 10,065 in the 1940s. This represented a 53 percent loss of Mexican-origin residents in Illinois.[49]

In 1941, the United States became engaged in World War II, once again finding itself with wartime labor voids and additional wartime industrial demands. The United States again eased on immigration restrictions; much in the same way as it did with the Puerto Rican government, it was now working with the Mexican government to contract labor. As a result of U.S.-Mexican negotiations over 15,000 guest workers, called braceros, arrived in Chicago from 1943 to 1945. Numerous braceros stayed and settled permanently after the expiration of their contracts. By the late 1940s, many had settled in Aurora, Joliet, Gary, and Blue Island. Among the settlers were Mexican Americans and Tejanos (Texans of Mexican origin).

Puerto Ricans

Many first-generation Puerto Rican migrants initially settled in various parts of the United States, particularly in Chicago and New York. The Jones Act of 1917 assured the inhabitants of the island of Puerto Rico U.S. Citizenship. The Puerto Rican influence in Chicago during the 1930s was minimal as there were only a few men and women who relocated from New York. Ultimately, the growth of Puerto Ricans settling in Chicago was sufficient to make an impact. The late 1940s saw a significant wave of Puerto Rican migration to Chicago.[51]

It is ironic that although Puerto Ricans from the island were U.S. citizens, Puerto Ricans from New York felt in competition with them for jobs. During this juncture, the Puerto Rican government did not want to get involved, but through contract labor it agreed to direct migrating Puerto Ricans to areas other than New York so as to avoid competition with local Puerto Ricans for jobs: "Through the 'advance-guardsmen' project, fluent English-speaking Puerto Ricans would be sent to previously agreed-upon towns and cities to lay the foundation to ease the migration of other Puerto Ricans into that area."[52] Ultimately, Puerto Ricans sought out larger cities such as Chicago, attracted by job opportunities. The migration of Puerto Ricans expanded as the immigration laws became unyielding, causing deportation of Mexican nationals as well as Mexican Americans.

During World War II, the need for labor again arose, and immigration laws were arbitrarily applied, luring foreigners to work in the United States. In the meantime, Puerto Ricans were being overlooked as viable members of the workforce. In 1946, after World War II, shady employment agents began offering Puerto Ricans employment in places where employment opportunities were scarce. Workers were transported to Chicago on cargo planes, were clearly overcharged for airfare, and were not allowed the customary luggage weight and capacity.

The new Puerto Rican migrants employed at the Chicago Hardware Foundry Company were underage, failed health exams, and worked in poor conditions. The U.S. Department of Labor went on record that these workers came of their own accord, and hence, it would not take action against the employers, unless there was a flagrant violation of contracts. The degree of violation would be later defined by the U.S. Department of Labor.[53]

Puerto Ricans were now working alongside the Mexican braceros. The braceros were hired initially to alleviate the need for laborers in the wartime relief effort. During this same period, an employment agency recruited women from Puerto Rico as domestic workers in the Chicago area. New Puerto Rican arrivals lived on the north side—in Lincoln Park, Uptown, and Near West Side. But that began to change in the 1960s, when Puerto Ricans began to claim their own environs concentrating in West Town and Humboldt Park.[54]

The growth in the Puerto Rican population was astounding. In 1950 the population was 8,000, for the entire Midwest. Due to the "advance guardsmen" program and to employment agency recruitment, by 1960 the Puerto Rican population in Chicago had grown to 32,000.[55] The most intense migration of Puerto Ricans from the island occurred after World War II, with over 2 million people migrating. Although the majority settled in New York, Chicago had the second-largest concentration of Puerto Ricans.[56]

Much like other Latinos, Puerto Rican migrant workers have suffered abuse in the workplace. For example, in 1946 an employment agency imported over 300 Puerto Rican girls to work as maids for about $60 a month. The agency then charged the girls a flat agency fee of $125.00 and paid them at the rate of $10 per month, while retaining additional funds in escrow for return flights. In another agency, over fifty Puerto Rican men were recruited for jobs at the North Chicago Hardware Foundry. They were paid approximately $30 weekly and then charged room and board, and employment agency fees. In addition, they had to pay for plane tickets to fly home.

The majority of Puerto Rican migrants were attracted to New York in the early years. By 1950 many had settled outside of New York. It is estimated that about 130,000 have settled in the Chicago area. Puerto Ricans, like many others, migrated to the United States to work. In the last several decades these U.S. citizens have filled labor shortages in many important mainland industries—the textile and garment industries in New York, the electronics industries in Illinois, the foundries in Wisconsin, the steel mills in Ohio, Indiana, and Pennsylvania, and the farms in the East and Midwest. This population is plagued by poverty and alienation.[57]

The first Puerto Rican Parade in Chicago was held on June 12, 1966. It was during this time that there was an upsurge of riots in the West Town community on Division Street. The riots were spurred by the shooting of a Puerto Rican man by the Chicago police. These riots lasted until June 14, 1966, and they highlighted the bleak social conditions of the Puerto Rican youth and the random spurts of police brutality. The Puerto Rican community and other Latinos were faced with racism, inadequate housing, inferior health care, and a poor educational system.

In 1968, ASPIRA Inc. of Illinois was established as a nonprofit organization in Chicago's West Town community to address the high dropout rates of Latinos and the growing social and educational needs in the Puerto Rican community. The first office was located on the third floor of a bank at the corner of Chicago and Ogden Avenues, in the community now known as River North. The first executive director of ASPIRA was Mirta Ramirez, who obtained funds to set up the first bilingual program in the public schools. She also founded the West Side Child Parent Bilingual Center, the first agency of its type in the nation. ASPIRA continues to thrive because of the perseverance and engagement of the Puerto Rican community.[58]

Two distinct migratory experiences and settlements between Puerto Ricans from Chicago and New York have been identified. The first migratory group, which is referred to as the "old migration," consisted mostly of those who were already living in other parts of the United States, such as New York, before settling in Chicago. Those who came from Puerto Rico as part of the old migration were usually university students pursuing an education in the United States. Puerto Ricans migrating directly from the island to Chicago as part of the second migratory group were mainly contract laborers recruited for domestic and foundry work via employment and government agencies.

One main difference between Puerto Ricans and Mexicans is that Puerto Ricans are not deportable because of their status as U.S. citizens. However, the status of U.S. citizenship has not shielded Puerto Ricans from prejudice and discrimination. They have endured a long history of being displaced from their homes because of gentrification projects in their neighborhoods.[59]

In Chicago, Division Street continues to symbolize the preferred destination for new Puerto Rican migrants. *Paseo Boricua,* better known as Puerto Rican Road, has an abundance of culturally friendly restaurants and shops on Davison Street between Western and California Avenues. In the last few decades, the Puerto Rican population within Chicago has continued to grow. Recently, Puerto Ricans have extended their influence to some of Chicago's suburbs, such as Naperville and Schaumburg.

Though the number of Puerto Ricans in white-collar or professional jobs is increasing, most continue to work as laborers and in domestic occupations.[60] There are many similarities between Mexican and Puerto Ricans migrants. Although the Jones Act of 1917 granted citizenship to Puerto Ricans, poverty, police brutality, discrimination, and poor living conditions have created situations similar to those experienced by Mexicans, which resulted in a better understanding on the part of Puerto Ricans of the daily lives of their Latino counterparts.

CUBANS

The history of Cubans in Illinois is poorly documented. Because of historical and geographical circumstances, Cubans represent a much smaller percentage of Latinos in Illinois. After Fidel Castro's coup in 1959, Chicago began to see its first significant influx of Cubans, composed of refugees, most of whom were professionals or paraprofessionals.

Cubans faced a different issue with their homeland than did Mexicans or Puerto Ricans: chances were that they would not be returning to Cuba because of the political situation there, whereas Puerto Ricans and Mexicans had the option to go back to their respective home countries. However, most in the latter group would probably not opt to return to their homeland.[61]

Over 1 million Cubans have entered the United States since the Cuban Revolution of 1959. The port of entry for Cubans has always been Florida. Cuba is located about 90 miles southeast of the tip of Florida, and refugees still attempt to enter the United States through the Atlantic waters. Puerto Ricans and Cubans have been settling in the mainland United States for centuries.

Unlike Mexican and Puerto Rican migration, Cuban migration involved noncitizen island-dwellers.[62] Cubans began to arrive in Chicago in the 1950s. Some came because of economic opportunities, but most were political refugees. Although some Cubans returned to the island after the Cuban Revolution in 1959, the majority stayed. Approximately 2,500 Cubans were living in Chicago in 1960. Between 1960 and 1973, approximately 20,000 Cubans arrived in the Chicago area. Many emigrated from Cuba because they opposed the Castro government.[63]

There were several waves of migration from Cuba. The first wave consisted largely of professionals. Doctors, engineers, teachers, and dentists were among this group. The second wave, which was referred to as the "freedom flights," allowed Cubans to reunite with their families in the United States. The third wave, known as the Mariel boatlift, arrived in 1980. This group was mainly made of young single men, poor and of color, who did not have any family in Chicago. The most recent wave, in the 1990s, consisted of the "boat people," or *balseros*. Most of these people, found by U.S. Coast Guard ships, were also poor. By the end of 1996 about 2,000 *balseros* had settled in the Chicago area, many of whom having been relocated to the city by Catholic charities.[64]

Unlike the Cuban migrants of the 1960s and the 1970s who entered the United States as political refugees, the Cubans forming the last several waves left for economic reasons. Since the 1980s, Cubans coming to Chicago have been younger and less educated. Cubans entering the United States after 1994 fall under revised U.S. immigration laws, that changed Cuban migrants' refugee status from political to economic. This new legal status in the United States meant that Cuban refugees received fewer benefits and support from the government.[65]

The majority of Cubans in the Chicago area live in Cook, DuPage, Kane, and Lake counties. Cubans are the largest Spanish-speaking group to migrate to the suburbs of Chicago and live in various Chicago neighborhoods, such as Albany Park and Logan Square.[66] Chicago Cubans are more apt to be business owners than other Latino groups, and Cuban women have a higher rate of participation in the labor force, with many of them in nontraditional careers such as dentistry and medicine.[67]

Salvadorans

The history of Salvadorans in Chicago can be traced back to the late 1920s, with a steady flow of migration beginning in the 1950s.[68] This first wave of migrants was mostly composed of upper- and middle-class students. The civil war in El Salvador spurred a second wave of Salvadoran migration to Chicago, from the 1970s through the 1990s. Initially, Salvadorans entered directly into the United States. However, as the civil war intensified, many Salvadorans migrated through Mexico to come to the United States, crossing over illegally.[69]

Archbishop Romero, an outspoken critic of the military in El Salvador, provided support for change and activism in Chicago. He was murdered by a gunman on March 24, 1980, while performing a memorial mass for a friend's mother.

His death became the impetus for the founding of Centro Romero in Chicago, whose mission is to address social injustice among Central Americans.[70] Chicago faith organizations formed the Chicago Metropolitan Sanctuary Alliance and unmistakably defied of the U.S. government, which continued to refuse political asylum to refugees. Without legal recourse, churches all over the United States began participating in a concerted effort to protect, aid, and shelter Salvadorans and others. The conglomeration of churches participating in this undertaking were known as the Chicago Religious Task Force on Central America. The task force established an "underground railroad," known to operate during 1983 and 1984. This underground railroad shuttled refugees from place to place, in secrecy, and through a network of churches and synagogues.[71]

Guatemalans

Similar to the Salvadorans, Guatemalans numbered very few in Illinois prior to the 1980s. A wave of migrants came to the United States and to the Chicago area, fleeing the intense and extreme violence of civil war.

The United States, in particular Chicago, played a vital role in aiding and providing shelter to Guatemalans seeking refuge from their war-torn country. In 1981 the government of Guatemala launched a scorched earth campaign that resulted in genocide, torture, and other war crimes against anyone suspected of participating in or empathizing with revolutionaries. This campaign continued into 1982, and it has been described as "the most intense years of the 36-year civil war."[72] During this time, the U.S.-based Sanctuary Movement offered protection to Central American refugees. Many Chicago-based churches and organizations provided assistance to Guatemalans and Salvadorans facing deportation.

Guatemalan refugees thus joined the Salvadorans who were fleeing their own political persecution. Refugees from various parts of Guatemala, and hailing from various ethnic groups, were part of the Sanctuary Movement and many of them had suffered torture and other unspeakable acts. During the 1990s there was another large wave of migrants from Guatemala, owing to extreme poverty and natural disasters. Various Chicago service organizations have estimated that Guatemalans in Chicago numbered up to 80,000 by 2000. The 2000 census reported 19,444 in the Chicago metropolitan area.[73]

Colombians

Colombians began migrating to Illinois decades before many of the other Latino groups. Colombia was embroiled in a civil war from 1948 to 1957. Therefore, the 1950s saw a large growth in their numbers in Illinois.[74] Since 1974 Colombianos Unidos Por Una Labor Activa (CUPULA) has been celebrating Colombian Independence Day (July 20th). A group of medical students from

Colombia started the tradition, and it is the largest annual Colombian celebration in the Midwest.[75]

ECUADORIANS

The presence of Ecuadorians in Chicago can be traced back to the mid-twentieth century. Ecuadorians came to Chicago primarily in two waves. Initially, they migrated to Chicago from the period between 1965 and 1976. They came from provinces such as Guayas, Pichincha, and Chimborazo, working primarily in, factories, retail, and the service industry. Ecuadorian businesses included travel and courier agencies, restaurants, and food and clothing stores, located primarily on Milwaukee, Division, and 26th Streets.

The second major wave of migration took place in the 1990s. These Ecuadorians came mainly from the highland provinces of Azuay and Cañar. This wave of Ecuadorians depended on networks of family and friends to secure jobs in the restaurant and hotel industry for the men, and housekeeping and garment industries for the women.[76]

In 2000 there were 8,941 Ecuadorians in Chicago, making them the fifth-largest Latin American group in the city. And after New York, Miami, and Los Angeles, Chicago is the fourth U.S. city with the largest number of Ecuadorians.[77] Ecuadorians live primarily in Logan Square, Albany Park, Uptown, and Lake View. There are smaller clusters in Irving Park, Belmont Cragin, Edgewater, and West Ridge. More recently, Ecuadorians have been moving to the suburbs of Skokie, Glenview, Des Plaines, Morton Grove, and Elgin.[78]

Ecuadorians have founded many organizations, such as the Ecuadorian Civic Society (founded in 1959), the Federation of Ecuadorian Entities, the Ecuadorian Lions Club, the Cotopaxi Foundation, the Social Association of Azuay, the Civic Society of Cañar, and the Alausí Foundation. Religion has played a major role in preserving Ecuadorian traditions. The Ecuadorian community hosts annual events that include cultural exhibits, picnics, and parades.

NOTABLE LATINOS

Parsons, Lucy (c. 1853–1942). Activist Lucy Parsons identified herself as an African American woman of Native American and Mexican descent. Parsons was an activist who stood up for the rights of poor people and workers for nearly 70 years. The Chicago Police Department described her as "more dangerous than a thousand rioters." Parsons married in 1870 and in 1873 came to Chicago, where she worked with unions and organized workers. Parsons led many workers on strike against poor working conditions. Parsons continued her activism until her death at 89 years old. In May 2004, Chicago Park District's board named a Chicago park at 4712 West Belmont Avenue after Parsons, notwithstanding strong opposition from local police union.[79]

Torriente, Cristóbal (1893–1938). Baseball player Torriente was born in Cienfuegos, Cuba. He played as a center fielder for the Chicago American Giants from 1918 to 1925. In 2006 the Special Committee elected him to the National Baseball Hall of Fame.[80]

Bithorn, Hiram (1916–1951). Puerto Rican who was drafted by the Chicago Cubs in 1942. Many consider Bithorn to have been the first to break the color line.

Hernandez, Irene C. (1916–). Hernandez was the first Latino elected to office when she became a member of the Cook County Board in 1974, representing the county's 7 million residents.[81]

Silva, Rufino (1919–). Rufino Silva was born in Puerto Rico and studied at the Chicago Art Institute from 1938 to 1942 on a fellowship from the Puerto Rican government. Silva taught at Milwaukee's Layton School of Art between 1946 and 1947. In the subsequent years Silva studied abroad, and upon his return he joined the faculty at the Chicago Art Institute, where he stayed until his retirement.[82]

Talip, Alfredo (1925–). Talip was born in San Fernando Tamalipas, Mexico, and he came to the United States in 1942. Talip has been one of the most involved political activists of his generation. His love for politics was spurred when his good friend Jack

John F. Kennedy campaigning in Aurora, Illinois, with Alfredo Talip, one of Kennedy's strongest supporters and campaign volunteer. Talip is in a white hat standing directly under "Viva Kennedy Club" poster (1960). Courtesy of the Alfredo Talip Family, Aurora, Illinois.

Hill ran for president of the AFL-CIO union. Talip later supported Hill's bid for state representative. He has been described as someone who has given to the Latino community unselfishly through his service and personal assets. In 1956, three years before becoming a legal resident alien, he was a volunteer driving people to polling places throughout the city of Aurora, and he continues this service to this day. In 1960 Talip helped establish a fraternal organization, the Latin American Club, whose purpose was to provide a place for Latino social events and a forum to raise the consciousness of Latino issues. He was a volunteer for President John F. Kennedy's campaign, and he has worked on voter registration drives. In 1970 Talip became a United States citizen, and he was proud that he could vote and affect the future of his family, community, and new country.

Ramirez, Mirta (1928–). The first executive director of ASPIRA Inc. of Illinois, Ramirez set up the country's first bilingual program in public schools. She also founded the West Side Child Parent Bilingual Center, the first agency of its type in the nation.

Jordan, Hector (1931–1970). Jordan was the first Latino to become a police officer in Aurora, Illinois, initially meeting with prejudice because of his Mexican heritage. During his tenure on the police force Jordan received many city commendations and was named Policeman of the Year. Later Jordan worked for the Federal Bureau of Narcotics and Dangerous Drugs (D.E.A.) and accepted a position with the D.E.A in Madrid, Spain, where he was murdered while off-duty. The Hispanic Illinois State Law Enforcement Association created the Hector Jordan Memorial Award.[83]

Gonzalez, Jose (1933–). Born in Iturbide, Nuevo Leon, Mexico, he has been a leader of the muralist movement in Chicago since the early 1970s. He devoted himself to the Chicano movement as a muralist, organizer of exhibitions, and founder of organizations such as Movimiento Artistico Chicano (MArCh) throughout the 1970s and 1980s. He graduated from the School of the Art Institute of Chicago in 1970 and received a master's of fine arts from the University of Notre Dame in 1971.[84]

Orozco, Raymond E. (1933–). Orozco was born in Chicago, joined the Chicago Fire Department in 1959, and rose through the ranks to become the head of the Chicago Fire Department. In 1979 he became battalion chief, in 1980 deputy district chief, and in 1981 executive assistant to the fire commissioner. On April 24, 1989, he became fire commissioner, retiring in 1996.[85]

Aparicio, Luis (1934–). Aparicio was born in Maracaibo, Venezuela, and played shortstop for the Chicago White Sox (1956–1962, 1968–1970). Aparicio led the American League in stolen bases for nine consecutive seasons, from 1956 to 1964. He won the Golden Glove Award eleven times, was named to eight All-Star teams, and was inducted into the Baseball Hall of Fame in 1984, 11 years after he retired. The White Sox retired his jersey number, No. 11.[86]

Welch, Raquel (1940–). The actress, a major sex symbol of the 1960s and 1970s, was born Jo Raquel Tejada, in Chicago. Welch's résumé includes over 45 films. Her father Armando was a Bolivian migrant and aerospace engineer.

López-Rivera, Oscar (1943–). Community activist Lopez-Rivera is serving a 70-year prison sentence for seditious conspiracy, which included the bombing of 28 targets in the

Chicago area. Lopez-Rivera was also involved in the Chicago Puerto Rican Riots of 1966. He is a founding member of the Rafael Cancel Miranda High School, now known as the Pedro Albizu Campos High School and the Juan Antonio Corretjer Puerto Rican Cultural Center. He was also active in the Northwest Community Organization (NCO), ASSPA, ASPIRA, and the 1st Congregational Church of Chicago. He helped to found FREE, a halfway house for convicted drug addicts, and ALAS, an educational program for Latino prisoners at Statesville Prison in Illinois. He is expected to be released in 2027.[87]

Andrade, Juan (1947–). Andrade heads the Chicago-based United States Hispanic Leadership Institute (USHLI). He is one of only two Latinos to receive the Presidential Medal for "the performance of exemplary deeds to the nation," which was presented to him by President Bill Clinton. Andrade received a PhD from Northern Illinois University, and a post-doctorate MA from Loyola University in Chicago. Now a weekly columnist for the Chicago Sun Times, he was a political commentator on ABC-7 television channel and on WGN radio, being the only Latino commentator in the nation appearing on English-language radio or television. Andrade has helped register more than 1 million new Latino voters throughout the United States. As a civics teacher just out of college, Andrade was arrested in his home state of Texas for teaching his students about the fundamentals of U.S. Democracy in his native tongue, Spanish, which then was a violation of state law.[88] The American G.I. Forum of Illinois named Andrade Man of the Year.[89]

Morton, Carlos (1947–). Morton was born in Chicago and is the most published Latino playwright in the United States. Morton's first book of poems, entitled *White Heroin Winter*, was published in 1971. His most famous play, *El Jardin* (The Garden), was published in 1974. He received a PhD degree in drama from the University of Texas in 1987. Morton's plays appear mainly in two collections, *The Many Deaths of Danny Rosales and Other Plays* (1983) and *Johnny Tenorio and Other Plays* (1991).[90]

Torrado, René (1947–). Torrado was the first Latino president of the Chicago Bar Association. He served as its general counsel from 1988 to 1995, and as its president in 1995 and 1996. Torrado currently chairs the CBA's Appellate Review Committee of the Judicial Evaluation Committee. In addition, Torrado is listed in the 2003–2004 edition of *The Best Lawyers in America*.[91]

Villa-Komaroff, Lydia (1947–). Dr. Villa-Komaroff, a physician, was employed at Northwestern University in Evanston, Illinois, as a professor of neurology and associate vice president for Research Administration. She later was appointed as vice president for Research. Some of Villa-Komaroff's career highlights include creating nine new research centers, the Office of Strategic Initiatives, and the Office of Clinical Research and Training. In 1998 Villa-Komaroff gained international recognition as a pioneer in the field of cloning and became faculty at Harvard University Medical School. Villa-Komaroff was also a founding member of the Society of the Advancement of Chicanos and Native Americans.[92]

Venegas, Aurora V. (1949–). Venegas is president of Azteca Supply Company, which is among the strongest and best-respected minority- and female-owned businesses in Illinois. Azteca supplies a variety of products and services of high quality, and it is a preferred supplier to its customers. Venegas actively supports such organizations as HACLA, the Illinois Hispanic Chamber of Commerce, and the Federation of Women Contractors. She gives back to the community by supporting the Boys Club, the Special Olympics, Hitzaba House, Pope John Paul II School, Alivio Medical Center, and Mujeres Latinas en Acción. She is a board member of Father Flanagan's Girls and Boys Town in Chicago.[93]

Del Valle, Miguel (1951–). Del Valle was the first Latino elected to the Illinois State Senate. He also became the first Latino ever to be appointed as City Clerk of Chicago by Mayor Richard M. Daley. Senator del Valle is the founder of the Illinois Association of Hispanic State Employees (IAHSE). He also cofounded numerous other Latino organizations, including the Illinois Legislative Latino Caucus, of which he is a cochair; the Illinois Latino Advisory Council on Higher Education (ILACHE); the Alliance of Latinos and Jews; the Illinois Hispanic Democratic Council (IHDC). He also developed the annual Department of Children and Family Services Hispanic Families Conference.[94]

Lozano, Rudy (1951–1983). Lozano was a community activist and the Midwest director of the International Ladies Garment Workers Union. Lozano arrived in Chicago with his family in the early 1950s and settled in Pilsen, a largely Mexican neighborhood. Lozano was on Mayor Harold Washington's transition team, whose goal was to unite Latinos and African Americans. He was also an organizer of the Independent Political Organization's Near Westside Branch. Lozano was murdered in his home, and in 1989 the Chicago Public Library opened its Rudy Lozano Branch.[95]

Maldonado, Roberto (1951–). In 1994 Maldonado was elected Cook County Commissioner, making him the first Puerto Rican in the nation to serve as a county commissioner. In this capacity, Maldonado is chairperson of the Stroger and Cermak hospitals, and of the Law Enforcement and Corrections Committee. Additionally, he serves on nine committees: Business and Economic Development; Contract Compliance; Labor; Real Estate; Department of Corrections; Health and Hospitals; Finance; Zoning and Buildings; and Roads and Bridges. Maldonado earned both his undergraduate and his master's degrees from the University of Puerto Rico, before heading north to Chicago. In Chicago, Maldonado continued his education at Loyola University, where he earned his PhD in clinical psychology.

Martínez, Oscar (1952–). Martinez is the founder of the Latin American Museum of Art in Chicago. He was appointed chair of Media Arts of the Illinois Arts Council. Martinez was also president of the Latino Institute of Chicago. He received a BS in medical art from the University of Illinois Medical Center. Martinez was born in Ponce, Puerto Rico, and currently resides in Chicago.[96]

Castillo, Ana (1953–). Author Castillo was born and raised in Chicago, Illinois. She earned her master's degree in Latin American and Caribbean studies from the University of Chicago. In 1991 she received her doctorate in American studies from the University of Bremen in Germany. In lieu of a traditional dissertation, she submitted essays later collected in her highly acclaimed work *Massacre of the Dreamers*.[97]

Gutierrez, Luis (1953–). In 1992, Gutierrez became the first Latino from the Midwest elected to Congress. By receiving 77 percent of the vote, he was able to win the 4th U.S. Congressional District seat. He received a BA from Northeastern Illinois University in 1974, and he worked as a social worker and teacher before being elected 26th Ward

Alderman to the Chicago City Council. In a survey of Hispanic voting patterns released in late 1999, Congressman Gutierrez was selected as the single leader most admired by Latino voters nationwide. The poll was commissioned by Univision, a nationwide Spanish-language television network.[98]

Martinez, Iris (1953–). Martinez is the first Latina in Illinois to be elected to the State Senate. She passed legislation that obligates health insurance companies to provide women with contraceptive coverage. In recognition of this legislation, Martinez received the Profile in Courage Award from Planned Parenthood. With the passage of yet another law Martinez targeted Illinois drivers with out-of-state reckless homicide and DUI convictions. This law ensures that convictions received in other states are not only included in Illinois driving records but also subject to state laws regarding further prosecution of these offenses. To help protect consumers from becoming victims of identity theft, Martinez helped pass a law requiring that all insurance cards be issued without a Social Security number.[99]

Cisneros, Sandra (1954–). Author Cisneros's first book of fiction, *The House on Mango Street*, was awarded the American Book Award by the Before Columbus Foundation in 1985. She received a Paisano Dobie Fellowship in 1986 and a second National Endowment for the Arts Award in 1988. Cisneros was awarded the Lannan Literary Award for fiction in 1991, an honorary doctor of literature degreed by the State University of New York at Purchase in 1993, and was named a MacArthur Fellow in 1995.[100]

Gonzalez, Michael W. (1955–). Gonzalez is chief executive officer of Maestros Ventures LLC. A licensed professional engineer, he was also cofounder and executive vice president of Primera Engineers Ltd and cofounder and president of Primera Hill, an affiliate of Primera Engineers. Gonzalez exemplifies Primera's commitment to the community by actively serving on the boards of Window to the World Communications Inc., the parent company of WTTW Channel 11 and WFMT 98.7; Latinos United; and ACE Technical Charter School. He also served two terms as president and more than 11 years as a board member of the Hispanic American Construction Industry Association. Gonzalez is treasurer of the Illinois Legislative Latino Caucus Foundation.

Delgado, William (1956–). Senator from the 2nd Legislative District, Delgado was born in Newark, New Jersey, but was raised in Chicago. He graduated from Tilden High School and Northeastern University, where he earned a bachelor's degree in criminal justice, with a minor in sociology. Delgado was first elected in 1998, and his top legislative priorities are education reform, economic development, and crime prevention. He is working to develop school safety initiatives to keep drugs and guns out of local classrooms. Delgado also supports reducing class sizes, improving classroom discipline, and increasing state support for school construction grant funding. Delgado also highlights his work as "champion of health and physical fitness issues." He has sponsored legislation to see that physical fitness is emphasized in schools statewide. Representative Delgado serves on seven committees: Appropriations for Elementary and Secondary Education; Fee for Service Initiatives; Human Services; Judiciary II-Criminal Law; KidCare; Managing Sex Offender Issues; and Registration and Regulation. William Delgado was appointed Illinois state senator by the former state senator Miguel del Valle.[101]

Hinojosa, Mark (1956–). Hinojosa has been the director of photography for the *Chicago Tribune* since 1994. Mr. Hinojosa is in charge of over 67 staff members, including photographers, photo editors, assignment editors, and lab personnel. In 1997, under the direction of Hinojosa, the *Tribune*'s photo department was awarded third place for best use of pictures in a newspaper. This was the very first time the newspaper had been recognized for this honor.

Mora, Antonio (1957–). The first Latino to serve as a main anchor in a mainstream Chicago network-owned station. Mora was born on December 14, 1957, in Havana, Cuba. Mora has worked as a news anchor at WBBM-TV in Chicago since 2002. Previously, Mora had worked at ABC as a news anchor for *Good Morning America*.[102]

Perez, Antonio (1962–). Perez was a full-time photographer for ¡Exito!, which is the Spanish-language publication in the *Chicago Tribune*. He currently works full time for the *Chicago Tribune*. He contributes photographs to several publications and has a private collection in the Museum of Contemporary Photography, at the Chicago Art Institute, as well as in the Stuart Baum Gallery.

Grillo, Fernando E. (1963–). Grillo was the head of the Department of Financial and Professional Regulation, making him the first Latino cabinet secretary in state history. Throughout the 1990s, he worked in public finance, serving as vice president of public finance for Samuel A. Ramirez & Co. Inc. from 1995 to 2000, and assistant vice president of public finance for Estrada Hinojosa & Company Inc. from 1993 to 1995. He worked in several capacities for the City of Chicago—in the Department of Consumer Services, the Park District, and the Department of Housing—between 1986 and 1992. Grillo grew up in Chicago's Logan Square neighborhood. He earned a bachelor's degree in history from Andrews University in Berien Springs, Michigan, and a law degree from John Marshall Law School. He is a member of the Puerto Rican Bar Association, the Puerto Rican Chamber of Commerce, and the Board of the Chicago Children's Advisory Center.[103]

Montes, Jorge (1963–). The first Latino chair of the Illinois Prisoner Review Board, Montes was nominated by Governor Rod Blagojevich and approved by the State Senate. The Illinois Prisoner Review Board is an independent entity that makes decisions on adult and juvenile prison inmate matters. One of the roles of the Prisoner Review Board is to make confidential recommendations to the governor on clemency petitions.[104]

Perez-Luna, Victor (1963–). Perez-Luna is an assistant professor of chemical and environmental engineering at the Illinois Institute of Technology. He is a member of the team of research scientists who have developed a new sensing device called the IIT ChemArray, which can detect and measure the presence of toxic agents in air, water, and food.

Lopez, Paul J. (1964–). Lopez is senior vice president and chief lending officer of Park Federal Savings Bank of Chicago. A banker for 24 years, Lopez's primary focus is neighborhood revitalization and community development. Born and raised in Chicago's Back of the Yards neighborhood, Mr. Lopez serves on Father Flanagan's Girls and Boys

Town of Chicago, Peace and Education Coalition of Back of the Yards, New Alliance Task Force, the Illinois Attorney General's Latino Advisory Council, Neighborhood Housing Services of Chicago, and many more. Lopez played a vital role in opening the first full-service bank branch in an Illinois high school, and he was honored by the City of Chicago for his relief efforts for the victims of Hurricane Katrina. Lopez serves as vice chair of the Illinois Legislative Caucus Foundation.

Osorio, Jose M. (1964–). Osorio has been employed as staff photographer at the *Chicago Tribune* since 1991. He has worked on many special projects, and he was awarded the 1997 Baseball Hall of Fame Feature Picture of the Year.

Gonzalez, Ramiro (1968–). Gonzalez became the first Latino town president of Cicero, a Chicago suburb made famous by Al Capone. His predecessor, Republican Betty Loren-Maltese, vacated the post to serve an 8-year prison term for bilking the town out of $12 million. Gonzalez moved with his family from Jalisco, Mexico, when he was 6 years old. He served on the Chamber of Commerce board and helped represent the U.S. Hispanic Chamber of Commerce at the local chamber.

Sosa, Sammy (1968–). In 1992 baseball player Sammy Sosa joined the Chicago Cubs, where he became an All-Star. In 1998 Sosa and Mark McGwire surpassed Roger Maris's record of 61 home runs. In that same year Sosa became known as Slammin' Sammy and won the Most Valuable Player Award. The next year, Sosa hit over 60 home runs in two seasons.

Lopez, Edwardo (1984–2006). Lance Corporal Edwardo Lopez was born in Aurora, Illinois, and graduated from high school in 2003. He enlisted in the Marines in 2004, and he was stationed and trained in Hawaii. Within four months, Lopez was deployed to Afghanistan for nine months. Lopez was a trained sniper for the U.S. Marines. Upon his return, Private Lopez was promoted to lance corporal. Shortly thereafter, Lopez was able to spend four months with his family in Aurora, Illinois. Lopez was recognized for being one of the best in his field. He was deployed to Iraq on September 8, 2006, and he was killed on October 19, 2006, in the Al Anbar Province of Iraq. Lopez was the recipient of a Purple Heart medal.

CULTURAL CONTRIBUTIONS

The cultural contributions of Latinas and Latinos in Illinois have had a tremendous impact on the lives of Illinoisans. The diversity and the complexity of Latino culture and traditions are not only rich in history but also intertwined in the fabric of daily life in Illinois.

In 1987 the Mexican Fine Art Center Museum opened its doors, receiving national acclaim for its art display and cultural celebrations. From Chicago to less populous rural towns, Mexicans and Mexican Americans celebrate Cinco De Mayo, 16 de Septiembre, Fiestas Patrias, and Día de Los Muertos. Hispanic Heritage Month celebrations in elementary and high schools are moving beyond tacos and other cultural foods to actually learning about Latino people.

The Segundo Ruiz Belvis Cultural Center was founded in the early 1970s to showcase the artistic work of Chicago's Puerto Rican community. The Puerto Rican community hosted its first Puerto Rican parade in Chicago on June 12, 1966. Many communities in Illinois celebrate Puerto Rican heritage with parades followed by music, food, and vendors selling Puerto Rico's flag and other artifacts.

Our Lady Charity is the patroness of the island of Cuba. In Chicago, Cubans celebrate the feat of Our lady Charity with masses on September 8. This day is so special that a Cuban priest is flown in from Miami or New York to be the main celebrant.

Guatemalan-based organizations and churches in different U.S. cities have played a critical role in the survival of Central Americans trying to escape torture in their mother countries. In the 1980s, the U.S.-based Sanctuary Movement offered critical protection to Central American refugees. A Sanctuary alliance of Chicago-based churches and synagogues provided aid and shelter to Guatemalans and Salvadorans facing deportation. In 1982, Chicago's Wellington Avenue United Church of Christ was the second church in the country to be declared a sanctuary.

Colombians celebrate Colombian Independence Day on July 20. Since 1974, Colombianos Unidos Por Una Labor Activa (CUPULA) has been celebrating this event. A group of medical students from Colombia started this tradition and it is now the largest annual Colombian celebration in the Midwest.

The Ecuadorian community holds organized events such as Ecuadorian Week, which involves cultural exhibits, a picnic, and a parade. Throughout the year, charity balls, beauty queen competitions, and fundraisers are held.

In the entertainment world, Illinois is the birthplace of Jo Raquel Tejada, better known as Raquel Welch. Welch is recognized as one of the most beautiful women of the 1960s and 1970s. Illinois is also home to Antonio Mora, the first Latino (Cuban) to serve as a main anchor at WBBM-TV in Chicago.

In the sports arena, Sammy Sosa, who some have described as one of the best baseball player ever, joined the Chicago White Sox in 1989, being traded to the Chicago Cubs in 1992. Sosa went on to become an All-Star, and in 1998 he won the Most Valuable Player of the Year Award. In 1999 Sosa became the first player ever to hit more than 60 home runs in two seasons.

NOTES

1. U.S. Census Bureau, 2000.
2. National Association of Latino Elected and Appointed Officials (NALEO) Educational Fund, 2006.
3. http://www.nd.edu/~latino/research/documents.
4. *Latino Research @ ND*, Vol. 1, May 2003, http://www.nd.edu/~latino/ils_publications.htm.
5. Vock, 2004.
6. The State of Latino Chicago, http://www.nd.edu/~latino/research/documents/StateofLatinofinal.pdf.

7. *Latino Research @ ND*, http://www.nd.edu/~latino/research.
8. http://www.illinois.gov/facts/history.cfm.
9. Illinois State Military Museum, http://www.il.ngb.army.mil/Museum/Illinois/ILMexicanWar.htm.
10. http://dig.lib.niu.edu/mexicanwar/overview.html.
11. http://dig.lib.niu.edu/mexicanwar/illinoisrole.html.
12. http://www.answers.com/topic/illinois.
13. http://www.spanamwar.com/1stillinois.html.
14. http://www.il.ngb.army.mil/museum/Historical Events/SpanishWar.htm.
15. http://www.spanamwar.com/1stillinois.html.
16. Acuña, 1998; Valdés, 1991; Saenz and Cready, 1997.
17. Valdés, 1991.
18. Saenz and Cready, 1997.
19. Arredondo, 2004; Hijar, 2006.
20. http://www.neta.com.
21. http://factfinder.census.gov.
22. National Center for Education Statistics, http://nces.ed.gov/pubs2005.
23. Jenkins and Kirsch, 2004.
24. Educational Attainment Census Brief of 2000.
25. http://www.ilache.com.
26. http://ilache.com/ibhefacultydiveristy.pdf.
27. http://www.heartlandalliance.org/Povertyreport2006lr.pdf.
28. http://www.dailysouthtown.com/news.
29. http://www.nwherald.com/articles/2006/11/17/news.
30. http://www.pbs.org.
31. http://www.wcvi.org/latino_voter_research/latino_voter_statistics.
32. Garcia, 1976; Bureau of the Census, 1900; Thirteenth Census, 1910; Fourteenth Census, 1920.
33. Valdés, 2000.
34. Kerr, 1976.
35. Clark, 1908; De Genova and Ramos-Zayas, 2003.
36. http://www.spartacus.schoolnet.co.uk/FWWusa.
37. Kerr, 1976.
38. Arredondo, 2004.
39. Rosales, 1998.
40. Saenz and Cready, 1997.
41. Acuña, 1988.
42. Jones, 1928.
43. Rosales, 1976.
44. Kerr, 1976.
45. De Leon and Griswold del Castillo, 1997.
46. Kerr, 1976.
47. Romo, 1975.
48. *New York Times*, 1931.
49. http://www.wtvs.org/archieve/our families/repatriation.

50. http://www.census.gov/prod/2001.
51. http://www.encyclopedia.chicagohistory.
52. Maldonado, 1979.
53. Maldonado, 1979.
54. http://www.encyclopeida.chicagohistory.org.
55. Badillo, 39.
56. De Wagenheim and Wagenheim, 1994.
57. Rodriguez, 2000.
58. http://www.Aspiral.about1.html. Aspira in Illinois.
59. Rúa, 2004.
60. http://www.encyclopedia.chicagohistory.org.
61. http://www.lib.niu.edu.
62. Kanellos, 1994.
63. http://www.encyclopedia.chicagohistory.org/pages/356.
64. http://www.encyclopedia.chicagohistory.org/pages/356.
65. http://www.encyclopedia.chicagohistory.org.
66. Latino Institute Data, 1995, http://www.encyclopedia.chicagohistory.org.
67. http://www.encyclopedia.chicagohistory.org.
68. http://www.encyclopedia. chicagohistory.org.
69. http://www.encyclopedia.chicagohistory.org/pages/1112.
70. Our Lady of Lourdes Parish, http://www.ourladyoflourdes.ca/parish_life/cultural_hispanic.htm.
71. http://www.encyclopedia.chicagohistory.org/pages/1112.
72. Kemp, 2002.
73. http://www.encyclopedia.chicagohistory.org/pages/556.
74. http://www.encyclopedia.chicagohistory.org/pages/313.
75. http://www.laraza.com.
76. http://www.encyclopedia.chicagohistory.org
77. http://www.encyclopedia.chicagohistory.org.
78. http://www.encycolpedia.chicagohistory.org.
79. http://www.lucyparsonsproject.org.
80. National Baseball Hall of Fame and Museum Inc., 25 Main Street, Cooperstown, New York.
81. Kerr, 1976.
82. Kanellos, 1994.
83. http://www.hislea.org/htm/hector/jordanbiography.htm.
84. Kanellos, 1994.
85. Kanellos, 1994.
86. Kanellos, 1994; Chicago Tribune, January and August 1984; Karst and Jones, 1973.
87. http://www.premium.caribe.net; www.prcc-chgo.org.
88. http://www.citizensmedal.com/JuanAndrade.htm.
89. http://www.ushli.org.
90. Kanellos, 1994.
91. http://www.lawyers.com.

92. Latinos in Hollywood, http://www.calstatela.edu/faculty/abloom/giselle.
93. http://www.ilcf.com.
94. State of Illinois, November 30, 2006.
95. Taller de Estudios Comunitarios, 1991; Sawyers, 1991.
96. http://www.uic.edu/~olm/martinez; www.oscarmartinez.com/aboutartist.htm.
97. http://www.uic.edu/~olm/martinez.
98. Kanellos, 1994; Chicago Tribune, November 5, 1992, 12; http://www.luisgutierrezhouse.gov.
99. http://www.luisgutierrezhouse.gov.
100. http://www.ilcf.com.
101. Governor's Office News Page, July 15, 2003.
102. http://abc7chicago.com.
103. Governor's Office News Page, July 15, 2003.
104. Springfield, press release, April 19, 2004.

BIBLIOGRAPHY

Abalos, David T. *Latinos in the United States: The Sacred and the Political.* South Bend, IN: University of Notre Dame, 1986.

Acuña, Rodolfo. *Occupied America: A History of Chicanos.* New York: Harper & Row, 1988.

Anrig Jr., Greg, and Tova Andrea Wang, eds. *Immigration's New Frontiers: Experiences from the Emerging Gateway States.* New York: Century Foundation, 2006.

Arredondo, Gabriela F. "Navigating Ethno-Racial Currents: Mexicans in Chicago, 1919–1939." *Journal of Urban History* 30 (2004): 399–427.

Badillo, D.A., ed. (2005) "Mexican Immigrants in Illinois History: Across Generations and Borders." *Journal of the Illinois State Historical Society* 98 no. 3, special issue (2005).

Cárdenas, Gilberto, ed. *La Causa: Civil Rights, Social Justice and the Struggle for Equality on Midwest.* Houston, TX: Arte Público Press, 2004.

Clark, Victor S. "Mexican Labor in the United States." *Bulletin of the U.S. Bureau of Labor* 78 (September 1908): 466–522.

De Genova, Nicolas. *Working the Boundaries: Race, Space, and "Illegality" in Mexican Chicago.* Durham, NC: Duke University Press, 2006.

De Genova, Nicolas, and Ana Y. Ramos-Zayas, eds. *Latino Crossings: Mexicans, Puerto Ricans, and the Politics of Race and Citizenship.* New York: Routledge, 2003.

De Leon, Arnoldo, and Richard Griswold del Castillo. *North to Aztlan: A History of Mexican Americans in the United States.* 2nd ed. Wheeling, IL: Harlan Davidson, 2006.

De Wagenheim, Olga Jiménez, and Kal Wagenheim, eds. *The Puerto Ricans: A Documentary History.* Princeton, NJ: Markus Wiener Publishing, 1994.

Dolan, Jay P. "Catholics in the Midwest." http://www.nd.edu/~jdolan/midwest.html.

Fernández, Lilia. "Latina/o Migration and Community Formation in Postwar Chicago: Mexicans, Puerto Ricans, Gender, and Politics, 1945–1975." PhD diss., University of California at San Diego, 2005.

Flores-Gonzalez, Nilda. "Paseo Boricua: Claiming a Puerto Rican Space in Chicago." *CENTRO Journal* XIII, no. 3, (Fall 2001): 8–23.

Garcia, Jerry, and Garcia, Gilberto, eds. *Memory, Community, and Activism: Mexican Migration and Labor in the Pacific Northwest.* East Lansing: Michigan State University, Julian Samora Research Institute, 2005.

Garcia, Juan R. "History of Chicanos in Chicago Heights." *Aztlán: A Journal of Chicano Studies* 7, no. 2 (Summer 1976): 141–336.

González-Pando, Miguel. *The Cuban Americans.* Westport, CT: Greenwood Press, 1998.

Hijar, Andres. *Mexican Immigration in Chicago, 1920–1960.* DeKalb: Northern Illinois University, 2006.

Jenkins, Lynn B., and Kirsch, Irwin S. Executive Summary from Adult Literacy in Illinois, Results of the National Adult Literacy Survey. http:///www.nces.edu.gov/NAALpdf/summaries/Illinois.pdf.

Jones, Lottie E. *Decisive Dates in Illinois History: A Story of the State.* Danville. Illinois Printing Company, 1904.

Kanellos, Nicolas. *The Hispanic Almanac: From Columbus to Corporate America.* Detroit, MI: Invisible Ink, 1994.

Karst, Gene, and Martin J. Jones Jr. *Who's Who in Professional Baseball.* New York: Arlington House, 1973.

Kemp, Susie. "20 Years Since Scorched Earth Policy in Guatemala." Justice and Reconciliation Program (DEJURE), Center For Human Rights Legal Action (CALDH). Press Release. March 25, 2002.

Kerr, Louise Año Nuevo. "The Chicano Experience in Chicago, 1920–1970." PhD diss., University of Illinois at Chicago Circle, 1976.

Maldonado, Edwin. "Contract Labor and the Origin of Puerto Rican Communities in the United States." *International Migration Review* 13, no. 1 (Spring 1979): 103–121.

Masud-Piloto, Felix. *From Welcomed Exiles to Illegal Immigrants: Cuban Migration to the U.S. (1959–1995).* Lanham, MD: Rowman & Littlefield, 1996.

Pérez-Firmat, Gustavo. *Life on the Hyphen: The Cuban-American Way.* Austin: University of Texas Press, 1994.

Romo, Ricardo. "Responses to Mexican Immigration, 1910–1930." *Aztlán: A Journal of Chicano Studies* 6, no. 2 (Summer 1975): 172–194.

Rodriguez, Clara E. *Changing Race: Latinos, the Census, and the History of Ethnicity in the United States.* New York: New York University Press, 2000.

Rosales, Francisco A. "The Regional Origins of Mexicano Immigrants to Chicago during the 1920s." *Aztlán: A Journal of Chicano Studies* 7, no. 2 (Summer 1976): 187–201.

Rúa, Mérida M. "Claims to 'The City:' Puerto Rican Latinidad amid Labors of Identity, Community, and Belonging in Chicago." PhD diss., University of Michigan, 2004.

Ruiz, Vicki L. "Nuestra América: Latino History as United States History." *The Journal of American History* 93, no. 3 (December 2006): 655–672.

Saenz, Rogelio, and Cynthia M. Cready. "The Southwest-Midwest Mexican American Migration Flows, 1985–1990." Paper presented at the Rural Sociological Society's 1996 annual meeting, Iowa, February 1997.

Sawyers, June Skinner. *Chicago Portraits: Biographies of 250 Famous Chicagoans.* Chicago, IL: Loyola University Press, 1991.

Sheppard, E. Donald. "DeSoto's Illinois Trails." http://www.floridahistory.com/illinois.html.
Valdés, Dennis N. *Al Norte: Agricultural Workers in the Great Lakes Region, 1917–1970*. Austin: University of Texas Press, 1991.
Valdés, Dionicio N. *Barrios Norteños: St. Paul and Midwestern Communities in the Twentieth Century*. Austin: University of Texas Press, 2000.
Vock, Daniel C. "Latino Power: A Rising Power is Pushing Political Change." *Illinois Issues*, May 2004. http://illinoisissues.uis.edu/features/2004may/latino.html.

15

Indiana

Segundo S. Pantoja

CHRONOLOGY

1890s	Thanks to railways, Mexican migrants start to participate in Indiana and other midwestern states' labor market.
1911	Manuel Lara is the first Mexican to settle in Gary.
1919	The nationwide steel workers strike marks the start of large scale hiring of Mexican-origin laborers in the Calumet region.
1924	Our Lady of Guadalupe Parish is created in Gary.
1925	The first Mexican Catholic parish is established in East Chicago, Indiana.
1932	The massive repatriation of Mexicans reaches its peak. During the Great Depression about half the people of Mexican descent residing in Indiana chose to return, or were deported, to Mexico.
1938	First Mexican American political club is established in East Chicago.
1948	First Puerto Rican contract workers arrive in northwest Indiana.
1957	Joe Maravilla becomes a member of the school board in East Chicago, which is a first step toward getting Latinos elected to public office in Indiana.
1960	Mexican Americans rally behind John F. Kennedy and organize Viva Kennedy! clubs, which is a significant show of allegiance to the Democratic Party in Indiana that lasts until today.
1963	Jesse Gomez is the first Latino elected to the City Council of East Chicago. Thereafter, Latino vote becomes a force to be reckoned with.
1972	The Concerned Latins Organization is founded to address issues of employment, education, housing, and government. It achieves important triumphs in areas of affirmative action and bilingual education.

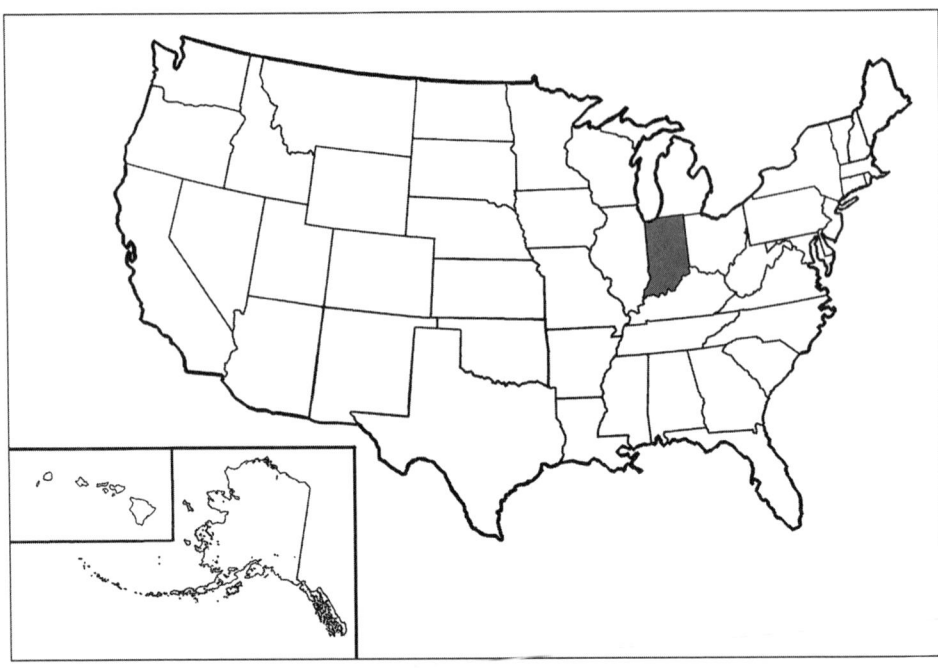

1973	The Chicano-Riqueño Studies program is established at Indiana University in Bloomington.
1999	The Institute for Latino Studies is established at the University of Notre Dame.
2003	The Commission on Hispanic/Latino Affairs is established by the state legislature to identify, measure, and review programs and legislation affecting the Latino community.
2004–2005	Construction and dedication of Our Lady of Guadalupe Church, Warsaw, Indiana. First new Catholic church to be built in the Diocese of Ft. Wayne-South Bend in 25 years.
2005	Mitch Daniels becomes the first governor of Indiana to create an Office of Latino Affairs. George Pabey makes history when he is elected the first Latino mayor of East Chicago.
2006	Mara Candelaria Reardon becomes the first Latina woman representative among the 150-member Indiana General Assembly.
2007	In Mishawaka, St. Joseph County, unprecedented massive raids in factories during March augur a nightmarish year for undocumented workers.

HISTORICAL OVERVIEW

Until recently Indiana had been a state with a solid white majority of over 90 percent. However, a steady shift in the demographic composition of the state has been taking shape since the last decades of the twentieth century. Between low fertility rates and out-migration, the percentages of Euro-Americans (also known as non-Latino whites or Anglos) have been descending, whereas those of Latinos and other groups have been rising. Since 1990 the total state population increased by 14 percent, whereas the Latino population rose by about 200 percent. The number of Latinos in Indiana has mushroomed since 1990, and it stood at 285,000 by 2005.[1] Not only are they numerous, but they are also young: half of all Latinos are under 24 years of age, in contrast to the rest of the state's population, whose median age is 35.[2] The young age of the Latino population calls for attention to key areas of investment, such as education, with a view to the potential contributions of Latinos in the coming years. Latino enrollment in public schools shot up by 119 percent between 1993 and 2002. In less than 10 years the number of Latino children in school increased by 23,143.[3]

Latinos are spreading throughout Indiana's geography, revitalizing with their presence the economies and declining demographics of many counties. Latinos are contributing more than just labor; they make up also a growing share of the consumers. A telling indicator is Latinos' significance to the real estate market. In 1990 only 12 percent of Indiana's Latinos owned homes; in 2000, that figure had climbed to 30 percent.[4] In 2002 Latinos owned 5,482 businesses, principally in construction and retail.[5] For most of their history Latinos remained concentrated within a cluster of towns in Lake County, northwestern Indiana, and a few miles from Chicago; but at least since the 1970s they have been fanning out in all directions, especially to the east and center of the state. By the 1990s, 82 percent of Latinos were found in Lake, Marion, Allen, St. Joseph, Porter, and Elkhart counties, which contain cities such as Gary, Hammond, East Chicago, Indianapolis, Fort Wayne, and South Bend.[6] Comparatively fewer Latinos live in rural areas, which are mostly to the south. Latinos have been attracted by opportunities in meatpacking plants and agriculture. In towns such as Logansport, the hog and chicken industries depend on their labor. Aware of this relationship, some companies—such as Logansport-based Iowa Beef Processing Company—instituted programs (for example, ESL classes) to ease the adaptation of Latinos to the area, provided free transportation, and even promoted home ownership for Latinos.

Latinos have come a long way, especially since World War II. In 1970 Latinos still represented less than 1 percent of the state's population. By 1980 they had increased their share to 1.5 percent of the total. In 1990 their participation inched slightly upwards to 1.8 percent, in a context of stagnant growth in Indiana's population (Indiana's total population went merely from 5,490,224 in 1980 to 5,544,159 in 1990). A significant break with that pattern occurred in the last 15 years, with Latinos constituting 4.5 percent of the state's 6.3 million people in

2005, figures which don't include the unknown but also growing number of unauthorized Latino migrants.[7] Among Latinos, Mexicans' share increased from two-thirds (67.6 percent) to almost three-quarters (71.3 percent) between 1990 and 2000. By contrast, the percentage of Puerto Ricans slipped down from 14.2 to 9.2 percent, as did that of Cubans (from 1.9 to 1.3 percent). The catchall category "Other Latino or Latino" increased during the same period from 16.4 to 18.2 percent. The growth in the latter category reflects the expanded numbers of migrants and the diversity of their origins in all the Americas—especially Central and, to a lesser extent, South America.[8]

THE ALLURE OF JOBS

Before Indiana in particular and the Midwest in general became known as the "rust belt," or a symbol of manufacturers' decline in the 1980s, great industrial complexes thrived in the northwest of the state, part of the Calumet region, near Chicago. This region had experienced dynamic growth since the last quarter of the nineteenth century. Oil, chemical, metal, and steel industries dominated economic activity, and in the 1920s Indiana boasted over 300 automobile companies. Northwest Indiana became a magnet for migrants. Migrants from eastern and southeastern Europe predominated from the late nineteenth century until the first two decades of the twentieth century. After the earlier waves of Germans, Irish, and other northern Europeans, Slovaks, Italians, Greeks, and Poles provided the bulk of the workforce that made possible the industrial expansion. Blacks from the South migrated to the Calumet region also in hopes of employment and better living conditions.

The history of Latinos in Indiana is less than 100 years old. Until World War II, it is for the most part the history of both Mexican migrants and people of Mexican descent born in the United States. (The latter are also known as Mexican Americans or Chicanos). Mexicans came following the railroad tracks which, in addition to transportation, were one of their main sources of jobs. Employment in manufacturing became the lure for the stream of Mexicans that was to grow from a mere trickle in 1911 to a considerable volume by the late 1920s. They concentrated in the industrial towns located along the southern shore of Lake Michigan. It was in cities such as Gary, Hammond, and East Chicago that they first lay down the foundations of the Latino communities.

The arrival of the first Mexicans coincided with the start of the Mexican Revolution (1910–1917). Many of those who migrated at the beginning of the decade were escaping the economic disruption and the violence spawned by the Mexican civil war. In the aftermath of the Mexican Revolution, another armed conflict—the Cristero Rebellion of the late 1920s—raged through parts of Mexico, which also sent a wave of migrants to the United States. Others, born in the United

States, came to Indiana in search of better opportunities after having lived in Texas, Oklahoma, Arkansas, Missouri, or Illinois. In 1919, during the nationwide strike of steel workers for better wages and working conditions, industrial companies such as Inland Steel and the U.S. Steel Corporation started the practice of recruiting Mexican workers for their plants. In an effort to break the strike and defeat the European migrant workers, the companies sent recruiters in search of laborers to the U.S. Southwest and as far as Mexico. By the late 1920s, the Mexican states of Guanajuato, Jalisco, and Michoacán had supplied about three-quarters of all Mexican workers.

The immigration laws approved by the U.S. Congress in 1921 and 1924 severely limited the numbers of workers coming from eastern and southern Europe.[9] Employers turned to Mexicans and blacks to make up the difference in the labor supply. Bringing in single men by the truckload created the phenomenon of the *solos,* or single male migrants. About 60 percent of Mexican workers were *solos.* They lived as lodgers in rooms shared by several men who took turns to sleep in the same bed. People referred to this practice as *camas calientes,* that is, warm beds. Over time, a significant number of these men either went back to Mexico to get married or sent for the families they had left behind. As the 1920s progressed, the percentage of Mexicans living in family units grew, and the population became more stable.

THE UGLY FACE OF RACISM

Mexicans' relationship with other groups was rocky from the start. During the 1919 strike, Mexican and black workers were introduced under the cover of night into the steel plants to take the place of the white workers. Thus was born the stereotype of these people as scabs. White workers' prejudice against Mexican and black laborers found in this experience a solid rationale. In the case of Mexicans, it would have to pass a generation before they were more or less accepted by the labor union movement. Racially speaking, Mexicans were wedged between the entrenched white-black extremes. Light-skinned Mexicans were spared some of the most blatant forms of racism, but the dark skin of the majority relegated them to a position closer to blacks than whites in the racial hierarchy. They felt the practical consequences of discrimination in the form of housing segregation and segregation in public places, such as movie theaters. In Gary, for example, Mexicans congregated in south side neighborhoods or *colonias,* in part because they sought each other's company, and in part because it was practically impossible to rent elsewhere. A Mexican migrant reported in the 1920s that "on the north side they will not rent to Mexicans."[10] The concentration of Mexicans in *colonias* favored the development of businesses that catered to their needs, such as tailor shops, groceries, barber shops, restaurants, and pool halls.

The difficulty for Mexicans to move up the occupational ladder at the workplace kept them stuck in the most dangerous and back-breaking jobs. White supervisors clearly preferred European laborers, allowing them to occupy skilled and managerial positions as they opened. On the streets and even in their neighborhoods Mexicans were harassed by the police. Encounters with Irish and Polish policemen left Mexicans frequently injured and sometimes dead. They received no sympathy from the judges or political authorities. After all, during these times Indiana was a hub of Ku Klux Klan activity around anti-immigrant, anti-Catholic, anti-Jewish and anti-black slogans.

The first phase of Mexican presence in Indiana came to a close with the Great Depression. The economic crisis that started in 1929 led to widespread unemployment and poverty. Even the U.S. Steel Corporation, one of the major employers of Mexicans, was operating at 10 percent of its capacity during 1932 and seldom at much more than 50 percent during the rest of the Depression. Mexicans were in a vulnerable position because few Mexicans at the time were U.S. citizens, and they lacked organization and political power. With a high unemployment rate and thousands seeking public relief during the 1930s, whites, blacks, employers, and politicians saw Mexicans as an undesirable competition for jobs, their children as a drain of public school funds, and the needy as an undeserving burden on government and private charity. Faced with tough circumstances and a hostile environment, unemployed Mexicans and their families thought they would be better in Mexico, especially when the Mexican government invited them back; others were cajoled by local authorities into accepting to return to their country. Whether by train or car, many left during the early 1930s; some paid their own way, whereas local governments and private donations footed the transport bill of the rest. Although the 1930 census had counted 9,007 Mexicans in Lake County, the repatriation campaign drastically reduced that number; Gary and East Chicago alone got rid of 3,600 Mexican residents during 1932. Eventually, Indiana, Michigan, and Illinois contributed 10.5 percent of the 500,000 Mexicans repatriated between 1929 and 1937.[11]

Indiana's economy recovered with World War II, attracting again Mexican and Mexican American workers to the state. Their numbers were added to those who had stayed and weathered the depression years. By the 1940s there was already a growing second generation of Mexican Americans born in Indiana; they were now true Hoosiers, as the natives of Indiana are called. Schools, sports leagues, U.S. music, and the media had helped Americanize the children of those who had migrated early in the century. An increasing number of high school graduates were moving up the occupational ladder, and many were serving their country in the armed forces. Since most of those of Mexican descent were still blue-collar workers, they contributed a large share of the industrial labor force. Others worked in the farms as part of the Bracero program, a United States–Mexico agreement to supply temporary agricultural workers that lasted from 1942 to 1964. With the employment opportunities created by the war and the support for unionization from President Franklin D. Roosevelt, Mexican American workers moved into good-paying industrial jobs protected by strong unions. Eventually, a few Mexican American workers figured prominently in the leadership of the unions too. A report from 1967 says that "Mexican-Americans appear to have made some progress in achieving status in the East Chicago unions, or in at least those locals that have a large Mexican-American membership."[12]

Puerto Ricans and Cubans Join the Mexicans

The United States emerged as a superpower after World War II. A period of rapid economic growth and modernization started at the end of the 1940s that would last until the mid-1970s. Faced with a shortage of workers, Indiana farmers and manufacturers turned to Puerto Rico as a source of laborers. Tapping Puerto Rico for cheap workers had been a well-established practice since 1898, when the United States took over that island. In subsequent decades, U.S. corporations contracted Puerto Ricans to work in such faraway places as Hawaii and Arizona. Thus, labor recruiters, with the help of the Puerto Rican government, set up offices in various towns throughout the island. Starting in 1948, hundreds of Puerto Ricans began to sign contracts that brought them to farms and factories in Indiana. U.S. Steel again played a leading role in importing workers by securing the services of Samuel J. Friedman Farm Labor Agency of Philadelphia, Pennsylvania. This company had been effective in bringing Puerto Rican workers to plants and farms not only in Pennsylvania, but also in New Jersey, Ohio, and other midwestern states. Though many came as farm workers, no sooner had they finished their contracts than they had moved to cities like Gary in search of industrial jobs, which offered higher wages and steadier employment. During the 1950s and 1960s the inflow of Puerto Ricans continued. Eventually, the Puerto Rican nation would lose about one-third of its population during the period 1946–1964 in what became known as the Great Migration. Puerto Ricans returned to their island in a proportion of between 15 and 25 percent, and for various reasons, which included homesickness, the harsh climate, or inability to adapt to night shifts.[13] However, the vast majority, especially those who were married, stayed and established the basis of a community that would expand later with the arrival of their relatives and fellow countrymen. Today, Latinos of Puerto Rican origin furnish a noticeable fraction of the middle class and of professional sectors, serving the community in various capacities and leadership positions; they are visible as business owners, teachers, social workers, deacons, and public officials.

The Cuban Revolution of 1959 generated a new influx of Caribbean migrants. Starting in that year and during the 1960s, the U.S. government welcomed thousands of Cubans as refugees and relocated them to the various states of the nation. The Cubans who came to Indiana were for the most part from middle- and upper-class background. With their superior skills and education, Cubans furnished a significant portion of the Latinos in the managerial, professional, and entrepreneurial sectors. The census of 1970 found that Indiana had 1,158 Cuban residents. They were in third place, after the Puerto Ricans, who numbered 9,269 and who, in turn, trailed the people of Mexican origin, who stood at 30,034 in 1970.[14] In total, Latinos were less than 1 percent of Indiana's population. Nevertheless, the convergence of most of these persons in a few cities and towns provided them the opportunity to learn about and from each other. Sharing common spaces and experiences allowed them to discover the common features in their respective cultural backgrounds as well as their different traditions.

The concentration of Latinos in manufacturing jobs allowed them to improve their living conditions during the period from the 1950s until the 1970s. Remarkably, data from those years reveal that the percentage of Latino households with incomes over $25,000 was the same as that of Anglos, namely 36 percent in 1980. Other indicators of social well-being, such as the percentage of Latinos residing in owner-occupied housing units, also showed progress in those decades. Post–World War II government policies expanded opportunities for home ownership, as did also the Civil Rights legislation of the 1960s. All such initiatives resulted in Latinos owning their homes in a proportion of 37 percent by 1980. Upward social mobility reflected a high degree of assimilation by Latinos. Over time they were becoming more like the rest of the state's population. The 1990 census found that five of every six Latinos (83.9 percent) residing in Indiana were U.S.-born, and about half (49.9 percent) were born in Indiana. It also found a high level of cultural integration. For instance, out of every five Latino married couples, three had one partner who was non-Latino. Latinos also reported that they preferred speaking English or that they spoke English well in a proportion of 80 percent.[15]

Latinos Adapt to a Changing Economy

In the meantime, the economy of Indiana was undergoing substantial change. Jobs in manufacturing were decreasing, whereas those in services were increasing. Indiana saw the number of manufacturing jobs decline by 11 percent between 1970 and 1988. Many Latinos lost good-paying jobs with the restructuring of the economy. By the end of the 1970s unemployment as well as poverty rates among Latinos were on the rise. The percentage of Latino households living with less than $10,000 stood at 32 percent, and around 17 percent of Latino families were receiving public assistance income. The 1990 census found Latino families' median income lower than the median for the rest of the population in Indiana ($34,187 vs. $40,096), but it was still higher than the median family income for Latinos nationwide ($24,156).[16]

The ability of Latinos to adapt to the economic changes and take advantage of the jobs being created by a service-and-knowledge-based economy was being hampered by their relative low levels of education. Adult Latinos had registered considerable, though still slow, gains in high school graduation rates between 1970 and 1980. The proportion of Latinos who completed high school had increased from 39 to almost 50 percent; but only in two cities, Fort Wayne and Indianapolis, did the rate exceed 50 percent. On the other hand, the rates of graduation among young Latinos offered more hope of educational progress for the forthcoming decades. For Latinos in the 18–24 years-of-age group the rate of high school completion was 60 percent. However, they were still lagging significantly behind whites (80 percent) and blacks (65 percent).[17] In the last three decades the number of Latinos attending college shows an upward trend. At Indiana University, in Bloomington, for example, there were 200 Latinos in attendance in 1975, but that number had changed to 800 by 2003.[18]

Religion Brings Latinos Together

Nationalism and religious beliefs have helped Mexicans, Puerto Ricans, and other Latinos forge a sense of community. Some of the first organizations that earlier Mexicans created were mutual aid societies. At a time when there was no government safety net—such as Social Security, Medicaid, pension funds, or labor unions—Mexicans relied on small self-help organizations to solve emergencies stemming from sickness, job loss, or death. But cultural survival was as important as material well-being. During the first decades of the twentieth century, most Mexicans saw their stay in Indiana as temporary. Few became U.S. citizens, and therefore the majority kept a strong allegiance to the Mexican nation. A considerable amount of organizing, energy, and resources went every year into the celebration of the *fiestas patrias* (festivals celebrating key holidays in the migrants' home country), commemorating Independence Day, on September 16, and glorious battles such as Cinco de Mayo, which celebrates the defeat of the French invaders on May 5, 1862.

Rivaling patriotic fervor were religious celebrations that marked the Mexican calendar with massive demonstrations of faith and piety during Holy Week processions, and the celebrations of the Day of Dead and the Feast of Our Lady of Guadalupe. Though on a smaller scale, *quinceañeras* (coming-of-age celebration for a girl on her fifteenth birthday), christenings, and weddings also provided opportunities for people to get together, celebrate, and renew their traditions and ties with one another. The Catholic churches provided a sense of coherence to the *colonias* from the beginning. In the Indiana Harbor section of East Chicago, for instance, Mexicans had their own Our Lady of Guadalupe parish since 1925. Throughout the ensuing decades, and especially during trying times such as the Great Depression, Mexicans found solace and support in their churches. Parish members were organized by gender and age for an array of devotional, civic, and recreational purposes. They formed Los Obreros, Madres Católicas, Las Guadalupanas, Legión de María, Junior and Senior Catholic Youth Organizations, and Our Lady of Victory Sodality, among other bodies, which instilled a sense of community among practicing Catholics. Mexicans in East Chicago had their first Catholic school founded in 1947.

When new national groups, such as the Puerto Ricans and Cubans, became part of the Latino community in Indiana, they also brought with them civic and religious holidays to celebrate. The Catholic background common to the majority of Latinos allowed them to share in each other's celebrations, so that to the Mexican Our Lady of Guadalupe, the Puerto Ricans added their patron saints, such as Our Lady of Divine Providence, Our Lady of Montserrat, and the Feast of Saint John the Baptist. For their part the Cubans brought later their cult to *Nuestra Señora de la Caridad del Cobre* (Our Lady of Charity).

The Catholic Church was the only institution familiar to Mexicans as they settled in Indiana. Their first experiences with the Church were unpleasant, though. They came from a Latino tradition that had little in common with the U.S. and European versions of Catholicism. Euro-American Catholics were resisting efforts by the clergy to assimilate the newcomers. There were few Spanish speaking priests in the beginning, and Mexicans were expected to contribute monetarily to the Church. Some preferred not to attend mass rather than part with a substantial share of their meager income. In the 1920s, a steel worker related that in Mexico "[we] just went to church and it didn't cost anything if we didn't have money. Here it cost twenty-five cents at the door and twenty cents in the plate."[19] Although most Catholic ethnic groups had their own parishes, Mexicans waited until 1924 to form their first congregation in Gary, when they built the parish of Our Lady of Guadalupe, under the auspices of Bishop Alerding.

Today as in previous decades the Catholic Church enjoys the trust of Latinos like no other U.S. institution. The dioceses of Indianapolis, Fort Wayne, South Bend, and Lafayette have been flooded with migrants. Therefore, the Church faces a grave responsibility with the sprouting of new and larger Latino settlements in the state. The mushrooming Latino population throughout Indiana demands pastoral care and assistance in solving urgent spiritual and material needs, especially services in Spanish, advocacy on immigration matters, and access to Catholic schools. However, the Church has neither moved fast enough to train its personnel, nor has it allocated the economic resources to adequately meet such needs. There are, for instance, 62 churches in the Diocese of Lafayette; however, parishioners may listen to Spanish mass in 16 of them. Not one Latino priest is found in the diocese, and two deacons are employed to serve Latinos in all 62 parishes. In response to the deficits in resources and human power, some initiatives are being developed by individual dioceses and branches of the Catholic Church. One example of these efforts is the Instituto Cultural del Medio Oeste, a program the Jesuits are implementing in several dioceses that seeks to prepare lay Latinos in leadership skills so that they organize themselves and start addressing their own needs within the Church and in the wider society.

Protestants have made inroads among the Mexican population since the beginning of their arrival in Indiana. At a time when migrants were vulnerable, Protestants approached Mexicans with offers of help in securing lodging and food. During the Great Depression they were instrumental in providing aid to the hungry and unemployed. Protestants also raised funds to defray travel expenses for those returning to Mexico during times of crisis such as the Great Depression. Although proselytism went hand in hand with the succor provided in times of need, few Mexicans seemed to have really abandoned their traditional faith.

Nevertheless, the number of Latino Evangelicals and Pentecostals expanded with the Puerto Rican migration. In contrast to Mexico, Puerto Rico was a place where certain types of Protestantism had been thriving since the beginning of the twentieth century. As Puerto Ricans started to make Indiana their home, they opened new Evangelical and Pentecostal churches, such as La Primera Iglesia Cristiana de Gary in 1956. Soon afterwards, other churches followed in East Chicago, and they have not stopped spreading to all areas of Latino settlement.

There is an ongoing tug-of-war between the Catholic and Protestant denominations. In recent years that competition has been heightened by the inability of the Catholic Church to reach out and serve adequately all the migrants who have come knocking at its doors. Christians of the Protestant varieties popular among Latinos require a short formal training to become pastors and little start-up capital to found a church, which can be established in a rented storefront and with few congregants, family members, and a few other believers. The Catholic Church's perception is that its insufficiency of personnel and resources leaves the flocks open to non-Catholic proselytism. Today's Catholic clerical and lay leaders couch their concerns in the language of competition; they feel that with every day that passes Evangelicals and Pentecostals are stealing from them a bigger share of the religious market.

Crawling Their Way into Politics

Before the 1940s, prejudice and discrimination prompted Mexicans to engage in self-defense and protest. The initial actions were usually formal complaints to local authorities and boycotts of businesses. As Mexican migrants became naturalized citizens and as their U.S.-born children came of age, they started voting in local and national elections. The experiences of participating in World War II helped many Mexican Americans realize that they had to get organized to address issues of equal access to better jobs, adequate housing, and quality education. They linked with Mexican Americans in other regions, especially in the Southwest, and became participants in networks such as the League of United Latin American Citizens (LULAC), which had been founded in 1929, and the Mexican-American Legal Defense and Education Fund (MALDEF), founded in 1968 as a result of the participation of Chicanos in the civil rights movement. A significant result of the mobilization started in the 1960s was the establishment of Chicano-and-Latino-based curricula in institutions of higher education such as Indiana University and the University of Notre Dame.

Latinos in Indiana have historically voted Democrat. They supported enthusiastically John F. Kennedy in 1960. During his campaign "Viva Kennedy Clubs" were organized in many states. The allegiance to the Democratic Party has been unwavering, especially among Mexican Americans who in the 2004 elections favored Kerry three to one over Bush. In fact, the few districts in Indiana carried by Kerry were those of heavy Latino concentration. Nevertheless, Latinos have been slow in reaching political office in Indiana, although some of them are being appointed to high posts. Examples of such appointments are Federico Thon, assistant to the Mayor of South Bend, and Juana Watson, Governor Daniels's senior advisor for Latino and Immigrant Affairs. Furthermore, Latina women are playing leading roles in the state: the executive director of the Ethics Commission in Indiana and the executive director of the Commission on Hispanic/Latino Affairs are Latina.

Among the reasons for the slow progress in electoral politics is that neither Black nor Latino voters make up the majority in any of Indiana's nine districts. As of 1990 only 10 Latinos were occupying elected seats at any level in the state. The city of East Chicago is the exception to the rule in that over half its population is Latino. Here there has been a history of Latinos being elected to local school boards and the City Council dating since at least 1957. More recently, George Pabey made history again in 2005 when he was elected the first Latino mayor of East Chicago. Indiana had one Latino state legislator as the Northwest Gary representative, John Aguilera, but he did not seek reelection in 2006. Instead, his seat was won by Mara Candelaria Reardon, who became the first Latina woman representative among the 150-member Indiana General Assembly. Few other success stories are known outside northwestern Indiana, but there are signs of change on the horizon, such as the 2006 election of the first Latino judge in central Indiana, José Salinas. Other Latinos have run for mayors and congressmen, but so far they have not been elected; Mark Leyva, for instance, has sought unsuccessfully to unseat incumbent Peter Visclosky in Indiana's 1st Congressional District.

There are two major Latino population layers in Indiana. One layer is formed by those whose roots stretch approximately from 1990 back to the beginning of the twentieth century; and the other is made up of the people whose presence stretches from 1990 to the present. This demographic split is significant because two-thirds of Latinos are recent settlers in the state; therefore, most have no age or legal qualifications to elect or be elected to political office. Furthermore, studies have shown that Mexican migrants have one of the lowest U.S. naturalization rates, a basic requirement for participation in electoral politics. People who want to become U.S. citizens have to go through stages. Becoming a legal resident (that is, getting a green card) is a condition which many will not meet. In addition, migrants who are legal residents wait on average 8 years before becoming naturalized citizens, but Mexicans wait 11 years; and when they do it, voting is not first on their list of motivations; the majority seek citizenship to ensure equal treatment, to fight discrimination, or to establish eligibility for government programs. Among Mexicans, their strong nationalism and expectations of return to Mexico constitute serious obstacles to naturalization and political participation.

Another obstacle to political involvement is the young age of U.S.-born Latinos. About 40 percent are less than 18 years old, the minimum age to vote. It is an established fact that citizens over 55 vote in higher proportion to younger groups. Because Latinos are concentrated in the age groups under 55, it is only natural that their participation in elections be low for now. The prospects for increased participation in a few years look brighter given the number of Latino children who are born and being schooled in Indiana. Organizations like the Indiana State Hispanic Chamber of Commerce and the Hispanic Leadership Coalition are targeting high school seniors and college students in their voter registration campaigns.

There are other indicators that political participation might be broadened in the coming years. In a way, grassroots organizations are laying the groundwork. Latino activists are meeting more frequently with public officials and organizing community dialogues to discuss issues that affect the Latino community and all residents. In addition to the traditional areas of Latino presence in northwest Indiana, committed community leaders are emerging in cities such as Indianapolis, Lafayette, Evansville, Angola, Ligonier, and Warsaw. Charles Garcia, for instance, is a recognized Latino business leader who was recently elected chair of the Greater Indianapolis Chamber of Commerce; he is also the first Latino to sit on the Federal Reserve Board representing Indiana. The business community has indicated that, as part of their agenda for the current decade, there is a plan to develop and elect Latino government officials.

Some of the most recent issues stirring Latinos to action include the need to address anti-immigrant legislation put forward by several legislators. Anglos and Latinos have rallied together, and a coalition was formed to distribute information and organize events. Also, a statewide Indiana Latino/Hispanic Association was created to monitor legislative measures that may adversely affect Latinos. Other groups form around specific interests, an example of this being the committee of Latino mental health professionals who want to ensure that culturally competent care be provided to people of color in the state. In the area of education, community leaders and universities are doing research and proposing policy initiatives to adequately integrate newcomers into the school system by sensitizing teachers and other school personnel to the language and sociocultural characteristics as well as the specific needs of Latino children.

NOTABLE LATINOS

Samora, Julian (1920–1996). As Notre Dame professor in the Department of Sociology from 1959 to 1985, Samora trained several generations of Latino researchers who went on to play leading roles in academia. The Julian Samora Research Institute at Michigan State University bears testimony to his contributions. Samora was cofounder of leading Latino organizations at the national level, such as La Raza and the Mexican American Legal Defense and Educational Fund. He also helped found the Southwest Voter Registration and Education Project. As a prominent scholar and activist, Samora also served on numerous governmental and private boards and commissions, including the U.S. Commission on Civil Rights, the National Institute of Mental Health, and the President's Commission on Rural Poverty.

Villa Parra, Olga (1944–). The daughter of farmworkers and a longtime local volunteer for various causes, Villa Parra began her activist career supporting Cesar Chavez's grape boycott in the 1960s. After working many years for the Lilly Endowment, a position from which she helped fund many Latino initiatives, Villa Parra continues her support and consulting for nonprofit and philanthropic organizations. Probably the most visible and respected Latina in Indiana, she keeps actively promoting Latino events, such as Cinco de Mayo festivities, that celebrate Latin culture.

Kanellos, Nicolás (1945–). Founder of Arte Público Press, the largest publisher of Latino literature in the United States. He is also the founder of *The Americas Review*, formerly *Revista Chicano-Riqueña*. Kanellos taught Latino Literature at Indiana University Northwest from 1973 until 1979. Among many awards, Kanellos has won the Latino Heritage Award for Literature in 1988; the American Library Association's Award for Best Reference Works of 1993, and the 1989 American Book Award for Publishing.

Garcia, Charles J. (1950–). Garcia's greatest contributions are his efforts to mentor aspiring entrepreneurs. His mentoring program has been adopted by the Greater Indianapolis Chamber of Commerce to assist minority- and women-owned businesses to grow at rates of 20 to 60 percent. Founder of the Indiana Hispanic Scholarship Foundation, Garcia has helped increase educational opportunities for first-generation college students. Garcia has received many awards, including the Small Business Association's (SBA) 1994 Regional Construction Company of the Year Award, the 1994 Ernst and Young Entrepreneur of the Year Award, the 2000 SBA Small Businessman of the Year

Award, the 1996–1999 Grow 100 Award Indiana, and the 2004 Center for Leadership Development Entrepreneur of the Year Award.

Cárdenas, Gilberto (1952–). Former graduate student of Notre Dame, Cárdenas returned to found and direct the Institute for Latino Studies (ILS) at that institution. In his work Cárdenas has demonstrated a commitment to Latino migrant workers. During his tenure as the head of the ILS, there has been a prolific production of knowledge on Latinos in the Midwest, which has had public policy repercussions. Cárdenas's contributions have earned him the honor of being named repeatedly among the 100 most influential Latinos in the country by the Latino Business Magazine.

Chapa, Jorge (1953–). Professor and founding director of Latino Studies at Indiana University in Bloomington from 1999 to 2006. He has scores of publications reflecting his research focus on the low rates of Latino educational, occupational, and economic mobility, and on the development of policies to improve these trends. He is currently director of the Center on Democracy in a Multiracial Society at the University of Illinois at Urbana-Champaign.

Watson, Juana (1955–). Indiana State's first senior advisor for Latino Affairs. She is the founder of two Latino community centers and a not-for-profit organization called Badges Without Borders. She has participated in organizations throughout the state helping develop programs regarding Latino cultural awareness.

Puente, Sylvia (1958–). Director of the Metropolitan Chicago Initiative for the University of Notre Dame's Institute for Latino Studies (ILS). In 2003, Puente was one of 25 Chicago area women named a Pioneer for Social Justice. Puente was introduced to a life of activism by her mother at the age of 13, when she joined her first picket line in support of the United Farm Workers. In 2005, Puente was listed among the nation's 100 most influential Latinos.

Thon, Richard William "Dickie" (1958–). Born in South Bend of Puerto Rican parents, "Dickie" Thon became an outstanding shortstop in Major League Baseball. His professional career started with the California Angels in 1975, reached its peak with the Houston Astros (1981–1987), and ended in 1993 with the Milwaukee Brewers. "Dickie" Thon was inducted to the Hispanic Heritage Baseball Museum's Hall of Fame in 2003.

CULTURAL CONTRIBUTIONS

Latinos moving into the state were quick to establish a rich community life in such cities as Gary and East Chicago. The maintenance of a Latino culture came to depend on several communication media such as newspapers and radio, as well as on leisure-time activities, sports, festivals, and dances. Dramatic performances were one of the visible art forms carried out in the community. At least five theater groups were active during the 1920s. They were associated to the two central institutions at the time: the Catholic Church and the Mutual Aid Society. The existence of the theater groups followed the ups and downs of the community, and thus they disappeared by the mid-1930s. A recovery of theatrical activity

"The Mexican Spirit Lives On." From author's personal collection. Courtesy of Julio Pantoja.

followed World War II, so that performances of Christmas plays and plays on the Guadalupe theme made a comeback in the 1950s and 1960s. By the early 1960s new groups had been formed, such as El Teatro Experimental Talia and El Club Artístico Guadalupano. With the advent of the civil rights movement, students and community activists used theater as a political tool to educate and discuss key issues affecting Latinos. El Teatro Desengaño del Pueblo is the best exponent of this type. Indiana audiences also enjoyed performances by groups such as El Teatro del Barrio, a Chicano group from South Chicago, and El Teatro de Artes Chicanos from San Antonio.

A new phase in the history of Indiana has started in the early 1990s. Their skyrocketing growth, owing mostly to migration from Mexico, has been impacting greatly the old and new areas of settlement. With their presence and bustling activity, Latinos have been transforming some institutions; both in their makeup as well as in the ways they function. In many districts Latino children are already half the school population. They are also changing the face of the Catholic Church, and Spanish-speaking priests are in short supply; three of every four baptized children are Latino, and classes for *quinceañera* celebrations are overbooked.

The growing numbers of Latinos and their concentration in cities such as Indianapolis, the state capital, have created markets for Spanish media—for example, *La Onda Latino Americana* newspaper, several radio stations, and Univision's WIIH TV station. In Indianapolis alone, where Latino residents are estimated to number 100,000, there are miles of commercial strips that cater to Latino customers including 100 Mexican restaurants, and several nightclubs advertising salsa dance nights.

Latinos participate in mainstream events such as the Indiana State Fair, and they also organize their own, such as Fiesta Indianapolis, the premier local Latino cultural event. These activities are in addition to the annual Puerto Rican Parade, Cinco de Mayo—which has become not just a Mexican, but also a Pan-Latino celebration—and other traditions such as the Day of the Dead, with its vigils, processions, parties, music, and food.

In other realms, Latinos hold also the potential to influence the host society with their values. Most of them come from rural areas imbued with traditions that rely on family cohesiveness and group solidarity. Strong work ethic and solid family principles remind many Hoosiers of their own cherished, but fading, conservative standards.

Latinos working within institutions of higher learning in Indiana are making intellectual contributions, particularly those in academic departments and research centers whose focus is the Latino experience. A case in point is the Institute for Latino Studies at the University of Notre Dame. The institute conducts demographic, economic, and political analyses. Its areas of study include also Latino art, spirituality, and literature. Their latest project, for instance, locates and surveys Latino art collections, museums, galleries, and cultural centers to produce a chronological survey of the history of Latino art in the Midwest.

NOTES

1. Indiana Commission on Latino/Latino Affairs, "2006 Demographic Overview of Latinos/Latinos in Indiana," http://www.in.gov/ichla/pdf/2006_Indiana_Latino-Latino_Overview.pdf.

2. http://quickfacts.census.gov/qfd/states/18000.html, accessed January 28, 2007.

3. Fry, "The Changing Landscape," Pew Latino Center, October 2006, 36, http://pewLatino.org/files/reports/72.pdf.

4. *Indianapolis Star,* "Real Estate Agents Court Latinos," February 20, 2005, http://www.mdrealtor.org/Tool_Kit/03_2_05.html, accessed November 22, 2006.

5. "Latino-owned Firms, 2002," http://www.census.gov/prod/ec02/sb0200chisp.pdf, 20, accessed February 28, 2007.

6. Aponte, "Latinos in Indiana," Statistical Brief No. 11, Julian Samora Research Institute, Michigan State University, July 1999, 22.

7. http://quickfacts.census.gov/qfd/states/18000.html, accessed January 11, 2007.

8. U.S. Census Bureau, Census 2000 Summary File 1, Matrix PCT11, http://factfinder.census.gov, accessed January 18, 2007.

9. The Emergency Quota Act of 1921 and the Immigration Act of 1924 cut the quotas for foreigners from 3 percent of persons of each nationality living in the United States to 2 percent, using as base the census of 1890. David Kennedy et al., *The Brief American Pageant*, 6th ed. (Boston, MA: Houghton Mifflin, 2004), 445.

10. Mohl, 1987, 94.

11. Mohl, 1987, 104.

12. Samora and Lamanna, 1987, 229.

13. Maldonado, 1987, 203–204.

14. Aponte, "Latinos in Indiana," Statistical Brief No. 11, Julian Samora Research Institute, Michigan State University, July 1999, 3.

15. Heartland Center. "On Many Edges," Winter 1996, ii.

16. Heartland Center. "On Many Edges," Winter 1996, iii–iv.

17. All figures in this paragraph taken from Anne M. Santiago, "Life in the Industrial Heartland: A profile of Latinos in the Midwest," Research Report No. 2, Julian Samora Research Institute, May 1990, 10–18, http://www.jsri.msu.edu/RandS?research/irr/rr02.html, accessed January 12, 2007.

18. De la Rosa, "Latinos at Indiana," *Latino Alumni Newsletter,* 4, http://alumni.indiana.edu/conpubs/archives/latino-spr03.pdf, accessed January 28, 2007.

19. Mohl, 1987, 96.

BIBLIOGRAPHY

Aponte, Robert. "Latinos in Indiana: On the Throes of Growth." Statistical Brief No. 11. Michigan State University, Julian Samora Research Institute, July 1999.

Badillo, David A. "The Catholic Church and the Making of Mexican-American Parish Communities in the Midwest." In *Mexican Americans and the Catholic Church, 1900–1965*. Eds. Jay P. Dolan and Gilberto M. Hinojosa. Notre Dame, IN: University of Notre Dame Press, 1994, 237–357.

De la Rosa, Belinda. "Latinos at Indiana: A Closer Look at the Numbers." *Latino Alumni Newsletter,* 4. http://alumni.indiana.edu/conpubs/archives/latino-spr03.pdf.

Fry, Richard. "The Changing Landscape of American Public Education: New Students, New Schools." Pew Latino Center, October 2006. http://pewLatino.org/files/reports/72.pdf.

Heartland Center. "On Many Edges—The Latino Population of Indiana." Heartland Center Reports. Hammond, Indiana, Winter 1996.

Indiana Commission on Latino/Latino Affairs. "2006 Demographic Overview of Latinos/Latinos in Indiana." http://www.in.gov/ichla/pdf/2006_Indiana_Latino-Latino_Overview.pdf.

Indiana Project for Latin American Competency Project. "Diversity Within: Latino Newcomers in Our Schools and Communities." Education Brief No. 1. School of Education, Indiana University, Bloomington, January 2007. http://www.indiana.edu/~iplacc/.

Indiana State History. http://www.infoplease.com/ce6/us/A0858787.html.

Kennedy, David, Lizabeth Cohen, and Mel Piehl. *The Brief American Pageant.* 6th ed. Boston, MA: Houghton Mifflin, 2004.

Lane, James B., and Edward J. Escobar, eds. *Forging a Community—The Latino Experience in Northwest Indiana, 1919–1975.* Chicago, IL: Calumet Regional Archives and Cattails Press, 1987.

Maldonado, Edwin. "Contract Labor." In *Forging a Community: The Latino Experience in Northwest Indiana, 1919–1975.* Eds. James B. Lane and Edward J. Escobar. Chicago: Calumet Regional Archives and Cattails Press, 1987, 203–204.

Millard, Ann V., and Jorge Chapa. *Apple Pie & Enchiladas: Latino Newcomers in the Rural Midwest.* Austin: University of Texas Press, 2004.

Mohl, Raymond A. *Steel City.* New York: Holmes & Meier Publishers Inc., 1987.

National Association of Latino Elected and Appointed Officials. http://www.naleo.org/downloads/3_NALEORacestowatch_fin_10-06.pdf.

Samora, Julian, and Richard A. Lamanna. "Mexican Americans in a Midwest Metropolis: A Study of East Chicago." In *Forging a Community: The Latino Experience in Northwest Indiana, 1919–1975.* Eds. James B. Lane and Edward J. Escobar. Chicago: Calumet Regional Archives and Cattails Press, 1987, 215–250.

Santiago, Anne M. "Life in the Industrial Heartland: A Profile of Latinos in the Midwest." Research Report No. 2. Julian Samora Research Institute, May 1990, 10–18. http://www.jsri.msu.edu/RandS?research/irr/rr02.html.

Taylor, D. Garth, María de los Angeles Torres, and Rob Paral. "The Naturalization Trail: Mexican Nationality and U.S. Citizenship." *Latino Research @ ND* 3, no. 2 (June 2006).

United States Latino Leadership Institute. http://ushli.org/pdf/2004%20presidential%20election2.pdf.

16

Iowa

Jerry Garcia

CHRONOLOGY

Pre-Contact	Approximately 17 different indigenous groups, including the Ioways, Sauks, Meskwakis, Santee Sioux, Winnebagos, Potawatomis, Missouris, and Otos inhabit the region of Iowa.
1542	Arrival of first Europeans. Spanish explorer Hernando de Soto explores the Mississippi reaching as far north as present day Iowa.
1673	First French explorers arrive in Iowa.
1762	Beginning of Spanish control over a region that includes Iowa.
1780s	Manuel Lisa, Spanish subject, marries a Sioux Indian and resides in what becomes Iowa. Lisa is possibly the first permanent Latino resident in the region.
1801	Spain relinquishes control of the region that includes Iowa to the French.
1803	The United States pays $11.2 million for the Louisiana Purchase from the French.
1803–1833	The United States removes most of the indigenous tribes from Iowa.
1833	First major groups of U.S. white settlers arrive in Iowa.
1846	Iowa becomes the 29th state.
1850	Census records 17 Latinos residing in Iowa.
1890	First Latino *colonia* (colony) is established at Fort Madison.
1920	U.S. census records 2,560 Latinos officially residing in Iowa, most arriving because of heavy recruitment of Mexican labor for sugar beet and railroad industries. Most believe there are hundreds of other Latinos not counted by the census.

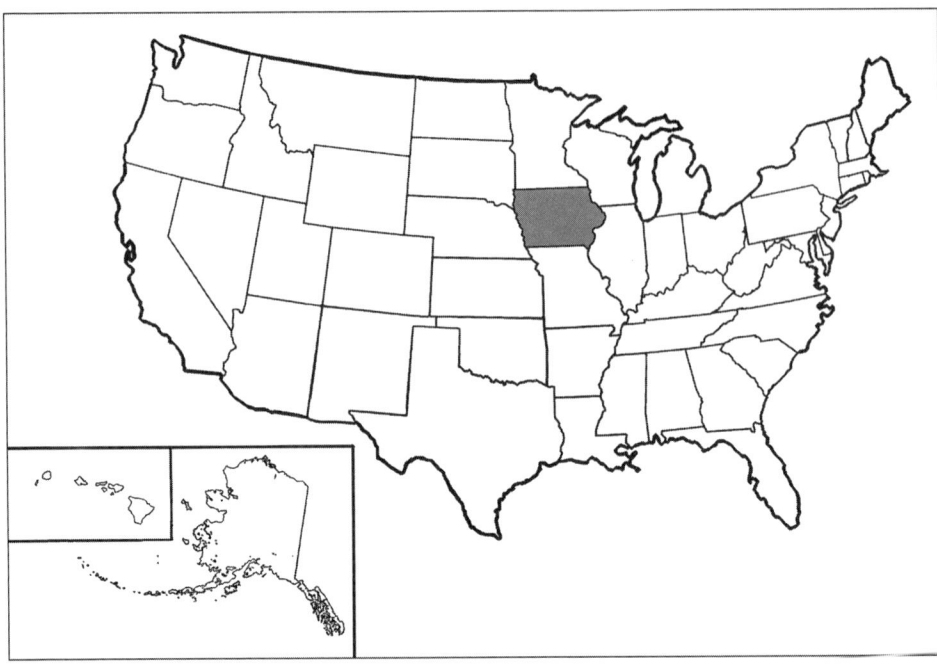

1930s	Great Depression; unconstitutional deportations of Mexicans take place nationwide. Many Iowa Latinos are forced to leave.
1938	Artist Lowell Houser completes "Evolution of Corn," which depicts Mayan Indians and the Mayan corn god on a mural in an Ames, Iowa, post office.
1940s	World War II and U.S. mobilization for the war. Nationally, 500,000 Latinos serve in the armed forces. Thirteen Latinos are awarded the Medal of Honor. Iowa Latinos/as serve the nation. Over 6,000 Mexican nationals (braceros) and Tejanos (Mexican Texans) are recruited to work in Iowa.
1950s	Operation Wetback rounds up 1.2 million Mexicans and has them deported (1953–1954). Fort Madison, Iowa LULAC Council #304, established in 1957, becomes the first in Iowa.
1960s–1970s	Iowa Latino population grows to approximately 30,000. Mexican American civil rights movement mobilizes Latinos in Iowa.
1980s	Iowa farm crisis: meatpacking industry expands and begins heavy recruitment of Latino labor, which increases the number of Latinos in Iowa.
1990s	Iowa experiences a large influx of Latinos.
2000	The release of the U.S. census reveals a 153 percent increase in the Latino population in Iowa since 1990.
2002	On October 14 the bodies of eleven Latinos are found in a train hopper car in Denison. These Mexican and Central American individuals were seeking work in the United States.
2007	Approximately 115,000 Latinos reside in Iowa.

HISTORICAL OVERVIEW

Ames, Iowa, home to Iowa State University, a land-grant institution, is an unlikely place to begin the history of Latinos in Iowa. Perhaps this could be said about Iowa in general. Nonetheless, Ames is the home to two remarkable representations of Latino history that illustrate the migration of Latino culture and people to the state of Iowa. The first, located in the main post office in Ames, is a 18' × 6' oil on canvas mural titled "Evolution of Corn," by Lowell Houser, a student of Grant Wood's who painted the mural in the 1930s. Maize (corn) originated in Mexico 9,000 years ago, became a main staple for almost all indigenous groups, and had profound religious significance. It did not reach the region of Iowa until late in the first millennium C.E. The mural by Houser prominently depicts a Mayan Indian harvesting corn; and in the foreground is the Mayan corn god holding the hieroglyph for corn in its hand. Although it was not his intent, Houser—in depicting the migration, legacy, and importance of corn to Iowa—may have been the first to illustrate the history of Latinos in that state with his representation of Mayan history and their contributions to the development of agriculture, while simultaneously depicting the indigenous roots of Latinos. What is not well known is that some of the descendants of the Mayans, the Mexicans, made a similar migration north, albeit thousands of years later.[1]

The second representation is located in the heart of the Iowa State University (ISU) campus. Just off the central mall area is a totem-like fiberglass and urethane statue standing approximately ten feet. This statue depicts a Latino man carrying his wife on his shoulders, and carefully bundled within the wife's *rebozo* (shawl) is an infant. At the base of the image is an inscription that partially reads *Border Crossing: Cruzando el Río Bravo* (*Border Crossing: Crossing the Río Bravo;* the Mexican name for the Rio Grande is actually Río Bravo del Norte). Originally, Luis Jimenez created this spectacular artwork in 1989 to honor the millions of Latinos who immigrated to the United States, including his father and grandmother, who came undocumented in 1924. Iowa State University invited Jimenez to campus in March 1999 to celebrate the resiliency of his family. What began as a temporary public art installation became a permanent fixture when the university reached an agreement to purchase the sculpture in 2000. The dedication and purchase of this art coincided with the establishment of the Latino Studies Program at Iowa State University and the release of census data indicating that the Latino population in Iowa had grown extensively. The objective of this entry is to illustrate the permanent presence since the mid-nineteenth century of Latinos in Iowa and their contributions to the development of the state.

DEMOGRAPHICS

In the contemporary period Latinos represent the largest minority group in the nation. The origins of Latinos can be traced throughout the world, but the majority is from Mexico, Central America, South America, the Caribbean, and southern Europe. The release of the 2000 U.S. census revealed a Latino population growing substantially and reaching beyond the traditional zone of the American Southwest. Nationally, between 1990 and 2000 the Latino population grew an astonishing 54 percent. Although the Latino diaspora is now more diverse than it was in the past, Latinos of Mexican origin remain the largest group. And during those same years Latinos of Mexican descent recorded the highest population increase among Latinos, at 52.9 percent, or from 13.5 million to 20.6 million. Nonetheless, nationwide other Latino groups experienced a significant increase in their populations, especially those from Central America. The 2006 U.S. census update revealed continued growth with an overall Latino population approaching 45 million. Although Mexicans remain demographically dominant, representing over 64 percent of all Latinos, immigration from El Salvador, Guatemala, Colombia, and Dominican Republic have statistically shown dramatic growth. Puerto Ricans (3,985,058) and Cubans (1,517,028) remain the second- and third-largest Latino groups in the United States. The current state population of Iowa is approximately 2,982,085, and it is 93 percent white (U.S. Census Bureau). Overall, Iowa is ethnically one of the least diverse states in the nation, has one of the slowest growth patterns, and has consistently lost people to other regions for the past three decades. One exception has been the growth of the Latino population.

Brief Background

The region that is now Iowa was quite diverse in the past. Iowa was inhabited by indigenous tribes—including the Ioways, Sauks, Meskwakis, Sioux, Potawatomis, Otos, and Missouris—long before the arrival of Europeans. Some sources indicate that the first Whites to travel in 1673 in what eventually became Iowa were French explorers. A critical mass of white settlers would not arrive until the Federal Government purchased, conquered, or appropriated by treaty land that belonged to the local Indians. Having been previously claimed by the French and the Spanish, Iowa was acquired through the Louisiana Purchase of 1803. Officially, 1833 is considered the year in which the first white settlers arrived in Iowa. And in 1838 the U.S. Congress created the Iowa Territory. By the 1840s the last remaining Indians were removed from their ancestral lands, allowing for the arrival of additional white settlers. Without Indians and with a critical mass of European Americans, the Iowa Territory petitioned for statehood, receiving it in 1846. The state of Iowa became a receiving state for large numbers of European migrants who arrived in the second half of the nineteenth century. This first wave of European migrants was mainly composed of English and German nationals; the second wave, in the early twentieth century, included Swedes, Danes, Dutch, and Italians. The African

American population also began to arrive in Iowa in the late nineteenth and early twentieth centuries, primarily to work in the coal mines.

Early Latino Settlers: Colonial Period to 1800s

There are many historical moments in which Latinos or their descendants explored, occupied, or settled in what is now Iowa. Perhaps the first Latino in the region was the Spanish explorer Hernando de Soto, who was the first European to see and explore the Mississippi in the early sixteenth century. De Soto's exploration of the Mississippi may have taken him north to the outer boundaries of Iowa. Maybe Manuel Lisa, owner-operator of a 1780s fur-trapping business who married a Sioux Indian, was the first Latino resident in what became Iowa. If Lisa did exist, then in 1803 he became one of the first U.S. citizens in Iowa.

During the period in which Spain controlled the region (1762–1801), it issued three land grants. However, the grants went to Spanish subjects of French ancestry. Nineteenth-century Mexican cowboys (vaqueros) also reached the southern and eastern boundaries of Iowa with the cattle drives into Nebraska. The 1850 U.S. census recorded 16 residents from Mexico and one from South America. It has been noted that when the railroad arrived in Muscatine in 1855, Mexicans helped build it, and a handful actually remained as permanent members of the community. In 1856 Iowa conducted a county-by-county census and found the following: one Venezuelan living in Butler County, one Mexican in Clinton County; one South American in Dubuque County, eight South Americans in Iowa City, and one Chilean in Marion County. The Iowa census of 1895 recorded an overall Latino population of 30 individuals; however, it is likely many more resided in the region, but census remunerators may have undercounted the Latino population. In the late 1890s one of the first Latino *colonias* (colonies) emerged in Fort Madison, as a result of the recruitment efforts by the Santa Fe Railroad. Lastly, Iowa made a permanent connection to Mexico by naming two of its counties, Cerro Gordo and Buena Vista, in honor of U.S. victories over the Mexican army during the Mexican-American War of 1846–1848.

The Spanish presence in Iowa is well known and well documented. Yet, the Spanish explorers left no long-term settlements. In their turn, the vaqueros and railroad workers were, by and large, transient until the late nineteenth century. Thus, Latinos in Iowa did not emerge as a significant and permanent population until the early twentieth century. Nevertheless, it is important to recognize and acknowledge the Spanish influence in the region as well as a small Mexican presence in Iowa starting in the mid-nineteenth century. The larger and more permanent movement of Latinos into Iowa began in the first and second decades of the twentieth century.

Latino Migration to Iowa: 1900-1920s

The movement and development of the Latino population in Iowa is primarily a Mexican affair until the late twentieth century. Several factors contributed to the movement of the first Latinos to Iowa. The migration of Mexicans beyond the borderland regions can be traced to the economy of Mexico—which drove down wages—at the beginning of the twentieth century, the displacement caused by the violent phase of the Mexican Revolution (1910-1920), increased demand for labor in the U.S.-Mexican border region, competition for labor along the border region, the development of the sugar beet industries in the northern plains, and the demand for labor in the railroad industry. As these factors coalesced in the early twentieth century, Latinos migrated and were recruited into places like Iowa.

Using a variety of sources such as municipal and church records, oral histories, census data, community studies, and local and regional newspapers, it is possible to determine the arrival of Latinos to Iowa. Historically there has been a trend in census data to undercount the Latino population, which is due to neglect and marginalization of that group. The U.S. census counted 509 first-generation Mexican Americans in Iowa in 1910, 616 Mexicans in 1915, and by 1920 the number has risen to 2,560. Fort Madison, located in southeastern part of Iowa, probably has one of the earliest Latino communities in the state, dating back to at least 1906, possibly even earlier. The *Fort Madison Daily Democrat* reported that on September 16, 1906, Latinos in the community celebrated Mexican Independence Day, and by 1922 fiesta committees were meeting on a regular basis. These types of celebrations indicate an organized and settled Latino population in Fort Madison. This period also coincided with the Santa Fe Railroad's chief recruitment of Mexican labor. Evidence also indicates that Latinos resided in Iowa prior to U.S. involvement in World War I (1917-1918). During this era newspaper articles reported that because of language barrier, some Latinos were unaware they were required to register for the draft, which included resident aliens. Although Latinos could be found working in a variety of sectors in Iowa during the early twentieth century, such as packinghouses and cement factories, two industries employed the largest number of Latino workers—namely, the sugar beet and railroad industries.

As the flow of migrants was disrupted and immigration restrictions were placed on Italians, Greeks, Poles, and Hungarians because of World War I, Latinos began to emerge in increasing numbers in the second decade of the twentieth century. In Iowa, Latinos were located in such places as Des Moines, Mason City, Davenport, Muscatine, Sioux City, Fort Madison, and Bettendorf. As early as 1915 The Bettendorf Company, which made train equipment, began to recruit and hire Latinos. Latinos worked in a variety of industries—such as steel mills, highway and building construction, tanneries, and brick houses. The first Mexican

The Diaz family is an excellent example of the early arrival of Mexicans in Fort Madison, Iowa, ca. 1920s. Courtesy of the Iowa Women's Archives, University of Iowa Libraries, Iowa City.

sugar beet workers in Iowa arrived in 1917, but they were more noticeable in the early 1920s. The American Sugar Beet Company recruited some of the first Mexicans to Mason City. The Iowa Valley Operating Company (formerly known as Iowa Valley Sugar Company) recruited Mexican workers to its Belmond sugar refinery. Indeed, these companies were partly responsible for creating the first permanent Latino communities in Iowa by encouraging the workers to remain throughout the year to save on recruitment and transportation costs. Take for example the family of Ila Plasencia, whose father came to Iowa in 1918 to work in the rock quarry in Earlham, Iowa. Ila was born February 18, 1927, in Earlham, and her family eventually moved to Des Moines when her father received work at Hawkeye Portland Cement. The family of Lucy Prado, who was born January 1, 1929, arrived in Fort Madison around 1918 from the state of Guanajuato. Her father, Manuel Salazar, and mother, Ezekia Mendes-Salazar, met in Fort Madison in the early 1920s. Manuel Salazar worked for the Santa Fe Railroad, a company that provided boxcars for individuals and families to live in.

By the early 1920s Mexican sugar beet workers could be found in Mason City, Belmond, Lakota, Fort Madison, and Britt. Many of these initial Latino workers were from Mexico, more specifically from the states of Michoacán, Guanajuato, Jalisco, Aguascalientes, Zacatecas, San Luis Potosí, Tamaulipas, Nuevo León, and Coahuila. However, a large segment of this population was U.S. born and arriving from Colorado, Texas, and New Mexico. According to one source 2,018 Latino workers were recruited to work in Iowa in 1926. At the local level, Mason City, located in north central Iowa, illustrates the movement of Latinos into the region. In 1920 Mason City had a Latino population of approximately 113 individuals; this number had increased to 455 by 1928, because of the need for labor in the sugar beet plantations, cement companies, and packinghouses. Mexicans also picked other crops. For example, in the Quad cities area of Iowa and Illinois (Davenport, Bettendorf, Moline, and Rock Island) onions were the prevalent staple harvest. In Pleasant Valley and Bettendorf, Iowa Mexicans worked on such farms as Shutter's, Clements's, and Blessing Garden.

Another strong indicator of a permanent Latino presence is the emergence and development of organizations catering to the community. The early twentieth century saw a number of organizations and government entities facilitate the transition for Latinos from transient to permanent members of the community. The most widespread type of such organizations was the mutual aid societies (*mutualistas*). Las *comisiones honoríficas* (honorary commissions) were organizations fostered by the Mexican consular office in order to keep pace with the growing Latino population in such places as Iowa. In many cases these *comisiones*—whose members were exclusively males—acted as de facto consular offices, addressing the needs of the community and looking into cases of discrimination, exploitation, and abuse. Another role of the *comisiones* was to teach Latinos how to adapt to their new environment. Several sources report the appearance of La Cruz Azul Mexicana (the Mexican Blue Cross) in the 1920s, a charitable organization run by females and the counterpart to the *comisiones*. The primary role of the Blue Cross was to raise money for financially needy Mexican families, ensure the welfare of the Mexican population that fell on hard times, and in some cases provide transportation back to Mexico.

A specific Iowa example of an honorary commission was the Bettendorf Latino community of the 1920s. Latinos living there celebrated religious and national holidays and created community institutions. David Macias arrived in Bettendorf in 1915 and became a community organizer and religious and social leader. Like the members of the *comisiones* and Cruz Azul, Macias understood the trauma of the recent Mexican migrant, and through personal involvement and the establishment of local organizations he helped ease the new arrivals into the community. By 1925 the overall Latino population in Iowa was approximately 2,597. By the late 1920s the Latino population had increased nationally and became more dispersed geographically. As the Great Depression settled in during the early 1930s Latinos became the scapegoats for the economic ills of the country. As panic set in, prejudices easily rose to the surface with local, regional, and national public officials, creating campaigns to drive Latinos out of their areas, including Iowa.

REPATRIATION AND RESISTANCE: 1930S

The removal of 500,000 Mexicans from the United States is well documented but not universally known. Indeed, few Americans realize that approximately 250,000 U.S. citizens of Mexican ancestry were either forced to "voluntary" remove themselves or deported to Mexico in the 1930s. The Great Depression, as a rationalization, does not explain the removal of U.S. citizens and their deportation to Mexico. A number of factors coalesced in the 1920s and 1930s that created fear, panic, and hysteria above and beyond the Great Depression. The assault on Latinos in general, and on Mexicans in particular, began after the incorporation of Mexican territory by the United States in 1848; and by the turn of the twentieth century U.S. perception of Mexicans was heavily pejorative.

In the early twentieth century, organizations and individuals drawing on the racist ideologies of social Darwinism and eugenics, which advocated white supremacy, viewed groups such as the mentally ill, those of mixed ancestry, and various immigrants as obstacles to the racial betterment of white society and as pollutants to European American ethos. These groups thus became targets for a number of official pogroms to eliminate their reproduction or movement into the United States. This gave rise to miscegenation laws, sterilization programs, and the exclusion of particular groups from immigrating to the United States. In general, Latinos were seen as a threat to U.S. society and often described as inassimilable, foreign, and criminally prone. The "Mexican problem" became a favorite expression during the 1920s and 1930s. Furthermore, public debates emerged as to why Mexicans were exempt from the 1924 National Origins Quota. As the debate leaned towards the inevitable, the Great Depression gripped the nation and provided a convenient mechanism for the repatriation and deportation of U.S. citizens of Mexican ancestry. After California, the Midwest was one of the hardest-hit regions regarding the removal of Mexicans, with thousands repatriated from Chicago, Milwaukee, Kansas City, and Detroit. Mexicans in Detroit became one of the largest enclaves removed during this period. Mexicans were also removed in substantial numbers from Illinois, Indiana, and Minnesota. Because the population of Mexicans living in Iowa was smaller than that in other northern Midwest states, Mexicans in that state were affected differently.

The removal of Mexicans from Iowa was primarily conducted through economic rationalization, nativist rhetoric, and coercion. The reason as to why roundups and deportation were not used can be explained by the small Mexican population in Iowa, making such tactics economically prohibitive. By the late

1920s and early 1930s a large portion of the Latino community in Iowa were working in agriculture. As the prices for commodities fell in the 1930s, so did wages. For example, the rate for working in sugar beets fell from $28 to $10 an acre. Economic necessity forced many Mexicans in Iowa to look for work in other regions. In many instances, employers in Iowa began to implement a "white workers only" policy in their hiring practices, regardless of legal status (Garcia, 1996). Furthermore, New Deal legislation had little to no impact on Mexicans in Iowa, because many were refused assistance and most Mexican Americans were never told they were eligible for relief programs. For those Mexicans repatriated from Iowa it was a demoralizing and humiliating experience.

Exact figures for the number of Mexicans who left Iowa during the 1930s are difficult to glean because they left under different circumstances. But regardless of how they left Iowa, they left in relation to the same sequence of events that saw thousands deported in the 1930s. An estimated 60 percent of all Mexican nationals from Midwest states such as Minnesota, Illinois, and Iowa had returned home by 1932. Affected by the rising tide of discrimination, they fled areas out of concern for their safety. One group of Mexican repatriates from Des Moines was forced to beg for food while waiting for transportation to their destination. Some Mexicans avoided deportation by sheer luck. For example, the family of John Ortega settled in Des Moines in the 1920s, in an area along the Des Moines River called Box Town. John Ortega believes his own family escaped deportation because they were very fair skinned and had blue-green eyes. Ortega also recalls he and his siblings were allowed to sit on the main floor of the theatre because of their light complexion, whereas darker-skinned Mexicans and "Negroes" were forced to sit in the balcony. Other Mexican American families experienced similar hardships. One example is the family of Estefania Rodriguez, who was born in Bettendorf, Iowa, in 1923. Estefania explains how her family survived by growing their own food and catching fish on the banks of the Mississippi. Her recollection of the relief and welfare programs was the allotment of a bag of flour to make tortillas. Estefania recalls being constantly hungry at the age of 10, her diet consisting mostly of beans and rice. During the Depression her father was able to find odd jobs in and around Bettendorf. The Rodriguez family is representative of some families who refused to leave the Midwest and like many other families in the 1930s eked out a living from wherever possible. Relief for Latinos, and the country as a whole, came in the late 1930s with the outbreak of World War II in Europe.

MEXICAN NATIONALS AND LATINOS: 1940s–1950s

The Latino experience in Iowa during 1940s included demographic growth, community building, and strong support for the Allied war effort when the United

States entered World War II in 1941. By the end of 1945 over 500,000 Latinos had served in the armed forces, many with distinction. In the 1940s close to 3,000 Latinos were residing in Iowa. Like other U.S. citizens, Latinos in Iowa volunteered and were drafted into the war. Others never returned, giving their life for liberty, democracy, and freedom. One such individual was Private John M. Piloto who entered the Army on March 3, 1942, being killed in action in Germany on February 10, 1945. Private Piloto was born in Fort Madison on March 21, 1923, and he spent his entire short life in Iowa.

Overall, Latinos are considered by many to have received the highest number of medals for valor of any ethnic group during World War II. According to one source Lando Valadez, from Des Moines, received one of the few Silver Stars awarded to Iowans. Latinas in Iowa played a vital role on the home front. Ila Plasencia had two brothers serving in World War II, and both were killed in action. One brother survived the Bataan Death March of 1942 in the Philippines, only to die as a prisoner of war. Ila, as a high school student, organized an all-Latina organization called the Twelve Stars, which performed community work. During World War II members of Twelve Stars wrote letters and sent care packages to servicemen. One of the other great contributions Latinos and Latinas made during the 1940s was their labor for the war effort.

In a twist of historical irony, as soon as the United States had deported nearly 500,000 Mexicans in the 1930s, almost an identical number was imported in the 1940s under a bilateral agreement. Historically, Latino labor has been viewed as tractable, expendable, and a necessary condition throughout the twentieth century. The movement of Latinos into Iowa during the 1940s is attributed to the global conflict that erupted in Europe and Pacific theatres of war that enveloped the United States in 1941. In short, because of a massive mobilization for the war effort, the United States found itself with a shortage of laborers in key areas, such as in agriculture and the railroad industries. One of the solutions for this dilemma was the development and implementation of the Emergency Farm Labor program in 1942 that advocated the use of multiple forms of labor to include children, prisoners, women, the elderly, as well as the importation of foreign labor. Overall, what became known as the Bracero program has been well documented for places such as California, Texas, Washington, Idaho, and Oregon, but no studies exist examining the use of Mexican nationals in Iowa.

By 1940 farmworkers in Iowa had declined by 10 percent, and seasonal workers by 35 percent. Iowa produced 10 percent of the nation's food in 1940. Iowa, synonymous with farming, has a proud heritage and history of farm operators with their families not only managing the farm, but also being its principal laborers. World War II changed this historical trajectory. From 1943 to 1947 Iowa growers utilized numerous forms of labor, including the importation of Mexican nationals and the recruitment of Mexican Americans primarily from Texas. During that period 6,395 Mexican nationals were imported into Iowa, and 1,670 Mexican Americans were recruited. These Latino workers were used in harvesting peas, nursery stock, and grain; cutting asparagus; and detasseling corn. The typical use and reaction to Mexican labor during this period is probably best exemplified by the following observations reported by the *Star Clipper* of Traer, Iowa, in 1943. Approximately 100 Mexican Americans born in Texas and Montana were recruited to work in Iowa. This group was brought into Iowa by the Pioneer Company to detassel corn in the town of Reinbeck. According to the article these Mexicans were to be segregated from the local workers, but the article does not state why. Furthermore, the Ladies Aid Society of the Methodist Church of Reinbeck took on the task of feeding the Mexicans three meals a day. By 1947 the importation of Mexican nationals was reduced, but the continued recruitment of Latinos was maintained. In fact, Iowa reported that for the 1947 Emergency Farm Labor program, Latin Americans comprised 2.1 percent of the overall workforce. For Iowa, the Bracero program came to an end in 1947, but nationally it continued until December 31, 1964. For the remainder of the twentieth century a steady stream of Latinos entered Iowa, and as the population grew, it became more visible and active within the state.

Overall, the permanent Latino population in Iowa during the 1950s was relatively small, probably not numbering over 4,000. However, several things hampered an accurate count. First, individuals of Latino background did not have a designator, and were put into the "white other" category. In the 1950s Iowa recorded 80 people under "other race." Also, during this time the majority of Latinos were counted under the "white" category because the nomenclature "Hispanic" was not available.

By the end of the 1940s and the beginning of the 1950s Latinos had been present in areas such as Fort Madison for almost 50 years. The Latino population was not evenly dispersed throughout the state, but it remained concentrated in regions where work was readily available—for example, in Fort Madison, Muscatine, Des Moines, Sioux City, Bettendorf, Davenport, and Mason City. A variety of indicators emerged in regards to the community formation that had taken place. As Latinos became established in their communities, organizations began to emerge that were initially social clubs. For instance, a Latin American organization was formed in Fort Madison that began as a culture conduit to the overall community. In fact, the Latin America Club of Fort Madison, founded in 1949, stressed the following points as an organization: religion, understanding, unity, and recreation. This organization eventually became the League of United Latin American Citizens (LULAC) #304. Similar organizations emerged in other communities throughout the state.

As the 1950s emerged, the United States found itself involved in the Korean War, which instigated another wave of Latinos to Iowa. Like World War II, the Korean War created the need for additional labor. Latinos heeded the call for help in Iowa and came seeking employment. One historian indicates that Iowans had a difficult time focusing on the war because farm issues—ranging from persistent droughts to debates over farm taxes and the introduction of margarine into the U.S. markets—were prevalent during the 1950s. Of course this was a major concern for Iowan farmers who marketed butter. For the Latino generation returning from World War II and the Korean Conflict, Iowa became the place where change was needed. The relatively small Latino population organized itself in a variety ways during the 1950s to not only take its place in society but also to demand the same rights that many had fought and died for in the European and Pacific theatres of war. LULAC organizations sprang up in Davenport, Des Moines, Fort Madison, and Mason City, among other places. LULAC was a quasi-civil rights organization with its origins in the late 1920s. A chapter of the American G.I. Forum was established in Bettendorf. The American G.I. Forum was created in 1948 in Texas after servicemen of Latino origin were denied their veteran's benefits. However, the G.I. Forum also demanded and fought for the basic rights of Latinos in the U.S. In general, the 1950s were a difficult period for many Latinos, especially for those who attempted to organize or were involved with unions. The communist scare of this era affected many Latino organizations by either driving them underground (which was due to government harassment) or in many cases by shutting them down, based on accusation of communism. The 1950s saw a new round of Mexican deportations under the military operational named Operation Wetback. During this three-year campaign approximately 1.2 million Mexicans were returned to Mexico.

Iowa's Mexican American generation paved the way for the next generation of Latinos. Furthermore, the late 1960s and early 1970s witnessed an increasing number of Latinos in Iowa that grew internally, but substantial growth came from migration, which created a more diverse Latino diaspora in regards to their place of origin.

CHICANOS IN IOWA AND A PAN-LATINO COMMUNITY: 1960S-1970S

According to the U.S. Census Bureau, by the end of the 1960s the Iowa Latino population had grown to over 21,000. Some sources stated that number was in fact closer to 30,000. The majority of Latinos resided in the following counties: Black Hawk, Cerro Gordo, Des Moines, Lee, Linn, Muscatine, Polk, Pottawattamie, Scott, and Woodbury. The 1970 census shows a Latino population working primarily in clerical, craftsman, factory, and laborer positions. A large number of transient migrant workers—estimated in 1970 to be approximately 3,000—and undocumented Latinos are not included in the census data. These migrants were mostly U.S.-born individuals coming from states such as Texas, Missouri, Florida, and Colorado. A significant change occurred within the Latino population. Civil wars in Nicaragua, El Salvador, and Guatemala created the displacement of a large number of individuals and families. As a result, a steady stream of migrants and political refugees began arriving in the United States. Iowa, a historical destination for migrant refugees, began receiving a significant number of Central Americans in the 1970s, which added to the diversity of the Latino community that had been, by and large, Mexican for most of the twentieth century.

In some ways Iowa was the same as the rest of the country during the 1960s. The civil rights movement was alive and well in Iowa, with numerous groups ranging from student activism against the Vietnam War to the Black Movement. Simultaneously, although the state had diversified its economy, Iowa continued to be a major agriculture producer, and this remained a top priority for the state. Latinos in Iowa were engaged in an Iowan version of the civil rights movement. The evidence suggests that Chicanos in Iowa were politically active during the 1960s on many fronts.[2]

Because Iowa has strong agricultural roots and employs a large number of Latinos in this industry, it is not surprising that this is one of the areas Latinos mobilized to boycott, strike, and demand equitable treatment. Although Latinos embraced and supported some of the national farmworker movements—such as Cesar Chavez's farmworkers movement and the Farm Labor Organizing Committee—Latinos had their local struggles in Iowa. For example, during the 1970s Davenport had a population of 3,000 Latinos. That city was the home of an Oscar Mayer processing plant that employed approximately 1,500 people, of whom only 18 had Latino background. Dolores Carrillo, a Davenport resident in the 1970s, had extensive experience working in factories, but was continually denied employment at the Oscar Mayer plant. Newspaper articles describe Carrillo's efforts to organize a boycott against Oscar Mayer because of unfair hiring practices and prejudice at the workplace. In 1976 LULAC filed a grievance with the Department of Defense against International Harvester Corporation for discriminatory hiring practices against Latino applicants. The Department of Defense found International Harvester in violation of numerous hiring procedures that adversely affected Latinos. What these cases reveal is a politically active Latino community—an activism that has its roots in the early twentieth century—and the maturation of such organizations as LULAC, which were willing to confront companies to ensure that Latino basic rights were protected. This type of activism and involvement did not define all Latinos in Iowa during the 1960s and 1970s, but it rather demonstrates a common history with other Latinos throughout the country that provides a common experience, albeit with Iowan twists. The political development of the Latino community prepared it for the influx of thousands of additional Latinos in the last two decades of the twentieth century. Indeed,

Iowa experienced one of the largest demographic changes in its Latino population in the country.

LATINOS IN IOWA, 1980–2000: CHANGES AND CHALLENGES

By the beginning of the 1980s the Latino population comprised over 26,000 people, and the region experienced the early signs of a Latino surge that increased in the coming two decades. Three developments explain why in the last two decades of the twentieth century Iowa experienced an increase in its Latino population. First, Iowa's agriculture industries went through a stage of deindustrialization created by the emergence of global competition. In the Iowan context this meant that many farmers in Iowa found it difficult to remain economically viable; thus, during the late 1970s and 1980s Iowa suffered a farm crisis, with many growers losing their farms, whereas large corporate entities increased. For Latinos this meant fewer jobs in agriculture. Since the ending of World War II farming in Iowa has become increasingly capital intensive and less labor intensive. Latinos as a whole shifted to the manufacturing and service sector for employment in the second half of the twentieth century, especially the food processing and packaging industries. Deindustrialization also meant that certain sectors of the manufacturing base adjusted to the global competition by moving their operations abroad, de-unionizing, de-skilling various industries, or going out of business. On the one hand Iowa's economy suffered a serious blow, but on the other, a number of large manufacturing and labor-intensive industries relocated to Iowa to take advantage of the low overhead cost and to attract a particular type of labor. As jobs in meatpacking became less desirable for native workers because of low pay, lack of benefits, and poor work conditions, immigrants, especially Latinos, began to fill those positions. Overall, Iowa also experienced a drop in its young population, which was due to the changes in its economy and to individuals leaving to find employment elsewhere.

The flight of Euro-American individuals and families from Iowa beginning in the 1980s explains the second factor for the rise in the Latino population in Iowa. The heavy recruitment and utilization of migrant labor by such companies as Iowa Beef Packers (IBP and now owned by Tyson Foods), ConAgra, Cargill, Hormel, and Swift, or the meatpacking industry in general, created a steady stream of Latinos into Iowa. The significance of these developments is that the Latino population in Iowa rose 27.8 percent between 1980 and 1990. The new Latinos consisted of Mexican nationals pulled by economic opportunities to the state, Latinos migrating from other states such as Texas and California—areas where jobs were becoming scarce because of an increase in the Latino population, which in turn increased competition—and Latino refugees fleeing war-torn regions of Central America. The final factor that contributed to the increase in the Latino population in Iowa was fertility rates. Nationally, the Latinos are one of the youngest population groups. The Latino population in Iowa increased substantially toward the end of the twentieth and beginning of the twentieth-first century.

At the national level, the overall Latino population increased from 22.4 million in 1990 to 35.3 million in 2000. Iowa followed a similar trend. Indeed, the 1990 U.S. census recorded approximately 32,643 Latinos residing in Iowa, and by 1998 that number had increased to 56,936, that is, by 74.4 percent. By the year 2000 the number of Latinos had reached 82,473, or 2.8 percent of the overall Iowan population. This represented a 169.2 percent increase in the Latino population from 1990 to 2000. Although individuals of Mexican origin remained the largest subgroup of Latinos, at 61,154 or 74.2 percent, other groups are clearly represented in Iowa: 2,690 Puerto Ricans; 1,298 Guatemalans; 1,470 Salvadorans; and 750 Cubans. Historical factors explain the large discrepancy in number between individuals of Mexican origin and their Central and South American counterparts.

2000–Present

The significant increase in the Latino population in Iowa was met with a variety of different perspectives. Iowa has never been a homogenous white state, as there has always been an indigenous population and a Black diaspora since its beginnings. However, what is apparent is a white hegemonic apparatus that has controlled the region since the nineteenth century. For most of the twentieth century the Asian, Native American, Black, and Latino populations remained exceptionally small, thus never challenging or threatening the dominance of the Anglo population until the late twentieth century. Because Iowa continually lost people for decades, there were many in the state who encouraged and welcomed the movement of Latinos. For example, in the 1990s Iowa grew only 3.3 percent, whereas the nation grew to 9.6 percent. Most of the growth in Iowa was due to the movement of Latinos into the state. In fact, by the late twentieth century then governor Tom Vilsack officially proclaimed Iowa open to immigrants by establishing New Iowan Centers in Muscatine and Sioux City to help migrants find jobs and settle in. There was a mixed reaction to these developments. Some openly opposed the invitation to migrants strictly on prejudicial grounds, but others were concerned that an unchecked and unplanned growth based on migration would create more problems that it would solve. In the end, the momentum that had began a decade earlier continued unabated. In the early twenty-first century Latinos remained the fastest-growing group both nationally and in the state of Iowa.

From 1990 to 2004, Iowa underwent a 221 percent increase in its Latino population, which contributed 97 percent of Iowa's population growth for this fourteen-year period. As of July 2006 there are approximately 114,700 Latinos in Iowa, constituting almost 5 percent of Iowa's population and representing a 28.1 percent increase from the 2000 census. Mexicans remain dominant at

74 percent, Central Americans at 5 percent, Puerto Ricans at 3 percent, South Americans at 2 percent, Cubans at 1 percent, and other Latinos at 15 percent. Many of the factors mentioned earlier that explain this growth remain the same. It should be noted that the median age of Iowa's Latino population is 24.6 years, whereas the overall median age for the state is 38.6. Occupationally, 37.1 percent of Latinos are employed in production, transportation, and material-moving positions. But a large percentage of Latinos are employed in the services industry, which has replaced agriculture as one of the main sectors of employment for Latinos. Yet, almost 20 percent of Latinos in Iowa are in managerial or professionally related occupations. Latinos also have a higher unemployment rate, at 7.7 percent, than the overall state rate of 5.3 percent; a significantly lower income, at $29,350, than the median income for the state of $43,609; and a much higher poverty rate, at 25.8 percent, than the state rate of 10.9 percent. Education remains a concern for Latinos: only 54.3 percent of Latinos age 25 and over have at least a high school education; 9.1 percent of Latinos age 25 and over have a bachelor's degree or higher; and approximately 1 percent had a master's, professional, or doctorate degree. As of 2006 Polk County had the largest population of Latinos, at 25,358.

Counties such as Marshall, Buena Vista, Muscatine, Woodbury, Scott, and Crawford have large concentrations of Latinos. At the city level Des Moines, Sioux City, Davenport, Marshalltown, Muscatine, Council Bluffs, Storm Lake, Cedar Rapids, Perry, and Iowa City have the largest population of Latinos in the state. At the current rate of growth the Latino population in Iowa is projected to reach 305,900 by 2030. This extraordinary growth has been met with resistance, acceptance, and tolerance, but it has not translated into a political voice.

Indeed, one consequence for Latinos was a nativistic reaction to their growth when in February 2002 the Iowa House of Representatives passed the English Language Reaffirmation Act. Governor Tom Vilsack signed the bill into law on March 1, 2002, thus making English the official language of the state. More importantly, as of 2005 there was only one Latino elected official in the entire state—a municipal official from Storm Lake. This is a most troubling fact, considering the high concentration of Latinos in certain counties and cities in Iowa. Thus, although Latinos are increasing their numbers and contributing to the growth and development of Iowa, they remain a politically marginalized group throughout the state. Latinos in Iowa recently surpassed the African American population to become the largest minority group in the state.

NOTABLE LATINOS

Lisa, Manuel (1772–1820). A well-known fur trader and explorer who founded the Missouri Fur Company, Lisa was born in New Orleans of Spanish parents (his father was a government official from Murcia). Lisa became involved in the fur trade while in his teens. By 1796 he had married a widow, Polly Charles Chew, and was operating a trading vessel along the Mississippi River. In 1799 he obtained a land grant and relocated to St. Louis, Missouri. By 1800 he was a preeminent trader in the fur business, and he was granted a monopoly by the Spanish government in 1802 for fur commerce with the Osage Nation. Lisa was also involved in the preparation for the journey of the Lewis and Clark Expedition in 1803–1804.

Plasencia, Ila (1927–). Widely regarded as the most prominent Latino political activist in Iowa, Ila Plasencia was born in Earlham, Iowa, on February 18, 1927. Plasencia had played a pivotal role in various community groups by her late teens. In 1957 she began a long-term career with LULAC (League of United Latin American Citizens), an organization devoted to the political and social advancement of Latino/as in the United States. She helped to establish the first women's LULAC council in Iowa, and in 1986 she became the first woman to hold the office of LULAC state director in the state of Iowa. In 1987 she became the first woman from Iowa to hold the office of LULAC national vice president for the Midwest (a 12-state region). Plasencia has also founded several Hispanic organizations and served as the first Latino in primary roles in a number of Latino organizations, including the Mexican American Bowlers League, the State of Iowa Spanish Speaking People's Commission (the precursor of the Iowa Commission on Latino Affairs), and the Midwest Educational Resources Development Fund. She has received numerous awards, including the Presidential Award in recognition of her untiring contributions to the Hispanic Community.

Vasquez Olvera, Mary (1927–). Political activist from Davenport, Iowa, who was involved in the Ladies Auxiliary of the Iowa chapter of the American GI Forum. She also cofounded the Quad Cities Viva Kennedy club with her husband.

Campos, Mary E. (1929–). Mary E. Campos, born in McAlester, Oklahoma, in 1929, is an advocate for women and children in Iowa. She has helped to establish better relationships between people of diverse ethnic backgrounds. Campos serves on numerous boards and councils as a champion for human rights, including the Community Housing Education Resources, Bidwell Riverside Community Center, Des Moines Human Rights Commission, Hispanic Education Resource Center, Council for International Understanding, Mid-City Vision Committee, Our Lady of Guadalupe Chapel, Hispanic Ministry, Senior Citizens Advisory Council, Adult and Youth Ministries Diocese of Des Moines Advisory Council, and the Des Moines Register Advisory Council. She has also served as president of the United Mexican-American Community Center. Campos has been active politically, serving as the Hispanic representative to the Iowa Democratic Party in 1983 and as the cochair of the Polk County Democratic County Convention in 1992. With the Latino population increasing in Iowa, Campos spends countless hours helping non-English speaking families who are relocating to Des Moines and Perry to become more informed about social and health issues. Campos was inducted into the Iowa Women's Hall of Fame in 1995. The Iowa Commission of Latino Affairs established an award named her honor. This first award was given to all the individuals who marched for immigrant rights in May 2006.

Rivera, Tomás (1935–1984). Author Rivera was born in Crystal City, Texas, to migrant farmworkers. In his youth, he accompanied his parents as they labored in various parts of the Midwest, including Iowa. These experiences had a discernable impact on his writing and his determination to succeed. The story "Tomás and the Library Lady" is based on his friendship as a child with a librarian in Iowa. Rivera is best known for *y no se lo tragó la tierra* (and the earth did not swallow him). In 1979 Rivera became the first minority to become chancellor in the University of California system (Riverside). The Tomás Rivera Policy Institute at the University of Southern California is named in his honor.

Aguilar, Maria (1936–). Factory worker who was among the first Latinas to be hired to work at the International Harvester Company (IHC) Farmall plant in Davenport, Iowa. In 1973 Maria Aguilera applied for a job at IHC Farmall, but she was denied work on the grounds that she was too short. Aguilera, suspecting discrimination, pressured the company, being finally hired to work on the assembly line. Aguilera worked for International Harvester Company Farmall until 1982, when the plant closed down.

Barceló, Nancy "Rusty" (1946–). Born in Merced, California, on June 5, 1946, activist and administrator Nancy "Rusty" Barceló earned a bachelor of arts degree in social welfare and corrections from Chico State University in 1969. Barceló arrived at the University of Iowa as a graduate student in 1970. In 1971 she and fellow students Antonio Zavalla and Ruth Pushetonequa founded the Chicano Indian-American Student Union (CIASU). Barceló earned her master of arts in recreational education in 1972. She left the University of Iowa to assume the position of coordinator of educational opportunity services at the University of Oregon, where she stayed from 1973 to 1975. After her time in Oregon, Barceló returned to the University of Iowa, where, in 1980, she became the first Mexican American to earn a doctoral degree from that university. Following her graduation, Barceló was hired by the University of Iowa, where she served as acting director of affirmative action (1982–1983), director of summer session (1981–1987), associate director at Opportunity at Iowa, (1987–1994), assistant dean (1981–1995), and assistant provost at Opportunity at Iowa (1995–1996). From 1996 to 2001, Barceló was associate vice president for multicultural affairs and the chair of the Chicana Studies Department at the University of Minnesota. She left that position in 2001 to become the vice president for minority affairs and diversity at the University of Washington in Seattle. In 2006, Barceló was appointed the University of Minnesota's first vice president and vice provost for equity and diversity. Barceló is responsible for developing and implementing a system-wide strategic plan for equity and diversity that is consistent with the university's strategic positioning efforts. Barceló is credited as the moving force behind the National Initiative for Women in Higher Education (NIWHE). She has chaired Mujeres Activas en Letras y Cambio Social (MALCS) and the Washington State Native American Advisory Board (NAAB). Her honors include establishment of the Rusty Barceló Award at the University of Minnesota, which honors faculty, staff, and students who, through their own work on campus, foster multicultural community building. In 2004, Barceló received the Ohtli Award, a special recognition presented by the Mexican government to Mexicans or Latinos whose work has benefited Mexicans living abroad.

Rundquist, Maria E. (1951–). Community volunteer Maria Eugenia Escamilla-Góngora Rundquist was born in 1951 to Addy Maria Luisa Góngora-Ceballos and Alberto Hernan Escamilla-Mendicuti, in Mérida, Yucatán, Mexico. She was one of six children.

In many of her positions she has used her bilingual skills (English and Spanish) and her multicultural experiences to improve the lives of Latinos in Iowa. She served on the board of both Latinos en Siouxland and La Casa Latina of Sioux City. Rundquist served on the Iowa Commission on Latino Affairs from 1993 to 1995, and she was appointed to the Sioux City Human Rights Commission in 2003.

CULTURAL CONTRIBUTIONS

Latinos in Iowa have been active in celebrating and integrating their unique and varied culture since their first arrivals to the state. Religious celebrations, media productions, and popular culture festivals continue to provide a venue for community solidarity among Latinos as an ethnic minority in the state.

Religion

Mexican Catholicism has been part of Iowa since the movement of Latinos into the region during the nineteenth century. The strongest symbol of Mexican Catholicism is la Virgen de Guadalupe (the Virgin of Guadalupe), whose apparition was seen in Mexico City in 1531. La Virgen de Guadalupe has become a singular source of faith and unity for Latinos. Her appearances to Juan Diego are celebrated from December 9 to 12. In 1948 Our Lady of Guadalupe Chapel was build at 801 Scott Avenue, Des Moines, Iowa, and it was used for decades as a parish and a center of activity for Latinos. Mexican Catholicism is also a transmitter of culture—ranging from traditional Latino weddings to baptisms, and the *quinceañera*, which is celebrated when Latina adolescents reach the age of fifteen—within the Mexican community. The origins of *quinceañera* are obscure, but it is likely a merging of indigenous and Christian religiosity that occurred after the conquest. And it has changed over the centuries. Traditionally, this rite of passage, for girls only, symbolized the age when a female accepted the Catholic Church as her faith and her entrance into womanhood. Today the celebration maintains its religious importance, but it also emphasizes a secular coming-of-age ritual. The celebration varies depending on the Latin American country or even the region of the United States. One major change from the past has been the willingness of churches to hold Spanish-only masses. Lastly, Latinos in the United States, including Iowa, for the last three decades have been leaving the Catholic Church for other denominations; however, most Latinos remain Catholic.

Spanish Language and Media

Over 90,000 Iowans age 5 and older in 2005 spoke Spanish at home. Among those who speak Spanish at home, more than half say they speak English "very well." Approximately 14,000 individuals were identified as English-language learners in Iowa's public and private schools during 2006–2007. This represents a 124.2 percent increase from the 1999–2000 school year. Throughout Iowa there are dozens of different media that caters to the Latino population, ranging from newspapers to magazines to radio. For example, *El Enfoque,* from Perry, Iowa, is a sports and soccer magazine catering to the interest of Spanish-speaking Latinos. Traditional Spanish-speaking newspapers such as *El Latino Newspaper* cover a wide area that includes Council Bluffs, Central and Eastern Iowa, and Omaha. *La Ley,* KBGG 1700 AM, is a Spanish-language radio station based out of Urbandale, Iowa. *VOCES,* a biweekly Spanish newspaper, covers a large portion of eastern Iowa.

Popular Culture

The oldest Latino festival in Iowa is perhaps the Mexican fiesta held annually in Fort Madison. It is at least 102 years old. The first-recorded Mexican fiesta took place in 1906 in celebration of Mexican independence. Overall, this festival celebrates Fort Madison's Latino heritage with food, music, dance, art, and fundraising for scholarships. Latino Iowans have also introduced such celebrations as Cinco de Mayo, which commemorates the Mexican army's victory over the French on May 5, 1862, in the Battle of Puebla. Each year between September 15 and October 15 Latinos and other Iowans celebrate Hispanic Heritage Month.

NOTES

1. Most scholars and scientists attribute the origins and cultivation of corn to central Mexico. As such, maize has been one of the primary staples of Mexican diet for over 9,000 years. Ceneotl and Chicomeocoatl represent the God and Goddess of corn, respectively, and they were worshipped by various indigenous groups in Central Mexico. I use Chicomeocoatl metaphorically, in conjunction with the immigration/migration of Mexicans to the state of Iowa, which happens to be synonymous with the cultivation of corn in the United States.

2. The term *Chicano* was adopted by many U.S. citizens of Mexican ancestry who were actively involved in their communities. The indigenous roots of Chicanos allowed many to embrace their Indian past with honor. Not all Mexican Americans embrace this term.

BIBLIOGRAPHY

Balderrama, Francisco, and Raymond Rodriguez. *Decade of Betrayal: Mexican Repatriation in the 1930s.* 2nd ed. Albuquerque: University of New Mexico Press, 2006.

Garcia, Jerry. *Mexicans in Iowa.* Unpublished manuscript.

Garcia, Juan R. *Mexicans in the Midwest, 1900–1932.* Tucson: University of Arizona Press, 1996.

Santillan, Richard. *A Social and Cultural History of the Midwest.* Unpublished manuscript.
Schwieder, Dorothy. *Iowa: The Middle Land.* Ames: Iowa State University Press, 1996.
Star Clipper, Traer, Iowa, 1943.
University of Iowa Libraries, Women's Archives, Mujeres Latinas Project.
Valdes, Dennis Nodin. *Al Norte: Agricultural Workers in the Great Lakes Region, 1917–1970.* Austin: University of Texas Press, 1991.
———. *Barrios Norteños: St. Paul and Midwestern Mexican Communities in the Twentieth Century.* Austin: University of Texas Press, 2000.
Vargas, Zaragosa. *Proletarians of the North: Mexican Industrial Workers of Detroit and the Midwest, 1917–1933.* Berkeley: University of California Press, 1999.

17

Kansas

David Knowlton

CHRONOLOGY

1541	Spanish conquistador Francisco Vázquez de Coronado and his troop enter Kansas, searching for the Pueblo Indian village Las Humanas, also known as Gran Quivira, thus starting Spanish involvement with Kansas.
1601	Juan de Oñate, governor of Spanish New Mexico, leads an expedition to Kansas.
1682	French explorer Robert LaSalle claims the land along the Mississippi River and its tributaries for France.
1720	The Pedro de Villasur expedition leaves Santa Fe and crosses Kansas to attack a Pawnee village allied with France. The expedition is defeated by the Pawnees.
1762	Spain acquires Kansas as part of the transfer of Louisiana from French to Spanish control.
1800	Louisiana and Kansas return to French control through a secret treaty between Napoleon and the King of Spain.
1803	France sells Kansas, as part of the Louisiana Purchase, to the United States.
1806	Facundo Melgares leads a Spanish expedition from New Mexico across Kansas to establish trade with Indians and to contest U.S. claims to the lands west of the Mississippi.
1821	The William Becknell expedition, from Missouri, reaches Santa Fe, New Mexico, and opens the Santa Fe Trail between Kansas City and Mexican Santa Fe.

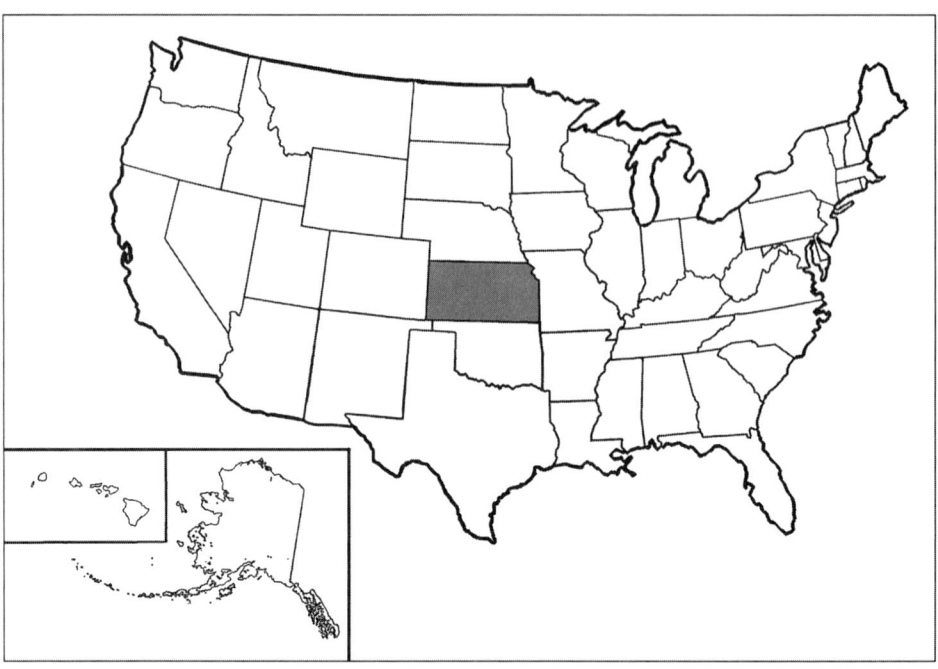

1862	President Abraham Lincoln signs the Pacific Railroad Bill, leading to massive building of railroads in Kansas.
1866	Beginning of the heyday of cattle drives from Texas to Kansas railheads, which depended on Latino vaqueros and survive in the folk song *Corrido de Kiansis*.
1905	Garden City Sugar Beet Company is founded and hires Mexicans to work in its large holdings of sugar beet fields in southwestern Kansas and in its beet processing factory. This leads to the foundation of a Latino *colonia* (colony) in Garden City.
1907	The Atcheson, Topeka, and Santa Fe Railway, along with other rail companies, actively recruits Mexican labor. The arrival of Mexican workers to Kansas prompts the establishing of Latino communities in every Kansas railroad town.
1918	Anglo parents in Emerson, Kansas, demand segregated schooling for Mexican students, which leads to the education of Latino children in school basements in Kansas.
1923	Clara Barton School, a public institution for Mexican children, opens in Argentine, Kansas, on the demand of Anglo parents for segregated education.
1924	Two hundred Anglo parents encircle the Major Hudson School in Kansas City, Kansas, to demand that four Mexican boys, who had been admitted, be removed from the school. This incident contributed to segregated elementary education for Latinos in Kansas.

1925	Saturnino Alvarado and other Kansas City parents begin a fight for their children to be admitted into Kansas City high schools when the Alvarado children and others are denied admission to 9th grade at the Argentine High School.
1926	Luz Alvarado, Jesús Alvarado, Marcos de León, and Victorina Pérez are admitted to Argentine High School.
1930	Luz Alvarado, Jesús Alvarado, and Marcos de León become the first darker-skinned Latinos to graduate from Argentine High School.
1942	Treaty between Mexico and the United States establishes the Bracero program, which leads to new migration to Kansas.
1970	First publication of the newspaper *Aztlán de Leavenworth* in the Leavenworth Federal Penitentiary with the poet Raúl R. Salinas as editor. Salinas also composed the important Chicano poem "Un Trip through the Mind Jail" while at Leavenworth.
1971	Formation of the Association of Mexican American Students—later Movimiento Estudiantil Chicano de Aztlán (MEChA), and then Hispanic American Leadership Organization (HALO)—at the University of Kansas.
1973	Paul Feleciano is elected to the Kansas state legislature.
1974	The Kansas Advisory Committee on Mexican American Affairs is founded by Kansas governor Robert Bennett. Its name was subsequently changed to Kansas Hispanic and Latino American Affairs Commission.
1975	El Centro Inc., the largest Latino service organization in Kansas, is founded.
1976	Paul Feleciano is elected to the Kansas state Senate.
1977	The Hispanic Chamber of Commerce of Greater Kansas City is founded by 25 Latino business leaders.
1987	The Kansas Advisory Committee on Hispanic affairs is founded by the Kansas state government. This organization later became the Kansas Hispanic and Latino American Affairs Commission.
2004	Governor Janet Sebelius signs into law legislation that enables illegal migrants who had graduated from Kansas high schools to pay in-state tuition, without being asked their immigration status. Delia García becomes the first Latina elected to the Kansas state legislature.
2007	Kansas governor Kathleen Sebelius signs HB 2140, the law that makes English the official language of Kansas, thereby requiring state agencies to carry out official business in English with limited exceptions.

HISTORICAL OVERVIEW

Early History

The Spaniard Francisco Vázquez de Coronado and his entourage were the first Europeans to enter the territory that became Kansas.[1] Coronado and his men left

Mexico City, traveled to New Mexico, and then headed northeastward onto the plains. In 1541 Coronado entered what is now Kansas, where he spent some three months before returning to Mexico. On this trip Vázquez de Coronado and his men were looking for Gran Quivira, a town on the plains about which the Pueblo Indians had told him. Gran Quivira was part of a network of trade that extended to Mexico.[2]

Five hundred years ago, central Kansas held Indian towns made possible by agricultural improvements and by trade routes that connected Pueblo Indians of the Southwest, the hunters and farmers of the plains, the riverine Indians of the east and south, and the civilizations of the Valley of Mexico.

As Spain consolidated its colonial empire, Kansas was further drawn into its domain. Spanish traders now joined the Indians working the networks to the north, as did occasional Spanish military expeditions. As a result people and products flowed between New Spain and Kansas. Indians who were detribalized (*genízaros*) through colonial warfare and slave trading not only formed an important population of the Spanish frontier but also drew Kansas's other Indians into the Spanish empire.

Juan de Oñate, the Spanish governor of New Mexico, entered Kansas with his army in 1601 to search again for Gran Quivira.[3] Other Spaniards entered Kansas to continue to colonize the Indians who had fled to Kansas after the sixteenth-century Pueblo Revolt. One such group, primarily from the pueblo of Taos, settled in western Kansas. The Spanish attacked their settlement, known as El Cuartelejo, several times.[4] The Pedro de Villasur expedition of 1720 crossed Kansas on its way to contemporary Nebraska to attack the Pawnee, who were allies of the French and who had defeated Villasur and his men. In 1806, the Facundo Melgares expedition crossed Kansas to foment trade with the Indians and to contest U.S. control of the land west of the Mississippi.[5]

Drawn into the conflicts of European and later U.S. governments, Kansas stood between the French and the Spanish. When in 1762 Spain acquired Louisiana from the French, Kansas was part of a massive Spanish land claim in North America. The rise of Napoleon led the king of Spain to return Louisiana to the French in a secret treaty known as the Treaty of San Ildefonso. In 1803 Napoleon sold Louisiana to the North Americans. Spain did not accept the North American claim to land west of the Mississippi. Nevertheless, Spain was soon caught up in the wars of independence in its own North American colonies, and that country could not push its claims, as U.S. power and presence grew.

Kansas became a border zone between the Anglo-Americans on the Mississippi and the Spanish in New Mexico. Building on earlier trading with Santa Fe, Anglo traders from Missouri established in 1821, the year of Mexican independence, the famous Santa Fe Trail that crossed Kansas to New Mexico.[6] From New Mexico the nineteenth-century Spanish trail Camino de California (now called the Old

Spanish Trail) continued to the California coast, opening trade with the Pacific.[7] Kansas lay near the eastern terminus of overland highways. Traders from the population mix of New Spain and then Mexico—European, Indian, and African—worked this trail, as did Anglo merchants. Although the United States established a presence in Kansas through settlers and built a new history, the old connections with Mexico were not long in reasserting themselves, even though in 1848 the United States took Mexico's northern territories.

THE PERIOD OF RAILROADS

Europe and the United States had a voracious appetite for the products from Kansas's plains. The acquisition of Kansas's goods and their movement to urban markets became ever more important. In 1862 President Lincoln signed the Pacific Railroad Bill to encourage the building of a transcontinental railroad as well as many regional rail connections.[8] Although the Civil War delayed construction, rail companies were chartered and received federal land grants for every mile of rail built. The railroads lowered costs of transportation, established rail ports for acquisition and shipment of goods, and opened land for colonization.[9]

As a result, beginning in 1860 herds of cattle that had flourished in Spanish—and then Mexican and Anglo—Texas were driven to Kansas's railheads such as Abilene and Dodge City. Entrepreneurial drovers would round up cattle and drive them to Kansas for sale in difficult and often dangerous cattle drives.[10] Many of the cowboys who worked the trails were Spanish-speaking Texans as well as people from across the new border with Mexico, where there was a long tradition of herding cattle. The traditions that gave rise to the North American cowboy developed in northern Mexico—an area which included Texas—from where they were passed on to Anglo Americans. The Latino cowboys had their own culture and traditions, and at the same time they were foundational in building this Anglo institution.[11]

In the cattle drives there was cultural conflict between Anglos and Latinos. As Anglos increased their social and economic dominance—with concomitant prejudice and discrimination—resentment and anger bloomed among Latinos. Both the drama of the drive and cultural conflict became part of the corrido, a foundational genre of Mexican American folk song, and hence Latino literature. The *Corrido de Kiansis* is an example of this type of song (Kiansis was the name used in local Spanish for what is now called Kansas).[12]

The *corrido*, a type of ballad sung in Spanish, is an important genre of folk song along the U.S.-Mexican border and in the *norteño* music that has accompanied Mexican migrants. In it the tensions of life as experienced by Spanish speakers and Latinos in the United States are narrated and examined. The *Corrido de Kiansis* is the earliest complete example of the *corrido* form recorded, although the *corrido* probably already existed among the Spanish-speaking population of Texas.[13]

The *Corrido de Kiansis* has many versions. In its classic form, instead of the conflict becoming violent, as in later *corridos*, it was generally resolved with the Spanish subjects of the *corrido* demonstrating their moral worth and physical prowess and skills as superior to those of the Anglos. For example, one version told how 30 North Americans could not control 500 steers; yet, once "five Mexicans arrived,/all of them wearing good chaps, and in less than a quarter-hour,/they had the steers penned up."[14] Hence, the *Corrido de Kiansis* presented a variety of ethnic triumph at a time of substantial ethnic conflict.

The cattle drives ended in the late 1880s, when costs of shipping cattle from Texas declined, barbed wire allowed the plains to be fenced, and quarantines were enforced against Texas cattle.

The railroads opened a new period of Kansas's Latino history. By 1890, the railroads extended into Mexico and connected with the U.S. rail network. Around the turn of the century the railroad companies began recruiting Mexican workers to fill the demand for lower-level workers.

The railroads enabled the development of agribusiness on the plains and thereby created a demand for farmworkers. Processing industries—such as the sugar beet processing plant in Garden City, Kansas, which also depended on Mexican labor—developed around agriculture.[15] The railroads facilitated the workers' recruitment in Mexico and transportation to the fields.[16]

As a result the first decade of the twentieth century saw Mexicans settle in almost every Kansas town and city that had a rail connection.[17] There the migrants formed neighborhoods and built local Latino culture. Initially, it was expected that both migrant farmworkers and rail workers would return to Mexico in the off-season, but the combination of farmwork and railroad work enabled Mexican families to settle in Kansas. By 1930 Mexicans and Mexican Americans formed 1 percent of the total Kansas population and, at the time, Kansas Mexicans were one of the larger Latino communities in the United States.[18] Mexicans were also the second-largest migrant group in Kansas, after the Germans.[19]

Kansas's population was highly rural, with only about 30 percent of the total population living in cities; yet, its Latino population was almost two-thirds urban.[20] Mexican *colonias* (neighborhoods) developed in cities despite the importance of Latinos as a migrant agricultural workforce.[21] The Catholic Church was a center of life, as were stores and other businesses that focused on the Mexican clientele. Newspapers, such as *El Cosmopolita* of Kansas City, were founded.[22] Parades and civic festivals—such as those celebrating Mexican Independence Day, the 16th of September, and Benito Juárez's birthday—were held. Local culture and language were built in these neighborhoods that continues to have resonance in contemporary Kansas Latino life.

Two central Mexican states of the Bajío, Michoacan and Guanajuato, dominated migration to Kansas.[23] People followed family members and others from their hometowns to settle in enclaves. From there they established connections back to their towns of origin, and people moved back and forth. A separate group of migrants passed through Kansas as part of the three main migrant farmworker streams that worked in the United States.

The Depression hit hard, and many Mexicans returned to Mexico because of the downturn and the dustbowl. As much as a quarter of the Latino population left.[24] Nevertheless, during World War II demand for Mexican labor increased once again.

Developing Diversity

Prior to World War II the Latino community of Kansas consisted almost entirely of a first generation of Mexican migrants and their children. With World War II the community developed connections beyond the boundaries of local neighborhoods and became more organizationally diverse.

During World War II the United States needed Mexican labor. As a result, in 1942 it signed the Bracero program, the first of several treaties with Mexico to import labor for short periods of time. Nevertheless, migration was not a strong factor in the growth of the Kansas Latino community after the war. The demand for farmworkers was met by migrants who came in a great stream from south Texas to Canada, following demand for work in the wheat fields and in the sugar beet fields, until this latter crop declined in the 1950s. Although some migrants did settle out, seasonal movement in search of work characterized this mid-century population.

The classic work *y no se lo tragó la tierra/And the Earth Did Not Devour Them* (1971), by the great Chicano writer Tomás Rivera, witnessed the experience of migrant labor in Kansas.[25] As a boy, Rivera and his family worked the fields as part of the migrant stream.

Nevertheless, the Bracero program and its social incentives for people to not return to Mexico but to settle in the United States, even without legal documentation, had a different impact in Kansas. Because a population of what is called undocumented workers, or illegal migrants, increasingly became a matter of political concern, the United States developed a bureaucracy to attempt to track and deport people who did not have proper documents. The transfer of the Immigration and Naturalization Service to the Justice Department of the Federal Government in 1940 marked the beginning of a political concern with controlling and limiting Mexican migration at a time when demand for workers increased. Migration, legal and otherwise, and the activities of "la Migra," as the INS was called in the Mexican community, became increasingly important in the consciousness of Kansas's Latino community.

The Latino community of Kansas became progressively differentiated by historical experience, time of migration, and generations in the United States.[26]

Although there was a trickle of migrants entering the Latino community at mid-century, Kansas's Latino community developed primarily in the succession of generations, from migrant parents who came in the early decades of the century to a war generation that grew up in the United States and whose children lived the social struggles that shook the country in the 1960s. Their lives were a successive struggle to gain access to mainstream society and to move up socially. Nevertheless, a great period of migration was to come in the last decades of the twentieth century, which was due to difficult conditions in Mexico and an increasing demand for Mexican labor in Kansas.

For example, Garden City, in southwest Kansas, developed an early, and important, Latino community because of sugar beet cultivation and processing as well as railroad work in the area.[27] Today the county in which it is found, Finney County, has the highest relative percentage of Latinos in Kansas, 43.5 percent.[28] This number is the result of almost 100 years of a community producing multiple generations and receiving new migration from Mexico and other countries in Latin America. This difference between those who had arrived earlier and those who have recently arrived in Kansas causes some tension within the community, which creates a separation of interest between new migrants, many of them undocumented, and long-time Garden City residents.

Southwestern Kansas, where Garden City is located, is one of the locations where a number of industrial meatpacking plants are concentrated in the United States (in fact, Southwestern Kansas may have the largest concentration of meatpacking plants in the United States).[29,30] Instead of being scattered across many states, or located in urban areas at centers of rail connections such as Kansas City or Chicago, this industry is now concentrated under a few corporations and in a few rural locations of the United States. The development of relatively inexpensive highway transportation of cattle, changes in the system of slaughter, and changes in conditions of labor enabled this concentration. The meatpacking industry actively courted refugee and migrant labor, and these new migrants entered Latino communities formed in earlier historical periods.

The United States needed Mexican American soldiers during World War II. Latino young men enlisted in the armed services in numbers that were proportionally far greater than their representation in the general population. For example, out of a total population of 800 persons, 52 Latino men from Florence, Kansas, joined the armed forces.[31] More than 300 men from the Latino community of Topeka enlisted.[32] In some cases all of the Latino young men of a given community were in the armed forces. Latinos enlisted for many reasons—for example, to demonstrate loyalty and commitment to the United States despite the discrimination they faced in their home communities. Enlisting was also a vehicle to citizenship for those who did not yet have it. Latinos received many honors for their wartime service.

While in the military, Kansas's Latinos met men from all over the country. Their consciousness was raised through sharing stories with other Latinos about discrimination and prejudice throughout the country. The recruits developed, as a result, an identity as a distinctive population in the United States, and not just in their local community, as well as a commitment to fight against the discrimination they faced at home. Besides developing a growing ethnic consciousness, they also formed networks of friends from many places. The veterans linked Kansas's scattered Latino communities to national networks of activists.[33]

Despite civic discrimination, during the war and after, Latinos saw opportunities for jobs open up for them outside of those they traditionally held. Nevertheless, they were limited by the barriers to education and, in the case of veterans, to full access to the benefits of the GI Bill. The postwar period was one of activism and formation of organizations to fight for social access and development. At first these were local fights, but then they became national. Latino communities as a result became more complex organizationally, and they also began to develop a generation of Latinos born to parents who themselves had been raised in the United States.

During the 1990s migration from Mexico increased, and, at the same time, the migrant stream diversified. More and more people came from southern Mexican states that previously had provided few migrants. Latinos from other countries were also migrating, some because of the civil wars in Central and South America, and some because of economic crisis. Almost 40 percent of the Latino population in Kansas is foreign born; of those in this group, 74 percent arrived between 1990 and 2005.[34, 35] This recent period of Latino migration and growth is comparable only to the first decade of the twentieth century. New migrants grapple with established Latino communities, as they build their own.

Most migrants came to places such as Kansas City because they already had family there, and these ties cut across lines of difference. Despite that, the new migrants found communities with their own languages—not the Spanish of Mexico, but languages heavily inflected by life in the United States. To these the migrants had to acculturate, and at the same time their own languages were a force for continued Mexican culture and influence. Instead of weakening, which happened to most migrant languages, Spanish continues nourished by the substantial stream of new migrants.

Community Organization

The Latino community of Kansas faced substantial discrimination in the early part of the century. They were segregated by residence and within many public facilities—such as churches, schools, and city parks. Anglos used many arguments for separation, including supposed linguistic and racial inferiority. Anglo ideas of race did not easily fit the Latino population, which had its own categories for racial and, thus, social distinction. Nevertheless, Anglos attempted to draw racial lines in accordance with their own notions; they separated lighter-skinned Latinos, who could pass as Spanish, from darker-skinned ones, who faced racial and cultural exclusion.

Within segregated neighborhoods, community organization flourished around businesses, sports, music, dance, celebrations, and religious devotion. The Latino community encouraged the Catholic Church to provide religious and other services to the predominantly Catholic Latinos. The Church, as a result, was a central place of social existence. For example, in Topeka in 1914 the parish of Our Lady of Guadalupe was formed following a conversation between a local Latino, Pedro López, and a Spanish speaking-priest, Rev. Epifanio Ocampo. Mutual aid societies were also formed—such as the Sociedad Morelos, the first formed in the Argentine neighborhood of Kansas City—or the Sociedad Mútua Benito Juárez in Garden City. Not only did these associations assist members in times of difficulty, but they also served, along with Catholic parishes, as an organizational base for the development of civic festivals. These festivities connected Mexican culture and history, including sacred history, with the lives of Latinos in Kansas. For example, in 1917 Chanute organized its fiesta to celebrate Mexican Independence Day and the Grito de Dolores—the shout of Father Hidalgo for Mexican independence—on September 16, when it is still celebrated. The Latino community in Kansas City held a parade to celebrate September 16. In 1922 Garden City's Latino community came out in great numbers to celebrate Benito Juárez's birthday, and as a result, in 1925 they initiated a fiesta that is ongoing. In Topeka the parish organized a fiesta in August 1932 to raise funds. Now celebrated in July, this fiesta is also ongoing.

The types of organization that developed in Kansas were somewhat different from those found in many other migrant communities. Instead of associations built on common place of origin and established to provide mutual assistance, in Kansas these associations developed around the Church, in an effort to present migrants as residents of the United States and not as foreign nationals.

The fight against prejudice also led to the creation of organizations that sought change. In Kansas City, *El Cosmopolita*, a Spanish-language newspaper, was founded in 1915 with the objective of unifying the community and obtaining political and social acceptance and respect for the Mexican community.[36] In the 1920s, darker-skinned Mexican children in Kansas City faced strenuous negative reactions from Anglo parents if they tried to attend public schools, especially in the neighborhoods with a greater concentration of Mexican migrants.[37] Lighter-skinned students were often classified as Spanish, thus being allowed admission. If admitted, the Mexican students were segregated in separate classrooms. Although the Catholic Church provided education for Mexican students, the fear of enrollment of Latino youths in public schools led Anglo parents of Argentine to pressure for the formation of a segregated Mexican school. In response, the Clara Barton School, specifically created for Mexican children, opened in 1923. It lasted until destroyed by the flood of 1951 and, although segregated, it was responsible for forming generations of upwardly mobile Kansas Latinos.[38]

However, there was no high school darker-skinned Mexican children could attend in Kansas. Saturnino Alvarado, from Michoacán, Mexico, wanted his children to be educated.[39] Along with other parents in the Argentine neighborhood of Kansas City, where there was a heavy concentration of Latinos because of proximity to the rail yards, Alvarado organized and took action to demand admission to high school for all Mexican children after his two children—Luz and Jesús, along with Victorina Pérez and Marcos de León—were removed from school because of pressure from Anglo parents. At the end of a two-year struggle the activists were successful, and they had broken a major social barrier in Kansas. In 1930, Luz, Jesús, and Marcos de León graduated from Argentine High School. There had been a small number of lighter-skinned, Anglicized Latinos who had graduated prior, but these three were the first to break the color and culture barrier in Kansas City schools. But in Kansas City the barriers to discrimination in public education for Latino students would not fall completely until a decade after World War II.

In the 1960s, as the civil rights movement demanded the removal of racial barriers, the Chicano movement exploded. Although Kansas is not one of the core settlement zones where the movement originated, important events took place in Kansas, and the Chicano movement led to greater social consciousness and the formation of social and political organizations that embraced both local national and concerns. During this period local Latino communities became connected with Chicano communities and with activists in the Southwest and elsewhere. A national consciousness of Latinos as Chicano was developing, although it had to compete with other local identities.

Kansas activists participated in national Chicano events. For example, Kansans attended the National Chicano Youth Liberation Conference in Denver, Colorado, in March 1969, organized by the activist and poet Rodolfo "Corky" Gonzales.[40] From the conference came the important *Plan Espiritual de Aztlán*, which presented a plan of action for the Chicano community. Surprised by the attendance of Chicanos from Kansas, the poet Alurista is reported to have said, "I didn't know there were any Mexicans in Kansas!"[41]

The ideas that emerged from national events such as the National Youth Conference and the writings of Chicano intellectuals found fertile soil in Kansas's Latino neighborhoods. There, local intellectuals and activists put together national thinking and local concerns and issues by writing in local daily and weekly publications. These newspapers and newsletters spread a national Chicano consciousness in Kansas that was connected with local concerns.

In 1971 Latino students at the University of Kansas formed the Association of Mexican American Students. In 1974 that association was renamed Movimiento

Estudiantil Chicano de Aztlán (MEChA).[42] By this change, members signaled a connection with Chicano consciousness and political action. MEChA is a national organization that developed out of preexisting California and Texas student organizations.

Ideas of Aztlán and Chicanismo took root in another Kansas institution a bit earlier. The Federal Penitentiary in Leavenworth, Kansas, had an important group of Latino prisoners. Like Latino prisoners, known as *pintos*, in other penitentiaries, many Latino prisoners at Leavenworth developed a political and literary consciousness, thus becoming important Chicano intellectuals while behind bars. Their physical imprisonment became a metaphor for the social confinement they felt as Chicanos. At Leavenworth, a group of prisoners influenced by a range of Third-World and other radical thinkers such as Frantz Fanon and Che Guevara explored issues of racism, colonialism, class analysis, and national liberation as a basis for activism. This group included Raúl R. Salinas, Ramón Chacon, Standing Deer, and Rafael Cancel Miranda.[43]

The broad ethnic, racial, and national interests and backgrounds of these prisoners built a critical context, both national and international, for thought. The inmates also organized themselves to fight for prisoners' rights, and they took control of their education. At their request a course was taught at the prison by Francisco Ruiz, of Penn Valley Community College, in Kansas City. This course was called Cultural History of the Southwest. From this class came the newspaper *Aztlán de Leavenworth*, in which Salinas's important poem "Un Trip through the Mind Jail" was first published. The group that created *Aztlán de Leavenworth* also organized the Chicanos Organizados de Rebeldes de Aztlán (C.O.R.A.), an association that worked to ensure prisoners' rights. Like in other states, the penitentiary became a breeding ground for Chicano activists and intellectuals. The publications by the prisoners were distributed widely in the community outside the prison's walls.[44]

The 1960s and 1970s brought not only activism connected with the Chicano movement but also attempts at community organization and social justice, as well as efforts by the Latino elite to claim a place in society. In 1963 Kansas veterans began chapters of the GI Forum, a national Chicano service and advocacy organization.[45] The League of United Latin American Citizens (LULAC) started its roots in Kansas around World War II, and it became a force in the state.[46] Local organizations, such as El Centro of Kansas City, were founded as nongovernmental entities, and they began seeking federal and state funding to provide social services.

Latino-owned businesses also felt the need to have a voice in Kansas's society. As a result the Latino business owners organized Hispanic chambers of commerce. The United States Hispanic Chamber of Commerce was founded in 1977, and it was located in Kansas City, from where it later moved to Washington, DC.[47]

In 2005 Kansas City native Michael L. Barrera became president and CEO of that national organization. His father, Richard Barrera, was one of 25 businessmen who started that Kansas City organization.[48]

Latinos also began to seek elected offices in Kansas. Jim Martínez, of Hutchinson, was the first Latino elected to a city council position in 1969. In 1970 he became mayor of that city.[49] Similarly, D.C. García was elected to the Garden City Council in 1970, before becoming mayor in 1974. In 1973 Paul Feleciano was elected to the lower house of the state legislature, before becoming a state senator in 1976. Currently, there are four Latinos in the state legislature, three Democrats and one Republican. Kansas Latino elected officials are also involved in national associations of Latino elected officials.

The Kansas native Janet Murguía, who began her political life as an aide in the U.S. Congress and in the White House, is currently the executive director of the National Council of La Raza. She is one of many Kansas Latinos who occupy leadership positions in the nation's Capitol, both in government and in nongovernmental organizations. Many Kansans are found in the ranks of government and business management.

On May 1, 2006, as in other states, Kansas experienced some of the largest demonstrations in Kansas history. Migrants and those who embrace their cause walked off work to ask for migration reform. Migration and the presence of a large Spanish-speaking community have become a difficult political issue in Kansas.

In 2004 Governor Janet Sebelius signed into law legislation that enables illegal migrants who had graduated from Kansas high schools to pay in-state tuition, without being asked their immigration status. This law has, along with similar legislation in several other states, become a lightning rod for anti-immigration activists. University of Kansas law professor Kris Kobach is a prominent opponent of such legislation, calling it unconstitutional and a violation of federal law. Nonetheless, a legal challenge to the law was dismissed in July 2005, when a federal judge ruled that plaintiffs had no standing to bring suit. Several other judicial challenges to the law are still active.

Sam Brownback, a Kansas Republican senator, was chair of the Senate Subcommittee on Immigration, where he shepherded legislation supporting refugee asylum cases. Senator Brownback cosponsored in 2003 an unsuccessful piece of legislation in the Senate known as the Dream Act, which would have provided the means for resident illegal migrants to pay resident tuition at institutions of higher education. Despite his strong conservative credentials, Senator Brownback has drawn the ire of many conservatives for his support of immigration legislation.

The Kansas state legislature has also taken on immigration. Besides unsuccessful efforts to overturn the state's law guaranteeing in-state tuition for resident immigrants regardless of legal status, the legislature has considered legislation that both restricts employment and provision of government services to undocumented migrants and requires proof of citizenship to vote. In March 2007 the legislature passed HB 2140, declaring English the official language of Kansas, with a margin of 114-7 in the House and 32-8 in the Senate, which requires government agencies to only provide services or published material in English, the only exceptions being those required by federal law. Governor Kathleen Sebelius signed the law into effect on May 11, 2007.

Republican Latino Representative Mario Goico was a prominent advocate of this English-only legislation. Born in Cuba, Representative Goico argued the importance of legislation to encourage migrants to learn English. "If you want to better yourself," Goico is reported to have said, "you'd better speak the English language." Professor Phillip De La Torre, of the University of Kansas Law School, came from Spanish-speaking parents and argued that the government should not "dictate what language we speak. It seems to me we should be able to make that decision by ourselves."[50] Most Latino advocacy organizations in Kansas were opposed to the legislation.

Population

The Latino population of Kansas is a complex one. Although mostly Mexican in origin, it has grown through native births and migration. By 1970, when the U.S. census began counting Latinos, there were 46,760 Latinos that comprised 2.1 percent of the total population. By 2000 the Latino population had grown to 188,252 persons, making up 7 percent of Kansas population. The U.S. census estimates that the Latino population now constitutes 8.4 percent (224,152 people) of the total state population.[51]

The growth rate of the Latino population has been increasing. In the decade between 1970 and 1980 it grew by 31.2 percent; between 1980 and 1990, 52.7 percent; and between 1990 and 2000 it more than doubled. The growth rate has slowed down in the first half of the current decade: by 2005 the population had grown by only 19.1 percent.[52]

The Latino population has had sustained growth from child births for a long time. In 1970 the median age of the Latino population was 19.9 years of age. In 2005 that number had risen to 25 years of age, whereas that of the general population was 36.1.[53]

Although the Latino population has been present in Kansas for more than a century, it also shows the heavy influence of recent migration, with some 62 percent of the Latino population being born in the United States and 38 percent being foreign born. Of this foreign-born Latino population, the vast majority came to the United States in the 15 years between 1990 and 2005; only some 26 percent entered the United States before 1990. During the 1990s, 42 percent of Kansas's Latino foreign-born population migrated to the United States. An additional 32 percent has come in the first five years of the current decade.[54]

This migrant Latin population is heavily Spanish-speaking—95 percent of its members speak Spanish at home; 67.2 percent report they speak English less than very well; and only 28 percent claim to speak English very well. Of this foreign-born, Spanish-speaking population, 26.3 percent is linguistically isolated; they do not have someone in their households older than 14 who can speak English very well.[55]

The 18-and-older Kansas Latino population shows an unequal distribution of men and women. Whereas the general Kansas population shows a slight majority of women, 50.5 percent, the Latino population is skewed heavily toward men: 53.9 percent are men and 46 percent are women. An important reason for this is the gender imbalance among migrants: of the foreign-born population, 57 percent are men and 43 percent are women.

According to the 2000 census, the Latino population of Kansas is 85.35 percent of Mexican origin,[56] and 7.14 percent falls in the category of "Other Hispanic or Latino." The remaining 7.5 percent shows increasing diversity. Almost 3 percent of Latinos are from the Caribbean (2.07 percent Puerto Rican; 0.75 percent Cuban; and 0.01% Dominican). A similar amount (2.9 percent) are from Central America, primarily from El Salvador, and 1.77 percent are from South America, primarily from Ecuador and Brazil. In brief, the foreign-born population is 86 percent Mexican and 14 percent from elsewhere in Latin America.[57]

Between 2000 and 2005 Kansas's population declined overall by almost 1 percent.[58] Yet, during that same period the Latino population grew by 19 percent.[59] This strong Latino growth slowed the state's overall population decline. As a result the relative percentage of Latinos for many Kansas counties is increasing.

Although it was believed that Latinos began the twentieth century in Kansas with a strong connection to employment in the railroads and in agriculture, the 2005 American Community Survey reveals a different picture.[60] Only 2.5 percent of employed Latinos worked in what the census labels "farming, forestry, and fishing occupations," whereas about 8 percent are employed in transportation. Management and professional occupations now claim 15 percent of the Latino workforce. Occupations in the service, sales, and clerical, construction, and production industries claim 20, 18, 17, and 20 percent of the Latino workforce, respectively.[61]

Latinos are not evenly distributed across Kansas. The counties with the highest relative percentages of Latinos are concentrated in the state's southwest, where there used to be sugar beet cultivation in the past and where there are meatpacking plants now. In 2000 Finney and Seward counties were 43 percent and 42 percent Latino, respectively. They are followed by Ford County at 38 percent, Grant County at 35 percent, Kearny County at 27 percent, and Wyandotte County (which is part of metropolitan Kansas City) at 16 percent.[62]

The development of a professional class is an important indicator of the development of a differentiated and stratified Latino community in Kansas. In 2005 management alone claimed 6 percent of the Latino workforce, and professional occupations alone claimed 8 percent. Of the Latino managers 5 percent are farmers or farm managers; 39 percent are in financial or business operations occupations; and 56 percent are in other management occupations. Of the professions, 37 percent are in education, training, and library occupations; 21 percent are in health care or in technical occupations; 13 percent are in community and social service occupations; and 12 percent are in architecture and engineering occupations. Of the remainder, 6 percent are in computer and mathematical occupations; 5 percent are in the in the arts, design, entertainment, sports, and media occupations; 4 percent are in legal occupations; and 2 percent are in the sciences.[63]

Latinos claim a substantially smaller percentage of their population as managers and professionals than does the dominant ethnic group of Kansas's society: whereas 15 percent of Latinos are managers or professionals, 35 percent of the non-Hispanic whites occupy positions in those fields.[64]

The Latino population has less educational attainment than the general population of Kansas, which is in part due to migration. Of the population 25 years of age and older, 2 percent have a graduate degree, 7 percent have a bachelor's degree, 4 percent have an associate's degree, 13 percent have some college without attaining a degree (these are grouped with those who have a college degree, totaling 26 percent). Of the rest of the Latino population, 25 percent has less than a 9th grade education, 20 percent has attended school to the 12th grade without obtaining a diploma, and 30 percent either have a high school diploma or have passed an equivalency test.[65]

These data reveal two things: the success and mobility of the native-born Latino population, and the lower educational level of the foreign-born migrants. Of the Kansas Latinos born in Latin America, 62 percent are less than high school graduates in educational attainment; 23 percent are high school graduates or the equivalent; 10 percent have an associate's degree; 3 percent have a bachelor's degree; and 1 percent have a professional degree.

As a result, the Latino population has a lower income than the general population of Kansas (especially the non-Hispanic white population). The median household income in Kansas for 2005, in inflation adjusted dollars, was $42,920, whereas for the non-Hispanic white population it was $44,839. In contrast, the Latino population had a median household income of almost $10,000 less, at $33,167.[66]

NOTABLE LATINOS

Feleciano, Paul (1942–). Democrat Paul Feliciano was elected in 1976 to the Kansas Senate, where he served for 28 years, after being in the House of Representatives for 3 years. In 2003 he resigned from the Senate to serve on the Kansas Parole Board. Born in 1942 in New York City, Feleciano graduated with an applied arts and science degree in petroleum geology from the New York City Community College. He served in the U.S. Air Force, and he is a longtime resident of Wichita, Kansas. Feleciano is CEO and president of Global One Technologies Ltd., and he has served two terms as president of the National Hispanic Caucus of State Legislators.

Goico, Mario (1945–). Cuban-born Mario Goico is a Republican member of the Kansas State House of Representatives, representing Kansas's District 100. He was elected to his first term in 2003. Prior to running for office, Goico was a pilot in the U.S. Air Force and in the Air National Guard, where he obtained the rank of colonel. Goico served in the Desert Shield-Desert Storm War. An engineer who spent 20 years with Boeing in Wichita, Kansas, Goico also worked for Boeing and Cessna as a part-time test pilot.

Torrez, Mike (1946–). A major league baseball player born in Topeka, Kansas, Mr. Torrez is well known for playing for both the Boston Red Sox and the New York Yankees.

Ruiz, Richard (1950–). A Kansas leader, activist, businessman, and cofounder and longtime executive director of El Centro Inc., Ruiz was born and raised in Kansas City. He graduated from Rosedale High School and, after years as the executive director of El Centro, graduated with an executive master's in business administration from Rockhurst University. He was also a member of the Kansas City Council from 1984 to 1992, and vice-mayor of that city from 1988 to 1991. He received the Ohtli Award from the Mexican government for his lifelong dedication to Mexican communities in the United States.

Ruiz, Louis (1953–). Louis Ruiz was elected in 2004 to the Kansas state legislature for the 32nd District. He is the first Latino from Kansas City to be elected to the State House of Representatives. Ruiz was born in Wyandotte County, in metropolitan Kansas City, where his family had resided for three generations. Ruiz made a career initially as a technical apprentice and then as a manager at Lucent Technologies. Active in the Communication Workers of America union, Ruiz also volunteered at a range of organizations over many years. He served as vice president of the Friends of National Public Broadcasting for two terms.

Sawyer, Tom (1958–). Tom Sawyer represents Wichita, the 95th District, in the Kansas House of Representatives as a Democrat. Sawyer was born in Wichita, and he graduated from Wichita State University with a bachelor's degree in business administration. In 1987 Sawyer was elected to the Kansas state legislature, where he served as his party's House Leader, both as a majority and a minority leader. Sawyer left the House when he won his party's nomination to run for governor in 1998. Unsuccessful in that election, Sawyer became the state chairman of the Kansas Democratic Party until 2002, when he was elected again to the Kansas legislature. By profession an accountant, Sawyer is a small-business owner as well as an adjunct professor of political science at Butler State Community College.

Murguía, Janet (1961–). Janet Murguía was raised in the Argentine neighborhood of Kansas City. After receiving a law degree from the University of Kansas, Murguía worked as a legislative counsel in the U.S. Congress. She also served as a deputy assistant to the president in the White House from 1994 to 2000. In 2001 she was named executive vice chancellor for university relations at the University of Kansas. She is the executive director of the National Council of La Raza, one of the nation's most important Latino advocacy groups.

García, Delia (1977–). In 2004 Delia García became the first Latina to serve in the Kansas state legislature. She is also the youngest woman ever elected to that body. García is a Democrat in the 103rd legislative District in Wichita, where she was born and raised in a family that started a restaurant. García graduated from Wichita State University and obtained a master's degree in political science from St. Mary's University, in San Antonio, Texas. García is also an adjunct professor of political science at Butler County Community College.

CULTURAL CONTRIBUTIONS

Massive public festivals—such as Topeka's Fiesta Mexicana, Garden City's Mexican Fiesta, and greater Kansas City's Hispanic Fiesta—are the most visible Latino contribution to Kansas's culture. These festivities are both social engines generating other contributions as well as consequences of a complex social history. They bring together hundreds of thousands of Kansans of diverse background to celebrate and experience an increasingly codified Latino culture in the United States; at the same time they are a source of pride and tradition for Kansas's Latino society.

These mass festivals are driven, in part, by trends for the celebration of ethnic diversity—as part of the visible and public culture of North American life and ideology—as well as the national trend towards the Cinco de Mayo (May 5) as the paradigmatic day of Latino festivals.[67] They also have roots that go deep into local communities. Mexicans who migrated to Kansas in the early twentieth century found themselves living near people who were both from their local communities of origin and from elsewhere. As people recreated their culture in Kansas, they found that they could not recreate the public, primarily religious, culture of fiestas and processions of their hometowns and villages because those are deeply tied to place.[68] As a result they developed more neutral public festivities, either in the local parish or during civic festivals celebrating Mexican national life. These local festivals provided people with community solidarity, a public presence, and the possibility of representing their community identity and culture to themselves and outsiders.[69] The festivities also delimited and made concrete a Mexican culture that could become a tradition and that could be preserved in the give-and-take of migrant life.

These public representations of concrete culture have spread to members of the broader Kansas's society in part through the fiestas. They now know and consume Mexican food and enjoy folk dance, arts, and music. In addition, the festivities developed and maintained a Kansas public culture of Latino identity into

Mexican Band, Wichita. Organizer and Director, Prof. A. De La Mara, 1924. Courtesy of Wichita-Sedgwick County Historical Museum.

which subsequent waves of migrants have been assimilated. At the same time these celebrations connect migrants with touring Latino performers and nationally recognized Latino identities.

NOTES

1. Vigil, Kaye, and Wunder, 1994.
2. Vehik, 2002.
3. Simmons, 1991.
4. Wedel, 1959, 424–468.
5. Weber, 1994.
6. Dary, 2002, 55–73.
7. Joseph Sanchez, 1997.
8. Moody, 1921, 121–153.
9. C.f. O'Brien, 1977.
10. Dale, 1960.
11. Clayton, Hoy, and Underwood, 2001.
12. Paredes, 1970, 228
13. Paredes, 1995, 140.
14. Peña, 1992, 191–225.
15. Ávila, 1997.

16. Mines, 1980.
17. Openheimer, 1985.
18. Openheimer, 1985, 431.
19. Openheimer, 1985, 431.
20. Openheimer, 1985, 431.
21. Ávila, 1997; Valerie Mendoza, 1997; Smith, 1989.
22. Smith, 1990.
23. Suarez Montero, 2006.
24. Openheimer, 1985.
25. Rivera, 1991.
26. Jiménez, 2005.
27. Ávila, 1997.
28. U.S. census, 2005.
29. Stull, 1990.
30. Benson, 1994.
31. Fredricksen, 2001.
32. Fredricksen, 2001.
33. Ramos, 1998.
34. U.S. census, 2005.
35. U.S. census, 2005.
36. Smith, 1990.
37. Cleary, 1981.
38. Cleary, 1981
39. Mary Sanchez, 2003.
40. Valerie Mendoza, 2000.
41. Valerie Mendoza, 2000.
42. HALO, 2007.
43. Louis Mendoza, 2006.
44. Louis Mendoza, 2003.
45. C.f. Ramos, 1998.
46. Gutierrez, 1995, 78; Navarro 2005, 208.
47. Maurilio Vigil, 1987, 129.
48. Cardinal, 2005.
49. Chacon, 1978, 111.
50. Quoted in James Carlson, "English-only Legislation Inspiring Heated Opposition," *Topeka Capital-Journal,* March 8, 2007.
51. 2005 American Community Survey.
52. Calculated on the basis of data from www.census.gov for the respective years.
53. U.S. census, 2005.
54. Calculated on basis of data from www.census.gov.
55. U.S. census, 2005.
56. U.S. census, 2000.
57. U.S. census, 2005.
58. U.S. census, 2000, 2005.

59. U.S. census, 2000, 2005.
60. U.S. census, 2005.
61. U.S. census, 2005.
62. U.S. census, 2000.
63. U.S. census, 2005.
64. U.S. census, 2005.
65. U.S. census, 2005.
66. U.S. census, 2005.
67. Carlson, 1998.
68. C.f. Williams and Fortuny, 2007.
69. Openheimer, 1985, 16, 19.

BIBLIOGRAPHY

Ávila, Henry J. "Immigration and Integration: The Mexican American Community in Garden City, Kansas, 1900–1950." *Kansas History: A Journal of the Central Plains* 20, no. 1 (1997): 22–37.

Benson, Janet E. "Staying Alive: Economic Strategies among Immigrant Packing Plant Workers in Three Southwest Kansas Communities." *Kansas Quarterly* 25, no. 2 (1994): 107–120.

Cardinal, Carmen. "Kansas City Leader Named as Head of National Hispanic Chamber." *Dos Mundos* 26, no. 25 (2005): 1, 2.

Carlson, Alvar. "America's Growing Observance of Cinco de Mayo." *Journal of American Culture* 21, no. 2 (1998): 7–16.

Chacón, José Andrés. *Hispanic Notables in the United States*. Phoenix, AZ: Saguaro Publications, 1978.

Clayton, Leonard, Jim Hoy, and Jerald Underwood. *Vaqueros, Cowboys, and Buckaroos: The Genesis and Life of the Mounted American Herders*. Austin: University of Texas Press, 2001.

Cleary, Robert M. "The Education of Mexican-Americans in Kansas City, Kansas 1916–1951." Master's thesis, University of Missouri at Kansas City, 1981.

Dale, Edward E. *The Range Cattle Industry: Ranching on the Great Plains from 1865 to 1925*. Norman: University of Oklahoma Press, 1960.

Dary, David. *The Santa Fe Trail: Its History, Legends, and Lore*. New York: Penguin, 2002.

Fredricksen, Lin. "'Fiesta, Kansas Style': A Moment in Time." Kansas State Historical Society, 2001. http://www.kshs.org/features/feat901.htm (accessed April 3, 2008).

Gutierrez, David G. *Walls and Mirrors: Mexican American Immigrants and the Politics of Ethnicity*. Berkeley: University of California Press, 1995.

HALO. "History: AMAS/MECHA/HALO." 2007. http://groups.ku.edu/~halo/history.html (accessed April 4, 2008).

Jiménez, Tomás R. "Immigrant Replenishment and the Continuing Significance of Ethnicity and Race: The Case of Mexican-Origin Population." Working paper 130. University of California, Center for Comparative Immigration Studies, San Diego, 2005.

Laird, Judith Fincher. "Argentine, Kansas: The Evolution of a Mexican American Community, 1905–1940." PhD diss., University of Kansas, 1975.

Mendoza, Louis. "The Re-Education of a Xicanindio: Raul Salinas and the Poetics of Pinto Transformation." *MELUS* 28, no. 1 (2003): 39–60.

———. "Raul Salinas and the Poetics of Human Transformation." In *Raúlrsalinas and the Jail Machine: My Weapon is My Pen.* Ed. Louis Mendoza. Austin: University of Texas Press, 2006, 3–30.

Mendoza, Valerie. *The Creation of a Mexican Immigrant Community in Kansas City: 1890–1930.* Berkeley: University of California Press, 1997.

———. Review of "Chicano! History of the Mexican American Civil Rights Movement." *Journal for MultiMedia History* 3 (2000). http://www.albany.edu/jmmh/vol3/chicano/chicano.html (accessed May 8, 2007).

Mines, Cynthia. "Riding the Rails to Kansas: The Mexican Immigrants." PhD diss., University of Kansas, 1980.

Moody, John. *The Railroad Builders: A Chronicle of the Welding of the States.* New Haven, CT: Yale University Press, 1921.

Navarro, Armando. *Mexicano Political Experience in Occupied Aztlán: Struggles and Change.* Walnut Creek, CA: Rowman Altamira, 2005.

O'Brien, Patrick. *The New Economic History of the Railways.* New York: St. Martin's Press. 1977.

Openheimer, Robert. "Acculturation or Assimilation: Mexican Immigrants in Kansas, 1900 to World War II." *Western Historical Quarterly* 16, no. 4 (1985): 429–449.

Ortiz, Leonard David. "La Voz de la Gente: Chicano Activist Publications in the Kansas City Area, 1968–1989." *Kansas History: A Journal of the Central Plains* 22, no. 3 (1999): 228–244.

Paredes, Américo. "*With His Pistol in His Hand*": *A Border Ballad and Its Hero.* Austin: University of Texas Press, 1958.

———. *Folklore and Culture on the Texas-Mexican Border.* Austin: University of Texas Press, 1995.

Peña, Manuel. "Música Fronteriza: Border Music." *Aztlán: A Journal of Chicano Studies* 21, nos. 1–2 (1992): 191–225.

Ramos, Henry. *The American G.I. Forum: In Pursuit of the Dream.* Houston, TX: Arte Público Press, 1988.

Rivera, Tomás. *y no se lo tragó la tierra/ And the Earth Did Not Devour Him.* Houston, TX: Arte Público Press, 1991.

Sanchez, Joseph P. *Explorers, Traders, and Slavers; Forging the Old Spanish Trail, 1678–1850.* Salt Lake City: University of Utah Press, 1997.

Sanchez, Mary. "KCK School to Salute Pioneering Parent." *Kansas City Star,* August 31, 2003. http://www.kckps.org/DISTHISTORY/dist-history/bios/arg-salvarado.html (accessed April 4, 2008).

Santillan, Richard. "Saving Private Jose: Midwestern Mexican American Men during World War II." 2001. http://www.csupomona.edu/~jis/2001/Santiallan.pdf (accessed April 3, 2008).

Simmons, Marc. *The Last Conquistador: Juan de Oñate and the Settling of the Far Southwest.* Norman: University of Oklahoma Press, 1991.

Smith, Michael M. "Mexicans in Kansas City: The First Generation, 1900–1920." *Perspectives in Mexican American Studies* 2 (1989): 29–57.

———. "The Mexican Immigrant Press beyond the Borderlands: The Case of El Cosmopolita, 1914–1919." *Great Plains Quarterly* 10, no. 2 (1990): 71–85.

Stanley, Kathleen. "Immigrant and Refugee Workers in the Midwestern Meatpacking Industry: Industrial Restructuring and the Transformation of Rural Labor Markets." *Review of Policy Research* 11, no. 2 (1992): 106–117.

Stull, Donald D. "I Came to the Garden: Changing Ethnic Relation in Garden City, Kansas." *Urban Anthropology* 19 (1990): 303–320.

Suárez Montero, Natalia. "El medioeste de Estados Unidos como una opción novedosa para la inmigración mexicana: los casos de Kansas y Missouri." Master's thesis. Universidad de las Américas, Puebla, México, 2006. http://catarina.udlap.mx/u_dl_a/tales/documentos/lri/suarez_m_n (accessed April 3, 2008).

United States Census, 2000. http://www.census.gov (accessed July 25, 2007).

United States Census, 2005. American Community Survey. http://www.census.gov (accessed July 25, 2007).

Vehik, Susan C. "Conflict, Trade, and Political Development on the Southern Plains." *American Antiquity* 67, no. 1 (2002): 37–64.

Vigil, Maurilio E. *Hispanics in American Politics: The Search for Political Power.* Lanham, MD: University Press of America, 1987.

Vigil, Ralph H., Frances W. Kaye, and John R. Wunder, eds. *Spain and the Plains: Myths and Realities of Spanish Exploration and Settlement on the Great Plains.* Boulder: University Press of Colorado, 1994.

Weber, David. *The Spanish Frontier in North America.* New Haven, CT: Yale University Press, 1994.

Wedel, Waldo R. *An Introduction to Kansas Archeology.* Washington, DC: United States Government Printing Office, 1959.

Williams, Philip J., and Patricia Fortuny Loret de Mola. "Religion and Social Capital among Mexican Immigrants in Southwest Florida." *Latino Studies* 5 (2007): 233–253.

18

Kentucky

Todd Hartch

CHRONOLOGY

1780s	Western Kentuckians move across the Mississippi River into Spanish Louisiana.
1787–1797	Spanish officials in New Orleans plot to detach Kentucky from the United States and to align it with Spain.
1822	Charles Todd, the original "Kentucky Colonel," is sent by the U.S. State Department to extend recognition to the newly independent nation of Colombia.
1823	Richard Anderson of Kentucky becomes the first minister plenipotentiary to Colombia, establishing the first U.S. legation to Spanish America.
1823–1829	As a U.S. Representative, Henry Clay plays a major role in the 1823 decision by the United States to recognize the independence of Brazil (the United States was the first nation to do so). As Secretary of State (1825–1829) he continued supporting Latin American independence.
1850	Kentucky filibusters under Cuban General Narciso López briefly invade Cuba.
1864–1865	William Preston of Louisville serves as the Confederacy's envoy to Mexico and plans to bring Confederate settlers to Mexico.
1918	Latino soldiers in the U.S. Army arrive at Fort Knox, near Louisville.
1950s	Students from Latin America begin to attend the University of Louisville in appreciable numbers.
1953	Henry Moreno (Mexican American) rides Dark Star to victory in the Kentucky Derby.

1956	Cuban investors purchase the Louisville Colonels, a minor league baseball team.
1958	Jockey Ismael Valenzuela (Mexican American) rides Tim Tam to victory in the Kentucky Derby. (He also rode a Derby winner in 1968.)
1960s	Cuban migrants arrive in Louisville.
1963	Cubans in Louisville erect a monument to José Martí in Shively Park.
1970s	The Latin American Club of Louisville is founded by Fortuna Gordon and Miguel Lagunas.
1980s	Mexican and Central American migrants begin working in tobacco, equine, and other agricultural enterprises.
2005	Latinos constitute 2 percent of the state population. The federal tobacco buyout pushes many Latinos out of agricultural labor and into urban service and industrial work.
2006	Approximately 5,500 Latinos demonstrate at the capitol in Frankfort for immigrant rights.

HISTORICAL OVERVIEW

Esteban Rodríguez Miró is not a household name in Kentucky, but if that Spanish governor of New Orleans's plans had succeeded, Kentucky might have seceded from the United States. Between 1787 and 1797 Rodríguez Miró and Lexington resident James Wilkinson, a general during the American Revolution, plotted with influential Kentuckians and with Spanish officials to detach Kentucky from the United States and to align it with Spain as a colony or a friendly independent nation. These plans resulted in little more than public scandal when Wilkinson exposed some of his fellow conspirators, but they do highlight the surprising fact that for four decades Kentucky bordered Latin America. During the years between 1763 and 1800, when Spain controlled the Louisiana territories, Kentuckians looked to Spanish officials in New Orleans as possible allies, and they could enter Spanish territory by crossing the Mississippi River from western Kentucky into what is today the state of Missouri. Some Kentucky trappers traveled into Spanish territory as far west as the Rio Grande in New Mexico, causing considerable notice in Taos with their overpowering stench. There was also some concern that many Kentuckians would be tempted to emigrate into Spanish territory and even a rumor that soldier and frontiersman George Rogers Clark had fallen in love with the daughter of Fernando de Leyba, the governor of upper Louisiana. But that era when Kentucky was on the forefront of Anglo-Latino relations soon faded as the Louisiana territory was transferred to France and then sold to the United States in 1803.

Instead of being on the frontier, Kentucky now found itself in the center of the nation—and Latinos would not show any great interest in the state for more than a century. The only significant way in which Kentucky engaged Latin America in the rest of the nineteenth century was through the actions of national politicians from Kentucky—such as Charles Todd, Richard Anderson, and Henry Clay—who figured prominently in the decisions of the United States to recognize and support newly independent Latin American nations between 1822 and 1826.

In fact, during the nineteenth century, there may have been more migration from Kentucky to Latin America than from Latin America to Kentucky. In 1865 Confederate General William Preston of Kentucky helped to organize a group of despairing Confederate generals, governors, and soldiers who attempted to start a settlement in Mexico. Almost all of the would-be settlers, who included at least three Kentuckians, had returned to the United States by 1867. Some Kentuckians also emigrated to Brazil, and they seem to have been more successful in adapting to their new culture.

Throughout the nineteenth century few parts of the United States had a lower Latino population than Kentucky. It simply had few industrial or agricultural draws; and what it did have was easily equaled by states that were much more accessible. In fact, the Latino presence in Kentucky was so minimal until recent years (unless one counts the Malungeons, a dark-skinned Appalachian population supposed by some to have Portuguese origins) that, other than in reference to the eighteenth-century intrigues mentioned above, a self-styled "new" history of Kentucky published in 1997 makes only one mention of Latinos, and that to say that there were "almost none" in the state.[1] Unlike much of the rest of the country, which was absorbing millions of migrants in the late nineteenth and early twentieth centuries, Kentucky attracted few newcomers. Some German and Irish migrants arrived in northern Kentucky and Louisville, and a few others went to the Appalachian mining region, but the migration to the north of many blacks in search of industrial jobs meant that the state became more ethnically homogenous during this period.

In Kentucky the civil rights struggles of the 1950s and 1960s were almost entirely a black-white issue. About the only Latino role in the struggle occurred in 1956, when a group of Cuban investors bought the Louisville Colonels, a minor league baseball team. The new owners fielded a team of black and white ballplayers and simultaneously tried to integrate the seating for fans in the Colonels' stadium. This gambit outraged many local whites and proved financially disastrous for the investors.

Everything changed in the late 1980s, when Mexican migrants began heading to states far from the Mexican border, including Georgia, New York, and Kentucky. For Kentucky, this trend increased dramatically in the late 1990s and early 2000s, especially in the Lexington and Louisville areas, the two major metropolitan areas in the state. In the 1990s single male Latino migrants—the large majority from Mexico (especially from the states of Durango, Michoacán, and Veracruz, and more recently, Oaxaca), and many also from Central America—increased their presence, working in tobacco farming, horse farms, and light industry. This influx of Latinos, many of whom came up the interstate highways in long haul trucks before transferring to smaller vehicles in Tennessee and Missouri, changed the labor demographics of Kentucky. Most notably, by 2002 80 percent of the workers on the famous horse farms in the Bluegrass area were Latinos.[2]

The Tobacco Transition Payment program (federal tobacco "buyout") in 2005 could have reduced the state's Latino population, as tobacco work was the initial draw for many Latinos. Many tobacco farmers accepted the buyout and traded tobacco for other less labor-intensive crops. However, even before the buyout, Latinos had begun to enter the urban service sector, particularly restaurants, in large numbers. The buyout did not begin this process, but it did hasten the transition of Kentucky Latinos from a largely rural to a largely urban population.

The growing Latino presence in Kentucky influenced policing in the state's two major cities. In 1994 Assistant Chief Fran Root began to take notice of the increased Latino presence in Lexington and of the growing communication problems that ensued when officers interacted with Spanish speakers. Root discovered that few cities anywhere were doing anything noteworthy to respond to larger Latino populations and that the police department would have to innovate. In 1999 the department began a partnership with the Kentucky Institute for International Studies (a consortium of university summer study programs) to send officers to Morelia, Mexico, for language and cultural training and for an exchange with Morelia's police.

Eventually, the program included 18 credit hours of college-level Spanish classes given in Lexington, followed by an additional 6 credit hours for those who completed the five-week immersion course in Morelia. The Spanish courses and the Morelia program won a 2002 award from a police association, and they have created a growing number of Spanish-speaking police officers who have been successful in connecting with Lexington's Latinos. In 2006 Louisville began a similar program for judges, county and state attorneys, and public defenders. Despite these innovations, Latinos still face serious hurdles in the justice system because of their undocumented status and the insufficient number of Spanish interpreters.

Other changes between 2000 and 2007 included more Latinos coming to Kentucky from other locations in the United States, such as Chicago and California, rather than directly from Latin America, because of safety concerns in those areas and the strong labor market in Kentucky. Another change was the gradual increase in the number of Latino families, as more families migrated together, and more women and children joined men already in the area. Counterintuitively, the larger presence of Latino women and children was probably a result of stricter enforcement at the United States–Mexico border: migrants could no longer depend on multiple crossings each year, and therefore they decided to unite their families in the north.

The rising number of families also raised issues about the children of undocumented migrants, many of whom had lived in Kentucky and attended local public schools for years by 2000. Without Social Security numbers they could not attend public universities in the state or apply for most financial aid programs. Because they had no great prospect of going to college, many dropped out of high school; especially in the years after 2001 some of these dropouts began to join groups of other disaffected youths. Los Angeles–style gangs had not yet entered the Bluegrass State, but clearly the potential existed. One bright spot for undocumented youths was the Bluegrass Community and Technical College (BCTC) in Lexington, which publicized an explicit policy of opening its doors to undocumented migrants in 2004, which led to an enrollment of more than 200 Latino students in 2007.[3] A 2004 state law and a 2005 administrative regulation of the state Council on Postsecondary Education made official the policy that undocumented graduates of Kentucky high schools would be treated as state residents eligible for in-state tuition at state colleges and universities. Four-year institutions then opened their doors to Latinos, with nine attending Kentucky State University and 120 at Northern Kentucky University in 2005. Both four-year institutions joined with BCTC in actively recruiting Latino students through the newly formed organization Educating Latinos for Kentucky's Future.

With at least 65,000 Latinos in the state according to the Pew Hispanic Center and more than 83,000 according to the U.S. Census Bureau, by 2005 Latinos made up between 1.5 percent and 2 percent of the state's population.[4]

With the majority of these Latinos living in Lexington, Louisville, and the Cincinnati suburbs, it might be expected that Latinos would have started to come into their own politically. However, because of the large percentage of undocumented migrants in the state's Latino population, in the period between 2000 and 2007 they found themselves an increasingly visible minority group that lacked even the beginnings of political power.[5] Without official documentation, the majority of Kentucky Latinos found themselves in a difficult and often dangerous legal twilight. Without the right to vote, most Latinos had little traction with local officials; without residency papers, many feared going to the police when they were attacked or threatened; and many were victimized because of their perceived vulnerability.

Latinos had begun lobbying the municipal and state governments for recognition and support in the late 1990s. In Lexington, the Lexington Hispanic Association/Asociación de Hispanos Unidos (AHU) and the Kentucky Migrant Network Coalition attracted the attention of the Lexington-Fayette Urban County Government in 1998. Mayor Pam Miller appointed the Lexington Hispanic Labor Task Force and followed its recommendations in hiring Abdón Ibarra as the city's first liaison to the growing Latino population and in helping to fund a new Hispanic Initiative Network (HIN). The HIN was able to provide bilingual social workers and translators for Latino patients in the health care system, but its grant money dried up after three years, in 2003.

The most impressive political action by Kentucky Latinos occurred in 2006, when a new organization, the Kentucky Coalition for Comprehensive Immigration Reform, organized thousands of Kentucky Latinos to take part in the National Day of Action for Immigration Rights on April 10. Organizer Freddy Peralta, who collected signatures from 5,500 Latinos (a significant percentage of the total Kentucky Latino population) at the rally, saw it as a turning point in the struggle for immigrant rights and evidence of heightened political will among Kentucky's Latinos. He seems to have been correct, for local politicians soon felt compelled to take stands on various immigrant issues.[6]

NOTABLE LATINOS

Cardenal, Ernesto (1925–). The Nicaraguan priest and poet spent some of his formative years at a Kentucky monastery. After supporting a failed revolt against dictator Anastasio Somoza in 1954, he left his country to join the Gethsemani Trappist monastery, south of Louisville, in 1957. At Gethsemani, Cardenal was mentored by Novice Master Thomas Merton, the renowned Roman Catholic author and poet. Merton and Cardenal developed a close relationship during Cardenal's three years in Kentucky. Cardenal considered Merton a lifelong influence; Merton tried unsuccessfully to gain permission from his abbot to found a new monastic community with Cardenal in Latin America. In addition to his continued work as a poet and a Roman Catholic priest, Cardenal founded the liberation theology–influenced community of Solentiname, in Nicaragua, and he served as the country's minister of culture from 1979 to 1987, during the Sandinista government of Daniel Ortega.

Lagunas, Miguel (1938–). The founder or cofounder of all major Latino organizations in Louisville migrated from Mexico City in 1956. He spent three years in the U.S. Army during the 1960s, graduated from the University of Louisville in 1969 with a degree in electrical engineering, and then worked for Louisville Gas and Electric until 1996. In the 1970s Lagunas emerged as the most important Latino leader in Louisville, eventually founding or helping to found all major Latino organizations in the city, including the Hispanic Business Association, Adelante Hispanic Achievers, El Club Latinoamericano de Louisville, the Hispano/Latino Coalition, the Liga Deportiva Latinoamericana, and the Police Academy for Hispanic Citizens. Since his retirement he has devoted his time to Latino charities and organizations in Louisville.

Cova, Antonio Rafael de la (1950–). Author of *Cuban Confederate Colonel: The Life of Ambrosio José Gonzales* and *The Moncada Attack: Birth of the Cuban Revolution*, de la Cova is Kentucky's most prominent Latino scholar. Born in Havana, de la Cova came to Louisville with his family and other Cuban refugees in 1963 and attended Butler High School. He has devoted his scholarly career to the complex relationships between Latin America, especially Cuba, and the United States. He has unearthed almost all there is known about the more than 260 Kentucky filibusters who invaded Cuba in 1850 under General Narciso López to end Spanish colonial rule. De la Cova has a PhD from West Virginia University, and he has taught Latin American and Latino history at the Rose-Hulman Institute and at Indiana University. In 2006 he was awarded the Annual Fellowship of the Kentucky Historical Society. He maintains a leading Web site for Latin American and Latino studies, "Latino Studies Resources" at http://www.latinamericanstudies.org/home2.htm.

Rodríguez, Glenn (c. 1950–). Rodríguez is the dean of Kentucky Campuses of McKendree College and a popular speaker on workplace diversity. He attained an MBA from Marshall University and a PhD in educational administration from the University of Louisville. As director of Papa John's Pizza in Latin America, he opened more than 80 new restaurants in several nations. Starting as an adjunct instructor in 1999, he worked his way to the top of McKendree College's Kentucky operations by 2005. The native of Puerto Rico also rose to the rank of lieutenant colonel in the Army Reserve.

Guzmán, Lila. (1952–). The author of children's literature books about Latinos earned her bachelor's degree at Western Kentucky University and her PhD at the University of Kentucky. Her series of historical novels on Lorenzo Bannister traces the considerable contributions of Latinos and Spaniards to the American Revolution. The Lexington native has also written biographies of famous Latinos and Latin Americans, including Frida Kahlo, Elena Ochoa, and Roberto Clemente.

Miranda, Marta (1954–). Miranda led the struggle for immigrant rights in Lexington from the late 1990s until 2005. After leaving Cuba at age 12, Miranda moved to New Jersey and then to southern Florida, where she earned a master's degree in social work from Barry University. Miranda came to Kentucky, which reminds her of rural Cuba, in

1990, and she has taught social work at Eastern Kentucky University since 1993. She organized the campaign for immigrant rights in Lexington in the period between 2000 and 2005. Since 2005 Miranda has served as the director of the Women's Studies program at Eastern Kentucky University.

García, Francisco (1981–). The University of Louisville basketball star was born in the Dominican Republic and raised in the Bronx. After arriving in Louisville in 2002, García's 16.4 points per game in the 2003–2004 season and 15.7 in the next season made him for a time one of the most prominent figures in Kentucky, a basketball-obsessed state with no major professional sports teams. After leading his team to the 2005 NCAA Final Four, García was drafted in the first round by the Sacramento Kings of the National Basketball Association.

CULTURAL CONTRIBUTIONS

As a border state between North and South that stretches from Appalachia to the Mississippi River, Kentucky has long had a complex and multifaceted culture that has been called southern, northern, midwestern, and western and that is probably best seen as a mixture. The arrival of large numbers of Latinos in the 1990s made the issue of culture even more complex. Much changed, most obviously in the arrival of Spanish as a second major media language: by 2007 Kentucky boasted eight Spanish-language newspapers and five Spanish-language radio stations. Mexican restaurants and grocery stores and Latin night clubs also changed the commercial landscape of not only the major cities but the smaller ones as well. Although many Kentuckians continued to see culture in terms of traditional categories such as the black-white racial dichotomy or of a regional perspective that, for instance, contrasted Appalachia with the Bluegrass, Latinos changed the whole equation.

Latino migration revitalized and transformed the Roman Catholic Church in the state. By 2003, 29 Kentucky parishes were offering masses in Spanish, and several urban churches had become predominantly Latino. St. Rita Catholic Church in Louisville, for example, became a center of Mexican-style religious devotion. Festivals in honor of the Day of the Dead and the Virgin of Guadalupe attracted hundreds of worshipers and brought media attention, not just in Louisville and Lexington but in smaller towns across the state. Meanwhile, Latino Protestant churches also sprang up throughout the state, including sixty Baptist, seven Assemblies of God, and dozens of independent Pentecostal congregations.

As in many parts of the country, Latinos in Louisville, Lexington, Shelbyville, and several other cities created soccer leagues that have become de facto Latino social networks. Less traditionally, the Las Americas baseball league of Lexington, started by Puerto Rican Omar Quintero in 1998, was the only adult hardball league in the city and therefore served non-Latinos who could not play the game anywhere else. Non-Latinos also responded enthusiastically to the annual Festival Latino de Lexington, which was attracting several thousand people by 2006.

Dance is the art most influenced by Latinos in Kentucky. In the 1990s, a number of Cuban migrants and Cuban Americans joined the Lexington Ballet, which closed in 1998 due to financial problems. Two of the Cuban dancers, Norbe Risco and Rafaela Cento Muñoz, formed a new company, the Kentucky Ballet Theatre, which featured four Cubans in leading roles. Dancer Orlando Viamontes extended the company's community impact by giving free salsa lessons at the public library in 2006. Mexicans also have contributed to dance in the state. Adalhi Aranda Corn founded and directed the Bluegrass Youth Ballet and choreographed a special Day of the Dead show in 2006. The Arcoiris dance group of Louisville performed its "Mexican Ballet Folclórico" piece 33 times in various locations around Kentucky and Indiana in 2006.

Churchill Downs, home of the state's most important sporting event, the Kentucky Derby, stands as an epitome of the profound cultural changes that Latinos have brought to Kentucky. Although the traditions of mint juleps and derby bonnets still prevail in the stands, behind the scenes is the track's "backside." There, hundreds of Latinos work and live; Spanish is the most common language; Mexican music wafts through the dormitories; worship services are held in Spanish; and so many are interested in soccer that there are entire leagues for track employees. In other words, at the heart of a Kentucky institution, perhaps *the* Kentucky institution, Latinos and Latino culture are increasingly evident and important.

NOTES

1. Harrison and Klotter, 1997, 437.
2. Kentucky Legislative Research Commission, "Immigration in Kentucky: A Preliminary Description," Research report No. 305 (Frankfort: Kentucky State Government, 2002), cited in Brian L. Rich and Marta Miranda, "The Sociopolitical Dynamics of Mexican Immigration in Lexington, Kentucky, 1997–2002: An Ambivalent Community Responds," in *New Destinations: Mexican Immigration in the United States*, eds. Victor Zuñiga and Rubén Hernández-León, (New York: Russell Sage Foundation, 2005), 214.
3. "Ky. College Reaches Out to Hispanic Students," Community College Week, May 24, 2004; Erin Howard, personal communication, March 23, 2007.
4. Pew Hispanic Center, "A Statistical Portrait of Hispanics at Mid-Decade, Table 10, Hispanic Population by State: 2000 and 2005," September 18, 2006, http://pewhispanic.org/reports/middecade/; U.S. Census Bureau, "Kentucky QuickFacts," January 12, 2007; http://quickfacts.census.gov/qfd/states/21000.html.
5. The Pew Hispanic Center estimated only 20,000 to 30,000 undocumented Hispanics in Kentucky in 2005 in Jeffrey Passel, "Estimates of the Size and Characteristics of the Undocumented Population," March 21, 2005, http://pewhispanic.org/files/reports/44.pdf, but other experts put the numbers much higher: Peter Laufer, "My New Kentucky Home," *Washington Monthly* 37, nos. 1–2 (January–February 2005): 26.

6. Steve Lannen and Todd Van Campen, "Thousands Rally Downtown: Protest Asserts Immigrant Rights, Opposes House Bill," *Lexington Herald-Leader,* April 11, 2006.

7. Peter Smith, "Faith Matters," *Courier-Journal* (Louisville), September 7, 2003.

8. Frank Lockwood, "My New Kentucky Home: Latino Workers Create a Community at Churchill," *Lexington Herald-Leader,* April 30, 2003.

BIBLIOGRAPHY

Allen, S.D. "More on the Free Black Populations of the Southern Appalachian Mountains: Speculation on the North African Connection." *Journal of Black Studies* 25, no. 6 (July 1995): 651–671.

Barrouquere, Brett. "Attorneys, Judges to Enter Spanish-Language Program." *Lexington Herald-Leader,* December 21, 2006.

Community College Week. "Ky. College Reaches Out to Hispanic Students." May 24, 2004.

Copley, Rich. "Dancing Life's Pas de Deux: We Love Ballet. We Love Each Other." *Lexington Herald-Leader,* February 8, 2004.

Council on Postsecondary Education. "Minutes." March 21, 2005. http://cpe.ky.gov/NR/rdonlyres/CE352A60-B836-4971-8851-00D7E27A06A2/0/32105CPE.pdf.

Cova, Antonio Rafael de la. "The Kentucky Regiment That Invaded Cuba in 1850." Forthcoming from the Register of the Kentucky Historical Society.

Cruz, Andrés. Interview. February 23, 2007.

Donís, José Neal. Interview. March 5, 2007.

Harrison, Lowell H., and James C. Klotter. *A New History of Kentucky.* Lexington: University Press of Kentucky, 1997.

Kentucky Legislative Research Commission. "Immigration in Kentucky: A Preliminary Description." Research report no. 305. Frankfort: Kentucky State Government, 2002.

Kentucky State University. "Common Data Set, 2005–2006." http://www.kysu.edu/about_ksu/president/oire/CDS_2005_2006.pdf.

Kleber, John, ed. *The Encyclopedia of Louisville.* Lexington: University Press of Kentucky, 2001.

Lagunas, Miguel. "Latin Americans." In *The Encyclopedia of Louisville.* Ed. John Kleber. Lexington: University Press of Kentucky, 2001, 500–501.

———. Interview. March 5, 2007.

Lannen, Steve. "Lexington Police Honored for Language Course." *Lexington Herald-Leader,* October 7, 2002.

———. "Who Speaks for Hispanics?" *Lexington Herald-Leader,* November 28, 2005.

Lannen, Steve, and Todd Van Campen. "Thousands Rally Downtown: Protest Asserts Immigrant Rights, Opposes House Bill." *Lexington Herald-Leader,* April 11, 2006.

Laufer, Peter. "My New Kentucky Home." *Washington Monthly* 37, nos. 1–2 (January–February 2005): 22–27.

Lexington Division of Police. 2005 Annual Report. www.lexingtonpolice.lfucg.com/PDFs/AR05%20web.pdf.

Lexington Herald-Leader. "Ancient Tradition is a Unique Way to Celebrate Loved Ones." November 3, 2006.

Lockwood, Frank E. "My New Kentucky Home: Latino Workers Create a Community at Churchill." *Lexington Herald-Leader*, April 30, 2003.

Marshall, William. "Baseball, Professional." In *The Encyclopedia of Louisville*. Ed. John Kleber. Lexington: University Press of Kentucky, 2001, 70–73.

Martin, Ernie Lee, and Joy Flynn, prods. "The Confederados." Kentucky Life, Program 822. Kentucky Educational Television. June 2002. One DVD.

Mateo, Darhiana M. "Dance Troupe in Demand." *The Courier-Journal* (Louisville), May 2, 2007.

Northern Kentucky University. "Common Data Set, 2005–2006." http://www.nku.edu/~oir/CDS/2005-2006/CDS_2005_06picsforwebpage_July25.pdf.

Novas, Himilce. *Everything You Need to Know about Latino History*. New York: Plume, 1994.

Passel, Jeffrey. "Estimates of the Size and Characteristics of the Undocumented Population." March 21, 2005. http://pewhispanic.org/files/reports/44.pdf

Pew Hispanic Center. "A Statistical Portrait of Hispanics at Mid-Decade, Table 10. Hispanic Population by State: 2000 and 2005." September 18, 2006. http://pewhispanic.org/reports/middecade/.

Rich, Brian L., and Marta Miranda. "The Sociopolitical Dynamics of Mexican Immigration in Lexington, Kentucky, 1997–2002: An Ambivalent Community Responds." In *New Destinations: Mexican Immigration in the United States*. Eds. Victor Zuñiga and Rubén Hernández-Léon. New York: Russell Sage Foundation, 2005, 187–219.

Rister, Carl Coke. "Carlota, a Confederate Colony in Mexico." *Journal of Southern History* 11, no. 1 (February 1945): 33–50.

Robinson, William Spence. "The First Legations of the United States in Latin America." *Mississippi Valley Historical Review* 2, no. 2 (September 1915): 183–212.

Rosenberg, G., and K.J. Luchok. "Steps in Meeting the Needs of Kentucky's Migrant Farmworkers." *Journal of Agromedicine* 4, nos. 3–4 (1997): 381.

Savelle, Max. "The Founding of New Madrid, Missouri." *Mississippi Valley Historical Review* 19, no. 1 (1932): 30–56.

Smith, Peter. "Faith Matters." *The Courier-Journal* (Louisville), September 7, 2003.

Spears, Valerie Honeycut. "Immigration: Candidates Can't Ignore It: Lexington Politicians Forced to Take Position on the Issue." *Lexington Herald-Leader*, May 3, 2006.

United States Census Bureau. "Kentucky QuickFacts." January 12, 2007. http://quickfacts.census.gov/qfd/states/21000.html.

Whitesell, Jesse. Letter to Henry F. Steagall, August 15, 1887. Confederados Collection, Auburn University. Also available at http://www.lib.auburn.edu/archive/find-aid/958/steagall-53.gif.

Zuñiga, Victor, and Rubén Hernández-Léon. "Introduction." In *New Destinations: Mexican Immigration in the United States*. Eds. Victor Zuñiga and Rubén Hernández-Léon. New York: Russell Sage Foundation, 2005, xi–xxi.

———, eds. *New Destinations: Mexican Immigration in the United States*. New York: Russell Sage Foundation, 2005.

19

Louisiana

Lázaro Lima

CHRONOLOGY

1814	After the British invade Louisiana, residents of the state from the Canary Islands, called *Isleños*, organize and establish three regiments. The *Isleños* had very few weapons, and some served unarmed as the state provided no firearms. By the time the British were defeated, the *Isleños* had sustained the brunt of life and property loss resulting from the British invasion of Louisiana.
1838	The first Mardi Gras parade takes place in New Orleans on Shrove Tuesday with the help and participation of native-born Latin Americans and *Isleños*.
1840s	The Spanish-language press in New Orleans supersedes the state's French-language press in reach and distribution.
1846–1848	Louisiana-born Eusebio Juan Gómez, editor of the eminent Spanish-language press newspaper *La Patria*, is nominated as General Winfield Scott's field interpreter during the Mexican-American War.
1850	The capital moves from New Orleans to Baton Rouge, where a new statehouse had been built with the help of Latin American and Caribbean immigrants.
1856	The Last Island Hurricane devastates Louisiana and destroys Last Island (also known as Derniere Island), interrupting commerce from Cuba to New Orleans for months.
1861	Cuban-born Loreta Janeta Velázquez enlists in the Confederate Army masquerading as a man, but she is ultimately discovered and discharged while in New Orleans.

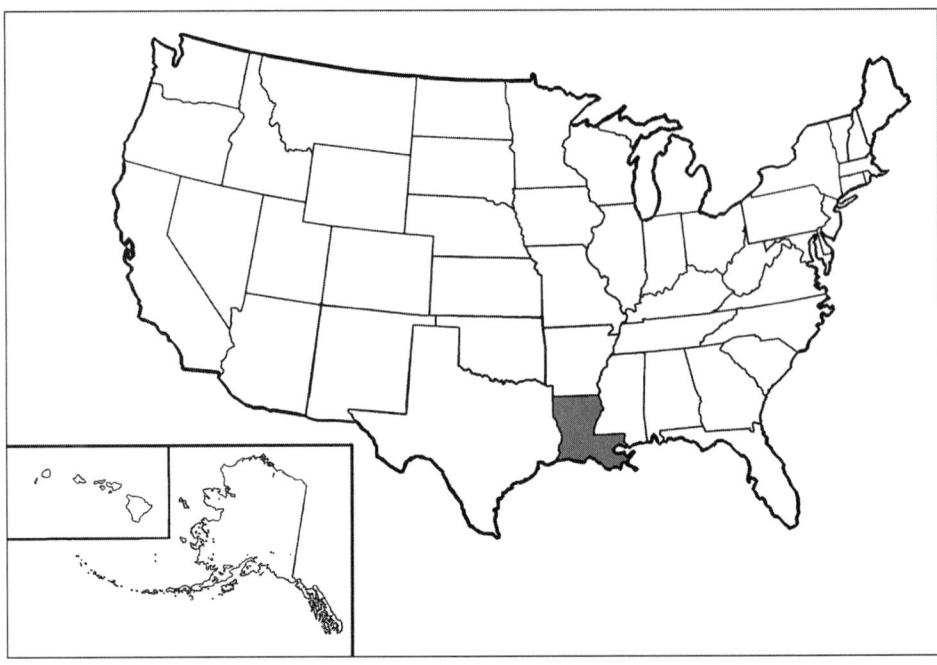

1861–1865	Various Louisiana regiments comprise Latinos fighting for the Confederacy, including the Chalmette Regiment Infantry of Louisiana and the "European Brigade." New Orleans is captured by Union forces in 1862.
1901	Latin American and Caribbean migrants are hired in Jennings after the first oil well establishes the importance of the state's oil industry.
1940s	United Fruit Company is headquartered in New Orleans. Hondurans begin to arrive because of the company's ties with their home country.
1942–1964	Bracero program brings Mexicans to the state.
1950s	Hondurans settle in New Orleans's Barrio Lempira, which will become the largest Honduran American community in the United States.
1953–1954	Ernesto Galarza of the National Farm Labor Union assists many sugarcane and strawberry pickers.
1959	Honduran Victor Herrera establishes the Asociación Hondureña de Nueva Orleans to help Honduran American migrants and other Latinos.
1962	The United States Catholic Conference in Miami resolves to open a Catholic Cuban Center in New Orleans to provide health care and resettlement assistance to Cuban exiles overwhelming resources in Miami.
1962–1963	Cubans exiles are encouraged to move to New Orleans to alleviate their settling exclusively in Miami.
1987	Cuban prisoners, known as Marielitos, take approximately 130 hostages in Oakdale.

1996	The Canary Islanders Heritage Society of Louisiana is created to preserve the history and culture of Spanish settlement in the state.
2005	The New Orleans Workers' Center for Racial Justice Coalition is established to address the working conditions of migrants and African Americans. In 2006 the coalition mobilizes 200 law school students to gather the stories of over 1,000 workers, and it authors one of the most comprehensive assessments of race and labor in the wake of Katrina.

HISTORICAL OVERVIEW

When Louisiana became the 18th state of the Union in 1812, the territory was already seeped in the linguistic, historical, and cultural antecedents that had made New Orleans, its most important city at the time, one of the first multilingual, multiracial, and multiethnic cosmopolitan centers in the United States. The origins of Spanish-speaking Latino Louisiana can be traced to the arrival of Alonso Álvarez de Pineda (c. 1492–1520) in 1519. Álvarez de Pineda sailed from Cuba to explore the uncharted territories between the Florida peninsula—modern-day Arkansas and Louisiana—and the southern Gulf of Mexico region. The purpose of his trip was to find a route to the Pacific Ocean and, in this sense, the trip can be said to have initiated the importance of Louisiana, and of New Orleans in particular, to the development of one of the first major commercial zones in the Americas. Though the Spanish were the first Europeans to explore Louisiana, the area was largely under the political control of the French until 1762, when it was briefly ceded to Spain. France, however, regained control of the region in 1800, with the Third Treaty of San Ildefonso, but less than 3 years later it sold the territory to the United States with the Louisiana Purchase of 1803. By the time it was incorporated into the Union, Louisiana had thriving communities of Spanish speakers composed of migrants from Latin American, Spain, and the Canary Islands.

The Canary Islanders—or *Isleños*, as they came to be known—migrated to Louisiana by way of Cuba between 1778 and 1783 to prosper economically and to protect the territory from English and French invasion. Scholars have referred to *Isleños* by the three distinct Spanish dialects that the latter developed in their cultural-geographic enclaves throughout the state of Louisiana. They are the *Isleños* proper, who have preserved the Spanish language with the lexical and syntactic patterns of the late colonial Spanish period, the *Bruli,* and the *Adaeseños*. The *Isleños* settled in St. Barnard Parish, near New Orleans; the *Bruli* settled throughout Iberville Parish, south of Baton Rouge; and the *Adaeseños* in Natchitoches and Sabine parishes, southwest of Shreveport.[1] Many of Louisiana's cities grew out of former settlements such as these and from Spanish posts throughout the state, including the cities of New Orleans, Donaldsonville, Alexandria, Marksville, Franklin, and Vidalia. Not surprisingly, New Orleans was the most significant city in the state given its strategic position on the Mississippi river. As early as 1820 New Orleans had already become a destination for visitors from around the globe, but especially from Latin America.

The importance of New Orleans to the state as the gateway to the Americas, not to mention the major inland shipping route through the Mississippi, also made the city one of the principal centers of Spanish-language print culture, with major newspapers circulating via ships through the Gulf of Mexico and by steamboats up and down the Mississippi River. By the 1840s the Spanish-language press in New Orleans was thriving, and it had superseded the French-language press not only in Hispanic expatriate communities but in Latin American and U.S. Latino communities as well. Many newspapers—such as *El Independiente, Diario del Gobierno, La verdad, La Patria*, and its predecessor *El Hablador*—were distributed throughout the United States via steamboats, trains, and the telegraph, so that by mid-nineteenth century New Orleans had at least 23 different Spanish-language newspapers and journals; New York, in comparison, had only thirteen.[2] Not surprisingly, the war with Mexico (1846–1848) was covered with singular interest in the Spanish-language press because many Latinos and Latin American expatriates, émigrés, and travelers saw the U.S. conquest of Mexico as but a precursor to U.S. expansion into the newly emerging Latin American republics.

During the Mexican-American War Latinos participated on both sides of the conflict. For example, the army nominated Eusebio Juan Gómez, editor of the eminent *La Patria* newspaper, as General Winfield Scott's field interpreter. Gómez was quickly commissioned as lieutenant colonel in the U.S. Army, until the Louisiana-born Gómez's position was rescinded because of allegations that he had leaked secret plans to the Mexicans. Manifest Destiny politics in the United States created the need to further justify the war with Mexico in an attempt to achieve geographic and political hegemony and to secure trade routes from the Atlantic to the Pacific seaboards. Native-born Louisiana Latinos such as Gómez were often assumed to be sympathetic to Mexico's plight and less American for their cultural, religious, and linguistic ties to Mexico—even if they were born in the United States.

Speakers of Spanish of various nationalities and political sympathies in Louisiana, as well as native-born Latinos, were often indistinguishable from each other in the English-speaking press and assumed to be Mexican, or at least sympathetic to Mexico during the war. Justifying the violence related to westward conquest—itself most often understood as "westward settlement"—required the denigration of conquered populations as "uncivilized mongrels." Given the racial diversity of Latinos and the need to justify the war against Mexico, many Latinos began to be classed along with blacks as the former's political and cultural influence diminished; still other Latino groups sought to assimilate by identifying positively with their European ancestry as Spaniards.⁴ However, determining race through ocular evidence was not always possible for such an ethnically diverse group as Latinos. Unlike the various *Isleño* communities who since their arrival in the late eighteenth century had always considered themselves European, most Latinos could not pass as European or as Anglo-Americans even if they wanted to do so. It was during this generative period that the importance of France to the region was exalted, and the notion of a French Louisiana grew in measure with the paradoxical representation of Latinos as foreign to the state. Indeed, even *Isleños* whose physical and cultural presence predated the arrival and settlement of Anglo-Americans began to emphasize their heritage as "pure" Spaniards in contradistinction to mixed-race Latinos in the region, who were increasingly classed as colored, foreign, or both.

Yet, many Louisiana Latinos saw themselves as part of the very fiber of the state and country. The Civil War (1861–1865) is a case in point. At the onset of the war in 1861 Louisiana seceded from the Union and joined the Confederacy. Estimates of Latino participation in the Civil War range as high as 9,500 nationally. In Louisiana, Latinos fought for the Confederacy in the Chalmette Regiment Infantry of Louisiana, as well as in the Zouaves First Florida Calvary of Louisiana.⁵ Louisiana's "European Brigade" alone had upwards of 800 "Spanish" soldiers, though it is not clear how many were actually Spanish nationals, given the pressure to assimilate and the collapsing of national distinctions for most speakers of Spanish in the public sphere. Other units such as Louisiana's William E. Stake Brigade included Cubans, Mexicans, Central Americans, as well as other Latin American nationals who suffered discrimination. For example, while in Maryland, the "foreign"-looking members of the Stake Brigade were signaled out and accused of looting and violence.⁶

Louisiana ultimately fell to Union forces early during the conflict when in 1862 Union admiral David G. Farragut, himself of Spanish ancestry, led the USS *Hartford* past the Chalmette batteries and took the port city of New Orleans by securing control of the Mississippi River, thereby effectively capturing the state for the Union. Economic recovery was slow in Louisiana after the Civil War, as slavery and the dependence on the plantation system were replaced with farm tenancy and sharecropping. The importance of the Mississippi River as a steamer commercial route was also diminished because of the emergence of railroad construction and related industries. Reconstruction in Louisiana, as in much of the South, was overseen by military governors who attempted to ensure, with limited success, that slaves would be freed and given suffrage, but literacy and poll tax laws aimed at former slaves disenfranchised them from the promise of political participation and cultural enfranchisement. Literacy laws, however, disenfranchised not only freed blacks but also Latinos. Recent arrivals to the region as well as established native-born Latinos who had found Louisiana's multilingual and ethnic diversity ideal for the maintenance of heritage traditions soon experienced how legalized discrimination prevented them from maintaining or achieving political relevance in the region. The landmark Supreme Court decision *Plessy v. Ferguson* (1896), which legally permitted segregation under the doctrine of "separate but equal" originated as a case in Louisiana, where the plaintiff was not allowed to sit in a "white" rail car because he was, in the parlance of the era, an "octoroon"; that is, a person who is one-eighth black. Ironically, common racial systems in Latin America—such as the *casta* divisions that created hierarchies based on race and ethnicity in Mexico and Peru—found their way into Louisiana law. To this day Louisiana is the only state that maintains earlier legal structures based on Spanish and Napoleonic code law as opposed to English common law, which forms the basis of the rest of the United States' legal system. Discrimination in Louisiana, as in much of the South, was systemic at the turn of the twentieth century.

Like blacks, Latinos fell victim to lynching mobs in Louisiana, though this fact has been largely elided in the history of lynching in the United States. The solidification of a rigid black and white binary in the post-Reconstruction imagination often meant that Latinos would be counted as white in the popular press in descriptions of lynching, often for reasons that had more to do with diminishing the onus of the South's lynching of blacks (as opposed to blacks *and* whites who were meted "justice") by collapsing other racial and ethnic distinctions. Such was the case on October 7, 1909, when a certain Mike Rodrigauez [sic] of Vernon Parish was lynched for an alleged robbery at the hands of "persons unknown." Indeed, the transliteration from Rodríguez to "Rodrigauez" is instructive of how English-language hegemony began to supplant multilingual Louisiana. In the process, Latinos became increasingly erased from the historical record, not only literally as in the case of lynchings, but symbolically, as the once multiracial, multiethnic, and plurilinguistic Louisiana began to be divided along black and white lines of racial affiliation under one language.[7]

Systemic discrimination was also part of the state's drive to delimit the cultural disenfranchisement of Latinos and blacks. In 1900 Louisiana stopped public schooling after fifth grade for blacks and native-born Latinos who were considered colored. It would not be until 1917 that Louisiana established a public high school for blacks or "students of color," after the state's Compulsory Education Act became effective in 1916. Not surprisingly, at the turn of the century thousands of blacks left Louisiana during the Great Migration to seek work and improve their lot in northern industrial cities. The migration of blacks to the North also partly explains the first wave of Latino migration to Louisiana at the turn of the century, as the region experienced a boom brought on by the discovery of natural gas and petroleum in the region.

The Mexican Revolution (1910–1920) also increased the number of Mexican nationals who fled their country to the United States for political and economic

Creole girls, Plaquemines Parish, Louisiana, c. 1935. Courtesy of the Library of Congress, Prints & Photographs Division, Reproduction Number LC-USF33-006159-M1.

reasons. Though most settled first in states across the border with Mexico, many traveled throughout the South in search of economic opportunity. It is estimated that this migration brought over 1 million Mexicans to the United States shortly after the revolution. These Mexicans eventually found work in U.S. farms, docks, railroads, as well as in the more traditional agricultural sectors of the economy. By 1911 the press of the period had noted how the increasing number of Mexican laborers to Louisiana allowed the Spanish language to be heard "almost as frequently as English on the docks where Mexican and Central Americans were often employed."[8] Indeed, by 1911 the United States Immigration Commission, also known as the Dillingham Commission, limited the immigration of southern and eastern Europeans and Asians who were deemed as "undesirable" as Mexicans; but because Mexicans were seen as temporary immigrants who would work for far less than other immigrants, it became expedient to make exceptions for them. The Dillingham Commission unwittingly set the stage for the arrival of Mexican migration through subsequent accords, as it noted that "'Mexican immigrants are providing a fairly acceptable supply of labor in a limited territory in which it is difficult to secure others . . . [w]hile Mexicans are not easily assimilated, this is not of very great importance as long as most of them return to their native land in a short time.'"[9] Not surprisingly, Mexican migration to Louisiana and the Southwest grew considerably because it was believed that their stay would be temporary.

This partly explains why even though Congress passed the Immigration Act of 1917 to prevent the immigration of "undesirables" during the height of World War I, itinerant agricultural workers from Mexico were exempted from the directive until 1923 in order to assist with the labor shortage occasioned by World War I. This concession to U.S. farmers brought over 200,000 migrants to states along the border with Mexico and throughout the South.[10] In Louisiana, Latino migrants worked in sugarcane fields and as strawberry and cotton pickers under oppressive conditions. Attempts to improve their lot were nearly nonexistent as unionizing became largely a clandestine operation that, if successful, ultimately required U.S. citizenship for membership. This was further hampered by the Louisiana Constitution of 1921 as it effectively sought to limit the enfranchisement of blacks and native-born Louisiana Latinos through voting roadblocks that required voters to complete voter registration cards without assistance, and to be able to both read and interpret any portion of the Constitution selected by the registrar of voters. Because Louisiana did not provide state schooling for "students of color" until 1917, the state's voter registration board effectively created a tiered democracy in the state.

The economic crisis brought on by the Great Depression ended these labor concessions and caused a backlash that resulted in the Mexican Repatriation, which deported over half a million Mexican Americans to Mexico, even though many were U.S. citizens. Yet, the experience provided a testing ground for the various guest worker accords that came to be known as the Bracero program, beginning during the height of World War II in 1942 and up until 1964.

Mexicans, however, did not provide the only source of migration-related labor in Louisiana. Hondurans also began to settle in New Orleans when the United Fruit Company, whose headquarters was in that port city, began shipping produce from their Honduran plantations for national distribution. The trade relationship that existed between Honduras and Louisiana ultimately made New Orleans the city with the largest Honduran American population in the United States.[11] Honduran immigration to Louisiana was also the result of political and economic disruptions exacerbated by U.S. capital and military interventions in Central America. When it was no longer possible to return to their country of origin, Honduran Americans settled in Louisiana, which led to one of the first permanent settlements of Honduran Americans in the state. During the early 1950s Hondurans settled in Barrio Lempira, near the lower Garden District of uptown New Orleans, and worked in agribusiness and related industries alongside other Latinos from various nationalities. By the end of that decade the Asociación Hondureña de Nueva Orleans "marked the official introduction of a Honduran identity to New Orleans."[12] The racialization of Hondurans prior to the civil rights movement in Louisiana was similar to that of many Latino groups. The white majority conferred a higher status to Creoles and Latinos who were lighter complected than darker-skinned blacks, as the "reality of racial ambiguity, a result of years of miscegenation, led the elite whites to make clear distinctions in order to guard their own white identity from the imminent black 'infiltration.'"[13] The term *Creole* itself (from the Spanish term *criollo*) became a euphemism for a person of Spanish or, in some instances, of Latin American lineage, and it signified affiliation with Spain, thus avoiding slippage into the more charged term of the era, *Negro*. Yet, unlike native-born Creoles and Latinos, more recent Latino arrivals had to contend with the added disadvantage of limited English-speaking skills, which made it difficult not only to get work but to demand humane working conditions.

The 1950s also marked concerted efforts by the white majority to limit the possibilities for Latinos to secure living wages. Latino populations in Louisiana were prevented from demanding work protections through Louisiana's right-to-work laws. The laws compromised the emerging strength of unions in the state by making it optional, rather than mandatory, to join labor unions. The laws effectively prevented many entry-level workers from establishing union ties, and they were eventually used as strike-braking measures. Ernesto Galarza of the National Farm Labor Union worked in Louisiana from 1953 to 1954 to assist sugarcane and strawberry pickers through organized protests against agricultural exploitation of Latino workers. Galarza's efforts resulted in the revision of many right-to-work laws through calls for the right to fair wages and safer working conditions.[14] Galarza's experiences in Louisiana and his native California led him to believe, however, that unionization would not provide the necessary safeguards and labor protections, because he saw the Bracero program as ultimately abusive of both braceros and native-born Latinos, who could not earn sustainable wages while the program was in place.[15] His living through the 1954 Operation Wetback, a program established to deport Mexican and Mexican Americans to Mexico, also made Galarza distrustful of unions' ability to protect workers. He was present in many congressional hearings on the Bracero program and eventually worked to end it. Just before the program was officially terminated in 1964—after its extension was denied by Congress—a Louisiana senator presciently noted, "I am certain that if the proposed extension is not granted, there may be a recurrence of conditions that existed . . . when Mexican labor came by the thousands."[16] Indeed, in 1970 less than 20 percent of Mexicans in the United States were born in their country of origin, whereas today over half of the Mexican population in the United States were born in Mexico.[17] Of course the end of the Bracero program did not end the pattern of itinerant and seasonal work to the state; only the designation of legal or undocumented workers changed.

The civil rights movement in Louisiana was largely dominated along the black/white divide. Latino rights struggles were most often associated with labor issues, whereas civil rights proper was something that Louisiana blacks were seeking. Unlike the states of California, New Mexico, and Texas, during the height of the civil rights movement Louisiana's established Latino communities—

composed chiefly, though not exclusively, of *Isleños*, Hondurans, and Mexican Americans—comprised U.S. citizens, either native born or naturalized, and the more recent arrivals at the time were working difficult jobs that left little opportunity to organize protests. Differences among and within various Latino groups in the state regarding questions of civil rights were also conditioned by class standing.

Because they had been residing in Louisiana for generations, Cuban Americans in Louisiana had ties to their U.S. identity that often superseded their relationship to more recent arrivals. Cuban Americans had long established ties to Louisiana prior to the Cuban Revolution of 1959. Cuba was the Port of New Orleans's leading customer prior to the revolution, and established Cuban American business interests were in place, as Cuban sugar producers sent their children to study agriculture and business at Louisiana State University. There was also an influx of post-1959 Cubans who settled predominately in New Orleans after the United States government "started to deny financial help to Cubans in Miami if they would not move to other cities"—New Orleans being one of the principal cities designated for Cuban resettlement.[18] However, already before the Cuban Revolution of 1959, Honduras had also become one of the largest trading partners of the Americas with Louisiana. From the mid-twentieth century to the present, Louisiana has had the highest number of Honduran Americans in the United States, with most settling near New Orleans. Native-born Honduran Americans, like Cuban Americans before them, also had a different relation to the civil rights movement and social inclusion, as their tight-knit communities provided much of the protections that were not available to more recent Latino arrivals.

Cubans reemerged as migrants to Louisiana in the 1980s though under quite different conditions from previous Cuban settlement in the state. The largest single number of arrivals to Louisiana in the 1980s was the nearly 2,400 Cuban refugees who were sent to the Oakdale Federal Detention Center in 1986. After the Port of Mariel boat exodus of 1980, during which over 125,000 Cubans sought political asylum in the United States, various detention centers were set up in the United States to house Cuban detainees who had criminal records or were considered mentally incompetent. The Marielitos, as they have come to be known, remained at Oakdale until in 1987, when, after being told that they would be returned to Cuba under a renegotiated immigration accord with Fidel Castro's government, they took approximately 130 hostages. The hostage crisis forced the United States to negotiate with the Cuban refugees and, with the help of various intermediaries, the latter agreed to release all hostages in return for an indefinite moratorium on their repatriation to Cuba and a review of their individual cases. (It was not until 2005 that the Supreme Court ruled that open-ended detention of Marielitos was illegal.) As these Cubans were processed and released, many stayed in the Bayou State, thereby changing the class dynamics of prior Cuban migration to Louisiana.

Census estimates for Latinos in Louisiana during the 1990s were upwards of 93,000, though the actual numbers were probably much higher, because of the undocumented Latinos in the state. By the 2000 census the total number of Latinos in the state had increased to over 107,700, reflecting an almost 16 percent population increase from the 1990 census. The highest concentration of Latinos from any single national group was composed of Honduran Americans, who accounted for 24 percent of the total Latino population in the state, with the Greater New Orleans metropolitan area serving as their principal enclave. This changed drastically after Hurricane Katrina hit the Gulf Coast region in 2005.

Hurricane Katrina has brought about profound ethnic and demographic shifts in Louisiana. Less than a year before the hurricane made landfall, the African American population in the Greater New Orleans metropolitan area alone had decreased from 37 to 22 percent.[19] The 2004 U.S. census update reported a Mexican American population of just below 2,000, whereas by 2006 estimates ranged from between 10,000 and 20,000 Mexican Americans in the region.[20] The astounding demographic shift in a state with a pre-Katrina Latino population of 3 percent was exacerbated by the suspension of the Davis-Bacon Act that had required contractors to pay prevailing local wages. The suspension of the Davis-Bacon Act allowed contractors to hire ready Latino laborers and exploit them in the process. As with previous informal and more formal Bracero accords with Mexico, Latinos of Mexican descent in the United States often perform the most dangerous work. In post-Katrina Louisiana alone, 80 percent of the debris and mold removal of hurricane-ravaged areas was undertaken by migrant Latino laborers, many of whom are undocumented. The unprecedented number of Mexican American laborers alone in the Greater New Orleans metropolitan area led city Mayor Ray Nagin to rhetorically ask, "How do I ensure that New Orleans is not overrun by Mexican workers?" in an utter collapse of all possible Latino American nationalities under the national signifier *Mexican*.[21] Nagin's inflammatory political rhetoric both fabricated scapegoats and elided the fact that the state itself had created the conditions for the arrival of contemporary forms of servitude that have profoundly benefitted the rebuilding efforts in Louisiana. In effect, the paradoxical verbal bashing of the very migrants who are rebuilding the region has created the conditions for the further dehumanization of Louisiana Latino laborers.

In August 2006 Latin American and Caribbean laborers on legal H-2B visas who were contracted to work in New Orleans hotels but denied their contractual right to work staged a protest in mock handcuffs in front of the hotels that had lured them from as far as Bolivia and as close as the Dominican Republic. With the assistance of the New Orleans Workers Center, the hotel workers sued their employers and won. They have since formed the country's first H-2B visa workers alliance. As one Dominican hotel worker put it, "Only by studying workers' experiences can government create adequate reform."[22] Supporting the struggles of

Latinos for social justice from the early nineteenth century to the present, the Latin American hotel laborers joined a long historical battle for the economic and human enfranchisement of Latinos in Louisiana.

NOTABLE LATINOS

Farragut, David G. (1801–1870). Union admiral of Spanish ancestry who led the USS *Hartford* past the Chalmette batteries and took the port city of New Orleans by securing control of the Mississippi River and effectively capturing the state for the Union.

Velázquez, Loreta Janeta (c. 1842–c. 1898). Cuban-born woman and Confederate Army soldier who was decommissioned in New Orleans after it was established the she was masquerading as a man.

Lázaro, Ladislas (1872–1927). The first Latino to serve in the United States House of Representatives, from 1908 until 1912. He attended Holy Cross College in New Orleans and later graduated from Louisville Medical College in Kentucky before practicing in Louisiana.

Pérez Sr., Leander Henry (1891–1969). Democratic "political boss" of Plaquemines and St. Bernard parishes in the first half of the twentieth century. Officially, Pérez served as district judge, as district attorney, and as president of the Plaquemines Parish Commission Council.

Gómez, Eusebio Juan (c. 1895–c. 1860). The editor of the eminent New Orleans newspaper *La Patria*. He served as a field interpreter for General Winfield Scott during the Mexican-American War (1846–1848).

Fernández, Joachim Octave (1896–1978). Democratic representative from Louisiana to the United States House of Representatives.

Pérez, Irvan (1923–2008). Famous *Isleño* singer of poetic compositions known as *décimas*. Pérez was featured in the PBS series *River of Song: A Musical Journey* (1999).

Herrera, Victor (c. 1926–c. 1985). Latino community health advocate and founder of the Asociación Hondureña de Nueva Orleans, in 1959.

CULTURAL CONTRIBUTIONS

The Latino presence in Louisiana predates and is coterminous with the economic and social development of the state. As one of the principal centers of journalistic and literary expression in the Spanish language during the nineteenth century, New Orleans alone has boasted a range of important newspapers and journals—including *El Independiente, Diario del Gobierno, La verdad, La Patria,* and its predecessor *El Hablador.* By the mid-nineteenth century New Orleans had over 23 different Spanish-language newspapers and journals in which the top figures of Latin American politics and culture of the period disseminated what has come to be known as Latino literatures and cultures of the United States. Given

New Orleans's unique location at the mouth of the Gulf of Mexico, the diffusion of Hispanic culture throughout the United States was literally carried up and down the Mississippi River and across the country.

Latinos in Louisiana have also infused the state's music with the ethnic and linguistic particularisms that have made the state a harbinger of the nation's musical heritage. Though Louisiana's importance to U.S. popular music is undisputed, it is an often ignored fact that Cuban commercial exchanges with New Orleans also facilitated the arrival of musical forms that informed and complemented one another. Scholars have noted how the emergence of the Cuban *danzón* and *son* is roughly coterminous with the emergence of ragtime and jazz. In literature the poetic composition known as *décima* emerged from *Isleño* communities, and it still survives as a popular form of entertainment and versification. Composed chiefly of 10 octosyllabic lines, the *décima* could also be said to share affinities with what came to be known as *corrido,* or border ballad, in Texas. Like the better known *corrido* tradition of southern Texas, the structure of the *décima* makes rote memorization easy, and its rhyme scheme allows for verbal play, double entendres, and the community-specific continuity of cultural memory. To this day *décimas* are sung at dances, community celebrations, and holidays, as well as during more intimate family events.

Latino arts have also flourished in Louisiana as Latino artists have found a visually and culturally diverse environment with an active plastic arts scene from the 1960s onward. Latino performance art has also emerged as an innovative and provocative form of cultural commentary and ethnic memory. For example, New Orleans–based José Torres Tama's performance piece "The Cone of Uncertainty: New Orleans After Katrina" critiques government ineptitude in the wake of Hurricane Katrina through spoken-word poetry as well as ritual movement and dance, through the voices of a myriad of characters that he channels in order to bear witness to the abandonment of displaced Latinos whose suffering and resilience have remained largely ignored by the mainstream English-speaking press. Local Latino stations such as Radio Tropical Caliente (KGLA), however, have kept Latino communities informed through Spanish-language programming. More recently, in 2007 Telemundo affiliate KGLA-DT has begun to offer sports coverage, talk-show entertainment, and more traditional cultural offerings such as *telenovelas* (soap operas), along with local programming and advertising, in addition to Telemundo's national coverage.

The region's cultural ties to Latino communities in the state and the Americas have been solidified through various educational and cultural industries. Important institutions—such as Tulane University and Louisiana State University—with historically close ties to the Caribbean and the Americas have established some of the country's premier research centers devoted to the study of Latino, Latin American, and Caribbean cultures. State institutions such as the New

Orleans Jazz and Heritage Foundation have also acknowledged the importance of Latino culture to the region and the country through extremely popular festivals such as the Fiesta Latina, where jazz and Latin rhythms are seen as culturally constitutive of the ethno-linguistic diversity of the region. More populist cultural events are showcased in other festivals—for example, the Carnival Latino—in which the region's heritage, as well as its present and future, are seen as imminently tied to Latino communities. Given the demographic explosion of Latino populations in the state, cities such as New Orleans are reclaiming their historical importance as the Gateway to the Americas.

NOTES

1. Armistead, 1992, 2.
2. For a discussion of Hispanophone print culture and New Orleans as its center in the nineteenth century, see Silva Gruesz, 2002, 108–120.
3. For a discussion of Hispanophone print culture and New Orleans as its center in the nineteenth century, see Silva Gruesz, 2002, 115.
4. Lima, 2007, 22–55.
5. For estimates of Latinos in the military during the Civil War and related history, see Thompson, 1976.
6. See Smith, 2005, 74.
7. Congressional Record—Senate, list of Louisiana victims of lynching, http://www.iconn.org/documents/s%20res39CongressionalRecord6-13-2005SenateComments.pdf (accessed December 12, 2007). Ken Gonzales Day's *Lynching in the West, 1850–1935* (2006) provides one of the few comprehensive attempts at documenting the historical erasure of Latinos from the history of lynching in the United States.
8. García, 1981, 62.
9. Tichenor, 2002, 168.
10. Monto, 1994, 55–57.
11. Fussell, 2006, 1.
12. Euraque, 2004, 10, 32–33.
13. Euraque, 2004, 32.
14. Chabran, 1985, 138.
15. Chabran, 1985, 139.
16. Cited in David M. Reimers, *Still the Golden Door: The Third World Comes to America* (New York: Columbia University Press, 1992), 59.
17. Gómez, 2007, 2.
18. Berchak, 2007, 51–52.
19. Berchak, 2007, 69.
20. Quinones, 2006, A10.
21. Fox Gotham, 2007, 201.
22. Fiedman-Rudovsky, 2007.

BIBLIOGRAPHY

Armistead, Samuel G. *The Spanish Tradition in Louisiana: Isleño Folkliterature*, Vol. I. Newark, DE: Juan de Cuesta, 1992.

Berchak, Katie Judith. "Nueva Orleans: Hispanics in New Orleans, the Catholic Church, and Imagining the New Hispanic Community." Master's thesis, Louisiana State University, 2007.

Chabran, Richard. "Activism and Intellectual Struggle in the Life of Ernesto Galarza (1905–1984)." *Hispanic Journal of Behavioral Sciences* 7, no. 2 (1985).

Euraque, Samantha. "'Honduran Memories': Identity, Race, Place, and Memory in New Orleans, Louisiana." Master's thesis, Louisiana State University, 2004.

Fiedman-Rudovsky, Jean. "Guest Workers Fighting Back." *Time Magazine*, March 14, 2007. http://www.time.com/time/nation/article/0,8599,1599032,00.html.

Fox Gotham, Kevin. *Authentic New Orleans: Tourism, Culture, and Race in the Big Easy.* New York: New York University Press, 2007.

Fussell, Elizabeth. "Latino Immigrants in Post-Katrina New Orleans." Unpublished paper presented at the Regional Seminar on Labor Rights, New Orleans, LA, October 19–22, 2006.

García, Mario T. *Desert Immigrants: The Mexicans of El Paso, 1880–1920.* New Haven, CT: Yale University Press, 1981.

Gómez, Laura E. *Manifest Destinies: The Making of the Mexican American Race.* New York: New York University Press, 2007.

Lima, Lázaro. *The Latino Body: Crisis Identities in American Literary and Cultural Memory.* New York: New York University Press, 2007.

Monto, Alexander. *The Roots of Mexican Labor Migration.* Westport, CT: Praeger, 1994.

Quinones, Sam. "Migrants Find a Gold Rush in New Orleans." *Los Angeles Times*, April 4, 2006, A10.

Reimers, David M. *Still the Golden Door: The Third World Comes to America.* New York: Columbia University Press, 1992.

Silva Gruesz, Kirsten. *Ambassadors of Culture: The Trans-american Origins of Latino Writing.* Princeton, NJ: Princeton University Press, 2002.

Smith, Derek. *The Gallant Dead: Union and Confederate Generals Killed in the Civil War.* Mechanicsburg, PA: Stackpole Books, 2005.

Smith, Michael M. "The Mexican Secret Service in the United States, 1910–1920." *The Americas* 59, no. 1 (July 2002): 65–85.

Thompson, Jerry D. *Vaqueros in Blue & Gray.* Austin, TX: Presidial Press, 1976.

Tichenor, Daniel J. *Dividing Lines: The Politics of Immigration Control in America.* Princeton, NJ: Princeton University Press, 2002.

Velázquez, Loreta Janeta. *Woman in Battle: A Narrative of the Exploits, Adventures, and Travels of Madame Loreta Janeta Velazquez, Otherwise Known as Lieutenant Harry J. Buford, Confederate States Army.* Ed. C.J. Worthington. Hartford, CT: T. Belknap, 1876.

20

MAINE

Phillip J. Granberry

CHRONOLOGY

1524	First Spanish exploration of the coast of Maine.
1940	The U.S. Census Department makes the first Latino population estimate (60) residing in Maine.
1990s	Latino businesses emerge in southern Maine.
2004	Portland's first Latino Youth Soccer Championship tournament is held.

HISTORICAL OVERVIEW

The 9,360 Latinos residing in Maine on April 1, 2000, ranked the state 48th in total Latino population. Latinos made up 0.7 percent of the state's population, which ranked Maine 49th in concentration of Latinos. Although the Latino population in the state is growing, it is doing so at a slower rate than New Hampshire and Vermont, states in the region with similarly small Latino populations. The first estimate of the Latino population in Maine was the 1940 U. S. census, which reported 60 Latinos living in the state. The 1970 U. S. census estimated that 2,433 Latinos resided in the state. By 1980 the Latino population was estimated to be 5,005, and in 1990, the estimate was 6,829, which was less than 0.5 percent of the state's population.

Long before today's Latino presence in Maine, the state was explored by early Spanish cartographers who sailed the eastern coast of the United States to map North America. Esteban Gómez was the first to sail the coast of Maine and travel inland, in 1524. Though no narrative or log of the journey exists, his detailed maps verify his exploration. He entered the Penobscot River and traveled to what

364 Latino America

is today the city of Bangor. He was unsuccessful in his attempt to find a direct passage to China, but he returned to Spain with slaves, some of whom were Algonquin Indians.[1]

Maine is home to an estimated 1.1 percent of all Latinos in New England. This small Latino population in Maine consists of people who have migrated to the southern part of state, where they are forming an emerging middle class. It also includes migrant and seasonal farmworkers who are employed in the state's blueberry, apple, eggs, Christmas wreath, tree-planting, and broccoli farms. Some of these workers stay year-round to work on the farms in the state. This trend is also occurring in the other New England states of New Hampshire and Vermont. Together with Maine, these two states are noted for having a small Latino population, as only 3.6 percent of all Latinos (regardless of place of birth) in the United States were residing in them in 2000.[2]

Latinos are an important demographic group to the region, which is experiencing limited population growth, because they are significant contributors to the region's population growth.[3] Latino population growth is driven almost equally by internal migration and births to resident Latinos, and not by migration from other countries, as only 16.7 percent of Maine's Latinos are foreign born.

Demographic and individual characteristics for Latinos in Maine are presented in this chapter to provide a portrait of this relatively small proportion of Maine's population that is increasingly making economic and cultural contributions to the state. Because of their small size and recent arrival to the state, Latinos historical contributions are limited, having occurred over the last 40 years. This chapter's demographic portrait provides a lens to document the contributions that Maine's emerging Latino population is making. In addition, examples of how Latinos are participating are added to support this demographic portrait.

Although an increasing number of Latino migrants are settling in nontraditional U.S. destinations such as New England, Maine has not attracted significant numbers of Latinos, unlike nearby Massachusetts.[4] Overall, Maine's population grew by 3.8 percent during the 1990s, from 1,227,928 in 1990 to 1,274,923 in 2000. Although only a small proportion of Maine's population is nonwhite (1.5 percent), Latinos form the second-largest ethnic minority group, having had a population increase of 37.1 percent in the 1990s, which was larger than that of Asians (34.9 percent), non-Latino blacks (25.3 percent) and non-Latino whites (1.8 percent). As of April 2000, Mexicans (3,649) and Puerto Ricans (2,561) represented the two largest Latino populations in Maine. Colombians (419), Cubans (323), and Dominicans (272) were the third, fourth, and fifth largest populations, respectively. Also included in the 10 largest Latino populations in the state were Guatemalans, Ecuadorians, Hondurans, Peruvians, and Salvadorans.

Latinos find Maine a welcoming place that offers support upon arrival and provides opportunities to integrate into the state's social and economic life. Latinos are attracted to Maine also because of its smaller cities with safer neighborhoods—which are seen as good places to live and raise families—because of opportunities for employment and entrepreneurship, and because of the overall good quality of life the state offers. Most Maine Latinos are U.S.-born people who have moved to that state from other northeastern states—such as Massachusetts and New York. The majority of Maine's Latinos live in the southern part of the state. In 2000 Cumberland County, where the cities of Portland and Brunswick are, was home to nearly a quarter of the state's Latino population, and nearby York County was home to nearly 15 percent of the state's Latino population.

Demographic Characteristics

Age distribution provides a possible insight into the economic contribution that Latinos are likely to make in the state. Latinos (37.3 percent) had greater proportions of their population under the age of 18, compared to non-Latino whites (23.2 percent). This suggests that in the short term Latinos are likely to impose relatively higher fiscal costs, similar to other minority groups; but in the medium and long terms, they are likely to begin working, paying taxes, and supporting the retiring non-Latino white population in the state. In contrast, Latinos had significantly lower percentages of their population who were age 65 and above (4.2 percent) than did non-Latino whites (14.7 percent). These percentages suggest that Latinos should not be incurring costs for elderly care, costs which the state needs to address in the short term.

Socioeconomic Characteristics and Educational Attainment

The socioeconomic portrait of Latinos in Maine supports the emergence of a Latino middle class. The Latino median household income in 1999 was $36,244. This group's household income was similar to that of Asians ($37,873) and non-Latino whites ($37,408), and it was well ahead of non-Latino blacks ($30,758). Latinos in Maine have high levels of education: Latinos 25 years of age and older have a high school or college degree (79.2 percent) at rates similar to those of non-Latino whites (85.5 percent).

Another factor influencing successful employment outcomes is language proficiency. The majority of Maine Latinos are fluent in English. Of the Latino migrants who report speaking only Spanish in the home, nearly three-quarters (72.4 percent) report speaking English very well. The public school systems in Maine appear to be addressing the needs of Latino children. For example, the Portland public schools has an Office of Multilingual and Multicultural Programs that offers technical assistance, training, and support to teachers of English as a Second Language (ESL). And besides providing professional development, diversity training, and support materials for all teachers and administrators within the school district, that office also assists other professionals in the area, offers support to the community to train people in cultural competency, and employs a parent-community specialist who provides outreach and support to Latino families whose children attend the city's public schools. Spanish is the third most spoken language in which service is provided in Portland's schools, behind Somali and Cambodian.

Citizenship status is thought to confer many benefits that should put migrant populations on a trajectory to the middle class. As previously noted, Latinos in Maine are predominantly born in the United States. Latinos speculate that there have been more foreign-born Latinos moving to the state since the 2000 census, but there is presently no quantitative evidence to demonstrate this. Of the 16.7 percent of Latinos who were foreign born in 2000, slightly over half (51.2 percent) were naturalized citizens.

However, concerns are being raised that unauthorized migration could interfere with Latinos' continued integration into the state's economic and social life. Latinos' growing presence in the state and the presence of unauthorized Latino migrants have become a concern to some Maine residents. In 2006, on three occasions, the police in Ellsworth apprehended and detained unauthorized Latino migrants. They subsequently turned them over to Immigration and Customs Enforcement (ICE) officials. In the December 2006 incident, three men were turned over to ICE officials after they were stopped for driving a motor vehicle with a broken window. The driver did not show a valid driver's license, and the police officer detained all men.[5] Some fear occurrences such as this highlight how concerns over unauthorized migration hinder the ability of Latinos to participate socially and economically in the state, even though the state's Latinos are overwhelmingly U.S. born and U.S. citizens.

BUSINESS DEVELOPMENT AND LABOR FORCE PARTICIPATION

Latinos have reported moving to Maine to experience a better quality of life. This included finding employment. Some Latinos have been successful in the labor market, whereas others have faced some problems finding employment. The labor force participation rates for Latinos age 16 to 64 years and not in school was similar to those for the general population, but they experienced higher rates of unemployment. Nearly 13.1 percent of Latinos were unemployed in 2000, compared to 5.2 percent of non-Latino whites. Over half (54.3 percent) of all Latinos worked in low-wage service-sector jobs. The few Dominicans in Maine demonstrated some success in the labor market, as 43.1 percent of them worked in white-collar jobs (executive, administrative, and managerial occupations, or professional specialty occupations).

Labor market participation can also be assessed by the number of workers in a family who are employed. Census data do not identify the number of jobs a person works, but they can be used to estimate the number of workers in a family. Latinos generally have a greater number of workers who are employed, compared to Anglo-Americans. However, this was not the case in Maine, where Latinos averaged 2.1 workers per family, and non-Latino whites averaged 2.2 workers.

Latinos, especially Mexicans, have traditionally come to Maine as migrant and seasonal farmworkers. They work in Maine's blueberry, apple, eggs, Christmas wreath, tree-planting, and broccoli farms. Many newly arrived Latinos from Mexico work in Maine's dairy farms.[6] The presence of low-income Latino workers has been strong enough to prompt the creation of the Maine Migrant Health Program, which provides primary and preventative health care services to migrant and seasonal farmworkers. In 2004 that program provided services to over 1,000 individuals. In addition, the city of Portland provides a Latino Community Health Outreach worker to assist Latinos in receiving adequate medical care.

Latinos have had some success starting new businesses in southern Maine. The 1997 U.S. Census Bureau's Economic Census reported that Maine had 545 Latino-owned businesses, which employed 677 workers. Most of these businesses are in the service industry, and two of the more prominent types of businesses are beauty salons and house-cleaning services.[7] *La Bodega Latina* is one of the largest and most visible Latino businesses in the state. It was started by a

Dominican migrant in Portland in 1997. The market specializes in Latino products from different Latin American countries. With its success, the owner started a restaurant with the same name in 2004. With Portland being home to a minor league baseball team that has a number of Latino baseball players, *La Bodega Latina* has become a favorite meeting place for Latinos in the area.

Latinos have received help from nonprofit organizations in starting new businesses. Costal Enterprises, a local community development agency, sponsors Start Smart, a program that provides technical assistance for migrants and refugees who are starting new businesses. The program started by assisting the owners of *Tu Casa*, a Salvadoran restaurant in Portland, who opened their restaurant out of their home in 1999. The owners received assistance initially from Start Smart's staff members, who helped with the permitting and licensing process and the establishing of good accounting procedures. This service proved invaluable for the owners of *Tu Casa* to make their business the thriving restaurant it is today.

Mobility and Homeownership

Latino migrants in Maine have been living in the United States for a substantial amount of time. Nearly 95.7 percent of Latinos had been living in the United States for at least 5 years prior to the 2000 census. However, Maine's Latinos were highly mobile: only 37.9 percent of Latinos were residing in the same location 5 years before the census, whereas 59.6 percent of non-Latino whites were residing in the same location 5 years earlier.

Home ownership is a way to demonstrate the commitment to remain in one location, and it has been shown to be important for building sustainable social networks and social capital. Maine Latinos (45.6 percent) had a home ownership rate identical to that of Latinos nationally (45.6 percent) but lower than the rate for non-Latino whites (72.2 percent).

In summary, the Latino population has grown slowly but steadily in Maine over the last 40 years. Latinos have found opportunities for employment and affordable housing. Maine's Latino population is located in the southern part of the state, whereas traditionally migrant and seasonal workers have been in the northern part of the state. The Latino population is growing more from internal migration than from international migration. Some anti-immigrant bias has surfaced in the state that has tarnished the rather positive reception that Latinos had initially received. Most people in Maine have welcomed Latinos and have been appreciative of their economic and social contributions. As the Latino population continues to grow, some believe that the conditions are positive for the Latino population to develop a strong middle-class presence in the state. The present concentration of Latinos in southern Maine could be a harbinger of increased internal and international migration to the state. As is the case in other regions of the United States, it is likely that beneficial socioeconomic integration will occur as both Latinos and others residing in Maine accommodate one another, rather than Latinos alone conforming to some imagined homogenous national identity.[8]

NOTABLE LATINOS

Yepes, Carlos (1952–). Carlos Yepes, the Peter M. Small associate professor of Romance languages at Bowdoin College, is the author of *Oficios del goce: Poesía y debate cultural en Hispanoamérica (1960–2000)*.

Faverón-Patriau, Gustavo (1967–). Gustavo Faverón-Patriau is the author of *Rebeldes: Sublevaciones Indígenas en Hispanoamérica en el Siglo XVIII*. He serves as an assistant professor of Romance languages at Bowdoin College.

CULTURAL CONTRIBUTIONS

Latinos in Maine have been increasingly making cultural contributions to the state. With a larger Latino population in the southern part of the state, Latino community leaders have focused on creating an internal organizational structure to develop activities to highlight the rich Latino culture. Their efforts are paying dividends as a number of Latino-focused programs and events are regularly held. For example, there are many opportunities to participate in Latino dance and music in the Portland area, and the local community radio station in Portland, WMPG, has a weekly Latino program.

Development of Latino Organizations

Latinos in Maine have begun to develop social institutions to help them keep a strong sense of identity. The Latin Community Council of Maine and the Centro Latino of Maine are two organizations in Portland that strive to improve the quality of life for Latinos. For example, the Centro Latino publishes *Mi Gente*, a bilingual directory of Latino-owned businesses, Spanish-speaking service providers, and community events and activities relevant to the Latino community. The Latin Community Council sponsors the annual Día de la Raza, a day for Latinos to connect with one another and enjoy Latino food, music, and dance. More importantly, these organizations provide Maine's Latinos with opportunities to develop connections with the established community structures. From these connections, Maine's Latinos are creating businesses and programs that highlight Latino contributions to the state.

The connections that have developed between Latinos and other Maine residents are important for the local community as well. The efforts of Maine's Latino leaders call attention to the needs and resources of the Latino community. They also demonstrate the willingness of those leaders to work in collaboration with

Marchers participating in the opening ceremony to the 2007 Portland Soccer Championship. Courtesy of the Portland Public Health Commission.

local institutions. For example, Portland's Public Health Commission sponsors an annual soccer championship to promote Latino health outreach programs. This event draws people to participate in the soccer tournament and allows Latinos to celebrate their culture with a parade and Latino food and dance. The event is also an opportunity for the Public Health Commission to provide health promotion materials for the growing Latino population in the area.

Churches and Religious Organizations

Churches are an important institution for Latinos, not only because they provide support, but also because they help keep Latino culture alive. Both Catholic and Evangelical Protestant churches reach out to the Latino community and offer opportunities for Latinos to celebrate their cultural and religious traditions. Sacred Heart Catholic Church in Portland has a full-time staff person who works with the Latino community. The church sponsors a women's group that has been successful in developing social activities and in incorporating many of the religious traditions from the different Latino populations. The church has also been successful in providing support for newly arrived Latinos. Immanuel Baptist Church in Portland has also developed Tengo Voz, a program that provides social and cultural support for Latinos. This church sponsors a women's group that helps its members promote their Latino identity.

NOTES

1. Weber, 1992.
2. P.J. Granberry, and E.A. Marcelli, "Latinos and Latinas in Vermont," In *Oxford Encyclopedia of Latinos and Latinas in the United States,* eds. S. Oboler and D. Gonzales (New York: Oxford University Press, 2005).
3. Marcelli and Granberry, 2006.
4. Singer, 2004.
5. Russell, 2006.
6. Grard, 2006.
7. U.S. Department of Commerce.
8. Suárez-Orozco and Páez, 2002.

BIBLIOGRAPHY

Grard, Larry. "Hard Work Pays Off." *Kennebec Journal* and *Morning Sentinel,* December 21, 2006.
Marcelli, E.A., and P.J. Granberry. "Latino New England: An Emerging Demographic and Economic Portrait." In *Latinos in New England.* Ed. A. Torres. Philadelphia, PA: Temple University Press, 2006, 25–52.
Russell, J. "Ellsworth: Police Detain Suspected Illegal Immigrants." *Bangor News,* 2006.
Singer, A. *The Rise of New Immigrant Gateways.* Washington, DC: Brookings Institution, 2004.
Suárez-Orozco, M.M. and M.M. Páez. "Introduction: The Research Agenda." In *Latinos: Remaking America.* Eds. M.M. Suárez-Orozco and M.M. Páez. Berkeley: University of California Press, 2002, 1–37.
U.S. Census Bureau (2001). Hispanic Economic Census. Washington, DC.
U.S. Department of Commerce.
Weber, David. *The Spanish Frontier in North America.* New Haven, CT: Yale University Press, 1992.

21

Maryland

Enrique S. Pumar

CHRONOLOGY

1500	The Juan de la Cosa map of the world (1500) indicates that John Cabot (Giovanni Caboto), the only explorer sailing the North American coast at that time under the British flag, may have coasted as far south as Cape Hatteras around 1498.
1572	Pedro Menendez de Aviles, Spanish governor of Florida, explores Chesapeake Bay.
1750s	Francisco de Miranda, a Venezuelan who later became one of that country's patriots during the independence struggle against Spain, plays a key role in obtaining supplies for the French admiral de Grasse, who then sailed to the Chesapeake Bay to help the Americans to capture Yorktown, Virginia.
1776	Maryland Convention delegates declare independence from Great Britain on July 4.
1960	With the outbreak of the Cuban Revolution, many Cuban exiles begin to settle in Maryland, along the DC metro area. Many Latin American political exiles trying to escape a new wave of dictatorships throughout Latin America settle in Maryland.
1970s	Economic crises and political instability in Central America increase Central American migrants in Maryland's DC metro area.
1979	The Salvadoran civil war and the Nicaraguan revolution contribute to the increase of these two Latino groups around Maryland's DC metro area.

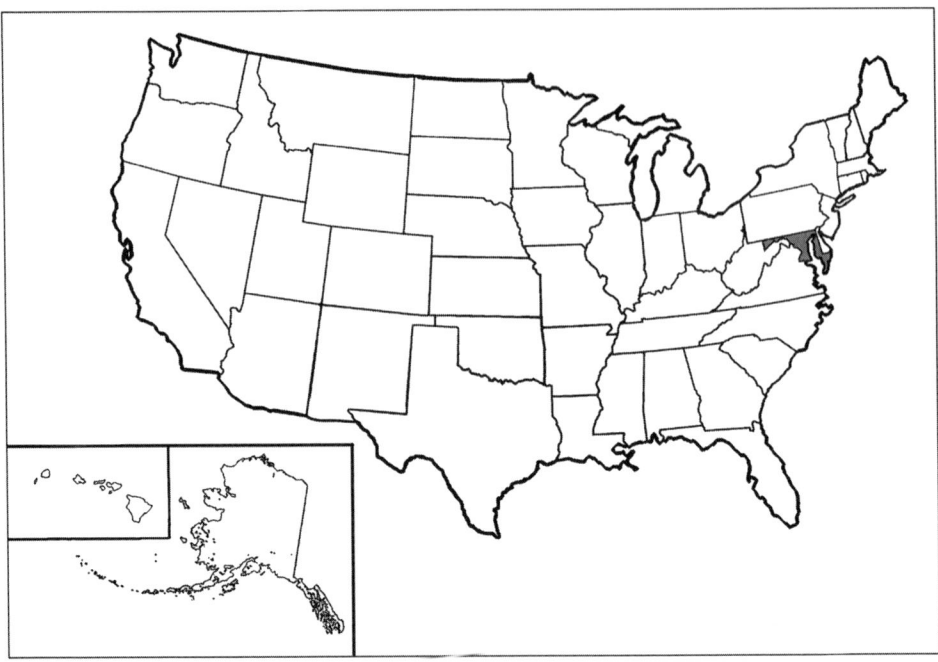

1980s	The years of the 1980s witness the largest wave of Latino migrants to Maryland. Between 1980 and 1990 the Latino population of Maryland rose by 93 percent, to more than 125,000.
1985	CASA de Maryland Inc., the largest Latino and migrant service and advocacy organization, is founded.
1986	The Hispanic Chamber of Commerce is founded, reflecting the increasing presence of Latinos in the business sector of the state and the purchasing power of this group.
1995	The Latino population in Maryland reaches 172,000.
2000	Statewide Latino groups form the Maryland Latino Coalition for Justice, an advocacy organization that scored various legislative victories, such as the legislation that requires state agencies to translate essential documents to Spanish.
2000–2005	The Latino population experiences the largest percentage growth of all ethnic groups in Maryland.

HISTORICAL OVERVIEW

Early History

As with other states along the eastern seaboard, Maryland's first contacts with Latinos came as a result of exploration. Governor Menendez the Aviles is said to have explored the Chesapeake Bay area in the late sixteenth century. However, unlike Florida, Maryland did not offer any strategic or known natural resource of value to Spaniards, and they did not establish any permanent settlements in the state. In fact, with the outgrowth of the British settlements in Virginia, settling in Maryland may have become a risk not worth pursuing.

With the expansion of British colonialism, the first settlement in Maryland was established in St. Mary's City in 1634, with 200 settlers, many of whom Catholics from northern Europe who had arrived in the lands granted to Roman Catholic Lord Baltimore by King Charles I. The economy of the state was soon to be dominated by tobacco, a crop that is not as labor intensive as sugar, which promoted the development of fiercely individualistic and relatively small settlements in the state.

During the American Revolution, Carlos III generously supported the rebel's call for independence, and many Latinos contributed money and supplies to the revolutionary effort. In addition, several Hispanic soldiers fought the British alongside the Americans. During the last major battle of the war, at Yorktown, Virginia, the French and American forces were able to sustain their triumphal efforts and pay for salaries, provisions, and ammunition, thanks in large measure to financial donations received from Latina women in Havana, Cuba. None of these events, however, resulted in the permanent settlements of Latinos in Maryland. In fact, by all accounts, the Latino population in the state was small enough not to merit an official count.

Recent Developments

Geography and the sparse communication between Maryland and Latin America contributed to the small number of Latinos settling in the state after the American War of Independence. Even throughout the first half of the twentieth century the Latino population in Maryland did not appear significant. This has to do with the slow demographic growth of the state, with an economy that has always been closely tied to both low labor-intensive forms of production and to the growth of the federal government, and with the fact that relatively close cities, such as Philadelphia and New York, have traditionally been magnets for Latino migration.

Like in most other states in the nation, the number, composition, and geographical distribution of the Latino community in Maryland have been in large part the result of transnational networks and events in Latin America. Before the 1980s, the Latino community in Maryland was primarily composed of a handful of professional and other political exiles who had left their countries to escape persecution; they took refuge in the counties of Prince George and Montgomery, along Maryland's DC metro area. For these migrants the major attractions the state offered were the abundance of professional and international jobs, its proximity to other major cities along the Washington, DC–New York corridor, and the relative low cost of living. This was the case, for instance, with the population of Cuban Americans who settled in the area after the Cuban Revolution.

THE GROWTH OF THE LATINO POPULATION

Starting in the 1980s the numbers and composition of the Latino community changed drastically. During this period the bulk of the Latino migration to Maryland came from Central America, primarily from El Salvador. The percentage of Latinos who identified themselves as Salvadorans in 1990 was 23 percent. The socioeconomic status of this new wave of migrants was also different. Besides professionals escaping civil wars and other political turmoil, Central Americans from lower socioeconomic strata arrived in the state, not only escaping the political instability of the region but also its economic devastation. When the effects of the debt crises throughout Latin America hit hard, working-class individuals also migrated and eventually settled in Maryland, this time attracted by the rapid explosion in the housing market and the booming construction job market in the state. By the end of the decade, the percentage of Latinos in Maryland jumped from 3 to 5 percent, and their median age was 27.4 years. By 2000 almost half of the Latinos residing in the Maryland–Washington, DC, metro area identified themselves as Central Americans.

Although Latinos in the Maryland–Washington, DC, area enjoyed a slightly higher standard of living than that of Latinos in the rest of the nation, this population confronted many of the same issues associated with the process of assimilation as many of their counterparts elsewhere in the nation. Almost half of the Latinos in Maryland are still not fluent in English, but they have a working command of the language. The majority is employed in the service sector. Despite the fact that the region's migrants live in middle-income neighborhoods, not the poorest, there is evidence of informal residential segregation. For instance, in Montgomery County, where about a quarter of the Latinos reside, the majority (77 percent) tend to congregate along with other working-class groups in the eastern half of the county, where there are more multifamily quarters available for rent.

In Maryland's eastern shore the Latino population is mostly composed of migrants who work in agriculture and the poultry industry. For instance, every summer hundreds of Mexicans and Guatemalans make the trip from Florida to work in the tomato harvest as migrant workers. As in other states throughout the nation, these workers are undocumented, they come without their families, and they constitute a very transient population whose stay is determined by the availability of work in the fields. Estimates set the Latino undocumented workers at about 50 to 60 percent of all the farm labor in the Delmarva region. When Mexican crews from Texas began to arrive in the early 1970s, the profile of migrant workers had a noticeable demographic shift in the agricultural labor market, as

Mexicans and other undocumented Latinos gradually replaced workers from Puerto Rico who had come in the 1960s, and African Americans who had come before that.

CONTEMPORARY ISSUES

The growth of the Latino community in Maryland has not been without controversy. The recent rise of ethnic tensions between Latinos and non-Latinos have manifested itself recently in two disturbing issues. The first issue is the so-called amigo shopping.[1] This practice refers to the assaults and robberies Latino service laborers suffer after they finish work late at night and are on their way home. Because most migrants use public transportation and walk to their homes after work, they are easy prey to robbers who steal their money hoping that the crime will never be reported for fear of deportation, or simply because the workers do not communicate fluently in English.

The second issue involves day laborers. In Maryland most day laborers are Central Americans working in construction-related jobs, such as construction proper, landscaping, and moving services. They are hired repeatedly by the same contractor or subcontractor, and they report incidents related to collecting their salaries. Besides the controversy regarding fair labor and hiring conditions, other minorities, primarily African Americans, have also accused day laborers of taking jobs away from them and lowering salaries in service jobs. Mainstream populations have complained that areas where day laborers congregate are usually unsafe. For these reasons, how to resolve problems with this sector of the Latino population has become a fierce political issue.

Yet, despite these obstacles, the Latino community has made tremendous strides in recent years. Politically, no gubernatorial candidate in the state can win without the Latino support. For this reason, both Republicans and Democrats are battling for the heart and soul of the Latino community. This is evident in the recent debate over illegal migration, in which Maryland officials have taken a less confrontational position than their counterparts in neighboring Virginia. In Baltimore, Montgomery, and Prince George counties Latino groups have established a presence that cannot be easily erased. The number of Latino organizations in Maryland listed in the National Directory of Hispanic Organizations is comparable to the number of such organizations in any other state in the nation.

NOTABLE LATINOS

Fernandez Cavada, Federico (1831–1871). A lieutenant colonel in the Union Army until his capture in the Battle of Gettysburg in 1863, Fernandez Cavada fought in the battles of Antietam, Fredericksburg, and Gettysburg. During the Battle of Gettysburg he was captured in Maryland and sent to Libby Prison, in Richmond. Later, he was appointed U.S. consul to Trinidad, Cuba, and in 1869 he resigned from his diplomatic appointment to fight in Cuba's 10-year war of independence. He was captured and executed in July 1871.

Perche Rivas, Emilio (1921–). Perche Rivas is the director of the Spanish Community of Maryland and an influential community leader in the creation and maintenance of educational programs for limited-English proficient students in the Montgomery County public schools. In 2006 then governor Robert Ehrlich awarded Perche Rivas a Lifetime Achievement Award.

Bustamante, Javier (1938–). Born in Seville, Spain, Bustamante resides in Baltimore, Maryland, where he has distinguished himself as a publisher, community and civic leader, and entrepreneur. He has participated in multiple commissions in Baltimore, and he has founded several Latino publications. Most notably, Bustamante has been the founder and president of the Club Andalucía, and founder and member of the board of the Baltimore Hispanic Chamber of Commerce. In 2007 he served as vice chairman of the Baltimore City Planning Commission. In that same year he was appointed commissioner of the Trial Courts Judicial Nominations by Governor Martin O'Malley, a position he holds to this day.

Iglesias Austrich, Jorge (1939–). Iglesias Austrich has been the director of business initiatives in the Governor's Office of Small Business Advocacy and Small Business Assistance since 1995.

Gutierrez, Ana Sol (1942–). Gutierrez has represented District 18 in the Maryland House of Delegates since January 8, 2003. Born in El Salvador, she has attended Pennsylvania State University, the American University, and George Washington University. She was president and chief operating officer at SOL Quality Systems Inc. from 1996 to 1999. Gutierrez has served in several community organizations, and local and state commissions. In 1997 she was awarded the Outstanding Contributions to Hispanic Community Award by the Maryland Hispanic Bar Association; in 1999 the Outstanding Achievement in Education and Politics Award by the Maryland State Teachers Association, and in 2002 the Political Leadership Award by the Hispanic Democratic Club.

Ruiz, Jose (1950–2006). Ruiz served as director of the Maryland Governor Commission on Hispanic Affairs from 1988 to 1995. In that capacity he organized a number of community programs to serve the Latino community in Baltimore—among them the Hispanic Chamber of Commerce of Maryland and the nonprofit Education Based Latino Outreach (EBLO). He was also instrumental in the growth of the Latino Festival in Baltimore.

Alonso, Andres (1957–). Alonso, a native of Cuba, is the chief executive officer of the Baltimore Public School System. He was deputy chancellor of the public school system in New York City before his current position. Alonso earned his bachelor magna cum laude from Columbia University and went on to earn law and EdD degrees from Harvard.

Barreiro, Mauricio (1958–). Barreiro is the chair of the Governor Commission of Hispanic Affairs. Born in Colombia, Barreiro has been a Maryland and DC licensed civil trial and business attorney since 1987. He graduated with a BA from West Chester State College, and a JD degree from the Georgetown University Law Center. In 2001 he formed his own law firm, Mauricio E. Barreiro LLC. Aside from the full-time law practice, Barreiro has been a consultant for many professional, social, and community organizations in the Baltimore metropolitan area.

Solis, Carlos (1959–). A community leader in Gaithersburg, Maryland, Solis is also a member of the Gaithersburg Policy Chief Advisory Committee and of the Mid-Atlantic Hispanic Chamber of Commerce, in addition to being the owner and manager of Family Dentistry of Gaithersburg. A native of Ecuador, Solis ran for the Gaithersburg City Council in 2007.

Lobo, Luis G. (1960–). A native of Alajuela, Costa Rica, Lobo is the chairman of the board of advisors of the Maryland Hispanic Chamber of Commerce and regional president of BB&T in Washington, DC, and chairman of BB&T's Hispanic Segment Task Force. His family migrated to the United States when he was 9 years old, and he was raised in Lincoln County, North Carolina. In 1983 he received a double major in economics and business administration from Belmont Abbey College and then earned a master's degree in business administration from Campbell University, in Buies Creeks, North Carolina. In 1998 Lobo received his graduate degree with honors from the American Bankers Association Stonier Graduate School of Banking at the University of Delaware. He graduated from the Advanced Management Program at the University of North Carolina at Chapel Hill in 1999.

Perez, Thomas E. (1960–). Perhaps the most successful elected leader in Maryland, Perez served from 2002 until 2006 as a member of the Montgomery County Council representing residents in Silver Spring, Kensington, Takoma Park, and Wheaton. He was the first Latino ever elected to the council and served as council president in 2005. From 2001 to 2007 he also served as professor at the University of Maryland School of Law. In January 2007 Perez was appointed secretary of the Department of Labor.

Torres, Gustavo (1960–). Executive director of La Casa de Maryland Community Organization, Torres was also the founding president of the Maryland Latino Coalition for Justice. He has served as a member of the executive committee of Prince George's County Chapter of the NAACP. In 2001 Torrez received the Leadership for a Changing World Award from the Ford Foundation, and in 2002 he was recognized as the Washingtonian of the Year. In September 2003 CASA received the Letelier-Moffitt Human Rights Award for its persistent fight for the fair treatment of migrants and refugees.

Aldunate, Wilson (1962–). Aldunate is the president and CEO of CompuData Systems Inc. and chairman of the Maryland Hispanic Chamber of Commerce. In 1981 Aldunate was awarded one of three scholarships allocated to Bolivia by the Institute of International Education (IIE) to study at the University of Kansas. In 1984 he received a BS in electrical engineering with a minor in digital telecommunications from the University of Kansas. In 1986 Aldunate worked as a full-time engineer at INTELSAT's Satellite Operations Department, and in 1987 at the Satellite Control Center. In 1995 he founded CompuData Systems Inc. (CSI), an information technology company that provides services to several federal agencies and public schools in the Washington metropolitan area.

Melnyck, Joseline Peña (1970–). Melnyck represents District 21 in the Maryland House of Delegates. She was an assistant U.S. attorney at the Office of the U.S. Attorney for the District of Columbia in the U.S. Department of Justice between 1997 and 1999. Born in the Dominican Republic, she graduated from Buffalo State College and received a degree in law from Buffalo Law School at the State University of New York in 1991. From 1991 to 1992 she was an attorney with the Defender Association of Philadelphia, Pennsylvania.

Ramirez, Victor (1974–). Ramirez has represented District 47 at the Maryland House of Delegates since 2003. Representative Ramirez was born in San Salvador, El Salvador, and attended Frostburg State University and St. Thomas University School of Law. He was admitted to the Maryland Bar in 2001, and he is a member of the American, Maryland State, Maryland Hispanic, and Prince George's County bar associations. He has been the co-chair of the Maryland Democratic Hispanic Caucus since 2004.

CULTURAL CONTRIBUTIONS

The close proximity and easy access to cultural organizations located in the District of Columbia overshadow some of the cultural contributions of the Latino population in Montgomery and Prince George counties, where most Latinos in the Washington, DC, metro area reside. The Maryland State Art Council lists 15 organizations and individuals who contribute to various forms of cultural expressions throughout the state. In addition, community organizations such as the Hispanic Cultural Association of Maryland and the East Baltimore Latino Organization provide a variety of cultural and educational programs.

All of the universities in the state support student cultural organizations. Of these institutions, the University of Maryland at College Park houses 11 Latino student organizations and several research centers promoting Latino culture in the state. The Latin American Studies Center, in collaboration with nearby community organizations, sponsors outreach programs to encourage first-generation Latino migrant students to attend college. Multiple community-based Latino associations run festivals to celebrate Latino culture and national identity. Two examples are the Fiesta de Sevilla, organized by the Andalucia Club of Maryland, which was founded in July 2000, and the Annual Gala, which has been sponsored by the Puerto Rican Club of Maryland for the past 28 years. There are three Spanish-language dailies published in Maryland.

The close cultural ties between the Latino community in Maryland and the rest of the Washington, DC, metro region can be illustrated by the work of the Ibero-American Cultural Attachés Association. Established in 1976 by cultural attachés from various Latin American embassies in Washington, the association has sponsored numerous activities to promote the rich Latino cultural heritage and its Latin American roots. In 1991 the association sponsored a symposium at the Library of Congress to commemorate the millennium of the Spanish language.

Latino commercial center in Wheaton. Courtesy of Enrique S. Pumar.

Later in 1988, it organized the first Ibero-American Chamber of Music Festival, and in 1992 the first of the Ibero-American Fine Arts Salon was held at the Venezuelan embassy. Today, one of its principal activities is the sponsorship of the Latin American Film Festival, held at the American Film Institute, in Silver Spring, Maryland.

Latinos in Maryland have also used art and culture as a medium to combat crime and other social problems affecting them. In 2005 the Latin American Youth Center of Washington, DC, expanded its operations into Maryland, opening offices and offering programs in Prince George and Montgomery counties to encourage youth development through art education. Named the Maryland Multicultural Youth Centers (MMYC), this center offers youth development programs modeled after those pioneered in the District for more than 30 years. To kick off its Maryland initiatives, MMYC offers an arts, media, and school beautification camp in Hyattsville, Maryland, in partnership with the Democracy Collaborative of the University of Maryland and the Boys & Girls Club of Greater Washington. In 2006 U.S. senator for Maryland Barbara Mikulski announced that the youth centers would receive $750,000 in federal funding to launch the Center for Educational Partnership, in association with the University of Maryland, to help combat gang violence in the state through such youth development programs as job training and placement, computer training, case counseling, arts activities, after-school programs, summer educational camps, and life-skills training.

A more sport-oriented leisure activity that also contributes to combat violence and other deviant behavior among Latino youth in the state is the soccer leagues where many Latino teams compete. In Maryland alone there are four well-established soccer leagues. For the Latino community in the state, soccer competition is more than just a sports event. It is regarded as a social networking opportunity and an occasion to reassert cultural identities, as many of the participating teams are organized along Latino nationalities and, in some cases, even along lineages and friendship ties from specific towns and neighborhoods in their native countries.

NOTE

1. *Washington Post*, October 26, 2007.

BIBLIOGRAPHY

Bean, Frank D., and Marta Tienda. *The Hispanic Population of the United States*. New York: Russell Sage Foundation, 1988.
Boswel, T.D., and J.R. Curtis. *The Cuban American Experience*. Totawa, NJ: Rowan and Allenheld, 1984.
Brugger, Robert J. *Maryland: A Middle Temperament, 1634–1980*. Baltimore, MD: Johns Hopkins University Press, 1988.
Fitzpatrick, Joseph P. *Puerto Rican Americans: The Meaning of Migration*. Englewood Cliffs, NJ: Prentice Hall, 1987.
Gómez-Quiñones, Juan. *Roots of Chicano Politics 1600 to 1940*. Albuquerque: New Mexico University Press, 1994.
Governors Commission of Hispanic Affairs. http://www.marylandhispanics.org.
Latino Health Initiative. "The Blueprint for Latino Health in Montgomery County, MD, 2002–2006." Montgomery County Department of Health and Human Services, May 2002.
Maryland Demographic Information. http://quickfacts.census.gov/qfd/states/24000.html.
Maryland Hispanic Chamber of Commerce. http://www.mdhcc.org/about/about_hispanics_in_maryland.asp.
Portes, Alejandro, and Robert L. Bach. *Latin Journey: Cuban and Mexican Immigrants in the United States*. Berkeley: University of California Press, 1985.
Renteria, Rose Ann. "A Vibrant Latino Presence in Washington, DC." *Footnotes*, May–June 2000.
Rochin, Refugio, and Lionel Fernandez. "US Latino Patriots: From the American Revolution to Afghanistan: An Overview." Pew Hispanic Organization. http://pewhispanic.org/files/reports/17.3.pdf.

Sanchez-Korrol, Virginia. *From Colonia to Community*. Westport, CT: Greenwood Press, 1983.
Singer, Audrey. *At Home in the Nation's Capital*. Washington, DC: Brookings Institution Center on Urban and Metropolitan Policy, 2003.
———. *The Rise of New Immigrant Gateways*. Washington, DC: Brookings Institution Center on Urban and Metropolitan Policy, 2004.
Valenzuela, Abel, Ana Luz Gonzalez, Nik Theodore, and Edwin Melendez. *In Pursuit of the American Dream: Day Labor in the Greater Washington D.C. Region*. Los Angeles: University of California, Center for the Study of Urban Poverty, 2005.

22
Massachusetts

Damian Nemirovsky

CHRONOLOGY

1890s	The Boston Independence Club Cuba-Borinquen advocates for Puerto Rican and Cuban independence.
1898	Massachusetts loses 292 men in the Spanish-American War.
1917	Congress naturalizes all Puerto Ricans through the Jones-Shafroth Act, facilitating the recruitment of individuals from the island by manufacturers and agriculturalists in Massachusetts.
1940s	Puerto Rican workers begin migrating to Massachusetts.
1950s	Puerto Rican agricultural workers begin staying year-round. Puerto Rican industrial workers greatly increase the Massachusetts Latino population.
1954	Eighteen hundred Puerto Rican farmworkers are recruited to work in Massachusetts.
1960s	Economic changes create large demand for Latino industrial workers in some areas, and the service sector begins to emerge.
1960s–1970s	Dominican workers begin migrating to Massachusetts.
1962	Rafael Benzan, the first Dominican to live in Cambridge, arrives.
1964	The Immigration and Naturalization Act restricts the use of foreign nationals in temporary agricultural work, increasing demand for Puerto Rican labor in many Massachusetts towns.
1968–1970	Cambridge implements rent control, preserving low-rent, affordable housing for low-income Latino families in the city.
1969	The Cambridge Spanish Council is established to fight for Latino rights in the city.

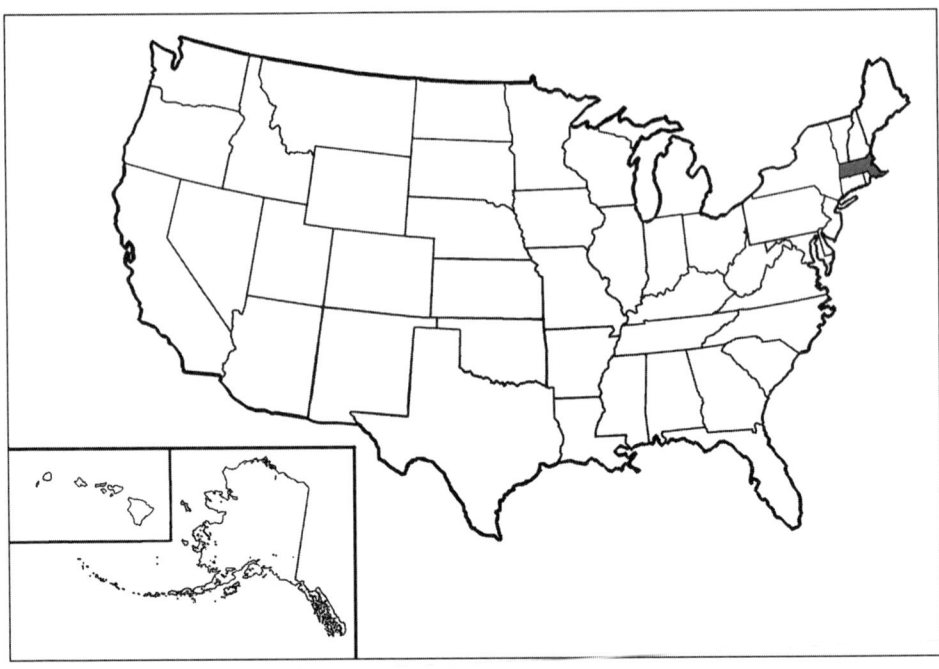

1972	Massachusetts passes the first mandatory bilingual education transition program in the United States as a result of demographic shifts and the work of activists in the Commonwealth.
1972–1994	Cambridge reimplements rent control, limiting the amount property owners can charge for rent and maintaining affordable housing for lower-income Latino families in the city.
1974	Judge W. Arthur Garrity Jr. of the Massachusetts U.S. District Court orders Boston public schools to be desegregated after finding a consistent and recurring pattern of racial discrimination against minority students.
1975	The Masters Parents Advisory Council (PAC) in Cambridge complains that the city is failing its responsibilities to Spanish-speaking students in bilingual programs.
1979	The Masters Parents Advisory Council faults the federal Department of Health, Education, and Welfare's Office for Civil Rights for violating the civil rights of bilingual students.
1983	Governor Michael Dukakis appoints a refugee advisory council. The following year, Cambridge becomes a sanctuary for Salvadoran refugees. As a result of the sanctuary offered to Central Americans by Massachusetts, the Latino population enters a period of great growth through immigration.
1984	Two days of riots break out between Latino and white youths in Lawrence as a result of that city's failure to incorporate the Latino population socially and economically.

1985	The *Harvard Journal of Hispanic Policy* is founded.
	The Cambridge Peace Commission proposes to the Cambridge City Council that city employees not ask individuals about their immigration status.
1987	San José Las Flores, El Salvador, becomes a sister city of Cambridge after a vote from the Cambridge Peace Commission, demonstrating the level of interest by non-Latinos in the cause of Latinos.
	Nelson Merced becomes the first Latino elected to a statewide office, representing the 5th Suffolk District in the Massachusetts House of Representatives.
1995	The Latino population in Massachusetts reaches 344,068.
1996	Federal welfare reform cuts public assistance funding and changes requirements for immigration requests, greatly impacting Massachusetts's Latino community.
1997	The Nicaraguan Adjustment and Central American Relief Act becomes a path for Guatemalans and Salvadorans in Massachusetts to attain permanent residence.
1998	Democrat Jarrett T. Barrios is elected to the Massachusetts House of Representatives.
	December 20 is the last day new Honduran migrants can qualify for temporary protected status. With the closing of this route for migration, Hondurans arriving after this date have much more difficulty attaining work, housing, and education.
2000	The Latino population in Massachusetts reaches 428,729.
2001	February 12 is the last day new Salvadoran migrants can qualify for temporary protected status. With the closing of this route for migration, Salvadorans arriving after this date have much more difficulty attaining work, housing, and education.
2002	Democrat Jarrett T. Barrios is elected to the State Senate in the Middlesex, Suffolk, and Essex districts.
	In November bilingual education is effectively ended by a vote on a referendum.
2003	Felix Arroyo becomes the first Latino elected to the Boston City Council.
	Democrat Jeffrey Sanchez is elected as a state representative in 2003.
2005	Latino population in Massachusetts reaches 490,839.
2006	On April 10, some 2,000 demonstrators protesting a bill that would make illegal immigration a felony march from Boston Common to Copley Square, forcing road closures.
	On May 1, as part of the Great American Boycott, about 2,500 people rally in Boston, and 5,000 in Chelsea, East Boston, and Somerville to protest proposed immigration policy changes.
	As he prepares for his presidential run, Governor Mitt Romney proposes a plan to use Massachusetts state police to detain illegal immigrants.

2007	Governor Deval L. Patrick rescinds former Governor Mitt Romney's immigration policy, and he changes and supplants it with one that deports the estimated 700 illegal immigrants sentenced to terms in state prisons.

HISTORICAL OVERVIEW

In spite of its small size and distance from Latin America, Massachusetts boasted the 12th largest population of Latinos in the United States in the year 2000. As of 2005, the 490,839 Latinos living in Massachusetts accounted for 7.9 percent of the commonwealth's population, making them the largest minority group there. Between 1990 and 2005 the population of Latinos increased by 203,290, or 70.7 percent. In addition, Massachusetts's Latino population has both diversified and spread throughout the commonwealth, increasing their economic and political importance. Although this demographic shift and its consequences occurred in the past few decades, Latinos have long affected and shaped the history of Massachusetts.

Early Latin Americans in Massachusetts

Latin American presence in Massachusetts dates back over a century. Accounts of Latinos in Massachusetts appeared as early as the 1890s, when Latin American migrants, advocating for the independence of Puerto Rico and Cuba, voiced their opinions. During this period the Latinos who arrived tended to come from the upper classes. The attraction for these individuals arose from Boston's prominent standing in the world and its renowned institutions of higher education, such as Harvard University and the Massachusetts Institute of Technology. These migrants, however, often returned to Latin America after realizing their educational or financial goals. Complementing the migration of upper-class Latinos was the small number of Latin Americans who migrated to Massachusetts searching for work in domestic service jobs. At the time, the limited number of Latin American migrants prevented them from having a collectively significant social impact and from creating a coherent Latino community.

One of the first mentions of Massachusetts's Latino community appeared in a newspaper article written by José Martí. Known for his poetry and journalism, Martí founded the Cuban Revolutionary Party in January 1892, and he was also the leader of the Cuban Independence movement. During his stay in the United States, where he lived between 1880 and 1894, he developed an affinity for Boston. Martí utilized his publications to spread a view of Cuba's northern neighbor that contradicted the monolithic perception held by his Latin American readers, namely that the United States had positive characteristics. One of these articles, published in the newspaper *Patria* on April 23, 1892, reported on his visit to the Boston Independence Club Cuba-Borinquen.

Pedro Albizu Campos, born in Ponce, Puerto Rico, migrated to New England and received a scholarship to study at the University of Vermont in 1912. The following year he attended Harvard University. His tireless work made a significant contribution to historical record of Latinos in Massachusetts. Taking advantage of his status as a Harvard student, Campos lectured about Latin American issues in a variety of venues both in and outside of Boston. He discussed and criticized issues such as the Monroe Doctrine, the silencing of Puerto Rican loyalty to the United States during World War I, and the ways in which the United States prevented Puerto Rican self-determination. The issue Campos worked hardest to achieve, Puerto Rican independence, led to his election as vice president of the Puerto Rican Nationalist Party in 1922 and as president in 1930. José Martí and Pedro Albizu Campos represent what scholar Andres Torres considers examples of the early and lasting presence of Latinos in Massachusetts.

The largest influx of Latinos into Massachusetts occurred after World War II. Prior to that period, the industrialization of Massachusetts depended on the arrival of European migrants. In the first period, between 1830 and 1890, migrants from Ireland, England, Germany, and French Canada provided the fundamental labor that supported industrialization. The recruitment of both these European migrants and rural farm girls from Massachusetts provided factories and mills with the cheap labor force that they needed, especially after the northern victory in the American Civil War and the subsequent industrial boom. As this period approached its end, migrants experienced an expansion of opportunities and success.

During a second industrial period, between 1890 and 1950, Massachusetts entered a process of industrial consolidation as larger manufacturers commenced absorbing smaller companies. This consolidation increased the demand for workers, whom the companies began recruiting from southern and eastern Europe. By the 1920s the manufacturing industry in Massachusetts began a noticeable decline, as companies moved either south or west. Even though World War II brought about a small boom to Massachusetts's manufacturing economy, deindustrialization and restructuring soon resumed. The beginning of deindustrialization coincided with both the commencement of large-scale Latin American migration to Massachusetts and the erosion of the opportunities which allowed previous generations of migrants to succeed.[1] The new conditions under which Latin American migrants arrived explain a great deal of the difficulty that the Latino community experienced in achieving the same success as past waves of migrants.

Post–World War II Latino Migration

Migration rates in Massachusetts dropped noticeably between the 1920s and 1960s, as the United States embraced tighter immigration laws that prevented

Farmworkers being recruited by labor boss in Caguas, Puerto Rico, to work on the mainland. No date. Courtesy of Archives of the Puerto Rican Diaspora, Centro de Estudios Puertorriqueños, Hunter College, CUNY.

industries from attracting the cheap labor source they had depended on throughout the previous century. The commonwealth's job market underwent a transformation, steadily losing employment opportunities to other locations. Even for newly formed migrant communities that had populated Massachusetts by 1960, including 5,217 Puerto Ricans, the success of the nineteenth century remained unattainable. New England lost, through both closures and failures, far more than did other industrial regions between 1955 and 1975. Furthermore, the manufacturing firms that remained were forced to reduce the number of people under employment to survive. Between 1967 and 1972 Massachusetts experienced a decline of 112,000 basic manufacturing jobs, demonstrating a pattern of decline in manufacturing that lasted until 1978. In spite of the declining availability of industrial jobs, however, there began a steady increase in the number of Latinos.

The first Latinos to arrive in large numbers in Massachusetts in the post–World War II period came from Puerto Rico. They differed from other Latin Americans in several ways, though primarily through their political status. In 1917, nearly two decades after Puerto Rico had become a U.S. territory, Congress passed the Jones-Shafroth Act, naturalizing all Puerto Ricans. As a result of this, Puerto Ricans emerged as a special case in the U.S. Latino population. Their status as U.S. citizens allowed them to travel freely throughout the nation, facilitating the process of recruitment by the struggling businesses in Massachusetts.

Initially, Puerto Rican migrants labored as seasonal agricultural workers in the Connecticut River Valley, western Massachusetts, and the rural region surrounding Boston. Many of them returned annually to the same farms they had worked at in prior years. The vast majority of these seasonal migrants were recruited either by the small local farmers seeking cheap labor or through the connection between the Shade Tobacco Growers Association and the government of Puerto Rico. The migrants were then contracted out as seasonal laborers to the large farms in the region—such as Reynolds Tobacco, Consolidated Tobacco, and other agricultural centers located throughout the Boston area—and to farms in western Massachusetts, the Connecticut River Valley, and portions of Rhode Island.

Slowly throughout the 1950s and early 1960s migrant workers began bringing their families to Massachusetts and settling permanently in the region, as they found a significant number of available unskilled labor jobs in the manufacturing industry and affordable housing. These migrants settled in a variety of locations ranging from larger cities, such as Boston and Cambridge, to smaller centers—such as Lowell, Lawrence, and Holyoke. During this period most Puerto Ricans who arrived in Massachusetts came directly from Puerto Rico, often recruited by individual companies searching for a cheap laborer willing to work the positions that the European migrants who had already assimilated into North American society refused to take.

Since the nineteenth century, Cambridge, Massachusetts, had been one of New England's three largest manufacturing centers and one of New England's busiest migrant access points, because of both the job opportunities located in the vicinity and the affordable cost of housing. These conditions that benefited the new generation of migrants resulted from the dispersal of the European migrants who predated early Latino migration in the 1950s. Much as other urban centers in the area, Cambridge began to see a shift in its composition as deindustrialization and the growth of suburban communities expanded, and the manufacturing jobs that had supported generations disappeared.

The Puerto Rican population in the area originated predominantly from the towns of Coamo and Jayuya. They arrived as a result of the communal and familial connections binding them to the Puerto Rican migrants who had already settled in the Cambridgeport area.[2] Through these connections, newcomers found it easier to locate both housing and employment in the region, thereby drawing more Puerto Ricans from both Coamo and Jayuya. Because of this network the Puerto Rican community grew from around 50 in the 1960s to thousands by the 1970s. They predominantly worked in older factories, such as those run by NECCO and Polaroid, though a few did work in the emerging technological companies that would soon dominate the labor market in the Cambridge region. The community, furthermore, began to form an identity as it expanded, organizing community sports teams and banding together to demand better schooling for their children and housing for their families, while increasing their visibility to the other groups in the area.

Early Latino Populations in Smaller Cities and Towns

Smaller cities in the commonwealth—such as Lowell, Lawrence, and Holyoke—also experienced a great deal of Puerto Rican migration, which in many ways paralleled that of Cambridge and Boston. In the case of Lowell, the initial group of Latinos came from the Puerto Rican towns of Comerio and Barranquitas, both located in the interior of Puerto Rico, toward the eastern side of the island. The earliest group arrived in Lowell as a result of direct recruitment by manufacturing companies that were finding it ever more difficult to employ a cheap workforce. These companies focused their recruitment on Comerio and Barranquitas because they owned manufacturing plants there. This link between the two regions facilitated the location and recruitment of workers because company branches in Massachusetts employed individuals in Puerto Rico. Through this network, 43 Puerto Ricans were living in Lowell by 1960.

Early Latino migrants to the city of Lawrence were also from Puerto Rico; however, these individuals tended to come from two coastal towns, Juana Diaz and Guayama. Numbering a mere 28 people by 1960, this group arrived as a result of familial and kin networks. Lawrence emerged as an attractive location for the same reasons as Boston, Cambridge, and Lowell. The restructuring in the manufacturing industry deeply affected the local labor situation, as more low-paying, unskilled jobs became available, because the existing regional population refused to work for those wages. Additionally, in both Lowell and Lawrence the lack of job stability—caused by the continual closing of factories and mills, paired with the difficulty that the community faced in integrating itself with the rest of the city's resident—led to the formation of a close-knit group.

Similarly to both Lowell and Lawrence, the city of Holyoke—located in south central Massachusetts, on the Connecticut River—flourished as a manufacturing center during the nineteenth and early twentieth centuries. Holyoke industries focused predominantly on the production of paper created in mills powered by the flow of the Connecticut River, but deindustrialization took a heavy toll on the manufacturing output of the city in the 1920s. Latinos, initially from Puerto Rico, began to arrive during the late 1950s as seasonal laborers working the local farms. At first recruited as agricultural workers, as the 1950s and 1960s proceeded, greater numbers of individuals stopped returning to their homes in Puerto Rico during the off-seasons, and they began setting up permanent residences in Holyoke, employed in either the agricultural sector or the dying manufacturing industry. Initially having a population of 99 Puerto Ricans in 1960, Holyoke now boasts the second-largest Puerto Rican concentration of any city in the United States.[3]

Dominicans and the Second wave of Latinos

As Puerto Rican migrants established themselves in Massachusetts through recruiting and kin connections, a second group of Latinos began migrating to the commonwealth in noticeable numbers. Beginning in the 1960s, Latinos from the Dominican Republic began arriving and settling within the communities previously established by Puerto Ricans. Dominicans utilized the same social networks as Puerto Ricans to migrate north and locate both housing and employment. Many Dominicans traveled through Puerto Rico en route to Massachusetts, and this more elaborate migratory path required greater financial resources. As such, Dominicans migrating to Massachusetts tended to come from wealthier families, compared with Puerto Ricans.

In addition to arriving through a more complex route, Dominicans faced greater adversity than Puerto Ricans as they attempted to become either U.S. citizens or permanent residents. Unlike their Caribbean neighbors, Dominicans attempting to escape from the tense political situation caused by the death of Rafael Trujillo in 1961, and the U.S. invasion that followed, were not naturalized by the Jones-Shafroth Act of 1917. They found it much harder to locate decent work, education, and health benefits because of their nationality.

Although tensions existed between the two groups, their relative isolation within a much larger non-Latino population forced Puerto Ricans and Dominicans to form a more encompassing community in which they bolstered each another. In the case of Cambridge both of these groups moved to the northern section of Cambridgeport. This region of the city contained a higher concentration of low-income, multifamily housing. As time passed, however, the Latin American community in Cambridge faced ever-growing problems. The unskilled-labor jobs that had supported Latinos began to give way to more skilled, technological jobs. Between 1950 and 1980, manufacturing jobs dropped from 30 percent of the total job market to less than 14 percent, and the manufacturing industries in the area began to disappear, replaced with technological research companies that required a higher degree of skill than pervious jobs. Exemplifying this trend, MIT converted several local manufacturing buildings into a nuclear-engineering center. The transition from manufacturing to technology caused demand for property in the area to increase, which subsequently raised the average housing costs.

The establishment of rent control between 1968 and 1970, followed by resurgence between 1972 and 1994, succeeded because of the combined efforts of the Latino community and the well-established progressive forces in the city. Thus, although housing continued to be available, traditional employment opportunities declined, and service-sector jobs emerged as the dominant job category in the area.

Migration of Central Americans

In the 1980s a new wave of migrants began to stream into Massachusetts from Central America as a result of the growing conflicts in the region. The roots of these conflicts traced back to well before World War II, when exploitation and domination of Central America by the Spanish gave way to control by the United States. Guatemalans, Hondurans, Nicaraguans, and El Salvadorans found that their countries' situation deteriorated particularly during the Reagan era. The Republican presidential victory of 1980 signified a break with the policies of the previous administration, as the United States officially shifted from a focus on human rights to a fight against insurgency and communism. The Reagan administration chose to ally itself with the very dictatorships it previously opposed, believing that they posed a lesser threat to U.S. global interests than did communist regimes. For this reason, Jeane Kirkpatrick, the U.S. ambassador to the United Nations during Ronald Reagan's presidency opted to support rulers such as Nicaragua's Anastasio Somoza in his struggle against the Sandinistas.

The conflict between the dictatorial governments and the various insurgent movements destroyed the local economies and forced many into exile. Between 1978 and the 1990s, some 300,000 people died in these conflicts, and in El Salvador alone 600,000 people were forced to leave their homes. These political developments led to a marked shift in the characteristics of Latino migrants to Massachusetts from Central America. Prior to 1980 the vast majority of the individuals that migrated from Central America to the United States came from the upper- and middle-classes. Predominantly arriving from more urban areas and with a higher level of education, Central Americans tended to possess the resources for a more comfortable transition, unlike the earlier migrants from Puerto Rico and the Dominican Republic. Demographic patterns of the new Central American migration proved difficult to discern because family units separated and migrated in unusual patterns that were difficult to categorize. Central American parents sometimes sent their children to the United States, while staying behind either in Mexico or in a Central American country; other times only one or both parents migrated to the United States, leaving their children behind.

The first Central Americans to arrive in the city of Cambridge, during the 1980s, emigrated as a direct result of the political turmoil prevalent throughout the region. These people received a great deal of help from the solidarity movements that existed within Cambridge. Due to the formation of a nascent kin and friendship network that facilitated the continued migration of others from the region, Cambridge soon attracted a large population of Central Americans. By this time the manufacturing jobs that attracted Puerto Ricans and Dominicans had diminished significantly, being supplanted by technological jobs. Fortunately for these new migrants, a wealth of low-skilled service-sector jobs accompanied the growth of the new technological industry. Unlike the Latino population in other cities in the commonwealth, however, Cambridge's Latino population underwent some particular shifts, because of the labor market and the termination of rent control in 1994. By 1990, Puerto Ricans accounted for only 28 percent of the Latino population in the city, as opposed to the 53 percent they constituted throughout the commonwealth.

Migration of Colombians and Mexicans

The latest groups of migrants to arrive in Massachusetts in significant numbers originate from Colombia and Mexico. Colombians began their migration to escape the violence in their home country. Much as the Central Americans during the 1980s, Colombians have migrated in response to political and social instability. The first migration to the United States resulted from the period know as *la Violencia*, which occurred between the 1950s and 1970s. Following this first migration, came a short period when middle- and upper-class Colombians emigrated, searching for better educational and professional opportunities. By the 1980s, however, the migration of elites had given way to a more generalized migration as drug-related violence spread throughout Colombia. This last group, still arriving at present from Colombia, began to appear in significant numbers beginning in the mid-1990s.

In contrast to the Central Americans who arrived in the 1980s and 1990s, and the Colombians who began arriving in the 1990s, Mexican migrants to Massachusetts did not migrate to the commonwealth to escape political violence. As of 1990, Mexicans represented the third-largest group of Latinos in the Commonwealth of Massachusetts, behind Puerto Ricans and Dominicans. They accounted for 4.7 percent of the Latino population and had the third-largest growth percentage, behind Salvadorans and Guatemalans, in the decade between 1990 and 2000.

Latinos as Political Refugees

Understanding the difficulties faced by the Latino community in Massachusetts first requires an analysis of the immigration procedure that this community faced beginning in the post–World War II era. Recently, the debate over so-called illegal immigration has focused on states such as California, Arizona, New Mexico, and Texas. As of January 2000, however, the Immigration and Nationalization Services (INS) estimated that 87,000 individuals resided in Massachusetts illegally, an increase of 60 percent from 1990. Both anecdotal and empirical evidence suggests that this figure is vastly underestimated. As a result a large portion of Massachusetts's residents encounter difficulties locating housing, employment, education, and healthcare, among other impediments. These issues compound the complexities of integrating into a society that does not speak the migrants' native language, demonstrates a great deal of discrimination, and views migrants' arrival as a cause for concern rather than as a vital economic force that bolsters local economies.

The 1917 Jones-Shafroth Act naturalized as U.S. citizens all Puerto Ricans who arrived in Massachusetts under one of four immigration categories: permanent legal residents, undocumented immigrants, refugees under the Nicaraguan Adjustment and Central American Relief Act (NACARA), or refugees under the Temporary Protected Statute (TPS). Latin American migrants under the first category, permanent legal residents, constitute the majority of first-generation Latinos in Massachusetts. In order to obtain this legal status, migrants had to qualify in one of the following categories: "family reunification, employment, investment, international adoptions, beneficiaries of the diversity lottery, and those designated refugees or asylees who have been in the United States for at least one year, among others."[4] This status allows individuals to become U.S. citizens and gain all legal rights granted by the government.

The second group, arriving without legal documentation, constitutes a much smaller portion of the first-generation Latinos in Massachusetts. These individuals often arrive with this status because of several reasons, including the long wait in receiving a visa granted to family members of migrants already living in the United States, the difficulty in finding sponsorship from a U.S. company, or the difficulty in gaining permanent residency through the diversity lottery. There are several programs offering citizenship to undocumented migrants of certain nationalities. These programs, however, offer help to a very limited number of people, leaving many with no avenue for legalization. Of the Latino community in Massachusetts, Colombians best exemplify this plight, as their only means for attaining permanent residency or citizenship in the United States is through a limited number of visas awarded yearly. As a result a large percentage of first-generation Colombians reside in Massachusetts illegally.

TPS and NACARA statuses awarded to Latino migrants are available only to Salvadorans, Hondurans, and Guatemalans. TPS applies only to Salvadorans and Hondurans, and it emerged as part of the Immigration Act of 1990. Eligible Salvadoran migrants need to have arrived prior to February 12, 2001, and eligible Hondurans prior to December 20, 1998. Furthermore, this status will not lead to U.S. citizenship, only to a 6- to 18-month-long permission to obtain work legally and prevent deportation. NACARA applies to Guatemalans and Salvadorans. Under this program, migrants who received asylum prior to 1990 or who arrived in the United States prior to 1990 and applied for TPS are eligible to receive permanent residency. As of 2003, some 200,000 Salvadorans and 50,000 Guatemalans qualified for NACARA. Both of these programs, however, leave migrants vulnerable to abuses that could lead to deportation if any little mistake occurs during the application and renewal processes.

EDUCATION IN GENERAL AND BILINGUAL EDUCATION

Latinos migrating to Massachusetts faced a plethora of difficulties, both when they arrived and as they tried to integrate themselves into the greater community. One of these difficulties with profound consequences was their experiences with public education. Prior to 1970 public schooling in Massachusetts failed to support the growing number of school-age Latino children settling in the commonwealth. The 1970 report "The Way We Go to School: The Exclusion of Children in Boston" made public the policies and actions that prevented a great number of students from attending Boston public schools. Among the groups it examined, "The Way We Go to School" report notes that 48 percent of eligible Latino children did not attend school. The report concludes that this resulted from a lack of programs intended to reach and incorporate Spanish-speaking students. The findings published in "The Way We Go to School" came as no surprise to Latinos living in Boston; however, the emergence of this report prompted Latinos to force change in the school system. The Massachusetts legislature passed the nation's first bilingual education law in 1970, and by the following year Boston's first bilingual elementary school had opened. It was named after Rafael Hernández, a Puerto Rican poet, composer, and musician.

Though the passing of this legislation signified a victory for the Latino community in the Commonwealth of Massachusetts, there remained a great deal of work in putting the new policy into practice. To achieve the ambitious goals of the new law, educators in Boston needed to create programs and make the most of their resources to incorporate Latinos into the classrooms. Furthermore, they needed to improve parent-school relations, place greater funding into facilities, strengthen the quality of curricula and teachers, and offer more support to students who appeared highly likely to drop out.

During the 1970s Latinos labored to maintain the effectiveness of transitional bilingual education programs in Massachusetts. After the 1974 ruling to desegregate the Boston school system their work became especially important in Boston, the city with the largest number of Latino students. Latinos labored to create space in a system based on a black/white dichotomy that failed to offer a voice to a community not defined by race, but by culture, national origin, and language. Within the city of Cambridge, Latinos faced similar problems, primarily the inability to obtain adequate funding. Frustration over the bilingual programs' deficiencies rose so high that in 1979 the Masters Parents Advisory Council (PAC) charged the federal Department of Health, Education, and Welfare's Office for Civil Rights for violating the civil rights of bilingual students. The PAC claimed that the city of Cambridge not only failed to provide classrooms and teaching materials to schools but also assigned students not in need of bilingual education to overcrowded programs solely because of their ethnicity.

Despite the initial difficulties Latinos had established themselves in the public school system by the following decade. Their achievement levels, however, remained far below those of other students in Massachusetts. In 1986 and 1987, when state officials first conducted a statistical analysis of dropout rates, Latino students as a group had the highest percentage of students failing to graduate. As the 1990s commenced, Massachusetts underwent a period of educational reform that should have benefited the most underserved students. Unfortunately, nearly 10 years after the implementation of educational reforms Latinos still lagged behind other groups. In 1998 the Massachusetts Department of Education estimated that 29 percent of Latinos beginning high school would not complete their education, whereas only one-third that many white students would dropout.

Massachusetts's bilingual education programs contained many faults, but in spite of this, it remained a vital tool for the transition of many Latinos. In November 2002, however, the commonwealth voted to end bilingual education. Though 93 percent of Latinos in Massachusetts voted to retain the program, 68 percent of the total votes favored ending bilingual education programs. This policy reversal illustrates an alarming trend in an area with a great influx of Latin American migrants. Behind this vote lays the fear that the large number of Spanish-speaking migrants can divide the United States into "two people, two cultures, and two languages."[5]

Migrant Rights

The years following the termination of bilingual education programs in Massachusetts saw an increase in anti-immigrant sentiment across the nation. As a result, pressure mounted in the commonwealth's House of Representatives to develop legislation aimed at limiting undocumented immigration, seen by some as both a national security threat and a financial burden on the nation. In 2005, in a vote that fell primarily along political party lines, the House of Representatives passed, by a vote of 239 to 182, Bill 4437—the Border Protection, Anti-terrorism, and Illegal Immigration Control Act. Among other provisions, if enacted, this piece of legislation would prohibit the aiding of undocumented immigrants and make it a felony to enter the United States without documentation.

Though this legislation targeted all undocumented migrants, it primarily affected the Latino community. Initial protests occurred throughout the nation on April 9 and 10, 2006, drawing a crowd of 8,000 in Massachusetts. A second national protest, planned to coincide with May Day in 2006, received very little coverage and attention in Massachusetts.[6] Regardless of the subdued showing in Boston, these protests pressured Congress to let the bill die on the Senate floor and demonstrated the activism of the Latino community both in Massachusetts and throughout the country.

NOTABLE LATINOS

Gastón, Mauricio Miguel (1947–1986). Mauricio Miguel Gastón played a very important role in the struggle for Latino rights in Massachusetts. Born in La Habana, Cuba, on September 10, 1947, Mauricio Gastón migrated to the United States shortly after the Cuban Revolution in 1960. He attended Princeton University, graduating in 1969 with a degree in architecture; he then attended the Harvard University School of Design. In 1981 he received a master's degree in city planning from the Massachusetts Institute of Technology. He joined the faculty at the Center for Community Planning of the University of Massachusetts College of Public and Community Service in 1980. As a faculty member his research focused on the patterns of investment that displaced the black and Latino communities from the areas where they lived. Gastón succumbed to AIDS in 1986. In 1989, the Mauricio Gastón Institute for Latino Community Development and Public Policy was founded at the University of Massachusetts Boston. Its goals have been to improve understanding of Latino experiences and living conditions in Massachusetts.

Merced, Nelson (1948–). Merced is a former executive director of Alianza Hispana of Boston, which provides social and educational services to the city's Latino population. He was a founding member and first president of the Dudley Street Neighborhood Initiative, a nationally recognized community development organization. Merced served as deputy director for policy and planning for the city of Boston and as a commissioner of the U.S. Commission on Immigration Reform, which made him the first Latino to hold statewide office in Massachusetts in 1987. While in public office, he served the most racially and ethnically diverse district in the commonwealth, wrote legislation creating the Urban Initiative Fund, and was a key legislative leader for the first bill that sought to establish community reinvestment mandates for the insurance industry.

Arroyo, Felix (1949–). Born in Puerto Rico and possessing a master's in education from the University of Puerto Rico, Arroyo became the first Latino elected to the Boston City

Council in January 2003. In November 2003, Councilor Arroyo was reelected to a second term, and then again to his third term in January 2005. Arroyo's electoral victory resulted from his cultivation of an expansive and progressive multiracial political base, transforming him into the biggest Latino vote getter in Massachusetts history.

Otero, Nora (1953–). Nora Otero has served the Latino community as a mental health worker in both the Greater Lawrence Family Health Center, in Lawrence, and the Massachusetts Mental Health Center (MMHC), in Boston. Born in Buenos Aires, Argentina, Nora Otero migrated with her family to the United States from Mexico in 1987. She has a master's degree in education, holds an appointment as a Harvard teaching fellow, and serves as both clinical instructor in psychiatry and team leader at the MMHC.

Barrios, Jarrett (1968–). Democrat Jarrett Barrios currently serves in the Massachusetts State Senate, where he represents Cambridge, Chelsea, Everett, Charlestown, Allston, and parts of Revere, Saugus, and Somerville. Barrios studied at Harvard and received a law degree from Georgetown University. In 1998 he began his legislative career in the Massachusetts House of Representatives. In 2002 he was elected to the state Senate, and he was reelected unopposed in both 2004 and 2006. Barrios is one of five openly homosexual members of the Massachusetts General Court. Elected as a state senator, he is among the most influential Latinos in Massachusetts politics. He is currently running for district attorney of Middlesex County, a position which is seen as a launching pad for statewide office.

Sánchez, Jeffrey (1969–). Jeffery Sánchez, a member of the Democratic Party, ran unopposed for the 15th District of Suffolk County in 2006. His election to the state legislature represents the first time that Latinos have had a voice in the Massachusetts State House of Representatives since Nelson Merced's term in the 1980s.

Martinez, Pedro Jamie (1971–). Pedro Jamie Martinez, born in Manoguayabo, Dominican Republic, was traded to the Boston Red Sox in 1997, and short thereafter he received the largest contract by any major league pitcher. With 200 wins, Martinez holds the highest-winning percentage for any major league baseball pitcher. He played a key role in the 2004 championship, when the Red Sox's 86-year-period with no national titles ended. He is considered one of the greatest pitchers in baseball history.

CULTURAL CONTRIBUTIONS

The growing population of Latinos in Massachusetts has added greatly to the commonwealth's diverse culture. Their influence can be seen in the arts, theater, music, food, and sports. The Institute of Contemporary Art houses several Latin American pieces in their permanent collection. From March to May 2004 this museum had a special exhibit entitled "Made in Mexico/Hecho en Mexico," showcasing the transnational aesthetics of the relationship between Mexico and the United States. Harvard's Fogg Art Museum serves as another example of Massachusetts's Latino influence in art collections. The Fogg Art Museum not only contains several Latino pieces, but from March 3 to October 21, 2001, it also displayed the "Geometric Abstraction: Latin American Art from the Patricia Phelps de Cisneros Collection," an exhibit that boasted works from Argentina, Brazil, and Venezuela.

Latino impact in theater, music, and dance is also abundant. In August 2005 the *Boston Globe* reported on the growing Latino nightlife. Dances such as salsa, merengue, and tango have become increasingly popular, resulting in new theatrical performances and a proliferation of dance instructors. Local community centers now hold weekly Latin dance nights, and mainstream nightclubs not only mix Latin music with other rhythms but even hold Latin nights.

Latin American restaurants and food shops are dispersed throughout the commonwealth. Examples range from major chains—such as Quedoba, Margaritas, and On the Border—to more local establishments—such as Tango, an Argentine restaurant in Arlington, and Casa de Nana, in Springfield. These businesses have expanded in tandem with the Latino population, though there are also many Latino businesses in regions with a low population of Latinos. They expose the Massachusetts community to a wide range of disparate foods from Latin American nations and provide an important link to Latino and Latin American culture.

Latinos have also played a prominent role on Massachusetts sports teams. Puerto Rican–native Ramon Rivas became the second player from Puerto Rico to play professional basketball in the United States, backing up Larry Bird and Kevin McHale of the NBA's Boston Celtics in 1988. Baldomero "Mel" Almada, the first Mexican-born player in major league baseball, began his career with the Red Sox in 1933 and continued with the team, playing center field, until 1937. Current and former Red Sox players such as Nomar Garciaparra, Pedro Martinez, Manny Ramirez, and David Ortiz have become household names and constant reminders of the way Latinos have integrated themselves not only into major league baseball but into Massachusetts's society as well.

Latinos are also represented in television, radio, and print. In 1993 WUNI, located in Worcester, became the first 100-kilowatt provider of Spanish-language television programming for New England, showing a range of local and national Spanish programs. The commonwealth also has six Spanish-language radio stations: WNNW-AM (800) in Lawrence, WAMG-AM (890) in Dedham, WSPR-AM (1270) in Springfield, WRCA-AM (1330) in Waltham, WLLH-AM (1400) in Lowell, and WAZN–AM (1470) in Marlborough. These stations add a sense of community by allowing for greater communication and social involvement by Latinos otherwise isolated from the more dense Latino cultural centers in the Greater Boston area, and in central and western Massachusetts.

In addition to television and radio media, periodicals in Spanish (and also in Portuguese) are readily available throughout Massachusetts. And several cities in Massachusetts publish periodicals such as the Boston-based *El Planeta*, the largest circulating Spanish-language weekly in New England, and the Springfield-based *El Diálogo*. Massachusetts is also the home base for *O Jornal*, a Portuguese-language weekly distributed in the area of New Bedford.

NOTES

1. Previous generations of migrants had benefited from the growth of the manufacturing industry and the expansion of the economy. Thus, although migrants faced difficult economic conditions, they were still able to improve their children's lives through education and better jobs. Additionally, as Ramón Borges-Méndez (1995, 48–50) states, "[Europeans] were allowed to preserve their physical community unthreatened by urban renewal or speculation in real estate markets with which no recent Latin American and Southeast Asian immigrant would have to contend."

2. Cambridgeport is a region of Cambridge, Massachusetts, that historically used to house a large portion of migrants living within Cambridge. It is bound by Massachusetts Avenue, Harvard University, MIT, and the Charles River. Most manufacturing companies were located near Cambridgeport, where rent was lower. Currently, Cambridgeport houses a mixture of students, longtime residents, and young professionals.

3. Holyoke has a Puerto Rican population concentration of 36.5 percent, second only to Yeehaw Junction, Florida. http://www.epodunk.com/ancestry/Puerto-Rican.html.

4. Uriarte, *Salvadorans, Guatemalans, Hondurans, and Colombians*, 2003, 8.

5. Torres, 2006, 274.

6. Observed in several European and Latin American countries, this is an international labor movement holiday.

BIBLIOGRAPHY

Borges-Méndez, Ramón F. "CBOs and Non-Profits in Policy Intermediation in New Latino Settlements: The Cases of Holyoke and Lawrence, Massachusetts." Paper presented at the 2006 ARNOVA Conference, November 17. http://www.naccouncil.org/pdf/Borges-Mendez%20ARNOVA2-1-4-07.pdf.

———. "Migration, Social Networks, Poverty, and the Regionalization of Puerto Rican Settlements: Barrio Formation in Lowell, Lawrence, and Holyoke, Massachusetts." *Latino Studies Journal* 4, no. 1 (May 1993): 3–21.

———. "Industrial Change, Immigration, and Community Development: An Overview of Europeans and Latinos." *New England Journal of Public Policy*, special issue (Spring–Summer 1995): 43–58.

Donghi, Tulio Halperín. *The Contemporary History of Latin America*. Durham, NC: Duke University Press, 1993.

Morales, Julio. *Puerto Rican Poverty and Migration: We Just Had to Try Elsewhere*. New York: Praeger Publishers, 1986.

Perez, Deborah Maira, and Melissa Lee. "The Evolution of the Latino Community in Cambridge, Massachusetts." Tufts University, Anthropology 183: Urban Borderlands, Spring 2002. http://repository01.lib.tufts.edu:8080/fedora/get/tufts:MS083.001.001.00013/bdef:TuftsPDF/getPDF (accessed February 2007).

Torres, Andres. *Latinos in New England*. Philadelphia, PA: Temple University Press, 2006.

U.S. Census Bureau. http://www.census.gov.

Uriarte, Miren. "Massachusetts." In *The Oxford Encyclopedia of Latinos and Latinas in the United States*. Eds. Suzanne Oboler and Deena González. New York: Oxford University Press, 2005, 87–88.

———. *Salvadorans, Guatemalans, Hondurans and Colombians: A Scan of Needs of Recent Latin American Immigrants to the Boston Area*. Boston, MA: Mauricio Gastón Institute for Latino Community Development and Public Policy, 2003.

Uriarte, Miren, and Lisa Chavez. *Latino Students and the Massachusetts Public Schools*. Boston, MA: Mauricio Gastón Institute for Latino Community Development and Public Policy, 2000.

Uriarte, Miren, Paul Osterman, Carol Hardy-Fanta, and Edwin Meléndez. *Latinos in Boston: Confronting Poverty, Building Community*. Boston, MA: Boston Persistent Poverty Project, 1992.

23

MICHIGAN

Jesse Hoffnung-Garskof

CHRONOLOGY

1846	Michigan senator Lewis Cass makes a speech before the Senate supporting the war against Mexico.
1876	Jose Celso Barbosa, the first Puerto Rican and the first Puerto Rican with African ancestry to study medicine in the United States, enrolls at the University of Michigan.
1897	Federal and state subsidies lead to the creation of Michigan's beet sugar industry, which would later employ thousands of Mexicans and Mexican Americans.
1915	First trainloads of Mexican-origin workers recruited to work in Michigan's beet fields.
1920–1921	The Mexican consulate helps to repatriate 1,500 Mexican citizens who were left unemployed by the cancellation of the beet harvest and by layoffs at automobile plants.
1926	The Comisión Honorífica Mexicana in Detroit begins to organize Cinco de Mayo and Independence Day festivals regularly.
1930–1933	Repatriation campaigns remove thousands of Mexicans and many Mexican Americans from Michigan.
1932	Mexican artists Diego Rivera and Frida Kahlo move to Detroit to work on murals at the Detroit Institute of Art which were commissioned by industrialist Edsel Ford.
1935	Blissfield beet workers, including both European and Mexican American migrants, go on strike for decent wages.

1942–1964	The Bracero program brings thousands of Mexican workers to the state.
1946	American Legion Post 505 is founded in Detroit by Mexican American veterans.
1947	Construction begins on the Lodge Expressway in Detroit, displacing Latino businesses and residents.
1950	Some 5,300 Puerto Ricans are airlifted to Michigan to harvest beet.
1952	Operation Wetback starts roundups of undocumented workers in Michigan.
1965	Michigan Migrant Opportunity Program is founded with a federal antipoverty grant.
1967	The March for Migrants goes from Saginaw to Lansing.
1968	The Cristo Rey Community Center is founded in Lansing to provide educational and social services as well as antipoverty programs to Latinos and other low-income residents.
1969	Latin Americans for Social and Economic Development, a community agency providing services to Latinos, is founded in Detroit.
1971–1972	Student protests and community activism create the Chicano-Boricua Studies program at Wayne State University.
1974	Michigan legislature recognizes the right to bilingual and bicultural education in the state.
1981	La Casa de la Unidad, a Latino arts organization, is founded in Detroit.
1984	The Latina/o Studies program is created at the University of Michigan.

1989	The Mexicantown Redevelopment Project is created in Detroit to promote alternatives to traditional urban renewal.
	The Julian Samora Research Institute is founded at Michigan State University.
1993	*El Vocero Hispano* (The Hispanic Voice) starts to be published in Grand Rapids.
2003	Ground is broken at Detroit's Mexicantown International Welcome Center and Mercado.
2006	Immigrant rights rallies mobilize 30,000 marchers in Detroit and 10,000 in Grand Rapids.

HISTORICAL OVERVIEW

The first Latinos to arrive in Michigan were Mexicans who came around 1915 to work in the state's sugar beet fields, railroad lines, and automobile plants. When Mexican workers arrived, political and economic elites and ordinary citizens perceived them, and the many thousands of European migrants in the state, as alien to their basic notion of "America." According to this thinking, Michigan, like the United States as a whole, was a racial and cultural entity defined as white, Anglo-Saxon, and Protestant. Less than a century earlier, when the United States first claimed the territory of Michigan, the residents were mostly Anishnabe (also often called Ojibwe), Ottowa, and Potowotomi. They had lived alongside French fur traders and culturally and racially mixed people (*métis*) for several hundred years. A boom in migration from the United States after the construction of the Erie Canal (1825) allowed Michigan to enter the Union in 1837. The newcomers defined both statehood and American nationality as Anglo-American, either by reconfiguring the local people as racial and cultural outsiders or, when more convenient, by absorbing them.

Michigan citizens, led by the expansionist senator Lewis Cass, participated in the war against Mexico in the 1840s, which was defined as a conflict against treacherous Spanish and mongrel Catholics. Michigan politicians participated in the compromises after the Reconstruction that stripped the basic citizenship rights from African Americans. In 1898, Michigan troops took part in the war against Spain and in the colonization of Puerto Rico and the Philippines, reviving the battle cry against the Spanish and asserting the right of the white United States to rule over inferior Caribbean and Pacific "races."

Each of these engagements contributed to the notion that Michigan was a white, Anglo-Saxon, Protestant place, defined in opposition to racial, cultural, and religious others. The idea that Mexicans were Latins out of place in an Anglo place derived from the struggle for white supremacy at home, and expansionist and imperialist projects abroad. To make matters worse, the first Mexicans arrived in Michigan just as the state's political elites started to become agitated because of the threat that migration posed to their racial vision of America.

Despite the worries of these immigration reformers, the state depended on imported labor for its prosperity. Since the 1890s migrant families from southern and eastern Europe had tended the state's sugar beets and staffed Detroit's assembly lines. During World War I an interruption in trans-Atlantic travel threatened this labor supply. In 1915 Michigan sugar companies began to recruit workers from the growing Mexican migrant population of south Texas. In 1917 the dozens of expanding automobile manufacturers in Detroit began recruiting Mexican workers from Michigan farms and directly from Mexico, along with the African American workers they brought in from the South. By the end of 1920 there were about 4,000 Mexican-born people living in Detroit. Living in a city with nearly 300,000 European migrants and 40,000 African American migrants, Mexicans escaped the notice of the worst anti-immigrant and white supremacist forces. Yet, like the European and African American workers they lived among, they were highly vulnerable to the whim of employers. Facing a severe recession, in the spring of 1920 sugar companies cancelled the beet season, leaving workers stranded in their camps with no work or wages. In Detroit the automobile industry laid off 80 percent of the workforce, including nearly all the Mexican workers. The Mexican consulate, Catholic Church, and local mutual aid societies raised money to help about 1,500 Mexicans living in Detroit to return to their families in Mexico.[1]

The 1920s

In 1921, in an effort to protect the supremacy of Anglo-Saxons in the United States, Congress passed a law to restrict new migration from Europe. As the postwar depression subsided, Michigan employers, unable to get new European workers, renewed their recruitment efforts in Texas. By 1927, some 20,000 Mexican-origin contract workers constituted three-quarters of the workforce in Michigan beet fields. Beet work stretched from May to November, but it included a dead period in August and September, between the last weeding of the beets and the harvest. During these months workers migrated to fruit- and vegetable-producing areas of Michigan to pick tomatoes, cucumbers, onions, apples, or cherries. Then in the winter they moved back to Texas to pick winter crops and cotton. Most Mexican migrants hailed from the states of Michoacán, Jalisco, and Guanajuato, areas torn by political and religious conflicts in the 1920s. But before coming to Michigan they lived in the Rio Grande Valley of south Texas, where they encountered the brutal legacies of U.S. conquest: segregation, lynching, and other campaigns of terror against local ethnic Mexican populations.

Although being in Michigan represented a welcome respite from violence in Mexico and south Texas, labor conditions for Mexican agricultural workers in that state were precarious in the 1920s. Some workers lived in trailers or camps provided by sugar companies, whereas others squatted in abandoned farmhouses. They had little access to basic sanitation or health care. The work itself required constant bending from the waist, which frequently led to chronic pain and disability. Wages were so low that families relied on the labor of children to ensure a minimum level of subsistence. The Texan-Mexican folk song "The Betabeleros ("The Beetworkers") recorded the disillusionment many migrant workers felt about their experiences in the Michigan beet fields.

These early migrant laborers lived in impoverished, often marginal, camps, but they were hardly marginal to the history of the state. To the contrary, the labor of Mexican sugar workers in Michigan contributed to one the most significant cultural transformations in the United States in the twentieth century, namely the rise of mass consumption. Sugar was the first commodity that reached all sectors of U.S. society, serving first as a cheap source of calories to feed a growing urban working class; then as a desirable product, as workers in the United States shifted from working to avoid starvation to working in order to consume more of the things they liked; in fact, Americans liked nothing so consistently or so voraciously as the sweetness of sugar. By the 1920s the residents of the United States consumed more than 100 pounds of sugar each year per capita, and the government saw the sugar supply as a matter of national security. Almost all of the sugar consumed in the United States came either from sugarcane in the Caribbean—worked by Puerto Rican, West Indian, Cuban, and Haitian laborers—or from beets in Michigan and other northern states, worked by Mexicans and Mexican Americans. Although the sugar industry helped usher in a new era of the citizen-consumer, most of the Caribbean or Latino migrant workers who produced sugar continued to labor, season to season, merely to avoid starvation.

It is no surprise, then, that when given the option, Mexican-origin workers in Michigan did not remain in the beet fields. As Michigan manufacturing grew in the 1920s, many migrant workers moved into cities in search of jobs in railroad maintenance, industry, or construction; others came directly from Mexico. By 1928 there were 15,000 Mexicans and Mexican Americans living in Detroit; outside the southwestern states only Chicago had a larger *colonia* (neighborhood). Mexican migrants working at the Michigan Central Railroad built camps near the train depot on Michigan Avenue in Detroit, and in the rail yards at Sixth Avenue and Plum Street. There they recycled empty boxcars into homes complete with porches and small vegetable gardens. Many factory workers either joined the Mexican migrants in the camps or settled in enclaves in the Irish neighborhood known as Corktown (along Michigan Avenue, just west of Woodward), in an area near Lafayette and Congress streets, as well as in Dearborn.

The growing Mexican population gave rise to a range of social and political institutions. Mexican parishioners collected the funds to build Our Lady of

Guadalupe Church in 1923, staffed by a Mexican priest. A Mexican grocery store opened in 1929, expanding within a few years into a chain of seven stores located in Detroit, Pontiac, and Saginaw, in Michigan, and Lorraine, in Ohio. Two mutual aid societies, the Circulo Mutualista Mejicano (founded 1923) and Sociedad Anahuac (1926) dedicated themselves to regular social events such as dinners and cultural acts. The members of these two organizations were the elite of the *colonia*: workers who had made their way up to high-prestige jobs in the auto plants and a few professionals. Workers with a more radical perspective founded the Obreros Unidos Mexicanos.

In 1926 the Mexican consulate convened the leadership of all social clubs in the *colonia* into a unified Comisión Honorífica Mexicana. The group began to celebrate patriotic festivals on September 16 and May 5. The main event of these festivals was a beauty pageant pitting the queens of the various clubs and organizations against each other to win the title of Queen of Beauty and Patriotism. These expressions of national pride fit closely with the general tenor of social life in Detroit, a city of migrant workers. National parades—Irish, Polish, Italian, Hungarian, or Mexican—were a way for ethnic leadership to build solidarity among constituents. The patriotic celebrations also fit more broadly with the efforts of the Mexican government in the 1920s to construct a national identity through public ritual. Mexican consulates and the expatriate middle classes did their best to extend this policy to Mexicans living abroad, hoping that a strong sense of patriotism might encourage emigrants to return to Mexico.[2] Mexican officials, especially, hoped that Mexicans who made it as far as Detroit factories might go back home, bringing with them the skills of modern industrial workers.

Despite these pressures to remain loyal to Mexico, many Mexican migrants and Mexican Americans in Detroit enthusiastically integrated themselves into U.S. consumer culture. As wages in Detroit rose, they bought cars and dressed themselves in the latest fashions. Mexicans in Detroit flooded into movie theaters to see silent Hollywood films. Many adopted the slicked-back hairstyle made famous by Rudolf Valentino, an Italian American actor famous for his depictions of Latin lovers. They also participated avidly in the tango craze that swept the United States in the 1920s, holding dances and crowning dance champions in their social clubs. It seems likely that both Valentino's Latin heroes and the Latin American origins of the tango held special significance for Mexican Detroiters who, otherwise, faced a constant stream of stereotyped Mexican villains and vixens in Hollywood westerns. Racial discrimination in Detroit also often prevented Mexican Detroiters' full integration into the U.S. working class. Segregation in Michigan was less formalized for Mexicans and Mexican Americans than it was in Texas; and it was certainly less severe for Mexicans and Mexican Americans than it was for African Americans. However, some dance halls, barbershops, workplaces, and landlords refused to admit Mexicans. These barriers tended to exclude Mexicans with dark skin. Those with lighter complexions often escaped discrimination by claiming Spanish, Italian, or even Native American heritage.

Depression, Repatriation, and War

During the Great Depression Michigan's farms and factories began to lay off workers, pushing thousands into homelessness and hunger. Meanwhile, across the United States the Depression gave new impetus to a movement to cleanse the country of foreigners, especially Mexicans. Michigan officials began espousing these ideas as the sharp rise in unemployment and extreme poverty overwhelmed state and local welfare agencies. Jobs and aid, they decided, should be reserved for Americans. Yet, they saw even U.S.-born people of Mexican descent as something less than fully American. Soon the Detroit welfare department and the federal government joined the Mexican consulate in offering to pay transportation costs to Mexico for unemployed workers, instead of providing standard relief. Trainloads carrying hundreds of Mexican nationals from Michigan, along with many U.S. citizens of Mexican ancestry and some non-Mexican husbands and wives of Mexican citizens, departed for the Texas border between 1931 and 1933. All told, between 1928 and 1936 the Detroit Mexican population shrank from more than 15,000 to about 1,200.[3] This was not quite the same thing as forced deportation. But it was a type of ethnic cleansing, nonetheless. When officials refused to grant public assistance to hungry and homeless people because of their Mexican origin, they made the choice something less than completely voluntary. The most notable and unusual aspect of the repatriation campaigns in Michigan was the involvement of two of the most famous Mexican visual artists of the twentieth century. Diego Rivera and Frida Kahlo moved to Detroit in 1932, when Edsel Ford commissioned Rivera to paint a fresco at the Detroit Institute of Arts depicting Ford's Rouge River automobile plant. Rivera, a communist, used both his fame and his money to help organize Mexicans in the state into the Liga de Obreros y Campesinos. In the Liga he articulated a sharp critique of U.S. capitalism, which, given the condition of Michigan's economy, appeared to be on the brink of collapse. He proposed that citizens of Mexico living in Detroit return to - Mexico, where the left-leaning government of Lázaro Cárdenas had promised to help returning workers build rural cooperatives. Rivera traveled around the state, organizing rural and urban workers in support of the plan and registering more than 5,000 for repatriation. When the first trainloads of repatriates left Detroit in November 1932, Rivera and Kahlo walked through the cars to bid farewell to their compatriots. Neither officials in Michigan, nor train companies, nor the Mexican government lived up to their promises, leaving repatriates stranded on trains or in border towns with little to eat and no place to resettle. Many repatriates, especially those born in the United States, eventually made their way back to Detroit.

Within a year, Rivera reversed his opinion on the repatriation program, arguing that Mexicans should stay in Michigan and organize themselves there.

The New Deal, World War II, and the Postwar Boom

Even before the Depression was over, employers again began to recruit Mexican-origin workers to the state. The New Deal helped to resuscitate the sugar industry in Michigan by guaranteeing prices and instituting new payments to sugar producers. In addition to its provisions for farmers, the New Deal began to defend the "freedom from want" for a broad section of the U.S. working class, including industrial workers in Detroit. Some rural workers made attempts to win the same rights. In 1935 eastern European sugar workers and members of the Liga de Campesinos y Obreros together successfully struck for higher wages in Blissfield. In 1937 labor and child protection activists within the Roosevelt administration tied sugar subsidies to minimum wages for all farmworkers, and eight-hour days for children over 14—which was the minimum age for a migrant worker to be legally employed)—working in migrant camps. But no permanent agency was put in place to enforce the rules. In response to the strikes and limited federal regulations, Michigan contractors paid truckers by the head to load up workers in San Antonio and smuggle them across state lines into Michigan. By the end of the 1930s Michigan manufacturers increasingly relied on few San Antonio firms, run by Mexican Americans, to contract and transport laborers to the state. Texicans, as local farmers called them, constituted about one-third of the workforce in Michigan agriculture throughout the Depression, working alongside white and black southern migrants.

New Dealers never guaranteed rights to social security, minimum wages, safe working conditions, unemployment insurance, and collective bargaining to these farmworkers. The state of Michigan imposed its own regulations on migrant labor in 1938 and 1939. These, however, were designed to protect Michiganders from the hazards of interstate migration rather than to benefit the migrants themselves. The state of Michigan sent Health Department officials to San Antonio during the spring contracting season, where they subjected potential migrants to inspections. Rather than offering treatment to the sick, they simply barred them from coming to Michigan. Only a few municipal governments in Michigan created clinics to provide medical services to migrants, but those clinics quickly ran out of money. In the early 1940s volunteers from local Protestant churches formed the Michigan Migrant Ministry to provide basic services and preach the Gospel in migrant camps. They sought to welcome workers on a temporary basis only, not to integrate them into Michigan society as full citizens.

The flow of migrant farmworkers to Michigan continued to grow in the 1950s and 1960s, bringing in as many as 106,000 seasonal workers in the peak summer of 1957. Many of these workers came through official government programs. Beginning in 1942 the federal government provided laborers to Michigan employers directly. Michigan was one of the states that received the most workers from the Bracero program—as many as 15,000 in the 1957 season.[4] During World War II, the War Manpower Commission also sent migrants from Arkansas, Missouri, and Texas to Michigan. Although the government served as a labor contractor, it made little attempt to regulate working conditions for any of these migrants. Braceros working for a railroad company in Ypsilanti, for instance, complained many times to the War Manpower Commission about the poor quality and scarcity of food in their boxcar camp. They received no attention until their complaint reached both the Mexican consulate and labor activist Ernesto Galarza, who visited the state in 1945. Children of all ages still worked on Michigan farms, and few migrant children had access to schools. Diphtheria outbreaks continued in migrant camps, and tuberculosis was widespread. When federal officials finally decided to regulate this labor market in the early 1950s, they defined the problem as an immigration control issue, not as a matter of labor and human rights. With a new nationwide outburst of racist anti-immigrant hysteria, the government sent a fleet of Army C-150s into the Midwest to round up undocumented workers and ship them to the Mexican border. This new repatriation campaign was called Operation Wetback.

That is not to say that migrants who moved between Texas and Michigan in the 1940s and 1950s were wholly docile, or that all Michigan employers offered the same subhuman treatment. When conditions on particular farms were bad enough, migrants often abandoned them mid-season. When rumors spread about bad employers in one northern state, migrants in Texas contracted to go to others. For instance, when Michigan health officials began their inspections in Texas, many migrants began to boycott Michigan labor contractors. Soon employers began to complain, and the state gave up on the inspections. On the other hand, migrants who found reasonable conditions on a particular farm often returned year after year, using the regular work in Michigan as a way to improve their lives in Texas. From 1940 to 1950 Candido Delgado, a bricklayer in San Antonio, came every summer with his family to work on the same Michigan beet farm. He could have worked the summer through in San Antonio, but he preferred to bring his family north. "You see," he explained in 1950, "we have got a lot of things to buy, and of course I figure the kids might have a house sometimes, so I just come here to make a little more." After paying back the sugar company for travel and living expenses, he and his three children ended the 1949 season with 1,500 dollars saved. Union membership in Texas would have made the trip unnecessary, but the bricklayer's union would not have him, so he chose to come to Michigan.[5]

The Boom in Urban Barrios

The cities of Michigan, meanwhile, recruited Texas migrants to settle and work in booming factories. Jane Gonzalez, who moved to Muskegon in 1946, later remembered that "the trucks would arrive and park themselves downtown in San Antonio. And there was a driver there who would give you the information, and the sign would say 'leaving for Muskegon, MI, . . . core-makers needed, welders needed.'"[6] Along with these direct recruits in Saginaw, Lansing, Muskegon, and Grand Rapids, many Mexican Americans settled out of the migrant stream, forming local barrios. The permanent Mexican-origin population of the state reached 65,000 in 1970, with almost all living in cities and working industrial jobs. More than 60 percent of the men in these communities were operatives in factories, and another 12 percent were craftsmen. More than half worked in motor vehicle or metal shops. Only in Detroit, with its earlier networks of migration directly from Mexico, were migrants from Mexico a large part of the growing Latino population. Overall, most of the new settlers were not migrants, but U.S. citizens. They maintained their ties to kin in the cities and towns of south Texas by sending a portion of their wages to relatives. Although they no longer returned to Texas for extended periods, many families in Michigan piled into cars for the drive to Texas to visit relatives during vacations. About 10 percent of Mexican American families that had settled in small and mid-sized Michigan cities by the 1960s owned property in Texas.[7]

These trips back south enabled Michigan settlers to compare their relative prosperity in Michigan with the violent segregation and widespread poverty suffered by their family members in south Texas. One member of the group Obreros Unidos in Detroit told a researcher in the early 1940s, "Detroit is better. . . . In Texas, especially in the small towns, people don't treat us good. In some of the restaurants and soda fountains they have signs like this: No Niggers or Mexicans Served Here. In Detroit, the people treat us better."[8] Yet, in Detroit, Latinos experienced the new, subtle, but equally destructive, forms of racial segregation that were emerging in American cities after World War II. Immediately after the war expressway construction cut through the center of Corktown, the commercial and social center of the growing Mexican *colonia*. Then, in 1957 and again in 1966, city planners razed more of the neighborhood to make way for a light industrial corridor. Barrio residents then started to shift westward, along the river, until the center of Latino commercial and residential life was in Southwest Detroit, in the shadow of the Fisher Freeway. The federal government provided subsidies for the construction and financing of new suburban homes for the many whites moving out of central Detroit in these years. But a range of practices kept these suburbs closed to African Americans and to most Latinos. The only public efforts at resettling residents displaced from the old barrio were two new public housing projects in Southwest

Detroit. Officials also built two projects in the nearby town of Ecorse, one to house Latinos and white Southerners, the other to house African Americans.

Mexican American workers joined unions in the postwar years, seeking the benefits of postwar industrial prosperity. By one estimate 75 percent of Mexican American men employed in Michigan cities were union members in 1967.[9] In many towns and plants, unions withheld leadership positions or preferred job categories from Mexicans in favor of white ethnic workers. The Latin American Steelworkers Club, founded in the 1950s at the Great Lakes Steel Plant, actively fought for, and won, inclusion in union leadership positions and contested on-the-job discrimination. With the new influx of Mexican Americans, the Catholic Church also returned to its prominent place in the Detroit *colonia*. In 1943 a Michigan-born priest named Clement Kern began offering Spanish-language masses at Holy Trinity Church. Padre Kern became one of the principal social and spiritual leaders of Mexican Detroit, helping to revive the older cultural and patriotic societies and setting up social services for the growing numbers of migrants moving from the fields into the city. Kern was also an outspoken defender of migrant workers in the state, testifying before Congress to denounce illegal labor practices and poor living conditions. The Holy Trinity Parish established a credit union in the late 1940s to help Mexican Americans buy homes. The parish also offered English, citizenship, and homemaking classes.

Mexican Americans in Michigan created an array of political organizations in the postwar period. Many of these groups, like similar groups in Texas, promoted Mexican American politics, emphasizing their citizenship and service to the United States and denouncing incidents of discrimination to local human relations committees. The American GI Forum, organized by Mexican American war veterans, had chapters in Detroit, Saginaw, Flint, and Adrian. The League of United Latin American Citizens also founded chapters in the state. The Federation for the Advancement of Mexican Americans operated in Adrian, and Latin Americans United for Political Action took root in Grand Rapids. In Saginaw, for instance, in the early 1960s Mexican American civil rights groups staged a successful boycott of a local agency to pressure for the hiring of Mexican American staff. The American GI Forum also sponsored Mexican American candidates for public office, mostly tied to the Republican Party. Leaders in the American Legion Post 505, founded by Mexican American veterans in 1946, also kept the Comité Patriótico Mexicano alive in Detroit, continuing to promote the public celebration of Mexican patriotic fiestas.

The Growth of Latino Diversity

Until 1950 nearly all Latinos in Michigan were either Mexican migrants or Mexican Americans. After mid-century other Latino groups began to arrive in the state. In 1950, federal policies designed to provide labor to Michigan employers and assist in modernization projects in Puerto Rico created the first major settlement of Puerto Ricans in the state. After five decades of U.S rule Puerto Rico suffered levels of unemployment and poverty worse than those in most of Latin America. Puerto Rican and federal officials hoped that by funneling the unemployed to the mainland, they could lighten the burden to create an industrial economy in Puerto Rico, raise living standards for Puerto Rican citizens, and demonstrate that U.S.-style capitalism could solve the problems of the Third World. Michigan congressman Fred Crawford was a leading proponent of migration as a solution to what he called "the pressure of population" in Puerto Rico. He was also a former beet sugar producer who knew about the seasonal market for farm labor in the Midwest. Along with the Migration Division of the Puerto Rican government, Crawford began, after the war, to promote Puerto Rican workers to midwestern farmers. When Texas officials warned that fewer Mexican Americans would be available for contracts in 1950, the Michigan Sugar Company arranged to airlift 5,300 Puerto Rican men to Saginaw for the beet harvest.

In their dealings with the Puerto Ricans, Michigan sugar contractors used the same systems of exploitation that they had practiced on Mexican American families for decades. They paid by the acre, passing much of the risk of losses on to workers; thus, if the weather was bad or if the fields were full of weeds, workers made less money per day. In 1950 both the weather and the fields were unusually bad, cutting workers income by more than half. Employers also held all wages until the end of the season to prevent workers from moving to better opportunities elsewhere in the state. Mexican American migrants survived this system by working as family units in the fields—men, women, and children. With everyone working, families could subsist on the credit offered by employers; and at the end of the season, after everything was discounted, these families received a modest amount from their employers. The Puerto Rican workers brought to Michigan were all men traveling without their families. Without women's unpaid labor, they needed to set aside food allowances to pay someone to clean the camps and cook. They needed wages sufficient for one worker in Michigan to support a whole family in Puerto Rico. And they needed regular paychecks in order to send money home to feed their wives and children before the end of the season.

Because employers were not willing to offer any of this, the airlift quickly turned into a humanitarian disaster. One airlifted worker, Santos Cintron, reported, "I have seven kids and my wife. They are buying in the grocery store on credit. I spoke with the man at the grocery store and asked him to give food to my wife and kids. Haven't sent one penny you see, in three months, because I haven't got it, the company hasn't paid. Now my wife writes that the grocery store stopped the credit."[10] Desperate, Cintron made his way to Detroit, where he found work in a steel plant. Foundry work was hot and dirty, but it paid him enough to send money home to his family every week. Other Puerto Ricans left the beet farms too, joining Mexican Americans in the growing barrio in the southwestern part of the city. There they became the pioneers of a growing Puerto Rican community in Detroit. Labor contractors continued to bring small numbers of Puerto Ricans to the state for the sugar harvest each summer. This helped build the permanent Puerto Rican population, but probably not as much as family ties did. Once established in Detroit, workers sent word to family and friends about jobs in their plants. In 1980 the federal census counted 12,425 Puerto Ricans in Michigan; in 2000 that number was 26,941.

Federal policies brought the first major settlement of Cubans to Michigan too, although under dramatically different circumstances. In the two years after the Cuban Revolution of 1959, several hundred thousand exiles arrived in south Florida. These exiles included supporters of the toppled Batista regime, business owners, professionals, and others threatened by the economic radicalism and shifting political repression in Cuba. U.S. officials waived visa requirements for refugees from Cuba, whom they saw as victims of a common communist enemy. The government also offered cash assistance, training, and other types of support to Cubans. Despite most Cubans' middle-class background and privileged status as refugees, many residents of south Florida chafed at the rapid growth of a new Latino population in their midst. In response the federal government worked with private church groups in an attempt to distribute the Cuban refugees around the country. These combined public and private resettlement programs had brought more than 1,700 Cuban refugees to Michigan by 1968.[11] By 1980, some 4,000 Cubans and Cuban Americans were living in the state. In the 1980s and 1990s, as new waves of refugees left Cuba, the Cuban ethnic population of Michigan grew to more than 7,000.

The arrival of Puerto Rican and Cuban migrants in Michigan raised a new set of questions: To what extent was there a Latino community in the state? And to what extent were there separate national communities—Mexican, Puerto Rican, and Cuban—simply imagined as homogeneous by outsiders? Because of their class status and because of the efforts made to distribute and integrate them into communities around the state, Cubans did not generally settle in urban neighborhoods occupied by other Latinos; nor, for that matter, did smaller numbers of Argentine and Brazilian professionals who came to the state to work at Ford and General Motors. Mexicans and Puerto Ricans shared the neighborhood of Southwest Detroit, but they did not necessarily share social institutions. Father Kern, of the Holy Trinity Church in Detroit, expressed frustration that Puerto Ricans did not attend mass in his church. The Episcopal Church of the Ascension in Detroit, on the other hand, saw a dramatic transformation in its membership in the late 1970s, becoming largely a Puerto Rican congregation. Puerto Ricans understandably showed little enthusiasm for celebrations of Mexican patriotic holidays, the primary spaces for celebrating Latino ethnicity since the 1920s. Rather than force their way into the existing festivals, newcomers set up separate Puerto Rican festivals in the early 1970s. Still, relations among these groups were not predominantly contentious. Not infrequently community activists from one national origin took up the cause of neighbors from unrelated backgrounds under the umbrella of a Latino community.

THE LONG MICHIGAN RECESSION

By the end of the 1960s Michigan industries again began laying off workers. Unlike the cyclical downturns of 1920 and the 1930s, the layoffs that struck in the 1960s and 1970s reflected a permanent shift of manufacturing out of Michigan and into the U.S. South, Asia, and Latin America. Things only got worse in the 1980s. The separation between middle-class suburbs and largely black cities that had begun in the 1940s reached a crisis as Michigan plunged into a deep recession. In Detroit the most recognizable symbol of this process was the widespread rioting in 1967. As African Americans revolted in response to their isolation in a decaying inner city, many Latinos retained an optimistic outlook. Migrants who left farmwork to take low- and middle-level industrial jobs in Michigan cities after World War II experienced a remarkable degree of social mobility. Interviewed in 1967, the vast majority of these industrial workers hoped that this rapid mobility would continue for their children. They wished for their sons to attend college and to make the leap to the status of professionals. Their ambitions for their daughters were more modest, reflecting the patriarchal expectations of the era. Yet, in fact, their children did not attend college in significant numbers. Only about 40 percent of Mexican American children were still in school at the age of 18. Only 7 percent continued in some kind of training or college after high school. This compared to 40 percent for the state as a whole. As a result Latino children were prepared mainly to continue in unskilled factory jobs, but these jobs were disappearing. According to an interviewed in the late 1960s most Latinos perceived themselves occupying an intermediate position between blacks and whites in Michigan. In practice they occupied small enclaves inside Michigan's struggling, mostly black inner cities.[12]

The combination of the emerging urban crisis and the federal War on Poverty program helped inspire a new kind of Latino politics in the state. In Detroit, city leaders planned a response to the riots that focused almost exclusively on the needs of African American city residents. This led the Latin American Steelworkers' Club, the American GI Forum, LULAC, and the Holy Trinity Church to create Latin Americans for Social and Economic Development, which became an outlet for antipoverty programs directed at Latinos. LA SED subsequently launched a campaign of rallies and demonstrations that won state recognition of a right to bilingual and bicultural education in 1974. In Lansing the Cristo Rey Community

Center grew in the late 1960s to provide a wide range of services to Latinos. Federal antipoverty grants also helped, after 1965, to create the Michigan Migrant Opportunity Program, a stable set of social programs for rural workers in the state, including daycare, schooling, and health clinics. These emerging, federally funded social agencies did not limit themselves to charity work. They became committed social organizations, fighting for labor rights among migrant workers in Michigan and seeking out and hiring leadership from within Latino communities.

The national context of Chicano and Puerto Rican nationalism and farmworker solidarity also helped to reshape Latino politics at the end of the 1960s. Across the state, local Mexican American activists and sympathetic Anglos organized boycotts of chain stores carrying California grapes and lettuce. These activists, led by United Farm Workers representative Julian Herrera, then joined in campaigns to benefit the tens of thousands of migrant farmworkers in Michigan. This effort included a 1967 march from Saginaw to Lansing, a 1974 Walk for Justice from Kalamazoo to Grand Rapids, as well as lawsuits against Michigan growers. Meanwhile, a group of Chicano nationalists in Lansing started publishing the newspaper *Sol de Aztlán*. Others founded a chapter of La Raza Unida Party. In Southwest Detroit two street gangs active since the 1950s transformed themselves into a chapter of the Brown Berets, taking part in rallies and demonstrations. Kalamazoo also had a Brown Beret chapter. At Wayne State University the Chicano-Boricua Collective, with the support of LA SED, began a series of demonstrations and protests eventually leading to the creation of a Chicano-Boricua Studies Program. Meanwhile, the Latin American Coordinating Council, led by Gloria López McKnight, organized residents in Southwest Detroit to resist further displacement by urban renewal. By the early 1980s, this group would not only give the Latino enclave in Southwest Detroit the name Mexicantown but also begin to build the Latino cultural character of the neighborhood into a plan for economic revitalization.

THE NEW MIGRANT BOOM

In the 1980s Michigan was unusual for its relatively slow-growing Latino population. As Michigan's economy slid into free fall, the systems of recruitment that pulled Latino workers from Mexico and from the migrant stream into permanent jobs in the state sputtered to a stop. New migration returned during the economic boom of the 1990s, most dramatically in southwest Michigan. By the end of the 1980s almost all of the farm labor in the area was done by Mexican or Central American workers who migrated between Michigan and Florida; many of these workers were undocumented. The economic expansion of the 1990s opened opportunities for these migrants to settle out of the migrant stream and move into service and factory jobs. Around the same time, many Dominicans living in New

York began fleeing drug-related crime, punitive welfare reform, and the harsh policing of the Giuliani administration. These Dominicans came to western Michigan because of ties to the Seventh Day Adventist Church, headquartered in Battle Creek. By 2005 Latinos were the largest ethnic minority in southwest Michigan, with large concentrations in Holland, Wyoming, and Grand Rapids. A similar process brought newcomers to Southwest Detroit, paving the way for new Spanish-language media, including a local affiliate of a national Spanish-language television network.

The sweat of Mexican beet workers in the 1920s had subsidized the early transformation of the United States into a consumer society by making sugar a cheap commodity. At the end of the twentieth century, as Michigan shifted from a landscape of urban factories to one of sprawling suburbs with bountiful shopping centers, Latino workers similarly subsidized the abundant fruits, vegetables, and meat on Michigan tables. They continued to work in fields and packinghouses for wages that were hardly above the bare minimum they needed to survive. At the same time many middle-class women in Michigan worked increasing hours outside their homes, the outcome of women's liberation struggles and of their families' rising consumer expectations. Because neither the government nor middle-class men stepped in to provide the household labor that women customarily performed, middle-class families increasingly relied on Latino, and especially Latina, migrants for tasks such as childcare and cleaning. Labor in homes, like labor in the fields, was poorly paid. In the first decade of the twenty-first century, in a country where expansive suburban consumption had become a key aspect of citizenship, this type of citizenship for some Michiganders still depended on the ability to pay Latinos very little for indispensable labor. As they had been doing for nearly a century in Michigan, Latinos took hold of opportunities to increase their own consumption, by moving from the worst jobs into slightly better ones. But the socioeconomic system relied on paying low wages for farm and household labor, so getting ahead was no easy task.

When the economic boom of the 1990s came to a shuddering halt after 2001, many politicians blamed Latin American migrants and progressive social programs for the state's economic woes. A ballot initiative passed in November 2006 banned the use of affirmative action in public universities. Meanwhile, the Bush administration directed Homeland Security officials in Michigan to round up what it called criminal aliens in dragnets called Operation Return to Sender. These sweeps often imprisoned and deported undocumented workers with no criminal record at all, or with minor offenses such as drunk driving. The result was widespread fear, a growing sense of community solidarity, and eventually mobilization in Detroit and southwest Michigan. In 2006 the U.S. House of Representatives passed a measure making immigration violations a felony offense thus turning all undocumented aliens into criminal aliens. The diverse Latino populations in Michigan took to the streets in protest. Ten thousand marched in Grand Rapids, and 40,000 marched in Detroit. These were by far the largest political demonstrations by Latinos in Michigan history.

NOTABLE LATINOS

Barbosa, Jose Celso (1857–1921). Puerto Rican intellectual and politician known for his position in favor of statehood, Barbosa lived in Michigan for 4 years, between 1876 and 1880, while he studied medicine at the University of Michigan. This made him the first Puerto Rican to receive a medical degree in the United States. The feat was more notable because Barbosa was of mixed African and European ancestry.

Gonzalez, Jane (1918–1977). City council member and community leader who migrated to Muskegon from Texas in 1946. After working as a court reporter, in the mid-1960s, Gonzalez headed migrant programs for the Office of Economic Opportunity. In 1964 she won a seat on the Michigan School Board, becoming one of the first Chicana women elected to public office in the United States. She later won election to the North Shore City Council, in Muskegon. In the 1970s Gonzalez served as chairperson of Midwest Mujeres de la Raza.

Benavides, Tony (1937–). Community leader and mayor of Lansing, Benavides migrated to Lansing from Mexico in 1952. He worked part-time in farm labor while studying in public schools and attending Lansing Community College and Lansing Business College. In 1969 he became executive director of Cristo Rey Community Center, a church-based social assistance agency providing services such as health clinics, employment programs, and youth activities. In 2003, while serving as president of Lansing City Council, he was elected mayor.

López McKnight, Gloria (1937–2003). The child of a Mexican American mother and a Mexican migrant father, she grew up in Los Angeles, where she became a designer of costume jewelry and an entrepreneur. She was road manager for singer Dinah Washington before moving to Detroit in 1963 to attend Wayne State University. She began working for the state's Department of Social Services in 1969. She led the movement to defend Southwest Detroit from urban renewal projects in the 1970s, and she testified before the U.S. Senate in 1972. As president of the Michigan chapter of LULAC in the 1980s, she organized protests to resist cuts in social programs.

Lozano, Raymond (1947–). Latino business owner and community leader in Detroit. The child of Mexican migrant workers who settled in the Midwest in the 1920s, Lozano attended Wayne State University and fought in Vietnam before becoming director of Latin Americans for Social and Economic Development in 1979. In 1980 he launched a professional and managerial career with DTE Energy. He became active in Latino business and civil rights organizations, eventually serving as executive director of the Michigan Hispanic Chamber of Commerce. He was on the board of directors and served as vice-chairman of the National Council of La Raza.

Abreu, Andres (1957–). Founder and editor of *El Vocero Hispano*, Abreu moved to Grand Rapids from Santo Domingo, Dominican Republic, in 1991. Trained as a journalist, he founded *El Vocero Hispano* in 1993, while working full-time at a local factory. Within a decade the newspaper grew to a circulation of 20,000. Taking active editorial positions, Abreu helped to elect the first Latino to the Grand Rapids school board and organized large demonstrations in Grand Rapids to support immigrant rights in 2006.

Herrada, Elena (1957–). Detroit community activist and historian, Herrada is the granddaughter of a Mexican revolutionary who fought with Emiliano Zapata before moving to Detroit to work in the automobile plants. Many of her family members moved to Mexico during the repatriations of the 1930s, but they soon returned to Detroit, where Herrada grew up. She worked as an advocate for prisoners in the early 1980s, and then as a labor activist with the Service Employees International Union. She created an oral history project to document the history of Mexican repatriation in Detroit. The resulting film, *Los Repatriados*, was released in 2000. After 2001 she helped create El Centro Obrero in Detroit, dedicated to defending the rights of migrant workers.

CULTURAL CONTRIBUTIONS

In beet fields, cherry orchards, auto plants, and suburban homes, Latino and Latina workers underwrote the transformation of Michigan into a consumer society, without usually enjoying full access to the evolving culture of plenty that they helped to create. This, in itself, is surely a remarkable cultural contribution to Michigan and the United States. When Latino and Latina artists and academics contribute to "high culture" in Michigan, they often choose to make migrant and factory workers the subjects of their work. The magnificent frescoes painted by Diego Rivera in 1932–1933 at the Detroit Institute of Arts, showing workers in Michigan factories and fields, are perhaps the best-known example. Similar themes appear in the work of Chicano muralists in Southwest Detroit, including George Vargas and Vito Valdez. The Latino Studies programs at Wayne State University and the University of Michigan, and the Julian Samora Research Institute at Michigan State support cultural and scholarly production, while working to preserve a place for Latino students in higher education. La Casa de la Unidad, a community-based organization in Detroit, works to bring arts to Latinos in Michigan and to promote artistic production by Latinos. The Fronteras del Norte Oral History Project collects the memories of early Latino settlers.

Latinos contributed to the cultural makeup of the state too, through efforts to build and develop their own community institutions. Since the 1920s, festivals and public celebrations have been important elements of Latino cultural life in Detroit. Representatives of the Mexican government encouraged the celebration of national holidays in an effort to bind migrants to the homeland. But these festivals continued through the 1950s, even as the local organizers grew apart from Mexican national politics, seeking to assert their U.S. citizenship through political action. The Comité Patriótico Mexicano and other clubs and organizations, such as the Caballeros Católicos and the American Legion, formed the backbone of the effort to promote holidays and festivals. Throughout the year these groups organized social dances and beauty pageants. Mexican national holidays, such as Cinco de Mayo, and regular dances and functions remained ways of uniting and consolidating an ethnic constituency in the 1960s. In the early years of the twenty-first century, as anti-immigrant forces gained strength nationally, Cinco de Mayo parades took on renewed significance as public demonstrations in defense of migrant rights.

Local Spanish-language radio broadcasts appeared sporadically the 1930s and 1940s, although none was ever able to succeed as a commercial venture. In the 1950s Javier Cárdenas, a migrant from Guadalajara by way of Brownsville, Texas, operated radio programs first in Pontiac, then in Ann Arbor, and then in Monroe, broadcasting Spanish-Language music and promoting patriotic and religious festivals in the *colonia*. Spanish-language newspapers also appeared and disappeared with regularity beginning in the 1930s. The ready availability of big-city newspapers—such as *La Prensa* from New York and *La Opinión* from Los Angeles—and a variety of papers from Mexico itself, meant that local publications had difficulty attracting readers and sustaining an advertising base. The first Spanish-language newspaper in the state to produce more than a handful of issues was *Renacimiento*, which began publication in Lansing in 1970 with a grant from Model Cities, a federal program. Not until the 1990s did self-sustaining Spanish-language newspapers appear: *Latino* in Detroit and *El Vocero Hispano* in Grand Rapids. In 2004 Univision created a Detroit affiliate of the national Spanish-language network. In television broadcasting, the power of national and international production over local content was still more overwhelming. Except for one half-hour news program, this network affiliate exclusively broadcast programming produced in the major markets of Miami, Los Angeles, New York, San Juan, and Mexico City. Although Latinos in Michigan continue to create their own cultural practices, they remain integrated in national and transnational industries that produce most of the news, music, and entertainment Latinos consume.

Since the early days of the Mexican *colonias,* Latino restaurants and grocery stores in towns and barrios around the state have provided local outlets for imported foodstuff and cultural products—from tortillas to flags to compact discs. With the arrival of Puerto Ricans and South and Central Americans, these stores began offering more diverse menus and products. Stores and restaurants provide links to homeland markets, familiar commodities, and even services to call or send money home. Public spaces welcoming to Latinos and Latino culture also formed the backbone of local popular culture and community identity. As a result, the threat to Latino establishments posed by freeway construction was a major concern of community leaders in the period after World War II, and the basis of community action in the early 1970s. In the 1980s a coalition of community activists, local entrepreneurs, and government agencies began to incorporate displays of ethnic distinctiveness, such as restaurants and festivals, into a campaign to draw tourists into Southwest Detroit, an area which was later renamed Mexicantown. To preserve the community they imagined ways in which institutions and products previously targeted only at the Latino community might also be marketed to outsiders. The centerpiece of this effort is the multimillion dollar Mexicantown International Welcome Center and Mercado, at the entrance of the Ambassador International Bridge. The center has space for cultural productions, ethnic shops, and places to eat Mexican food. Planners hope that this investment in a monument to Latino culture will contribute to presenting a new and improved city of Detroit to the millions of visitors who enter the United States through this bridge each year.

NOTES

1. For number of Mexicans and number of Mexicans repatriated, see Vargas, 1999, 75, 84. On ethnic Detroit, see Kenneth Waltzer, "East European Jewish Detroit in the Early Twentieth Century," *Judaism*, 2000.

2. Gamio, 1930, 86.

3. Oral history (originally collected by Ciro Sepúlveda) and statistics on repatriation are from Vargas, 1999, 187, 189.

4. Badillo, 2003, 38.

5. President's Comission on Migratory Labor, Stenographic Report, 1950, 477–478.

6. Clive, transcript of interview with Jane González, 1973.

7. For employment statistics and ties to Texas, see Choldin and Trout, 1969, 82–86, 194–200.

8. Humphry, 1944, 332.

9. Choldin and Trout, 1969, 25.

10. President's Comission on Migratory Labor, Stenographic Report, 1950, 451.

11. Wenk, 1968, 38–49.

12. Choldin and Trout, 1969, 49–50.

BIBLIOGRAPHY

Baba, Marietta L., and Malvina Hauk Abonyi. *Mexicans of Detroit*. Detroit, MI: Wayne State University, 1979.

Badillo, David. *Latinos in Michigan*. East Lansing: Michigan State University Press, 2003.

Carmichael, Karen. "Americanization and Mexican Immigrants." Honors essay, University of Michigan, 2007.

Choldin, Harvey M., and Grafton D. Trout. *Mexican Americans in Transition: Migration and Employment in Michigan Cities*. East Lansing: Michigan State University, Rural Manpower Center, 1969.

Faiver, Cristina. "A History of Mexicans and Mexican Americans in Lansing, Michigan." Honors essay, University of Michigan, 2007.

Gamio, Manuel. *Mexican Immigration to the United States.* Chicago, IL: University of Chicago Press, 1930.

González, Jane. Interview by Alan Clive. 1973.

Herrada, Elena. *Los Repatriados: Exiles from the Promised Land.* Detroit, MI: Fronteras Norteñas, 2000.

Humphry, Norman. "The Detroit Mexican Immigrant and Naturalization." *Social Forces* 22, no. 3 (1944): 332–335.

———. "Mexican Repatriation from Michigan: Public Assistance in Historical Perspective." *Social Service Review* 15 (1941): 497–513.

Julian Samora Research Institute. Research and Publications. http://www.jsri.msu.edu/RandS/research/index.html.

Maldonado, Edwin. "Contract Labor and the Origins of Puerto Rican Communities in the United States." *International Migration Review* 13, no. 1 (1979): 103–121.

Michigan Latino History Project. Online Resources. http://sitemaker.umich.edu/michiganlatinos.

President's Commission on Migratory Labor. Stenographic Report of Proceedings Held at Saginaw, Michigan, Tuesday, September 12, 1950. Washington, DC: Ward and Paul, 1950.

Skendzel, Eduard Adam. *Detroit's Pioneer Mexicans.* Grand Rapids, MI: Littleshield Press, 1980.

Thaden, John F. *Migratory Beet Workers in Michigan.* East Lansing: Michigan State College Agricultural Experiment Station, 1942.

Valdés, Dennis Nodin. *El Pueblo Mexicano En Detroit Y Michigan.* Detroit, MI: Wayne State University, College of Education, 1982.

Vargas, Zaragosa. *Proletarians of the North: A History of Mexican Industrial Workers in Detroit and the Midwest, 1917–1933.* Berkeley: University of California Press, 1999.

Waltzer, Kenneth. "East European Jewish Detroit in the Early Twentieth Century." *Judaism*, 2000.

Wenk, Michael G. "Adjustment and Assimilation the Cuban Refugee Experience." *International Migration Review* 3, no. 1 (1968): 38–49.

24
MINNESOTA

Leah Schmalzbauer

CHRONOLOGY

1860	Luis Garzón, an upper-class Mexican musician, is the first recorded Latino to settle in Minnesota. Although Garzón lived in Minneapolis, he was a leader in the Mexican community that developed on the west side of St. Paul.
1910	The first wave of Latinos, most of whom are Mexican, arrives in Minnesota. They settle on the west side of St. Paul and work in the sugar beet fields of greater Minnesota.
1920s	In the late 1920s Mexicans are doing most of the work in Minnesota's sugar beet fields. Mexicans also work for the railroads and in the meat-packing industry in south St. Paul.
1932	In response to the Great Depression, American Crystal Sugar Company, the largest employer of Latinos in Minnesota, stops guaranteeing wages or transportation for its field workers. On November 10, eighty-six Mexicans are repatriated to Mexico, many of whom are U.S. citizens who had never been to Mexico. Although many Mexicans volunteered to go to Mexico, some were forced to do so.
1934	Governor Elmer Benson attempts to deport 1,500 Mexicans. His efforts met with opposition.
1940	The Neighborhood House and Our Lady of Guadalupe Church, both on the west side of St. Paul, help Mexicans in Minnesota register with the Immigration and Naturalization Service (INS) as part of the Alien Registration Program. All Mexicans who could prove they had been residing in the United States since July 1, 1924, were eligible to become citizens.

1943–1947	Approximately 8,000 Mexicans come to Minnesota through the Bracero program to work in the sugar beet fields, for the railroads, in the canneries, and in the slaughterhouses. During this time many Tejanos (Mexican Americans from Texas) also come to Minnesota.
1952	A flood destroys many Mexican homes and businesses on the lower west side of St. Paul, an area commonly known as the Flats. Soon thereafter the lower west side is targeted for urban renewal, which uproots many more families. Most of those displaced move to the upper west side.
1962	Ballet Folklórico Guadalupaño is founded on the west side.
1968	Mexican Americans on the west side organize to build the Torre de San Miguel, a cooperatively owned housing project for Mexican families.
1970s	Minnesota sees a surge in its Latino population. The majority are migrant farmworkers.
1972	A total of 142 private family units are opened in Torre de San Miguel housing project. The same year the Department of Chicano Studies is founded at the University of Minnesota.
1974	La Clinica, Minnesota's first bilingual health clinic, opens in St. Paul. That same year Governor Wendell Andersen establishes the Minnesota Office of Migrant Affairs.
1976	Centro Cultural Chicano, the first bilingual social service agency, opens in Minneapolis. That same year Conrad Vega becomes the first Latino elected to the Minnesota legislature. He went on to serve as a Democratic Farm Labor (DFL) senator for Dakota County for 10 years.
1990	*La Prensa*, Minnesota's first Spanish-language newspaper is founded.

1999	Mercado Central, a cooperatively owned marketplace and community center for Latino entrepreneurs, opens in South Minneapolis.
2000	Local Latino businesspeople found the Hispanic Chamber of Commerce of Minnesota with 200 members.
2003	A segment of Concord Street on the west side of St. Paul is renamed Cesar Chavez Street.
2004	Mexican president Vicente Fox visits Minnesota.
2005	The 46th Mexican consulate in the United States opens in St. Paul.
2006	Approximately 40,000 Minnesotans, the majority Latinos, march in protest to proposed immigration reform, which imposes punitive measures on undocumented migrants. Later that year, on December 12, the U.S. Department of Homeland Security's Immigration and Customs Enforcement (ICE) raids the Swift and Company meat processing plant in Worthington, Minnesota. Some 230 migrants are arrested, the majority from Mexico. Other Latinos arrested are from Honduras, El Salvador, Guatemala, and Peru.

HISTORICAL OVERVIEW

The history of Latinos in Minnesota is in large part the history of Mexicans in Minnesota. Currently, there are 15 times more Mexicans in Minnesota than the

"The Heroes of Freedom, Justice, and Peace" mural, painted by Teens Networking Together and artist Craig David in 1995 on the wall of the popular west side restaurant El Burrito Mercado. The west side of St. Paul: "The Ellis Island of Minnesota." Photo by Leigh Roethke. Courtesy of Afton Historical Society Press: Afton, MN.

second-largest Latino group, Puerto Ricans, and 40 times more than the third group, Ecuadorians. The disproportionate numbers of Mexicans in comparison to other Latino groups has been the case since Latinos first began to arrive in Minnesota in the late 1800s, although in the past decade Latinos from Central and South America have started to come to Minnesota in large numbers. Latinos from several nations now live throughout the St. Paul and Minneapolis metro area as well as in several towns in rural Minnesota.

The First Wave of Latino Migration

The first wave of Latinos began to arrive in Minnesota in the late 1800s. The majority of them were Mexican Americans recruited from South Texas, Kansas, and Nebraska to work in the sugar beet fields of the American Crystal Sugar Company. Latino workers received piece rate pay, and the work was temporary and seasonal. As such, only a minority of this first wave of Latinos remained in Minnesota permanently. The fact that the sugar beet fields were located in homogenous rural areas with no history of non-European migration further discouraged Latino settlement. Yet, economic forces would soon alter this demographic trend.

By 1928 more than 7,000 Mexican migrants were working in the fields of the Minnesota Red River Valley, making the sugar industry the first in Minnesota in which Latinos, specifically Mexicans, dominated. In order to encourage workers to stay in Minnesota year-round, Crystal Sugar began to offer higher wages. This strategy was successful. Workers soon thereafter began to put down roots in Minnesota, migrating within Minnesota in the off-season from rural areas such as the Red River Valley to the Twin Cities. At the same time, Crystal Sugar was able to boost its profits, as it no longer had to transport workers from Mexico and the Southwest to Minnesota and back again.

Already poor and disenfranchised, Latinos in Minnesota were hit hard by the Great Depression. Yet, few sought public assistance, and little assistance was available for those who did seek it. A strong work ethic, coupled with general condemnation for anything deemed a "free ride," motivated Latinos to struggle to make it on their own, despite the incredible hardships they encountered.[1] Pride in providing for one's family gave many Latinos the strength to endure difficult and often dangerous working conditions, low wages, and the stigma of being a migrant in an often unfriendly place. Despite the challenges resulting from the Great Depression, the Mexican population in Minnesota grew rapidly during this time. In the 1930s a surplus of workers in the sugar beet industry prompted more Latinos to move to the Twin Cities in search of other employment.

On August 4, 1942, the U.S. government instituted the Bracero program. This guest worker program recruited skilled workers from Mexico to come to the

United States on temporary visas to labor in the fields, factories, and on the railroads, essentially filling the void created by the thousands of workers who left their jobs to fight in World War II. The program continued until 1964, when the immigration system was overhauled.

The contribution of braceros to the economies of the United States and Minnesota cannot be understated. Between 1943 and 1947 nearly 8,000 braceros worked in Minnesota agriculture and industry. The abuse of Braceros, especially those who worked in agriculture, is well documented. For example, many field workers were forced to work with a short-handled hoe, literally making the work backbreaking.

During this time many Tejanos also came to work in Minnesota, seeking to escape discrimination and the surplus of Latino workers in Texas. Not bound by migration restrictions, Tejanos were able to remain in Minnesota year-round, and many settled permanently. By 1951, Tejanos outnumbered Mexican braceros by about four to one.

THE WEST SIDE OF ST. PAUL: "THE ELLIS ISLAND OF MINNESOTA"

The west side of St. Paul is commonly considered the birthplace of Minnesota's vibrant Latino community. Most Mexicans who came to Minnesota to work for the railroad and in the packinghouses and slaughterhouses of St. Paul, as well as those who worked in the sugar beet fields of greater Minneapolis, made their first permanent home on the west side of St. Paul.

The west side of St. Paul, like many migrant communities of the time, was impoverished, and as such, life for Latinos living there was difficult. Most Latinos made their homes in the low-lying area on the banks of the Mississippi River called the Flats. Residents of the Flats lived in ramshackle dwellings, many of which lacked heating and indoor plumbing. A 1926–1927 study by the Department of Labor concluded that the worst lodging in the United States was found in St. Paul's west side "slums," where Mexican workers lived in old boxcars. Twenty years later, not much had changed; a study by the International Institute concluded that Mexicans on the west side lived in the worst housing in St. Paul.

In addition to the poverty that characterized life on the west side of St. Paul, Latino migrants met with discrimination and racism. In 1932, for example, a Minnesota deportation drive resulted in the removal of 15 percent of the Mexicans living there. Although the drive was officially voluntary, it is now known that many Mexicans were forced to leave, and that some of them had never before lived in Mexico. The latter were born in the United States and were by most traditional definitions American. Yet, their skin color and ethnic heritage marked them as foreigners, and thus they were vulnerable to expulsion from the community.

Those Latinos who remained on the west side of St. Paul made great strides in building a thriving community. Neighborhood House, founded in 1897, was the Latino community's cultural center. The focus of Neighborhood House beginning in the early years of the 1900s was to serve the residents of the Flats, all of whom were poor and most of whom were Mexican migrants. Neighborhood House provided English classes, day care, and a space for youth and adults alike to gather. During the Depression, Neighborhood House administered Works Progress Administration projects, as well as food drives and benefit dances to support programs for the poor.

Another Mexican institution was Our Lady of Guadalupe Church and Mission. This church, which held its first bilingual mass on February 22, 1931, was considered by many to be the spiritual center of the west side neighborhood.[2] In addition to providing a place for Latinos to worship, Our Lady of Guadalupe raised money to assist the poor and infirm.

In 1952 the Mississippi River flooded, wiping out most of the housing in the Flats. The city of St. Paul responded with an urban renewal plan that leveled the Flats and displaced hundreds of Latino families. Most families and businesses rebuilt their homes and storefronts on a nearby hill. The destruction of the oldest and most significant Latino community in Minnesota sparked anger and resistance, and it seemingly fueled the determination of those on the west side to recreate a stronger and more politicized community.

The urbanization of the Flats and the demolition of its houses and businesses also launched Chicanismo in Minnesota, a movement for Chicano pride and dignity. Chicanismo was most clearly symbolized by the formation of the Minnesota Brown Berets. Gilbert de la O, a community leader on the west side, headed the organization in St. Paul, which not only was involved in political activism and education but also provided many services to Mexican families. At its high point, the Brown Berets had approximately 50 active members fighting for social justice for Chicano workers in the Twin Cities. In the 1960s the Brown Berets aligned themselves with the United Farm Workers of America to support Latinos laboring in the sugar beet fields of rural Minnesota. Many of those migrant workers were abused and exploited, and the Brown Berets struggled to reverse this trend. They also lent their solidarity to the cause of migrant agricultural workers outside of Minnesota. In 1966, for example, they organized a boycott of Twin Cities' grocery stores that were selling grapes picked by nonunionized migrants in California.

The Brown Berets were committed to empowering and educating Latinos, and especially Chicanos, about their culture and about their history of exploitation and struggle. Their commitment to this cause fueled a major campaign that resulted in the formation of the Chicano Studies Department at the University of Minnesota in 1972. Years later, in 1995, St. Cloud State University followed suit, inaugurating their own Chicano Studies Department and hiring several Chicano and Latino professors.

The energy spawned by the community efforts of the Brown Berets, Neighborhood House, and Our Lady of Guadalupe Church led to other great achievements on the west side of St. Paul. Their efforts can be credited with the opening of La Clinica in 1974, the first bilingual health center in Minnesota. La Clinica, which is now called the West Side Community Clinic, served over 35,000 patients in 2005, most of whom were Latino. Other achievements of the community include the institutionalization of a Cinco de Mayo festival and the creation of the Guadalupe Area Project in 1969, an alternative school that continues to serve and empower troubled urban Latino youth.

In the 1980s the west side Latino community began to diversify beyond its historical Mexican roots, welcoming a growing number of Cubans and Puerto Ricans. These two new communities fused traditions and celebrations with the existing Mexican community. The expansion of the west side community soon came to include Central Americans and South Americans.

Today, although the Latino communities on the east side of St. Paul and in south Minneapolis are the largest and fastest growing in the Twin Cities, the west side of St. Paul continues to be an important Latino hub. Whereas poverty in the area persists, Mexican-owned businesses and restaurants, many of which were started by first-generation Latino migrants, flourish. Neighborhood House and Our Lady of Guadalupe continue to provide services and support to the Latino community, and several colorful murals symbolize the community's historical and current significance.

Minnesota as an Emerging Gateway

Though Latinos have been in Minnesota since the end of the nineteenth century, it is only recently that the population has increased at a notably rapid rate. Minnesota is still a predominantly white state. As of the year 2000, 88 percent of the state's residents were non-Hispanic whites, and 85 percent had European ancestry. Yet, the rate of increase in Minnesota's foreign-born population has been among the highest in the nation. In the past 15 years the number of Latinos in Minnesota has increased by over 500 percent, accounting for 24 percent of the growth in the state's labor force. As such, Minnesota has been characterized as a reemerging migrant gateway, a state that was at one time a migrant hub but that until recently has had very little migration activity.[3] At the beginning of the twentieth century Minnesota was a pull for northern European migrants, but migration waned for decades until the recent influx of Latinos, Southeast Asians, Somalians, and Ethiopians.

The growth of Minnesota's migrant population, and particularly of the Latino population, has occurred in response to shifts in Minnesota's economy, specifically the expansion of low-wage jobs in manufacturing, construction, services, and food processing. Whereas manufacturing, construction, and services have drawn Latinos to the Twin Cities, the food processing industry has recruited thousands of Latinos to small towns in rural Minnesota. As a result of the latter, Latinos have become much more visible in places that have a history of European migration. Moreover, there has been a dramatic decline in the number of large farms in many of these areas, which has spurred the out-migration of white residents and which has further increased Latino visibility.

As an example of the changing demographics of rural Minnesota, in the 1990s, 16 to 25 percent of the populations of Worthington, Willmar, St. James, and Madelia were Mexican. These numbers have likely grown since. Another demographic shift spurred by migration has been the expansion of Latinos into the suburbs of the Twin Cities. Latino neighborhoods are now well established in Shakopee, New Hope, Crystal, Chaska, South St. Paul, and Inver Grove Heights.

The majority of Latino arrivals to Minnesota continue to be Mexican, most originating from the rural states of the Mexican central plateau. Others are Mexicans who have migrated from California, Texas, or other midwestern agricultural states. In 2000 there were 42,000 Mexicans in Minnesota. This number continues to increase rapidly. According to the Minnesota State Demographic Center, in 2004 there were 175,000 Latinos in Minnesota, the majority Mexican. This number is most definitely low, as it excludes the undocumented.

Minnesota's response to and reception of the growing Latino population has been mixed. Though Latinos report feeling an overall sense of welcome by Minnesotans, they also report incidents of discrimination and racism.[4] Much of the racism and discrimination is rooted in the beliefs that Latinos are taking Minnesotans' jobs, abusing the welfare system, and changing the traditional culture. Negative feelings and actions toward Latinos have emanated from civil society as well as from local political leadership. In the 1990s, for example, political leaders in Willmar and Moorhead introduced legislation to curb welfare use by Latinos. In Moorhead this was accompanied by a spate of racist attacks aimed at Latinos, including the painting of swastikas and other racist graffiti in public places.

In 1992 racial tension around the issue of Latino newcomers was exacerbated by an INS raid of Heartland Foods in Marshall, which resulted in the deportation of many workers. Though this specific raid did receive support from around the state, it also met with vocal and active resistance from the Latino community. Specifically, in 1993 a strike and protest by Heartland workers against unethical compensation practices resulted in the company agreeing to release the paychecks of deported workers to their families.

Discrimination against Latinos continues. A 2001 Minnesota state study found that Mexicans were stopped, fined, searched, and frisked by police more often than other groups. In fact, Latino complaints about police treatment have been registered throughout Minnesota.[5] Discrimination has also been cited in the housing market. In 2004 a study by the Association of Community Organizations for Reform Now (ACORN) found that Latinos are three times more likely than whites to be denied mortgages in the Twin Cities, which has led to a sharp difference in home ownership between these two groups.[6]

Racial tension and discrimination exist not only between white Minnesotans and Latinos; problems also exist within the diverse Latino community. For example, on the west side of St. Paul, Latinos who have been in Minnesota for generations, and who are thus English-Speaking citizens, are often hostile toward the newly arrived Spanish-speaking Latinos. This hostility is most often directed toward poor and undocumented newcomers. Our Lady of Guadalupe Church, for example, has a bilingual and a Spanish-language mass, and attendance is segregated; longtime Latino residents usually attend the bilingual mass, whereas the newly arrived residents attend the Spanish-only mass. In another example, in September 2006 Neighborhood House hosted a rally in support of migrants rights, but only a few longtime residents showed up to lend their support. The trend was similar throughout Minnesota. Indeed, few Latinos who are now citizens participated in the protests against proposed anti-immigrant legislation.[7] Furthermore, a study by HACER of Latinos in rural Minnesota found that there is a high level of mistrust between Latinos who have been in the area for a long time and those who have recently arrived. This mistrust has been a barrier to implementing supportive services for the community.

Yet, despite these challenges, Minnesota's Latino community has achieved notable economic and cultural representation in the state. For example, *La Prensa*, Minnesota's first Spanish-language newspaper, now has a circulation of over 14,000. In Minneapolis, Latino entrepreneurs sell their wares in the cooperatively owned Mercado Central, the commercial heart of the large south Minneapolis Latino community. In addition to the economic contributions and media presence of Latinos in Minnesota, several large Latino service organizations—including Comunidad de Latinos Unidos En Servicio (CLUES), Centro Cultural Chicano, La Oportunidad, and Centro Campesino—defend the interests of the Latino community. The strength of Minnesota's Latino community has also attracted attention from abroad. In 2004 Mexico's former president Vicente Fox visited Minnesota, and in 2005 the 46th Mexican consulate in the United States opened in St. Paul.

LATINOS IN THE LABOR FORCE

Whereas the demographics of Minnesota's Latino population have changed since the late 1800s, what attracts Latinos to the state remains the same. Family and kin networks fuel the growth of the community, but employment is the initial draw. Latinos first came to Minnesota to work in the sugar beet fields, in the packinghouses, and for the railroad. More recently Latinos have come to

Minnesota to work in food processing, agriculture, construction, and the thriving service industry.

In 2000 there were over 42,000 Mexicans in Minnesota, and over 132,000 native speakers of Spanish. Most in both groups are migrant workers. In addition to being drawn to Minnesota's burgeoning industries, Latino labor migrants are attracted by Minnesota's relatively low cost of living. Industrial and agricultural jobs in rural Minnesota offer an appealing combination of the two. For these reasons employers throughout Minnesota, but especially in rural Minnesota, have been able to recruit thousands of Latino workers.

Although their labor participation rates are high, Latinos are positioned near the bottom of Minnesota's socioeconomic hierarchy. Latinos are much more likely than other Minnesotans to hold low-wage jobs, and therefore they have a much higher poverty rate than other minority groups. Latino mobility is hindered by their means of incorporation into U.S. economy. Work as they may, Latinos often find themselves in low-wage jobs, with little chance of promotion.

Sociologist Michael Piore has asserted that capitalist economies are structured by a dual labor market with a primary and secondary sector.[8] The primary sector—which encompasses business, finance, science, academia, and government—employs a highly skilled, high-wage workforce. Economic mobility within this sector is high. The secondary sector, on the contrary, demands a low-skill, low-wage workforce, and mobility within it is restricted. Historically, the secondary sector has included the most vulnerable workers, essentially migrants who are relegated to a permanent discriminatory status because of their incapacity to negotiate with employers. This incapacity is compounded by one's undocumented status. In fact, undocumented migrants are among the most vulnerable workers to date.

Latinos in Minnesota are most often employed in the secondary sector of the economy. Few have benefits or earn a living wage, and many cite abuses at the workplace. Recently, migration raids of workplaces throughout the country have heightened fear among all migrants, especially the undocumented, further stifling their demands for fair treatment. Minnesota has been the site of several migration raids, the most recent occurring in December 2006.

Barriers to the socioeconomic mobility of Latinos also include language, education, and history. Many Latinos who come to the United States do not speak English and have very low levels of education. In Minnesota only 71 percent of Latinos who are 25 years and older have a high school diploma. A study by the Center for Rural Policy and Development, at Minnesota State University at Mankato, of Latino communities in rural Minnesota found that education is one of the most pressing concerns.[9] A consistently high number of Latino youths drop out of high school; in addition, there are many barriers to first-generation Latino migrants learning English. The task is all the more difficult when one is not educated in their native language, a common characteristic of Latino migrants. Further barriers to upward mobility and assimilation include the legacy of poverty and oppression that many Latino migrants carry with them from their home countries; history weighs heavily on them and can perpetuate their discrimination and stagnation. Latinos in Minnesota face all of these barriers, but they continue to struggle to achieve the American Dream.

Latinos in the Rural Sector

Although Latinos have always had a presence in rural Minnesota, it is only in the past two decades that they have filled positions in the rural industry. This is due to major shifts in Minnesota's economy in general and in the state's rural economy in particular. Rural Minnesota has seen a decline in agriculture and high-wage manufacturing jobs, and an increase in service and low-wage industrial jobs. Many of the large farms that used to dominate the landscape of southwestern Minnesota have disappeared, and the remaining industrial jobs have become less desirable because of their low-wages and lack of benefits. As a result many local residents of the region have left.

Paralleling this out-migration, food processing companies have moved into the area in an attempt to lower their production costs. They are initially attracted by the weak labor unions and accompanying low wages of rural areas. The ruralization of the industry has been further encouraged by tax breaks given by small towns to food processing companies to locate there. As a result of these incentives Minnesota has become one of the nation's leaders in processing foods such as turkey and sweet pea. Farmland Foods, Midwest Foods, Hormel, Jennie-O, Schwan, Swift and Company, Monfort Pork, and Campbell Soup either have headquarters or production hubs in rural Minnesota.

With the relocation of food processing factories, new jobs were created in rural Minnesota. Yet, towns had difficulty filling these jobs because they are low paying and unappealing, and because they often entail dangerous working conditions. As a result, in the 1980s food processing companies began to recruit migrants to fill their demand for workers. Little knowledge of English is necessary to work in food processing factories, which makes the jobs attractive to the poorest and least educated Latinos.

Besides participating in Minnesota's rural food processing industry, Latinos continue to work on the farms. A report by the Wilder Research Center estimated that in 2003 there were between 1,200 and 10,000 migrant farmworkers in Minnesota.[10] These numbers only include those who are actually working in the fields—that is, they exclude family members accompanying the workers.

As was the case in the early 1900s, when Mexicans and Tejanos first came to Minnesota to work in the sugar beet fields, life for contemporary migrant farmworkers is difficult, and exploitation is common. Workers are hard pressed to meet even their most basic needs. Housing is a good example. Few employers provide housing for their migrant workers. In 2002 a study of migrant housing in southern Minnesota by the Hispanic Advocacy and Community Empowerment through Research

(HACER), at the University of Minnesota, found that housing is such a great problem that some migrants resort to living in their cars.[11] When the option is available, workers commonly choose to live in employer-provided barracks, which are essentially mobile trailers. Still, living conditions in these trailers are far from ideal. Up to 15 workers live in a single gender-segregated trailer, many of which do not have bathrooms. Other housing options include mobile homes or hotels. Migrant living conditions are substandard across the board. In addition, Latinos report persistent discrimination when trying to find housing on the private market.

Many migrant farmworkers must piece together work to make ends meet. This means that they often work in both agriculture and industry. Most have to commute to the workplace. Because employers do not provide transportation, workers must have access to a car. HACER reports that the average commute by workers in southern Minnesota is six miles, and that this distance between home and work adds to the costs and challenges of migrant life.

As a result of the massive influx of Latino workers into the poultry, meat, and food processing industries, scholars and policy makers have been paying the industry much attention.[12] Researchers have found that dangerous working conditions, low pay, and labor abuse are common among migrant workers in Minnesota. Research also reveals that Latino workers—especially those who move to small towns that don't have a history of non-European migration—commonly face discrimination that permeates their work and social lives.

Undocumented Latino Workers

According to research done by HACER in 2000, there are between 18,000 and 48,000 undocumented migrants working in Minnesota, most of whom are Mexican. Analyses of current undocumented migration to the United States suggest that this number is now much higher.

Undocumented workers in the United States are most commonly found in the following industries: seasonal agricultural work, textiles, manufacturing, personal service, janitorial services, hotel and restaurants, food service, and construction. Undocumented Latinos in Minnesota work in significant numbers in all of these industries, save in textiles. In addition, undocumented Latinos in Minnesota are present in the rural industry, more specifically in food processing.

At the same time that hostility toward undocumented Latinos is growing in the United States, so too is the economic demand for their labor. This paradox also exists in Minnesota. A study of the economic impact of undocumented workers in Minnesota concluded that undocumented labor in the industries cited above contribute between $1.5 billion and $4 billion in added value to Minnesota's economy each year.[13] Similarly, if undocumented workers were removed from Minnesota's economy, economic growth would be reduced by 40 percent. Finally, it was estimated that the presence of undocumented labor in Minnesota resulted in the generation of approximately $1 billion in tax revenue. Thus, contrary to popular belief, undocumented migrants in Minnesota provide a net gain, not a net loss, to tax payers.

Despite their contribution to Minnesota's economy, undocumented migrants in the state are vulnerable to discrimination and deportation. On December 12, 2006, Immigration and Custom Enforcement (ICE) agents raided Swift and Company meat processing factories in six states, including the one in Worthington, Minnesota. Some 230 migrants, documented and undocumented, were arrested. Most of them were from Mexico; others were from Honduras, El Salvador, Guatemala, and Peru. Many of the workers were separated from their children because of subsequent deportation.

For obvious reasons, following the Swift and Company raid, fear permeated Minnesota's rural Latino communities. The Center for Human Rights and Constitutional Law reported that the raids sent many Latinos in the region into hiding. The raids also affected business. Swift and Company was forced to suspend operations in the days following the raids, which is yet another indicator of the centrality of undocumented Latinos to the economy.

Many of Minnesota's political and religious leaders, along with local residents, condemned the raids and subsequent detention of the Swift workers. Perhaps the most vocal in their opposition to the raids were seven Minnesota Catholic bishops representing Winona, St. Cloud, Crookston, New Ulm, Duluth, St. Paul, and Minneapolis. They issued the following statement:

> As the Catholic Bishops of the State of Minnesota, we are distressed and disheartened by the workplace raids that took place in Worthington, Minnesota, and other communities this past week . . . The raids did nothing to advance needed reform. Instead, the raids heartlessly divided families, disrupted the whole community of Worthington, and undermined progress that that city had made toward bridging racial and cultural differences.[14]

Despite support from many segments of society, Latinos in Minnesota, especially those who are undocumented migrants, will likely continue to struggle for acceptance and social justice. Yet, all Latinos—residents, citizens, and migrants alike—have contributed a great deal to the economy and to the political and social landscape of the state of Minnesota.

NOTABLE LATINOS

Garzón, Luis (1867–1954). Luis Garzón was the first Latino to settle in Minnesota. Although he lived in Minneapolis, he was a leader in the west side community. He opened Tienda de Abarrotes, the first Mexican grocery store in Minnesota, which was also an information center for the community. Garzón also helped found the Sociedad Mutua Beneficia Recreativa Anahuac in 1922, which helped first-generation Mexicans settle into their new neighborhood.

Rangel, Ray (1932–). A member of Mexican American Veteran's Post #5, Ray Rangel has successfully brought attention to the contribution of Minnesota's Mexican Americans to the U.S. military. Following a major organizing effort, he has recently been able to get an area on Harriet Island, in St. Paul, dedicated for a memorial to Minnesota's fallen Mexican American soldiers.

Gomez-Bethke, Irene (1935–). The daughter of migrant farmworkers, Irene Gomez-Bethke has been involved in social justice issues for most of her life. In the late 1970s she sat on both the Hispanic Advisory Committee, representing Minneapolis mayor Don Fraser, and the Spanish-Speaking Affairs Council. In 1982 she became commissioner for Minnesota's Department of Human Rights. She has also served as state chair of the Hispanic American Democrats, and she has been a member of the board for the Harriet Tubman Center and of the Chicana Caucus. Gomez is also cofounder of Centro Cultural Chicano in Minneapolis and executive director of the Instituto de Arte y Cultura. Her son Jesse Bethke Gomez is the president of CLUES (Comunidades Latinas Unidas en Servicio), the state's largest Latino service organization.

Calderon, Maria Elena (1936–). Maria Elena Calderon was the first Latino administrator in the St. Paul school district. She arrived in Minnesota from El Salvador in 1968, and she was one of the first Central Americans to settle in Minnesota. A teacher and single mother of four children, she earned her PhD in education.

Vega, Conrad (1938–). Conrad Vega was the first Latino elected to the Minnesota legislature, in 1976. He served as a Democratic senator for Dakota County for 10 years.

O, Gilbert de la (1945–). Gilbert de la O was the head of the Brown Berets in Minnesota and a celebrated community leader. Born in New Ulm, Minnesota, his parents migrated to Minnesota from Texas to work in the sugar beet fields. In addition to his political work, his service work with youth on the west side has earned him notoriety. Included in his many service awards are the Martin Luther King Community Legend Award for the Twin Cities, and his induction into the Neighborhood House Alumni Hall of Fame, in Washington, DC.

Silva, Maria (1947–) and Tomas (1944–). In 1979 Maria and Tomas Silva opened up El Burrito restaurant on the west side of St. Paul. El Burrito has since expanded its services to include a grocery store, a bakery, and a factory that produces wholesale foods, which are distributed throughout Minnesota and the Midwest. The Silvas employ over 100 Latinos and remain dedicated to running a business that gives back to the Twin Cities' Latino community.

Cervantes, Manuel (1951–). The first of seven children of migrant farmworkers, Manuel Cervantes is a judge and the first Chicano attorney for the city of St. Paul. Previous to his service as city attorney, he served as a judge on the State Workers' Compensation Court, as a referee in Ramsey County District Court, and as a judge in Minnesota's Family and Juvenile Court. He remains very active in the Latino community.

CULTURAL CONTRIBUTIONS

Latinos have contributed to Minnesota's culture through music, food, and commodity production. Beginning in the 1950s Latin music could be heard throughout the Twin Cities. In this era the west side of St. Paul was the hub for several popular Mexican American groups, including Las Hermanas Rangels, Los Rumbaleros, the Augie Garcia Quintet, and the Orquesta Tejana, all of which gained state and regional notoriety. In 1956 the Augie Garcia Quintet opened for Elvis Presley at the St. Paul Auditorium.

In 1962 the Ballet Folklórico Guadalupaño was founded on the west side. The dance company has performed throughout the Twin Cities, incorporating the talents of local Latino youth. Today, Latin music and dance continue to be popular in Minnesota. The Latin dance craze has led many Twin Cities' nightclubs to dedicate one or two weekend nights every week to Latin sound.

Latinos have also contributed to education in Minnesota. In 1971 the Mexican American Cultural and Educational Center opened on the west side of St. Paul. The purpose of the center was to provide additional Latino-focused curriculum to the St. Paul public school system. Classes on culture, history, folk and regional dance, and boxing helped youth learn about and celebrate Latino culture. The center offered a tutorial program for struggling students and housed a Latino Credit Union and the Minnesota Migrant Council until it was forced to close in 1974.

Food is another means through which Latinos have enhanced Minnesotan culture. Latino restaurants and *panaderías* (bakeries) in the Twin Cities and throughout Minnesota attract a diverse customer base. For example, at lunchtime every table is full at El Burrito Mercado, a popular restaurant and bakery on the west side of St. Paul. There the local Latino community mixes with non-Latinos who go to the eatery for great Mexican food. El Burrito Mercado also houses a Latino grocery store that has a special section of Mexican arts and crafts. The salsa made at El Burrito has become so popular that it will soon be distributed by Target and CUB food stores.

When walking through the west side of St. Paul, it is difficult not to be taken in by the colorful murals that decorate several walls and buildings. The murals are a reminder of the long and powerful history of Latinos in the Twin Cities and of how much they have contributed economically and culturally. Annual Cinco de Mayo and Día de los Muertos celebrations confirm the vibrancy of Latino culture in Minnesota.

NOTES

1. Interview by Leah Schmalzbauer with Gilbert de la O, in St. Paul, MN, February 2007.
2. Roethke, 2007.

3. Singer, 2004, 1–34.
4. Fennelly, *Immigration and Poverty*, 2005; Wilder Foundation, 2004.
5. Bushway, 2001.
6. ACORN, 2004.
7. Interview by Leah Schmalzbauer with Gilbert de la O, in St. Paul, MN, February 2007.
8. Piore, 1975, 67–79.
9. Bushway, 2001.
10. Owen, Ulstad, Shardlow, Shelton, and Cooper, 2004.
11. Ziebarth and Byun, 2002.
12. Ziebarth and Byun, 2002.
13. Kielkopf, 2000.
14. Minnesota Catholic Conference, www.mncc.org.

BIBLIOGRAPHY

ACORN. *Separate and Unequal: Executive Summary Minneapolis-St. Paul*. St. Paul: Minnesota ACORN, 2004.

Amato, Joseph. *To Call It Home: The New Immigrants of Southwestern Minnesota*. Marshall, MN: Crossing Press, 1996.

Bushway, Deborah. *The Vitality of Latino Communities in Rural Minnesota*. Mankato, MN: Center for Rural Policy and Development, 2001.

Fennelly, Katherine. *Immigration and Poverty in the Northwest Area States*. Working paper no. 65. East Lansing: Michigan State University, Julian Samora Research Institute, 2005.

———. "Latinos, Africans, and Asians in the North Star State: Immigrant Communities in Minnesota." In *Beyond the Gateway: Immigrants in a Changing America*. Eds. Elizabeth Gozdziak and Susan Martin. Boulder, CO: Lexington Books, 2005, 111–136.

———. "Prejudice toward Immigrants in the Midwest." In *New Faces in New Places: The Changing Geography of American Immigration*. Ed. Douglas Massey. New York: Russell Sage, 2008.

Kielkopf, James. *The Economic Impact of Undocumented Workers in Minnesota*. Minneapolis, MN: HACER, 2000.

Massey, Douglas. "International Migration in a Globalizing Economy." *Great Decisions*, 2007, 41–52.

McMurry, Martha. "Minnesota Labor Force Trends 1990–2000." Minnesota State Demographic Center, OSD-02-101. December, 2002.

Mines, R., S. Gabbard, and A. Steirman. "A Profile of U.S. Farmworkers: Demographics, Household Composition, Income, and Use of Services." National Agricultural Workers Survey. Research report 6. Washington, DC: U.S. Department of Labor, Office of Program Economics, 1997.

O, Gilbert de la. Interview by Leah Schmalzbauer. St. Paul, MN. February 2007.

Owen, G., K. Ulstad, B. Shardlow, E. Shelton, and T. Cooper. "Migrant Workers in Minnesota: A Discussion Paper." Unpublished study by the Wilder Research Center. St. Paul, MN, 2004.

Piore, Michael. "Unemployment and the Dual Labor Market." *Public Interest*, 1975, 67–79.

Roethke, Leigh. *Latino Minnesota*. Afton, MN: Afton Historical Society Press, 2007.

Schmalzbauer, Leah. *Striving and Surviving: A Daily Life Analysis of Honduran Transnational Families*. New York: Routledge, 2005.

Singer, Audrey. *The Rise of New Immigrant Gateways*. Living Cities Census Series. Washington, DC: Brookings Institution, 2004.

Valdés, Dionicio. *Mexicans in Minnesota*. St. Paul: Minnesota Historical Society Press, 2005.

Wilder Foundation, Anti-Racism Research Team. *An Assessment of Racism in Dakota, Ramsey, and Washington Counties: Executive Summary*. St. Paul, MN: Wilder Research Center, 2004.

Ziebarth, Ann, and Jaehyun Byun. *Migrant Worker Housing: Survey Results from South-Central Minnesota*. Minneapolis, MN: HACER, 2002.

25

Mississippi

Julie M. Weise

CHRONOLOGY

1908	Mexican workers are recruited to Lumberton.
1925	Thousands of Mexicans pick cotton in the Mississippi Delta. Priests observe that all plantations in the Clarksdale area have Mexican workers.
1926	Gunnison schools' board of trustees rules that Mexicans cannot attend Gunnison Consolidated School. Some Mexicans attend a separate Mexican school on the plantation of J.G. McGehee.
1928–1929	Mexican children attending white schools of Cleveland are forced out.
1930	Community leader Rafael J. Landrove and the New Orleans Mexican consulate gain readmission of Mexicans in white schools.
1931–1932	Cotton prices crash, which causes Mexicans to repatriate and Mexican Americans to return to Texas at their own expense.
1942–1964	Tejanos and Mexican braceros pick cotton in the Mississippi Delta.
1977	BC Rogers poultry processing plant in Morton tries to recruit Mexican Americans from Texas. Few stay in Mississippi.
1993	BC Rogers begins its Hispanic Project. At its height, the project buses in 80 Mexican, Caribbean, and Central American workers per week from Miami or Texas
1997	The Immigration and Naturalization Service opens an office in Jackson. Before this date, Mississippi was one of seven U.S. states with no INS office.
2000	Mississippi Immigrants' Rights Alliance (MIRA!) is formed in Jackson.

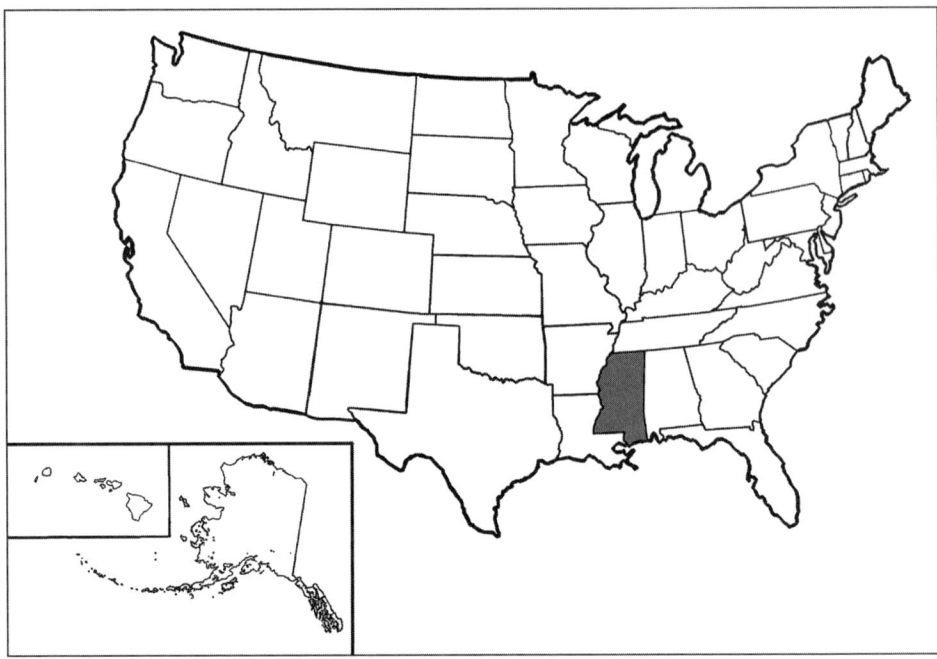

2001	*La Noticia* becomes Mississippi's first major Spanish-language newspaper, quickly circulating more than 2,000 copies in Jackson, Biloxi, Carthage, Kosciusko, and Forest.
2004	The Mississippi Baptist Convention elects its first Latino officer.
2005	Hurricane Katrina strikes Mississippi's Gulf Coast. In the subsequent year, south Mississippi's Latino population increases nearly fivefold.
2006	African American and Latino leaders organize pro-immigrant marches in Jackson, Gulfport, and Laurel.
2007	Mississippi state politicians make illegal immigration a top campaign issue.

HISTORICAL OVERVIEW

Though the Spanish had a colonial presence in Mississippi, Latinos had little influence on Mississippi culture until the 1920s. Then, Mexican and Mexican American workers came to northwest Mississippi's Delta region, recruited from Texas, to pick cotton. They negotiated their in-between racial status and ultimately secured their children's admission to Gunnison's white school. Although the Depression forced most back to Texas and Mexico, Mexicans and Mexican Americans continued to come to the Mississippi Delta as migrant workers through the 1960s.

When cotton farmers completed their transition to mechanized picking in the 1960s, Mississippi became largely a way station for Latino workers traveling

"Mexican and Negro cotton pickers inside plantation store, Knowlton Plantation, Perthshire, Mississippi Delta. This transient labor is contracted for and brought in from Texas each season." October 1939. Photograph by Marion Post Wolcott. Courtesy of the Library of Congress, Prints & Photographs Division, FSA-OWI Collection, Reproduction Number LC-USF34-052248-D DLC.

between Texas and Florida. Yet, as the state's agricultural economy shifted from small-scale farming to industrialized production, so too did Latinos' role in the economy. Though attempts to recruit Latinos to the industry's growing poultry industry faltered during the 1970s and 1980s, by the 1990s their numbers were on the rise.

The new center of Latino migration in the 1990s was central Mississippi, most prominently in and around Scott County. There, Latinos joined an overwhelmingly African American labor force in the state's poultry processing plants. They negotiated harsh working conditions and racial and language barriers in their attempts to settle in Mississippi and improve their lives there.

Concurrently, Latinos had begun to move to the Gulf Coast to work in the casino and construction industries. Through Hurricane Katrina devastated the lives of Gulf Coast Latinos in 2005, thousands of others saw the region's reconstruction work as an economic opportunity. As construction work subsided and Latino workers got tired of its exploitative conditions, some left the state, whereas others settled in casino or service jobs.[1]

COLONIAL MISSISSIPPI

Even though the Spanish were the first to explore Mississippi in the 1500s, France first claimed and settled the area. Battles for control amongst France,

Spain, and Britain concluded in 1763, with Britain controlling the area east of the Mississippi River, and Spain the Natchez colony. Yet, by the late 1700s British colonists were the Natchez colony's most numerous, with few Frenchmen and almost no Spaniards among its population. Spain's governor, Manuel Luis Gayoso, had no choice but to rule through accommodation to British colonists, even appointing British settlers to top posts. Making little attempt to Hispanicize its new subjects, the Spanish Crown encouraged Anglo settlement in Natchez and eventually ceded the area to the United States through the Treaty of San Lorenzo. By 1798 the Mississippi Territory was part of the United States.

As Spain's overseas empire crumbled, the English-speaking residents of the Mississippi Territory, and later the state of Mississippi, retained little active memory of their Spanish past. During the nineteenth century, Mississippi's Gulf Coast attracted a few Latino merchants, as it was in contact with Mexico, the Caribbean, and Central America via maritime trade.

MEXICANS IN THE INTERWAR DELTA

Latinos did not again settle in Mississippi until the twentieth century, when agricultural labor brought them to the state in large numbers. Since Reconstruction, rural Southern elites had sought migrants—previously Chinese and Italian—to break blacks' dominance over the rural labor market. Though the lumber industry in south central Mississippi recruited Mexican laborers as early as 1908, World War I and the Great Migration of blacks to northern and western cities most acutely forced the Delta's white planters to confront the dilemma of their dependence on blacks, and to think seriously about recruiting Mexican workers as an alternative. By the mid-1920s Mexicans could earn more picking cotton in Arkansas, Louisiana, Alabama, and Mississippi than anywhere else in the country, as farmers there paid Mexicans an average of $4 per day for picking cotton, as compared to $1.75 in Texas and $3.25 in California.

In 1925, Mexican migration to Mississippi reached its peak. As the cotton-picking season arrived that fall, the Catholic priest at Clarksdale claimed that 5,000 "Mexicans"—as he called Mexicans and Mexican Americans alike, without regard to citizenship—were picking cotton on plantations in Clarksdale, Greenwood, Greenville, Cleveland, Tunica, and Hollandale. And "more are coming every day," he wrote.[2] Indeed, at the end of 1925, when the priest paid a visit to every plantation in his Clarksdale Parish, he found Mexicans—and presumably, Texas-born Mexican Americans—on all of them.

These workers were predominantly Mexican migrants who had left during the Mexican Revolution, spent some time in Texas, and then moved on. In this sense their profile mirrored that of the era's Mexican and Tejano migrants overall. Though they had first lived in south Texas locales such as Crystal City, Pearsall, San Antonio, Mercedes, and San Benito, five-sixths of ethnic Mexican household heads, wives, and boarders enumerated by census takers in the Delta's Bolivar County during the 1930 planting season were Mexican-born, whereas only one-sixth were Texas born. A quarter had first crossed the border before the Mexican Revolution (1910–1917), some as early as the 1880s; half had crossed during the revolution; and a quarter had crossed after the revolution's end. Most had first spent some time in Texas.

Though most Mexicans and Mexican Americans would leave the Delta after the last of the cotton crop had been picked in December, many would try to stay in Mississippi. From March to December they would plant, cultivate, and pick cotton in family groups. Those who remained through the winter bought a few chickens, hogs, and cows, which would provide meager food. Others, such as A. González, left their wives and children in Mississippi and migrated elsewhere for temporary work, at the end of the cotton harvest. Living even more precariously than he had in Mississippi, González's tertiary migration ended in tragedy. He was accidentally run over while asleep on the railroad tracks in Middlesboro, Kentucky, in November 1930.

Many Mexican families in Mississippi sent their children to school there, but a 1926 ruling of the Bolivar County Schools Board of Trustees prohibited them from attending the Gunnison Consolidated School along with white children. Instead, the county paid a Mexican community leader to offer instruction at a separate Mexican school on the plantation of J.G. McGehee. However, by 1928 the Mexican teacher had left the area, the number of Mexican children had dwindled, and the county was unable to convince a young Tejana woman to assume the role of teacher at the Mexican school. Hortensia Landrove, daughter of local community leader Rafael Landrove, and her young uncle George thus attended the white school for a few weeks during the winter of 1928–1929. The following year, the Robledo children enrolled in the second grade once the cotton was picked. Though Telesforo and María Robledo pulled their son Freddo out in February to help seed the next crop, their daughter Jubertina finished the school year, struggling with English but otherwise earning As and Bs. She was promoted to the third grade at the end of the year, even as many of her peers were left behind. She became the first Mexican to complete the academic year in the white elementary school of Gunnison, Mississippi.

In early 1930, however, school officials decided to enforce the 1926 school board ruling, telling Mexican families their children could not attend the white school. Landrove appealed to the Mexican consulate in New Orleans for help, and the consulate in turn asked Governor Theodore Bilbo to intervene. Comparable court cases that year in Del Rio, Texas, and Lemon Grove, California, argued that U.S. law did not permit discrimination against Mexicans because they were entitled to all the rights of other Caucasian citizens. In Mississippi, however, the consul did not appeal to U.S. law or to ideas about Mexicans' racial categorization, but rather to "the desire to strengthen the cordial relations that fortunately now exist between [the United States and Mexico]."[3]

By April, the governor's intervention had resolved the matter in Landrove's favor, and the following school year Hortensia Landrove, her uncle George Pérez, and Telesforo Robledo's son Trinidad once again enrolled in the white school after the cotton was picked. All three finished the academic year and passed on to the next grade. The victory was crucial for Landrove. His children would be educated at a white school in the Delta, leaving open the possibility of gaining economic stability and culturally becoming middle class in the future.

However, Mexicans had entered sharecropping in the Delta at the beginning of its end. As cotton prices crashed from 16.78 cents per pound in 1929 to 5.66 cents per pound in 1931, white, black, and Mexican sharecroppers found themselves unable to pay the debts they had incurred by purchasing seed and equipment, let alone turn any profit. For most of the Delta's Mexicans, the experiment with Mississippi was over. Neither deported by local officials nor able to secure consular help in repatriating, the destitute Mexican sharecroppers of the Mississippi Delta were effectively abandoned, left to finance their own return to Mexico or Texas.

Though their numbers were diminished, Mexican workers continued to come to Mississippi's cotton fields seasonally throughout the 1930s and early 1940s. As World War II accelerated migration from rural to urban areas and increased wages off the farm, the Delta's planters once again looked to Texas and Mexico for labor.

Tejanos and Braceros, 1940s–1960s

Though Mississippi farmers were comparatively slow to take advantage of the guest worker program that would come to be known as the Bracero program, their fates were tied to it. The influx of Mexican laborers into Texas after 1942 made it easier for Mississippi farmers to recruit Tejanos for the picking season. Soon, Mississippi farmers tried to free themselves from dependence on Texan farmers' leftover labor, and in 1947 they began recruiting braceros of their own. Though Mississippi farmers never received nearly as many braceros as their counterparts in the Arkansas Delta, in some years the mid-South employed significant shares of the bracero labor force. For example, in the fall of 1954, the states with the highest number of contracted braceros were Texas (345,500), California (277,800), Arkansas (149,400), Mississippi (119,900), and Louisiana (107,700). The leadership of the Mississippi Delta Council actively lobbied Congress for the program's continuation and the minimization of its financial requirements, and Congress's Agriculture Committee put Greenville on its itinerary for farm labor hearings in 1950.

Yet, bracero contracting required organized farmers' associations, minimum standards for housing and wages, and the threat of supervision and intervention from the Mexican consulate. Thus, for most of the era, Mississippi's cotton farmers preferred to bring Tejanos up to the Delta. In so doing, they took advantage of Texan farmers' bracero recruitment, and of Mississippi's slightly later picking season, to recruit Texas's surplus labor. Mexican Americans from Texas picked cotton alongside African Americans, German POWs, and braceros during the war years. During the 1950s, hundreds of Tejano families settled in the Delta, where they performed agricultural labor until they were slowly replaced by mechanical cotton pickers.

Although braceros and Tejanos labored in the same fields, their lives were markedly different. Braceros came as single men; Tejanos were more likely to come as families. Braceros remained only seasonally, whereas many Tejanos stayed in the area for longer periods of time or even settled there. Braceros were almost entirely isolated on plantations, whereas many Tejanos had their own cars and trucks, which made it possible for them to join their families on the weekend. Bracero Luís Gutiérrez Velásquez, who worked in Mississippi during 1947–1948, picked cotton alongside 60 other braceros, half of whom were from his small town in Durango, Mexico. So isolated was the work crew that during his time in Mississippi, Gutiérrez saw not a single black person. Other braceros sometimes went to town on Saturdays, but Gutiérrez saw only rows of cotton during his weeks of picking.

Though Tejanos led a largely private cultural and communal life, many found a limited acceptance from whites in the Delta, particularly if they had some education. The Soto family, for example, arrived to Rosedale in 1962, having heard that Mississippi would be a welcome escape from the abysmally low wages and Anglo-Mexican tensions of Texas. They were not disappointed: the father, Daniel, a trained electrician, found well-paid work in his profession—something the anti-Mexican racism of Texas had never allowed him. In Texas, Soto had "worked out in the field sometimes. He didn't make any money there," recalled his wife Alice, "maybe 5 dollars a day. Here [in Mississippi] it was $1.25 an hour. We felt rich!"[4] Their daughter, a high school student, felt shunned by whites in Texas; in Mississippi, she became friends with them.

Yet, Mexican Americans' limited possibilities for assimilation were not without condition, and they most typically avoided association with blacks. The feeling may have been mutual; the Sotos remembered being turned away from a black lunch counter they had entered by mistake. "This is the black side, you go to the white side," they were told.[5] Intermarriage between Mexican Americans and whites was acceptable in the Delta by this era, whereas other Tejanos married each other or the children of Mexican migrants who had come to the area in the interwar years. As the civil rights movement began to build in the Mississippi Delta during the 1950s, the region's Mexican Americans remained silent, at the sidelines. By the time the movement flourished in the early 1960s, most Tejanos had moved on. Displaced by the mechanical cotton picker, they went to pick fruit in Florida's orchards.

Isolated Migrations in the 1970s–1980s

Mechanical cotton pickers notwithstanding, there was still much low-wage labor to be performed in Mississippi—this time, in more industrialized sectors, such as poultry processing. As the civil rights movement expanded beyond the notion of equal rights to include the struggle for economic advancement, mere inclusion in Mississippi's poultry labor force was no longer enough for blacks. As black labor unionism strengthened in the poultry plants during the 1970s, some owners attempted to import Mexican labor into the industry. For example, in 1977 the B.C. Rogers Poultry plant in Morton began to recruit Mexican Americans from El Paso. Company officials targeted agricultural migrant workers during the off-season. Though a few of these Mexican American workers remained in Mississippi, most did not, and the poultry industry quickly reverted to its status quo of a predominantly African American labor force.

Isolated groups of Latinos in other regions and industries also dotted Mississippi during these decades. For example, government subcontractors charged with seasonal tree planting in Homochitto National Forest employed Mexican migrant workers, many of them undocumented. These workers lived in tents in the forests where they worked, cooking game on kerosene stoves and remaining entirely hidden from public view. Their situation was emblematic of the period's small Latino migrant population: isolated, invisible, and soon to emigrate from Mississippi entirely.

Latino Boom: The 1990s

If attempts to recruit Mexicans as a permanent labor force largely failed in the 1970s, in the 1990s they were successful, as their scope expanded to all Latino groups. Whereas some Latinos came to work in traditional agricultural jobs, such as the sweet potato harvest in Vardaman or the Delta's cotton gins, more came for the service and construction industries, particularly casinos in Tunica and along the coast. The greatest number, however, came to work in industrialized agriculture: catfish, lumber, and, most importantly, poultry processing. In 2000 the U.S. census counted 39,569 Latinos in Mississippi, nearly three times as many as were residing there in 1990.

Initially, native-born Mississippians assumed the Latino presence would be temporary, as it had been in previous decades. "I think most people thought that this was a temporary thing," said the Chamber of Commerce director in Forest, "that they came and were going to go away—that this was not going to happen to our community."[6] As Mississippians adjusted themselves to the new reality of Latino migration, the state's relative inexperience with this population led to misconceptions about immigration law, violations of immigrants' rights, and ad hoc policy making toward the newcomers. On the other hand, many public agencies and businesses actively sought to build their Spanish-language capacity and reach out to Latinos.

Because churches were the only institutions interacting with Latinos for most of the 1990s, officials and employers who would violate immigrants' rights typically faced no legal opposition. Immigration raids during the 1990s often occurred based on dubious causes, such as a raid in Pelahatchie prompted by complaints from locals that migrants had caused a shortage of rental housing. In an echo of earlier Southern practices of discrimination, in 2002 the Scott County Circuit Clerk began requiring proof of legal presence for those seeking marriage licenses. Though the state's attorney general affirmed that the law made no such requirement, the county clerk continued to deny marriage licenses to undocumented migrants. Some migrants went to other counties for marriage licenses, and local churches agreed to wed couples who had been denied a license on grounds of immigration status. Shortly after Hurricane Katrina, Latino leaders in affected areas alleged that some stores flatly refused to sell gasoline and supplies to Latinos, stating clearly, "We are not serving Mexicans."[7]

In another incident, the Peco Foods poultry processing plant in Canton fired 200 migrant workers after receiving no-match letters from Social Security—despite the fact that the letters specifically stated that workers should not be fired without a thorough investigation into why their social security numbers did not match federal records. Though many of the fired workers paid union dues, they claimed union officials did little to aid their cause; indeed, the union lacked sufficient Spanish-speaking organizers and experience with the immigration issues of the newly arrived Latino workforce. When the company finally agreed to reinstate the fired workers months later, most of the affected workers had either moved away or disappeared into the shadows.

If the seemingly sudden arrival of so many Latinos spawned creative ways to exclude migrants, so too did it encourage creative ways to include them. Churches both Catholic and Protestant became the first local institutions to reach out to Latinos in Mississippi. Indeed, many came to serve as all-purpose help for migrants, with bilingual church employees ministering not only to migrants' spiritual needs but also to their practical ones. In 2004, Mississippi's Southern Baptist Convention elected its first Latino officer, Joel Medina, pastor of several Spanish-language churches in Carthage.

Given the lack of a bilingual second-generation to serve newly arrived migrants, white and African American businesspeople and law enforcement officials began enrolling in Spanish classes to better communicate with Latino migrants. Describing her students, one Spanish teacher commented, "They're by and large people who feel that Spanish is here and it's now."[8]. As of 2003, 20 of the state's 152 school districts had hired a translator or designated a bilingual school employee specifically to aid the Latino migrant population. Of course, Latinos generated their own communication media not reliant on translators, and by 2001 Memphis's emerging Spanish-language press, as well as Mississippi's *La Noticia*, was providing news to Latino Mississippians in Spanish.

The Poultry Industry

As the state's most important employer of Latinos during the 1990s, the poultry industry provides a useful window into the critical issues affecting Latinos in the state. Scott County in central Mississippi exemplifies this trend. Despite their failure to retain Latino workers recruited from Texas during the late 1970s, B.C. Rogers Poultry executives in the 1990s once again turned their attention to Latinos. In 1993 the company began Hispanic Project. That year, company officials regularly traveled to Miami to recruit Cuban and Central American workers; in 1994, they opened an office there. At its height, the Hispanic Project bused in approximately 80 workers per week from Miami and later from south Texas. Of these workers, company officials estimate that 20 to 40 percent remained in Mississippi.

By the mid-1990s B.C. Rogers poultry executives estimated that 400 of the plant's 600 workers were Latino. The practice of recruiting Latinos to work in the chicken plants spread through the local industry, and by the late 1990s many of the area's poultry processors were recruiting workers from Miami, south Texas, and even Mexico and Peru. The census recorded 141 "Hispanics" in Scott County in 1990, and in 2000 there were 1,660.

African Americans and Latinos

Poultry is just one area in which the histories of Mississippi's Latinos and African Americans have intersected. Mississippi has a higher percentage of African American residents (36 percent) than any U.S. state or territory but the District of Columbia. As throughout the South—but perhaps nowhere more than in Mississippi—African Americans' economic and political activities have affected the lives of Latinos. Though media reports have focused on animosity between African Americans and Latinos, in Mississippi the story has been one of both conflict and alliance. Broadly speaking, the state's established African American politicians have taken a position of support toward Latinos and their nascent political activity. On the other hand, racial and language barriers have created obstacles to alliance and understanding among African American and Latino workers, whose labor conditions and wages are directly impacted by each other's.

On the level of state politics, African Americans have spoken out prominently and unequivocally in favor of migrants' rights. Though mostly white anti-immigrant activists criticized migrants' use of the Freedom Rides metaphor during a protest in 2003, African American leaders defended the analogy. "They have the same problems we had in the 1960s as to finding jobs, living wages, and places to live," said state National Association for the Advancement of Colored People (NAACP) officer Eddie R. Smith.[9] African American leaders also helped organize Mississippi's pro-immigrant marches in 2006. State Representative Jim Evans

(D-Jackson), president of Mississippi's Southern Christian Leadership Council, evoked the importance of defending the human rights of all—a significant departure from African American civil rights leaders' traditional reliance on the rhetoric of equal citizenship for all Americans.

Notably, however, African American voting rights activist Hollis Watkins spoke through a translator at the 2006 rally, expressing his regret that more blacks had not attended the event. Indeed, though their politicians spoke the language of human rights and mutual struggles, African American and Latino workers faced considerable barriers to working together for better wages and conditions in the workplace. Scholars conducting fieldwork with poultry workers have found that many adopted mainstream discourses, which reinforced distinctions between African American and Latino workers. Black workers commonly expressed that "Hispanics are too willing to work for nothing," and "they're taking our jobs and forcing us to work harder"—the flip side of local whites' discourses praising Latinos for working harder than blacks.[10] Meanwhile, Latinos described their African American co-workers as being lazy and as not having discrimination problems. Efforts at cross-racial organizing have attempted to identify common elements of the two groups' histories and positions within the global economy—for example, by encouraging Latino workers to consider the history of racism against African Americans in the United States, while showing African Americans that a low wage in Mississippi might translate into subsistence for an entire family living off remittances in Latin America. The relationship between African Americans and Latinos in Mississippi would continue to prove critical as the next wave of Latinos arrived.

Hurricane Katrina

On the one hand Hurricane Katrina devastated south Mississippi's Latinos; on the other it provided job opportunities for thousands of would-be newcomers. Those who did not speak English likely did not hear any warning of the storm before its arrival. Latino migrants who survived the storm proved reluctant to seek aid and relief services because of fears of immigration enforcement. And if Latinos with limited roots in Mississippi had little access to resources immediately following the storm, newly arrived workers reconstructing the coast found themselves even more disenfranchised.

Though it is difficult to establish exact numbers, observers estimate that 30,000 to 60,000 Latinos moved to the Gulf Coast to work on reconstruction efforts within the first three months after the hurricane, bringing the state's post-Katrina total to 100,000 Latinos. These new arrivals were not only from Mexico but also from Guatemala, Honduras, Peru, Argentina, and Puerto Rico. Though low-wage migrant workers are vulnerable throughout the country, the exploitation of Latino migrant reconstruction workers was endemic in Mississippi—even more so than in Louisiana. The state of Mississippi has no department of labor, creating a climate in which abuse is routine. Working largely for subcontractors, Mississippi's Latino reconstruction workforce widely reported nonpayment of wages, threats of deportation to avoid paying migrants, toxic work sites with inadequate protective gear, and deplorable housing conditions. Some workers reported going hungry for days, or being suddenly and unfairly evicted from their housing. Though it had no office in Mississippi, the National Council of La Raza sent its head, Janet Murguia, to the coast in late 2005 to call attention to the abuse of Latino workers.

Hurricane Katrina also had ramifications for Latinos' participation in Mississippi's workforce overall. The number of Latinos on the coast peaked in the months after Katrina but subsided somewhat within a year, as migrants got tired of the rampant abuse by contractors and the lack of housing. Though some left the state altogether, many who came for construction work ultimately went to work in the poultry or service industries. For example, an organizer at Sanderson Farms' poultry plant in Collins estimated that before Katrina the plant's workforce had been 30 percent Latino; and that since the storm Latinos have composed about 45 percent of the plant's workers.[11]

ORGANIZING FOR CHANGE

Mississippi's Latinos have not been able to use the traditional bases of Latino political power in the United States. No national Latino advocacy organization has offices there, and until Hurricane Katrina the state received little attention from these groups. Furthermore, in this right-to-work state, the labor movement historically has been weak, limiting Latinos' possibilities for gaining power through organized labor as they have done elsewhere. Thus, Latinos' political strategies have been uniquely Mississippian—that is, based on religious institutions, limited union activity, and attempts at alliance with African Americans.

Churches were Latinos' first and only line of defense in the 1990s. Though church workers, some themselves Latinos, sometimes chose to intervene in particular troubles with bosses or landlords, on their own they could do little to address the systemic concerns of this newly arrived, largely undocumented migrant population.

In 2000, church groups joined forces with union, African American, and social service groups to form the Mississippi Immigrants' Rights Alliance (MIRA!). MIRA! has focused largely on state and local policy advocacy on behalf of migrants. As rallies in favor of immigrants' rights swept the United States in 2006, MIRA! worked with religious and African American leadership to organize rallies in Jackson, Gulfport, and Laurel. Approximately 500 people attended each event. Casting the rallies in the tradition of the state's history of civil rights struggle, organizers led marchers in a Spanish-language version of "We Shall Overcome"—"Juntos Venceremos."

Though Jackson is the state's capital, central Mississippi has been the locus of an equally dynamic migrant workers' movement centering around the concerns of poultry workers. Given traditional poultry unions' initial failure to reach out to Latinos, organizers have created alternative strategies. Helping Latino and African American workers find common ground has been a central concern of MPOWER (formerly the Mississippi Poultry Workers' Center), in Morton. Working in collaboration with civil and immigrants' rights organizations, religious leaders, labor unions, and other community groups, MPOWER focuses on worker education. It works across race lines to build a climate of political consciousness among central Mississippi's poultry workers. In part because of these efforts, Latino migrants in the area responded in large numbers to the national call for an immigrant strike on May 1, 2006. Sanderson Farms' poultry plant in Laurel, for example, became so short-staffed on that day that it had to cut back from two production shifts to one.

In other parts of the state, middle-class Latino professionals have improvised as needed to provide basic services, advocacy, and translation for newly arrived Latinos. In 2002 middle-class Latino leaders on Mississippi's Gulf Coast founded the Gulf Coast Latin American Association, whose goal is to help the poorer, more recent arrivals from throughout Latin America to the coast.

NOTABLE LATINOS

Landrove, Rafael J. (1893–1976). By drawing New Orleans's Mexican consulate into the daily struggles of the Delta's Mexican migrants in the 1920s–1930s, Landrove became its most prominent community leader. Literate and nurturing middle-class aspirations, he sought to utilize the profits of sharecropping and the in-between status of Mexicans in the Delta to advance into its middle class. When his children and the Robledos' were denied admittance to Gunnison's white school in 1929, Landrove penned an appeal to the Mexican consulate, which eventually resulted in the children's admittance to the school. Together with Manuel Solis, he also organized a *comisión honorífica*, or honorary commission, to both foster Mexican patriotism and organize the Mexicans in the area to regulate the cotton market and prevent a disaster in the next harvest because of plummeting cotton prices. The Depression, however, would ultimately thwart Landrove's goals. The Landroves outlasted most other Mexican families in the Delta, remaining there at least through 1934. They eventually left Mississippi and returned to the Southwest.

Longoria, Valerio (1924–2000). Though this pioneer of Tejano conjunto music grew up in south Texas, he actually was born to migrant farmworker parents on a cotton plantation in Clarksdale. The first to combine lyrics with accordion music and to introduce Colombian *cumbia* to the conjunto genre, Longoria is known as the "genius of conjunto." He spent his life playing in a band with his family, bringing this south Texas musical tradition to Mexican and Mexican American audiences throughout the country. The Mississippi birthplace of this Tejano icon demonstrates both the centrality of south Texas to the pre-1970 Mississippi Latino experience, and the influence of Mississippi, however peripheral, in the lives of the thousands of Tejanos and Texas-based Mexicans who worked the Delta's cotton plantations as migrants.

Echiburu, Tito (1944–). As one of the few Latinos in central Mississippi in the 1970s, Echiburu used his Latin American connections and language skills to spearhead the first successful effort to recruit Latinos to central Mississippi's poultry industry. He had first come to Mississippi State University from Chile on a tennis scholarship in 1962, and he later returned to the region in 1973 to take a position as chief financial officer of B.C. Rogers Poultry. In 1993 after the plant's owner, John Rogers, saw a news report about high Latino unemployment in Miami, he sent Echiburu there to recruit workers for the difficult-to-fill night shift. Recruiting mostly Cubans, Dominicans, and Central Americans, Echiburu filled bus after bus with Latino workers bound for the Rogers plant in Mississippi. Thus began B.C. Rogers's Hispanic Project. Soon, a Mexican American man from California took over the project, recruiting more Mexican workers from south Texas. As other poultry plants followed suit, bringing workers from as far as Argentina, Colombia, and Peru, Central Mississippi's diverse Latino community was born.

Thompson, Marie (1957–). A third-generation Latino American with family roots in south Texas and Peru, Thompson arrived in Vicksburg in 2001. There, she found that recent Latino migrants to the area assumed she spoke Spanish because of her appearance. Dusting off a language she had not used since childhood, Thompson became the unofficial translator and advocate for the area's burgeoning Latino population. However nascent the immigrants' rights movement in central Mississippi may be, Vicksburg is a decade behind. Working as welders and laborers for a large oil rig manufacturing company and its subcontractors, the area's Latino workers have no formal organizations representing them. Thus, Thompson tries to balance advocacy with reality: if she pushes employers too far, they may refuse to deal with her. Working alone to help Latino workers communicate with employers, doctors, and city officials, she also distributes pamphlets originally produced by organizations representing central Mississippi's poultry workers.

Medina, Joel (1968–). In 2004 Medina became the first Latino officer in Mississippi's Southern Baptist Convention. Originally from Puerto Rico, Medina worked at an auto parts shop and as a bank teller after arriving to Scott County in 1996. Though most Latin Americans are Catholic, Protestantism dominates the rural South, and Protestants have long spotted an opportunity for evangelism among Latino newcomers. Noticing Medina's nascent ministry work in the late 1990s, Southern Baptists invited him to start a church of his own in Carthage. They provided him with a trailer and some funds, and thus began the Iglesia Internacional las Américas. Like other clergy in the area, Medina ministers mostly to poultry workers and their families, and he provides an array of supports, such as English classes and emergency food supplies, in addition to spiritual leadership. Medina also works as a chaplain at the Tyson poultry processing plant.

Salvador, Natanael (1968–). A leader of Mam-speaking indigenous Guatemalans in Carthage, Salvador was among the first group of Latinos recruited to the area's poultry processing plants. After crossing the border to pick oranges in Florida, Salvador followed the lead of some Cubans who recruited him to work in Mississippi in 1995. Though turnover among the area's early Latino workers was extraordinarily high, Salvador remained in the area. Despite his limited English skills, he quickly became a resource for newly arrived workers, particularly Mam speakers, helping them navigate the health care, school, and court systems of rural Mississippi. He has also served as a union steward in the chicken plant where he works.

CULTURAL CONTRIBUTIONS

Latino culture in Mississippi has been both visible and invisible, mainstream and separate from the culture of white and black Mississippians. The signature Mississippi hot tamale is perhaps the best-known cultural contribution of Latinos to the state. Though theories on the tamale's arrival to Mississippi abound, food historians suggest that tamales became popular in the 1920s as a result of the influx of Mexican migrant workers to the area. Memories of tamales' presence in the Delta date back to the 1910s, and since then there has been a dynamic relationship between the Delta's Mexican and non-Mexican tamale producers. Because the tamale stayed warm all day, it proved particularly well suited for the cool fall days of cotton picking in the Delta. Working alongside Mexicans, the Delta's African American cotton laborers soon adopted tamales as their own.

Yet, the Mississippi hot tamale did not develop entirely in isolation from its Mexican cousin. Capitalizing on Mississippians' fondness for the tamale, Mexicans in the area during the 1940s and 1950s once again sold tamales to eager customers. Today, dozens of Mississippi establishments serve Mississippi's unique brand of hot tamale. Ironically, though the Mexican migrants of the 1920s and 1930s left a lasting mark on Mississippi culture, their isolation on separate plantations made the establishment of a communal cultural life of their own exceedingly difficult.

The Tejanos who came to the Delta during the 1940s and 1960s enjoyed a richer cultural life than their Mexican-origin predecessors of the 1920s and 1930s. Improved roads and looser labor controls enabled a community life that had been difficult for the earlier, isolated Mexican workers to achieve. Other than the ubiquitous tamale, this period saw little crossover between Latino culture and that of native Mississippians. Tejanos from around the Delta would travel up to 20 miles each Saturday night to gather in private homes. There, they would dance all night to the sounds of Tejano bands that would come up to Mississippi for the weekend. Neither native Mississippians nor braceros participated in these festivities.

Though the most recent Latino migrants to Mississippi have established stores, bars, and faith communities apart from those of white and black Mississippians, overall the period has brought a new interaction between Latino and Mississippian cultures. In many ways, Mississippi's rural landscape has proved particularly fertile for Latino cultural influences. Unlike in southwestern or northeastern states, where Latino culture is ubiquitous, in Mississippi natives have received Latino culture as an international novelty and unique opportunity to forge a new, more cosmopolitan identity. For example, in the small town of Newton, population 3,700, Mexican migrant entrepreneurs organized an authentic Mexican bullfight—purportedly the state's first—in a 4,000-person arena in 2005. Locals flocked to the event, and the Newton Chamber of Commerce embraced and promoted the bullfight, hoping it would draw tourists from throughout the South. Officials correctly predicted that bullfighting would become an important local attraction, putting Newton on the itinerary of visitors to nearby Indian casinos.

Given Mississippians' longstanding love of tamales, white and black Mississippians have been particularly receptive to the arrival of dozens of new Mexican restaurants since the 1990s. Though they are mostly run by migrants, the restaurants' novelty has attracted a mostly non-Mexican clientele. For example, native-born residents of Cleveland, a Delta town, fiercely debate which Mexican restaurant on Route 61 is the best: Guadalajara or La Cabaña.

NOTES

1. Due to the near invisibility of Latinos in Mississippi until very recently, there were no published academic works to draw upon in the writing of this chapter. For the period 1908–1960s, I have drawn upon my own original research as well as that of Richard Enriquez. For the post-1970 period, I have drawn upon the unpublished original research of Angela Stuesse, Anita Grabowski and Laura Helton. All information on this latter period is therefore based on these scholars' research, in addition to newspapers and oral history interviews. I thank them for giving me permission to include their work in this chapter.

2. Weise, 2005; Weise, "Mexicans and Mexican Americans in the Mississippi Delta," 2007.

3. Weise, "'Different . . . from That Which Is Intended for the Colored Race,'" 2007.

4. Enriquez, interview with Mrs. Daniel (Alice) Soto, 1991.

5. Enriquez, interview with Mrs. Daniel (Alice) Soto, 1991.

6. John, 1998.

7. Davis Maute, 2005.

8. Lindsay, 2003.

9. Brown, 2003.

10. Steusse, 2008.

11. Davis Maute, 2006.

BIBLIOGRAPHY

Brown, Riva. "Immigrants in U.S. Pay Hefty Price." *Clarion-Ledger*, 2003.

Davis Maute, Nikki. "Hispanic Leader Says Stores Discriminated." *Hattiesburg American*, September 25, 2005.

———. "Program Helps Verify Immigrants' Status." *Hattiesburg American,* April 20, 2006.

Grabowski, Anita M. "La Pollera: Latin American Immigrant Workers at the Koch Foods Poultry Plant in Morton, Mississippi." Master's thesis, University of Texas, 2003.

Helton, Laura E., and Angela Stuesse. "Race, Low-Wage Legacies and the Politics of Poultry Processing: Intersections of Contemporary Immigration and African American Labor Histories in Central Mississippi." Paper presented at the Southern Labor Studies Conference, Birmingham, AL, April 15–17, 2004.

John, Butch. "Diluted Dreams of Milk and Honey." *Clarion-Ledger,* January 18, 1998.

Lindsay, Arnold. "Learning Spanish Good for Business." *Clarion-Ledger,* April 27, 2003.

Soto, Mrs. Daniel (Alice). Interview by Richard Enriquez. Audio tape. Delta State University Archives. Cleveland, MS. 1991.

Southern Foodways Alliance. "The Mississippi Delta Hot Tamale Trail." http://www.tamaletrail.com.

Steusse, Angela. "Race, Migration, and Labor Control: Neoliberal Challenges to Organizing Mississippi's Poultry Workers." In *Latinos in the Contemporary U.S. South.* Eds. Elaine Lacy and Mary Odem. Athens: University of Georgia Press, 2008.

Weise, Julie. "Mexicans and Mexican Americans in the Mississippi Delta, 1908–1939." Paper presented at the Huntington-USC Institute on California and the West Brown Bag Series in U.S. Western/Borderlands History, Los Angeles, April 23, 2007.

———. "'Different . . . from That Which Is Intended for the Colored Race': Mexico and Mexicans in the Mississippi and Arkansas Deltas, 1908–1964." Paper presented at the Southern Historical Association, Richmond, VA, November 1, 2007.

———. "Al Sur: Mexicans and Mexican-Americans in the U.S. South, 1918–1935." Paper presented at the Pacific Coast Branch of the American Historical Association, Corvallis, OR, 2005.

Woodruff, Nan Elizabeth. "Pick or Fight: The Emergency Farm Labor Program in the Arkansas and Mississippi Deltas during World War II." *Agricultural History* 64, no. 2 (1990): 74–85.

26

Missouri

Brittney Yancy

CHRONOLOGY

1541	Spanish explorer Hernando de Soto visits the Missouri area in 1541.
1770	The Spanish government takes control of the Territory of Louisiana.
1821	Captain William Becknell develops the Santa Fe Trail.
1825	Former Missouri senator Thomas Benton petitions the U.S. government to survey the Santa Fe Trail.
1846	The beginning of the Mexican-American War. On May 11 Congress passes a resolution, and President James Polk summons 50,000 troops and appropriates $10 million for the war. Missouri sends 2,000 men to the front.
1865	Major General Sterling Price, Missouri's highest-ranking military officer, leads his army to Mexico, to the colony of Confederate exiles at Carlota, in the state of Veracruz.
1885	After the Alien Labor Act of 1885, Latino migrants replace Chinese migrant workers in the railroad industry and agriculture.
1923	Cuban veteran baseball star Jose Menendez becomes the manager of the Kansas City Monarchs and leads the team to a league championship.
1960	The Cuban Revolution and the rise of communism ignite mass migration of Cubans to the United States, including Kansas City and St. Louis.
1970s	Latinos laborers begin to find work in Missouri's meat processing industry.
1977	The Hispanic Chamber of Commerce of Greater Kansas City is established by 25 Latino business leaders.
1980s	Latino workers begin supplying labor on farmlands in the southwest and boot heel of Missouri.

1990	Yolanda Jorge establishes Grupo Latinoamericano, an organization of Latin American migrants in southwest Missouri that celebrates folk tradition from Latin American countries.
1998	On December 15, four senators and four state representatives form the Joint Interim Committee on Immigration to provide social services to immigrants.
2000	The U.S. census reports that Latino numbers in Missouri, estimated at 118,592, are much higher than anticipated.
2001	The University of Missouri at Kansas City creates a research organization, the Alianzas Alliances Project, for the study of the Latino presence in Missouri and across the Midwest.
2002	The Mexican consulate moves to Kansas City from St. Louis.
2004	Governor Matt Blunt creates the Commission on Hispanic Affairs. A community of scholars, activists, professors, and students creates the Cambio Center de Colors at the University of Missouri at Columbia.
2005	Governor Matt Blunt replaces the Missouri Governor's Commission on Hispanic Affairs with the Hispanic Business, Trade, and Culture Commission.
2006	Alianzas Alliances meets in Guanajuato, Mexico, to establish a partnership with its sister city, San José Iturbide.

HISTORICAL OVERVIEW

The history of Latinos in Missouri is a narrative of community creation and cultural reinvention, as well as a search for identity, equality, and economic security in the face of adversity. From international students and CEOs to exiles and undocumented workers, Latinos have shaped the cultural, social, economic, and political landscape of Missouri in particular, and the United States in general.

Newcomers: Latino Presence in Missouri, 1500s–1800s

The history of Latinos in Missouri dates back to the sixteenth century, when Spanish conquistador Hernando de Soto led his army across the present-day Midwest. In the spring of 1541, de Soto left the southeast, marched through Kentucky and Indiana, and headed up toward Chicago. After failing to locate a route to China for trade, de Soto retreated southwestward through Illinois and Missouri. According to Hernando de Soto's secretary, "On Tuesday, the sixth of September [1541, de Soto's army] departed from Coligua, Illinois [Kaskaskia] and crossed the [Mississippi] river another time into present-day Ste. Genevieve, Missouri, precisely on the Full Moon."[1] De Soto and his army encountered five tribal villages of Native Americans in Missouri: Calpista, Palisema, Quizila, Tutilcoya, and Tancio. De Soto died upon his departure from Tancio, Missouri, and his army continued south into Harrison, Arkansas.

In 1800, France reclaimed the Louisiana Territory (including Missouri), and sold it to the United States in the Louisiana Purchase in 1803. By the 1830s the Santa Fe Trail connected Missouri to Mexico. New Mexico, which was then a northern province of Mexico, hungered for goods not regulated by the Spanish Crown's repressive trade policies. Kansas City, Missouri, was the endpoint of this lucrative commercial traffic and benefited greatly from this trade.[2] Throughout the nineteenth century, Missourians engaged in many war efforts within the Spanish territory.

Missouri's relationship with Latin America intensified during the United States' nineteenth-century imperial expansion in countries such as Mexico, Cuba, and Puerto Rico. The Mexican-American War began in April 1846. On May 11, the U.S. Congress passed a resolution to summon 50,000 troops and appropriate $10 million for the war. Missouri sent over 2,000 male volunteers from eight Missouri counties: Jackson, Lafayette, Clay, Saline, Franklin, Cole, Howard, and Callaway. Beyond Missouri's connection to Mexico, Cuba has had an important place in the state's history. On April 25, 1898, the Spanish-American War began, and Missouri provided infantry and light artillery. Battery A of light artillery was sent to Puerto Rico as part of the First Army Corps.[3] By the end of this war, demand for cheap labor had brought migrants from Latin America to Missouri.

Latinos in the Show-Me State

The Mexican Revolution forced Mexicans who wanted to improve their lives to flee their homeland. Mexican migrants, in particular, were initially attracted to jobs in the agriculture, railroad, and meatpacking industries. During the Great

Depression (1929–1939), Spanish-speaking populations in Missouri grew slowly, forming enclaves in major cities such as Kansas City and St. Louis.

World War II prompted the U.S. government to work with its Mexican counterpart to develop the Bracero program, a contract labor program that officially hired Mexican laborers to work in the United States. Braceros worked in the railroad and agriculture industries in Missouri and throughout the Midwest. Wartime employment brought better jobs and allowed some mobility for Mexican laborers. Missouri received the highest number of Latinos after 1950; the majority of migrants settled into agriculture, manufacturing, and domestic service jobs. In addition, following the Cuban Revolution, the federal government and Catholic churches resettled Cuban refugees in various cities in Missouri. Over the last 40 years Latinos have changed Missouri's cultural, social, political, and economic landscape. From business owners to professional baseball players, Latinos have established themselves as prominent leaders of the state.

From the 1960s to the present, Latinos have increased their presence in Missouri, mainly through labor migration. The University of Missouri's Office of Social and Economic Data Analysis (OSEDA) reported that the Latino population in the 1960s totaled 60,000 people. The postwar era and the expansion of the meatpacking industry have precipitated nearly a half century of demographic transformation characterized by racial stratification and significant Mexican migration. If in the 1980s and 1990s African Americans and non-Latino whites were the predominant ethnic groups in Missouri, by 2000 the number of Missouri Latinos had doubled to an estimated 120,000 people. In 2000 the Census Bureau announced that Latinos had surpassed African Americans as the largest minority population; and in 2003 the OSEDA announced that Missouri's Latino population had increased slightly, by 10.4 percent, totaling 131,000 Latino residents.

A New Generation of Latino Americans

Motivated by economic security, education, and democracy, Latinos migrated to the United States. Over the past 40 years Latinos have composed 2.7 percent of Missouri's population, but their growth rate has outpaced that of Anglos and African Americans by far. Latino settlement in Missouri takes place largely in urban areas. Missouri's Latinos have been consistently settling in Missouri's metropolitan areas of Kansas City and St. Louis.

Kansas City

Kansas City has the most established Latino population in Missouri, according to the 2000 census, with a population of 92, 910.[4] Kansas City became an important transportation, commercial, and industrial center. The first Mexican settlement in Kansas City dates back to 1905, when a barrio developed in the flood-prone

Argentine area. This settlement was made up mostly of boxcars, provided by the Santa Fe Railroad, and of segregated boarding houses. Two hundred of the 300 Mexicans living in Argentine worked for the railroad, and of this amount 12 percent were women and 12 percent were children.[5]

By the 1920 census, Kansas City had become an important destination for Mexican laborers seeking work in the Midwest. The settlement process of Mexican workers was interrupted at two major points: during the Great Depression (1929–1939), when U.S. citizens falsely argued that Mexicans were taking away jobs, and during World War II, when Mexicans were deported as threats to U.S. national security. Postwar official policies uprooted many Mexican families, including children born in the United States. However, many resisted, and they were aided by employers in several instances. Three to four generations later, the descendants of these settlers now form the core of Kansas City's Mexican American community. The importance of Kansas City to Missouri's Latino population was implicitly recognized by the move of the Mexican consulate's office to Kansas City in August 2002. In the last decade Kansas City's metropolitan area has experienced the greatest growth in the state in the number of Latinos (55,243).

Kansas City has benefited from Latino-led nonprofit groups working to rehabilitate run-down homes and to reinvest in new construction in the inner city. The Latino population has expanded beyond the boundaries of the old barrio, and Latinos are now present everywhere in the Kansas City metro area. Throughout Kansas City suburbs the Latino population grew by 33 percent, reflecting a national trend of Latinos moving out of segregated inner-city neighborhoods as their economic fortunes improve. The northeast side, formerly predominantly Italian American, is increasingly becoming Latino; in fact, Latinos now represent approximately 30 percent of the population in that area.

Kansas City Latinos are finding employment in landscaping, distribution centers, and construction. First- and second-generation Latinos create a dynamic community that has become culturally and politically engaged in advancing. However, Kansas City, like other cities with big Latino communities, faces the challenge of defining a unified Latino agenda and going beyond that to exercise statewide and national leadership.

St. Louis

St. Louis, also known as the melting pot city, has a Latino community dating back to the 1920s. The community is substantial but relatively small within St. Louis, amounting to approximately 20,000 Latinos in the inner city and 40,000 in the metropolitan area.[6] For the past decades Latinos have ranked economically between the working poor and the middle class. They have established enclaves across the metropolitan areas, and they have formed groups such as the Hispanic Leaders Group of Greater St. Louis, which came to prominence during the early 1990s, and La Clínica, a public health clinic established in the late 1990s to provide free health care to the Latino community in St. Louis.[7] Creating a unified *latinidad* (Latin-ness) has been difficult, as Latinos in St. Louis are heterogeneous, coming not only from Mexico but from a variety of places in Latin America, including Puerto Rico, Cuba, and South America.

Rural Missouri

Latinos in rural Missouri have a very different profile. Most are first-generation migrants who speak Spanish only, earn low wages, and are young and with children. Other areas that showed exceptionally high numbers of Latinos in 2000 are the southwest and central rural counties of the state, including Sullivan, Moniteau, Pettis, Lawrence, Saline, Taney, Dunklin, and Jasper.

Labor and Industry

After the Alien Labor Act of 1885, which further barred Chinese migrants from entering the United States, Latino migrants became the source of cheap labor in Missouri. Throughout the early twentieth century, U.S. employers recruited Mexican workers in El Paso and transported them by railroad to jobs in Missouri, Kansas, and elsewhere in the Midwest (e.g., Illinois, Michigan, and Ohio), where they found jobs on railroads, in meat processing plants, and in sugar beet fields. In the early decades of the twentieth century, these Mexican workers may have gone back to Mexico and Texas in the winter, but as circular migration increased between Missouri and Mexico, more Latino settlements began to emerge. Latino farmworkers tended the western apple farms, and the southeastern cotton, soybean, wheat, and rice farms. More recently the increased demand for workers in the meatpacking industry has influenced migration of Latinos to Missouri.

Third-generation Latinos and educated Latino migrants have diverted from agriculture to entrepreneurship. In 1977 the Hispanic Chamber of Commerce was formed to represent Latino business interests before the public and private sectors. Currently, the organization aims at developing a network that would bring cohesion to the Latino business community, and at promoting economic growth and development of its member businesses and their communities.

Missouri Latino Politics

Though Latinos in Missouri have always been concerned with citizenship and labor and civil rights, scholars have failed to acknowledge the presence of Latino activism. The historical record has not fully developed a narrative of Latino politics in the state of Missouri. In recent years, new legislative initiatives have

Board members of the St. Louis Hispanic Chambers of Commerce. Courtesy of Hispanic St. Louis and Joe Bomarrito.

attracted Latino political activists to the state's capital. Under the leadership of Representative Deleta Williams and Senator Harold Caskey, the state legislature formed the Joint Interim Committee on Immigration (HCR 10) that met during 1998 and 1999.[8] The committee examined, through a series of statewide hearings, the effect of migration on community social services. In 2002 the first annual Hispanic Legislative Day brought Latinos to the state capital to inform legislators of relevant issues, such as bilingual education, wages, and political disenfranchisement. In 2004 Governor Matt Blunt created the Missouri Governors' Committee on Hispanic Affairs (later known as Hispanic Business, Trade, and Culture Commission) to provide guidance on issues affecting the Latino community.

Statewide, Missouri's large and small cities and rural counties have seen the growth of the Latino population in their communities. Latinos of all backgrounds have regained a sense of identity through various cultural activities. There are positive forces at work in Missouri: faith-based organizations, multicultural and community-based groups, the charitable dedication and leadership of individual Missourians, and the work of the men and women who work for Missouri's state universities and government.

NOTABLE LATINOS

Bommarito, Dinorah (1936–). Born in Santurce, Puerto Rico, Bommarito, a prominent Latina community activist, came to St. Louis in July 1960, after marrying Joe Bommarito, a veteran. In the 1960s Bommarito worked with numerous Latino organizations and the St. Margaret of Scotland Church as a translator for Cuban refugee families, helping them adjust to their new environment. Bommarito has earned several degrees and worked at various universities in the St. Louis area. Currently, she works at St. Louis Community College. As a community leader, Bommarito serves on numerous boards and committees for several Latino organizations, including the HLG, Older Women's League, and the Bellas Artes Multicultural Center and Art Gallery. For 6 years, Bommarito has been a St. Louis's Hispanic Leaders' delegate. In that capacity, she was selected to visit Missouri representatives while they were in session in Jefferson City, Missouri.

Cepeda, Orlando (1937–). Baseball player Orlando Cepeda's conflicts with the Giants' management, in San Francisco, sent him to the St. Louis Cardinals in 1966. Known as Cha-Cha because of his love for salsa, Orlando Cepeda led the Cardinals to the World Series championship in 1967.

Miranda-Yuen, Celia (1946–). Businesswoman Yuen-Miranda migrated to Missouri from Brazil. Miranda-Yuen earned an undergraduate degree in economics from the Catholic University in Brazil in 1988, and a master's degree in finance from the Business Management University in Brazil in 1990. In St. Louis, Miranda-Yuen earned a master's in business administration from Webster University in May 2001. Miranda-Yuen has recently established Bellas Artes—a not-for-profit arts and events gallery and cultural center celebrating Latino heritage—of which she is the director.

Pinela, Gilberto (1964–). From San Juan, Puerto Rico, to New York City, media figure Pinela has traveled a long, and ultimately fulfilling, road to St. Louis. As the founder and president of Pinela Communications, he has been working in conjunction with UPN 46 to present a block of programming aimed at the Latino market. In the fall of 2004 Pinela produced and hosted a Spanish-language variety television program, *Entérate*, for UPN. Pinela has also hosted the first Spanish-language televised variety show in Missouri, *Ahora San Luis*, since 2001.

Desarden, Arnette (1974–). Born in Puerto Rico, Desarden is a prominent Latina activist in the St. Louis area. Desarden earned her bachelor's in communication from Universidad Del Sagrado Corazon, San Juan, Puerto Rico, in 1997. After moving to Missouri, Desarden earned a bachelor's in industrial engineering from the University of Missouri at Columbia in 2003. She is working on her MBA at Lindenwood University. Aside from her civil involvement, she is the founder and past president of the St. Louis chapter of the Gateway Society of Hispanic Professional Engineers.

CULTURAL CONTRIBUTIONS

In response to the rapid growth of Latinos in the state, the Catholic Church—particularly through the St. Louis Archdiocese and the Diocese of Kansas City and St. Joseph—has historically aided the Latino community, and it has been involved in acknowledging the diversity of Latino culture. In 1919 the Guadalupe Center Inc., which was named after the patron saint of Mexico, became the cornerstone of the Latino community within Kansas City. On the west side of Kansas City, different catholic organizations in the early 1920s established volunteer schools and clinics for disenfranchised Mexican migrants. During the 1960s, the St. Margaret of Scotland Church, in south St. Louis, brought Cuban refugee families to live and work in St. Louis.

Spanish-language magazines as well as Latino sports leagues, festivals, parades, and cultural institutions date back to the early 1930s in Missouri's history. For example, in May 1936 a group of Mexicans formed the Sociedad Mexicana Benito Juárez de St. Louis—named after the late Mexican president—to promote and preserve Mexican tradition and culture through Mexican national fiestas such as Cinco de Mayo and Independence Day (September 16). Over the decades, the community has addressed the increase in the size and prominence of its Latino population by creating social and cultural organizations, including the Sociedad Hispano-Americana de St. Louis, that stabilize Latino community life in the state.

In 1990 Yolanda Jorge, a Mexican-born migrant, created a local nonprofit organization, Grupo Latinoamericano, in the southwest of Missouri. Grupo Latinoamericano currently provides volunteer and education services to Latino communities in the region. Yolanda Jorge and Frank Soriano created the first Latino magazine in Missouri, *Enfoque*.

Several key organizations have formed to address the needs of Latinos communities such as the ALIANZAS project at the University of Missouri at Kansas City, the League of Latin American United Citizens (LULAC) Regional Office, La Council de la Raza, Hispanic Leaders Groups of St. Louis, and grassroots groups such as the Hispanic Economic Development, Westside CAN, and the Council of Hispanic Organizations (COHO). Bilingual magazines such as the Kansas City–based *Dos Mundos* have emerged across the state.

The academic community responded to the demographic changes by convening an annual conference—Cambio de Colores (Changes of Colors)—in Columbia, Missouri. Participants from across the region have gathered since 2002 to engage in intellectual debates about the needs and issues concerning migrants of Latin American descent. In 2004 the Cambio Center was established as a research institution at the University of Missouri at Columbia.

Latino students at Missouri's universities have organized to provide a social and cultural environment for Latino students and to increase awareness of the Latino community through several organizations, including the Hispanic American Leadership Organization (HALO), the Cuban American Students Undergraduate Association, and the Society of Professional Hispanic Engineers.

From 1871 to 1950, there were only 54 Latin Americans playing professional baseball in the United States.[9] But in the 1950s, African American Jackie Robinson's participation in the National Baseball League prompted team owners to recruit outside the United States, notably in Latin America and the Caribbean. In Missouri the St. Louis Cardinals and the former Kansas City Monarchs recruited a number of Latinos from Puerto Rico, the Dominican Republic, and Cuba.

NOTES

1. Sheppard, 1993, 50–52.
2. The earliest record of a Mexican national working in Kansas City dates back to 1861, when Miguel Antonio Otero founded the largest land freight company then in existence in the United States. Driever, 1996.
3. Driver, 1996.
4. In 2000, Kansas City and its environs counted 35,150 Latinos, and St. Louis 21,850, for a total of 57,000, or 48 percent of the total Latino population in the state. Hobbs, 2002.
5. Hobbs, 2002.
6. Suro and Singer, 2002.
7. Corey, 2000.
8. Lazos-Vargas and Jeanetta, 2002, 19.
9. Regalado, 2002, 162–176.

BIBLIOGRAPHY

Baldassaro, Lawrence, and Richard A. Johnson. *The American Game: Baseball and Ethnicity*. Carbondale: Southern Illinois University Press, 2002.

Corey, Andrea. "La Clinica Offers Health Care to Hispanic Community." *St. Louis Business Journal*, February 4, 2000.

Driever, Steven L. "Midwest." In *The Latino Encyclopedia*. Eds. J. Ramírez-Johnson and R. Chabrán. New York: Marshall Cavendish, 1996, 1019–1021.

Fredericksen, Lin. "'Fiesta, Kansas Style': A Moment in Time." Kansas State Historical Society, September 2001. http://www.kshs.org/features/feat901.htm.

Hobbs, Daryl J. "Overview of Missouri Hispanics—2000." Changing Colors in Missouri Conference, University of Missouri. Columbia, MO, March 13–15, 2002. http://www.oseda.missouri.edu/presentations/hispanic_conf_mar02.ppt.

Lazos-Vargas, Sylvia R., and Stephen C. Jeanetta. *Cambio de Colores: Immigration of Latinos to Missouri*. Columbia: University of Missouri Press, 2002.

Mendoza, Valerie M. "They Came to Kansas: Searching for a Better Life." *Kansas Quarterly* 25 (1994): 97–106.

Regalado, Samuel O. "The Latin Quarter in the Major Leagues: Adjustment and Achievement." In *The American Game: Baseball and Ethnicity*. Eds. Lawrence Baldassaro and Richard A. Johnson. Carbondale: Southern Illinois University Press, 2002. 162–176.

Sheppard, Donald E. *The De Soto Chronicles: The Expedition of Hernando De Soto to North America in 1539–1543*. Tuscaloosa: University of Alabama Press, 1993.

Suro, Robert, and Audrey Singer. "Latino/a Growth in Metropolitan America: Changing Patterns, New Locations." Washington, DC: Brookings Institution, Center on Urban and Metropolitan Policy, and Pew Hispanic Center, July 2002. http://www.brook.edu/dybdocroot/es/urban/publications/surosinger.pdf.

Wirth, Jim. *The Story of the Hispanic/Latino Experience in Southwest Missouri: Surveys of Latino Adults, Latino Youth, and Non-Hispanic Service Providers/Community Residents.* Springfield, MO: University of Missouri Outreach and Extension, Alianzas Project Surveys of the Southwest Region of Missouri, 2002.

Discarded

University of Cincinnati
Blue Ash College Library